If you're wondering why you should buy this new edition of *Global Political Economy*, here are ten good reasons!

1. Discussions of **globalization** throughout the text make understanding economic interdependence easier.

2. Chapters 1 and 2 provide an overview of the **international economic system** and explain the importance of IPE theory in interpreting economic events.

3. Chapter 3, "The Realist Perspective," has a more detailed discussion of the status of U.S. hegemony to help you understand **the role of the United States in the world.**

4. Chapter 5, "Critical Perspectives," now includes **important theories and perspectives,** you will cover in your course including constructivism, rational choice feminism, and environmentalism.

5. Chapter 6, "International Monetary Relations," takes a hard look at the consequences and future of **financial globalization.**

6. Chapter 7, "Global Trade Relations," now explores the **domestic politics of trade** and the relationship between trade and the environment.

7. Chapter 10, "International Development," now discusses microfinance and other **development strategies** in use throughout the world.

8. Chapter 11, "Foreign Debt and Financial Crises," now includes analysis of the current **global financial crisis** and compares it with previous crises.

9. Chapter 12, "Current Trends in the Global Political Economy," has been updated to discuss **globalization in the context of the current financial crisis.**

10. Each chapter now includes **suggested readings with annotations** to help you learn more about International Political Economy and complete your course assignments.

PEARSON

GLOBAL POLITICAL ECONOMY

THEORY AND PRACTICE

Fifth Edition

Theodore H. Cohn
Simon Fraser University

Longman
New York   San Francisco   Boston
London   Toronto   Sydney   Tokyo   Singapore   Madrid
Mexico City   Munich   Paris   Cape Town   Hong Kong   Montreal

To Shirley

Acquisitions Editor: Vikram Mukhija
Marketing Manager: Lindsey Prudhomme
Editorial Assistant: Toni Magyar
Production Manager: Kathy Sleys
**Project Coordination, Text Design, and Electronic
  Page Makeup:** Shiny Rajesh/Integra Software Services Pvt. Ltd.
Design Director: Jayne Conte
Cover Designer: Bruce Kenselaar
Cover Illustration/Photo: Corbis/Veer
Printer, Binder and Cover Printer: R.R. Donnelley & Sons, Inc.

Library of Congress Cataloging-in-Publication Data
Cohn, Theodore H.
   Global political economy: theory and practice/Theodore H. Cohn.—5th ed.
      p. cm.
   Includes bibliographical references and index.
   ISBN-13: 978-0-205-74234-9 (alk. paper)
   ISBN-10: 0-205-74234-3
   1. International economic relations.   2. International trade.   3. International finance.   I. Title.
HF1359.C654 2010
337—dc22

                                                                                    2009018919

1 2 3 4 5 6 7 8 9 10—DOH—12 11 10 09

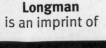
Longman
is an imprint of

www.pearsonhighered.com

ISBN-13: 978-0-205-74234-9
ISBN-10:   0-205-74234-3

BRIEF CONTENTS

CONTENTS

PREFACE

While I was revising this book for the fifth edition, "subprime" lending to U.S. borrowers who did not qualify for market interest rates became a subprime mortgage crisis. The borrowers could not repay their loans, and it was not long before the mortgage crisis evolved into a financial crisis with global dimensions. This crisis illuminates many of the key issues I discuss in the current edition. First is the globalization issue, one of the main themes of this text. Financial globalization has reached the point that banking and financial crises today often have global effects. The second issue relates to the close ties between domestic and international issues in international political economy (IPE). As this book discusses, the subprime crisis began at the domestic level, but it always had international elements; and the global repercussions have been felt domestically by investors, consumers, and workers around the world. The third issue relates to the changing role of the United States as the leading economic power (or "hegemon"). Although the subprime crisis demonstrates the centrality of the U.S. position, it also shows that the United States is becoming more dependent on others in areas such as finance. This book examines the changing U.S. position in the major areas of IPE. The fourth issue relates to the question of who is responsible for the crisis. As with most IPE issues, the allocation of "blame" depends on one's theoretical point of view. Different theorists blame the mortgage lenders; the mortgage borrowers; and the regulatory failings of the U.S. Federal Reserve, Securities and Exchange Commission, and state insurance regulators. Some theorists also blame China for manipulating its currency, sending its surplus earnings into the United States, and creating a "mortgage bubble," and others blame our capitalist-oriented global system. Some assert that no one is to blame because the crisis resulted from unanticipated domestic and international events, while others argue that all of the above groups are to blame because they (like economists who did not predict the crisis) assumed that the market would regulate itself.

This book introduces undergraduate and beginning graduate students to the complex and important issues of global political economy. I wrote the book because of a conviction that students can understand the broader implications of IPE issues only by examining them in a theoretical context. Without the organizing framework of theory, it is difficult to make sense of the growing body of facts and statistics in the global political economy. Theory helps us identify a degree of order in the complex world of IPE and enables us to go beyond description and engage in causal explanations and modest predictions. Thus, the text takes a comprehensive approach to the study of IPE, focusing on both theory and practice. To help draw connections between theory and the substantive issues, the book focuses on three major themes: globalization, North–North relations (among developed countries), and

North–South relations (among developed and developing countries). Considerable space is also devoted to the transition economies of China, Eastern Europe, and the former Soviet Union (FSU) countries, which are becoming increasingly integrated in the capitalist global political economy.

Although globalization is a major theme of the text, I do *not* claim that it is leading to a world society or world government. Indeed, considerable space is devoted to the importance of regional blocs and organizations such as the European Union (EU) and the North American Free Trade Agreement, and Chapter 8 focuses on the subject of regionalism. Furthermore, I discuss the interconnections between economic and security issues and domestic and international issues. Domestic–international interactions are generally more important in IPE than in security issues.

FEATURES

An important distinguishing feature of this book is its emphasis on the interaction between theory and practice. I believe that students understand theory better when they see its practical applications and that theory in turn gives meaning to substantive IPE issues. Chapters 3–5 provide a comprehensive overview of the most important theoretical perspectives in IPE, and Chapters 6–11 examine monetary relations, global and regional trade, multinational corporations, international development, and foreign debt and financial crises. Most importantly, Chapters 6–11 include many references to the theoretical perspectives, and each of these chapters concludes with a boxed item on "Considering IPE Theory and Practice." Another distinguishing feature of this book is its emphasis on the role of formal and informal institutions in IPE. As a result of globalization, there is a much greater need for global governance in IPE. However, it is becoming more difficult to manage the global economy, and formal and informal institutions such as the International Monetary Fund (IMF), World Bank, World Trade Organization (WTO), Group of 8 (G8), and Group of 20 (G20) are subject to numerous criticisms. In some critical areas of IPE such as the relations between states and multinational corporations, there is a notable lack of global governance. Chapter 2 introduces the institutional framework for managing the global economy, and basic organizations such as the IMF, World Bank, and WTO are discussed throughout the book. Considerable emphasis is also given to the role of private actors such as multinational corporations, nongovernmental organizations, and civil society groups in global economic governance.

A third important feature of this book is its emphasis on the historical evolution of issues. The book assumes that some historical background provides us with a better understanding of contemporary IPE issues. For example, knowing the history of the informal General Agreement on Tariffs and Trade (GATT) helps explain why the major trading countries replaced it with the formal WTO in 1995, and knowing the history of the 1980s foreign debt crisis helps explain why some developing countries are still plagued with foreign debt problems. A fourth feature is this book's treatment of North–South issues between developed and developing countries. In addition to devoting Chapters 10 and 11 mainly to North–South issues (international development, and debt and financial crises), I integrate the discussion of North–North and North–South issues throughout the book. This reflects the fact that most developing countries are becoming increasingly integrated in the capitalist global economy, and that some Southern states such as China, India, and Brazil are becoming major actors. A fifth feature is the emphasis on regional as well as global relations in IPE. One of the most controversial issues in IPE today is the proliferation of regional trade agreements, and Chapter 8 is devoted to this subject; regionalism is also discussed in other chapters. A sixth feature is the emphasis on domestic–international interactions in IPE, for example, in Chapter 4 on liberalism and Chapter 7 on global trade. One effect of globalization is the blurring of boundaries between international and domestic relations. Finally, this book discusses the broad range of IPE economic concepts as clearly as possible for students new to the subject, without oversimplifying them. To make the concepts more "user-friendly," examples are often provided. Other efforts to make this complex subject understandable to students include study and research aids such as sample questions and detailed suggestions for further reading at the end of Chapters 1–11.

NEW TO THIS EDITION

The fifth edition of this book has extensive revisions, reflecting the major changes in the global political economy (such as the current financial crisis) and the newer theoretical developments in IPE. The factual material and statistics are fully updated, and a section on *Further Reading* is now included after the Study Questions at the end of Chapters 1–11. The Further Reading section provides detailed recommendations to students and is designed to provide them with more guidance to the important literature in the field than the Bibliography provided in earlier editions.

This edition contains substantial revisions to the theoretical chapters (3–5). The chapters now compare two methods of theory construction: rational choice and constructivism. Chapter 3 on realism has a more detailed discussion of the challenge that the EU, China, and Japan pose to U.S. hegemony. Chapter 4 on liberalism contains more discussion of domestic–international interactions and two-level game theory and a revised discussion of prisoners' dilemma. The most extensive theoretical changes are in Chapter 5, which is now entitled "Critical Perspectives." The critical perspectives discussed include historical materialism, constructivism, feminism, and an entirely new section on environmentalism. Environmental theory is also applied to issues in some of the substantive chapters in Part 3.

The substantive chapters also contain major revisions. Chapter 6 on international monetary relations has a more detailed discussion of financial globalization, the future of the U.S. dollar as the key currency, and the possible future role for the euro. The chapter also introduces the issue of sovereign wealth funds and addresses the implications of the 2008 global financial crisis for U.S. foreign debt (this issue is examined in more detail in Chapter 11). Chapter 7 is now on global trade relations. It provides a clearer discussion of some trade theories (e.g., the theory of comparative advantage) and devotes more attention to the domestic politics of trade. The chapter also examines the relationship between trade and the environment and introduces the subject of "fair trade" for marginalized workers. The final section of Chapter 7, "Considering IPE Theory and Practice," focuses on competing theoretical explanations for the breakup of the WTO Doha Round, which has major implications for global trade relations. Chapter 8 on regionalism and global trade discusses fewer regional trade agreements, but provides more in-depth discussion of them. The chapter also introduces three theoretical approaches to European integration: neofunctionalism, liberal intergovernmentalism, and constructivism. The "Considering IPE Theory and Practice" section focuses on whether regional trade agreements are stepping stones or obstacles to global free trade. This is a highly contentious issue because of the collapse of the WTO Doha Round talks and the proliferation of regional trade agreements.

Chapter 9 on multinational corporations (MNCs) now discusses the corporate social responsibility concept and the relationship between foreign investment and sovereign wealth funds. The "Considering IPE Theory and Practice" section discusses competing theoretical views of corporate social responsibility. Chapter 10, on international development, adds a discussion of "bottom-up" approaches to development such as microfinance. The section on official development assistance now explores the long-term debate regarding the value versus pitfalls of foreign aid. This edition moves the discussion of foreign debt and financial crises from Chapters 7–11, because it is easier for students to understand these crises after they have read about theories of international development (now Chapter 10). Chapter 11 on foreign debt and financial crises updates the discussion of foreign debt. Most importantly, the chapter compares the recent 2008 global financial crisis with earlier financial crises.

In sum, the fifth edition of this text is fully updated and contains extensive revisions that reflect the many changes occurring in the global political economy and in the academic study of IPE.

SUPPLEMENTS

Longman is pleased to offer several resources to qualified adopters of *Global Political Economy* and their students that will make teaching and learning from this book even more effective and enjoyable.

For Instructors

MYPOLISCIKIT VIDEO CASE STUDIES FOR INTERNATIONAL RELATIONS AND COMPARATIVE POLITICS Featuring video from major news sources and providing reporting and insight on recent world affairs, this DVD series helps instructors integrate current events into their courses by letting them use the clips as lecture launchers or discussion starters.

For Students

LONGMAN ATLAS OF WORLD ISSUES (0-321-22465-5)   Introduced and selected by Robert J. Art of Brandeis University and excerpted from the acclaimed Penguin Atlas Series, the *Longman Atlas of World Issues* is designed to help students understand the geography and major issues facing the world today, such as terrorism, debt, and HIV/AIDS. These thematic, full-color maps examine forces shaping politics today at a global level. Explanatory information accompanies each map to help students better grasp the concepts being shown and how they affect our world today. Available at no additional charge when packaged with this book.

NEW SIGNET WORLD ATLAS (0-451-19732-1)   From Penguin Putnam, this pocket-sized yet detailed reference features 96 pages of full-color maps plus statistics, key data, and much more. Available at a discount when packaged with this book.

THE PENGUIN DICTIONARY OF INTERNATIONAL RELATIONS (0-140-51397-3) This indispensable reference by Graham Evans and Jeffrey Newnham includes hundreds of cross-referenced entries on the enduring and emerging theories, concepts, and events that are shaping the academic discipline of international relations and today's world politics. Available at a discount when packaged with this book.

RESEARCH AND WRITING IN INTERNATIONAL RELATIONS (0-321-27766-X) Written by Laura Roselle and Sharon Spray of Elon University, this brief and affordable guide provides the basic step-by-step process and essential resources that are needed to write political science papers that go beyond simple description and into more systematic and sophisticated inquiry. This text focuses on the key areas in which students need the most help: finding a topic, developing a question, reviewing literature, designing research, analyzing findings, and last, actually writing the paper. Available at a discount when packaged with this book.

CAREERS IN POLITICAL SCIENCE (0-321-11337-3)   Offering insider advice and practical tips on how to make the most of a political science degree, this booklet by Joel Clark of George Mason University shows students the tremendous potential such a degree offers and guides them through: deciding whether political science is right for them; the different career options available; job requirements and skill sets; how to apply, interview, and compete for jobs after graduation; and much more. Available at a discount when packaged with this book.

ACKNOWLEDGMENTS

I am grateful for the comments, advice, and support of a number of individuals in writing and revising this book. First, I want to thank Michael Webb of the University of Victoria for giving me extensive feedback and advice, especially for the first, fourth, and fifth editions. I also want to thank Mark Zacher of the University of British Columbia, and Benjamin Cohen of the University of California–Santa Barbara for providing helpful advice and comments. In addition, it is important to note that the emphasis of this IPE text on international institutions and governance owes a great deal to the interest I developed in the subject years ago when the late Professor Harold K. Jacobson was my Ph.D. supervisor. I am also indebted to the following external reviewers, whose helpful comments contributed to the various editions of this book: Sherry L. Bennett, Rice University; Vicki Birchfield, Georgia Institute of Technology; Kurt Burch, University of Delaware; Jeffrey Cason, Middlebury College; Robert A. Daley, Albertson College; Vincent Ferraro, Mount Holyoke College; David N. Gibbs, University of Arizona; Vicki L. Golich, California State University–San Marcos; Robert Griffiths, University of North Carolina at Greensboro; Beverly G. Hawk, University of Alabama at Birmingham; Michael J. Hiscox, University of California–San Diego; Tobias Hoffman, College of William and Mary; Matthias Kaelberer, University of Northern Iowa; Quan Li, Florida State University; Waltraud Q. Morales, University of Central Florida; Thomas Oatley, University of North Carolina at Chapel Hill; Howard Richards, Earlham College; David E. Spiro, University of Arizona; Kenneth P. Thomas, University of Missouri–St. Louis; John Tuman, University of Nevada, Las Vegas; Robert S. Walters, University of Pittsburgh; and Jin Zeng, Florida International University. In addition, thanks are due to several colleagues at Simon Fraser University, including James Busumtwi-Sam, Anil Hira, Stephen McBride, David Laycock, Sandra MacLean, Tsuyoshi Kawasaki, and Michael Howlett. I also want to thank Joel Fox for his assistance in preparing the tables and figures for the fifth edition.

The competent editorial staff at Longman Publishers has given active support to this book. I especially want to thank Vikram Mukhija, Toni Magyar, Kathleen Sleys, Shiny Rajesh, and Elizabeth Daniel for their time and assistance with the fifth edition. Eric Stano has been helpful and supportive for all five editions of this book, and I also want to thank Lindsey Prudhomme and Wendy Gordon. I appreciate the work that Megan Galvin-Fak, Jennie Errickson, Ellen MacElree, Anita Castro, Edward Costello, Sarah Orzalli, Ken Harrell, and Kent Martin put into earlier editions.

My acknowledgments would not be complete without mentioning the important role of my students over the years in asking insightful questions, raising important issues, and providing feedback on the aspects of IPE they found clear or confusing. I also want to thank Pierre Dansereau, Marco Lilliu, and Kenneth Abramson for computer and other help at various junctures. My sons Daniel and Frank gave me assistance in various areas, and I appreciate their patience over the years with my extended working hours. Finally, I am dedicating this book to my wife Shirley, for her caring advice, support, and encouragement. She makes it all seem so much more meaningful and worthwhile.

Theodore H. Cohn

ACRONYMS AND ABBREVIATIONS

ACP: African, Caribbean, and Pacific

ADD: antidumping duty

AFTA: ASEAN Free Trade Area

AID: Agency for International Development

AIDS: acquired immunodeficiency syndrome

ASEAN: Association of Southeast Asian Nations

BIS: Bank for International Settlements

BITs: bilateral investment treaties

BRIC: Brazil, Russia, India, and China

CACM: Central American Common Market

CAP: Common Agricultural Policy

CARICOM: Caribbean Community and Common Market

CDF: Comprehensive Development Framework

CEECs: Central and Eastern European countries

CFIUS: Committee on Foreign Investment in the United States

CIS: Commonwealth of Independent States

CMEA: Council for Mutual Economic Assistance

COCOM: Coordinating Committee

CPE: centrally planned economy

CRTA: Committee on Regional Trade Agreements

CU: customs union

CUSFTA: Canada–U.S. Free Trade Agreement

CVD: countervailing duty

DC: developed country

DISC: Domestic International Sales Corporation

EBRD: European Bank for Reconstruction and Development

EC: European Community

ECB: European Central Bank

ECSC: European Coal and Steel Community

ECU: European currency unit

EDF: European Development Fund

EFTA: European Free Trade Association

EMS: European Monetary System

EMU: European Economic and Monetary Union

ERM: exchange-rate mechanism

EU: European Union

Euratom: European Atomic Energy Community

FDI: foreign direct investment

FIRA: Foreign Investment Review Agency

FSU: former Soviet Union

FTA: free trade area

G5: Group of Five

G7: Group of Seven

G8: Group of Eight

G10: Group of 10

G20: Group of 20

G24: Group of 24

G77: Group of 77

GAB: General Arrangements to Borrow

GATS: General Agreement on Trade in Services

GATT: General Agreement on Tariffs and Trade

GDP: gross domestic product

GNI: gross national income

GNP: gross national product

GSP: generalized system of preferences

HDI: human development index

HIPC: heavily indebted poor countries

HIV: human immunodeficiency virus

IBRD: International Bank for Reconstruction and Development (World Bank)

ICSID: International Centre for Settlement of Investment Disputes

IDA: International Development Association

IDB: Inter-American Development Bank

IFC: International Finance Corporation

IMF: International Monetary Fund

IO: international organization

IPE: international political economy

IR: international relations

ISI: import substitution industrialization

ITO: International Trade Organization

KIEO: keystone international economic organization

LAFTA: Latin American Free Trade Association

LDC: less-developed country

LIC: low-income country

LLDC: least developed country

M&As: mergers and acquisitions

MAI: Multilateral Agreement on Investment

MDRI: Multilateral Debt Relief Initiative

Mercosur: Southern Common Market Treaty

MFA: Multi-Fiber Arrangement

MFN: most favored nation

MIC: middle-income country

MIGA: Multilateral Investment Guarantee Agency

MNC: multinational corporation

MTN: multilateral trade negotiation

NAFTA: North American Free Trade Agreement

NATO: North Atlantic Treaty Organization

NEM: New Economic Mechanism

NEP: National Energy Program

NGO: nongovernmental organization

NIE: newly industrializing economy

NIEO: New International Economic Order

NTB: nontariff barrier

ODA: official development assistance

ODF: official development finance

OECD: Organization for Economic Cooperation and Development

OEEC: Organization for European Economic Cooperation

OPEC: Organization of Petroleum Exporting Countries

PPP: purchasing power parity

PRC: People's Republic of China

R&D: research and development

RTA: regional trade agreement

RTAA: Reciprocal Trade Agreements Act

SAL: structural adjustment loan

SAP: structural adjustment program

SDRs: special drawing rights

SDT: special and differential treatment

SEA: Single European Act

STABEX: Stabilization of Export Earnings

TAN: transnational advocacy network

TFN: transnational feminist network

TOA: Treaty of Asunción

TRIMs: Trade-Related Investment Measures

TRIPs: Trade-Related Intellectual Property Rights

UN: United Nations

UNCTAD: United Nations Conference on Trade and Development

UNCTC: United Nations Center on Transnational Corporations

UNDP: United Nations Development Program

USTR: U.S. Trade Representative

WEF: World Economic Forum

WTO: World Trade Organization

PART ONE

Introduction and Overview

Many personal decisions we make have economic importance for us, whether we are choosing a career, investing in stocks, or purchasing goods. Collective political decisions also affect us economically. For example, government decisions may affect tax rates, welfare payments, and the priority given to economic, social, and environmental goals. As global interdependence has increased, decision making by **multinational corporations (MNCs)** and international organizations such as the **World Trade Organization (WTO)** also has a greater economic impact on us. Thus, *international political economy (IPE)* is an important area of study. Chapter 1 introduces the subject of IPE, the IPE theoretical perspectives, and the main themes of this book. Chapter 2 provides an overview of global economic relations before World War II, and the postwar institutional framework developed to manage the global economy. For ease of reference, all terms defined in the glossary are initially in **bold print,** while terms defined only in the text are in *italics*.

CHAPTER 1

Introduction

The study of IPE requires factual knowledge in a wide range of areas such as trade, monetary relations, foreign investment, and development. However, people interpret the "facts" quite differently depending on whether they view them "from a bank office in Zurich, a *maquiladora* [border factory] in Mexico, a shantytown in Peru, a rice paddy in Sri Lanka . . . [or] a trade office in Washington, D.C."[1] Our interpretation of the facts also depends on our theoretical views, and the only choice is whether these views are implicit or whether we explicitly examine the theories we use to interpret issues and events. Our theoretical views also determine what facts we consider important. For example, realist theorists often focus on the power relations among developed countries (DCs) in the North, while many critical theorists argue that the North's exploitation of less-developed countries (LDCs) in the South is a more pressing issue. Although people tend to interact with those who share their views, becoming familiar with other perspectives gives us a more complete picture of the world. Thus, the development of knowledge in IPE has been shaped by some "great debates" among theorists.[2] This book emphasizes the juxtaposition between the theory and practice of IPE; theory shapes the practice of IPE, and practical experience leads to a reassessment of theory. Before introducing the main theoretical perspectives and themes of this book, we address the question "what is IPE?"

WHAT IS INTERNATIONAL POLITICAL ECONOMY?

IPE is concerned with the interaction between the **state,** a sovereign territorial unit, and the **market,** a coordinating mechanism where buyers and sellers exchange goods and services at prices and output levels determined by supply and demand. We normally associate the state with the political pursuit of power, and the market with the economic pursuit of wealth. However, the state also has an interest in accumulating wealth, and the market is not totally removed from power considerations. An inherent tension exists between the state and the market because the market's association with economic openness and the removal of state barriers poses a threat to state sovereignty.[3] For example, the 1988 **Canada–U.S. Free Trade Agreement (CUSFTA)** established an open market between the two countries, which some Canadians considered a threat to their national sovereignty in energy, foreign investment, and cultural industries. When the **North American Free Trade Agreement (NAFTA)** replaced CUSFTA in 1994, Mexicans were concerned that it would encroach on their sovereignty in energy and agriculture, and many Americans feared that NAFTA would limit their control over employment and the environment. Despite the tension between states and markets, they also have a complementary relationship. Domestically, states protect private property rights and provide **infrastructure** such as transportation and communications required for market transactions. Internationally, states form agreements and organizations to promote economic openness and stability; and wealthier states with larger markets often have more military and political power. As interdependence has increased, states have been drawn into the competitive forces of the world economy. Thus, *competition states* seek to increase their competitiveness by restructuring industry, deregulating financial markets, and supporting research and development (R&D) in high-technology sectors.[4] As we discuss, the rapid economic growth of Japan and the East Asian newly industrializing economies (NIEs) from the 1960s to 1980s was related to their symbiotic relationship with the competitive marketplace.

Although most scholars treat state–market interactions as the core IPE issue, they are also interested in other types of relationships. Primary among these is the interaction between the state and the multinational corporation (MNC), the main nonstate actor with which the state must contend. In 2006 there were about 70,000 MNCs with 780,000 foreign affiliates, whose sales were greater than $25 trillion. Almost a third of world exports take place within the networks of MNC foreign affiliates.[5] As is the case with states and markets, state–MNC relations are marked by both cooperation and conflict (see Chapter 9). Whether we focus on state–market or state–MNC relations, IPE is interdisciplinary and draws on contributions from political scientists, economists, sociologists, anthropologists, historians, and geographers. In their effort to cross disciplinary boundaries, IPE theorists criticize some economists for **economism** (i.e., for focusing too much on economics and too little on politics) and some political scientists for **politicism** (i.e., for devoting too much attention to politics and too little to economics).[6] In addition to doing interdisciplinary work at the international level, IPE scholars must also devote considerable attention to domestic–international linkages. Whereas domestic groups generally leave decision making on security matters to the government "experts," they demand a greater role in economic decision making because they view trade and foreign investment as "bread and butter issues" that affect their economic welfare. In sum, IPE scholars have the daunting task of focusing on both international and domestic relations and of crossing disciplinary boundaries.

THE IPE THEORETICAL PERSPECTIVES

Many students tend to avoid "theory," but without it we are unable to assess the broader implications of our statistical and factual studies. (We discuss the purpose of theory in greater detail in the introduction to Part II.) IPE has been marked by a growing diversity of theories, and some critics point to our failure to develop an all-embracing theory to explain events. However, the existence of different theoretical perspectives should not be viewed as a weakness. Social science theory "is always *for* someone and *for* some purpose,"[7] and the IPE theoretical perspectives will never be entirely compatible because they are based on different sets of values. When IPE emerged as a major field of study in the 1970s, the three dominant perspectives were realism (or economic nationalism), liberalism, and Marxism, and IPE theorists tended to view them as separate "ideologies."[8] This book adopts a more updated approach to IPE theory in several respects. First, we do not view the IPE perspectives as separate ideologies, and we examine how they overlap and influence each other over time. Second, we view Marxism as less important today and supplement the third perspective with several "critical" perspectives. Some theorists question the value of using this typology for examining IPE theory today, but we believe it is still useful because realism and liberalism continue to be the two mainstream perspectives with the most influence on the practice of IPE.[9] Chapters 3 and 4 of this book focus on realism and liberalism, and Chapter 5 examines several perspectives that are critical of the two mainstream IPE perspectives.

Realists consider the state to be the principal actor in international relations (IR). IR is a "self-help" system without a centralized authority in which states must build up their power or form alliances to prevent being dominated by others. Thus, realists often see IR as a *zero-sum game,* in which one state's gain is another state's loss, and they emphasize *relative gains* or the gains a state achieves in relation to the gains of other states. In IPE each state will try to manipulate the market to capture relative gains. Although realism traditionally has been the most important IR perspective, liberalism is the most important IPE perspective. To avoid confusion, we should note that the term *liberal* is used differently in IPE and in U.S. domestic politics. In the United States, "liberals" support greater government involvement in the market to prevent inequalities and stimulate growth, while "conservatives" support free markets and minimal government intervention. Orthodox liberals in IPE are more akin to U.S. conservatives, because they favor free markets, private property rights, and only a limited government role in economic activities. However, Keynesian liberals are more accepting of government intervention (see Chapter 4). Liberals are more optimistic than realists about the prospects for cooperation among states, and they believe that international institutions can help promote cooperation. Thus, liberals view economic relationships as a *positive-sum game,* in which all states benefit, even if they do not benefit equally.

Chapter 5 of this book introduces several *critical perspectives* that are critical of the mainstream liberal and realist perspectives. They question the mainstream's view of the world, and see the mainstream as favoring some groups or issues and marginalizing others. The *historical materialist* perspective encompasses the largest group of critical theories. Stemming partly from Marxism, historical materialism is "historical" because it examines structural change over time, with an emphasis on class and sometimes North–South struggles. The perspective is "materialist" because it examines the role of material factors, especially economic factors, in shaping society.[10] The current system is marked by the dominance of capitalism, with the capitalist class (the bourgeoisie) exploiting the workers (the proletariat). In addition to historical materialism, Chapter 5 also discusses the *social constructivist, feminist,* and *environmental perspectives.*

Although the realist, liberal, and critical perspectives provide us with alternative lenses for viewing IPE issues (such as trade and monetary relations), it is important to note that the margins separating these perspectives have become blurred as they have evolved and influenced each other over time. Hybrid theories and approaches such as regime theory, hegemonic stability theory, and constructivism are also linked with more than one perspective. Furthermore, the literature examining the relationship between domestic institutions and IPE does not fit easily into any one of the three perspectives. In addition to the three main theoretical perspectives, this book discusses the hybrid theories and approaches, and domestic–international interactions.

PURPOSES AND THEMES OF THIS BOOK

This book provides a comprehensive approach to the study of IPE. Part II discusses the theoretical perspectives, and Part III examines substantive issues including global and regional trade, monetary relations, investment, development, and foreign debt and financial crises. To understand the broader implications of these issues, the chapters in Part III direct the reader to the interaction between theory and practice. To help draw connections between theory and the substantive issues, this book focuses on three major themes: globalization, North–North relations, and North–South relations.

Globalization

The first theme of this book is *globalization,* which involves the broadening and deepening of interactions and interdependence among peoples and states. Broadening refers to the extension of geographic linkages to encompass virtually all major societies and states, so that policies and events in one part of the world can have a significant impact on distant locations. Deepening refers to the greater frequency and intensity of state and societal interactions. Although the state continues to be the most important actor in IR, modern telecommunications and rapid transportation have increased connections among people with less regard to territorial boundaries. Thus, states are confronting a more complex environment in which international organizations (IOs), MNCs, and nongovernmental organizations (NGOs) have important roles. Theorists do not define globalization in a consistent manner, and they have differing views regarding the causes and effects of globalization. Whereas some theorists argue that globalization stems from technological advances, others emphasize the role of the state, the capitalist mode of production, and cultural and social-psychological factors.[11] We discuss the different definitions of globalization here, and focus more on the causes and effects of globalization in Chapters 3–5.

At one end of the spectrum are *extreme* or *hyper-globalists,* who believe that globalization involves the creation of a "borderless world" in which national economies are being subsumed under regional and global markets, and MNCs are losing their national identities. For example, Kenichi Ohmae asserts in *The End of the Nation-State* that "traditional nation states have become unnatural, even impossible, business units in a global economy."[12] When there is no longer state interference, Ohmae argues, MNC decisions and consumer choices will result in the rational allocation of global resources. We devote more attention to the views of *internationalists* and *moderate globalists* than to hyper-globalists, because there is little evidence that globalization is causing the state to wither away.[13] *Internationalists* are at the other end of the spectrum from hyper-globalists. Although they recognize that interdependence is increasing and that nonstate actors have a role in IPE, they see the world as being no more international than it was in some earlier periods such as the nineteenth century. The international economy in the view of internationalists "is still fundamentally characterized by exchange between relatively distinct and national economies."[14] Although some internationalists acknowledge that globalization today may be different because of the greater speed and volume of transactions, they see globalization mainly as an economic phenomenon and argue that "in most areas of world politics . . . states are still the principal authorities."[15] Internationalists view the disastrous events of September 11, 2001 and the subsequent increase in U.S. unilateralism as evidence that globalization has not produced significant change, and that geopolitics, violence, and the national interest continue to be central concerns.[16]

Moderate globalists take a position between hyper-globalists and internationalists. Although they reject the hyper-globalist view that the state is no longer a viable actor, they differentiate IR among states from global relations that take place without regard to territorial boundaries. Global linkages in finance, trade, investment, and communications have existed in the past, but they now occur more frequently, intensely, and on a wider scale. For example, the Internet provides instantaneous linkages around the world; MNCs control economic resources greater than those of many states; and global problems such as ozone depletion, climate change, money laundering, and market volatility are increasing. Although states continue to be important, they must share the stage with private actors such as MNCs and NGOs, and with systems of transnational, global, and regional governance. Nevertheless, the world is *globalizing,* rather than fully *globalized,* and territorial and supraterritorial relations coexist today.[17]

This book provides evidence that both the internationalist and moderate globalist positions have some validity, depending on the issue areas and countries being studied. Relying on these two approaches, we briefly discuss some important points about globalization:

- Globalization is not a uniform process throughout the world. Its effects are more evident in major urban centers than in rural areas, remote islands, and the poorest countries.
- Globalization is *not* causing the state to wither away. Although the state's autonomy is eroding in some important respects, states are adopting new and more complex functions to deal with an interdependent world and they continue to have choices in responding to globalization.[18]
- Globalization can result in fragmentation and conflict as well as unity and cooperation; for example, an increase in global **competitiveness** has led to the formation of regional economic blocs in Europe, North America, and East Asia. Although competitiveness is a "contested concept" with various meanings, this book shows that it causes states to be concerned with their relative positions in the global economy.[19]
- Interdependence and globalization are not unique to the present-day world, and it is possible that international events could reverse the current moves toward globalization. For example, there was a high degree of interdependence in trade and foreign investment before World War I which declined during the interwar period and began to increase again after World War II.

Despite the historical fluctuations, globalization is more encompassing today than it was at any time in the past. With advances in technology, communications, and transportation, state activities are being internationalized to a degree not previously experienced. For example, the cost of international telephone calls fell by more than 90 percent from 1970 to 1990, shipping costs fell by more than two-thirds between 1920 and 1990, and airline operating costs per mile fell by 60 percent from 1960 to 1990.[20] Global interdependence today is also *qualitatively* different than previously. Although a number of corporations globalized their activities during the nineteenth century, the role of MNCs in generating foreign investment, trade, and technology is a modern-day phenomenon.[21] The geographic reach of the capitalist economic system is also encompassing the entire globe, with LDCs and the transition economies of Eastern Europe and the former Soviet Union (FSU) becoming more involved in the global economy. For the first time, membership in the IMF, World Bank, and WTO is becoming truly global.[22] This book examines the implications of these changes and the differing views as to whether globalization is a positive or negative process.

North–North Relations

The second theme of this book concerns relations among the DCs in the North. The DCs in Western Europe, North America, and Japan are the only group of states with the wealth and power to look after international management of the global economy. Thus, international management has been primarily a North–North issue, even though emerging LDCs in the South such as China, India, and Brazil are posing a challenge to Northern management in some areas such as international trade. This book discusses two factors that contribute to international economic management: hegemony and international institutions.

The United States was the undisputed leader or *hegemon* in the early post–World War II period because of its economic and military power. An important measure of economic power is the **gross domestic product (GDP),** the total value of goods and services produced within a country's borders during a given year. The GDP records income in terms of where it is earned rather than who owns the factors of production. Thus, a country's GDP includes the interest and profits domestic and foreign companies and individuals earn in the country; it does *not* include income the country's residents earn abroad. In contrast to the GDP, the **gross national product (GNP)** records income according to who owns the factors of production rather than where the income is earned. Thus, the GNP is the total value of goods and services produced by domestically owned factors of production in a given year. GNP is derived by adding the income a country's residents earn from foreign activity to the GDP and subtracting the income foreigners earn from activity in the country. For example, the income a U.S. resident earns in France is part of the U.S. GNP but not the U.S. GDP. On the other hand, this income is included in the French GDP but not in the French GNP. A number of states and IOs now use a third indicator of total output, the **gross national income (GNI),** instead of the GNP. In practical terms *the GNI is equal to the GNP*—it simply measures the income produced by the GNP rather than the value of the product itself.[23] This book usually uses the GDP, because most countries use the GDP as their main measure of national economic activity. However, a country's GDP and GNI (or GNP) normally do not differ greatly, and we use all of these measures, depending on the source of the data. Whether we use the GDP or GNI, the United States was clearly the economic hegemon after World War II. During the war the U.S. GDP had increased by about 50 percent, whereas Western European states had lost one-quarter of their GDPs on average and the Soviet Union and Japanese economies were severely damaged. In 1950 the U.S. GDP was about 3 times larger than the Soviet Union's, 5 times larger than Britain's, and 20 times larger than Japan's. Western Europe and Japan were also highly dependent on U.S. aid and foreign investment for postwar reconstruction.[24]

During the 1960s the United States' *relative* economic position vis-à-vis other DCs began to decline as Western Europe and Japan recovered from the war. The extent of the U.S. economic decline and the possibilities for U.S. hegemonic renewal are matters of intense debate, partly because IR theorists often focus on different aspects of hegemony. In the *security* area, for example, U.S. hegemony has clearly increased since the breakup of the Soviet bloc and Soviet Union. However, most would agree that the relative *economic* power of the United States has declined since the end of World War II. In 1971 the United States shifted from having annual balance-of-trade surpluses to having balance-of-trade deficits (i.e., imports greater than exports), the United States has become a major recipient as well as a source of foreign direct investment, and the euro is posing a challenge to the U.S. dollar's supremacy as the top international currency. The United States remains a major force in the global economy, and in 2004 it accounted for about 25 percent of world GDP.[25] However, this book discusses the fact that the relative U.S. economic decline has resulted in a gradual shift from unilateral U.S. to collective management of the global economy.

The second factor in global economic management is the role of international institutions. Under U.S. and British leadership, three international economic organizations were established in the 1940s to help manage the global economy: the **International Monetary Fund (IMF),** the International Bank for Reconstruction and Development (IBRD or World Bank), and the **General Agreement on Tariffs and Trade (GATT).** The DCs were the dominant economic powers in these organizations, and they also created some smaller institutions largely limited to DC membership, including the **Organization for Economic Cooperation and Development (OECD)** and the **Group of Seven (G7)/Group of Eight (G8).** In 1995 the WTO replaced the GATT as the main global trade organization. This book examines the role of these institutions in managing the global economy.

Despite the joint efforts of DCs to manage the global economy, they also have some significant differences. Three major economic blocs have emerged in Europe, North America, and East Asia with the decline of U.S. economic hegemony and the demise of the Cold War. The competitiveness among these three blocs has major consequences for the future of the global economy because they encompass much of the world's economic, technological, scientific, and military power.[26] Differences over security issues such as the 2003 U.S.-led war against Iraq have further exacerbated the divisions among DCs on economic issues. Thus, the second theme of this text concerns the linkages and divisions among the DCs of the North.

North–South Relations

The third theme of this book concerns North–South relations. The South includes almost all the countries of Latin America and the Caribbean, Asia and Oceania, and Africa and the Middle East. These countries are mainly LDCs with colonial histories and lower levels of economic and social development. In 1950 the South accounted for almost 65 percent of the total world population, and by 1996 this figure had climbed to almost 80 percent of the world total. A number of previously Communist states in Eastern Europe and the FSU are now receiving foreign debt and development financing from the DCs and are, in effect, also a part of the South. When we speak of the world, we therefore must give a great deal of attention to the South.[27]

Economically, LDCs generally have lower per capita incomes, inadequate infrastructure (e.g., transportation and communications), and limited access to modern technology. Many LDCs also have lower levels of social development such as inadequate educational facilities, health and sanitary facilities, and literacy rates. Assessing political development in a country is a difficult and contentious issue; but LDCs are more likely than DCs to have unstable and authoritarian governments.[28] LDCs also have less influence in most international economic organizations such as the IMF, World Bank, and WTO. It is important to note that many IOs and development theorists prefer the term *developing countries* to *LDCs* because they believe the *LDC* term suggests that these countries are inferior or are expected to follow the same path to development as the DCs. However, LDC is used as an abbreviation in this book simply to indicate that these countries are *economically* less developed. LDCs may have histories and cultures as rich or richer than those of DCs.

As this book shows, LDCs in fact have become a highly diverse group of countries with major differences in income and economic development. Some analysts therefore question whether it is meaningful to speak of the South or LDCs as a single group. On the one hand, the East Asian NIEs—South Korea, Taiwan, Singapore, and Hong Kong—have relatively high per capita incomes and literacy rates and are quite competitive with DCs in some areas. Some of the larger LDCs and transition economies such as the *BRIC economies*—Brazil, Russia, India, and China—also have a growing degree of political and economic influence. On the other hand, the UN list of 50 *least developed countries (LLDCs)*—mainly in Sub-Saharan Africa and Central Asia—have extremely low per capita incomes, literacy rates, and shares of manufacturing. One analyst argues that 4 billion of the 5 billion people in LDCs today live in countries that are in fact developing. However, the "bottom billion" people in the world—most of whom are in LLDCs—are caught in a "development trap" and falling further behind.[29]

Despite the South's socioeconomic disparities, we can generalize about LDC development problems because a major characteristic of the global economy is the inequality in wealth and power between DCs in the North and most LDCs in the South. The 1 billion people in DCs account for about 80 percent of the world's GDP, and the 5 billion people in LDCs account for the remaining 20 percent.[30] Although a number of LDCs have been developing, most have been frustrated in their efforts to exert more influence and close the economic gap with the North. Furthermore, the East Asian success stories are unusual in several respects. Singapore and Hong Kong are so small geographically that they are more akin to city-states, Hong Kong was a British crown colony before being incorporated into mainland China, and Taiwan and South Korea are contested territories. Although China, India, and Brazil have growing economic and political influence, they have major problems to overcome; even the East

Asian NIEs have been vulnerable to financial crises (see Chapters 10 and 11). Thus, in 2005 the United Nations Development Program reported that

> most developing regions are falling behind, not catching up with, rich countries. Moreover, convergence is a relative concept. Absolute income inequalities between rich and poor countries are increasing even when developing countries have higher growth rates—precisely because the initial income gaps are so large. . . . If average incomes grow by 3 percent in Sub-Saharan Africa and in high-income Europe, for example, the absolute change will be an extra $51 per person in Africa and an extra $854 per person in Europe.[31]

This book explores the strategies LDCs have employed to promote economic development and increase their influence.

Although we focus mainly on inequalities between the North and the South, the global economy is also marked by differences of wealth and power *within* states. Brazil has one of the largest income gaps among LDCs, with the per capita income of the richest 10 percent of the population 32 times higher than that of the poorest 40 percent.[32] As Chapter 10 discusses, some groups within LDCs such as women and children are especially disadvantaged. (Disparities in wealth are of course also present within DCs.) This book discusses the effects of changes in the global economy on inequalities between rich and poor both among and within states. We also devote considerable space to the transition economies that are liberalizing as a result of the breakup of the Soviet bloc and Soviet Union. However, East–West relations are not a major theme of this book because the Cold War has virtually ended and the transition economies are becoming more integrated in the capitalist global economy. Chapters 3–5 show that IPE theorists have different interpretations of the main themes in this book. In regard to North–North relations, liberals are more inclined than realists or critical theorists to see international institutions as having a positive role in promoting international economic cooperation. In regard to North–South relations and gender-based relations, critical theorists place more emphasis than liberals or realists on inequalities and exploitation. In regard to globalization, realists emphasize the centrality of the state; liberals believe that globalization is an important and beneficial process; and historical materialists also view globalization as significant, but as having negative consequences for poorer people, LDCs, and those marginalized because of gender, race, and ethnicity.

FOCUS OF THIS BOOK

This book introduces undergraduate and graduate students to the study of IPE, and some of its distinguishing features have already been discussed. First, it provides an in-depth background to IPE theory, current IPE issues in historical perspective, and the interplay between theory and practice. Without the organizing framework of theory, discussions about trade, foreign investment, and development become simply a series of disparate facts. Although we devote considerable attention to the mainstream perspectives of liberalism and realism, we do not accept the view that the breakup of the Soviet bloc marked an "end of history" leading to "the universalization of Western liberal democracy as the final form of human government."[33] Thus, we also examine critical perspectives such as historical materialism. Second, we focus on three themes relating to globalization, North–North relations, and North–South relations. Third, we emphasize the role of global organizations such as the WTO, IMF, and World Bank, and regional organizations such as the **European Union (EU),** NAFTA, and **Mercosur** (the Southern Common Market Treaty). Early scholarship on international organization had a strong idealistic and legal focus on the bodies and rules of the League of Nations and United Nations, and post–World War II realists pointed out that these studies did not deal with the real world of power politics. In recent years, scholars have recognized the need to study IOs as part of the realities of international politics, and we devote attention to the limitations as well as the strengths of international economic organizations.[34] IOs are to a large degree creatures of the states that created them, and they are having difficulty managing the international economy in an age of globalization. Indeed, the daily flows of foreign exchange on global markets are much greater than the total resources of the United Nations, World Bank, and IMF. Despite their limitations, IOs are important forums for negotiation that assist in upholding the principles, norms, and rules of the global economy.

Fourth, this book emphasizes regional as well as global relations in IPE. The current trends toward regionalism inevitably affect the management of the global economy, and this book devotes Chapter 8 to regionalism and globalism in trade. With the formation of NAFTA, "the trade and economic relations of the two largest markets in world trade—the European Community and the United States—are increasingly conditioned by regional agreements."[35] LDCs have also established regional trade agreements (RTAs), and two of the largest South American countries, Brazil and Argentina, are members of Mercosur. In addition to these larger RTAs, countries ranging from the United States to Japan and Singapore are negotiating a number of bilateral free trade agreements. Although liberal scholars believe that RTAs such as the EU and NAFTA may be "stepping stones" to global free trade, they fear that the many smaller bilateral RTAs could impede global trade liberalization. Chapter 8 discusses the debate on this issue, and other chapters examine regional trends in monetary relations, foreign investment, and international development. Of particular interest is the *relationship between* regionalism and globalism in IPE.

Fifth, this book focuses on North–South issues, and it integrates the North–North and North–South discussions as much as possible for several reasons. The IPE theoretical perspectives should be assessed in terms of their approach to *all* countries, and Chapters 3–5 therefore discuss each perspective's approach to North–South as well as North–North issues. Part III also integrates the discussion of North–North and North–South relations because globalization in trade, foreign investment, and monetary relations is affecting the entire world. Two chapters are devoted mainly to the South: Chapter 10 examines LDC strategies to promote economic development, and Chapter 11 on foreign debt and financial crises focuses mainly on LDCs, but it also discusses the North and the former Soviet bloc countries. Sixth, this book discusses the "transition economies" of Eastern Europe, the FSU, and China, which are in transition from centrally planned to market economies. They are establishing closer economic ties with the DCs and becoming more active members of international economic organizations. Seventh, this book examines the challenges civil society groups and NGOs are posing to globalization and the policies of the IMF, World Bank, and WTO. Finally, we devote some attention to the linkages between international economic and security issues. Events such as the end of the Cold War and the 2001 terrorist attacks on the U.S. World Trade Center highlight the degree to which security and economic issues are often closely intertwined.

Chapter 2 provides an overview of the history and institutions of the postwar international economic order; Chapters 3–5 discuss the basic assumptions and historical evolution of the IPE theoretical perspectives; and Chapters 6–11 cover monetary relations, global trade, trade regionalism, MNCs, international development, and foreign debt and financial crises. Study questions at the end of Chapters 1–11 cover the main issues in each chapter.

Questions

1. What is IPE, and why have IPE scholars criticized some economists and some political scientists?
2. What is the relationship between "the state" and "the market"?
3. What is the importance of theory, and what are some of the main theoretical perspectives in IPE?
4. What are the hyper-globalist, moderate globalist, and internationalist views of globalization? Which group's views do you find most convincing?
5. Why has the North been so important in the management of the global economy?
6. What are the East Asian NIEs, the BRIC economies, and the LLDCs? What do these groups tell us about economic disparities *within* the South?

Further Reading

A groundbreaking study in IPE is Robert Gilpin with Jean M. Gilpin, *The Political Economy of International Relations* (Princeton, NJ: Princeton University Press), 1987.

Two useful studies on approaches to theorizing in IPE and IR are Thomas J. Biersteker, "Evolving Perspectives on International Political Economy: Twentieth-Century Contexts and Discontinuities," *International Political Science Review* 14, no. 1 (January 1993), pp. 7–33; and James N. Rosenau and Mary Durfee, *Thinking Theory Thoroughly,* 2nd ed. (Boulder, CO: Westview Press, 2000), chs. 1 and 9.

Recent studies on globalization from different perspectives include Jagdish Bhagwati, *In Defense of Globalization* (New York: Oxford University Press, 2004); Martin Wolf, *Why Globalization Works* (New Haven, CN: Yale University Press, 2004); David Held and Anthony McGrew, *Globalization/Anti-Globalization: Beyond the Great Divide,* 2nd ed. (Malden, MA: Polity Press, 2007); David Held and Anthony McGrew, eds., *Globalization Theory: Approaches and Controversies* (Malden, MA: Polity Press, 2007); Jan Aart Scholte, *Globalization: A Critical Introduction,* 2nd ed. (New York: Palgrave Macmillan, 2005); Michael M. Weinstein, *Globalization: What's New* (New York: Columbia University Press, 2005); Ngaire Woods, *The Globalizers: The IMF, the World Bank and Their Borrowers* (Ithaca, NY: Cornell University Press, 2006); and Linda Weiss, *The Myth of the Powerless State* (Ithaca, NY: Cornell University Press, 1998).

Notes

1. James A. Caporaso, "Global Political Economy," in Ada Finifter, ed., *Political Science: The State of the Discipline II* (Washington, D.C.: American Political Science Association, 1993), p. 451.
2. Ole Wæver, "The Sociology of a Not So International Discipline: American and European Developments in International Relations," *International Organization* 52, no. 4 (Autumn 1998), p. 715; Margaret G. Hermann, "One Field, Many Perspectives: Building the Foundations for Dialogue," *International Studies Quarterly* 42, no. 4 (December 1998), pp. 605–624.
3. Robert Gilpin, with Jean M. Gilpin, *The Political Economy of International Relations* (Princeton, NJ: Princeton University Press, 1987), pp. 8–11.
4. Philip G. Cerny, *The Changing Architecture of Politics: Structure, Agency and the Future of the State* (London: Sage, 1990), pp. 228–229; Philip G. Cerny, "Paradoxes of the Competition State: The Dynamics of Political Globalization," *Government and Opposition* 32, no. 2 (April 1997), pp. 251–274.
5. United Nations Conference on Trade and Development (UNCTAD), *World Investment Report 2007* (New York: United Nations, 2007), pp. xvi and 9; Lorraine Eden, "Bringing the Firm Back In: Multinationals in International Political Economy," in Lorraine Eden and Evan H. Potter, eds., *Multinationals in the Global Political Economy* (New York: St. Martin's Press, 1993), p. 26.
6. Richard K. Ashley, "Three Modes of Economism," *International Studies Quarterly* 27, no. 4 (December 1983), p. 463; Colin Hay and David Marsh, "Introduction: Towards a New (International) Political Economy?" *New Political Economy* 4, no. 1 (1999), pp. 9–10.
7. Robert W. Cox, "Social Forces, States and World Orders: Beyond International Theory," *Millennium* 10, no. 2 (1981), p. 128. See also Roger Tooze, "Perspectives and Theory: A Consumer's Guide," in Susan Strange, ed., *Paths to International Political Economy* (London: Allen & Unwin, 1984), pp. 3–4.
8. Robert Gilpin is credited with identifying these three perspectives in IPE. See Robert Gilpin, *U.S. Power and the Multinational Corporation: The Political Economy of Foreign Direct Investment* (New York: Basic Books, 1975); Gilpin, *The Political Economy of International Relations,* ch. 2.
9. For example, see Matthew Watson, "Theoretical Traditions in Global Political Economy," in John Ravenhill, ed., *Global Political Economy,* 2nd ed. (New York: Oxford University Press, 2008), pp. 27–66.

10. Mark Rupert and Hazel Smith, eds., *Historical Materialism and Globalization* (New York: Routledge, 2002). Some historical materialists are interested in the relationship between ideas and material circumstances. See Robert W. Cox with Michael G. Schechter, *The Political Economy of a Plural World: Critical Refllections on Power, Morals and Civilization* (New York: Routledge, 2002), pp. 26–27.
11. Jan Aart Scholte, *Globalization: A Critical Introduction,* 2nd ed. (New York: Palgrave Macmillan, 2005); Aseem Prakash and Jeffrey A. Hart, "Globalization and Governance: An Introduction," in Aseem Prakash and Jeffrey A. Hart, eds., *Globalization and Governance* (London: Routledge, 1999), pp. 4–17.
12. Kenichi Ohmae, *The End of the Nation State: The Rise of Regional Economies* (New York: Free Press, 1995), p. 5.
13. Linda Weiss, ed., *States in the Global Economy: Bringing Domestic Institutions Back In* (Cambridge: Cambridge University Press, 2003), p. 3, ch. 1.
14. Paul Hirst and Grahame Thompson, *Globalization in Question: The International Economy and the Possibilities of Governance,* 2nd ed. (Cambridge, MA: Polity Press, 1999), p. 7.
15. Buzan in Barry Buzan, David Held, and Anthony McGrew, "Realism vs Cosmopolitanism," *Review of International Studies* 24, no. 3 (July 1998), p. 392.
16. David Held and Anthony McGrew, *Globalization/Anti-Globalization: Beyond the Great Divide,* 2nd ed. (Malden MA: Polity Press, 2007), pp. 6–8.
17. Scholte, *Globalization: A Critical Introduction,* pp. 59–75.
18. Philip G. Cerny, "Globalization and Other Stories: The Search for a New Paradigm for International Relations," *International Journal* 51, no. 4 (Autumn 1996), pp. 617–637.
19. David P. Rapkin and Jonathan R. Strand, "Competitiveness: Useful Concept, Political Slogan, or Dangerous Obsession?" in David P. Rapkin and William P. Avery, eds., *National Competitiveness in a Global Economy* (Boulder, CO: Rienner, 1995), pp. 1–20.
20. United Nations Development Program (UNDP), *Human Development Report 1997* (New York: Oxford University Press, 1997), p. 83; Buzan, Held, and McGrew, "Realism vs Cosmopolitanism," p. 389.
21. John H. Dunning, *Multinational Enterprises and the Global Economy* (Wokingham, MA: Addison-Wesley, 1993), pp. 14–15.
22. Russia is not yet a WTO member.
23. On the GNP and GNI, see Organization for Economic Cooperation and Development, *System of National Accounts, 1993—Glossary* (Paris: OECD, 2000), p. 23; World Bank, *World Development Report—2003* (Washington, D.C.: World Bank, 2003), pp. 233, 245.
24. Joseph S. Nye, Jr., *Bound to Lead: The Changing Nature of American Power* (New York: Basic Books, 1990), p. 70.
25. For more on the GDP and GNP, see Paul R. Krugman and Maurice Obstfeld, *International Economics: Theory and Policy,* 7th ed. (New York: Pearson Addison-Wesley, 2006), pp. 11–14 and 280–283.
26. Lester Thurow, *Head to Head: The Coming Economic Battle among Japan, Europe, and America* (New York: Morrow, 1992).
27. Mike Mason, *Development and Disorder: A History of the Third World Since 1945* (Toronto: Between the Lines, 1997), p. 1.
28. Howard Handelman, *The Challenge of Third World Development* (Upper Saddle River, NJ: Prentice-Hall, 1996), pp. 3–10.

29. Paul Collier, *The Bottom Billion: Why the Poorest Countries are Failing and What Can Be Done About It* (New York: Oxford University Press, 2007).

30. United Nations Department of Economic and Social Affairs, *The Inequality Predicament: Report on the World Social Situation 2005* (New York: United Nations, 2005), p. 1.

31. United Nations Development Program (UNDP), *Human Development Report 2005,* p. 36, http://hdr.undp.org/reports/global/2005, p. 37.

32. United Nations Department of Economic and Social Affairs, *The Inequality Predicament,* p. 49.

33. Francis Fukuyama, "The End of History?" *The National Interest* 16 (Summer 1989), p. 4.

34. On the inadequate attention given to IOs, see J. Martin Rochester, "The Rise and Fall of International Organization as a Field of Study," *International Organization* 40, no. 4 (Autumn 1986), pp. 777–813.

35. World Trade Organization, *Regionalism and the World Trading System* (Geneva: WTO, April 1995), p. 27.

CHAPTER 2

Managing the Global Economy Since World War II: The Institutional Framework

In July 1944 delegates from 44 countries convened the *Bretton Woods Conference,* and within 22 days they endorsed a framework for international economic cooperation after World War II. Two international economic organizations resulted from the Bretton Woods Conference—the International Monetary Fund (IMF) and International Bank for Reconstruction and Development (IBRD) or World Bank—and in 1948 the General Agreement on Tariffs and Trade (GATT) became the main global trade organization. These organizations were part of a complex institutional framework to help manage the postwar global economy. Although the Bretton Woods negotiations were "the first successful attempt . . . by a large group of nations to shape and control their economic relations,"[1] only a small number of states had a critical role in the process. The three years of prenegotiations before Bretton Woods and the conference itself were "very much an Anglo-American affair, with Canada playing a useful mediating role,"[2] and the chief conference planners were Harry Dexter White of the U.S. Treasury and John Maynard Keynes of Britain. Although French delegates participated in the conference, France was still occupied by Germany; and Germany, Italy, and Japan as enemy states were not represented. Despite some basic differences of outlook, the Western DCs generally agreed on the postwar institutional order. Above all, they wanted to avoid repeating the disastrous events of the interwar period, when exchange controls and trade protectionism contributed to the 1930s Great Depression and World War II.

After providing some background on economic relations before World War II, this chapter introduces the postwar institutional framework that the North developed to manage the global economy. The chapter also focuses on two other groups of states that had only a limited role in establishing the postwar economic order and at times sought to form an alternative order: the

South and the former East bloc led by the Soviet Union. Although 27 LDCs (19 of them Latin American) were at the Bretton Woods Conference, their role was marginal, and for many years the South had little influence in the major postwar economic institutions. The Soviet Union also had only a limited role in the Bretton Woods Conference, and it refused to sign the final agreements. Instead of joining the IMF, World Bank, and GATT, the Soviets established their own economic institutions. This book examines how globalization has contributed to the gradual integration of the South and the former East bloc with the dominant liberal economic order. Finally, this chapter discusses the role of nongovernmental actors (business groups and NGOs) in the liberal economic order. We organize this chapter according to the three major themes of the book—globalization, North–North relations, and North–South relations.

GLOBAL ECONOMIC RELATIONS BEFORE WORLD WAR II

This section introduces some general historical benchmarks before World War II, and Chapters 6–11 provide historical background on each issue area such as trade and monetary relations.

The Mercantilist Period

The origins of IPE are closely associated with the development of modern European states and their global markets.[3] The modern European state gained official recognition at the 1648 Treaty of Westphalia, which marked the defeat of the Catholic Hapsburg countries by mostly Protestant countries in Northern Europe. The Peace of Westphalia upheld state sovereignty and territorial integrity by institutionalizing changes to prevent external religious and secular authorities (e.g., the Pope, Holy Roman Emperor, and other states) from interfering in a state's internal affairs. A major factor enabling the state to establish its authority vis-à-vis internal and external forces was the development of **mercantilism.** Adam Smith, an eighteenth-century liberal economist who was highly critical of the mercantilists, first used the term in reference to much of the economic thought and practice in Europe from about 1500 to 1750.[4] Mercantilists were acutely aware of the linkage between politics and economics, viewing both power and wealth as legitimate goals of national policy. Mercantilist states could use their wealth to build up their armed forces, hire mercenaries, and influence their enemies and allies. Thus, they accumulated gold and silver by increasing their exports and decreasing their imports of higher value manufactured goods, they restricted raw material and technology exports to prevent others from developing manufacturing capabilities, and they only imported raw materials that would reduce costs for their own manufacturers. Colonialism was central to mercantilism, because the colonies provided the metropole with raw materials and served as markets for its manufactures; thus, manufacturing in the colonies was usually prohibited. Although Smith criticized mercantilists for following beggar-thy-neighbor policies that would lead to conflict, mercantilism's emphasis on national power was an important contributor to state authority and territorial unification.[5] The European state system in turn contributed to the development of the global political economy.[6]

Although sovereignty in principle gives states supreme authority within their own territory, there is a pecking order in which some states are more powerful than others. A number of scholars have examined the role of dominant or *hegemonic* powers in leading the international system, and Chapter 3 discusses hegemonic stability theory. Some scholars have examined the role of "world powers" such as Portugal, Spain, the Netherlands, and Britain during the mercantilist period, but there is considerable debate as to whether these states were dominant enough to be hegemonic.[7] Most hegemonic stability theorists refer to only two global hegemonic periods, both of them after the mercantilist period: under Britain in the nineteenth century and the United States in the twentieth century.

The Industrial Revolution and British Hegemony

Mercantilism, as the term is used in this book, is a preindustrial doctrine. The Industrial Revolution began about 1780, affected only some manufactures and means of production, and initially progressed from region to region rather than involving entire countries. However, Britain became the hegemonic power in the nineteenth century because it was the first state to industrialize. By 1860 Britain accounted for about 37 percent of European industrial production, 20 percent of world industrial production, and 80 percent of newer technology industries.[8] In view of its competitive edge, Britain shifted from mercantilist policies toward free trade. It removed most of its industrial trade restrictions by the 1830s, and in 1846 it abolished its *Corn Laws,* which had restricted agricultural imports. These policies contributed to an extended period of free trade during the nineteenth century.[9] Both domestic and external factors accounted for Britain's decision to liberalize agricultural trade. Domestically, industrial groups gained seats in the British Parliament at the expense of landed agricultural groups through legislative and demographic changes, and the agricultural elite could no longer prevent the repeal of the Corn Laws. Externally, Britain opened its markets to agricultural and raw material imports so that foreign countries would accept its manufactured goods. The division of labor served Britain's hegemonic interests, because it specialized in industrial exports. Other states oriented their production in line with Britain's preferences because it was the largest market for their exports. In addition to the repeal of the Corn Laws, another free-trade landmark was the British-French *Cobden–Chevalier Treaty* in 1860, which resulted in a network of commercial treaties lowering tariff barriers throughout Europe.[10]

The Decline of British Hegemony and World War I

The growth of trade began to falter in the late nineteenth century because of depressed economic conditions, industrial protectionism on the European continent, and a decline of British hegemony. A decrease in Britain's productivity relative to the United States and Germany made it less competitive in trade and less able to serve as a market for other countries' exports. Banks and the state (including U.S. state governments) helped promote U.S. and German productivity through investment in industrial production and infrastructure such as railroads and canals, and the two countries built up their infant industries through trade protectionism so they could challenge British industry in global markets. Whereas Britain's share of world trade fell from 24 percent in 1870 to 14.1 percent in 1913, Germany's share rose from 9.7 to 12.2 percent and the U.S. share rose from 8.8 to 11.1 percent. On the eve of World War I, the United States had become the largest industrial power, accounting for about 32 percent of world industrial output.[11] However, Britain continued to dominate in international finance until World War I. The city of London was the main center of the international financial system, the British pound was the international currency, and in 1913 Britain accounted for about 43 percent of the world's foreign investment. Whereas Britain's foreign liabilities increased during World War I, the United States emerged as a net creditor and financial preeminence shifted from London to New York.[12]

The Interwar Period

The United States emerged from World War I as the world's largest industrial power and the only major net creditor. Although it lent about $10 billion to cash-short countries during the 1920s, some U.S. policies did not facilitate a return to an open, liberal economy. For example, the United States initially insisted that its close allies Britain and France repay all their war debts, and it imposed import barriers that made it difficult for Europeans to gain needed revenues from exports. The 1922 Fordney–McCumber Act raised U.S. customs duties, and when the U.S. economy moved into depression after the 1929 stock market crash, the 1930 Smoot–Hawley Act increased U.S. tariffs to their highest level in the twentieth century. European states retaliated with their own import restrictions, and world trade declined from $35 billion in 1929 to $12 billion in 1933.[13] The disastrous experience of the interwar period resulted partly from a lack of economic leadership, and hegemonic stability theorists argue that a global hegemon increases the prospects for a stable, open international economy. Whereas Britain was the global hegemon in the nineteenth century, during the interwar period Britain was no longer able, and the United States was not yet willing, to assume the hegemon's role.[14] (Chapter 3 assesses the validity of hegemonic stability theory.) Other theorists argue that domestic politics was a major factor explaining the economic disarray. The U.S. Constitution gives Congress authority to regulate foreign commerce, but as a large unwieldy body subject to special interests, Congress could not resist constituent demands for protectionism. Thus, U.S. tariffs increased because of domestic politics despite the growing economic power of the United States.[15]

In efforts to reverse the damage caused by the Smoot–Hawley tariff, the U.S. Congress passed the *Reciprocal Trade Agreements Act* (*RTAA*) in 1934. The RTAA delegated tariff-setting policy to the president, who could resist special interest pressures and negotiate tariff reductions more effectively than Congress. However, the RTAA reflected a conviction that the reduction of tariffs through bilateral bargaining would help restore U.S. export markets, and "protection at home remained an important goal of American trade strategy."[16] Although the RTAA agreements resulted in a substantial reduction of some tariffs, tariff rates were so high in the early 1930s that the agreements were not sufficient to stem the forces of protectionism.

The Institutional Framework Before World War II

Most IOs formed from 1815 to 1914 were composed mainly of European states and were designed to utilize technological innovations and promote economic regulation and commerce. For example, the Central Commission for the Navigation of the Rhine was created in 1815 to gain commercial advantages from the development of the steamship, the International Telegraph Union was formed in 1865 to benefit from the invention of the telegraph, and the Universal Postal Union was established in 1874 to promote speed and efficiency in postal deliveries.[17] The first financial IO, the **Bank for International Settlements** (**BIS**), was established in Basle, Switzerland, in 1930. The BIS was formed to oversee the settlement of German reparations after World War I, but its main purpose was to promote cooperation among central banks in developing financial policies (see Chapter 6).[18] Other than the BIS, economic IOs in the interwar period were mainly concerned with developing international standards for facilities, equipment, and installations required for the functioning of the global economy. These organizations were *not* able to deal with major economic problems such as the Great Depression. As economic differences increased in the 1920s–1930s, several international conferences were convened to confront the trade and financial problems. For example, a 1922 conference in Genoa, Italy, pressured central banks to manage currency exchange rates and use currencies that were convertible into gold. However, these conferences failed to resolve the problems of war reparations and debt, disorderly currency exchange conditions, and a decline in world trade. In 1936 Britain, the United States, and France finally reached an agreement that recognized international responsibility for exchange rates. This experience demonstrated the need for international arrangements to support open and stable economic relations, and after World War II the IMF, World Bank, and GATT were established to promote international economic collaboration.[19]

THE FUNCTIONS OF THE IMF, WORLD BANK, AND GATT

The United States emerged as a more mature power after World War II than during the interwar period, both willing and able to lead. Under U.S. leadership, the major powers established institutions to develop a liberal economic order and prevent a recurrence of the interwar problems. Although some writers refer to the IMF, World Bank, and GATT as the Bretton Woods institutions, GATT was formed several years after the Bretton Woods Conference. We refer to these IOs as *keystone international economic organizations* (*KIEOs*) because of their central role in international trade, development, and monetary relations.[20] The IMF was created to monitor a system of pegged or **fixed exchange rates,** in which each currency had an official exchange rate in relation to gold and the U.S. dollar. This system was designed to avoid the competitive devaluation of currencies that led to trade wars during the interwar period. **Devaluation** refers to a reduction in the official rate at which one currency is exchanged for another. States with **balance-of-payments** deficits (i.e., with more money leaving than entering the country) are inclined to devalue their currencies because their imports become more expensive and their exports less expensive to foreigners. Thus, the IMF provided short-term loans to help states deal with temporary balance-of-payments deficits and maintain the fixed exchange rates of their currencies. In contrast to the IMF's short-term loans, the IBRD or World Bank provided long-term loans for postwar reconstruction in Europe and economic development in LDCs to avoid the financing problems that developed after World War I. The GATT lowered tariffs in multilateral trade negotiations, established rules for conducting international trade, and developed procedures for settling trade disputes. These functions were designed to avoid the protectionist barriers of the interwar period.

The functions of the KIEOs evolved as events unfolded after World War II. For example, European reconstruction was a larger task than anticipated, and the United States established the European Recovery Program (the Marshall Plan) in 1948 to give **bilateral aid** to Western Europe. The World Bank therefore had only a minor role in European reconstruction, and shifted its loans to LDCs for economic development. The IMF lost one of its main functions when the fixed-exchange-rate system for currencies collapsed in the 1970s and was replaced by **floating exchange rates.** However, the IMF's role increased again in the 1980s and 1990s when it became the lead international agency for the foreign debt and financial crises (see Chapter 11). GATT was formed under special circumstances that affected its evolution. After the Bretton Woods Conference, negotiations were held to create an international trade organization (ITO) comparable in strength to the IMF and World Bank. However, the U.S. Congress refused to support the formation of the ITO, and the "temporary" GATT which had initiated postwar trade negotiations became our global trade organization by default (see Chapter 7). States joining GATT were "contracting parties" rather than formal members because it was designed to be a provisional treaty (this book uses the term *GATT members* for the sake of brevity). Despite its humble origins, GATT was quite effective in liberalizing trade; but its dispute settlement system was weak, its regulations were often circumvented, and it was unable to deal with new areas of trade. Thus, the formal WTO superseded the informal GATT as the global trade organization in 1995. Unlike GATT, the WTO deals not only with trade in goods but also with trade in services, intellectual property rights, and trade-related investment measures (see Chapter 7).

INTERNATIONAL ECONOMIC ORGANIZATIONS AND THE UNITED NATIONS

Figure 2.1 shows that the IMF and World Bank are *specialized agencies* and that the World Bank is in fact a **World Bank group** of five institutions (see Chapter 10). As specialized agencies, the IMF and World Bank are autonomous organizations created by separate treaties and affiliated with the United Nations. Although they report to the Economic and Social Council (ECOSOC)—a principal UN organ—once a year on their activities, the United Nations has little authority over them. Indeed, the United Nations signed an agreement with the World Bank (and a similar one with the IMF), acknowledging that "it would be sound policy to refrain from making recommendations to the Bank with respect to particular loans or with respect to terms or conditions of financing."[21] The UN General Assembly has at times tried to influence World Bank lending decisions, but it has been largely unsuccessful.[22] When the WTO was established in 1995, the members decided it should be a "related organization" rather than a specialized agency, so it does not even issue a yearly report to the ECOSOC (see Figure 2.1).[23]

A major reason for the lack of UN leverage is that the IMF, World Bank, and WTO do not seek UN funds. In September 1995 the United Nations even indicated it might deal with its deficits by borrowing money from the World Bank, but some major UN members vetoed this idea. The DCs have directed most of their funds for multilateral economic management to the IMF and World Bank because they prefer their weighted voting systems to the one-nation, one-vote system of many UN bodies (see Chapters 6 and 10).[24] Despite the United Nations' limited leverage, it has sometimes induced the KIEOs to revise their policies and adopt new programs. Examples include the UN role in the World Bank's creation of a soft-loan agency (see Chapter 10), the IMF's establishment of a compensatory financing facility (see Chapter 6), and IMF and World Bank decisions to introduce human and social dimensions in their lending programs. The World Bank has also cooperated with UN bodies in providing development assistance.[25]

POSTWAR ECONOMIC INSTITUTIONS AND THE NORTH

The North's role in the global economy is marked by several characteristics:

• The United States continues to be the most powerful single state, but its economic hegemony is giving way to a *triad* composed of North America, Western Europe, and East Asia.

The United Nations System

Trusteeship Council

Security Council

General Assembly

Subsidiary Bodies

Military Staff Committee

Standing Committee and ad hoc bodies

Peacekeeping Operations and Missions

Counter-Terrorism Committee

International Criminal Tribunal for the former Yugoslavia (ICTY)

International Criminal Tribunal for Rwanda (ICTR)

Subsidiary Bodies

Main committees

Human Rights Council

Other sessional committees

Standing committees and ad hoc bodies

Other subsidiary organs

Programmes and Funds

UNCTAD United Nations Conference on Trade and Development

    ITC International Trade Centre (UNCTAD/WTO)

UNDCP[1] United Nations Drug Control Programme

UNEP United Nations Environment Programme

UNICEF United Nations Children's Fund

UNDP United Nations Development Programme

    UNIFEM United Nations Development Fund for Women

    UNV United Nations Volunteers

    UNCDF United Nations Capital Development Fund

UNFPA United Nations Population Fund

UNHCR Office of the United Nations High Commissioner for Refugees

Advisory Subsidiary Body

United Nations Peacebuilding Commission

WFP World Food Programme

UNRWA[2] United Nations Relief and Works Agency for Palestine Refugees in the Near East

UN-HABITAT United Nations Human Settlements Programme

Research and Training Institutes

UNICRI United Nations Interregional Crime and Justice Research Institute

UNITAR United Nations Institute for Training and Research

UNRISD United Nations Research Institute for Social Development

UNIDIR[2] United Nations Institute for Disarmament Research

UN-INSTRAW United Nations International Research and Training Institute for the Advancement of Women

Other UN Entities

UNOPS United Nations Office for Project Services

UNU United Nations University

UNSSC United Nations System Staff College

UNAIDS Joint United Nations Programme on HIV/AIDS

Other UN Trust Funds[8]

UNFIP United Nations Fund for International Partnerships

UNDEF United Nations Democracy Fund

NOTES: Solid lines from a Principal Organ indicate a direct reporting relationship; dashes indicate a non-subsidiary relationship.

[1] The UN Drug Control Programme is part of the UN Office on Drugs and Crime.

[2] UNRWA and UNIDIR report only to the GA.

[3] The United Nations Ethics Office, the United Nations Ombudsman's Office, and the Chief Information Technology Officer report directly to the Secretary-General.

[4] In an exceptional arrangement, the Under-Secretary-General for Field Support reports directly to the Under-Secretary-General for Peacekeeping Operations.

[5] IAEA reports to the Security Council and the General Assembly (GA).

[6] The CTBTO Prep.Com and OPCW report to the GA.

[7] Specialized agencies are autonomous organizations working with the UN and each other through the coordinating machinery of the ECOSOC at the intergovernmental level, and through the Chief Executives Board for coordination (CEB) at the inter-secretariat level.

[8] UNFIP is an autonomous trust fund operating under the leadership of the United Nations Deputy Secretary-General. UNDEF's advisory board recommends funding proposals for approval by the Secretary-General.

FIGURE 2.1 The United Nations System

Source: Adapted from the U.N. Chart, December 2007. http://www.un.org/aboutun/chart_en.pdf

Economic and Social Council

Functional Commissions

Commissions on:
  Narcotic Drugs
  Crime Prevention and Criminal Justice
  Science and Technology for
    Development
  Sustainable Development
  Status of Women
  Population and Development
Commission for Social Development
Statistical Commission

Regional Commissions

Economic Commission for Africa (ECA)
Economic Commission for Europe (ECE)
Economic Commission for Latin
  America and the Caribbean (ECLAC)
Economic and Social Commission for
  Asia and the Pacific (ESCAP)
Economic and Social Commission for
  Western Asia (ESCWA)

Other Bodies

Permanent Forum on Indigenous Issues
United Nations Forum on Forests
Sessional and standing committees
Expert, ad hoc and related bodies

Related Organizations

WTO World Trade Organization

IAEA[5] International Atomic Energy
  Agency

CTBTO Prep.Com[6] PrepCom for the
  Nuclear-Test-Ban Treaty Organization

OPCW[6] Organization for the
  Prohibition of Chemical Weapons

International Court of Justice

Specialized Agencies[7]

ILO International Labour
  Organization

FAO Food and Agriculture
  Organization of the United Nations

UNESCO United Nations
  Educational, Scientific and Cultural
  Organization

WHO World Health Organization

World Bank Group

  IBRD International Bank
    for Reconstruction and
    Development

  IDA International Development
    Association

  IFC International Finance
    Corporation

  MIGA Multilateral Investment
    Guarantee Agency

  ICSID International Centre for
    Settlement of Investment
    Disputes

IMF International Monetary Fund

ICAO International Civil Aviation
  Organization

IMO International Maritime
  Organization

ITU International Telecommunication
  Union

UPU Universal Postal Union

WMO World Meteorological
  Organization

WIPO World Intellectual Property
  Organization

IFAD International Fund for
  Agricultural Development

UNIDO United Nations Industrial
  Development Organization

UNWTO World Tourism
  Organization

Secretariat

Departments and Offices

OSG[3] Office of the
  Secretary-General

OIOS Office of Internal Oversight
  Services

OLA Office of Legal Affairs

DPA Department of Political Affairs

UNODA Office for Disarmament
  Affairs

DPKO Department of Peacekeeping
  Operations

DFS[4] Department of Field Support

OCHA Office for the Coordination
  of Humanitarian Affairs

DESA Department of Economic and
  Social Affairs

DGACM Department for General
  Assembly and Conference
  Management

DPI Department of Public Information

DM Department of Management

UN-OHRLLS Office of the High
  Representative for the Least
  Developed Countries, Landlocked
  Developing Countries and Small
  Island Developing States

OHCHR Office of the United
  Nations High Commissioner for
  Human Rights

UNODC United Nations Office on
  Drugs and Crime

DSS Department of Safety and
  Security

ⓒ☙ⓔ

UNOG UN Office at Geneva
UNOV UN Office at Vienna
UNON UN Office at Nairobi

- The DC-led triad is responsible for the largest share of international economic transactions, including foreign investment, trade in manufactures and services, and **capital** flows.
- Countries within the triad conduct most of their international economic transactions with each other, especially in foreign direct investment and intra-industrial trade.[26]

Thus, the DCs occupy the dominant position in the global political economy. Some LDCs are increasing their role, most notably China and other East and Southeast Asian LDCs, India, Brazil, and Mexico. However, the DCs as a group continue to have the greatest influence in most international economic institutions.

The IMF, World Bank, and WTO

DCs provide most of the funding for IMF and World Bank loans, and the countries with the most votes in these institutions are the United States, Japan, Germany, Britain, and France. Although the WTO has a one-nation, one-vote system, the major trading nations which are mainly DCs have the largest role in setting the agenda in multilateral trade negotiations. The North also has a dominant position in the bureaucracies of these institutions. By tacit agreement, the World Bank president has always been American, and the IMF managing director has always been European. All the GATT/WTO directors general were from DCs from 1948 until 2002 when Supachai Panitchpakdi of Thailand became the first WTO director general from an LDC. The South has also been underrepresented on the professional staffs of all three KIEOs, and most Communist states were not KIEO members from the 1940s to the 1970s.[27]

The Bretton Woods institutions are often credited with contributing "to almost unprecedented global economic growth and change over the past five decades."[28] However, the type of growth these institutions foster has closely followed the prescriptions of the United States and other DCs. The KIEOs support a liberal economic approach, which holds that the free flow of goods and capital throughout the world promotes prosperity. (Critical theorists by contrast argue that the liberal economic approach benefits some states and individuals at the expense of others.) The KIEOs in the 1950s and 1960s contributed to economic liberalization, growth, and stability for several reasons. First, the Cold War increased U.S. determination to cooperate economically with Western Europe and Japan; vigorous economic recovery was viewed as a prerequisite for a strong anti-Soviet alliance. Second, the United States as global hegemon helped establish principles and rules for the conduct of postwar trade, financial, and monetary relations, and the major DCs generally accepted U.S. leadership. Third, the KIEOs enabled governments to abide by international rules and obligations without jeopardizing domestic policy objectives such as full employment.[29]

Despite their early effectiveness, the KIEOs encountered serious problems in the 1970s for several reasons. First, the United States became less supportive of economic liberalism as its economic dominance declined; for example, U.S. protectionism increased after its balance of trade shifted to a deficit position in 1971. Europe and Japan also began to question U.S. leadership, and the decline of the Cold War permitted frictions among DCs to increase. Second, the *Organization of Petroleum Exporting Countries (OPEC)* limited the supply of oil after the October 1973 Middle East War, and oil prices increased by more than 400 percent; this disrupted the global economy and challenged the management capabilities of the KIEOs. Third, the KIEOs had difficulty in managing the forces of globalization. The KIEOs' economic resources "pale in comparison to daily market-driven foreign exchange cash flows," and no IO oversees the activities of MNCs and international banks which are major contributors to these capital flows.[30] Finally, the growing membership of the KIEOs with the influx of LDCs and transition economies has also interfered with their management capabilities. In May 2008 there were 185 members of the IMF and World Bank and 153 members of the WTO. Whereas some argue that the KIEOs must become more broadly representative, others note that their large, diverse memberships interfere with consultation, coordination, and decision making.

Although the IMF, World Bank, and WTO continue to have important functions, their large memberships have led some analysts to argue that "they must be led by a much smaller core group whose weight confers on them the responsibility of leadership."[31] The decline of U.S. economic hegemony has also contributed to the need for collective leadership, and DCs often confer among themselves before seeking endorsement of their policies by the KIEOs.[32] As Figure 2.2 shows, the smaller DC-led groups include the Organization for Economic Cooperation and Development (OECD), **Group of Ten (G10)**, and **Group of Seven (G7)**. Although the G7 superseded the **Group of Five (G5)** in 1986, the G5 is included in Figure 2.2 because its members still have a major role in the IMF and World Bank. These groups permit the DCs to coordinate their policies without sharing information with the LDCs. Whereas liberal economists believe these groups promote economic leadership and stability, critical theorists argue that they exclude LDCs from the decision-making process.

The OECD

The OECD, which is located in Paris, has 30 mainly DC members that produce about two-thirds of the world's goods and services (see Figure 2.2). When the OECD was created in 1961, Americans viewed it as "a forum where they, the Europeans and other 'industrial democracies' could sit down together on equal terms" and share responsibilities for economic management.[33] The OECD is committed to liberalizing international transactions such as trade and capital flows, and in this sense it has been an agent of globalization. The OECD also serves as a forum for the North to discuss members' economic policies and common problems and promote policy coordination. In an age of globalization, a

ORGANIZATION FOR ECONOMIC COOPERATION AND DEVELOPMENT
(YEAR OF ADMISSION)

Australia	1971	Hungary	1996	Poland	1996
Austria	1961	Iceland	1961	Portugal	1961
Belgium	1961	Ireland	1961	Slovak Republic	2000
Canada	1961	Italy	1962	South Korea	1996
Czech Republic	1995	Japan	1964	Spain	1961
Denmark	1961	Luxembourg	1961	Sweden	1961
Finland	1969	Mexico	1994	Switzerland	1961
France	1961	Netherlands	1961	Turkey	1961
Germany	1961	New Zealand	1973	United Kingdom	1961
Greece	1961	Norway	1961	United States	1961

SMALLER GROUPS

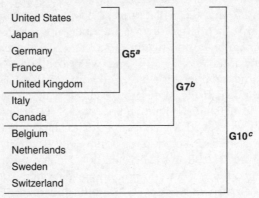

[a]The G5 has been superseded by the G7.
[b]The G8 also includes Russia, but Russia is not in the G10 or OECD.
[c]The G10 has 11 members.

FIGURE 2.2   Groups of Developed Countries

state's domestic policies often have international consequences, and OECD members seek to reach a consensus on domestic policies that will minimize conflict. The OECD usually operates through a system of mutual persuasion, in which members exert peer pressure on each other to meet their commitments.[34]

The North also uses the OECD to develop a more unified position on issues in the IMF, World Bank, and WTO. For example, the OECD's work on services trade helped the North legitimize the idea that the WTO should include rules for trade in services as well as goods.[35] Although the OECD normally maintains a low profile, its efforts to negotiate a Multilateral Agreement on Investment (MAI) in the 1990s were highly controversial. The MAI would have provided much more protection for Northern investors than for Southern recipients, and the negotiations were suspended in 1998 because of divisions among OECD members and strong opposition by LDCs and civil society groups (see Chapter 9). Although OECD membership has generally been limited to DCs, a decision in the early 1990s opened the organization to some enlargement. Figure 2.2 shows that six countries outside the industrial core group became OECD members, including Mexico in 1994; the Czech Republic in 1995; Hungary, Poland, and South Korea in 1996; and the Slovak Republic in 2000. At the beginning of the twenty-first century, OECD members accounted for about 75 percent of global trade, 59 percent of the world's GNI, 51 percent of carbon dioxide emissions, and 95 percent of official development assistance. However, the relative economic importance of OECD members has declined vis-à-vis emerging powers such as China, India, and the Asian NIEs. Some members believe that further enlargement is necessary if the OECD is to remain relevant, and in May 2007 the OECD invited Chile, Estonia, Israel, Russia, and Slovenia to open discussions for membership; the OECD also offered enhanced engagement to Brazil, China, India, Indonesia, and South Africa with a view to possible membership. However, critics argue that further enlargement would jeopardize the OECD's strength as an organization of like-minded members. If the emerging economies joined the OECD, China and Russia would not meet the democratic requirements of OECD members, South Africa's human rights record could pose problems, and India's capital controls would conflict with the OECD Codes on Liberalization. Some also argue that too much enlargement would turn the OECD into a mini-United Nations.[36]

The G10, G5, G7, G8, and G20

These groupings, like the OECD, indicate a shift from unilateral U.S. management to collective management. The G10, which was formed in 1962, now includes 11 countries: the United States, Japan, Germany, France, Britain, Italy, Canada, Belgium, the Netherlands, Sweden, and Switzerland (see Figure 2.2). The IMF lacked sufficient funding in the early 1960s to meet its members' borrowing requirements (discussed in Chapter 6). In 1962 the G10 countries therefore established the General Arrangements to Borrow (GAB), which would provide the IMF with supplementary loans in the G10 currencies. This represented a shift from U.S. management to collective management on monetary issues, because the G10 had to approve each IMF request for supplementary support.[37] Although the OECD and G10 continue to coordinate DC economic policies, the main focus of policy coordination shifted in the 1970s to two smaller groups, the G5 and G7, which had some special advantages.

- They were flexible groupings without formal constitutions.
- They included the most powerful DCs in the global economy.
- Top political leaders with authority to implement agreements often attended their meetings.[38]

The G5 included the finance ministers and **central bank** governors of the five largest DC economies with the most votes in the IMF and World Bank: the United States, Japan, Germany, France, and Britain (see Figure 2.2). After informally discussing international monetary issues from 1967, the G5 began to hold more formal summit meetings to discuss international economic issues in 1975. When Italy and then Canada were invited to attend the G5 summits, the G7 was created. The G7 summits stemmed from the move toward collective leadership with the decline of U.S. economic hegemony, the growing interdependence among DCs, the 1973–1974 OPEC oil crisis, and the world economic recession. G7 members use the summits to reach a consensus on key issues at the highest political level. From 1975 to 1986 the G5 and G7 met as largely separate entities, but the G7 superseded the G5 in 1986, and today the G7 has two layers: At the top are heads of state or government who meet in annual summits, and at the second level are finance ministers and central bank governors. In 1991 the G7 invited Russia to the summit to help it come to terms with its loss of superpower status and to encourage it to continue with economic and political reforms. Russia gradually became more involved, and the G7 has become a **Group of Eight (G8)**. However, Russia is more involved in political than economic discussions, and in some areas such as finance the G7 countries continue to be the main actors.[39]

In view of its informality, most analysts consider the G8 to be a forum or think tank of individual leaders rather than an institution. It has no constitution or legal status, no headquarters or formal meeting place, no formal rules of membership, and no means to enforce its decisions. The main G8 objectives are "to raise consciousness, set an agenda, create networks, prod other institutions to do things that they should be doing, and in some cases to help create institutions."[40] The G8 has been quite successful in some areas such as managing the end of the Cold War and addressing the issue of debt relief for LDCs. However, the G8's influence has declined because of growing DC divisions with the demise of the Cold War and the difficulties in coping with globalization; for example, massive international capital flows interfere with the ability of G8 monetary authorities to influence currency markets. Thus, the G8 must make a fuller transition from U.S. leadership to collective leadership, with the U.S. sharing decision making and Japan and Germany assuming more global responsibilities. Even if this transition occurs, G8 members must confront the fact that, other than Russia, they do not include important emerging powers such as China, India, and Brazil. Without these powers, the G8's influence will continue to decline. The DCs in the G7 accounted for about 65 percent of global output from 1965 to 2002, but by 2008 their share had fallen to 52 percent, and it is estimated that their share of global output will fall to 37 percent by 2030 and to 25 percent by 2050. Thus, a new group formed in 1999, the **Group of 20 (G20)**, has an increasingly important role on the world stage. The G20 finance ministers and central bank governors hold an annual summit to discuss key issues in the global economy, and also meet on extraordinary occasions such as the April 2009 meeting to address the global financial crisis. The G20 is a diverse group that includes five countries from Asia, three from Latin America, two from the Middle East, and one from Africa.[41] The G7/G8 is likely to continue to play an important role for like-minded DCs, but in terms of changing global power shifts a group such as the G20 is likely to become more influential over time. The main question is whether a group as large and diverse as the G20 can form a consensus on actions to deal with critical global issues such as financial crises.

POSTWAR ECONOMIC INSTITUTIONS AND THE SOUTH

The Bretton Woods system and its institutions are often credited with contributing "to almost unprecedented global economic growth and change over the past five decades."[42] However, this economic growth has not been shared by all. Poverty, disease, and hunger are prevalent in much of the world, and there is a major gulf between the North and the South. The most common measure economists use to compare the economic development of states is *per capita GDP* or *per capita income* (a country's GDP or national income divided by its population). **Exchange rates,** or the rates at which currencies are exchanged for one another, are used to convert per capita GDP figures in other currencies into the U.S. dollar. However, comparing countries' per capita GDPs does not tell us fully about their relative standards of living because the exchange rate does not accurately reflect the *purchasing power* of the local currency in each country. Price levels of comparable goods differ significantly in different countries, and price levels are generally lower in LDCs than in the United States. In comparing per capita GDPs, IOs therefore often convert the figures into **purchasing power parity (PPP)** based exchange rates. PPP rates are "the number of units of a country's currency required to buy the same amount of goods and services in the domestic market as a United States dollar would buy in the United States."[43] For example, *The Economist* magazine has used a "Big Mac index" to compare PPP rates for hamburgers. If a Big Mac costs 2.75 euros in countries using the euro and $2.65 in the United States, the PPP exchange rate for Big Macs would be 2.75/2.65, or 1.0377.[44] The PPP rate differs for different goods and services, and goods and services are weighted according to their importance in the economy. PPP exchange rates have limitations because they are based on price comparisons of "comparable items" even though the quality of items may differ across countries. Nevertheless, PPP rates are more accurate in comparing living standards, and this book sometimes provides per capita GDP figures in PPP terms (e.g., see Table 2.1).

Even PPP-weighted per capita GDP figures are an imperfect indicator of well-being because they do not take account of income inequalities, leisure time, and quality of the environment. For example, a country in which a small percentage of people are extremely rich and most are extremely poor has less well-being than a country with the same GDP per capita that has less extreme wealth and poverty.[45] Furthermore, PPP-adjusted per capita GDP figures only measure a country's *economic* development. Since 1990 the United Nations Development Program (UNDP) has published a *Human Development Report*

TABLE 2.1   Human Development Index (HDI), GDP per Capita, and GDP per Capita Rank Minus HDI Rank, 2005

Country	HDI Value (and Rank)	GDP per Capita (PPP[a] U.S.$)	GDP per Capita (PPP[a] U.S.$) Rank *Minus* HDI Rank
Iceland	0.968 (1)	36,510	4
Australia	0.962 (3)	31,794	13
Canada	0.961 (4)	33,375	6
Japan	0.953 (8)	31,267	9
United States	0.951 (12)	41,890	−10
Germany	0.935 (22)	29,461	−2
Republic of Korea	0.921 (26)	22,029	6
Poland	0.870 (37)	13,847	11
Mexico	0.829 (52)	10,751	7
Saudi Arabia	0.812 (61)	15,711	−19
Russian Federation	0.802 (67)	10,845	−9
Brazil	0.800 (70)	8,402	−3
China	0.777 (81)	6,757	5
Iran	0.759 (94)	7,968	−23
Indonesia	0.728 (107)	3,843	6
South Africa	0.674 (121)	11,110	−65
India	0.619 (128)	3,452	−11
Bangladesh	0.547 (140)	2,053	0
Nigeria	0.470 (158)	1,128	4
Niger	0.374 (174)	781	−1
Sierra Leone	0.336 (177)	806	−5

[a]Purchasing power parity

Source: United Nations Development Programme, *Human Development Report 2007/2008* (New York: Palgrave Macmillan, 2007), Table 1, pp. 229–232. http://hdr.undp.org/en/reports/global/hdr2007-2008

with a **human development index (HDI)**, which measures social as well as economic development. The HDI focuses on three dimensions: a long life measured by life expectancy at birth, knowledge measured by adult literacy rates and school enrollments, and a decent standard of living measured by PPP-adjusted per capita GDPs. A major problem with the HDI is collecting data; for example, the 2007/2008 *Human Development Report* does not provide an HDI for 17 UN member states because of a lack of reliable data.[46]

Table 2.1 compares HDI values and per capita GDPs for a number of countries during 2005. The first column lists the countries' HDI values and rank, the second lists their PPP-adjusted per capita GDPs, and the third lists their per capita GDP rank minus their HDI rank. For example, in 2005 Iceland ranked first (of 177 countries) in HDI and fifth in GDP per capita; so its figure in the third column is (5 − 1) or 4. Some countries have HDI rankings that are considerably lower than their per capita GDP rankings. For example, Table 2.1 shows that South Africa's and Iran's GDP per capita rankings exceeded their HDI rankings by 65 and 23, respectively. Lower-than-expected HDI rankings (relative to the per capita GDP) may result from specific problems such as the high incidence of HIV/AIDS (human immunodeficiency virus/acquired immunodeficiency syndrome) in South Africa, or from domestic policy problems that limit opportunities in health and education. For example, Saudi Arabia has a lower-than-expected performance on education and literacy, and the United States has shorter life expectancy rates than some countries with lower per capita GDPs.[47] Despite the disparities between the HDI and per capita GDP rankings, Table 2.1 shows that both HDIs and per capita GDPs tend to be higher for DCs than LDCs. The six DCs on the list (Iceland, Australia, Canada, Japan, United States, and Germany) have the highest HDIs as well as per capita GDPs; and the four LDCs with the lowest per capita GDPs on the list (Bangladesh, Nigeria, Niger, and Sierra Leone) also have the lowest HDI values. This is not surprising, because the poorest LDCs have less funding available for health care and education.

HDI values have some limitations in measuring well-being; for example, the HDI does not fully measure the effects of rapid socioeconomic and political change. Although Russia's 2005 HDI rank was nine points below its GDP per capita rank (see Table 2.1), this understates the fact that Russia has been undergoing a "mortality crisis" in human terms. Life expectancy for Russian men was 59 years in 2003, down from 65 years in the mid-1960s. Russians have high rates of cardiovascular disease, tuberculosis, HIV/AIDS, and homicide and suicide. Although scholars often relate these figures to Russia's instability during transition from Communism to a free market system, life expectancy in some other transition economies such as Poland has been increasing.[48] This book discusses some of the reasons for the differences among transition economies. Another shortcoming of the HDI is that it does not measure political aspects of human rights such as free speech and free elections. Table 2.1 shows that China's HDI rank exceeds its per capita GDP rank (by 5), whereas India's HDI rank is lower than its per capita GDP rank (by 11); these figures do not reflect that fact that India has a more democratic political system than China. The HDI, like other rankings, is also not always a good predictor of the future. Although Iceland had the highest HDI in 2005, it was one of the countries most severely affected by the 2008 global financial crisis! Despite its shortcomings, the HDI is important because it takes account of social as well as economic aspects of development.

In some respects, LDC socioeconomic conditions have improved on average in recent years. For example, since 1990 life expectancy in the South has increased by two years, 3 million fewer children are dying annually and 30 million fewer children are out of school. Indeed, all LDC regions except Sub-Saharan Africa have had increasing HDI scores. The colonial experience, economic reversals, and the human costs of conflict have had some role in the declining fortunes of Sub-Saharan Africa, but the primary factor has been the catastrophic effect of HIV/AIDS. High income growth in China and India has been a powerful factor behind the improving LDC income poverty figures overall, but this tends to mask the lack of progress in Sub-Saharan Africa and many countries in other regions. For example, 18 countries—most in Sub-Saharan Africa—had lower HDI scores in 2004 than in 1990. Three million people died from AIDS in 2005 alone, and more than 39 million are infected with HIV. The following examples show that a wide North–South socioeconomic gap continues to exist:

- Forty percent of the world's population lives on less than $2 a day and accounts for only 5 percent of global income. The richest 10 percent of the world's population by contrast accounts for 54 percent of global income.
- Ninety percent of the people in OECD countries are in the top 20 percent of the global income distribution.
- The average life expectancy gap between low- and high-income countries is about 19 years. Japan's life expectancy is 35 years longer than Burkina Faso's and the United States' is 14 years longer than India's.
- About 20 percent of the 57 million deaths worldwide in 2002 were children less than five years old. Almost all child deaths occur in the South, while most of the funds to prevent child deaths are spent in the North.[49]

Although the North–South gap is the most significant division, there are also major differences *within* the South. Table 2.2 shows that Latin American, East Asian, and Arab states generally score higher in terms of socioeconomic indicators than South Asian and Sub-Saharan African states. For example, in

TABLE 2.2   Human Development Indicators

LDC Region	HDI Value 2005	GDP per Capita (PPP[a] U.S.$) 2005	GDP per Capita Annual Growth Rate 1975–2005	GDP per Capita Annual Growth Rate 1990–2005	Life Expectancy at Birth (years) 2005	Adult Literacy Rate (%) 1995–2005[b]
Latin America and Caribbean	0.803	8,417	0.7	1.2	72.8	90.3
East Asia and Pacific	0.771	5,100	6.1	5.8	71.7	90.7
Arab States	0.699	6,604	0.7	2.3	67.5	70.3
South Asia	0.611	3,416	2.6	3.4	63.8	59.5
Sub-Saharan Africa	0.493	1,998	−0.5	0.5	49.6	60.3

[a]Purchasing power parity
[b]Data refer to national literacy estimates from surveys conducted between 1995 and 2005.
Source: United Nations Development Programme, *Human Development Report 2007/2008* (New York: Palgrave Macmillan, 2007), Table 1, p. 232 and Table 14, p. 280, http://hdr.undp.org/en/reports/global/hdr2007-2008

2005 the HDI index ranged from 0.803 in Latin America and the Caribbean to 0.493 in Sub-Saharan Africa; life expectancy ranged from 72.8 years in Latin America and the Caribbean to 49.6 years in Sub-Saharan Africa; the adult literacy rate ranged from 90.7 percent in East Asia and the Pacific to 59.5 percent in South Asia; and the PPP-adjusted GDP per capita ranged from $8,417 in Latin America and the Caribbean to $1,998 in Sub-Saharan Africa. Although the Latin American and Caribbean region had the highest GDP per capita on average ($8,417), the East Asian newly industrializing economies (NIEs) had higher incomes than any Latin American state in 2005. For example, the per capita GDPs for Hong Kong, China; Singapore; and South Korea were $34,833, $29,663, and $22,029, respectively. This compared with per capita GDPs for Argentina, Chile, and Mexico of $14,280, $12,027, and $10,751, respectively. Table 2.2 also shows that East Asia and the Pacific have had higher annual GDP per capita growth rates (6.1 and 5.8 percent) than other LDC regions. Chapters 10 and 11 discuss the reasons for the economic prosperity of the East Asian NIEs. In marked contrast to East Asia and Latin America is Sub-Saharan Africa, which scores lowest in HDI value, GDP per capita, GDP per capita growth rate, and life expectancy (see Table 2.2). A variety of reasons account for Sub-Saharan Africa's problems, ranging from the colonial experience to regional conflicts; but HIV/AIDS has been the most significant factor:

> Twenty years ago somebody born in Sub-Saharan Africa could expect to live 24 fewer years than a person born in a rich country, and the gap was shrinking. Today, the gap is 33 years and growing. HIV/AIDS is at the heart of the reversal.[50]

In 1971 the United Nations compiled a list of 24 least developed countries (LLDCs), which has now grown to 50 countries. The United Nations describes the LLDCs as having low per capita incomes; weak human assets (i.e., nutrition, health, school enrollment, and adult literacy); and high economic vulnerability (i.e., instability of production and exports, and lack of economic diversification). Thirty-four of the 50 LLDCs are in Africa, 10 are in Asia, 5 are in the Pacific, and 1 is in the Caribbean. Fifteen of the LLDCs are landlocked, and 10 are small island states.[51] Table 2.3 shows that 24 of the 39 LLDCs for which data are available had *negative* GDP per capita growth rates for the 1980–1990 period; 18 of 46 had negative rates for 1990–2000; and 15 of 46 had negative rates from 2000 to 2004. The figures show that the number of LLDCs with negative growth rates is declining, and many LLDCs have increased their exports and economic growth rates in recent years. However, this growth does not seem to be leading to poverty reduction and a greater sense of well-being. Most LLDC growth is fragile because it depends on commodity prices, external finance, and weather conditions. In 2000–2003, primary commodities accounted for almost two-thirds of LLDC merchandise exports. Growth collapsed in many LLDCs in the late 1970s and 1980s, and LLDCs have been highly vulnerable to the 2008 financial crisis.[52]

TABLE 2.3   Development Indicators of the Least Developed Countries (LLDCs)

LLDCs	2004 GDP per Capita (in 2004 Dollars)	Annual Average Growth Rates of per Capita Real GDP (%)		
		1980–1990	1990–2000	2000–2004
Afghanistan	—	—	—	—
Angola	1,298	0.4	−1.1	5.1
Bangladesh	408	1.3	2.6	3.1
Benin	498	−0.9	1.4	1.2
Bhutan	751	5.4	3.4	3.6
Burkina Faso	376	0.9	1.2	1.9
Burundi	90	1.1	−3.8	−0.2
Cambodia	333	—	4.2	3.5
Cape Verde	1,915	3.7	3.5	2.3
Central African Republic	334	−1.1	−0.3	−2.7
Chad	454	3.3	−1.1	10.3
Comoros	472	−0.3	−1.6	−0.5
Democratic Republic of the Congo	118	−1.4	−7.5	0.7
Djibouti	851	−6.7	−3.7	0.6
Equatorial Guinea	6,572	−0.7	18.4	9.3
Eritrea	219	—	3.8[a]	−1.2
Ethiopia	107	−1.1	1.1	1.2
Gambia	281	−0.1	−0.5	0.8
Guinea	381	1.6	1.2	0.7
Guinea-Bissau	182	1.5	−1.8	−4.1
Haiti	421	−2.5	−2.9	−2.4
Kiribati	636	−1.2	3.2	−0.3
Lao PDR	416	1.1	3.9	3.3
Lesotho	765	2.3	2.6	3.1
Liberia	138	−8.3	−0.2	−9.6
Madagascar	241	−1.7	−1.0	−1.9
Malawi	144	−1.9	1.8	−0.5
Maldives	2,345	—	5.6	4.1
Mali	371	−1.6	1.3	3.2
Mauritania	455	−0.5	1.7	2.2
Mozambique	286	−1.0	3.2	6.3
Myanmar	—	—	—	—
Nepal	252	2.2	2.4	0.4

TABLE 2.3   Continued

LLDCs	2004 GDP per Capita (in 2004 Dollars)	Annual Average Growth Rates of per Capita Real GDP (%) 1980–1990	1990–2000	2000–2004
Niger	228	−3.2	−1.0	0.6
Rwanda	208	−1.3	−1.4	4.4
Samoa	1,978	—	3.0	2.6
Sao Tome and Principe	407	−0.6	0.0	1.9
Senegal	673	0.1	0.9	2.1
Sierra Leone	202	−1.9	−5.9	11.0
Solomon Islands	519	3.2	−0.4	−2.8
Somalia	—	—	—	—
Sudan	551	—	3.0	4.0
Timor-Leste	382	—	−12.2	−5.7
Togo	344	−1.9	0.4	−0.2
Tuvalu	—	—	—	—
Uganda	246	−0.7	3.8	2.3
United Republic of Tanzania	288	1.9	0.1	4.7
Vanuatu	1,526	−0.3	1.1	−2.7
Yemen	631	—	1.9	−0.4
Zambia	469	−2.2	−1.9	2.6

[a]1993–2000.

Source: United Nations Conference on Trade and Development, *The Least Developed Countries Report 2006* (New York: United Nations, 2006), Annex Table 1, p. 311.

It is also important to consider inequities *within* states. Statistics show that within-country income inequality declined from the 1950s to 1970s in most DCs, LDCs, and centrally planned economies (CPEs). However, this decline slowed beginning in the 1980s, and income inequality has been increasing in many states in recent years.[53] Within-country inequities stem from such factors as difference in educational opportunities, gender, race and ethnicity, and region of birth. For example, there are persistent gender gaps in access to education, employment, and equitable pay for work. Women account for about two-thirds of adult illiteracy today—the same as in the 1990s. Although the number of women in the workforce has increased in many LDCs, their jobs usually have lower pay and poorer working conditions. Some areas such as rural China and northwest India have significantly more boy than girl infants because of sex-selective abortion and differential care after birth.[54] Although this book discusses within-country inequities and inequities among LDCs, it gives more emphasis to North–South inequities. Some LDCs have improved their socioeconomic positions, but many have been frustrated in their efforts to promote development and exert more influence. Because most LDCs are in a weak position individually, only collective action provides some opportunity to extract concessions from the North. From the South's perspective, some KIEO policies pose major obstacles to economic development. This chapter briefly discusses the **United Nations Conference on Trade and Development (UNCTAD)**, which gives priority to the interests of LDCs (see also Chapter 7).

In the 1960s many LDCs gained political independence, and the number of African and Asian states in the United Nations increased from 10 in 1955 to 55 in 1966. In 1964, the 77 LDCs in the United Nations from Africa, Asia, and Latin America ("the Third World") met to express their dissatisfaction with the KIEOs, and this LDC caucus, which now has 130 members, is still referred to as the **Group of 77 (G77)**.[55] The G77 was highly critical of GATT, which it viewed as a rich countries' club, and it was instrumental in organizing the first United Nations Conference on Trade and Development, or UNCTAD I, in March 1964. UNCTAD subsequently became a permanent forum or conference under the UN General Assembly, with facilities to do research and policy analysis (see Figure 2.1). Unlike the KIEOs, UNCTAD depends on UN funding for its operating budget and its technical cooperation activities. Although all UN members are in UNCTAD, its secretariat openly supports LDC trade interests, and the UNCTAD secretary general has always been from the South. UNCTAD established some international commodity agreements and has induced the GATT/WTO to give more priority to Southern trade interests (see Chapter 7). However, the DCs refused to accept UNCTAD as a major forum for trade negotiations, and the WTO continues to be the unrivaled global trade organization. In recent years, UNCTAD's critical approach has been replaced by a greater acceptance of orthodox liberalism, and the South has had to function within the institutional framework of the KIEOs. Nevertheless, UNCTAD continues to have important roles as a pressure group for Southern interests and a source of technical expertise. For example UNCTAD has assisted LDCs with the complex process of joining the WTO.

POSTWAR ECONOMIC INSTITUTIONS AND THE CENTRALLY PLANNED ECONOMIES

All states can become members of the IMF, World Bank, and WTO, which are universal membership organizations.[56] However, for many years the CPEs of Eastern Europe, the Soviet Union, and China were nonmembers or had a very limited role. At the end of World War II, the United Nations focused mainly on political security and the KIEOs on economic cooperation, but security issues were inevitably a factor in the KIEO deliberations. The Western allies thought that universalism would create a more secure environment, and the U.S. negotiator Harry Dexter White wrote in his 1942 draft Bretton Woods plan that to exclude "Russia would be an egregious error. Russia, despite her socialist economy could both contribute and profit by participation."[57] The allies also assumed that the Eastern European states would become KIEO members. Although the Soviet Union feared capitalist encirclement, it participated in the Bretton Woods Conference and wanted financial aid to reconstruct its war-damaged economy. As the only Communist state at Bretton Woods (Poland and Czechoslovakia were not yet Communist), the Soviet Union was critical of IMF and World Bank voting procedures, policies regarding state-trading countries, and the information they would require from members. Although the West made limited concessions to the Soviet Union and it signed the Bretton Woods agreements, the Soviets continued to oppose the IMF and World Bank voting systems, the transfer of gold to U.S. territory, and the IMF conditions on loans. Cold War issues also intruded (e.g., disputes over Berlin and the Soviet occupation of Eastern Europe), and the Soviet Union decided not to become a member of the KIEOs.[58]

In 1947, the United States responded to Western Europe's lack of foreign exchange reserves with the *European Recovery Program* or *Marshall Plan*. Although U.S. Secretary of State George C. Marshall invited the Soviet Union and Eastern Europe to participate, the Soviets refused and vetoed the idea of East European participation. They objected to provisions that the United States have advisory authority over the internal budgets of Marshall Plan recipients, that European states cooperate with each other in using Marshall Plan aid, and that most of the aid be used to purchase U.S. exports. Only Western Europe participated in the Marshall Plan, and the Soviets established the *Council for Mutual Economic Assistance* (*CMEA*) in 1949 as a counterweight. Composed of the Soviet Union and Eastern European states other than Yugoslavia, CMEA solidified the East–West economic and political divisions.[59] CMEA's strategies to promote economic cooperation sharply differentiated it from the market-oriented Bretton Woods system. For example, CMEA emphasized central economic planning, nationalization of the factors of production such as capital and natural resources, the collectivization of agriculture, and insulation of the domestic economy from external economic influences. CMEA's main goals were to reorient Eastern European trade away from the West and to solidify Soviet–East European economic linkages. However, CMEA performed poorly because it contributed to bilateralism, inward-looking policies, and a currency (the ruble) with unrealistic conversion rates that limited trade.[60] The growing East–West economic rift resulted from U.S. as well as Soviet policies. For example, the United States restricted trade with Communist countries and pressured its allies to participate in the *Coordinating Committee* (*COCOM*), which organized Western embargoes of strategic goods to the Soviet bloc. The liberal economic orientation of the KIEOs also contributed to the East–West split. Although the IBRD Articles of Agreement state that "only economic considerations shall be relevant" to the Bank's decisions,[61] the KIEOs in fact base their decisions on political and ideological as well as economic factors. The values of the KIEO professional staffs, who have received their education mainly in Western countries, also affect the decision-making process.[62]

In view of the East–West divisions, most linkages between Communist states and the KIEOs were severed. Czechoslovakia, Poland, Yugoslavia, China, and Cuba were founding members of the IMF and World Bank, but their membership ended or their status changed after they became Communist (the sole exception was Yugoslavia). As Table 2.4 shows, Poland withdrew from the IMF and World Bank in 1950 charging that the U.S. government controlled these institutions, and the World Bank and IMF expelled Czechoslovakia in 1954 ostensibly for failing to pay its capital subscription.[63] The only Eastern European state remaining in these institutions in the 1950s was Yugoslavia, which was a special case because of its independence from the Soviet Union. Taiwan occupied the China seat in the IMF

TABLE 2.4   Membership of Transition Economies in the Keystone International Economic Organizations

	IMF	World Bank	GATT/WTO
1946	Poland, Czechoslovakia, Yugoslavia, China (founding members of IMF/World Bank)		
1948			Czechoslovakia and China (founding Members)
1950	Poland withdraws from IMF/World Bank		Republic of China (Taiwan) withdraws from GATT
1954	Czechoslovakia ousted from IMF/World Bank		
1966			Yugoslavia
1967			Poland
1971			Romania
1972	Romania	Romania	
1973			Hungary
1980	People's Republic of China (replaces Taiwan in IMF/World Bank)		
1982	Hungary	Hungary	
1986	Poland	Poland	
1990	Czech and Slovak Federal Republic Bulgaria	Bulgaria	East Germany Accedes to GATT due to German reunification
1991	Albania, Lithuania	Albania, Czech and Slovak Fed. Republic	

TABLE 2.4   Continued

	IMF	World Bank	GATT/WTO
1992–1997	Russian Federation, other FSU[a] republics, Croatia, Slovenia, Macedonia, Bosnia and Herzegovina, Czech Republic, Slovak Republic (IMF/World Bank)		Bulgaria, Czech Republic, Slovak Republic, Slovenia Mongolia
1998–2001	Serbia/Montenegro (IMF/World Bank)		Kyrgyz Republic, Estonia, Croatia, Albania, Georgia, Latvia, Lithuania, Moldova, China
2002			Chinese Taipei (Taiwan)
2003			Armenia, Macedonia
2007	Montenegro (IMF/World Bank) (Serbia continues membership of former Serbia/Montenegro)		
2008			Ukraine

[a]FSU = Former Soviet Union republics

Sources: IMF Annual Report (Washington, D.C.: IMF, various years); *World Bank Annual Report* (Washington, D.C.: World Bank, various years); http://www.org/english/thewto_e/whatis_e/tif_e/org6_e.htm

and World Bank after the People's Republic of China took over the mainland in 1949 and Fidel Castro's Cuba withdrew from the Bank in 1960 and the IMF in 1964. As for the GATT, Table 2.4 shows that China and Czechoslovakia were founding members in 1948, but the Chiang Kai-shek government (which had fled to Taiwan) withdrew from GATT in 1950, purportedly on behalf of China. Czechoslovakia remained in GATT, but its membership was inactive for many years. This was possible because of GATT's status as an informal organization.

The Soviet bloc countries as nonmembers of the KIEOs joined the South in supporting alternative organizations such as UNCTAD. However, Eastern Europe became more interested in the KIEOs by the late 1960s because of its increased economic problems, its growing dependence on Western markets for its exports, its efforts to gain more independence from the Soviet Union, and East–West détente. Thus, Table 2.4 shows that Poland, Romania, and Hungary joined the KIEOs beginning in the late 1960s, and the People's Republic of China replaced Taiwan in the IMF and World Bank in 1980. The most dramatic change occurred in the early 1990s after the breakup of the Soviet Union, when Russia and other FSU republics joined the IMF and World

Bank and a number of former East bloc countries joined GATT. Other major changes occurred when China, Taiwan, and Ukraine became WTO members in 2001, 2002, and 2008, respectively. However, Russia has not yet become a WTO member. Later chapters discuss both the opportunities and difficulties presented by the transition economies' membership in the KIEOs.

NONSTATE ACTORS

Over the last two decades, a wide range of nonstate actors have had a growing presence in IPE. Whereas some nonstate actors (e.g., many business groups) support the neoliberal globalization process, others are strongly opposed. Business firms are the most influential nonstate actors in the global economy; they have established their own business institutions, influenced the policies of the KIEOs, and interacted with governments and IOs in the **World Economic Forum (WEF)**. The WEF's origins stem from the *European Management Forum,* a group of European business leaders that began meeting in Davos, Switzerland, in 1971 to help Europe reclaim some leadership of the international business community from the United States. The group gradually shifted to a global focus, changed its name to the WEF in 1987, and became a venue in which business executives, political leaders, and multilateral institutions discuss global socioeconomic and political problems. The WEF's core members are the top 1,200 global firms and banks in terms of global sales or capital. In addition to its annual meeting in Davos, the WEF holds regional summits and issues influential publications such as the *Global Competitiveness Report* and the *Global Information Technology Report.* Although the WEF is a private institution with no publicly-sanctioned authority, it has a public agenda and considerable influence in the public sphere. For example, the Mexican President initiated discussions at the WEF in 1990 that led to negotiation of the NAFTA.[64] Many liberals believe that business entrepreneurs in the WEF are acting in the global public interest, and they note that the WEF's founder (Klaus Schwab) adheres to a *multistakeholder model* that takes account of the interests of a wide range of private and public actors. Critical theorists by contrast argue that NGOs account for less than 2 percent of those at the Davos meetings, and that members of the WEF governing boards are "overwhelmingly male, predominantly white and substantially from the wealthiest nations of Europe, North America and Japan."[65]

In contrast to global business firms, NGOs and social movements focusing on labor, women, the environment, development, and human rights have been largely excluded from positions of power. These diverse groups are often categorized together as *civil society,* which can be defined as a wide range of nongovernmental, noncommercial groups that seek to either reinforce or alter existing norms, rules, and social structures. Scholars discuss three types of civil society orientations in terms of objectives and tactics: conformist, reformist, and transformist or rejectionist.[66] Although much of the literature focuses on civil society protests aimed at the IMF, World Bank, WTO, and other symbols of neoliberal globalization, most civil society organizations (CSOs) are conformists "that seek to uphold and reinforce existing norms."[67] Conformist CSOs include many professional associations, business lobbies, philanthropic foundations, some research groups such as the Institute for International Economics and the Brookings Institution, and the WEF, which has official NGO consultative status with the UN ECOSOC.[68] Reformist CSOs want the KIEOs to become more democratic, transparent, and open to participation by underrepresented groups, but they do not seek to replace the underlying structure of capitalism.[69] Reformists often engage in peaceful protest such as passive marches, but they also interact with the KIEOs through lobbying, discussions, briefing sessions, and negotiations. Transformist or rejectionist CSOs seek "a comprehensive change of the social order (whether in a progressive or a reactionary fashion)."[70] Leftist rejectionists adopt an anti-capitalist position and see the KIEOs as unreformable. Although rejectionists employ a diversity of tactics, they are generally committed to confrontational and disruptive actions; extreme rejectionists such as anarchists may engage in property destruction, clashes with the police, and violence. Some scholars refer to rejectionists as "anti-globalizers" because they oppose international trade and financial integration, but others argue that rejectionists are not opposed to globalization *per se;* they oppose the neoliberal terms of globalization.[71]

A major obstacle to scholarly analyis of civil society groups is that "civil society" is a vague term used in "many different theoretical, practical, and historical contexts."[72] A number of scholars find the term **transnational advocacy networks** (**TANs**) more useful for analyzing the relations between NGOs and other actors. A TAN "includes those relevant actors working internationally on an issue, who are bound together by shared values, a common discourse, and dense exchanges of information and services."[73] TANs advocate for value-laden causes and they are particularly important in areas related to the environment, women, infant health, and indigenous peoples. However, they have also been involved with economic matters, and we will examine the position of TANs on trade, development, and foreign debt issues. NGOs have a central role in most TANs, but they may also include social movements, the media, trade unions, consumer organizations, religious institutions, intellectuals, parts of IOs, and various branches of governments.[74]

CONCLUSION

This chapter has examined the institutional framework for managing the postwar global economy in terms of the themes of North–North relations, North–South relations, and globalization. Subsequent chapters discuss the role of the KIEOs and other economic institutions in greater detail. The DCs at the Bretton Woods Conference had faith in the ability of international institutions to promote economic stability and growth, and the three KIEOs have contributed to postwar prosperity. However, there is a hierarchy of states in the IMF, World Bank, and WTO, and postwar prosperity has not been equally distributed. The LDCs have less power and wealth in the global political economy, and they have tried to alter the KIEOs and establish alternative organizations such as UNCTAD. However, their gains have been limited, and the foreign debt and financial crises have induced many LDCs to become more closely integrated with the KIEOs (see Chapter 11). For many years the centrally planned economies did not participate in the KIEOs, and the Soviet Union established the CMEA as an alternative organization. However, these countries began to join the KIEOs because of growing economic problems and dependence on the West. The breakup of the Soviet bloc and Soviet Union sped up this integration process.

The KIEOs are therefore becoming universal membership organizations, but it is increasingly difficult for them to reach a consensus and manage global economic relations. The KIEOs are also affected by civil society groups and TANs that criticize them for subordinating "issues such as environmental protection, gender equality, and labour rights to a liberalization drive."[75] Although many reformist civil society groups are engaging in dialogue with the KIEOs, dialogue with the rejectionists is virtually impossible because they consider the IMF, World Bank, and WTO to be unreformable. The KIEOs are also finding it difficult to manage the globalization process; for example, it is difficult to promote financial stability because MNCs and international banks are moving more capital around the world than the economic resources available to the KIEOs. The DCs have turned to smaller groupings such as the OECD and G8 to bolster their management capabilities, but these groups also have limitations, partly because important economic actors such as China, India, and Brazil are not members. In view of the growing importance of these emerging powers, it is likely that the G20, which is composed of major LDCs as well as DCs, will have growing influence. However, the question remains whether the G20 is too large and diverse to form a consensus on critical global economic issues. In sum, this chapter has examined the role of the postwar institutions in promoting globalization and the complexities globalization is presenting for their management capabilities. The next three chapters examine the IPE theoretical perspectives.

Questions

1. Why were the IMF, World Bank, and GATT/WTO created, and why are they called the "keystone international economic organizations"?
2. What is the role of smaller organizations and groups such as the OECD, G7/G8, and G20? Why was the G20 formed, and do you think it is likely to displace the G7/G8?
3. What are the advantages of using PPP-adjusted per capita GDP figures, and what are the shortcomings of the PPP-adjusted figures?
4. What is the human development index, and what are its strengths and weaknesses?
5. Why were the G77 and UNCTAD formed, and how successful have they been?
6. How has the relationship changed between the former centrally planned economies and the KIEOs?

7. What is the World Economic Forum, and in what way does it contribute to a blurring of lines between "public" and "private" in the global political economy?
8. What are civil society groups, and how are they differentiated in terms of their tactics and goals? What are TANs?

Further Reading

Recent studies with alternative perspectives on the keystone international economic organizations include Gustav Ranis, James Raymond Vreeland, and Stephen Kosack, *Globalization and the Nation State: The Impact of the IMF and the World Bank* (New York: Routledge, 2006); Ngaire Woods, *The Globalizers: The IMF, the World Bank, and Their Borrowers* (Ithaca, NY: Cornell University Press, 2006); Richard Peet, *Unholy Trinity: The IMF, World Bank and WTO* (New York: Zed Books, 2003).

A classic study of the Group of Seven is Robert D. Putnam and Nicholas Bayne, *Hanging Together: Cooperation and Conflict in the Seven-Power Summit,* rev. ed. (London: Sage, 1987); a more updated study on the G7/G8 is Hugo Dobson, *The Group of 7/8* (New York: Routledge, 2007). John J. Kirton has also been series editor for a number of books dealing with the G8 and global governance.

A recent study of the role of LDCs in UNCTAD is Ian Taylor and Karen Smith, *United Nations Conference on Trade and Development* (New York: Routledge, 2007). For an intellectual history of UNCTAD see Shigehisa Kasahara and Charles Gore, eds., *Beyond Conventional Wisdom in Development Policy: An Intellectual History of UNCTAD 1964-2004* (New York: United Nations, 2004). On the poorest developing countries (or LLDCs), see Paul Collier, *The Bottom Billion: Why the Poorest Countries are Failing and What Can Be Done About It* (New York: Oxford University Press, 2007).

For differing views on the World Economic Forum, see Geoffrey Allen, *The World Economic Forum: A Multi-Stakeholder Approach to Global Governance* (New York: Routledge, 2007); Jean-Christophe Graz, "How Powerful are Transnational Elite Clubs? The Social Myth of the World Economic Forum," *New Political Economy* 8, no. 3 (November 2003), pp. 321–340.

A good study of transnational advocacy groups and social movements is Sanjeev Khagram, James V. Riker, and Kathryn Sikkink, eds., *Restructuring World Politics: Transnational Social Movements, Networks, and Norms* (Minneapolis, MN: University of Minnesota Press, 2002). A study that compares the role of business and NGOs in trade policy is Brian Hocking, "Changing the Terms of Trade Policy Making: From the 'Club' to the 'Multistakeholder' Model," *World Trade Review* 3, no. 1 (2004), pp. 3–26.

Notes

1. Armand Van Dormael, *Bretton Woods: Birth of a Monetary System* (London: Macmillan, 1978), p. ix.
2. Richard N. Gardner, "The Political Setting," in A. L. Keith Acheson, John F. Chant, and Martin F. J. Prochowny, eds., *Bretton Woods Revisited* (Toronto: University of Toronto Press, 1972), p. 20.

3. Herman M. Schwartz, *States versus Markets: The Emergence of a Global Economy,* 2nd ed. (New York: St. Martin's Press, 2000), p. 11.

4. Adam Smith used the term *mercantile system,* German writers used the term *Merkantilismus,* and only later did the term *mercantilism* become standard. Jacob Viner, "Mercantilist Thought," in David L. Sills, ed., *International Encyclopedia of the Social Sciences,* vol. 4 (New York: Free Press, 1968), p. 436; David A. Baldwin, *Economic Statecraft* (Princeton, NJ: Princeton University Press, 1985), p. 72.

5. Adam Smith, *The Wealth of Nations,* vol. 1 (London: Dent, Everyman's Library no. 412, 1910), bk. 4, p. 436.

6. On mercantilism, see Eli F. Heckscher, *Mercantilism,* vols. 1 and 2, rev. 2nd ed., transl. Mendel Shapiro (London: George Allen & Unwin, 1955); and Jacob Viner, *Studies in the Theory of International Trade* (New York: Augustus M. Kelley, 1965), chs. 1 and 2.

7. For differing views on world powers during the mercantilist period, see George Modelski, "The Long Cycle of Global Politics and the Nation-State," *Comparative Studies in Society and History* 20, no. 2 (April 1978), pp. 214–235; Joshua S. Goldstein, *Long Cycles: Prosperity and War in the Modern Age* (New Haven, CT: Yale University Press, 1988), pp. 99–147.

8. Paul Kennedy, *The Rise and Fall of the Great Powers: Economic Change and Military Conflict from 1500 to 2000* (New York: Random House, 1987), p. 151; Paul Bairoch, "International Industrialization Levels from 1750 to 1980," *Journal of European Economic History* 11, no. 2 (Fall 1982), pp. 291–292.

9. Some writers argue that Britain's contribution to freer trade in the nineteenth century is overestimated. See Timothy J. McKeown, "Hegemonic Stability Theory and 19th Century Tariff Levels in Europe," *International Organization* 37, no. 1 (Winter 1983), pp. 73–91.

10. Edward John Ray, "Changing Patterns of Protectionism: The Fall in Tariffs and the Rise in Non-Tariff Barriers," *Northwestern Journal of International Law & Business* 8 (1987), pp. 294–295; Stephen D. Krasner, "State Power and the Structure of International Trade," *World Politics* 28, no. 3 (April 1976), pp. 330–335.

11. David A. Lake, *Power, Protection, and Free Trade: International Sources of U.S. Commercial Strategy, 1887–1939* (Ithaca, NY: Cornell University Press, 1988), pp 30–32; Bairoch, "International Industrialization Levels from 1750 to 1980," pp. 292–293, 297.

12. Kennedy, *The Rise and Fall of the Great Powers,* p. 230; Albert Fishlow, "Lessons from the Past: Capital Markets during the 19th Century and the Interwar Period," *International Organization* 39, no. 3 (Summer 1985), p. 390; David A. Lake, "British and American Hegemony Compared: Lessons for the Current Era of Decline," in Michael Fry, ed., *History, The White House and The Kremlin: Statesmen as Historians* (London: Pinter, 1991), p. 108.

13. Sally Marks, *The Illusion of Peace: International Relations in Europe 1918–1933* (New York: St. Martin's Press, 1976), p. 47; Charles P. Kindleberger, *The World in Depression 1929–1939,* rev. ed. (Berkeley: University of California Press, 1986), pp. 23–26; Robert A. Pastor, *Congress and the Politics of U.S. Foreign Economic Policy, 1929–1976* (Berkeley: University of California Press, 1980), p. 78.

14. See Kindleberger, *The World in Depression 1929–1939.*

15. The classic study of domestic pressures on the U.S. Congress during the interwar period is Elmer E. Schattschneider, Politics, Pressures and the Tariff: A Study of

Free Private Enterprise in Pressure Politics, as Shown in the 1929–1930 Revision of the Tariff (Hamden, CT: Archon Books, 1963).

16. Lake, *Power, Protection, and Free Trade,* p. 204.

17. Harold K. Jacobson, *Networks of Interdependence: International Organizations and the Global Political System* (New York: Alfred A. Knopf, 1979), pp. 230–231.

18. On the BIS, see Age F. P. Bakker, *International Financial Institutions* (New York: Longman, 1996), ch. 6; Hazel J. Johnson, *Global Financial Institutions and Markets* (Oxford: Blackwell, 2000), pp. 410–411.

19. Margaret G. de Vries, "The Bretton Woods Conferences and the Birth of the International Monetary Fund," in Orin Kirshner, ed., *The Bretton Woods-GATT System: Retrospect and Prospect After Fifty Years* (Armonk, NY: M. E. Sharpe, 1996), pp. 3–4; Arthur Stein, "Coordination and Collaboration: Regimes in an Anarchic World," in David A. Baldwin, ed., *Neorealism and Neoliberalism: The Contemporary Debate* (New York: Columbia University Press, 1993), pp. 41–45.

20. The term *KIEOs* is used in Harold Jacobson and Michel Oksenberg, *China's Participation in the IMF, the World Bank, and GATT: Toward a Global Economic Order* (Ann Arbor, MI: University of Michigan Press, 1990).

21. Quoted in Sidney Dell, "Relations Between the United Nations and the Bretton Woods Institutions," *Development* 4 (1989), p. 28.

22. See Samuel A. Bleicher, "UN v. IBRD: A Dilemma of Functionalism," *International Organization* 24, no. 1 (Winter 1970), pp. 31–47.

23. Communication from a Counsellor, External Relations Division, WTO, November 8, 2001.

24. "United Nations-Bretton Woods Collaboration: How Much Is Enough?" *Report of the Twenty-Sixth United Nations Issues Conference* (Muscatine, IA: Stanley Foundation, February 24–26, 1995), p. 18.

25. Dell, "Relations Between the United Nations and the Bretton Woods Institutions," pp. 27–38; Edward S. Mason and Robert E. Asher, *The World Bank Since Bretton Woods* (Washington, D.C.: Brookings Institution), pp. 566–576.

26. UNCTAD, *World Investment Report 1996* (New York: United Nations, 1996), pp. 239–247; World Trade Organization, *WTO Annual Report 1996,* vol. 2 (Geneva: WTO, 1996), pp. 24, 67.

27. Miles Kahler, *Leadership Selection in the Major Multilaterals* (Washington, D.C.: Institute for International Economics, 2001); Theodore Cohn, "Developing Countries in the International Civil Service: The Case of the World Bank Group," *International Review of Administrative Sciences* 41, no. 1 (1975), pp. 47–56.

28. Bretton Woods Commission, *Bretton Woods: Looking to the Future* (Washington, D.C.: Bretton Woods Committee, 1994), p. B–3.

29. Barry Eichengreen and Peter B. Kenen, "Managing the World Economy under the Bretton Woods System: An Overview," in Peter B. Kenen, ed., *Managing the World Economy: Fifty Years After Bretton Woods* (Washington, D.C.: Institute for International Economics, 1944), pp. 5–6; John G. Ruggie, "International Regimes, Transactions, and Change: Embedded Liberalism in the Postwar Economic Order," in Stephen D. Krasner, ed., *International Regimes* (Ithaca, NY: Cornell University Press), pp. 195–231.

30. "United Nations-Bretton Woods Collaboration: How Much Is Enough?" p. 2; Aaron Segal, "Managing the World Economy," *International Political Science Review* 11, no. 3 (1990), p. 367.

31. C. Fred Bergsten and C. Randall Henning, *Global Economic Leadership and the Group of Seven* (Washington, D.C.: Institute for International Economics, 1996), p. 15.

32. On the smaller DC-led groups see Theodore H. Cohn, *Governing Global Trade: International Institutions in Conflict and Convergence* (Burlington, VT: Ashgate, 2002).

33. Nicholas Bayne, "Making Sense of Western Economic Policies: The Role of the OECD," *The World Today* 43, no. 2 (February 1987), p. 27. The European Union is a special member of the OECD.

34. Organization for Economic Cooperation and Development, *The OECD in the 1990s* (Paris: OECD, 1994), p. 9; David Henderson, "The Role of the OECD in Liberalising International Trade and Capital Flows," in Sven Arndt and Chris Miller, eds., special issue of *The World Economy* on "Global Trade Policy" (1996), pp. 11–28.

35. William J. Drake and Kalypso Nicolaïdis, "Ideas, Interests, and Institutionalization: 'Trade in Services' and The Uruguay Round," *International Organization* 46, no. 1 (Winter 1992) pp. 37–100.

36. Richard Woodward, "Global Governance and the Organization for Economic Cooperation and Development," in Glenn D. Hook and Hugo Dobson, eds., *Global Governance and Japan: The Institutional Architecture* (New York: Routledge, 2007), pp. 59–75.

37. Bergsten and Henning, *Global Economic Leadership and the Group of Seven*, pp. 22–23; Peter B. Kenen, *The International Financial Architecture: What's New? What's Missing?* (Washington, D.C.: Institute for International Economics, 2001), p. 4.

38. Michael C. Webb, *The Political Economy of Policy Coordination: International Adjustment Since 1945* (Ithaca, NY: Cornell University Press, 1995), pp. 176–177.

39. Robert D. Putnam and Nicholas Bayne, *Hanging Together: Cooperation and Conflict in the Seven-Power Summits,* rev. ed. (London: Sage, 1987), pp. 150–154; Nicholas Bayne, *Hanging in There: The G-7 and G-8 Summit in Maturity and Renewal* (Burlington, VT: Ashgate, 2000), pp. 116–118.

40. Michael R. Hodges, "The G8 and the New Political Economy," in Michael R. Hodges, John J. Kirton, and Joseph P. Daniels, eds., *The G8's Role in the New Millennium* (Brookfield, VT: Ashgate, 1999), p. 69; Hugo Dobson, *The Group of 7/8* (New York: Routledge, 2007), pp. xv–xvii.

41. The G20 members are Argentina, Australia, Brazil, Canada, China, France, Germany, India, Indonesia, Italy, Japan, Mexico, Russia, Saudi Arabia, South Africa, South Korea, Turkey, United Kingdom, United States, and the EU. James D. Wolfensohn, "The Summit's Promise," *Washington Post,* November 14, 2008, p. A19; David Akin, "G-20 Mission: Save World From Deep Recession," *Vancouver Sun,* November 14, 2008, p. H7.

42. Bretton Woods Commission, *Bretton Woods,* p. B–3.

43. World Bank, *World Development Indicators— 2001* (Washington, D.C.: World Bank, 2001), p. 293. On the use of PPP rates by international organizations, see Ian Castles and David Henderson, "International Comparisons of GDP," *World Economics* 6, no. 1 (January–March 2005), pp. 75–80.

44. For example, see "Big MacCurrencies," *The Economist,* April 11, 1998, p. 58.

45. "Grossly Distorted Picture," *The Economist,* February 11, 2006, p. 72; Organization for Economic Cooperation and Development, *Going for Growth—2006* (Paris: OECD, 2006), pp. 135–136.

46. United Nations Development Program, *Human Development Report 2007/2008* (New York: Palgrave Macmillan, 2007), p. 221. The 17 excluded countries are listed on p. 233 of the report.

47. UNDP, *Human Development Report 2006* (New York: Palgrave Macmillan, 2006), p. 264.
48. Graeme Smith, "Russians Dying of AIDS, Drugs, and Despair," *Globe and Mail,* April 24, 2006, pp. A12–A13; UNDP, *Human Development Report 2005* (New York: UNDP, 2005), p. 23.
49. UNDP, *Human Development Report 2006,* pp. 265–269; UNDP, *Human Development Report 2005,* p. 3–4, 25–27.
50. UNDP, *Human Development Report 2005,* p. 26.
51. UNCTAD Secretariat, "Statistical Profiles of the Least Developed Countries," United Nations, New York, 2005, pp. 5–6.
52. UNCTAD, *The Least Developed Countries Report 2006* (New York: United Nations, 2006), ch. 1.
53. See United Nations Department of Economic and Social Affairs, *The Inequality Predicament: Report on the World Social Situation 2005* (New York: United Nations, 2005), pp. 47, 79–80.
54. UNDP, *Human Development Report 2006,* p. 267; United Nations Department of Economic and Social Affairs, *The Inequality Predicament,* p. 4; World Bank, *World Development Report 2006* (Washington, D.C.: Oxford University Press, 2005), pp. 4–6.
55. David A. Kay, *The New Nations in the United Nations, 1960–1967* (New York: Columbia University Press, 1970), pp. 2–3.
56. Harold K. Jacobson, *Networks of Interdependence: International Organizations and the Global Political System* (New York: Knopf, 1979), p. 13.
57. Quoted in Joseph Gold, *Membership and Nonmembership in the International Monetary Fund: A Study in International Law and Organization* (Washington, D.C.: International Monetary Fund, 1974), p. 129.
58. Valerie J. Assetto, *The Soviet Bloc in the IMF and the IBRD* (Boulder, CO: Westview Press, 1988), pp. 56–66, 185; Jozef M. van Brabant, *The Planned Economies and International Economic Organizations* (Cambridge, UK: Cambridge University Press, 1991), pp. 45–48.
59. Michael Kaser, *Comecon: Integration Problems of the Planned Economies* (London: Oxford University Press, 1965), pp. 9–12.
60. Klaus Schröder, "The IMF and the Countries of the Council for Mutual Economic Assistance," *Intereconomics* 2 (March/April 1982), p. 87; Brabant, *The Planned Economies and International Economic Organizations,* p. 70.
61. *IBRD—Articles of Agreement,* as amended effective February 16, 1989 (Washington, D.C.: International Bank for Reconstruction and Development, August 1991), Article 4, section 10.
62. David A. Baldwin, "The International Bank in Political Perspective," *World Politics* 18, no. 1 (October 1965), pp. 68–81; Theodore H. Cohn, "Politics in the World Bank Group: The Question of Loans to the Asian Giants," *International Organization* 28, no. 3 (Summer 1974), pp. 561–571.
63. Gold, *Membership and Nonmembership in the International Monetary Fund,* pp. 342–379; Assetto, *The Soviet Bloc in the IMF and the IBRD,* pp. 69–93.
64. Geoffrey A. Pigman, *The World Economic Forum: A Multi-Stakeholder Approach to Global Governance* (New York: Routledge, 2007), p. 15.
65. Quoted in Mark Rupert and M. Scott Solomon, *Globalization and International Political Economy: The Politics of Alternative Futures* (Lanham, MD: Rowman & Littlefield, 2006), pp. 59–61.
66. See Jan A. Scholte, "Civil Society and Democracy in Global Governance," *Global Governance* 8 (2002), pp. 281–304; Jeffrey M. Ayres, "Global Governance and

Civil Society Collective Action: The Challenge of Complex Transnationalism," *International Journal of Political Economy* 33, no. 4 (Winter 2003–2004), pp. 84–100.

67. Scholte, "Civil Society and Democracy in Global Governance," p. 284.
68. Pigman, *The World Economic Forum,* p. 58.
69. Scholte, "Civil Society and Democracy in Global Governance," p. 284.
70. Scholte, "Civil Society and Democracy in Global Governance," p. 284.
71. Ayres, "Global Governance and Civil Society Collective Action," pp. 92–94; Leslie E. Armijo, "The Terms of the Debate: What's Democracy Got to Do with It?" in Leslie E. Armijo, ed., *Debating the Global Financial Architecture* (Albany, NY: State University of New York Press, 2002), pp. 51–53.
72. Mark N. Jensen, "Concepts and Conceptions of Civil Society," *Journal of Civil Society* 2, no. 1 (May 2006), p. 39.
73. Margaret E. Keck and Kathryn Sikkink, *Activists beyond Borders: Advocacy Networks in International Politics* (Ithaca, NY: Cornell University Press, 1998), p. 2.
74. Sanjeev Khagram, James V. Riker, and Kathryn Sikkink, eds., *Restructuring World Politics: Transnational Social Movements, Networks, and Norms* (Minneapolis, MN: University of Minnesota Press, 2002).
75. Robert O'Brien et al., *Contesting Global Governance: Multilateral Economic Institutions and Global Social Movements* (New York: Cambridge University Press, 2000). p. 21.

PART TWO

Theoretical Perspectives

Before turning to the theoretical perspectives, it is important to discuss the role of theory and methodology in the study of IPE. Theory helps us identify meaningful patterns and a degree of order in the complex world of IPE. Theory also enables us to go beyond description and provide causal explanations and modest predictions. For example, one scholar might hypothesize that free trade contributes to an increase in average real incomes, while another might hypothesize that free trade results in greater economic inequality. Some theorists use mathematical and statistical techniques to test hypotheses such as these, while others rely on historical or comparative studies that are qualitative (i.e., nonquantitative) in nature. A third group of theorists questions whether value-free theorizing is even possible, because the work of all scholars is affected by the historical and cultural setting in which operate (see the discussion of constructivists in Chapter 5). Despite these differences, most theorists agree that theory helps us deal with the wide array of IPE issues and events by focusing on some and disregarding others. (Theorists from different perspectives do *not* agree on which issues are most and least important!)[1]

This book focuses on theories within the realist, liberal, and critical perspectives, and also on two methodologies or methods of theory construction: **rational choice** and **constructivism.** We discuss rational choice here because it is most closely associated with the mainstream liberal and realist assumptions that individuals and states are rational actors with specified interests. In contrast to rational choice theorists, constructivists see reality as being socially constructed. Although there are both critical and conventional (or liberal) versions of constructivism, we discuss constructivism in Chapter 5 with the critical perspectives because even conventional constructivists are critical of the rationalist assumptions of many liberals and realists.

Both supporters and opponents of rational choice analysis would agree that it is a highly influential method of theory construction. Indeed, one scholar has described rational choice as "the most powerful paradigm in the political science discipline, especially in the United States."[2] (*Rational choice* is the favored term of political scientists, while economists prefer the term *public choice*.) Rational choice theorists apply an economic model of human behavior to the social, political, and economic spheres, and develop propositions presenting simplified versions of the real world that can be tested through quantitative methods. (Although mathematical models are often central, they are not a *necessary* feature of rational choice.)[3] Rational choice theorists also assume that individuals have goals and some freedom of choice, and that they take actions they believe will achieve their goals. Individuals are "utility maximizers" who seek to maximize or optimize their self-interest by weighing the expected costs versus the expected benefits of their actions. For example, political leaders weigh the benefits and costs of adopting particular policies in terms of their re-election (i.e., political survival); and individuals weigh the benefits of voting (having some effect on the election results) against the costs (the effort involved in going to vote). Although the pure rational choice model posits that rational individuals obtain an *optimal* amount of information before making decisions, "rationality applies only to endeavor not to outcome; failure to achieve an objective because of ignorance or some other factor does not invalidate the premise that individuals act on the basis of a cost/benefit or means/ends calculation."[4] Thus, many studies assume that individual actions produce *satisfactory* rather than optimal outcomes. The actions available to individuals also have limits because they make choices under conditions of scarcity. For example, an individual may decide to rent a house because she is unable to purchase one.[5] Although rational choice is grounded in the liberal perspective with its emphasis on the individual, some realists use it to explain the international behavior of states, and some critical theorists also use it.[6] Rational choice has contributed to theoretical and empirical analysis in many areas of IPE.

In a number of cases individuals might behave the way the rational choice model predicts; for example, politicians may support policies strongly favored by their constituents to increase their chances for re-election. However, rational choice analysis has been criticized on a number of grounds. Some critics argue that politicians may take actions that rational choice analysts would not consider "rational"; for example, they may oppose policies that go against their ethical principles even if this decreases their chances for re-election. Some politicians may also feel obliged to honor prior commitments to support less popular policies, and this could also decrease their re-election chances. Thus, the rational choice model does not explain all the choices of political actors. Critics also point out that rational choice analysis assumes a rational, self-interested actor who makes decisions without regard to historical and cultural context. It takes individual preferences as a "given" without judging the worthiness of the preferences or seeking to explain why an individual or state has some preferences rather than others. It simply assumes that a state or individual's preferences reflect rational choices under conditions of scarcity. Some other IPE approaches such as constructivist theory take more account of historical and sociological factors (see Chapter 5). Constructivists seek to explain why actors have particular norms, values, beliefs, perceptions, and preferences, and how these affect actions and outcomes. This book examines several areas where rational choice is explicitly applied to the study of IPE. For example, Chapter 3 discusses public goods theory, and Chapter 4 discusses a type of game theory—prisoners' dilemma. In game theory two or more people interact, with each person acting according to the rational choice model (see Chapter 4).[7]

Several other points should be emphasized before we discuss the theoretical perspectives. First, the perspectives are *not* mutually exclusive ideologies; the margins between them are sometimes blurred, and they influence each other over time. Many IPE theories such as hegemonic stability and regime theory are hybrids that draw on more than one perspective. Second, no theoretical perspective explains all phenomena in IPE, and the success of one theory is not necessarily tied to the failure of another. Different theoretical perspectives are useful for explaining various issues and events, and "our empirical task is to sort out under what condition each logic operates—including the recognition that they operate together in some circumstances."[8] Third, there is a wide diversity of writings within each theoretical perspective. Despite this diversity, however, authors within each perspective generally agree on a core set of assumptions. Chapters 3–5 begin with a discussion how the theoretical perspectives deal with four key questions: (1) What is the role of domestic actors? (2) What are the nature and purpose of international economic relations? (3) What is the relationship between politics and economics? (4) What are the causes and effects of globalization? The chapters then examine the historical development of the perspectives, with particular emphasis on the diversity of views within each perspective.

Notes

1. James N. Rosenau and Mary Durfee, *Thinking Theory Thoroughly: Coherent Approaches to an Incoherent World,* 2nd ed. (Boulder, CO: Westview Press, 2000), ch. 1.
2. John S. Dryzek, *Deliberative Democracy and Beyond: Liberals, Critics, Contestations* (New York: Oxford University Press, 2000), p. 31.

3. Duncan Snidal, "Rational Choice and International Relations," in Walter Carlsnaes, Thomas Risse, and Beth A. Simmons, eds., *Handbook of International Relations* (Thousand Oaks, CA: SAGE, 2002), p. 77.

4. Robert Gilpin, *War and Change in World Politics* (New York: Cambridge University Press, 1981), p. x.

5. Stephen Parsons, *Rational Choice and Politics: A Critical Introduction* (New York: Continuum, 2005), pp. 1–23.

6. George T. Crane and Abla Amawi, eds., *The Theoretical Evolution of International Political Economy* (New York: Oxford University Press, 1997), pp. 21–22.

7. See Lisa J. Carlson, "Game Theory: International Trade, Conflict and Cooperation," in Ronen Palan, ed., *Global Political Economy: Contemporary Theories* (New York: Routledge, 2000), pp. 117–129.

8. Snidal, "Rational Choice and International Relations," p. 80.

CHAPTER 3

The Realist Perspective

Realism emphasizes power and the national interest and generally directs more attention to security than economic issues. Liberalism, which is more concerned with socioeconomic issues, has therefore been the dominant perspective in IPE. We nevertheless begin with the realist perspective for several reasons. First, realism is the oldest school of thought in international relations (IR). Thucydides (ca. 471–400 B.C.E.) is often credited with being the first realist author and also with writing the first important work on IR—*The History of the Peloponnesian War,* on war between the Greek city-states.[1] Second, classical realism was the dominant approach to IR for so long that it "provides a good starting point and base line for comparison with competing models."[2] Third, realism is an important approach to IPE today because of ongoing concerns about U.S. hegemony and the changing distribution of economic power, and because of debates regarding the relative merits of the developmental state versus market approaches to development.

Two major strains of realism are relevant to the study of IPE. The first strain, which largely neglects economics, was evident in the views of Niccolò Machiavelli (1420–1527), an Italian philosopher and diplomat who is best known for his classic work *The Prince*. Machiavelli saw little connection between economics and politics, writing that "as I do not know how to reason either about the art of silk or about the art of wool, either about profits or about losses, it befits me to reason about the state."[3] Machiavelli also considered military strength to be more important than wealth in making war because "gold alone will not procure good soldiers, but good soldiers will always procure gold."[4] As this chapter discusses, American realists after World War II, like Machiavelli, devoted little attention to economics. The second strain of realism, stemming from Thucydides and the mercantilists, is more attuned to economic–political interactions. In *The History of the Peloponnesian War,* Thucydides attributed war among the Greek city-states to several economic changes, including the growth of trade and the emergence of new commercial powers such as Athens and Corinth. Unlike Machiavelli, Thucydides viewed wealth as a critical source of military strength, and he wrote that "war is a matter not so much of arms as of money, which makes arms of use."[5] Although Thucydides often referred to economic matters, the mercantilists of the sixteenth to nineteenth centuries were the first to engage in *systematic* theorizing on IPE issues from a realist perspective.[6]

BASIC TENETS OF THE REALIST PERSPECTIVE

The Role of the Individual, the State, and Societal Groups

Realists assert that the international system is "anarchic," because there is no central authority above the state. Unlike most domestic societies, IR is a self-help system in which each state must look after its own interests. Thus, realists see the state as the principal actor in IR, and they emphasize the need to preserve national sovereignty. A state has internal sovereignty when it has a monopoly on the legitimate use of force within its territory, and it has external sovereignty when it is free of control by outside authorities. Some realists give top priority to power and others to security, but both are necessary for the state to survive and pursue its national interest. Realists see the state as a unitary actor, with subnational and transnational actors operating within the rubric of the state in IR. Realists also describe states as rational actors that seek to maximize the benefits and minimize the costs of pursuing their objectives. States may settle for *value-satisfying* rather than *value-maximizing* decisions, because policy makers have biases and misperceptions and may lack information and capabilities needed to make optimal choices. Nevertheless, the state according to realists is basically a rational decision maker.[7] The assumption that states are rational, unitary actors enables realists to be *parsimonious* theorists who explain numerous phenomena with a small number of concepts and variables.

The Nature and Purpose of International Economic Relations

In a self-help system such as IR, a *security dilemma* results because the actions a state takes to bolster its own security may increase the fear and insecurity of others; thus, even if a state arms itself for defensive purposes, this may raise fears and contribute to an arms race. In view of the security dilemma, realists see each state as being most concerned with *relative gains*, or its position vis-à-vis other states. Even if two states are "gaining absolutely in wealth, in political terms it is the effect of these gains on relative power positions which is of primary importance."[8] The realist emphasis on relative gains stems from their view that IR is a *zero-sum game*, in which one group's gain equals another group's loss. Liberals by contrast focus on *absolute gains*, in which each state seeks to maximize its own gains and is less concerned about the gains of others; and liberals see IR as a *variable-sum game,* in which groups may gain or lose together. Liberal and realist views of international institutions are a prime example of this difference in outlook. Whereas liberals see the IMF, World Bank, and WTO as politically neutral organizations that benefit all states adhering to their liberal economic guidelines, realists see these IOs as "arenas for acting out power relationships" in which the most powerful states shape the rules to fit their national interests.[9]

Despite their concern with relative gains, realists focus on the redistribution of power *within* the capitalist system, whereas historical materialists believe that a more equitable distribution of wealth and power is not possible with unfettered capitalism. In the view of historical materialists, there are "two main modes of development in contemporary history: capitalist and redistributive," and realism fits with liberalism in the capitalist mold.[10]

The Relationship Between Politics and Economics

Realists give priority to politics over economics and generally view "the economy as a creature of the state."[11] This was especially the case during the height of the Cold War when American realist scholars focused almost exclusively on political security issues and largely ignored economics (see discussion in this chapter). Realists also believe that the distribution of political power has a major effect on international economic relations. Thus, this chapter discusses "hegemonic stability theory," which examines the effect of a predominant state (Britain in the nineteenth century and the United States in the twentieth century) on the global political economy.

The Causes and Effects of Globalization

Realists see globalization primarily as an economic process that does not affect the basic international political structure in which states are predominant. Thus, globalization increases only when states permit it to increase. The largest states can either open or close world markets and can use globalization to improve their power positions vis-à-vis weaker states. In regard to the effects of globalization, realists see

> no evidence that globalization has systematically undermined state control. . . . Transnational activities have challenged state control in some areas, but these challenges are not manifestly more problematic than in the past.[12]

Whereas liberals believe that globalization is imposing pressures on states to adopt a single model of capitalism, realists argue that different national capitalisms can continue to exist in a world of separate states. For example, the state has generally had a greater role in socioeconomic affairs in France, the Scandinavian countries, Japan, South Korea, and Taiwan than it has had in the United States, Britain, and Canada.[13] Some realists argue that globalization has "enabling" as well as "constraining" effects on the state. Thus, many states have "increased direct tax yields, maintained or expanded social spending, and devised more complex systems of trade and industrial governance in order to cope with deepening integration."[14]

THE MERCANTILISTS

Adam Smith, the eighteenth-century liberal economist and philosopher, used the term **mercantilism** to refer to economic thought and practice prevalent in Europe from about 1500 to 1750.[15] As discussed in Chapter 2, mercantilism's emphasis on national power played an important role in state building after the demise of feudalism. Mercantilists believed that a state could use the gold and silver it accumulated to increase its power by building up its armed forces, hiring mercenaries, and influencing its enemies and allies. Mercantilist states therefore took all necessary measures to accumulate gold by increasing their exports and decreasing their imports. Because it is impossible for all states to have a balance-of-trade surplus, mercantilists viewed conflict as central to IR and relative gains as more important than absolute gains.[16] In the late eighteenth century, important critics argued that mercantilism encouraged states to encroach on individual freedom and engage in the continuous cycle of European wars. For example, Adam Smith asserted that mercantilism encouraged states to "beggar . . . all their neighbours" and caused trade and commerce to become a "fertile source of discord and animosity."[17] These criticisms were highly effective, and liberal views of free trade became dominant in England—the major power of the time—for much of the nineteenth century. We should note that some authors use *mercantilism* as a general term in reference to realist thought and practice in IPE, and they refer to some states today as being "neomercantilist." To avoid confusion, this book uses the term *realism* in reference to the IPE perspective and the term *mercantilism* only in reference to the period when states sought to increase their national power in the sixteenth to eighteenth centuries.

REALISM AND THE INDUSTRIAL REVOLUTION

Mercantilism was a preindustrial doctrine, and the Industrial Revolution gave new impetus to realists who viewed industrialization as essential for a state's military power, security, and economic self-sufficiency. Foremost among the realist thinkers at this time were Alexander Hamilton (1755–1804), the first U.S. Secretary of the Treasury, and Friedrich List (1789–1846), a German civil servant, professor, and politician who was imprisoned and exiled for his dissident political views. Hamilton's 1791 *Report on the Subject of Manufactures* "contains the intellectual origins of modern economic nationalism and the classic defense of economic protectionism."[18] The report argued that the

United States could preserve its independence and security only by promoting economic development through industrialization, government intervention, protectionism, and economic self-sufficiency. Industrialization was especially important because the "independence and security of a Country, appear to be materially connected with the prosperity of manufactures,"[19] and U.S. government intervention was necessary to establish an industrial base because Britain had discouraged manufacturing in its colonies. To counter Britain's industrial advantages, the U.S. government had to promote the use of foreign technology, capital, and skilled labor and adopt protectionist policies such as tariffs and quotas to bolster its fledgling industries.

List, who was influenced by Hamilton's ideas, also emphasized the importance of manufacturing for a state's economic development. In *The National System of Political Economy* (1841), List wrote that "a nation which exchanges agricultural products for foreign manufactured goods is an individual with *one* arm, which is supported by a foreign arm."[20] Thus, Germany and the United States could catch up with the British only by providing protection for their infant industries. Britain itself had attained manufacturing supremacy by adopting protectionist policies, and it did not turn to free trade until the nineteenth century to retain its lead in manufacturing; thus, Britain traded industrial products for U.S. wool and cotton. National unity was also important because a strong, unified state could impose external trade barriers, launch national projects such as building railroads, and promote the development of "human capital" (e.g., human skills, training, and enterprise). List argued that governments had responsibilities to educate their citizens because Britain's leadership in manufacturing stemmed largely from the superiority of its educational system.[21]

As realists, Hamilton and List criticized liberal economists who favored a division of labor and free trade. In List's view, liberals overemphasized the existence of natural peace and harmony, and underestimated the importance of national rivalries and conflict. However, Hamilton and List were "benign" rather than "malign" economic nationalists. Whereas malign nationalists seek "national goals relentlessly, even at the expense of others," benign nationalists identify their "own national interest with an interest in the stability of the overall international system."[22] Although List argued that protectionism could be used to promote industrialization, he criticized the mercantilists for supporting agricultural protectionism; and he considered free trade to be valuable in the long term for states that had achieved industrial supremacy. The United States and Germany had to adopt protective trade policies to increase their productive potential, but after they were "raised by artificial measure," List wrote, "freedom of trade" could then "operate naturally."[23]

REALISM IN THE INTERWAR PERIOD

Although Britain ushered in a period of free trade with the repeal of its Corn Laws in 1846, changes in the late nineteenth century caused trade liberalization to lose some of its appeal (see Chapter 2). Under the pressures of World War I and the economic crises of the interwar years, there was a virtual breakdown of cooperative relations based on liberalism. Scholars wrote many books and articles on economic nationalism during the interwar period, and states sought to protect their national interests with trade barriers, competitive currency devaluations, and foreign exchange controls.[24] The dire economic conditions also encouraged extreme ideologies such as fascism, which "took advantage of the economic dislocation to attack the entire liberal-capitalist system and to call for assertive 'national' policies, backed if necessary by the sword."[25] The extreme nationalism and protectionism contributed to the Great Depression and World War II and gave leaders at Bretton Woods the impetus to establish a liberal economic system. In the postwar international *political* system, however, realist thought was to reign supreme.

REALISM AFTER WORLD WAR II

Although Thucydides, the mercantilists, Hamilton, and List had been highly attuned to economic issues, U.S. realist scholars after World War II focused almost exclusively on security issues. Security was the major concern with the emergence of the Cold War, and economic issues seemed to have less political importance. A consensus was formed under U.S. leadership at Bretton Woods that ushered in a period of economic stability and prosperity, and LDCs that felt their interests received too little attention were unable to exert much influence. The Cold War was also largely excluded from the postwar economic system because most Soviet bloc countries were not members of the IMF, World Bank, and GATT. These organizations functioned well without the Soviet bloc because it accounted for only a small share of global economic transactions. Thus, realist scholars considered economic issues to be "low politics" and not worthy of much attention.[26] Postwar realists were also influenced by liberal views on the separability of economics and politics. However, unlike liberals such as Adam Smith who favored a laissez-faire economy free of political constraints, realist scholars emphasized politics and largely ignored economics. The United States views that the state *should be* separated from the economy also influenced postwar realists. Whereas U.S. government involvement in military defense matters was accepted, government involvement in the economy was considered less legitimate. Finally, America's superpower status led U.S. realists to focus so firmly on the struggle with the Soviet Union that they "overlooked the economic relations beneath the flux of political relations."[27] Thus, liberalism and Marxism clearly overshadowed realism as IPE perspectives during the 1950s and 1960s.

THE REVIVAL OF REALIST IPE

In the 1970s and 1980s, theorists such as Robert Gilpin and Stephen Krasner returned "to a realist conception of the relationship of economics and politics that had disappeared from postwar American writings."[28] Two factors contributed to the revival of realism as an IPE perspective. First, the decline of the Cold War and increasing disarray in the global economy forced many realists to broaden their focus beyond security issues. Although Western economic relations had prospered under U.S. leadership during the 1950s and 1960s, major changes in the 1970s and 1980s—such as the OPEC price increases, the relative decline of U.S. hegemony, and the foreign debt crisis—destabilized the global economy. These new sources of instability forced realists to revise their view that economic issues were low politics. Second, realists returned to IPE because they considered liberal and Marxist studies to be *economistic;* that is, they exaggerated the importance of economics and underestimated the importance of politics. A number of postwar developments demonstrated the need for realist studies focusing on the role of the state. For example, the "Keynesian Revolution" caused DC governments to become heavily involved in **macroeconomic management,** the breakdown of colonialism led to the creation of newly independent states that differed from the Western liberal democratic model, and growing international competition in the 1970s and 1980s put pressure on states to promote industry and technology. Thus, realists had to "bring the state back in" to the study of IPE.[29]

The newer realists challenged liberal interpretations of economic change. Whereas liberals believed that postwar international economic relations had flourished because of the growth of interdependence, realists argued that *the distribution of power among states* was a more important factor than interdependence. A major issue was whether there was a global hegemonic state with predominant power willing and able to provide leadership. Thus, the newer realists strongly supported hegemonic stability theory. Although hegemonic stability theory is closely tied with realism, it is a hybrid theory that also draws on liberalism and historical materialism. However, we discuss hegemonic stability theory here because it has been central to the realist approach to IPE.

HEGEMONIC STABILITY THEORY AND DEBATES OVER U.S. HEGEMONY

Hegemonic stability theory asserts that the international economic system is more likely to be open and stable when a dominant or hegemonic state is *willing* and *able* to provide leadership and when most other major states view the hegemon's policies as relatively beneficial. When a global hegemon is lacking or declining in power, economic openness and stability are more difficult—but not impossible—to maintain. Scholars generally agree that Britain was a global hegemon during the nineteenth century and the United States was a hegemon after World War II. Some scholars assert that there were other world powers before the nineteenth century such as Portugal, Spain, the United Provinces or present-day Netherlands, and (again) the British.[30] However, most scholars believe the influence of these states was not comparable with British and American influence during the nineteenth and twentieth centuries.

Hegemonic stability theory spawned a vast array of literature and "remained atop the agenda of IPE in the United States" for two decades.[31] Scholars critiqued virtually all aspects of the theory, and many of the criticisms were based on empirical grounds. For example, critics questioned whether theorists could draw meaningful conclusions about hegemonic behavior from the experience of only two global hegemons during limited historical periods. Theorists also did not have consistent definitions and measures of hegemony, with different authors focusing on the military, political, economic, and/or cultural aspects. Thus, there was no consensus on when British hegemony declined, and on whether—or by how much—U.S. hegemony was declining. Some critics questioned a basic premise of the theory: that a global hegemon contributes to economic openness and stability. As a result of these criticisms, U.S. scholars gradually became less interested in hegemonic stability theory. However, as an important critic of the theory has noted, "the hegemonic stability research program has sensitized the current generation of scholars to the international political underpinnings of the international economy. This insight should be preserved and built upon, not abandoned."[32] Furthermore, scholars have continued to debate whether or not U.S. hegemony has declined in response to such events as the breakup of the Soviet bloc and Soviet Union in the 1980s and 1990s, and the decline of the U.S. dollar followed by the global financial crisis in 2008. This section therefore focuses on some key questions related to hegemonic stability theory and on the current status of the debate regarding U.S. hegemony:

1. What is hegemony?
2. What are the strategies and motives of hegemonic states?
3. Is hegemony necessary and/or sufficient to produce an open, stable economic system?
4. What is the status of U.S. hegemony?

What Is Hegemony?

The term **hegemony** refers to an extremely unequal distribution of power, and realists view hegemony as a state-centric concept. For example, one realist scholar describes the international system as hegemonic when "a single powerful state controls or dominates the lesser states in the system."[33] However, this definition does not tell us how much control a state must have to be a hegemon. Can a state with military or economic power alone have hegemony, or must it predominate in both areas? Most theorists have stringent conditions for hegemony and believe that only two or three states have been hegemons. Thus, one definition limits hegemony to a relationship in which one state "can largely impose its rules and wishes (at the very least by effective veto power) in the economic, political, military, diplomatic and even cultural arenas."[34]

Although most theorists define hegemony in state-centric terms, *Gramscian* theorists use the term in a cultural sense to connote the complex of *ideas* social groups use to exert their authority; for example, Gramscians refer to the hegemony of ideas such as capitalism and to the global predominance of American culture (see Chapter 5). According to Gramscians, the capitalist class provided subordinate social classes with some concessions such as welfare payments, unemployment insurance, and the rights to unionize; in return, the subordinate classes viewed the capitalist class's hegemony as perfectly legitimate. This hegemony is difficult to overcome because subordinate classes are not aware they are being oppressed. Neo-Gramscians assert that globalization in trade, foreign investment, and finance is enabling a "transnational capitalist class" to establish its hegemony and remove all impediments to the free flow of capital.[35] Althought the Gramscian views alert us to other aspects of hegemony, mainstream scholars usually define hegemony only in state-centric terms.

What Are the Strategies and Motives of Hegemonic States?

Hegemonic stability theorists have differing views of the hegemon's strategies and motives. One model portrays the hegemon as benevolent in both its methods and goals; it promotes general benefits rather than its self-interest and relies on rewards rather than threats to ensure compliance by other states. A second, mixed model portrays the hegemon as seeking both general and personal benefits, and as relying on both threats and rewards to achieve its goals. A third model portrays the hegemon as exploitative; it exerts leadership out of self-interest and uses coercion to enforce compliance. Benevolent hegemons focus on absolute gains, coercive hegemons seek relative gains, and hegemons with mixed motives and methods are interested in both absolute and relative gains.[36]

Liberals view the hegemon in benevolent terms as willing to "take on an undue share of the burdens of the system" by providing public goods to help create open, stable economic regimes.[37] **Public goods** (or *collective goods*) are *nonexcludable* and *nonrival*. Nonexcludability means that others can benefit from the good, even if they do not contribute to its provision. For example, a sidewalk is nonexcludable because individuals who do not help pay for it through taxes are free to use it. Nonrivalness means that a state's (or individual's) use of the good does not decrease the amount available to others. Again, a sidewalk is nonrival because many individuals can benefit from using it. In the liberal view, a benevolent hegemon provides public goods to ensure there is economic openness and stability. At the end of World War II, the United States provided security as a public good through the U.S. nuclear umbrella so that Western Europe and Japan could focus on economic recovery. The United States as a global hegemon also permitted its currency to be used as the main reserve asset, supplied U.S. dollars to facilitate international trade, provided finance for LDC economic growth, and maintained an open market for other countries' exports. (In reality, there are very few *pure* public goods because a hegemon may at least partially exclude some countries.) Rational choice theorists point out that public goods are underproduced even though rational individuals would benefit from cooperating in providing them because states receive public goods even if they are noncontributors or *free riders*. To convince states that they will benefit from contributing to the provision of public goods it is necessary to overcome *collective action problems*. Liberals assume that the hegemon is more likely to rely on rewards rather than coercion in encouraging others to contribute.[38]

Realists are more inclined than liberals to portray the hegemon as further-ing its national interest rather than the general good. Realists expect a rising hegemonic state to prefer an open international system because this contributes to its economic growth, national income, and political power.[39] They also often portray the hegemon as coercive, threatening to cut off trade, investment, and aid to force other states to share the costs of providing public goods. However, many realists believe that hegemonic states have mixed motives and that the effects of hegemony may be beneficial. Thus, one realist writer asserts that

> the creation of a system of multilateral trade relations was in the interests of the United States. . . . It does not follow from this fact, however, that American efforts to achieve such a system were solely self-serving. . . . Nor does it follow that what is good for the United States is contrary to the general welfare of other nations.[40]

Historical materialists are the least likely to view a hegemon as benevolent. Some historical materialists see the hegemon as coordinating the actions of DCs in the core of the global economy, ensuring their dominance over LDCs in the periphery. Only when the hegemon declines is there disarray among the lead-ing capitalist states, which undermines their ability to extract surplus from the periphery. Gramscian theorists encourage disadvantaged groups to develop a "counterhegemony" as a means of extricating themselves from subservience to hegemonic forces in the core.[41]

Is Hegemony Necessary and/or Sufficient to Produce an Open, Stable Economic System?

Hegemonic stability theorists believe that the international economy is more likely to be open and stable if there is a hegemonic state. A hegemon promotes openness and stability by helping create liberal international **regimes,** or "sets of implicit or explicit principles, norms, rules, and decision-making procedures around which actors' expectations converge in a given area of international relations."[42] The regime concept refers to the fact that a degree of governance exists above the nation-state in the absence of a centralized world government. For example, WTO members abide by certain trade regime principles, norms, and rules. The United States as the postwar global hegemon helped create and maintain open and stable monetary, trade, and aid regimes by providing pub-lic goods and using coercion when necessary. Hegemonic stability theorists make several assertions about the effects of British and U.S. hegemony:

• British hegemony was a major force behind trade liberalization in the nineteenth century.

- Britain's hegemonic decline after 1875 led to an increase in trade protectionism.
- Protectionism increased between World Wars I and II because there was no hegemon willing and able to lead.
- The United States as global hegemon after World War II helped create open and stable international regimes.

Despite these claims, a number of empirical studies question whether hegemony is in fact necessary or sufficient to produce economic openness. For example, some critics argue that World War I, *not* Britain's hegemonic decline after 1875, "sounded the death knell for liberalized international trade."[43] Some liberal critics also argue that a hegemon's decline will not necessarily weaken open international regimes, even though the hegemon helped create them. Other states that benefit from open regimes may collectively maintain them even after the hegemon declines. Thus, it is important to ask not only whether there is a hegemon to *supply* open regimes, but also whether there is sufficient *demand* to maintain those regimes in a posthegemonic period.[44] Some liberal theorists go even further and argue that hegemony is not necessary for the creation of regimes. *Negotiated regimes* may arise among states that are relatively equal in stature, and *spontaneous regimes* may arise when countries' expectations converge even without negotiating an explicit agreement.[45]

Others point out that hegemonic states are not always committed to open economic regimes because domestic groups may favor barriers to the free flow of goods, services, or capital. Although the United States generally supported an open international trade regime in the 1940s, it joined European countries in supporting national controls on capital flows. Even in the trade area the United States was not uniformly liberal; in response to domestic interests it insisted that GATT treat agriculture as an exception and it supported a Multi-Fiber Agreement limiting textile imports (see Chapter 7).[46] Some writers assert that factors other than hegemony can account for economic openness and stability. Whereas world prosperity can result in open economic regimes, economic downturns may cause states to adopt protectionist policies. Furthermore, industries tend to support trade openness during periods of shortages and trade protectionism when surpluses accumulate.[47] In sum, while there may be some connection between hegemony and economic openness, critics question whether hegemony is necessary and/or sufficient to create and maintain open, stable economic regimes.

What Is the Status of U.S. Hegemony?

Scholars have had vigorous debates on the status of British and U.S. hegemony. Whereas some authors assert that Britain's hegemony in trade was already declining in 1875, others argue that Britain maintained its hegemony in finance until World War I (see Chapter 2).[48] Some theorists are "declinists," who believe that hegemony is inherently unstable. Declinists predict that the hegemon will overextend itself in military and economic terms (*imperial overstretch*), that free riders will gain more than the hegemon from economic openness, and that dynamic economies will arise to challenge the hegemon's predominant position.[49] Thus, an historian writes that "the only answer to . . . whether the United States can preserve its existing position is 'no'—for it simply has not been given to any one society to remain *permanently* ahead of all the others"; and a political scientist claims that "one of the most important features of American hegemony was its brevity."[50] Pitted against declinists are "renewalists" who question whether the United States is declining. Although most renewalists concede that U.S. economic power has declined in a *relative* sense since 1945, they argue that U.S. hegemony remains largely intact. U.S. predominance at the end of the war was so great that its relative position had to decline with economic reconstruction in Europe and Japan. However, U.S. economic power continues to be "quite enormous when compared to that of any other country, and has an international aspect which gives the U.S. government a unique prerogative *vis-à-vis* the rest of the world."[51] As evidence of its continued hegemony, renewalists point to U.S. *structural* or *soft power;* that is, it can persuade "other countries to *want* what it wants."[52] Thus, the United States has a major role in setting the global agenda. Renewalists also criticize declinists for disregarding noneconomic factors such as U.S. military supremacy and cultural influence through television, movies, and magazines.[53] Events in the late 1980s and 1990s resulted in an upsurge of renewalist writing. In the security sphere, the end of the Cold War led some scholars to argue that we were entering a "unipolar" period with the United States as the only superpower.[54] The 1990s East Asian financial crisis and Japan's inability to revive its lackluster economy led renewalists to argue that the United States was also regaining its economic predominance.

Declinists and renewalists can be found on all ends of the political spectrum. Prominent among the renewalists are U.S. "neoconservatives," who called for greater U.S. activism when the Soviet bloc and Soviet Union imploded in the late 1980s and 1990s. For example, Robert Kagan and William Kristol argued that

> the United States achieved its recent position of strength not by prac-
> ticing a foreign policy of live and let live, nor by passively waiting
> for threats to arise, but by actively promoting American principles of
> governance abroad—democracy, free markets, respect for liberty.[55]

Although Kagan and Kristol have cautioned that "no doctrine of foreign policy can do away with the need for judgment and prudence," they support a more activist U.S. foreign policy "premised on American hegemony."[56] The tragic terrorist events in the United States on September 11, 2001 increased the resolve of neoconservatives to follow an activist foreign policy combining moral purpose with the national interest. For example, after 9/11 Charles Krauthammer wrote that "the new unilateralism argues explicitly and unashamedly for maintaining unipolarity, for sustaining America's unrivaled dominance for the foreseeable future."[57] However, the results of the Iraq War show that neoconservatives overestimated the United States' ability to replace coercive regimes in complex developing societies with Western-style governments; and the United States' growing economic problems (discussed in this book) show the pitfalls of defining unipolarity mainly in security terms. Thus, a scholar previously identified with neoconservatism now argues that "the neoconservative moment appears to have passed."[58]

In assessing the declinist–renewalist debate, it is important to consider soft as well as hard power. During the Cold War, Western Europeans "welcomed the United States as their protector against the other superpower," but after the Cold War, Europeans responded to the possibility of unrivalled U.S. power by strengthening their "military capacity, and forging an inner core within an enlarged European Union, as a balance to American power."[59] Thus, Joseph Nye advises U.S. leaders to use "hard power in a manner that does not undercut . . . [their] soft power."[60] It is also important to consider economic as well as military power, because renewalist arguments that the United States is the unchallenged hegemon are less convincing in the economic sphere. For example, the EU is a larger international trading entity than the United States and the adoption of the euro by 16 EU members "offers the prospect of a new bipolar international economic order that could replace America's hegemony since World War II."[61] Some analysts argue that U.S. economic decline is due less to imperial overstretch than to domestic factors such as a

> low savings rate, poor educational system, stagnant productivity, declining work habits . . . [and] the low tax ideology of the 1980s, coupled with America's insatiable desire for yet higher standards of living without paying any of the cost.[62]

The U.S. subprime mortgage crisis in 2008 added weight to these arguments.

This book discusses the sources of U.S. strength and also the challenges the EU, Japan, and the BRIC economies (Brazil, Russia, India, and China) pose to U.S. hegemony. For example, we discuss the challenge the euro is posing to the U.S. dollar, the decline of U.S. hegemony in the global trade regime, and the growing importance of non-U.S. multinational corporations. A cursory look at U.S.–China relations shows that both declinists and renewalists offer important arguments. (Part III discusses China's position in greater detail.) After China began to reform its economy in 1978, it averaged a 9.4 percent annual GDP growth rate, and its foreign trade increased from $20.6 billion in 1978 to $851 billion in 2005. China's massive trade surplus with the United States and the United States' dependence on China's purchase of its government bonds to deal with U.S. foreign debt contribute to both interdependence and tension in their relationship. However, China's economy is only one-seventh the size of the United States' and it ranks about 100th in the world in per capita income. China's large population is also putting great pressure on its natural resources, which could impose limits on its economic development. Whereas China was East Asia's largest oil exporter 20 years ago, it is now the world's second largest oil importer. Despite its limitations, China has great economic potential, and its policies can have a major effect on the United States.[63] In assessing the debate between declinists and renewalists, both economic and security issues must be considered. On the one hand, renewalists who write about U.S. unipolarity have devoted too little attention to economic issues. On the other hand, declinists who see the euro as posing a serious challenge to the U.S. dollar sometimes devote too little attention to the EU's weak position in the political and security spheres. For example, the EU is often divided on major political issues, only 16 of the EU's 27 members have adopted the euro, and about 40 percent of EU oil and gas depends on Russia or territories controlled by Russia.

REALISM AND NORTH–SOUTH RELATIONS

Although realists focus on relative gains, their preoccupation with power and influence leads them to emphasize distributional issues among the most powerful states. In security studies, realists during the Cold War were less concerned about conflicts in the South (Korea, Vietnam, and the Middle East were exceptions) than about possible conflict in Europe, where fear of major "East-West confrontations prevented even the most minor form of warfare between the two power blocs."[64] In IPE, the realist tendency to ignore Southern interests was especially evident in earlier years. For example, Friedrich List believed that the United States and Germany should adopt protectionist policies to develop their manufacturing industries so they could compete with Britain, but he ruled out industrialization for the South. Northern states were "specially fitted by nature for manufacturing," in List's view, whereas Southern states should provide the North with "colonial produce in exchange for their manufactured goods."[65] Realist scholars have shown more interest in the South in recent years, but they are usually most interested in those LDCs that pose a challenge to the power position of the North. In the 1970s, for example, realists became interested in OPEC when it wrested control over oil prices from the international oil companies and launched "the most effective exercise of power by the South against the North since the conclusion of the Second World War."[66] When OPEC supported the G77's demands in the United Nations for a **New International Economic Order (NIEO),** realists examined the NIEO's possible impact. In the 1980s and 1990s, realists devoted attention to the East Asian NIEs, which posed a new economic challenge to the North. More recently, realists have focused on the challenge posed by China and India. Realists by contrast do not have a sustained interest in the poorest LDCs and the poorest groups within LDCs.

The realist and liberal perspectives on North–South relations differ in several respects. Whereas liberals see LDCs as seeking economic growth and prosperity, realists argue that LDCs seek increased power as well as wealth to decrease their vulnerability to the North. In the realist view, LDC problems result not only from their poverty but also from their weak position in the international system. Thus, even when LDCs experience absolute economic gains they feel vulnerable because of their weak position vis-à-vis the North.[67]

Realists refer to several strategies LDCs employ to decrease their vulnerability. First, in line with Hamilton and List's assumption that late industrializers require state involvement, LDCs depend on government involvement to help promote their development.[68] As discussed in Chapter 10, LDCs have often adopted policies such as import substitution and export-led growth in which the government supplements the market. An important realist contribution in this regard has been the concept of the *developmental state* which has helped promote economic development in several East Asian NIEs in the 1970s and 1980s (see Chapters 10 and 11).[69] A second LDC strategy is to use their greater numbers to engage in collective action because they lack power individually. For example, the G77 has been a major vehicle for Southern pressure on the North (see Chapter 2). Third, LDCs try to alter international economic regimes and organizations. At the end of World War II, the United States as hegemon helped establish liberal economic regimes, but LDCs would prefer more authoritative, less market-oriented regimes in which IOs would redirect some power and wealth from the North to the South.[70]

Although realists focus on the North–South struggle for a redistribution of power and wealth, they assume that such a redistribution is possible within the capitalist system. Thus, both realists and liberals generally accept capitalism as the most desirable system for conducting economic relations. As discussed in Chapter 5, historical materialists by contrast believe that a significant redistribution of power and wealth between the North and the South can only occur under socialism.

CRITIQUE OF THE REALIST PERSPECTIVE

Realists often pride themselves on being parsimonious theorists, and their simplifying assumptions regarding the rational, unitary state have enabled them to develop some elegant theories. Realists also sharply differentiate domestic and international politics, anticipating that states as unitary actors will respond to external threats by protecting their borders with armed forces and tariffs. In assuming that states respond to external challenges as rational unitary actors, realists devote little attention to the internal structures of societies and to partisan politics. The history, social structure, and cultural values of a state are of little interest to realists, and they also have little interest in the views of individuals who do not have some authority over state policy making. This is a major shortcoming of realism, because to understand state decision making it is necessary to delve into the social, economic, and cultural interests within the state. State boundaries today are also more porous than realists indicate, and domestic groups such as business firms and NGOs have numerous transnational linkages with the outside world. Transnational actors such as MNCs and international banks are particularly important in IPE, so the parsimonious habits of realists limit their analyses of economic issues. To understand state decision making in IPE it is necessary to recognize that a state's policies are shaped by a wide range of domestic and international economic and societal interests. In recent years, some realists have developed a theory of state action that takes account of domestic as well as international variables.[71] However, liberal IPE theorists are more attuned than realists to domestic variables.

Realists often correctly criticize both liberals and historical materialists for "economism," or for overestimating the importance of economics; but realists by contrast tend to overemphasize the centrality of politics. The preoccupation of U.S. realists in the early postwar period with security issues and their neglect of economic issues was a prime example of this error. Since the 1970s and 1980s, some realists have "returned to" economic issues with studies of hegemonic stability theory and the role of the state in IPE. Nevertheless, these theorists often downgrade the importance of economic issues that are not related to realist concerns with power, security, and relative gains. For example, realists do not have a sustained interest in the effects of IPE on the poorest LDCs in the South. Realists also place more emphasis on relative gains because of their concern with state survival and security in an anarchic self-help system. Relative gains are of primary concern in some interstate relationships, such as U.S.–Soviet relations during the Cold War; but absolute gains are often of greater concern in interdependent relationships among states that do not threaten each other with force. Even when realists study international economic organizations, they are more attuned to relative than to absolute gains. For example, one realist study of the EU concludes that the weaker members "will seek to ensure that the rules" give them the opportunity "to voice their concerns and interests and thereby prevent their domination by stronger partners."[72] The preoccupation of realists with relative gains causes them to be highly skeptical about the influence of international institutions. If states are always fearful of gaining less than others, they will not transfer significant authority to IOs. However, the IMF, World Bank, WTO, EU, and NAFTA all have a significant effect in IPE. Despite the realist perspective's influence in IR, its preoccupation with security issues and relative gains has limited its influence in IPE. This book now turns to liberalism, the most important IPE theoretical perspective.

Questions

1. What were the similarities and differences between the mercantilists and Friedrich List in their approach to IPE?
2. Why did realists devote little attention to IPE issues after World War II, and why did this change in the 1970s and 1980s?
3. What is hegemony, and how do theorists differ in their views regarding the strategies and motives of hegemonic states?
4. What are "public goods," why are they necessary for the functioning of the global economy, and why does their provision present "collective action" problems? What is the relationship between hegemony and public goods?
5. Is a hegemon necessary to create and maintain open, stable economic regimes?
6. How and why do theorists differ in their views regarding the current status of U.S. hegemony? Is any other actor likely to replace the United States as the global hegemon?

7. What aspects of North–South relations are of most, and least, interest to realists?

8. What are the strengths and weaknesses of the realist approach to IPE?

Further Reading

A study that applies rational choice to IPE is Bruno S. Frey, *International Political Economics* (New York: Basil Blackwell, 1984). For rational choice analysis from a liberal perspective, see Robert O. Keohane, *After Hegemony: Cooperation and Discord in the World Political Economy* (Princeton, NJ: Princeton University Press, 1984); from a realist perspective, see Robert Gilpin, *War and Change in World Politics* (New York: Cambridge University Press, 1981); from a critical perspective, see John Roemer, "'Rational Choice' Marxism: Some Issues of Method and Substance," in John Roemer, ed., *Analytical Marxism* (New York: Cambridge University Press, 1986), pp. 81–113.

Declinist literature on U.S. hegemony includes *After Hegemony: Cooperation and Discord in the World Political Economy* (Princeton, NJ: Princeton University Press, 1984); Paul Kennedy, *The Rise and Fall of the Great Powers: Economic Change and Military Conflict from 1500 to 2000* (New York: Random House, 1987); and David Calleo, *Beyond American Hegemony: The Future of the Western Alliance* (New York: Basic Books, 1987). Renewal literature on U.S. hegemony includes Susan Strange, "The Future of the American Empire," *Journal of International Affairs* 42 (Fall 1988), pp.1–17; Samuel P. Huntington, "The Lonely Superpower," *Foreign Affairs* 78, no. 2 (March/April 1999), pp. 35–49. On neoconservativism and U.S. renewal, see Robert Kagan and William Kristol, eds., *Present Dangers: Crisis and Opportunity in American Foreign and Defense Policy* (San Francisco, CA: Encounter Books, 2000); and Francis Fukuyama, "After Neoconservatism," *The New York Times Magazine*, February 19, 2006, pp. 62–67. On soft versus hard power, see Joseph S. Nye, Jr., *The Paradox of American Power: Why the World's Only Superpower Can't Go It Alone* (New York: Oxford University Press, 2002).

On realist views of the role of the state in IPE, see Jonathan Perraton and Ben Clift, eds., *Where are National Capitalisms Now?* (New York: Palgrave Macmillan, 2004). Realist studies on the developmental state include Linda Weiss, "Guiding Globalization in East Asia: New Roles for Old Developmental States," in Linda Weiss, ed., *States in the Global Economy: Bringing Domestic Institutions Back In* (New York: Cambridge University Press, 2003), pp. 245–270.

On realist views of North–South relations, see Stephen D. Krasner, *Structural Conflict: The Third World Against Global Liberalism* (Berkeley, CA: University of California Press, 1985); and David A. Lake, "Power and the Third World: Toward a Realist Political Economy of North-South Relations," *International Studies Quarterly* 31, no. 2 (June 1987), pp. 217–234.

Notes

1. Laurie M. Johnson Bagby, "The Use and Abuse of Thucydides in International Relations," *International Organization* 48, no. 1 (Winter 1994), pp. 131–153; Jonathan Monten, "Thucydides and Modern Realism," *International Studies Quarterly* 50, no. 1 (March 2006), pp. 3–25.

2. Ole R. Holsti, "Theories of International Relations and Foreign Policy: Realism and Its Challengers," in Charles W. Kegley, Jr., ed., *Controversies in International Relations Theory: Realism and the Neoliberal Challenge* (New York: St. Martin's Press, 1995), p. 36.

3. Quoted in Albert O. Hirschman, *National Power and the Structure of Foreign Trade,* exp. ed. (Berkeley, CA: University of California Press, 1980), p. xv.

4. Niccolò Machiavelli, *The Prince and the Discourses* (New York: Modern Library, 1940), pp. 308–310.

5. Thucydides, *The History of the Peloponnesian War,* transl. Richard Crawley (London: Dent, Everyman's Library, 1910), p. 41; Robert G. Gilpin, "The Richness of the Tradition of Political Realism," *International Organization* 38, no. 2 (Spring 1984), p. 293.

6. Thomas J. Biersteker, "Evolving Perspectives on International Political Economy: Twentieth-Century Contexts and Discontinuities," *International Political Science Review* 14, no. 1 (1993), p. 25.

7. Herbert A. Simon, "A Behavioral Model of Rational Choice," in Herbert A. Simon, ed., *Models of Man: Social and Rational* (New York: John Wiley & Sons, 1957), pp. 20–21; Robert Gilpin, *War and Change in World Politics* (New York: Cambridge University Press, 1981), pp. 20–21.

8. Robert Gilpin, *U.S. Power and the Multinational Corporation: The Political Economy of Foreign Direct Investment* (New York: Basic Books, 1975), p. 34; Kenneth N. Waltz, *Theory of International Politics* (Reading, MA: Addison Wesley, 1979), p. 126; Joseph M. Grieco, "Anarchy and the Limits of Cooperation: A Realist Critique of the Newest Liberal Institutionalism," *International Organization* 42, no. 3 (Summer 1988), p. 498.

9. Tony Evans and Peter Wilson, "Regime Theory and the English School of International Relations: A Comparison," *Millennium* 21, no. 3 (Winter 1992), p. 330.

10. Robert W. Cox, *Production, Power, and World Order: Social Forces in the Making of History* (New York: Columbia University Press, 1987), p. 6.

11. Hannes Lacher, "Putting the State in Its Place: The Critique of State-Centrism and Its Limits," *Review of International Studies* 29 (2003), p. 526; Janice E. Thomson, "State Sovereignty in International Relations: Bridging the Gap between Theory and Empirical Research," *International Studies Quarterly* 39, no. 2 (June 1995), pp. 213–233.

12. Stephen D. Krasner, *Sovereignty: Organized Hypocrisy* (Princeton, NJ: Princeton University Press, 1999), p. 223.

13. Jonathan Perraton and Ben Clift, *Where Are National Capitalisms Now?* (New York: Palgrave Macmillan, 2004).

14. Linda Weiss, "The State-Augmenting Effects of Globalisation," *New Political Economy* 10, no. 3 (September 2005), p. 352; "Realism vs Cosmopolitanism: A Debate between Barry Buzan and David Held, Conducted by Anthony McGrew," *Review of International Studies* 24, no. 3 (July 1998), p. 394.

15. Smith used the term *mercantile system*, and German writers used *Merkantilismus* to describe this doctrine. Only later did *mercantilism* become a standard English term. See Jacob Viner, "Mercantilist Thought," in David L. Sills, ed., *International Encyclopedia of the Social Sciences,* vol. 4 (New York: Free Press, 1968), p. 436; David A. Baldwin, *Economic Statecraft* (Princeton, NJ: Princeton University Press, 1985), p. 72.

16. Eli F. Heckscher, *Mercantilism,* vol. 2 (London: Allen and Unwin, 1934).

17. Adam Smith, *The Wealth of Nations,* vol. 1 (London: Dent & Sons, Everyman's Library, 1910), bk. 4, p. 436.
18. Robert Gilpin with Jean M. Gilpin, *The Political Economy of International Relations* (Princeton, NJ: Princeton University Press, 1987), p. 180.
19. Alexander Hamilton, "The Report on the Subject of Manufactures," in Harold C. Syrett, ed., *The Papers of Alexander Hamilton, December 5, 1791*, vol. 10 (New York: Columbia University Press, 1966), p. 291.
20. Friedrich List, *The National System of Political Economy,* transl. Sampson S. Lloyd (London: Longmans, Green 1916), p. 130.
21. David Levi-Faur, "Friedrich List and the Political Economy of the Nation-State," *Review of International Political Economy* 4, no. 1 (Spring 1997), pp. 154–178.
22. Benjamin J. Cohen, *Crossing Frontiers: Explorations in International Political Economy* (Boulder, CO: Westview Press, 1991), p. 47; David Levi-Faur, "Economic Nationalism: from Friedrich List to Robert Reich," *Review of International Studies* 23, no. 3 (July 1997), pp. 367–369.
23. List, *The National System of Political Economy,* p. 107.
24. Levi-Faur, "Economic Nationalism," p. 359. Scholarly writing during the interwar period included John Maynard Keynes, "National Self-Sufficiency," *Yale Review* 22 (1933), pp. 755–769; Jacob Viner, "International Relations between State-Controlled Economies," *American Economic Review* 34, no.1 supplement (March 1944), pp. 315–329; Lionel Robbins, *Economic Planning and International Order* (New York: Macmillan, 1937).
25. Paul Kennedy, *The Rise and Fall of the Great Powers: Economic Change and Military Conflict from 1500 to 2000* (New York: Random House, 1987), p. 283.
26. Although U.S. government officials helped create the KIEOs, they subordinated their economic goals to security goals. U.S. realist scholars, by contrast, largely ignored economic issues. See Michael Mastanduno, "Economics and Security in Statecraft and Scholarship," *International Organization* 52, no. 4 (Autumn 1998), p. 835.
27. Gilpin, "The Richness of the Tradition of Political Realism," p. 294.
28. Gilpin, *The Political Economy of International Relations,* p. xii.
29. Theda Skocpol, "Bringing the State Back In: Strategies of Analysis in Current Research," in Peter B. Evans, Dietrich Rueschemeyer, and Theda Skocpol, eds., *Bringing the State Back In* (New York: Cambridge University Press, 1985), pp. 6–7.
30. George Modelski, *Long Cycles in World Politics* (Seattle, WA: University of Washington Press, 1987), ch. 2; Joshua S. Goldstein, *Long Cycles: Prosperity and War in the Modern Age* (New Haven, CT: Yale University Press, 1988), pp. 126–133.
31. Benjamin J. Cohen, *International Political Economy: An Intellectual History* (Princeton, NJ: Princeton University Press, 2008), p. 67.
32. David A. Lake, "Leadership, Hegemony, and the International Economy: Naked Emperor or Tattered Monarch with Potential," *International Studies Quarterly* 37, no. 4 (December 1993), p. 485.
33. Robert Gilpin, *War and Change in World Politics* (New York: Cambridge University Press, 1981), p. 29.
34. Immanuel Wallerstein, "The Three Instances of Hegemony in the History of the Capitalist World-Economy," in Immanuel Wallerstein, ed., *The Politics of the World-Economy: The States, the Movements and the Civilizations* (London: Cambridge University Press, 1984), p. 38.
35. Stephen Gill, ed., *Gramsci, Historical Materialism and International Relations* (New York: Cambridge University Press, 1993).

36. Duncan Snidal, "The Limits of Hegemonic Stability Theory," *International Organization* 39, no. 4 (Autumn 1985), pp. 585–586.

37. Charles P. Kindleberger, *The World in Depression 1929–1939* (Berkeley, CA: University of California Press, 1973), p. 28. On the collective goods version of the theory see Michael C. Webb and Stephen D. Krasner, "Hegemonic Stability Theory: An Empirical Assessment," *Review of International Studies* 15 (Spring 1989), pp. 184–186.

38. Snidal, "The Limits of Hegemonic Stability Theory," pp. 590–592; Robert O. Keohane, *After Hegemony: Cooperation and Discord in the World Political Economy* (Princeton, NJ: Princeton University Press, 1984), p. 65; Mancur Olson, *The Logic of Collective Action: Public Goods and the Theory of Groups* (Cambridge, MA: Harvard University Press, 1965), pp. 14–15.

39. Stephen D. Krasner, "State Power and the Structure of International Trade," *World Politics* 28 (April 1976), p. 322.

40. Robert Gilpin, "The Politics of Transnational Economic Relations," in Robert O. Keohane and Joseph S. Nye, Jr., eds., *Transnational Relations and World Politics* (Cambridge, MA: Harvard University Press, 1972), p. 58.

41. Wallerstein, "The Three Instances of Hegemony in the History of the Capitalist World-Economy," pp. 44–46; Robert W. Cox, "Gramsci, Hegemony and International Relations: An Essay in Method," in Stephen Gill, ed., *Gramsci, Historical Materialism and International Relations* (New York: Cambridge University Press, 1993), pp. 64–65.

42. Stephen D. Krasner, "Structural Causes and Regime Consequences: Regimes as Intervening Variables," in Stephen D. Krasner, ed., *International Regimes* (Ithaca, NY: Cornell University Press, 1983), p. 2.

43. Arthur A. Stein, "The Hegemon's Dilemma: Great Britain, the United States and the International Economic Order," *International Organization* 38, no. 2 (Spring 1984), p. 373.

44. Keohane, *After Hegemony;* Robert O. Keohane, "The Demand for International Regimes," in Stephen D. Krasner, ed., *International Regimes* (Ithaca, NY: Cornell University Press, 1983), pp. 141–171.

45. Oran R. Young, "Regime Dynamics: The Rise and Fall of International Regimes," in Stephen D. Krasner, ed., *International Regimes* (Ithaca, NY: Cornell University Press, 1983), pp. 98–101.

46. Eric Helleiner, *States and the Reemergence of Global Finance: From Bretton Woods to the 1990s* (Ithaca, NY: Cornell University Press), p. 4; Theodore H. Cohn, "The Changing Role of the United States in the Global Agricultural Trade Regime," in William P. Avery, ed., *World Agriculture and the GATT, International Political Economy Yearbook,* vol. 7 (Boulder, CO: Rienner, 1993), pp. 20–24; Vinod K. Aggarwal, *Liberal Protectionism: The International Politics of Organized Textile Trade* (Berkeley, CA: University of California Press, 1985), pp. 77–81.

47. Timothy J. McKeown, "Hegemonic Stability Theory and Nineteenth Century Tariff Levels in Europe," *International Organization* 37, no. 1 (Winter 1983), p. 89; Peter F. Cowhey and Edward Long, "Testing Theories of Regime Change: Hegemonic Decline or Surplus Capacity?" *International Organization* 37, no. 2 (Spring 1983), pp. 157–188.

48. David A. Lake, *Power, Protection, and Free Trade: International Sources of U.S. Commercial Strategy, 1887–1939* (Ithaca, NY: Cornell University Press, 1988), pp. 30–32; Albert Fishlow, "Lessons from the Past: Capital Markets during the

19th Century and the Interwar Period," *International Organization* 39, no. 3 (Summer 1985), p. 390.

49. Samuel P. Huntington, "The Lonely Superpower," *Foreign Affairs* 78, no. 2 (March/April 1999), pp. 35–49.

50. Kennedy, *The Rise and Fall of the Great Powers,* p. 533; Robert O. Keohane, *After Hegemony: Cooperation and Discord in the World Political Economy* (Princeton, NJ: Princeton University Press, 1984), p. 139.

51. Stephen Gill, "American Hegemony: Its Limits and Prospects in the Reagan Era," *Millennium* 15, no. 3 (Winter 1986), p. 331.

52. Joseph S. Nye, Jr., "Soft Power," *Foreign Policy* 80 (Fall 1990), p. 166.

53. Bruce Russett, "The Mysterious Case of Vanishing Hegemony; or, Is Mark Twain Really Dead?" *International Organization* 39, no. 2 (Spring 1985), p. 230.

54. Charles Krauthammer introduced the idea of U.S. unipolarity in "The Unipolar Moment," *Foreign Affairs* 70, no. 1 (1990/1991), pp. 23–33.

55. William Kristol and Robert Kagan, "Toward a Neo-Reaganite Foreign Policy," *Foreign Affairs* 75, no. 4 (July/August, 1996), pp. 21–22.

56. William Kristol and Robert Kagan, "Introduction: National Interest and Global Responsibility," in Robert Kagan and William Kristol, eds., *Present Dangers: Crisis and Opportunity in American Foreign and Defense Policy* (San Francisco, CA: Encounter Books, 2000), p. 13.

57. Charles Krauthammer, "The Unipolar Moment Revisited," *The National Interest* 70 (Winter 2002/2003), p. 17.

58. Francis Fukuyama, "After Neoconservatism," *The New York Times Magazine*, February 19, 2006, p. 67.

59. "Which Way Now for French Policy?" *The Economist*, July 26, 2003, pp. 47–48; Huntington, "The Lonely Superpower," p. 43.

60. Joseph S. Nye, Jr., *The Paradox of American Power: Why the World's Only Superpower Can't Go It Alone* (New York: Oxford University Press, 2002), pp. 140–141.

61. C. Fred Bergsten, "America and Europe: Clash of the Titans?" *Foreign Affairs* 78, no. 2 (March/April 1999), p. 20.

62. Krauthammer, "The Unipolar Moment," pp. 26–27.

63. Zheng Bijian, "China's 'Peaceful Rise' to Great-Power Status," *Foreign Affairs* 84, no. 5 (September/October 2005), pp. 18–24; David Zweig and Bi Jianhai, "China's Global Hunt for Energy," *Foreign Affairs* 84, no. 5 (September/October 2005), pp. 25–38.

64. Amitav Acharya, "Beyond Anarchy: Third World Instability and International Order after the Cold War," in Stephanie G. Neuman, ed., *International Relations Theory and the Third World* (New York: St. Martin's Press, 1998), p. 165.

65. List, *The National System of Political Economy,* p. 154.

66. Stephen D. Krasner, *Structural Conflict: The Third World Against Global Liberalism* (Berkeley, CA: University of California Press, 1985), pp. 108–109.

67. Krasner, *Structural Conflict,* p. 3; Robert L. Rothstein, *The Weak in the World of the Strong: The Developing Countries in the International System* (New York: Columbia University Press, 1977), p. 8.

68. On the government involvement in late industrializers, see Alexander Gerschenkron, *Economic Backwardness in Historical Perspective: A Book of Essays* (Cambridge, MA: Harvard University Press, 1962).

69. Chalmers Johnson, "Introduction—The Taiwan Model," in James C. Hsiung et al., eds., *Contemporary Republic of China: The Taiwan Experience 1950–1980* (New York: Praeger, 1981), pp. 9–18.

70. Krasner, *Structural Conflict*, p. 7.

71. See Michael Mastanduno, David A. Lake, and G. John Ikenberry, "Toward a Realist Theory of State Action," *International Studies Quarterly* 33, no. 4 (December 1989), pp. 457–474.

72. Joseph M. Grieco, "The Maastricht Treaty, Economic and Monetary Union and the Neo-realist Research Programme," *Review of International Studies* 21 (January 1995), p. 34.

CHAPTER 4

The Liberal Perspective

Liberalism is the most influential perspective in IPE. Most international economic organizations and the economic policies of most states today are strongly influenced by liberal principles. However, the term *liberal* is used differently in IPE and in U.S. politics. Whereas U.S. conservatives support free markets and minimal government intervention, U.S. liberals support greater government involvement in the market to prevent inequalities and stimulate growth. Liberal economists, by contrast, have many similarities with U.S. conservatives; they emphasize the importance of the free market and private property and seek to limit the government's role in economic affairs. However, there are also variations among economic liberals. Although some liberal economists favor as little government involvement as possible, others believe that some government intervention is necessary for the effective functioning of markets.

BASIC TENETS OF THE LIBERAL PERSPECTIVE

It is easier to provide a single "core statement" in realism and Marxism than in liberalism, because realists and Marxists place more emphasis on developing parsimonious theories that rely on a small number of concepts and variables.[1] In contrast to realists who focus on the rational unitary state, and Marxists who view the world in terms of class relations, liberals deal with a wider range of actors and levels of analysis. Although this broader outlook enables liberals to capture complexities that realists and Marxists overlook, it also hinders the development of a coherent liberal international theory. This chapter focuses on three variants of liberalism relevant to IPE: orthodox, interventionist, and institutional liberalism. *Orthodox liberals* promote "negative freedom," or freedom of the market to function with minimal interference from the state. *Interventionist liberals* believe that negative freedom is not sufficient because the market does not always produce widespread benefits; thus, they support some government involvement to promote more equality and justice in a free **market economy.** *Institutional liberals* also believe that some outside involvement is necessary to supplement the market, and they favor strong international institutions such as the WTO, IMF, and World Bank. In addition to these three variants of liberalism, liberals also have different views regarding the best method of studying IPE. As discussed in Chapter 3, there are liberal *rationalists* and liberal *constructivists*. We discussed rationalism or rational choice in Chapter 3, and we discuss constructivism in Chapter 5 because liberal (or conventional) as well as critical constructivists are critical of the rationalist assumptions of most liberals and realists.

The Role of the Individual, the State, and Societal Groups

Liberals take a bottom-up approach to IPE and give primacy of place to the individual consumer, firm, or entrepreneur.[2] Thus, liberals focus more than realists on domestic–international interactions in IPE. Liberals believe that individuals have inalienable rights that must be protected from collectivities such as labor unions, churches, and the state. Thus, the orthodox liberal Adam Smith (1723–1790) argued (in his discussion of the "invisible hand") that the welfare of society depends on the individual's ability to pursue his/her interests:

> Every individual is continually exerting himself to find out the most advantageous employment for whatever capital he can command. It is his own advantage, indeed, and not that of the society, which he has in view. But the study of his own advantage naturally, or rather necessarily, leads him to prefer that employment which is most advantageous to the society.[3]

Because the hidden hand of the market performs efficiently, society can regulate itself best with minimal interference from the state. Some liberals even reject the idea that the state is an autonomous actor and see public policy as resulting from a struggle among private interests. Interventionist liberals, however, foresee some role for the government because of the market's limitations in dealing with problems such as unemployment.

The Nature and Purpose of International Economic Relations

The KIEOs—the IMF, World Bank, and WTO—uphold liberal economic principles, and liberals therefore have a positive view of international economic relations as currently structured. They assert that the KIEO liberal principles are politically neutral and that states benefit from economic growth and efficiency when their policies conform to these principles. If international relationships do not result in growth and the efficient allocation of resources, the problem is not with the global economic system but with government unwillingness to pursue liberal economic policies. Liberals also assume that international economic interactions can be mutually beneficial, or a positive-sum game, if they operate freely. All states are likely to gain from open economic relationships, even if they do not gain equally. Thus, liberals are often less concerned with *distributional* issues and less likely to differentiate between rich and poor or large and small states. Although liberalism encompasses a range of views on distributional issues, with interventionist liberals emphasizing equality and social democracy as well as liberty and efficiency, all liberals believe that the international economic system functions best if it ultimately depends on the price mechanism and the market.

Many liberals assume that the South faces basically the same challenges that the North did during the nineteenth century. Unlike the nineteenth century, however, the South benefits from the North's diffusion of advanced technology and modern forms of organization. Integration with the DC centers of activity therefore spurs LDC economic growth, whereas isolation from these centers results in LDC backwardness. The purpose of international economic activity, according to liberals, is to achieve optimum use of the world's scarce resources and to maximize economic efficiency and growth. Thus, liberals view aggregate measures of economic performance such as the growth of GDP, trade, foreign investment, and per capita income as more important than relative gains among states.

The Relationship Between Politics and Economics

Liberals tend to view economics and politics as separate and autonomous spheres of activity. Many liberals believe that governments should not interfere in economic transactions and that their role should be limited to creating an open environment in which individuals and private firms can freely express their economic preferences. Thus, the state should prevent restraints on competition and provide public goods such as infrastructure (roads and railways) and national defense to facilitate transportation and production. If governments permit the market to operate freely, a natural division of labor develops in which each state produces goods for which it has a comparative advantage and everyone benefits from the efficient use of the world's scarce resources. As this chapter discusses, interventionist liberals accept a greater degree of government involvement.

The Causes and Effects of Globalization

Whereas realists emphasize the role of the state, liberals attribute globalization to technological change, market forces, and international institutions. For example, one liberal argues that "our new international financial regime . . . was not built by politicians, economists, central bankers or by finance ministers. . . . It was built by technology."[4] Some liberals argue that technological advances in transportation and communications are shrinking time and space so rapidly that governments can do nothing to stop the globalization process. Other liberals believe that governments have choices but that technological progress makes it more costly for them to close their economies. In addition to technology, liberals attribute globalization to the competitive marketplace and to legal and institutional arrangements. Thus, liberals examine the role of the KIEOs in facilitating globalization.[5] In regard to the effects of globalization, Kenichi Ohmae argues that globalization is leading to the demise of the state, but this is an extreme view (see Chapter 2). Most liberals argue that the state lacks the capacity to deal with many global issues ranging from climate change to capital mobility and financial crises. Thus, globalization is constraining the state and forcing it to vie with other significant actors such as MNCs, IOs, and NGOs. Liberals generally view these changes as positive developments, but this chapter discusses the fact that there is a range of liberal views.

ORTHODOX LIBERALISM

The liberal tradition dates back at least to John Locke (1632–1704), who argued that the state's primary role was to ensure the "*Preservation* of . . . [peoples'] Lives, Liberties and Estates, which I call by the general Name, *Property*."[6] Locke predated Adam Smith by almost a century, but Smith was more associated with the orthodox liberal approach to political economy because he opposed mercantilism and favored laissez-faire economics (see Chapter 3). Whereas the mercantilists assumed that a state could gain wealth and power only at the expense of other states, Smith cautioned that

> By such maxims as these . . . nations have been taught that their interest consisted in beggaring all their neighbours. Each nation has been made to look with an invidious eye upon the prosperity of all the nations with which it trades, and to consider their gain as its own loss. Commerce, which ought naturally to be . . . a bond of union and friendship, has become the most fertile source of discord and animosity.[7]

Thus, Smith opposed mercantilist state barriers against the free exchange of goods. Although he realized that merchants might favor protectionism to preserve their advantages, he differentiated such specific groups from the general populace who would benefit from freer trade. Smith's free-trade arguments were based on the principles of the division of labor and interdependence. Each state in an unregulated international economy would find a productive niche based on **absolute advantage;** that is, it would benefit by specializing in those goods it produced most efficiently and by trading with other states. David Ricardo (1772–1823) strengthened the free-trade defense by arguing that two states would benefit from trade based on **comparative advantage.** Even if a state had no absolute advantage in producing any good, it should specialize in products for which it had a *relative* advantage, or the least cost disadvantage. (We explain absolute and comparative advantage in detail in Chapter 7.)

Although Smith strongly supported free trade, he did not view it as a unilateral or unconditional policy. For example, a state should be able to retaliate against unfair trade restrictions, and it might implement free trade gradually to give domestic industry and labor groups time to adjust to international competition. Smith was also open to limited government intervention because of political realities; he indicated that a state should be able to engage in national defense, protect individuals from injustice or oppression, and provide public works and institutions that private actors would not provide on their own.[8] Despite his openness to some role for the government, Smith as an orthodox liberal believed it should be limited mainly to actions that promoted the functioning of the market.

THE INFLUENCE OF JOHN MAYNARD KEYNES

The ideas of John Maynard Keynes (1883–1946) greatly influenced the theory and practice of political economy, and some scholars view him as "the most influential economist of his generation."[9] Although Keynes strongly opposed the extreme nationalism of the interwar years, he also viewed the Great Depression as an indication that orthodox liberals overestimated the degree of convergence between self-interest and the public interest. In contrast to the orthodox liberal view that markets contribute to a socially beneficial equilibrium, Keynes argued that a market-generated equilibrium might occur at a point where labor and capital are underutilized. For example, he noted that economic adjustment often resulted in unemployment rather than wage cuts because labor unions resisted the downward movement of wages; this unemployment in turn led to decreased demand and a reduction in production and investment. Thus, Keynes wrote in *The General Theory of Employment, Interest, and Money* that "the central controls necessary to ensure full employment will, of course, involve a large extension of the traditional functions of government."[10] He called on governments to implement fiscal policies (and to a lesser extent monetary policies) to increase demand, and he supported government investment when necessary in public projects. Keynes's view that the state should intervene in the economy differed from the laissez-faire doctrine of orthodox liberals.

Keynes's support for government involvement resulted in a greater "willingness to accept public sector deficits in order to finance public works or other spending programs designed to lower unemployment."[11] His emphasis on full employment also caused him to place less priority than orthodox liberals on specialization and international trade. Thus, he argued that limits on imports were sometimes justifiable to bolster domestic employment, even if the goods could be produced more cheaply abroad. When unemployment reached record highs in the 1930s, Keynes wrote that goods should "be homespun whenever it is reasonably and conveniently possible."[12] After World War II, Keynes supported internationalist solutions at Bretton Woods, largely because of his preference for planning on a global scale (the United States overruled this idea) and because of Britain's financial problems. As Britain's chief postwar negotiator he pressured the Labour government to pursue open liberal policies, and in return the United States provided the British with $3.75 billion in loans.[13]

Keynes's support for national and international economic management had a major impact on liberal economic thought. Keynes called for the state to help combat unemployment because markets often behaved differently than orthodox liberals predicted. Despite his divergence from liberal orthodoxy, as an economic liberal he believed in the importance of individual initiative and the efficiency of the market. Greater management, in Keynes's view, would facilitate the efficient functioning of market forces. Thus, he favored government intervention, not to replace capitalism but to rescue and revitalize it; his views gave rise to interventionist liberalism.[14]

LIBERALISM IN THE POSTWAR PERIOD

The ideas of Karl Polanyi as well as Keynes were important for avoiding a recurrence of the economic problems of the interwar years. In *The Great Transformation,* Polanyi warned that the orthodox liberal commitment to the "self-regulating market" had produced disasters such as the Great Depression, and he predicted that society would move to protect itself from unregulated market activities.[15] Influenced by the ideas of Keynes and Polanyi, the postwar planners designed the international economic order on the basis of an interventionist or "embedded liberal compromise." "Embedded liberalism" refers to the fact that postwar efforts to maintain an open liberal international economy were embedded in societal efforts to provide domestic security and stability for the populace.[16] Thus, policies to promote openness in the global economy included measures to cushion domestic economies, and policies to provide domestic stability in turn were designed to minimize interference with expansion of the global economy. In trade policy, for example, Western leaders called for multilateral tariff reductions, but they permitted states to use safeguards when necessary to protect their balance of payments and promote full employment. Underlying the interventionist liberal compromise was a domestic class compromise between business and labor. Labor unions tempered their demands that the economy be socialized, and in return they benefited from collective bargaining and the welfare state. By acceding to some of labor's demands, business won broad acceptance of trade liberalization, private ownership, and the market.[17] In sum, most postwar liberals favored government intervention to counter socially unacceptable aspects of the market, but they opted for government measures that would reinforce the market.

A RETURN TO ORTHODOX LIBERALISM

Although postwar policy makers supported interventionist liberalism, orthodox liberals continued to have influence in some circles. In 1947 Friedrich Hayek organized what became known as the Mont Pelerin Society, a private transnational forum of scholars and political figures committed to orthodox liberalism. Prominent members such as Hayek, Ludwig von Mises, and Milton Friedman favored competitive markets, the efficient allocation of resources, and a strict separation between politics and economics.[18] Thus, Friedman wrote in 1962 that "the kind of economic organization that provides economic freedom directly, namely, competitive capitalism, also promotes political freedom because it separates economic power from political power."[19] Milton Friedman and Rose Friedman also strongly criticized state interference with the market:

> Wherever we find any large element of individual freedom, some measure of progress in the material comforts at the disposal of ordinary citizens, and widespread hope of further progress in the future, there we also find that economic activity is organized mainly through the free market. Wherever the state undertakes to control in detail the economic activities of its citizens . . . ordinary citizens are in political fetters, have a low standard of living, and have little power to control their own destiny.[20]

Despite the persistence of orthodox views, most Western leaders followed interventionist liberal policies during the expansive years of the 1950s and 1960s. However, the 1973 OPEC oil price shock and the prolonged global recession after 1974 made welfare and full-employment policies more costly for governments, and the contradictions between capital accumulation and the redistribution of wealth became more evident. Thus, the writings of Hayek and Friedman had more influence on government policies in the late 1970s and 1980s. Foremost among political leaders pushing for this revival were British Prime Minister Margaret Thatcher and U.S. President Ronald Reagan. Critics argued that the Thatcher–Reagan policies revitalized business confidence by rejecting the attempt to ease the effects of liberalism on vulnerable groups; these policies resulted in open conflict with government employees, trade unions, and welfare recipients. As these changes became more widespread, governments felt growing pressure to adopt orthodox liberal policies such as privatization, deregulation, and free trade and foreign investment.[21] In contrast to the liberalism of Adam Smith, the return to orthodox liberalism has been global in extent, for several reasons:

- Advances in technology, communications, and transportation have enabled MNCs and international banks to shift their activities and funds around the world.
- The IMF, World Bank, and DCs have provided LDC debtors with financing since the 1982 foreign debt crisis, but the conditions on this financing have included privatization, deregulation, and liberalization of the LDC economies.
- With the breakup of the Soviet bloc, orthodox liberal pressures have also spread to the transition economies.

To differentiate this new liberal orthodoxy from the liberalism of Smith and Ricardo, scholars often use the term *neoliberalism*.

LIBERALISM AND INSTITUTIONS

As discussed in Chapter 1, "hegemony" and "institutions" are important mechanisms for managing the global political economy. International regimes and IOs are types of institutions, and IR scholars have applied regime theory to the study of institutions.[22] A liberal scholar first used the *regime* term in an IPE context, and a realist scholar edited a definitive volume on regimes.[23] However, we discuss institutions in this chapter because liberals attach more importance to them than realists. International regimes promote cooperation in areas such as trade and monetary relations where there is a high degree of interdependence. Before turning to regimes, we therefore discuss the liberal approach to interdependence and cooperation in IPE.

Interdependence Theory

Interdependence can be defined as "mutual dependence," in which "there are reciprocal (although not necessarily symmetrical) costly effects of transactions."[24] Although theorists have written on interdependence since the early 1900s, Richard Cooper's *The Economics of Interdependence* (1968) is the first systematic study of economic interdependence among states.[25] Cooper argues that growing interdependence as a result of advances in transportation, communications, and technology "negates the sharp distinction between internal and external policies," and limits the ability of states "to achieve their desired aims, regardless of their formal retention of sovereignty."[26] States should respond to interdependence in Cooper's view by coordinating their policies in "taxation, the regulation of business . . . [and] the framing of monetary policy."[27] However, Cooper does not consider how *political* conditions affect international cooperation. In *Power and Interdependence* (1977), Robert Keohane and Joseph Nye analyze how interdependence transforms international politics:

> Asymmetrical interdependence [i.e., mutual dependence that is not evenly balanced] can be a source of power. . . . A less dependent actor in a relationship often has a significant political resource, because changes in the relationship . . . will be less costly to that actor than to its partners.[28]

Nevertheless, Keohane and Nye have a rather benign view of the effects of asymmetrical interdependence on smaller states. For example, they conclude that Canada often can successfully confront the United States in conflicts because of the highly interdependent relationship between the two countries. In their view, Canada benefits from "complex interdependence" with the United States, in which multiple channels (nongovernmental as well as governmental) connect societies, there is an absence of hierarchy among issues (military security does not dominate the agenda), and one government does not use military force against another.[29] However, critics of the Keohane–Nye study argue that the United States as the larger power does not let market transactions dictate its interdependence with Canada and instead demands a wide array of "side payments." For example, Canadian side payments in NAFTA include concessions to U.S. demands regarding sharing of energy resources and openness to foreign investment (see Chapter 8).[30]

Interdependence theorists question the realist assumptions that states are rational unitary actors, that states are the only important actors in IR, and that states can rely on military force to promote their national interest. Military force is of little use in dealing with interdependence issues such as environmental pollution, human rights, immigration, monetary and trade relations, and **sustainable development.** Interdependence theorists note that these issues are also more *intermestic* (domestic as well as international) than traditional security issues, and they criticize realists for overemphasizing the division between international and domestic politics.[31] Despite these criticisms, interdependence theorists view their model as supplementing rather than replacing realism. Whereas realism is the best model for studying security issues, interdependence theory is best for studying international economic issues.

The Liberal Approach to Cooperation

Liberals are interested in how states can cooperate in an anarchic international system, and a particular type of game theory called **prisoners' dilemma** examines how states can achieve a better collective outcome through cooperation. *Game theory* investigates the interaction of two or more individuals or states, in which each individual or state is acting according to rational choice; it seeks to explain how the actors' decisions are interrelated and how these decisions affect outcomes.[32] Prisoners' dilemma is a "mixed-motive game," in which two players can benefit from mutual cooperation but have an incentive to "defect" or cheat on each other and become free riders. The term *prisoners' dilemma* derives from the story used to describe the game: The police arrest two individuals, A and B, for committing fraud, and they suspect that A and B have also committed robbery but cannot prove it. To get A and B to confess, the police put them in different cells so they cannot communicate with each other, and question them separately. In Figure 4.1, prisoners A and B "cooperate" with each other if they do not confess to committing robbery, and they "defect" (or cheat on each other) if they confess. The sentences the prisoners receive depend on the decisions they make. The numbers in bold at the top right-hand corners of the squares are A's years in prison, and the numbers at the bottom left-hand corners are B's years in prison. The police make a tempting offer to induce A to confess (i.e., defect). They inform A that conviction for fraud is certain and will result in a two-year sentence for both prisoners if they do not confess (square I in Figure 4.1). However, if A confesses to robbery

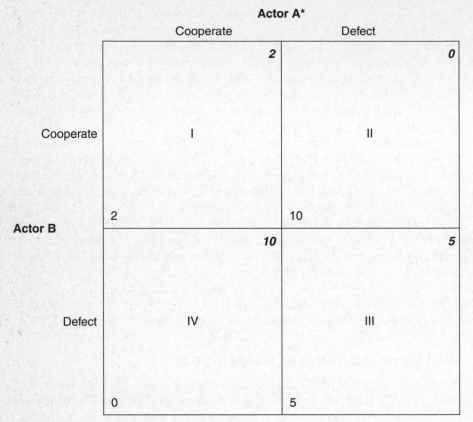

*Actor A's years in prison in bold and italics

FIGURE 4.1 Prisoners' Dilemma

(i.e., defects) and B does not (i.e., cooperates), A will go free and B will get 10 years in prison (square II). If both A and B defect and confess to robbery, they will get a reduced sentence of five years (square III). Finally, if A does not confess (i.e., cooperates) but B confesses (i.e., defects), A will get 10 years in prison and B will go free (square IV). The police provide the same offer to B.

What will the prisoners do? According to *individual* rationality, if B defects, A is better off defecting (5 years in prison) than cooperating (10 years). If B cooperates, A is also better off defecting (goes free) than cooperating (2 years in prison). Thus, *individual* rationality pushes A to defect regardless of what B does, and the same reasoning applies to B! Furthermore, A and B mistrust each other, and they both fear that they will receive the worst possible penalty by cooperating (10 years) if the other prisoner defects. A and B therefore are both likely to defect and end up with five years in prison (square III), even though both would get only two years (square I) if they cooperated. Square I is the best *collective* outcome or the **Pareto-optimal** outcome for A and B, because no actor can become better off without making someone else worse off (i.e., if

A confesses and goes free, B will get 10 years in prison). Square III is an inferior collective outcome or *Pareto-deficient* outcome because both actors (A and B) would prefer another outcome (square I).

As is the case for the provision of public goods (see Chapter 3), prisoners' dilemma presents a *collective action problem* in rational choice analysis, because rational actors may "find themselves unable to reach a Pareto-optimal solution, despite a certain degree of convergence of interests between them."[33] The dilemma in both the provision of public goods and the prisoners' dilemma game is that *individual* rationality differs from *collective* rationality: The decision of rational, self-interested states to become "free riders" may interfere with the provision of public goods, and the decision of rational, self-interested prisoners to defect may lead to a Pareto-deficient outcome (square III in Figure 4.1) for both prisoners.[34] In IPE we ask how states can move from a Pareto-deficient (mutual defection or DD) to a Pareto-optimal outcome (mutual cooperation or CC). In the liberal view, "cheating" or free riding by states can inhibit cooperation, and mutual cooperation is possible if cheating can be controlled. A global hegemon can prevent cheating by providing public goods and coercing other states to abide by agreed rules and principles. Institutions such as IOs can also prevent cheating by bringing states together on a regular basis. A state that interacts regularly with others is less likely to cheat because the other states have many opportunities to retaliate. International institutions also enforce principles and rules to ensure that cheaters are punished and they collect information on members' policies, increasing transparency or confidence that cheaters will be discovered. Finally, international institutions contribute to a learning process in which states become aware that mutual gains can result from cooperation.[35] Realists are more skeptical than liberals that international institutions can help move states to a Pareto-optimal (CC) outcome because they believe that institutions serve the interests of the most powerful states. Realists also argue that state concerns with *relative gains* pose a major obstacle to cooperation. Even when two states have common interests, they may not cooperate because of each state's concern that the other will receive greater gains. Institutions may promote cooperation, according to realists, only if they can ensure that members' gains are balanced and equitable; but this is difficult to achieve because gains are rarely equal. Some realists concede that institutions may have an important role when they "do not infringe on the security interests of powerful states."[36] However, realists are less inclined than liberals to attribute an important role to international institutions.

Regime Theory

Regime theory first developed from efforts to explain why international interactions are more orderly in some issue areas than in others. *Regimes* are "sets of implicit or explicit principles, norms, rules, and decision-making procedures around which actors' expectations converge in a given area of international relations."[37] Regime *principles* and *norms* refer to general beliefs and standards of behavior that guide relations in specific areas; for example, principles of the global trade regime include trade liberalization, reciprocity, and nondiscrimination. Rules and decision-making procedures stem from the broader principles and norms; for example, to promote the "trade liberalization" principle, the WTO has rules and decision-making procedures that limit protectionism and increase transparency. International regimes are normally associated with IOs; the WTO, for example, is embedded in the global trade regime, and the IMF is embedded in the global monetary regime.

Regime studies focus on several themes. One theme concerns the *formation* of international regimes. Researchers disagree as to whether a hegemon is necessary for the creation of regimes (see Chapter 3), and they also examine the strategies and processes that lead to successful regime creation and the role of IOs in the creation of regimes. A second theme concerns the *maintenance* of regimes. Many theorists are impressed by the durability of regimes even after the interest and power structures that led to their creation have changed. Thus, some writers argue that it is easier to maintain regimes than to establish them and that states benefiting from a regime may collectively maintain it even after a hegemonic state declines (see Chapter 3).[38] Others relate the durability of regimes to their adaptability and examine the changes in regimes over time. A third theme relates to the *results* of regimes, or whether regimes "make a difference" in IR. Initially there was a "relative absence of sustained discussions of the significance of regimes," but in more recent years theorists have examined regime significance in a wide range of areas such as global debt, the environment, transportation, and communications.[39] In assessing regime results, researchers examine whether states regularly abide by regime principles, norms, and rules; whether regimes effectively manage international problems; and whether regimes cause states to broaden their perceptions of self-interest.[40]

Traditional realists believe that states participate in regimes to improve their relative positions because they are mainly concerned with survival, security, and power; thus the regimes become arenas for acting out power relationships. The most powerful states establish regime principles, norms, and rules that further their national interests, and they do not adhere to the principles, norms, and rules when they conflict with their interests. For example, one realist asserts that "all those international arrangements dignified by the label regime are only too easily upset when either the balance of bargaining power or the perception of national interest (or both together) change among those states who negotiate them."[41] As global interdependence increased, some "modified" realists such as Stephen Krasner acknowledged that regimes may be important in certain areas (e.g., trade and monetary relations). However, they continue to emphasize the centrality of the state and national power and see regimes as existing only under rather restrictive conditions. Liberals by contrast are more likely to view regimes as a pervasive and significant phenomenon in IR.[42]

This book assumes that regimes have a significant impact on international behavior in certain areas. Regime principles, norms, and rules can increase understanding and cooperation and help establish standards that states and nonstate actors use to assess each others' behavior. Regimes can also induce states to follow consistent policies, limit actions that adversely affect others, and become less responsive to special interests. To say that regimes and their IOs influence behavior does not indicate that their effect is always positive. As realists and historical materialists point out, a regime's principles, norms, and rules may further the interests of the most powerful actors, and pressure may be greatest on the least powerful to abide by them. Despite the value of regime analysis, even liberal theorists argue that it has some serious shortcomings, and many now focus instead on *global governance*. The next section discusses the problems with regime analysis and compares the regime and global governance concepts.

LIBERALISM, GLOBAL GOVERNANCE, AND REGIMES

Governance refers to formal and informal processes and institutions that organize collective action, and **global governance** describes formal and informal arrangements that produce a degree of order and collective action above the state in the absence of a global government.[43] As globalization has increased, global governance has become a central issue in IPE because states have more difficulty managing their economic affairs individually, and actions states take in their self-interest have a greater effect on others. Some liberal theorists believe that the global governance concept avoids the limitations of regime analysis. First, most regime studies are state-centric, devoting too little attention to nonstate actors. Global governance studies by contrast assess the degree to which authority is being relocated from states to subnational, transnational, and supranational actors.[44] Second, the issue-area focus of regimes causes analysts to overlook broader aspects of global management; for example, most regime studies do not examine the crucial linkages between the global trade and environmental regimes. Global governance by contrast is a more encompassing concept that examines the linkages among issue areas. Third, regime theorists are criticized for assuming that "everyone wants . . . more and better regimes" and "that greater order and managed interdependence should be the collective goal."[45] Global governance studies are less obsessed with order and cooperation among states and more open to NGO demands for greater equity and justice.[46]

Despite the advantages of the global governance concept, it also has shortcomings. The most important problem with the global governance literature is that it does *not* offer a consistent theoretical framework for testing the coherence or utility of its ideas; instead, it addresses a wide array of diverse issues and uses a number of theoretical approaches.[47] Furthermore, regime theorists have altered their studies in response to the criticisms of regime analysis. For example, some analysts examine private and transnational regimes, in which nongovernmental actors agree on principles, norms, rules, and decision-making procedures to regulate their interactions in particular areas.[48] Some regime analysts have also broadened their studies and devoted more attention to the linkage among issue areas. Thus, "the concept of international regimes is not . . . , incompatible with the concept of global governance; on the contrary, although they differ in emphasis, both concepts recognize the significance of nonstate actors and the relationships between issue areas."[49] Part III of this book relies on regime theory because it permits us to analyze specific issue areas. However, we are attuned to the criticisms of regime analysis and also refer to some of the broader issues of global governance.

LIBERALISM AND DOMESTIC–INTERNATIONAL INTERACTIONS

IPE scholars focus on domestic–international interactions because domestic groups often see a close relationship between international economic issues such as trade and their own economic welfare. Literature on domestic–international interactions cannot be categorized under a single IPE perspective, but we discuss this issue here because liberals have a particular interest in the role of domestic societal pressures on the state. Realists devote less attention to domestic issues with their emphasis on the rational, unitary state. (Some Marxists view the state as an "instrument" of the dominant capitalist class; see Chapter 5.) Although many IPE scholars recognize the importance of understanding domestic–international interactions, integrating the domestic and international areas is a difficult process. This section examines the theoretical advances in this area, and the chapters in Part III give examples in specific IPE issue areas. Domestic–international interactions have most often been examined in the area of international trade, but monetary relations are also beginning to receive more attention.[50]

IPE theorists have a particular interest in domestic–international interactions in foreign economic policy making. In a 1977 study, Peter Katzenstein and others identified domestic political structure as a factor explaining differences in national responses to international economic events. For example, some analysts argued that more centralized states such as Japan and France respond more decisively than decentralized states such as the United States to events such as the 1973 OPEC oil price increase. The U.S. separation of powers between the president and Congress and the division of powers between the federal government and the states make the U.S. government more vulnerable to interest group pressures and less able to respond promptly to international economic events.[51] Although the strong state/weak state distinction may help us compare national policies in a general sense, later studies found that states are not uniformly strong or weak across different issue areas or time periods.[52] Thus, the U.S. executive has more leeway in making monetary than trade policy because societal groups see their economic fortunes as being more affected by trade. More centralized states such as Japan also do not act decisively on every economic issue. When a financial crisis affected East and Southeast Asia in the late 1990s, Japan had great difficulty in adopting the bold policy measures required to alleviate the crisis (see Chapter 11).

Scholars have also examined the effect of domestic producers and the general public on a state's foreign trade policy. Consumers may benefit from lower prices and a greater variety of goods if import tariffs are abolished, but local producers may suffer because of increased competition from imports. Although consumers greatly outnumber producers, the gains of free trade to consumers are more *diffuse,* whereas the losses to producers are more *concentrated.* Thus, local producers are often more united and vociferous in demanding protection than consumers are in seeking free trade. Rational choice theorists argue that concentrated protectionist industries have more influence over policy makers than the diffuse free-trade interests of consumers, because politicians adopt policies that improve their chances for reelection.[53] However, it is not sufficient to simply distinguish between concentrated and diffuse domestic interests for several reasons. First, concentrated interest groups do not necessarily have common interests. Concentrated "anti-protection interests" such as exporters, import-using industries, retailers, and multinational corporations often counteract the influence of concentrated protectionist interests.[54] Second, concentrated producer interests do not in all cases exert more influence than the general public, because the public sometimes reacts strongly to policies affecting employment, taxation, and inflation, and threatens to express its views in the ballot box. In sum, it is *not* true that "debates over foreign economic policy always pit concentrated interests against the public or that the mass electorate is always bested by concentrated interests."[55]

A country's domestic governmental institutions can have a significant effect on the influence private interest groups are able to exert. For example, members of the U.S. Congress who are elected by constituencies are more susceptible to pressure from concentrated protectionist interests than the U.S. president who is elected by the entire voting public. Concentrated groups can often exert strong protectionist pressures because the U.S. Constitution gives Congress the sole power to regulate commerce and impose tariffs. As Chapter 7 discusses, the change in U.S. trade policy from protectionism to free trade was made possible by Congressional delegation of trade negotiating authority to the president. In contrast to the U.S. presidential system, parliamentary systems with strong party discipline are better equipped to limit protectionist forces, but parliamentary systems with weaker party discipline provide more leeway for legislators to respond to protectionist interests. A country's trade policies of course are determined not only by domestic interests and institutions but also by the country's position in the international system.[56] Peter Gourevich and others focus on domestic structure as a *consequence* as well as a *cause* of foreign economic policy making. For example, interdependence and globalization have altered domestic structure, causing governmental actors to share power with private actors such as MNCs.[57]

Two-level game theory, a term coined by Robert Putnam, highlights the complexity of domestic–international interactions.[58] For example, theorists often view international negotiations as a two-level game involving the relationship between a state's international interests and obligations (level 1) on the one hand and domestic interactions within the state (level 2) on the other. At the international level, state representatives bargain with each other to reach an agreement. At the domestic level, these representatives bargain with domestic actors whose concurrence is needed to give the agreement legitimacy and effectiveness. A degree of consistency must develop between the state's international interests at level 1 and the domestic interests of groups within the state at level 2 if an agreement is to be signed and implemented. Game theorists are interested in discovering "win-sets," or all possible level 1 agreements that would win ratification at level 2. Executives negotiating international agreements are aware that legislative concurrence may be a necessary part of their win-sets, because legislatures can sometimes block or limit the implementation of agreements even if they do not require formal legislative approval; as Chapter 7 discusses, this is often the case in the U.S. presidential system.

Two-level game theory is also used to assess the leverage states have in negotiations. For example, Putnam notes the irony that "the stronger a state is in terms of autonomy from domestic pressures, the weaker its relative bargaining position [may be] internationally."[59] A democracy can claim more easily than a dictatorship that domestic pressures prevent it from signing a disadvantageous agreement. When an executive leader's options are limited domestically, others must recognize that he has more restricted domestic win-sets. For example, if an international agreement requires legislative ratification and the legislature strictly limits the agreements it will approve, this may give a negotiator more bargaining leverage. Chapter 7 shows that the U.S. Congress's constitutional powers on trade often limit the executive's options and give the president more leverage in international trade negotiations. A minority government in a parliamentary system may also have more leverage if it can convince others that its win-set is limited domestically by its minority position.

The substantive chapters in Part III provide more examples of domestic–international interactions in specific issue areas.

LIBERALISM AND NORTH–SOUTH RELATIONS

Liberals see the key factors in development as the efficient use of scarce resources and economic growth, which is often defined as an increase in a state's per capita income. Beyond these broad areas of agreement, the liberal development school "lacks a central unifying, theoretical argument."[60] The division between orthodox and interventionist liberals is evident among development theorists.

Orthodox Liberals and North–South Relations

Orthodox liberals devote little attention to North–South distributional issues because they assume that international economic relations are a positive-sum game and that interdependence has a mutually beneficial effect on states. Indeed, orthodox liberals often argue that North–South linkages provide more benefits to LDCs than to DCs. The sections that follow outline the orthodox liberal views regarding domestic and external determinants of development.

DOMESTIC DEVELOPMENT FACTORS   Orthodox liberals assume that development problems stem largely from inefficient LDC policies. Although liberal *modernization theory* of the 1950s and 1960s was considered to be passé by the 1970s, its precepts continue to influence orthodox liberal thought. Modernization theory asserts that the DCs achieved economic development by abandoning traditional practices and that LDCs must also replace their traditional practices with Western norms and institutions if they are to achieve development; for example, a system of rewards for innovation is essential because it helps generate surpluses that contribute to increased investment and self-sustaining growth. Although the changes required may produce dislocation and hardship, there are great rewards and opportunities for societies that successfully modernize.[61] Today most scholars would concede that the terms *traditional* and *modern* are imprecise and that "modern" values and practices are not always superior to "traditional" ones. However, orthodox liberals continue to believe that the main factors hindering LDC development are domestic. For example, they argue that Western states that protected private property rights successfully industrialized and that LDCs that do not enforce these rights hinder foreign investment and development. LDCs should permit private producers to operate freely through the price mechanism and should rely on governments only to provide national security, education, and services to improve the functioning of markets.[62]

PATHS TO DEVELOPMENT   Although some modernization theorists suggested that LDCs might follow different routes to development, most modernization theorists were deterministic, advising the South to follow the same path to development that the North had taken.[63] For example, one theorist wrote that the Western development model "reappears in virtually all modernizing societies of all continents of the world, regardless of variations of race, color, or creed."[64] Walt Rostow's book *The Stages of Economic Growth* was highly deterministic, claiming that societies move through five stages on the path to modernity: traditional society, the preconditions for takeoff, the takeoff, the drive to maturity, and the age of high mass consumption.[65] Despite the initial appeal of this model, Rostow's predictions regarding LDC growth were overly optimistic, and it was difficult to apply his stages to specific LDCs. For example, Rostow argued that an LDC's growth would become self-sustaining when it reached the takeoff stage; this prediction raised false hopes that LDC development was readily achievable and irreversible. Critics of modernization theory point out that the challenges facing LDCs today are very different from those confronting early developers. Southern development cannot be a repetition of the earlier Western model because of globalization, MNCs, and the difficulty in competing with the North.[66] Despite these criticisms, orthodox liberals continue to view the Western model as the only legitimate path to development. In the late 1980s, one liberal wrote that "third-world countries are much like those of the first world and will, with a modicum of external aid and internal stability, follow in the path of their predecessors," and another predicted that "what we may be witnessing is not just the end of the Cold War" but "the universalization of Western liberal democracy as the final form of human government."[67]

EXTERNAL DEVELOPMENT FACTORS Internationally, orthodox liberals view North–South relations as a positive-sum game that benefits the South, and they often argue that "the late-comers to modern economic growth tend to catch up with the early-comers."[68] The South requires foreign investment, the diffusion of advanced technologies, and export markets. Thus, LDCs that achieve development are integrated in the global economy through freer trade and capital flows, whereas the least developed LDCs have few trade and investment linkages with the North. In the orthodox liberal view, the East Asian NIEs developed rapidly in the 1960s–1980s because of their market orientation. Thus, Milton Friedman and Rose Friedman wrote in 1980 that "Malaysia, Singapore, Korea, Taiwan, Hong Kong, and Japan—all relying extensively on private markets, are thriving," while "India, Indonesia, and Communist China, all relying heavily on central planning, have experienced economic stagnation and political repression."[69] Realists by contrast see government–business cooperation and selective government involvement as the key to East Asian economic development. Chapter 10 examines the liberal–realist debate on this issue.

Interventionist Liberals and North–South Relations

Interventionist liberals, like orthodox liberals, believe that LDCs with efficient, market-oriented policies are most likely to achieve economic growth. However, interventionists point to the pronounced inequalities between the North and the South, and some interventionists argue that "economic forces left entirely to themselves tend to produce growing inequality."[70] Interventionists therefore call on the North to consider the special needs of the South, and they recommend changes that involve some intervention in the market. For example, they recommend that DCs remove trade barriers to LDCs, permit some protectionism for LDC industries, provide IMF and World Bank financing to indebted LDCs, and ensure that MNCs do not take advantage of LDC needs for foreign investment and technology. Interventionists believe that DC assistance to LDCs is a matter of enlightened self-interest because "the countries of the North, given their increasing interdependence with the South, themselves need international economic reform to ensure their own future prosperity."[71] Although interventionists argue that reforms are needed to provide for the South's special needs, they believe that the necessary changes can occur within the liberal order and that a radical redistribution of wealth and power between North and South is not necessary. They also believe in private enterprise and agree with orthodox liberals that many LDC development problems stem from domestic inefficiencies.[72]

CRITIQUE OF THE LIBERAL PERSPECTIVE

As this chapter notes, orthodox liberals believe that all states benefit from free trade, foreign investment, and other economic linkages in a competitive market. Because these linkages produce mutual benefits, orthodox liberals are not concerned about the fact that all states do not benefit equally. Interventionist liberals note that unemployment can occur under market conditions and that LDCs may require special treatment, but they believe that these problems can be remedied by supplementing rather than replacing the liberal economic system. Both realists and historical materialists criticize liberals for their inattention to power and distributional issues. Realists argue that relative gains are more important than absolute gains, because the most powerful states capture the largest share of the benefits. Economic exchanges are rarely free and equal, and bargaining power based on monopoly and coercion can have important political effects. Thus, powerful states can harm weaker states simply by reducing or terminating trade, aid, and investment.[73] Historical materialists accuse liberals of seeking to legitimize inequality and exploitation. Domestically, liberals mislead the working class into believing that it will benefit from economic prosperity along with the capitalist class, and internationally, liberals disguise exploitation and dependency relations under the cloak of "interdependence."

Critics also question the liberal view that advances in technology, transportation, and communication rather than global redistribution can solve the world's most urgent economic and environmental problems. Even with technological advances, the liberal international order that seemed so positive-sum in the immediate postwar years is becoming more competitive as global resources such as energy, water, and food become less abundant. Furthermore, technological advances may in fact contribute to greater North–South inequalities. **Endogenous growth theory** posits that technological change is not simply the result of fortunate breakthroughs in knowledge exogenous to the factors of production. Instead, technological knowledge is an important endogenous factor of production along with labor and capital. In other words, technological progress depends on investment in science and education, and on research and development (R&D). Because DCs and their firms have more resources than LDCs to subsidize education and R&D, they can continue to increase the productivity of capital and labor and "grow indefinitely at a faster pace" than small and poor economies.[74] Although some claims of endogenous growth theorists are controversial, they raise important questions about the orthodox liberal assumption that "the late-comers to modern economic growth tend to catch up with the early-comers."[75]

Orthodox liberals also simply assume that open economic policies and interdependence will improve LDC opportunities, without considering North–South political power relationships. Aside from aberrant cases such as OPEC and the East Asian NIEs, North–South relations are highly asymmetrical. Thus, in 1979 Tanzania's President Julius Nyerere remarked to a G77 ministerial meeting,

> . . . What we have in common is that we are all, in relation to the developed world, dependent—not interdependent—nations. Each of our economies has developed as a by-product and a subsidiary of development in the industrialized North, and is externally oriented.[76]

This dependent relationship provides the North with a potent source of power over the South. Economic liberals tend to discount the effects of this power asymmetry by arguing that North–South relations are a positive-sum game in which everyone benefits. One liberal assessment of NAFTA, for example, indicates that the United States, Canada, and Mexico agreed to "a partial surrender of autonomy in order to achieve the benefits that are available from mutual relaxation of protectionism."[77] However, orthodox liberals avoid asking whether Southern states (i.e., Mexico in NAFTA) must surrender more autonomy than Northern states (the United States and Canada). Liberals are also criticized for putting too much faith in the market and for disregarding the role of the state. Interventionist liberals such as Keynes have viewed states as performing various corrective functions, but even interventionists are criticized for undertheorizing the role of the state. Thus, realists argue that we should "bring the state back in" to our research because of its central role in policy making.[78]

Whereas liberals and realists accept the capitalist system as a given, historical materialists view capitalism as an exploitative system that should—and will—eventually be replaced by socialism. It is to the historical materialists and other critical theorists that this book now turns.

Questions

1. What are the similarities and differences among orthodox, interventionist, and institutional liberals?
2. Why did "embedded liberalism" become so important after World War II, and how did it draw upon the ideas of John Maynard Keynes and Karl Polanyi?
3. When did neoliberalism (or a "return" to orthodox liberalism) emerge, and why? How did it draw on the ideas of Milton Friedman? How did it differ from the liberalism of Adam Smith?
4. In what way do both the provision of public goods and prisoners' dilemma demonstrate "collective action problems"? How and why do liberals and realists differ in their views regarding the possibilities for cooperation under prisoners' dilemma?
5. What are international regimes, and what are the views of regime theorists regarding the formation, maintenance, and results of regimes?
6. What are the major criticisms of regime theory, and to what extent has the global governance literature dealt with the problems of regime theory?
7. In what ways have studies of foreign economic policy making, concentrated and diffuse domestic interests, and two level game theory increased our understanding of domestic–international interactions in IPE?
8. How do orthodox and interventionist liberals approach the issue of North–South relations?

Further Reading

Basic studies on game theory and prisoners' dilemma include Robert Axelrod, *The Evolution of Cooperation* (New York: Basic Books, 1984); and Kenneth A. Oye, ed., *Cooperation under Anarchy* (Princeton, NJ: Princeton University Press, 1986).

Basic studies on regime theory include Stephen D. Krasner, ed., *International Regimes* (Ithaca, NY: Cornell University Press, 1983); Stephan Haggard and Beth A. Simmons, "Theories of International Regimes," *International Organization* 41, no. 3 (Summer 1987), pp. 491–517; and Volker Rittberger with Peter Mayer, eds., *Regime Theory and International Relations* (New York: Oxford University Press, 1993). On private regimes, see Virginia Haufler, "Crossing the Boundary between Public and Private: International Regimes and Non-State Actors," in Volker Rittberger with Peter Mayer, eds., *Regime Theory and International Relations* (New York: Oxford University Press, 1993), pp. 94–111; and A. Claire Cutler, "Private International Regimes and Interfirm Cooperation," in Rodney B. Hall and Thomas A. Biersteker, eds., *The Emergence of Private Authority in Global Governance* (New York: Cambridge University Press, 2002), pp. 23–40.

The literature on global governance in IPE includes Miles Kahler and David A. Lake, eds., *Governance in a Global Economy: Political Authority in Transition* (Princeton, NJ: Princeton University Press, 2003); Rorden Wilkinson and Steve Hughes, eds., *Global Governance: Critical Perspectives* (New York: Routledge, 2002); and David Held and Anthony McGrew, eds., *Governing Globalization: Power, Authority and Global Governance* (Malden, MA: Polity, 2002).

On domestic–international interactions, see Peter J. Katzenstein, ed., "International Relations and Domestic Structures: Foreign Policies of the Advanced Industrial States," special issue of *International Organization* 31, no. 4 (Autumn 1977); G. John Ikenberry, David A. Lake, and Michael Mastanduno, eds., "The State and American Foreign Economic Policy," special issue of *International Organization* 42, no. 1 (Winter 1988); Robert O. Keohane and Helen Milner, eds., *Internationalization and Domestic Politics* (New York: Cambridge University Press, 1996). On two-level game theory, see Robert D. Putnam, "Diplomacy and Domestic Politics: The Logic of Two-Level Games," *International Organization* 42, no. 3 (Summer 1988), pp. 427–460; Peter B. Evans, Harold K. Jacobson, and Robert D. Putnam, eds., *Double-Edged Diplomacy* (Berkeley, CA: University of California Press, 1993); and William P. Avery, ed., *World Agriculture and the GATT* (Boulder, CO: Lynne Rienner, 1993).

On liberalism and North–South relations, see Lloyd G. Reynolds, *Economic Growth in the Third World, 1850–1980* (New Haven, CT: Yale University Press, 1985); Walt W. Rostow, *Why the Poor Get Richer and the Rich Slow Down* (Austin, TX: University of Texas Press, 1980); and Independent Commission on International Development Issues, *North-South, A Program for Survival* (Cambridge, MA: MIT Press, 1980). On endogenous growth theory, see Paul M. Romer, "Endogenous Technological Change," *Journal of Political Economy* 98, no. 5 (October 1990), pp. S71–S102; and Philippe Aghion and Peter Howitt, *Endogenous Growth Theory* (Cambridge, MA: MIT Press, 1998).

Notes

1. Robert. D. McKinlay and Richard Little, *Global Problems and World Order* (London: Pinter, 1986), p. 41.
2. Andrew Moravcsik, "Taking Preferences Seriously: A Liberal Theory of International Politics," *International Organization* 51, no. 4 (Autumn 1997), p. 517.

3. Adam Smith, *The Wealth of Nations,* vol. 1 (London: Dent, Everyman's Library no. 412, 1910), bk. 4, p. 398.

4. Walter Wriston, "Technology and Sovereignty," *Foreign Affairs* 67, no. 2 (Winter 1988–1989), p. 71.

5. Geoffrey Garrett, "The Causes of Globalization," *Comparative Political Studies* 33, no. 6/7 (August/September 2000), pp. 941–991.

6. John Locke, *Two Treatises of Government* (Cambridge, UK: Cambridge University Press, 1964), ch. 9 of the Second Treatise, p. 368. Locke believed governments should be able to levy taxes and require military service.

7. Smith, *The Wealth of Nations,* p. 436.

8. Smith, *The Wealth of Nations,* vol. 2, bk. 4, pp. 180–181. For an alternative view see Andrew Wyatt-Walter, "Adam Smith and the Liberal Tradition in International Relations," *Review of International Studies* 22, no. 1 (1996), pp. 142–172.

9. Peter A. Hall, "Introduction," in Peter A. Hall, ed., *The Political Power of Economic Ideas: Keynesianism across Nations* (Princeton, NJ: Princeton University Press, 1989), p. 4.

10. John M. Keynes, *The General Theory of Employment, Interest, and Money* (New York: Harcourt, Brace & World, 1936), pp. 378–379.

11. Hall, "Introduction," p. 7.

12. John M. Keynes, "National Self-Sufficiency," *The Yale Review* 22 (1933), p. 758. On Keynes's changing view of trade protection, see Barry Eichengreen, "Keynes and Protection," *Journal of Economic History* 44, no. 2 (June 1984), pp. 363–373.

13. Fred L. Block, *The Origins of International Economic Disorder: A Study of United States International Monetary Policy from World War II to the Present* (Berkeley, CA: University of California Press, 1977), pp. 62–69.

14. Anthony Arblaster, *The Rise and Decline of Western Liberalism* (New York: Basil Blackwell, 1984), p. 292; Donald Winch, "Keynes, Keynesianism, and State Intervention," in Peter A. Hall, ed., *The Political Power of Economic Ideas: Keynesianism across Nations* (Princeton, NJ: Princeton University Press, 1989), pp. 109–110.

15. Karl Polanyi, *The Great Transformation* (Boston, MA: Beacon Press, 1965).

16. The *embedded liberalism compromise* term was coined by John G. Ruggie in "International Regimes, Transactions, and Change: Embedded Liberalism in the Postwar Economic Order," in Stephen D. Krasner, ed., *International Regimes* (Ithaca, NY: Cornell University Press, 1983), pp. 204–214.

17. Peter Gourevitch, *Politics in Hard Times: Comparative Responses to International Economic Crises* (Ithaca, NY: Cornell University Press, 1986), pp. 166–169; Adam Przeworski, *Capitalism and Social Democracy* (New York: Cambridge University Press, 1985), pp. 205–211.

18. Hayek gave priority to social as well as economic relationships. See Walter Block, "Hayek's Road to Serfdom," *Journal of Libertarian Studies* 12, no. 2 (Fall 1996), p. 365; Charles R. McCann, "F. A. Hayek: The Liberal as Communitarian," *Review of Austrian Economics* 15, no. 1 (2002), pp. 5–34.

19. Milton Friedman, *Capitalism and Freedom* (Chicago, IL: University of Chicago Press, 1962), p. 9.

20. Milton Friedman and Rose Friedman, *Free to Choose: A Personal Statement* (New York: Harcourt Brace Jovanovich, 1980), pp. 54–55.

21. Robert Cox, *Production, Power, and World Order: Social Forces in the Making of History* (New York: Columbia University Press, 1987), pp. 286–288; Alain Lipietz, *Towards a New Economic Order: Postfordism, Ecology and Democracy,* trans. Malcolm Slater (New York: Oxford University Press, 1992), pp. 30–31.

22. Robert Keohane identifies three types of international institutions—IOs, regimes, and conventions—in "Neoliberal Institutionalism: A Perspective on World Politics," in Robert O. Keohane, ed., *International Institutions and State Power: Essays in International Relations Theory* (Boulder, CO: Westview Press, 1989), pp. 3–4.

23. John G. Ruggie first used the *regime* term in IPE in "International Responses to Technology: Concepts and Trends," *International Organization* 29, no. 3 (Summer 1975), pp. 570–573. Stephen Krasner edited *International Regimes.*

24. Robert O. Keohane and Joseph S. Nye, *Power and Interdependence,* 2nd ed. (Glenview, IL: Scott, Foresman, 1989), pp. 8–9.

25. Richard N. Cooper, *The Economics of Interdependence: Economic Policy in the Atlantic Community* (New York: McGraw-Hill, 1968). Earlier studies include Sir N. Angell, *The Foundations of International Polity* (London: Heinemann, 1914); William A. Brown, Jr., *The International Gold Standard Reinterpreted, 1914–1934,* 2 vols. (New York: National Bureau of Economic Research, 1940); Albert O. Hirschman, *National Power and the Structure of Foreign Trade* (Berkeley, CA: University of California Press, 1945).

26. Richard N. Cooper, "Economic Interdependence and Foreign Policy in the Seventies," *World Politics* 24 (January 1972), p. 179.

27. Cooper, "Economic Interdependence and Foreign Policy in the Seventies," pp. 170–171.

28. Keohane and Nye, *Power and Interdependence,* p. 11.

29. See Keohane and Nye, *Power and Interdependence,* pp. 24–29, and ch. 7.

30. Ricardo Grinspun and Maxwell A. Cameron, eds., *The Political Economy of North American Free Trade* (Montreal, QC: McGill-Queen's University Press, 1993). Some Canadian analysts go even further and characterize Canada's relationship with the United States as dependence rather than interdependence. See Glen Williams, "On Determining Canada's Location within the International Political Economy," *Studies in Political Economy* 25 (Spring 1988), pp. 107–140.

31. Bayless Manning coined the term *intermestic* in "The Congress, The Executive and Intermestic Affairs: Three Proposals," *Foreign Affairs* 55 (June 1977), pp. 306–324.

32. James D. Morrow, *Game Theory for Political Scientists* (Princeton, NJ: Princeton University Press, 1994), pp. 1–8.

33. Robert O. Keohane, *After Hegemony: Cooperation and Discord in the World Political Economy* (Princeton, NJ: Princeton University Press, 1984), p. 68.

34. Robert Axelrod, *The Evolution of Cooperation* (New York: Basic Books, 1984), p. 9. The terms *Pareto-optimal* and *Pareto-deficient* are named after an Italian sociologist, Vilfredo Pareto (1848–1923).

35. Keohane, "Neoliberal Institutionalism," pp. 1–20; Robert Axelrod and Robert O. Keohane, "Achieving Cooperation Under Anarchy: Strategies and Institutions," in Kenneth A. Oye, ed., *Cooperation Under Anarchy* (Princeton, NJ: Princeton University Press, 1986), pp. 226–254.

36. Robert Gilpin with Jean M. Gilpin, *Global Political Economy: Understanding the International Economic Order* (Princeton, NJ: Princeton University Press, 2001), p. 83, fn. 13.
37. Stephen D. Krasner, "Structural Causes and Regime Consequences," in Stephen D. Krasner, ed., *International Regimes* (Ithaca, NY: Cornell University Press, 1983), p. 2; Mark W. Zacher with Brent A. Sutton, *Governing Global Networks: International Regimes for Transportation and Communications* (New York: Cambridge University Press, 1996), p. 1.
38. Keohane, *After Hegemony,* pp. 49, 244–245.
39. Oran R. Young, *International Cooperation: Building Regimes for Natural Resources and the Environment* (Ithaca, NY: Cornell University Press, 1989), p. 206.
40. Olav S. Stokke, "Regimes as Governance Systems," in Oran R. Young, ed., *Global Governance: Drawing Insights from the Environmental Experience* (Cambridge, MA: MIT Press, 1997), pp. 27–63.
41. Susan Strange, "Cave! Hic Dragones: A Critique of Regime Analysis," in Stephen D. Krasner, ed., *International Regimes* (Ithaca, NY: Cornell University Press, 1983), p. 345.
42. See Krasner, "Structural Causes and Regime Consequences," pp. 5–10.
43. Oran R. Young, *Governance in World Affairs* (Ithaca, NY: Cornell University Press, 1999), p. 2.
44. John Vogler, "Taking Institutions Seriously: How Regime Analysis Can be Relevant to Multilevel Environmental Governance," *Global Environmental Politics* 3, no. 2 (May 2003), pp. 32–35; James N. Rosenau, "Governance in the Twenty-first Century," *Global Governance* 1, no. 1 (Winter 1995), pp. 18–20.
45. Strange, "Cave! Hic Dragones," p. 345.
46. Anil Hira and Theodore H. Cohn, "Toward a Theory of Global Regime Governance," *International Journal of Political Economy* 33, no. 4 (Winter 2003–2004), pp. 9–11.
47. For other criticisms of the global governance literature, see Hira and Cohn, "Toward a Theory of Global Regime Governance," pp. 12–16.
48. See Further Readings in this chapter for examples.
49. Stokke, "Regimes as Governance Systems," p. 31.
50. Jeffry Frieden and Lisa L. Martin, "International Political Economy: Global and Domestic Interactions," in Ira Katznelson and Helen V. Milner, eds., *Political Science: The State of the Discipline* (New York: W.W. Norton, 2002), pp. 118–120.
51. Peter J. Katzenstein, ed., "International Relations and Domestic Structures: Foreign Policies of the Advanced Industrial States," special issue of *International Organization* 31, no. 4 (Autumn 1977); Benjamin J. Cohen, *International Political Economy: An Intellectual History* (Princeton, NJ: Princeton University Press, 2008), pp. 124–129.
52. G. John Ikenberry, David A. Lake, and Michael Mastanduno, eds., "The State and American Foreign Economic Policy," special issue of *International Organization* 42, no. 1 (Winter 1988).
53. Bruno S. Frey, "The Public Choice View of International Political Economy," *International Organization* 38, no. 1 (Winter 1984), pp. 207–214; Guido Pincione and Fernando R. Tesón, *Rational Choice and Democratic Deliberation* (New York: Cambridge University Press, 2006), pp. 5–7.
54. I. M. Destler and John S. Odell, *Anti-Protection: Changing Forces in United States Trade Policy* (Washington, D.C.: Institute for International Economics, 1967), pp. 125–128.

55. Frieden and Martin, "International Political Economy," p. 130.
56. Frieden and Martin, "International Political Economy," pp. 132–136.
57. Peter Gourevitch, "The Second Image Reversed: The International Sources of Domestic Politics," *International Organization* 32, no. 4 (Autumn 1978), pp. 881–912.
58. Robert D. Putnam, "Diplomacy and Domestic Politics: The Logic of Two-Level Games," *International Organization* 42, no. 3 (Summer 1988), pp. 427–460.
59. Putnam, "Diplomacy and Domestic Politics," p. 449.
60. David A. Lake, "Power and the Third World: Toward a Realist Political Economy of North-South Relations," *International Studies Quarterly* 31, no. 2 (June 1987), p. 218.
61. Cyril E. Black, *The Dynamics of Modernization: A Study in Comparative History* (New York: Harper & Row, 1966), p. 27; Daniel Lerner, "Modernization: Social Aspects," in David Sills, ed., *International Encyclopedia of the Social Sciences,* vol. 10 (New York: Macmillan, 1968), pp. 386–388.
62. Robert Wade, *Governing the Market: Economic Theory and the Role of Government in East Asian Industrialization* (Princeton, NJ: Princeton University Press, 1990), pp. 11–14.
63. Less deterministic studies include Gabriel A. Almond and James S. Coleman, eds., *The Politics of the Developing Areas* (Princeton, NJ: Princeton University Press, 1960); Samuel P. Huntington, *Political Order in Changing Societies* (New Haven, CT: Yale University Press, 1968); Alexander Gerschenkron, *Economic Backwardness in Historical Perspective: A Book of Essays* (Cambridge, MA: Harvard University Press, 1962).
64. Daniel Lerner, *The Passing of Traditional Society: Modernizing the Middle East* (New York: Free Press, 1964), pp. viii–ix. (This quotation appears in the preface to the paperback edition.)
65. W. W. Rostow, *The Stages of Economic Growth: A Non-Communist Manifesto* (Cambridge, UK: Cambridge University Press, 1960), pp. 4–92.
66. Alejandro Portes, "On the Sociology of National Development: Theories and Issues," *American Journal of Sociology* 82, no. 1 (July 1976), p. 60.
67. Lloyd G. Reynolds, *Economic Growth in the Third World, 1850–1980* (New Haven, CT: Yale University Press, 1985), p. 6; Francis Fukuyama, "The End of History?" *The National Interest* 16 (Summer 1989), p. 4.
68. W. W. Rostow, *Why the Poor Get Richer and the Rich Slow Down* (Austin, TX: University of Texas Press, 1980), p. 259.
69. Friedman and Friedman, *Free to Choose,* p. 57.
70. Independent Commission on International Development Issues (henceforth, Brandt Commission I), *North–South, A Program for Survival* (Cambridge, MA: MIT Press, 1980), pp. 103–104.
71. Brandt Commission I, *North–South,* p. 33.
72. Stephen D. Krasner, *Structural Conflict: The Third World Against Global Liberalism* (Berkeley, CA: University of California Press, 1985), pp. 22–25.
73. Charles E. Lindblom, *Politics and Markets: The World's Political–Economic Systems* (New York: Basic Books, 1977), p. 48.
74. Michael Burda and Charles Wyplosz, *Macroeconomics,* 4th ed. (New York: Oxford University Press, 2005), pp. 65–66.
75. Rostow, *Why the Poor Get Richer and the Rich Slow Down,* p. 259.
76. "Address by His Excellency Mwalima Julius K Nyerere, President of the United Republic of Tanzania, to the Fourth Ministerial Meeting of the Group of 77,"

Arusha, 12–16 February 1979, in Karl P. Sauvant, *The Group of 77: Evolution, Structure, Organization* (New York: Oceana Publications, 1981), p. 133.

77. Steven Globerman and Michael Walker, "Overview," in Steven Globerman and Michael Walker, eds., *Assessing NAFTA: A Trinational Analysis* (Vancouver, BC: The Fraser Institute, 1993), p. ix.

78. Theda Skocpol, "Bringing the State Back In: Strategies of Analysis in Current Research," in Peter B. Evans, Dietrich Rueschemeyer, and Theda Skocpol, eds., *Bringing the State Back In* (New York: Cambridge University Press, 1985), p. 6.

CHAPTER 5

Critical Perspectives

This chapter is more broad ranging than Chapters 3 and 4 because it discusses four *critical perspectives* that do *not* agree on a core set of assumptions: historical materialism, constructivism, feminism, and environmentalism. Their main common feature is that they are all critical of the traditional mainstream liberal and realist perspectives. However, the "mainstream" is not static, and we will discuss the fact that there are liberal as well as critical constructivists, feminists, and environmentalists. This chapter devotes more attention to the basic tenets of historical materialism than to the tenets of the other critical perspectives because it encompasses the largest group of critical theories, including Marxism, dependency theory, world-system theory, and Gramscian analysis. Although all these approaches have some roots in Marxism, they often diverge substantially from classical Marxist ideas. The *historical materialist* perspective is "historical" because it examines structural change in terms of class and sometimes North–South struggles over time, and it is "materialist" because it examines the role of material (especially economic) factors in shaping society.[1]

BASIC TENETS OF HISTORICAL MATERIALISM

The Role of the Individual, the State, and Societal Groups

Marxists see "class" as the main factor affecting the economic and political order. Each mode of production (e.g., feudalism and capitalism) is associated with an exploiting nonproducing class and an exploited class of producers. Classes are absent only in the simplest primitive-communal mode of production and the future Communist mode. Thus, Karl Marx and Friedrich Engels wrote that modern bourgeois society "has not done away with class antagonisms. It has but established new classes, new conditions of oppression, new forms of struggle in place of the old ones."[2] Marx and Engels usually depict the state as being an agent of the bourgeoisie, which uses it as an instrument to exploit wage labor. Although the state may have some autonomy from a dominant class during transition periods when the power of warring classes is more equally balanced, the state cannot escape from its dependence on the capitalist class in the longer term.[3] Only when the proletarian revolution eliminates class distinctions based on private ownership will the state no longer be an instrument of class oppression. A number of scholars criticize Marx and Engels' position that state actions simply reflect the views of the dominant class (see the following discussion).

The Nature and Purpose of International Economic Relations

Historical materialists view economic relations as basically conflictual, with "the exploitation of one part of society by the other."[4] It is well known that the views of historical materialists evolved along with changes in the international system. Thus, Marx and Engels predicted that contradictions within capitalism would contribute to poverty of the working class, surplus production, economic downturns, and the collapse of capitalism. Lenin then cited *imperialism* to explain why capitalism survived, asserting that colonies provided the "metropole" states with a cheap source of agricultural and raw materials and a market for the metropoles' surplus production.[5] When capitalism persisted after decolonization, historical materialists explained this as *neocolonialism:* Although the imperial powers ceded *political* control, they continued to have *economic* control over their former colonies.[6] As this chapter discusses, dependency, world-system, and Gramscian theorists offer other explanations for the persistence of capitalism. Historical materialists favor a redistribution of power and wealth, but unlike realists they do not believe that such a redistribution can occur with unfettered capitalism. Although historical materialists advocate for the poor and less powerful, they take different approaches to dealing with capitalism's inequities. Some accept certain elements of market capitalism while others totally reject it, some want LDCs to become socialist while others seek the overthrow of the capitalist system, and some believe in evolutionary reform while others advocate revolution.

The Relationship Between Politics and Economics

Marx describes history as a dialectical process in which there is a contradiction between the economic mode of production (e.g., feudalism, capitalism, and socialism) and the political system. This contradiction is resolved when changes in the mode and relations of production eventually cause the political "superstructure" to change. Thus, Marx provided the foundation for **instrumental Marxism,** which—like liberal pluralism—sees government (i.e., politics) as responding in a rather passive manner to socioeconomic pressures.[7] Liberals, however, see any societal group as having political influence, whereas instrumental Marxists believe that a state's policies reflect the interests of the capitalist class. To support this position, instrumental Marxists point to personal ties between capitalists and public officials and to the movement of individuals between business and government.[8] After World War II, many scholars criticized instrumental Marxism because DCs adopted welfare and unemployment insurance policies *despite* the opposition of major business groups. As a result, **structural Marxism** emerged, which sees the state as relatively autonomous from direct political pressure of the capitalist class. Although some capitalists may oppose state policies benefiting workers, they do not realize that these policies serve their long-term interests. By providing welfare and other benefits, the state placates the workers and gains their support for the continuance of capitalism.[9] Structural Marxists differ from realists even though they both see the state as somewhat autonomous. In the structural Marxist view, the bourgeoisie does not *directly* control the state, but the two are committed to the survival of capitalism. Realists, by contrast, see the state as acting independently of the economic interests of any societal group to further the "national interest."

The Causes and Effects of Globalization

In the Marxist view, the bourgeoisie promote globalization because it increases their profits and gives them more resources and power vis-à-vis the proletariat. Marxists agree with liberals that technological advances can facilitate globalization. However, liberals see these technological advances as resulting from natural human drives for economic progress, while Marxists assume that they result from "historically specific impulses of capitalist development."[10] Historical materialists agree with liberals that globalization is a pervasive force, but unlike liberals they see it as a negative process that prevents states from safeguarding domestic welfare and employment. Adjustment to global competitiveness is the new imperative, and states must adapt to the needs of the global economy; for example, indebted LDCs must impose adjustment measures on vulnerable groups such as women and children to become more globally competitive. Globalization is also increasing the structural power of capital vis-à-vis labor. Because states depend on business confidence and investment, they respond to business demands by disciplining trade unions and pressuring for lower wages. A new transnational managerial class has also divided the labor force by shifting production from the mass production factory to many small component–producing and servicing units. Historical materialists also see globalization as a cause of the polarization of wealth and poverty, environmental degradation, money laundering and the illegal drug trade, intra-ethnic and fundamentalist conflict, and civil society protests. Whereas some historical materialists oppose globalization in general, most focus their criticisms on capitalist globalization.[11]

EARLY FORMS OF HISTORICAL MATERIALISM

Karl Marx and IPE

Although Karl Marx (1818–1883) did not write systematically about IR, his theory of capitalism and class struggle provided the basic framework for historical materialism in IPE. Marx wrote many articles about the effect of Western capitalism on non-European areas, but he had only limited information on the subject.[12] He believed that capitalism emerged in Europe when private feudal landholdings were converted into private bourgeois property. India and China by contrast had an "Asiatic" mode of production that Marx viewed as outside the mainstream of Western development. The state's presence was much greater in the Asiatic mode, with the Chinese and Indian central governments developing large public work projects to provide water over extensive land areas. At the local level India and China had small, self-sufficient village communities with communal rather than individual ownership. In view of this communal property (locally) and public property (centrally), Marx saw no basis for a transformation to private capitalist holdings in the Asiatic mode. Thus, Marx believed that external pressure from Western imperialism was necessary if China and India were to progress to capitalism and then to socialism.[13]

Marx harshly criticized England for destroying India's handicraft textile industry by preventing it from exporting cotton to Europe and by inundating it with British textiles; but he also criticized India for lacking capitalism's capacity for development.[14] In contrast to stagnating Asiatic societies, Marx viewed capitalism as a dynamic, expansive system with a historic mission to move development throughout the world. Thus, Marx believed that England performed a dual function in India: destroying the old society and providing the foundation for Western society, which would in turn provide the conditions for a Communist revolution in Asia:

> Can mankind fulfill its destiny without a fundamental revolution in
> the social state of Asia? If not, whatever may have been the crimes
> of England, she was the unconscious tool of history in bringing
> about that revolution.[15]

Marx's analysis of Asia had major defects due to his lack of firsthand knowledge and his Eurocentric prejudices, and later in life he repudiated some of his own ideas regarding the Asiatic mode of production.[16]

Marxist Studies of Imperialism

Despite Marx's writing on Western capitalism and non-European societies, systematic studies of imperialism depended on later writers. Theories of imperialism portray the world as hierarchical, with some societies engaging in conquest and control over others. John Hobson (1858–1940), a non-Marxist English economist, developed an influential economic theory of imperialism that identified three major problems of capitalist societies: low wages and underconsumption by workers, oversaving by capitalists, and overproduction. Because private owners increase their profits by paying low wages, workers have limited purchasing power and the capitalists must look to countries abroad as an outlet for their surplus goods and profits; this gives rise to imperialism.[17] Despite Hobson's influence, Vladimir Lenin's (1870–1924) *Imperialism: The Highest Stage of Capitalism* became the most widely cited work in this area.[18] Lenin focused on the expanded imperialism of the late nineteenth century "in which the dominance of monopolies and finance capital established itself" and "the division of all territories of the globe among the great capitalist powers [was] . . . completed."[19] Although Hobson and Lenin agreed that imperialism resulted from low wages and underconsumption by workers, they offered different solutions. As a liberal, Hobson assumed that imperialism would no longer be needed as an outlet for surpluses if workers' wages increased *within* the capitalist system. As a Marxist, Lenin by contrast viewed exploitation of the workers and imperialism as *inevitable* outcomes of capitalism.

Lenin also turned to imperialism to explain why the revolution had not occurred as Marx predicted. The export of capital and goods to colonial areas provided new "superprofits," which capitalist firms could use to bribe the working class in their home countries with higher wages. However, imperialism did not mark an end to capitalism's underlying contradictions, and the revolution was still inevitable. Once the capitalist states had divided the globe into colonial areas, competition among them would lead to interimperialist wars and the downfall of capitalism. Lenin's position on the effects of colonialism was somewhat ambivalent. Although he believed that capitalist states would oppose industrialization in the colonies and use them as sources of raw materials, like Marx he viewed colonialism as a progressive force essential for Southern development. Western exports of capital and technology to their colonies would help create foreign competitors with lower wages, and the increased economic competition between rising and declining capitalist powers would eventually lead to imperial rivalries and conflict. However, colonialism did not bring industrialization and development to the colonies as Marx and Lenin had predicted. Even after Latin American colonies gained their independence in the nineteenth century, they depended on external capital and technology and continued to produce more primary products than industrial goods. The failure to bring about capitalist development led to major rifts among Marxists, with some arguing that imperialism was economically regressive.[20] As the following discussion shows, dependency theorists turned Marxism on its head and focused on capitalism's role in hindering rather than facilitating LDC development.

Dependency Theory

Dependency theory, the dominant approach to development among Latin American intellectuals during the 1960s, rejects the optimism of liberal modernization theorists (see Chapter 4) and argues that advanced capitalist states either underdevelop LDCs or prevent them from achieving genuine autonomous development. The following discussion examines the origins, basic tenets, and criticisms of dependency theory.

Dependency theory is based on two theoretical traditions: Marxism and Latin American structuralism. Like Marxists, dependency theorists focus on capitalist development and adopt terms such as *class, mode of production,* and *imperialism.* Dependency theorists and Marxists also are committed to political action and support the replacement of capitalism with socialism. However, dependency theorists reject Marxist views that DCs perform a service to LDCs in the long term by contributing to the spread of capitalism. Dependency theory is also based on the ideas of the Argentinian economist Raúl Prebisch and other Latin American "structuralists," who focused on structural obstacles to LDC development. Prebisch rejected liberal assumptions regarding the benefits of free trade and argued that LDCs in the periphery suffer from declining **terms of trade** with DCs in the core. The South is hindered by its dependence on primary product exports because people demand more finished goods as their incomes increase, but *not* more primary products. If LDCs try to raise prices for their raw materials, the North can develop substitute or synthetic products. Thus, Prebisch argued that LDCs should adopt **import substitution industrialization (ISI)** policies to protect their infant industries, imposing trade barriers and producing manufactures domestically to satisfy demand previously met by imports.[21] In the 1950s and 1960s many LDCs adopted ISI, but it contributed to numerous problems and growing balance-of-payments deficits (see Chapter 10). Scholars challenged Prebisch's views from the right and the left, and many leftists turned to dependency theory. Unlike Prebisch, dependency theorists argue that the core will never permit LDCs to achieve genuine, autonomous development.[22]

There are two major strains of dependency theory. The first, inspired by André Gunder Frank's *Capitalism and Underdevelopment in Latin America,* takes a more doctrinaire position on the impact of dependency, and the second, inspired by Fernando Henrique Cardoso and Enzo Faletto's *Dependency and Development in Latin America,* takes a less doctrinaire approach.[23] Dependency theorists see the global capitalist economy as responsible for constraining the South's development. Whereas the North benefits from global capitalist linkages and dynamic development based on internal needs, the South's development is severely constrained because of its interaction with the North. However, Cardoso and Faletto were more inclined than Frank to reject the idea that "external factors or foreign domination were enough to explain the dynamic of societies," and they examined the relationship between "internal and external processes of political domination."[24] For example, dependency theorists in the Cardoso–Faletto strain contend that elites in the South (*compradores*) have alliances with foreign capitalists in the North and often take actions that reinforce the pattern of LDC dependency. Dependency theorists in the Frank strain also argued that the development of capitalist economies in the core *required* the underdevelopment of the periphery. Although LDCs may have been *un*developed in the past, they became *under*developed as a result of their involvement with core countries.[25] Theorists in the Cardoso–Faletto strain took a more nuanced approach, arguing that "associated dependent development" was sometimes possible in the periphery.[26] The Cardoso–Faletto view gained support over time because industrialization *was* occurring in some LDCs, and many dependency studies in the 1970s and 1980s focused on "dependent development" rather than "underdevelopment."[27] Frank's views evolved, and even he began writing about dependent development in the East Asian NIEs. Dependent development, however, differs from genuine autonomous development, because workers in the periphery produce less technologically sophisticated goods, and the production of capital goods in the periphery depends on imports of machinery, technology, and foreign investment from the core.[28]

Dependency theory became a target of criticism in the 1970s and 1980s. A major criticism is that dependency theorists do not adequately define their concepts; they see states as either dependent or not dependent, and do not measure different levels of dependence. Furthermore, "core" and "periphery" are overly broad categories. How do we justify including Haiti with Brazil in the periphery, or Portugal with the United States in the core? Second, the only form of exploitation dependency theorists discuss is capitalism. Critics argue that the most important factor in dependency is not capitalism *per se* but unequal power among states; thus, capitalism and Soviet communism were both marked by "asymmetric and unequal linkages between a dominant center and its weaker dependencies."[29] Third, dependency theorists often prescribe a breaking of linkages with the core and a socialist revolution to bring about social justice and equality. However, critics note that cutting linkages with the core does not ensure that there will be social justice. Dependency theorists can only hope that an end to dependent linkages will lead a country to "emphasize distribution and participation rather than accumulation and exclusion."[30] Fourth, dependency theorists focus so much on the international system as the source of LDC problems that they do not adequately explain why LDCs may respond differently to similar external constraints. Even the Cardoso–Faletto strain gives primacy to external factors.[31] Fifth, dependency theory's predictions regarding development are simply incorrect. For example, theorists held up China as a model of agrarian self-reliance, but in 1976 it turned to a policy of openness that contributed to its rapid economic growth. Some of the strongest criticisms come from Marxists, who assert that dependency theorists are overly nationalistic. Whereas dependency theorists see the central problem as *foreign* control or domination, Marxists see it as *private* control of the means of production. Thus, dependency theorists give more emphasis to "relations of exchange" (between core and peripheral states) than to "relations of production" (between classes).[32] Although these criticisms contributed to the decline of dependency theory, they were often aimed at the more radical version and did not do justice to the less extreme Cardoso–Faletto strain.[33] Writers today rarely identify themselves as dependency theorists, but development theorists in fact continue to draw on aspects of the theory because there are "many issues and areas of development where dependency plays a major role."[34]

WHITHER THE HISTORICAL MATERIALIST PERSPECTIVE?

With the breakup of the Soviet bloc and the end of the Cold War, some mainstream theorists see historical materialism as no longer relevant. For example, one liberal theorist argues that "the implosion of the Soviet Union, and domestic changes in Eastern Europe, have eliminated the significance of the socialist economic model," and another claims that we are witnessing the "victory of economic and political liberalism."[35] However, historical materialism has not disappeared and there are reasons to expect a renewed interest in it in future years. First, the breakup of the Soviet bloc enables theorists to express Marxist ideas without having to defend the heavy-handed actions of governments such as the Soviet Union. Second, Marxist analyses of capitalism's contradictions have gained some support from the 1980s foreign debt crisis, the 1990s East Asian financial crisis, and the 2008 global financial crisis. A number of LDCs and transition economies have been disillusioned with liberal market reforms, and some analysts warn that "Latin America is swerving left, and distinct backlashes are under way against the predominant trends of the last 15 years: free-market reforms, agreement with the United States on a number of issues, and the consolidation of representative democracy."[36] A 2005 UN Report helps explain this leftward shift: "Historically, the highest levels of income inequality have been found in Africa and Latin America, and in the 1980s and 1990s the situation deteriorated even further."[37] Historical materialism continues to have appeal because of its focus on the poor, the weak, and distributive justice issues. The following sections discuss some contemporary theories with links to historical materialism.

World-System Theory

World-system theory is more broad ranging than dependency theory. Whereas dependency theorists focus on core-periphery relations, world-system theorists focus on the entire world-system, including relationships among core states and the rise and decline of hegemons.[38] The following discussion refers mainly to the writings of Immanuel Wallerstein, who founded world-system theory, but we sometimes discuss areas where other theorists diverge from Wallerstein's views. The main unit of analysis in world-system theory is the *world-system,* which has "a single division of labor and multiple cultural systems."[39] There are two types of world-systems: *world-empires,* which have a common political system, and *world-economies,* which have many political systems. In a world-empire, a single political entity (such as ancient Rome) often uses coercive power to control the economic division of labor between the core and the periphery. The modern world-system is a world-economy, because no single state has conquered the entire core region. Instead, states engage in a "hegemonic sequence," in which various hegemonic states (the Netherlands, Britain, and the United States) rise and fall. Today the capitalist world-economy is the only world-system. Although states in this world-economy establish a power hierarchy through market mechanisms, the core states may use force when peripheral states challenge the market rules that sustain the core's dominance. Wallerstein asserts that the capitalist world-economy emerged in Europe during the "long" sixteenth century (1450–1640), but some other theorists argue that it originated earlier in the Middle East or Asia.[40] The capitalist world-economy's main features are production for the market to gain the maximum profit and unequal exchange relations between core and peripheral states.[41]

Because the world-economy is their unit of analysis, world-system theorists do not consider states to be meaningful actors apart from their position in the world-economy; thus, long before the breakup of the Soviet Union, Wallerstein wrote that there are "no socialist systems in the world-economy any more than there are feudal systems because there is *one* world-system" that is capitalist in form.[42] They also believe that a state's internal and external strengths cannot be viewed separately from its position in the world-economy; core states are strong and peripheral states are weak. World-system theorists introduced the *semiperiphery* as a third category between the periphery and the core to account for the fact that some LDCs—East Asian and Latin American NIEs—were industrializing. Some states have moved up or down on the core/semiperiphery/periphery hierarchy, but world-system theorists are more pessimistic than liberals about the prospects for today's LDCs. Although some semiperipheral states *seem* to be models of economic success, they are simply "the more advanced exemplars of dependent development."[43] Thus, the core, the periphery, and the semiperiphery are enduring features of the capitalist world-economy. The semiperiphery divides the periphery so the core states do not face a unified opposition, and the semiperipheral states view themselves "as better off than the lower sector rather than as worse off than the upper sector."[44] Thus, the semiperiphery stabilizes the capitalist world-economy. Despite this apparent stability, capitalism has contradictions that could threaten its long-term survival, and world-system theorists raise the prospect of its replacement by socialism.

Many theorists have criticized world-system theory. Some classical Marxists charge that (like dependency theory) it puts more emphasis on "relations of exchange" among core, semiperipheral, and peripheral states than on "relations of production" between capitalists and workers. Realists see world-system theory as undertheorizing the role of the state. In their view, Wallerstein's interest in individual states "is limited to showing how they are incorporated into" the world-economy, and he simplistically assumes that "strong states" are in the core and "weak states" are in the periphery.[45] As realists point out, in the sixteenth century some strong states—Spain and Sweden—were in the periphery, while the core states—Holland and England—had relatively weak state structures. Indeed, late industrializers often require strong state leadership to promote their development.[46] Despite its shortcomings, world-system theory provides an alternative approach to IPE that offers a long-term historical view of socioeconomic and political change. Many liberals by contrast underestimate the importance of historical differences between industrializing countries in the past and LDCs today, and the realist approach is often ahistorical. World-system theory also avoids a problem with dependency theory by asserting that states can sometimes ascend from the periphery to the semiperiphery and core. However, world-system theorists avoid the over-optimism of liberals regarding LDC development prospects. Unlike realists and liberals, world-system theorists focus on the poorest and weakest in society and on the core's exploitation of the periphery. Although world-system theorists overestimate the degree to which external exploitation causes LDC problems, orthodox liberals err in the opposite direction by downplaying the role of external exploitation in the capitalist world-economy.

Gramscian Analysis

Gramscian IPE, which emerged in the 1980s, draws on the writings of Antonio Gramsci (1891–1937), a theorist and social activist who was a former leader of the Italian Communist party. Despite his Marxist linkages, Gramsci saw Marxism as unable to explain crucial aspects of Italian politics and society such as the role of Catholicism and the rise of Mussolini because it was *economistic* (it exaggerated the importance of economics). To discuss capitalist domination and the reorganization of society under socialism, it is necessary to examine the interaction between economics on the one hand and politics, ideology, and culture on the other.[47] Whereas realists identify hegemony solely with the power of a predominant state, Gramscians view hegemony in terms of class. A dominant class that rules only by coercion is not hegemonic in Gramscian terms because its power does not extend throughout society and it can be overthrown simply by physical force. To attain hegemony, the dominant class must gain the active consent of subordinate classes on the basis of shared values, ideas, and material interests. For example, the bourgeoisie gained the support of subordinate classes for its leadership by offering concessions such as economic benefits and the acceptance of labor unions. Gramscians use the term *historic bloc* to refer to the congruence between state power and the ideas that guide the society and economy; it is difficult for subordinate groups to replace the bourgeois historic bloc because it is supported by the power of ideas as well as physical power. Like classical Marxists, Gramsci was committed to political action, and called for building a *counterhegemony*—an alternative ethical view of society—to challenge capitalism. The decline of government economic benefits in this age of global competitiveness could eventually cause subordinate classes to develop a counterhegemony.[48]

Whereas Gramsci focused on the domestic level, neo-Gramscian scholars such as Robert Cox apply his ideas to IPE. For example, Cox writes that postwar institutions such as the UN Security Council, IMF, World Bank, and GATT upheld liberal norms and legitimized U.S. hegemony with a minimal amount of force. Cox also sees a *transnational historic bloc* composed of the largest MNCs, international banks, business groups, and economic organizations as extending class relations to the global level. A crucial part of this historic bloc is the power and mobility of transnational capital, which is extending neoliberalism on a global scale. The ability of transnational capital and MNCs to shift location from one state to another enables them to play off relatively immobile national labor groups against one another. Workers employed by MNCs also identify their interests with transnational capital, and this divides the working class and limits its ability to build a counterhegemony. Further solidifying this transnational historic bloc is a hegemonic ideology that sees capital mobility as contributing to economic efficiency, consumer welfare, and economic growth.[49] Despite the solid foundations of this transnational historic bloc, civil society dissatisfaction could eventually stimulate a counterhegemony. Civil society refers to both "the realm in which the existing social order is grounded" and "the realm in which a new social order can be founded."[50] In supporting bourgeois hegemony, civil society is part of a top-down process in which the capitalist class gains acquiescence from the population. As part of a counterhegemony, civil society is part of a bottom-up process in which disadvantaged people try to displace the capitalist order. Although civil society protests at IMF, World Bank, and WTO meetings have "not attained the status of a counterhegemonic alliance of forces on the world scale," they demonstrate considerable concern about the effects of neoliberal globalization on people's lives today.

Critics charge that neo-Gramscians are so preoccupied with capitalist hegemony that they do not explore the problems of dominance and subordination in other systems such as socialism. Neo-Gramscians avoid some of the pitfalls of classical Marxists who predicted the early downfall of capitalism. However, neo-Gramscians provide little guidance as to when a counterhegemony might develop and what form it might take; thus they are better at pointing to problems with capitalism than in offering solutions. Many Marxists criticize neo-Gramscians for focusing so much on ideology and culture that they underestimate the centrality of economics. Furthermore, some critics question the degree to which Gramsci's analysis of domestic issues "can be adapted for use in the international domain."[51] Despite these criticisms, Gramscian analysis has many strengths. As discussed, realists and liberals define hegemony in state-centric terms, and their ability to examine the effects of hegemony is limited to a small number of relatively brief historical periods. Gramscians, by contrast, use the term *hegemony* in a cultural sense to connote the complex of *ideas* social groups use to assert their legitimacy and authority, and they extend the concept of hegemony to include nonstate actors such as MNCs and international banks as well as states. Thus, the Gramscian concept of hegemony can be applied to a much wider range of relationships in the global economy. We now turn to a discussion of constructivism, which has growing influence with liberal as well as critical IPE theorists.

CONSTRUCTIVISM

Constructivism is a social theory rather than a substantive theory. Whereas substantive theories such as realism, liberalism, and historical materialism offer specific explanations and predictions that we can test in social science research, constructivism provides "a framework for thinking about the nature of social life and social interaction."[52] In IR and IPE, constructivism is concerned with conceptualizing the relationship between *agents* (states) and *structures* (the international system). Constructivists devote considerable attention to the role of social or collectively held ideas in IR. They see reality, or what we accept as knowledge, as socially constructed, and they are interested in how our sense of identity and our interests become established as *social facts*. Social facts, or the meanings people attach to objects, are the product of collectively held (or "intersubjective") beliefs, and they exist only because everyone agrees they exist. For example, shared understandings that a country's monetary reserves have value determine that they are not simply worthless pieces of paper. Social facts differ from *material facts,* the physical properties of objects that exist regardless of shared beliefs about their existence. Constructivists do not reject material reality, but they note that its meaning and construction depend on ideas and interpretation.

The mainstream liberal and realist theories have traditionally been committed to rationalism and *materialism,* the view that international constraints on state behavior stem from material factors such as the distribution of power, wealth, technology, and geography. Constructivists by contrast attribute more importance to *normative* elements such as ideas, values, and rules and devote more attention to how actors formulate preferences and the processes by which they make and implement decisions. Instead of assuming that an actor's preferences reflect rational choices, constructivists examine the beliefs, traditions, roles, ideologies, and patterns of influence that shape preferences, behavior, and outcomes. Although constructivism can be traced back to the writings of Immanuel Kant (1724–1804), it did not emerge as a social theory in IR until the 1980s, and Nicholas Onuf coined the term in 1989.[53] Constructivists began to critique the mainstream rationalist and materialist approaches, with some willing to engage in a dialogue with the mainstream and others taking a more extreme position. Those engaging in dialogue have increased their influence in the mainstream, and "constructivism has flowered today into one of the main analytic orientations for mainstream IR research."[54] Whereas the most prominent debates in IR theory in the 1980s and 1990s were between variants of realism and liberalism, some argue that the most important IR mainstream debate today is between rationalism and constructivism.[55]

Scholarly work in some areas such as epistemic communities has enabled liberals who do research on international regimes to benefit from the insights of constructivists.[56] An *epistemic community* is "a network of professionals with recognized expertise and competence in a particular domain and an authoritative claim to policy-relevant knowledge within that domain or issue-area."[57] The epistemic community literature explores the role of knowledge-based experts (e.g., economists, physicists, and environmentalists) in helping states identify their interests and in framing international issues. For example, an epistemic community helped shape the Bretton Woods order discussed in Chapter 2. Whereas U.S. State Department officials wanted an open-trading system, British cabinet officials favored a preferential trading system that would ensure full employment and economic stability. A set of policy ideas inspired by Keynesianism and supported by an epistemic community of U.S. and British government specialists and economists helped create a new system of interventionist capitalism acceptable to both the United States and Britain, which John Ruggie labeled "embedded liberalism" (see Chapter 4). In sum, material interest–based explanations for the establishment of the postwar economic order underestimate the important role an epistemic community played in devising a U.S.-British agreement based on shared ideas and values.[58]

Despite the influence of constructivism on mainstream IR, many U.S. scholars in particular are uncomfortable with an approach that devotes more attention to "social facts" than "material facts" and does not adhere to the systematic and objective testing of hypotheses. Even those who agree that ideas, cultures, and identities affect political actors assume that *economic* actors rationally pursue *material* interests. Thus, security specialists have been more open to accepting constructivism than IPE specialists. Furthermore, critical constructivist theorists are less willing to engage in a dialogue with the mainstream. They seek to "deconstruct" what mainstream theorists assume are givens, and they advocate a change in social structures and relationships.[59] We therefore discuss constructivism in this chapter on critical perspectives. As with other IPE theoretical approaches, it is important to note that the boundaries between constructivism and materialism are sometimes blurred. For example, although Robert Cox has labeled his neo-Gramscian approach as "historical materialist," the Gramscian emphasis on hegemonic ideas has similarities with constructivist thought. Constructivists ask whose interests and ideas shape the rules and norms of the system, and Gramsci viewed the hegemon as achieving its goals not only through coercion but also through consent. A hegemon in the Gramscian sense promotes institutions and ideas that help persuade others that it has common interests with them. The following examples of constructivist reasoning show that social facts and social interaction have a major effect on many aspects of IPE.

Constructivists point out that basic IPE concepts such as the gross domestic product (GDP) are not as objective as we think because they are based on shared ideas and values. Although the GDP would seem to be a "material fact" that measures the output of goods and services, it is also a "social fact," because shared values determine what is included and not included. Whereas goods and services with market values are included in the GDP, economic activities within households are excluded. Feminist scholars point out that this decision reflects the downgrading of the role of women (who do most of the household work) in the economy. Shared values also determine that environmental measures are not included in the GDP. Although environmental degradation may have detrimental effects on a state's economic productivity, the GDP does not include a measure of whether the state is pursuing environmentally sustainable policies.[60]

Constructivists also believe that "national identities influence how societies interpret the material facts of their foreign economic relations."[61] For example, scholars have examined the divergent policies states have followed after the breakup of the Soviet Union in 1991. Whereas some former Soviet republics viewed economic dependence on Russia as a threat to national security, others saw it as a reason for closer ties with Russia. These policy makers observed the same material fact regarding the world economy (economic dependence), but they disagreed on its meaning. Thus, some former Soviet republics adopted a Western orientation in finance and trade, while others joined Russia in the new Commonwealth of Independent States (CIS). Constructivists attribute these differences to each new state's sense of self, arguing that states with a stronger sense of national identity were more inclined to distance themselves from the CIS.[62] Scholars have also examined the effects of national identity on economic policies and processes for other parts of the world.[63]

This book does not delve deeply into constructivism, but we provide some discussion of the role of culture and ideas in IPE.

FEMINISM

This section provides a brief introduction to the relationship between feminist theory and IPE, and it cannot possibly cover the range and scope of feminist research. One classification, for example, divides feminist thought into liberal, radical, Marxist and socialist, psychoanalytic, existentialist, postmodern, multi-cultural and global, and ecofeminist variants.[64] This wide range of approaches reflects the fact that as a group that is often marginalized in IR and IPE, feminists are open to a diversity of thought and reject the idea that they should develop a single IR theory. We discuss feminist thought in this chapter because feminist theorists have generally been critical of the mainstream perspectives for their inattention to gender issues. In contrast to sex, which refers to biological differences between male and female, feminist scholars view *gender* mainly as a constructivist concept, which can be defined as "a structural feature of social life" that "shapes how we identify, think, and communicate."[65] Whereas men are associated with the public sphere as wage earners, women are associated with the private sphere as housewives, mothers, and caregivers. When women work outside the home they often receive lower wages than men for similar work, because their pay is seen as supplemental to family income.[66] Although there are major differences in the economic position of women based on their class, race, and nationality, they are located disproportionately on the lower end of the socioeconomic scale. Thus, feminist scholarship critically examines "the unequal gender hierarchies that exist in all societies and their effects on the subordination of women and other marginalized groups with the goal of changing them."[67]

Feminist studies came much later to IR than to some other academic disciplines, partly because IR specialists after World War II focused mainly on the "high politics" of diplomacy, war, and statecraft. Scholars simply assumed that the political and military leaders and soldiers involved in high politics were male. When IPE emerged as a discipline in the 1970s, its emphasis on international finance, trade, and production, and its rationalist methodologies, also left little room for the study of gender relations. Thus, the first major studies on feminist IR were published in the 1980s. Development theory was the one exception to this generalization, but the literature on women and development was "marginalized from mainstream theories of political and economic development."[68] A major theme of the women and development literature is that pre-existing gender relations affect the outcome of development policies. For example, as Chapter 10 discusses, IMF and World Bank structural adjustment loans required indebted LDCs to reduce spending on social services such as health care, education, and food subsidies, and this downloaded more responsibility to women as the main caregivers in households. Other than the early writing on women and development, the focus of IPE on the impersonal structure of states and markets generally does not take account of the degree to which women's activities are devalued and relegated to the private sphere. Thus, feminist scholars often ask "Where are the women?" in accounts of IR and IPE.[69] Liberal feminists basically accept the existing liberal institutions and propose that the greater inclusion of women in positions of influence is the best way to address the problem of gender inequality. Critical feminists by contrast believe that inequality and exclusion are inherent characteristics of liberal institutions, and see the replacement of these institutions with more egalitarian models (in terms of class, gender, race, and ethnicity) as the only way to move beyond patriarchy based on the oppression of women.

Feminist scholars often point out that the main IPE perspectives largely ignore the role of women. Liberalism measures production and participation in the labor force only in terms of the market, or working for pay or profit. However, women often work in the subsistence sector of LDC economies or provide basic needs in the household. Because this work does not involve payment for goods and services, these women are considered "nonproducers" who should not expect to share in the benefits resulting from global economic production.[70] Deregulation, privatization and other neoliberal restructuring strategies have been especially damaging to women because of their dependence on the state for public services such as child care and elder care that support families. Realism views the state as the main unit of analysis, but in many respects the state is a gendered construct. Survival and security are the main state objectives according to realists, and men are normally responsible for defining and advancing the state's security interests. States also relegate women to an inferior position by sanctioning gender differences in inheritance rights and wages for comparable work, and by tacitly accepting or even condoning domestic and sexual violence.[71] Realism also gives priority to maximizing wealth and power, but it does not consider the effects on women who are often near the bottom of the socioeconomic scale. Historical materialism focuses on class-based oppression of workers and on the core's oppression of the periphery, but it does not consider patriarchy-based oppression of women. The emphasis on the working class overlooks the fact that there is also considerable inequality based on gender differences. Feminist scholars point out that by ignoring gender, historical materialism "mirrors the tactics that have so commonly been wielded by the mainstream against the fringes."[72] Some believe that the main IPE perspectives do not address gender because they are "gender neutral, meaning that . . . the interaction between states and markets . . . can be understood without reference to gender distinctions."[73] However, feminists argue that those who ignore gender distinctions simply reinforce the unequal economic relations between men and women. The emphasis of the mainstream perspectives on rationalist and materialist methodologies is also not sufficient, and it is necessary to focus on subjective factors such as culture and ideology. Thus, many feminist theorists take a constructivist or postmodern approach to increase our understanding of "subjectivity, reflexivity, meaning, and value."[74]

Feminist theorists have examined the gendered effects of a number of IPE processes such as global restructuring and the changing international division of labor, the tourism industry, labor migration, and IMF and World Bank structural adjustment loans (discussed in Chapter 10). These studies tend to be highly normative in their commitment to achieving gender equality, and they are also often concerned with issues involving the entire society that have implications for men as well as women. In view of their commitment to activism, feminist scholars have an interest in women's movements such as *transnational feminist networks (TFNs),* which are "structures organized above the national level that unite women from three or more countries around a common agenda, such as women's rights, reproductive health and rights, violence against women, peace and antimilitarism, or feminist economics."[75] Although the results of such activism "have been uneven, in many ways insufficient, and often contradictory," IR and IPE feminists "will continue to challenge disciplinary boundaries and methods that, they believe, impose limitations on the kinds of questions that can be asked and the ways in which they can be answered."[76]

ENVIRONMENTALISM

Traditionally IR specialists devoted little attention to the environment, but it has become a more central issue because of concerns about environmental degradation, resource scarcity, global warming, population growth, and nuclear accidents. International gatherings such as the 1972 Stockholm Conference and 1992 Rio Conference have also linked environmental concerns with development and the global economy. Thus, the environment is an important aspect of the study of IPE. Environmental theory is discussed in this chapter on critical perspectives because environmentalists have criticized the major IPE perspectives for their inattention to environmental concerns. However, environmental theorists are a diverse group, with some identifying more closely with mainstream IPE theorists and others identifying with critical theorists. This discussion examines the approach of realists, liberals, and critical theorists to environmental issues.

Realists have devoted little attention to environmental issues, because they view them as not being relevant to the protection of national security. However, "security" is a contested concept which liberal and critical theorists have broadened in recent years to include environmental issues. For example, a *cooperative security* concept emerged in the post-Cold War era to indicate that security issues require cooperative approaches rather than unilateral action. Cooperative security depends on collaborative rather than confrontational relations, and extends beyond the military to include environmental, demographic, and other common threats to humanity.[77] Another important concept is *human security,* which broadens the traditional focus on the state to include the security of people and the planet. The *Human Development Report* describes "human development" as the process of increasing the range of people's choices, and "human security" as people's ability to exercise those choices freely and safely.[78] International cooperation is necessary to deal with human security problems such as pollution, famine, disease, terrorism, and drug trafficking, because they cannot be contained within national boundaries. Environmental theorists use the term *environmental security* to examine more explicitly the relationship between security and global environmental politics. However, realists fear that broadening the security concept to include the environment and other general welfare issues provides little specific guidance for policy formation and weakens the resolve to deal with "real" national security threats. Extending the security concept to the environment in the realist view goes "far beyond what has usually been defined and claimed as the security sector in international politics."[79] Thus, liberal and critical theorists have contributed more than realists to the development of theory on the environment and IPE.

Liberals are optimistic about peoples' ability to improve environmental conditions through progress in science and technology, but they have a range of views regarding the role of the government and institutions. Chapter 4 discussed orthodox, interventionist, and institutional liberals, and these three "model" types are also evident among environmental theorists.[80] Orthodox liberals believe that economic growth increases peoples' incomes, giving them the ability and incentive to improve the environment. Even if the profit-oriented policies of some business firms adversely affect air and water quality in the short term, they contribute to economic growth which will improve environmental conditions over time. Thus, the best policy for the environment is to promote economic growth through open trade and foreign investment policies without government interference. Interventionist liberals also prefer market-based solutions to environmental problems, but they favor some government involvement to address the market's inadequacies and ensure that business firms follow environmentally-friendly policies. Although governments should avoid mandatory policies, they should use market-based strategies whenever possible to protect the environment such as environmental taxes, tradable pollution permits, and market incentives to encourage firms to produce environmental products. Governments should also encourage firms to adopt voluntary measures to improve environmental conditions. Institutional liberals like other liberals prefer market-based solutions, but they call for strong global institutions to channel and coordinate efforts to deal with environmental degradation, pollution, and resource scarcity. Thus, they support efforts of the World Bank, United Nations Environment Program, and Global Environment Facility to provide technology, finance, and knowledge to help LDCs promote *sustainable development;* that is, development that "meets the needs of the present without compromising the ability of future generations to meet their own needs."[81] Institutional liberals also call for the creation of effective environmental regimes to promote cooperative efforts to improve the environment. For example, Oran Young and others have examined the effectiveness of international environmental regimes in dealing with oil pollution, the management of fisheries, and acid rain.[82]

Critical environmental theorists, whom we refer to as the *greens,* often argue that economic growth is a *cause* of global environmental problems; that DCs follow environmentally exploitative practices; and that environmental degradation affects some more than others because of globalization, domination, and inequality. Some greens are historical materialists, arguing that capitalism is the main source of environmental degradation. Thus, greens are critical of the World Bank, IMF, and WTO and call for a radical restructuring of the global economy. Many greens reject economic globalization and favor a return to autonomy for local and indigenous communities.[83] The greens believe that overconsumption of resources threatens the earth's ability to support life, but that it is difficult to limit resource use. The concept of "common property goods" is central to this problem. Figure 5.1 lists four types of goods. We discussed *public goods,* which are nonexcludable and nonrival, in Chapter 4. *Private goods* are excludable and rival; for example, I must have money to buy food and clothing (they are excludable), and I must purchase some items that are in short supply before someone else does (they are rival). *Club goods* are excludable but not rival; for example, cable television and private golf club memberships are usually not rival, but the fees charged make them excludable. The greens (and some liberal institutional theorists) argue that major problems stem from *common property goods,* which are rival but nonexcludable. Resources such as the air, water, fish outside territorial waters, and outer space can be exploited for private gain (they are rival), but no one owns them (they are not excludable). Common property goods present a collective action problem because no single individual benefits from conserving the resource; but we all lose when the resource is depleted. Garrett Hardin described this as the "tragedy of the

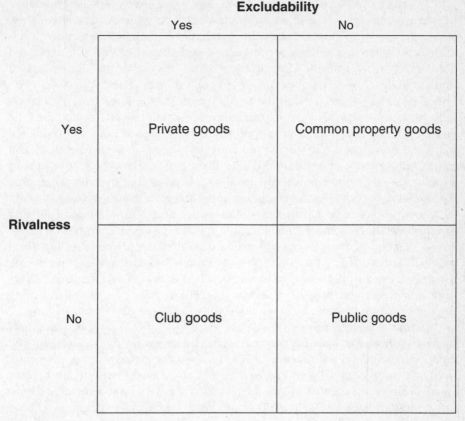

Excludability

	Yes	No
Yes	Private goods	Common property goods
No	Club goods	Public goods

Rivalness

FIGURE 5.1 Types of Goods

commons."[84] Comparing the unregulated use of the atmosphere and the oceans to the pre-industrial overuse of the English commons, Hardin predicted this would be detrimental to all. In terms of prisoners' dilemma (Chapter 4), individual rationality leads us to deplete our common property resources. To avoid this outcome, the greens call for limits on population growth and on economic growth.[85]

CRITIQUE OF THE CRITICAL PERSPECTIVES

It is difficult to provide a general critique of the critical perspectives (historical materialism, constructivism, feminism, and environmentalism), because they do not agree on a core set of assumptions. However, all of these perspectives in some way are critical of the traditional mainstream realist and liberal perspectives. It is important to assess the validity and importance of their arguments, and whether they provide viable alternatives to the mainstream perspectives in IPE.

A major criticism of historical materialism relates to its repeated tendency to overestimate the degree to which capitalism is in decline. As discussed, Marx and Engels predicted that contradictions within capitalism would lead to its collapse, and when this did not occur, Lenin asserted that *imperialism* explained the survival of capitalism. After decolonization, historical materialists argued that capitalism persisted because it benefited from *neocolonialism*. The breakup of the Soviet bloc and the Soviet Union led the liberal analyst Francis Fukuyama to declare that the capitalist liberal system had triumphed, but the world-system theorist Wallerstein went to the opposite extreme and predicted that the end of the Cold War would lead to "the collapse of liberalism and our definitive entry into the world 'after liberalism.'"[86] However, in efforts to explain the continued survival of capitalism, world-system theorists argue that the *semiperiphery* divides the periphery and prevents it from replacing the capitalist core. Neo-Gramscian theorists refer to the need for a counterhegemony to topple the hegemony of capitalism, but they rarely venture to guess when— or if—this counterhegemony will ever materialize. More recently, historical materialists have reacted to the 2008 global financial crisis by again predicting the end of capitalism. In sum, one can ask whether historical materialist predictions regarding the demise of capitalism (like Fukuyama's predictions regarding the final triumph of capitalism) are affected by a degree of wishful thinking.

Some mainstream theorists also argue that the critical perspectives are of limited significance, because they have little influence on the mainstream IPE perspectives and on the practice of IPE. Of the critical perspectives discussed, only constructivism has been involved in one of the major mainstream debates (rationalism versus constructivism). Many critical theorists would concede that to this point they have had little effect on the mainstream. For example, a feminist theorist asserts that "in spite of the consistently high quality and quantity of gender analysis, gender has not been able to achieve more than a marginal status in International Political Economy (IPE)."[87] When critical perspectives do manage to enter the mainstream arena, they often must do so on the mainstream's terms. For example, Steven Bernstein argues that "liberal environmentalism legitimates the primacy of the global marketplace . . . rather than adapting the marketplace to operate in sympathy with requirements of ecological integrity and sustainability."[88] The World Bank, WTO, OECD, UNCTAD, and the United Nations Development Program (UNDP) have become lead organizations on global environmental issues; but they generally give priority to economic over environmental concerns.

Critics also question whether the critical perspectives can provide viable alternatives to the mainstream perspectives, because the critical approaches are marked by major divisions. Although feminists, constructivists, and others view this multiplicity of views as being consistent with their acceptance of a diversity of marginalized voices, mainstream theorists often question whether such a diversity of voices can offer coherent and meaningful alternatives. Indeed, theorists from different critical perspectives, and within the same critical perspective, often vehemently criticize one another. For example, within historical materialism Marxists criticize dependency and world-system theorists for giving priority to relations of exchange (between North and South) over relations of production (between classes). Feminists, on the other hand, argue that many Marxists are so focused on class that they give little attention to gender issues. Thus, one feminist scholar asserts that "while it is perhaps not so surprising that mainstream IPE explicitly marginalizes gender, critical IPE's reluctance to engage fully with gender is perhaps more startling."[89]

Although the mainstream has devoted little attention to most of the critical perspectives, it is important to note that critical theorists play a vital role in the study of IPE. Constructivists increase our awareness of the effects of historical and social contexts on our preferences and decisions; historical materialists and feminists give a voice to poorer and more marginalized people and states; and environmentalists alert us to the risks of ignoring the long-term effects of the environment on the economy. Furthermore, current instability in financial, trade, and foreign investment relations indicates that global capitalism has been functioning poorly, and that alternatives are necessary to the dependence on the unrestrained market in recent years. Although some critical theorists advocate the replacement of the capitalist global economy, others seek to make it more socially responsible.[90]

Questions

1. What are the similarities and differences between Marxism, dependency theory and world-system theory?
2. What are the main features of Gramscian analysis and how does it differ from classical Marxism?
3. How does the constructivist approach differ from the rationalist approach to IPE?
4. In what ways do the mainstream IPE perspectives not adequately address gender issues, and how do you think gender issues should be dealt with in IPE?
5. What are the views of liberal and critical environmental theorists? How do realists view environmental issues? How important do you think environmental issues are to the study of IPE?
6. What is the difference between public goods, private goods, club goods, and common property goods? In what way do common property goods present a collective action problem?
7. Do you believe that historical materialism is passé as a result of the breakup of the Soviet bloc and the end of the Cold War?
8. What are some of the criticisms of the critical perspectives, and how valid do you think they are?

Further Reading

Useful studies of Marxism and historical materialism include Anthony Brewer, *Marxist Theories of Imperialism: A Critical Survey,* 2nd ed. (New York: Routledge, 1990); and Mark Rupert and Hazel Smith, eds., *Historical Materialism and Globalization*

(New York: Routledge, 2002). A good introduction to world-system theory is Thomas R. Shannon, *An Introduction to the World-System Perspective,* 2nd ed. (Boulder, CO: Westview Press, 1996). Studies on Gramscian theory include Stephen Gill, ed., *Gramsci, Historical Materialism, and International Relations* (New York: Cambridge University Press, 1993); and Randall D. Germain and Michael Kenny, "Engaging Gramsci: International Relations Theory and the New Gramscians," *Review of International Studies* 24, no. 1 (January 1998), pp. 3–21.

Good overviews of contructivism include John G. Ruggie, "What Makes the World Hang Together? Neo-Utilitarianism and the Social Constructivist Challenge," *International Organization* 52, no. 4 (Autumn 1998), pp. 855–885; Martha Finnemore and Kathryn Sikkink, "Taking Stock: The Constructivist Research Program in International Relations and Comparative Politics," *Annual Review of Political Science* vol. 4 (Norwood, NJ: Ablex, 2001), pp. 391–416; and Emanuel Adler, "Constructivism and International Relations," in Walter Carlsnaes, Thomas Risse, and Beth A. Simmons, eds., *Handbook of International Relations* (London: SAGE, 2002), pp. 95–118.

Books focusing on gender and IPE include Sandra Whitworth, *Feminism and International Relations: Towards a Political Economy of Gender in Interstate and Non-Governmental Institutions* (London: Macmillan, 1994); Elisabeth Prügl, *The Global Construction of Gender: Home-Based Work in the Political Economy of the 20th Century* (New York: Columbia University Press, 1999); Marianne H. Marchand and Anne S. Runyan, eds., *Gender and Global Restructuring: Sightings, Sites and Resistance* (New York: Routledge, 2000); and V. Spike Peterson, *A Critical Rewriting of Global Political Economy: Integrating Reproductive, Productive and Virtual Economics* (New York: Routledge, 2003). A useful general study of feminist theory is J. Ann Tickner, *Gendering World Politics: Issues and Approaches in the Post-Cold War Era* (New York: Columbia University Press, 2001).

A valuable introduction to environmentalism and IPE that includes all major perspectives is Jennifer Clapp and Peter Dauvergne, *Paths to a Green World: The Political Economy of the Global Environment* (Cambridge, MA: MIT Press, 2005). An important work on liberal environmentalism with a strong IPE emphasis is Steven Bernstein, *Compromise of Liberal Environmentalism* (New York: Columbia University Press, 2001). A useful edited collection on environmentalism and IPE from a critical perspective is Dimitris Stevis and Valerie J. Assetto, *The International Political Economy of the Environment: Critical Perspectives* (Boulder, CO: Rienner, 2001).

Notes

1. Mark Rupert and Hazel Smith, eds., *Historical Materialism and Globalization* (New York: Routledge, 2002).
2. Karl Marx and Friedrich Engels, *The Communist Manifesto* (New York: International Publishers, 1948), p. 9.
3. Bob Jessop, *The Capitalist State: Marxist Theories and Methods* (Oxford, UK: Martin Robertson, 1982), pp. 1–31.
4. Marx and Engels, *The Communist Manifesto,* p. 29.
5. V. I. Lenin, *Imperialism: The Highest Stage of Capitalism,* rev. trans. (New York: International Publishers, 1939).

6. Jack Woddis, *An Introduction to Neo-Colonialism* (London: Lawrence & Wishart, 1967); Harry Magdoff, "Imperialism Without Colonies," in Roger Owen and Bob Sutcliffe, eds., *Studies in the Theory of Imperialism* (London: Longman, 1981), pp. 144–169.
7. Some authors argue that Marx was not a strict economic determinist. See David McLellan, *Marx*, 7th ed. (London: Fontana/Collins, 1980), p. 41.
8. On instrumental Marxism, see David A. Gold, Clarence Y. H. Lo, and Erik O. Wright, "Recent Developments in Marxist Theories of the Capitalist State," *Monthly Review* 27, no. 5 (October 1975), pp. 32–35.
9. On structural Marxism, see Gold, Lo, and Wright, "Recent Developments in Marxist Theories of the Capitalist State," pp. 35–40; Pat McGowan and Stephen G. Walker, "Radical and Conventional Models of U.S. Foreign Economic Policy Making," *World Politics* 33, no. 3 (April 1981), pp. 357–360.
10. Jan A. Scholte, *Globalization: A Critical Introduction,* 2nd ed. (New York: Palgrave Macmillan, 2005), pp. 128–130.
11. Robert W. Cox, "Structural Issues of Global Governance: Implications for Europe," in Stephen Gill, ed., *Gramsci, Historical Materialism and International Relations* (New York: Cambridge University Press, 1993), pp. 259–262; Jackie Smith and Hank Johnston, eds., *Globalization and Resistance: Transnational Dimensons of Social Movements* (Lanham, MD: Rowman & Littlefield, 2002).
12. For Marx's writings on non-European areas, see Shlomo Avineri, ed., *Karl Marx on Colonialism and Modernization: His Dispatches and Other Writings on China, India, Mexico, the Middle East and North Africa* (Garden City, NJ: Doubleday, 1968).
13. Brendan O'Leary, *The Asiatic Mode of Production: Oriental Despotism, Historical Materialism and Indian History* (New York: Basil Blackwell, 1989), p. 263; Lawrence Krader, *The Asiatic Mode of Production: Sources, Development and Critique in the Writings of Karl Marx* (The Netherlands: Van Gorcum & Comp., 1975).
14. Karl Marx, "The British Rule in India," in Shlomo Avineri, ed., *Karl Marx on Colonialism and Modernization: His Dispatches and Other Writings on China, India, Mexico, the Middle East and North Africa* (Garden City, NJ: Doubleday, 1968), pp. 86–88.
15. Marx, "The British Rule in India," p. 481.
16. B. N. Ghosh, *Dependency Theory Revisited* (Aldershot, UK: Ashgate, 2001), p. 19.
17. John. A. Hobson, *Imperialism: A Study* (Ann Arbor, MI: University of Michigan Press, 1965), p. 81.
18. For differing views of Lenin's contribution see Anthony Brewer, *Marxist Theories of Imperialism: A Critical Survey,* 2nd ed. (New York: Routledge, 1990), p. 116; Tom Kemp, "The Marxist Theory of Imperialism," in Roger Owen and Bob Sutcliffe, eds., *Studies in the Theory of Imperialism* (London: Longman, 1972), pp. 26–30.
19. Lenin, *Imperialism,* p. 89.
20. Thomas Biersteker, "Evolving Perspectives on International Political Economy: Twentieth-Century Discontinuities," *International Political Science Review* 14, no. 1 (January 1993), p. 12.
21. Raúl Prebisch, "The Economic Development of Latin America and Its Principal Problems," *Economic Bulletin for Latin America* 7, no. 1 (February 1962), pp. 1–22 (first published in Spanish in May 1950).
22. Joseph L. Love, "The Origins of Dependency Analysis," *Journal of Latin American Studies* 22 (February 1990), pp. 143–160.

23. André G. Frank, *Capitalism and Underdevelopment in Latin America: Historical Studies of Chile and Brazil* (New York: Monthly Press, 1967); Fernando H. Cardoso and Enzo Faletto, *Dependency and Development in Latin America*, trans. Marjory M. Urquidi (Berkeley, CA: University of California Press, 1979).

24. Cardoso and Faletto, *Dependency and Development in Latin America*, p. xviii.

25. André G. Frank, "The Development of Underdevelopment," *Monthly Review* 18, no. 4 (September 1966), pp. 17–31.

26. Cardoso and Faletto, *Dependency and Development in Latin America*, p. 174.

27. Peter Evans, *Dependent Development: The Alliance of Multinational, State, and Local Capital in Brazil* (Princeton, NJ: Princeton University Press, 1979); Gary Gereffi, *The Pharmaceutical Industry and Dependency in the Third World* (Princeton, NJ: Princeton University Press, 1983); Thomas B. Gold, *State and Society in the Taiwan Miracle* (Armonk, NY: M.E. Sharpe, 1986).

28. André G. Frank, "Asia's Exclusive Models," *Far Eastern Economic Review* 116, no. 26 (June 25, 1982), pp. 22–23.

29. Cal Clark and Donna Bahry, "Dependent Development: A Socialist Variant," *International Studies Quarterly* 27, no. 3 (September 1983), p. 286; Colin Leys, "Underdevelopment and Dependency: Critical Notes," *Journal of Contemporary Asia* 7, no. 1 (1977), pp. 92–107. Although some dependency theorists acknowledge that dependent relationships can exist between socialist states, they focus on capitalism.

30. Evans, *Dependent Development,* p. 329.

31. Tony Smith, "The Underdevelopment of Development Literature: The Case of Dependency Theory," *World Politics* 31, no. 2 (January 1979), pp. 257–258.

32. Ernesto Laclau, "Feudalism and Capitalism in Latin America," *New Left Review* 67 (May–June 1971), p. 25.

33. Peter Evans, "After Dependency: Recent Studies of Class, State, and Industrialization," *Latin American Research Review* 20, no. 2 (1985), p. 158.

34. Ghosh, *Dependency Theory Revisited,* p. 133.

35. John G. Ruggie, "Multilateralism: The Anatomy of an Institution," in John G. Ruggie, ed., *Multilateralism Matters: The Theory and Praxis of an Institutional Form* (New York: Columbia University Press, 1993), p. 33; Francis Fukuyama, "The End of History?" *The National Interest* 16 (Summer 1989), pp. 3, 11.

36. Jorge G. Castañeda, "Latin America's Left Turn," *Foreign Affairs* 85, no. 3 (May/June 2006), pp. 28–29.

37. United Nations Department of Economic and Social Affairs, *The Inequality Predicament: Report on the World Social Situation 2005* (New York: UN, 2005), p. 49.

38. On the differences between dependency and world system theory, see Peter Evans, "Beyond Center and Periphery: A Comment on the Contribution of the World System Approach to the Study of Development," *Sociological Inquiry* 49, no. 4 (1979), pp. 15–20.

39. Immanuel Wallerstein, "The Rise and Future Demise of the World Capitalist System: Concepts for Comparative Analysis," in Immanuel Wallerstein, *The Capitalist World-Economy* (New York: Cambridge University Press, 1979), p. 5.

40. Janet L. Abu-Lughod, *Before European Hegemony: The World System A.D. 1250–1350* (New York: Oxford University Press, 1989); Andre G. Frank and Barry Gills, eds., *The World System: Five Hundred Years or Five Thousand?* (London: Routledge, 1996).

41. Wallerstein, "The Rise and Future Demise of the World Capitalist System," pp. 18–19.

42. Wallerstein, "The Rise and Future Demise of the World Capitalist System," p. 35.

43. Evans, *Dependent Development,* p. 33.

44. Immanuel Wallerstein, "Dependence in an Interdependent World: The Limited Possibilities of Transformation Within the Capitalist World-Economy," in Immanuel Wallerstein, *The Capitalist World-Economy* (New York: Cambridge University Press, 1979), p. 69.

45. Gold, *State and Society in the Taiwan Miracle,* pp. 13–14.

46. Theda Skocpol, "Wallerstein's World Capitalist System: A Theoretical and Historical Critique," *American Journal of Sociology* 82, no. 5 (March 1977), pp. 1084–1088; Alexander Gerschenkron, "Economic Backwardness in Historical Perspective," in Alexander Gerschenkron, *Economic Backwardness in Historical Perspective: A Book of Essays* (Cambridge, MA: Belknap Press of Harvard University Press, 1962), pp. 16–21

47. Antonio Gramsci, *Selections from the Prison Notebooks of Antonio Gramsci,* ed. transl. Quintin Hoare and Geoffrey N. Smith (New York: International Publishers, 1971).

48. Robert W. Cox, "Gramsci, Hegemony and International Relations: An Essay in Method," *Millennium* 12, no. 2 (1983), pp. 162–175.

49. Robert W. Cox, "Social Forces, States and World Orders: Beyond International Relations Theory," in Robert O. Keohane, ed., *Neorealism and Its Critics* (New York: Columbia University Press, 1986), pp. 204–254; Stephen Gill and David Law, "Global Hegemony and the Structural Power of Capital," in Stephen Gill, ed., *Gramsci, Historical Materialism and International Relations* (New York: Cambridge University Press, 1993), pp. 93–124.

50. Robert W. Cox, "Civil Society at the Turn of the Millennium: Prospects for an Alternative World Order," *Review of International Studies* 25 (1999), p. 4.

51. Randall D. Germain and Michael Kenny, "Engaging Gramsci: International Relations Theory and the New Gramscians," *Review of International Studies* 24 (1998), p. 20; Andreas Bieler and Adam D. Morton, "A Critical Theory Route to Hegemony, World Order and Historical Change: Neo-Gramscian Perspectives in International Relations," *Capital & Class* 82 (Spring 2004), pp. 85–113.

52. Martha Finnemore and Kathryn Sikkink, "Taking Stock: The Constructivist Research Program in International Relations and Comparative Politics," *Annual Review of Political Science* 4 (2001), pp. 392–393.

53. See Nicholas G. Onuf, *World of Our Making: Rules and Rule in Social Theory and International Relations* (Columbia, SC: University of South Carolina Press, 1989).

54. Benjamin J. Cohen, *International Political Economy: An Intellectual History* (Princeton, NJ: Princeton University Press, 2008), p. 132.

55. On the earlier realist-liberal debates, see David A. Baldwin, ed., *Neorealism and Neoliberalism: The Contemporary Debate* (New York: Columbia University Press, 1993); Charles W. Kegley, Jr., ed., *Controversies in International Relations Theory: Realism and the Neoliberalism Challenge* (New York: St. Martin's Press, 1995).

56. Jeffrey T. Checkel, "The Constructivist Turn in International Relations Theory," *World Politics* 50, no. 2 (January 1998), p. 329.

57. Peter M. Haas, "Introduction: Epistemic Communities and International Policy Coordination," *International Organization* 46, no. 1 (Winter 1992), pp. 2–3.

58. G. John Ikenberry, "Creating Yesterday's New World Order: Keynesian 'New Thinking' and the Anglo-American Postwar Settlement," in Judith Goldstein and

Robert O. Keohane, eds., *Ideas and Foreign Policy: Beliefs, Institutions, and Political Change* (Ithaca, NY: Cornell University Press, 1993), pp. 57–86.

59. On constructivism as critical theory, see Richard Price and Cristian Reus-Smit, "Dangerous Liaisons? Critical International Theory and Constructivism," *European Journal of International Relations* 4, no. 3 (1998), pp. 259–294. On the different types of constructivism, see Emanuel Adler, "Seizing the Middle Ground: Constructivism in World Politics," *European Journal of International Relations* 3, no. 3 (1997), pp. 335–336.

60. Rawi Abdelal, Mark Blyth, and Craig Parsons, "Constructivist Political Economy," January 14, 2005. http://www.jhfc.duke.edu/ducis/GlobalEquity/pdfs/ABP.pdf

61. Rawi Abdelal, *National Purpose in the World Economy: Post-Soviet States in Comparative Perspective* (Ithaca, NY: Cornell University Press, 2001), p. 151.

62. See Abdelal, *National Purpose in the World Economy;* Andrei P. Tsygankov, *Pathways after Empire: National Identity and Foreign Economic Policy in the Post-Soviet World* (Lanham, MD: Rowman & Littlefield, 2001).

63. See Eric Helleiner and Andreas Pickel, eds., *Economic Nationalism in a Globalizing World* (Ithaca, NY: Cornell University Press, 2005).

64. Rosemarie P. Tong, *Feminist Thought: A More Comprehensive Introduction,* 2nd ed. (Boulder, CO: Westview Press, 1998).

65. V. Spike Peterson, *A Critical Rewriting of the Global Political Economy: Integrating Reproductive, Productive and Virtual Economies* (New York: Routledge, 2003), p. 31.

66. See Elisabeth Prügl, *The Global Construction of Gender: Home-Based Work in the Political Economy of the 20th Century* (New York: Columbia University Press, 1999).

67. J. Ann Tickner, "On the Frontlines or Sidelines of Knowledge and Power? Feminist Practices of Responsible Scholarship," *International Studies Review* 8, no. 3 (September 2006), p. 386.

68. J. Ann Tickner, *Gender in International Relations: Feminist Perspectives on Achieving Global Security* (New York: Columbia University Press, 1992), p. 70.

69. Cynthia Enloe, *Bananas, Beaches and Bases: Making Feminist Sense of International Politics,* updated ed. (Berkeley, CA: University of California Press, 2000), p. 11.

70. Marilyn Waring, *Counting for Nothing: What Men Value and What Women Are Worth,* 2nd ed. (Toronto: University of Toronto Press, 1999), p. 1.

71. Jill Steans, *Gender and International Relations: An Introduction* (Cambridge, UK: Polity Press, 1998), p. 149.

72. Penny Griffin, "Refashioning IPE: What and How Gender Analysis Teaches International (Global) Political Economy," *Review of International Political Economy* 14, no. 4 (October 2007), p. 735. See also Georgina Waylen, "You Still Don't Understand: Why Troubled Engagements Continue between Feminists and (Critical) IPE," *Review of International Studies* 32, no. 1 (January 2006), pp. 145–164.

73. Tickner, *Gender in International Relations,* pp. 69–70.

74. Peterson, *A Critical Rewriting of Global Political Economy,* pp. 22–25. On feminism and constructivism, see Elisabeth Prügl, *The Global Construction of Gender: Home-Based Work in the Political Economy of the 20th Century* (New York: Columbia University Press, 1999).

75. Valentine M. Moghadam, *Globalizing Women: Transnational Feminist Networks* (Baltimore, MD: Johns Hopkins University Press, 2005), p. 4.

76. Lourdes Benería, *Gender, Development, and Globalization: Economics as if All People Mattered* (New York: Routledge, 2003), p. xii; J. Ann Tickner, *Gendering World Politics: Issues and Approaches in the Post-Cold War Era* (New York: Columbia University Press, 2001), p. 146.

77. David Dewitt, "Common, Comprehensive, and Cooperative Security," *Pacific Review* 7, no.1 (1994), pp. 7–9; Ashton B. Carter, William J. Perry, and John D. Steinbruner, "A New Concept of Cooperative Security," *Brookings Occasional Papers* (Washington, D.C.: Brookings Institution, 1992).

78. United Nations Development Program, *Human Development Report—1994* (New York: Oxford University Press, 1994), pp. 22–25.

79. Lorraine Elliott, *The Global Politics of the Environment,* 2nd ed. (New York: Palgrave Macmillan, 2004), p. 222.

80. Jennifer Clappe and Peter Dauvergne, *Paths to a Green World: The Political Economy of the Global Environment* (Cambridge, MA: MIT Press, 2005), pp. 3–9.

81. World Commission on Environment and Development, *Our Common Future* (New York: Oxford University Press, 1987), p. 8.

82. Oran R. Young, ed., *The Effectiveness of International Environmental Regimes: Causal Connections and Behavioral Mechanisms* (Cambridge, MA: MIT Press, 1999).

83. Clappe and Dauvergne, *Paths to a Green World,* pp. 11–16.

84. Garrett Hardin, "The Tragedy of the Commons," *Science* 162, no. 3859 (December 1968), pp. 1243–1248.

85. Clappe and Dauvergne, *Paths to a Green World,* pp. 9–11.

86. Francis Fukuyama, "The End of History?" *The National Interest* 16 (Summer 1989), p. 4; Immanuel Wallerstein, *After Liberalism* (New York: New Press, 1995), p. 1.

87. Penny Griffin, "Refashioning IPE: What and How Gender Analysis Teaches International (Global) Political Economy," *Review of International Political Economy* 14, no. 4 (October 2007), p. 719.

88. Steven Bernstein, "Environment, Economy, and Global Environmental Governance," in Richard Stubbs and Geoffrey D. Underhill, eds., *Political Economy and the Changing Global Order,* 3rd ed. (New York: Oxford University Press, 2006), p. 246; Steven Bernstein, *The Compromise of Liberal Environmentalism* (New York: Columbia University Press, 2001).

89. Griffin, "Refashioning IPE," p. 735.

90. See Jeffry A. Frieden, *Global Capitalism: Its Fall and Rise in the Twentieth Century* (New York: W.W. Norton, 2006), ch. 20.

PART THREE

The Issue Areas

Part III focuses on the substantive issue areas in IPE. Chapter 6 begins with a discussion of international monetary relations, because most transactions in the international economy including trade, investment, and finance depend on the availability of money and credit. Chapter 7 examines trade relations at the global level and the emergence of the WTO. Although regional issues are discussed throughout Part III, Chapter 8 focuses specifically on trade relations at the regional level. Chapter 9 deals with the most important private actor in the global economy, the MNC and its relationship with globalization, international competitiveness, and the state. Whereas most chapters in Part III devote some attention to the South, Chapter 10 focuses specifically on alternative strategies for promoting LDC economic development, and Chapter 11 deals with foreign debt and international financial crises. The World Bank is the most important IO for development, and the IMF is the lead IO dealing with foreign debt and financial crises. The final section of each chapter in Part III draws linkages between the issue areas and the main themes and IPE theoretical perspectives.

CHAPTER 6

International
Monetary Relations

International monetary relations are a central part of IPE because the most important transactions in the global economy depend on the availability of money and credit. As one IPE scholar has noted, "it is impossible to understand the operation of the international economy without also understanding its monetary system."[1] Although monetary issues are difficult for students to master, some background in this area provides a sound basis for understanding other IPE issues such as trade and investment. International monetary and financial transactions have a major role in reshaping the global economy. Indeed, the amount of money foreign exchange markets handle *daily* increased from negligible amounts in the late 1950s, to $590 billion in 1989, $1.5 trillion in 1998, and $1.9 trillion in 2008.[2] Realists and liberals have different interpretations of these increased financial flows. Realists argue that financial transactions have increased with the permission and sometimes encouragement of the most powerful states and that these states continue to dictate the terms for such transactions. Liberals by contrast assert that the increased transactions result from advances in communications, technology, and transportation and that it is difficult for states to regulate financial activities.

Realists also point to the fact that international monetary transactions still rely mainly on separate national currencies, even though 16 EU members now use the euro. However, a liberal monetary specialist argues that the concept of one state, one currency is a myth today, because "international relations . . . are being dramatically reshaped by the increasing interpenetration of national monetary spaces."[3] About 29 percent of the world's circulating currency is located outside the country issuing it, and during the mid-1990s at least $300 billion of the three top currencies at the time (the U.S. dollar, German deutsch mark, and Japanese yen) were circulating outside the country of origin. Cross-border currency competition is a reality today, and a prime example is the challenge the euro is posing to the U.S. dollar.[4] Although monetary flows and cross-border currency competition are eroding some governmental powers, monetary relations continue to function in a world of states. It is therefore necessary to discuss the balance of payments, which tells us about a state's overall financial position.

THE BALANCE OF PAYMENTS

The **balance of payments** records the debit and credit transactions that residents, firms, and governments of one state have with the rest of the world, normally for a one-year period; it is composed of two main items: the **current account,** which includes all transactions related to a state's current expenditures and national income, and the **capital account,** which includes all movements of financial capital into and out of a state. As Table 6.1 shows, the current account comprises four types of transactions:

1. *Merchandise trade,* or trade in tangible goods. The difference between the value of merchandise exports and merchandise imports is the *merchandise trade balance.*
2. *Services trade,* or trade in intangible items such as insurance, information, transportation, banking, and consulting. A state's merchandise and services exports minus imports (items 1 and 2 in the table) are equal to its *balance of trade.*
3. *Investment income and payments* measure interest and dividend payments on investments by citizens of a country to foreigners and by foreigners to citizens of the country.
4. *Remittances and official transactions* include income that migrant workers or foreign companies send out of a country, military and foreign aid, and salaries and pensions paid to government employees abroad.

Table 6.1 shows that in 1992 Japan had a current account *surplus* of $117.64 billion (U.S.) and the United States had a current account *deficit* of $66.30 billion. The critical item for both countries was the merchandise trade balance: Japan had a merchandise trade *surplus* of $132.40 billion and the United States had a merchandise trade *deficit* of $96.14 billion. As Chapter 7 discusses, the United States has had merchandise trade deficits since 1971, and its largest trade deficits have often been with Japan, and more recently with China. Table 6.1 shows that in contrast to merchandise trade, the United States had a positive *services* trade balance in 1992 (plus $42.32 billion). The strong U.S. export position in services results from its skilled consultants and its highly developed markets in insurance and banking. Thus, the United States applied pressure to include services trade in the GATT and the NAFTA. The balance on U.S. investment income and payments was also positive in 1992 (plus $20.40 billion) because of interest and dividend payments received on past investments. However, the positive balances on services trade and investment income were not sufficient to overcome the large U.S. merchandise trade deficit. Thus, the U.S. current account balance was negative (minus $66.30 billion) in 1992.

TABLE 6.1 Balance-of-Payments Data, 1992 (Billions of U.S. Dollars)

	United States	Japan
Current account		
1. Merchandise trade		
Exports	+440.14	+330.87
Imports	−536.28	−198.47
Merchandise trade balance	−96.14	+132.40
2. Services trade		
Credit	+159.40	+48.31
Debit	−117.08	−89.73
Services trade balance	+42.32	−41.42
Balance of trade (1 + 2)	−53.82	+90.98
3. Investment income and payments		
Credit	+130.95	+145.75
Debit	−110.55	−114.47
Balance	+20.40	+31.28
4. Remittances and official transactions	−32.88	−4.62
Current account balance	**−66.30**	**+117.64**
Capital account		
5. Direct investment and other long-term capital	−17.61	−30.78
6. Short-term capital	+54.19	−75.77
Capital account balance	**+36.58**	**−106.55**
Statistical discrepancy	**−12.34**	**−10.46**
Total	**−42.06**	**+0.63**
Change in reserves[a]	**+42.06**	**−0.63**

[a] Increase in reserves, −; decrease in reserves, +.

Source: International Monetary Fund, *Balance of Payments Statistics Yearbook,* vol. 44, part 1, 1993 (Washington, DC: IMF, 1993), pp. 366, 742.

The second major item in the balance of payments is the *capital account,* which measures long- and short-term capital flows (items 5 and 6 in Table 6.1). A country's capital exports are *debit* items because they involve the purchase of financial assets from foreigners, and its capital imports are *credit* items because they involve the sale of financial assets to foreigners. (This is the opposite of merchandise trade, in which exports are credits and imports are debits.) Short-term investments normally have a maturity of less than one year, and long-term investments extend beyond this period. Long-term capital flows are further subdivided into foreign direct investment (FDI) and portfolio investment. FDI is capital investment in a branch plant or subsidiary of an MNC in which the investor has some operating control. **Portfolio investment,** by contrast, refers to the purchase of stocks and bonds that does not involve operating control.

A country often seeks to offset a current account deficit with foreign investment or an inflow of funds into its capital account; a current account surplus by contrast permits a country to have a capital account deficit through investment abroad or the purchase of foreign assets. As Table 6.1 shows, Japan (with a current account *surplus*) had a capital account *deficit* of $106.55 billion in 1992, and the United States (with a current account *deficit*) had a capital account *surplus* of $36.58 billion. In addition to the current and capital accounts, the balance of payments includes two less important items. The *statistical discrepancy* item results partly from errors in data collection but mainly from a government's failure to include all the goods, services, and capital that cross its borders. The final item is the *change in official reserves.* Each country has a **central bank** (e.g., the U.S. Federal Reserve or the Bank of Canada) that holds foreign exchange and gold reserves. When a country has a deficit in its current *and* capital accounts (the "Total" item in Table 6.1), it loses reserves, and when a country has a surplus in its current and capital accounts, it adds to its reserves. The total of a country's current account, capital account, statistical discrepancy, and change in reserves always equals zero, hence the term *balance of payments.* Note in Table 6.1 that, by standard accounting procedures, a *minus* figure equals an *increase* in reserves and a *plus* figure equals a *decrease* in reserves. This is merely a bookkeeping exercise so the balance of payments will equal zero. Thus, in 1992 U.S. reserves *declined* by $42.06 billion, and Japanese reserves *increased* by $0.63 billion.

Although the balance-of-payments account always balances (i.e., equals zero) in a bookkeeping sense, countries can have payments difficulties. When a country has a *balance-of-payments surplus* or a *balance-of-payments deficit,* these terms refer only to the current and capital accounts and exclude any changes in official financing. A government with a balance-of-payments surplus reduces its liabilities and/or adds to its official reserves, whereas a government with a balance-of-payments deficit increases its liabilities and/or reduces its official reserves. The main body of the balance of payments therefore informs us about a state's overall financial position.

GOVERNMENT RESPONSE TO A BALANCE-OF-PAYMENTS DEFICIT

A country with large balance-of-payments surpluses may feel some pressure to correct its imbalances in the longer term. Large payments surpluses can force up the value of its currency making its exports more expensive for foreigners, and excessive official reserves can lead to inflationary pressures and rising domestic prices. However, countries with payments deficits feel more pressure to correct the imbalances than countries with surpluses, because a deficit country's reserves can be depleted but a surplus country can increase its reserves indefinitely. Thus, surplus countries normally view their payments disequilibrium as an economic asset, and we focus here on a country's response to a payments deficit. A government with a payments deficit has two policy options: to *finance* the deficit or *adjust* to it. Adjustment measures have political risks because some societal groups must bear the adjustment costs in the present; thus, governments often prefer financing measures that defer the adjustment costs to the future.[5]

Adjustment Measures

Governments opting for adjustment rely on monetary, fiscal, and commercial policy instruments. **Monetary policy** influences the economy through changes in the money supply. A central bank uses monetary policy to deal with a balance-of-payments deficit when it limits public access to funds for spending purposes and makes such funds more expensive. For example, a central bank raises interest rates to make borrowing more costly, decreases the amount of money available for loans by requiring commercial banks to hold larger reserves, and sells government bonds to withdraw money from the economy. These policies can lower the payments deficit through a contraction of the economy and decreased spending on goods and services. A government uses **fiscal policy** to deal with a payments deficit when it lowers government expenditures and raises taxes to withdraw purchasing power from the public. (Countries with payments surpluses by contrast often seek to expand the money supply, increase the budget deficit, and inflate the economy.) *Commercial policy* lowers a country's payments deficit through trade by increasing its exports and decreasing its imports.

The combination of monetary, fiscal, and commercial policies depends on whether a government opts for external or internal adjustment measures. *External adjustment measures* impose most of the adjustment costs on foreigners. For example, tariffs, import quotas, export subsidies, and currency devaluation are used to decrease imports and foreign investment outflows and increase exports and foreign investment inflows. Because external adjustment measures are aimed at foreigners, others often retaliate—and everyone loses in the long run. The competitive devaluation of currencies, with every country trying to lower the relative price of its exports, is an example of the results of such retaliation. Although a government may adopt external measures to avoid politically unpopular decisions, even external measures impose costs on some domestic groups. For example, a reduction of imports adversely affects importing businesses and the products available to consumers. *Internal adjustment measures* cause individuals and groups at home to pay more of the adjustment costs. These are usually deflationary monetary and fiscal policies to slow business activity and decrease the deficit; examples include higher taxes and interest rates to reduce spending by individuals, business, and the government. The domestic costs of internal adjustment include unemployment, lower living standards, business bankruptcies, and fewer publicly financed programs. However, internal adjustment can also affect foreigners by deflating the economy and lowering the demand for imports.

Financing

A country may also seek *financing* for its balance-of-payments deficit by borrowing from external sources or decreasing its foreign exchange reserves. Financing is often the preferred option when access to credit is available because it is easier to postpone difficult adjustment measures. However, financing may not be available over the long term; a country's reserves may be depleted, and foreigners are reluctant to invest in a country with chronic foreign debt problems. The United States has depended mainly on financing through its capital account (plus $36.58 billion in 1992, in Table 6.1) to counter its current account deficit (minus $66.30 billion in 1992). As Table 6.2 shows, the U.S. current account deficit has increased almost every year, and in 2006 it was $856.7 billion. Japan, China, and Russia by contrast had current account *surpluses* of $170.4 billion, $238.5 billion, and $95.6 billion, respectively, in 2006 (see Table 6.2). The main factor in the U.S. current account deficit is its balance-of-trade deficit, which rose to $765.3 billion in 2006. As a result of its chronic current account deficits, the United States changed from being a net creditor of $300 billion in 1980 to a net debtor of $1.5 trillion in 1998, and its net external liability position was almost $3 trillion in 2007, about 25 percent of its GDP.[6]

Some analysts have argued that the U.S. deficits are not a major concern for several reasons. First, the negative U.S. trade balance is no longer a valid measure of U.S. competitiveness because corporate America "has never been better positioned to compete in the global marketplace."[7] U.S. firms often sell goods abroad through their foreign subsidiaries rather than exporting them from the United States; in 1998, for example, U.S. global exports of $933 billion were far less than U.S. foreign affiliate sales of $2.4 trillion. Second, the United States often has higher trade and current account deficits when U.S. productivity is increasing at a faster rate relative to others. For example, the United States had growing current account deficits while Japan and the euro area had current account surpluses in the late 1990s. The 1990s was a decade when the United States had sustained economic expansion, EU economic growth was largely stalled, and the Japanese

---

TABLE 6.2   Current Account Balances (Billions of U.S. Dollars)

	1999	2000	2001	2002	2003	2004	2005	2006
United States	−299.8	−415.2	−389.0	−472.4	−527.5	−665.3	−791.5	−856.7
Euro Area[a]	22.4	−41.3	3.2	42.2	35.5	97.5	8.1	−29.1
Japan	114.5	119.6	87.8	112.6	136.2	165.7	163.9	170.4
China	15.7	20.5	17.4	35.4	45.9	68.7	160.8	238.5
Russia	24.6	46.8	33.9	29.1	35.4	58.6	83.3	95.6

[a] Euro Area: The 12 countries in the EU that used the euro to 2006. (Slovenia joined the euro zone in 2007, Cyprus and Malta joined in 2008, and Slovakia joined in 2009.)

Source: International Monetary Fund, *World Economic Outlook, April 2007* (Washington, D.C.: IMF, 2007), Table 25, p. 247 and Table 28, p. 251.

economy was often in recession. Thus, the trade and current account deficits indicate that a vibrant U.S. economy is serving as the largest market for other countries' exports. Third, some argue that the United States attracts so much foreign capital because others want to invest in the country. In view of this positive balance on its capital account, the United States balances its payments by incurring a deficit on its current account. Central banks in Europe and Asia will continue to buy U.S. dollars indefinitely, so there is no effective constraint on U.S. borrowing.[8]

A balance of trade surplus is certainly not the only measure of economic health, as Japan's economic problems demonstrate (see Chapter 10). However, arguments that the U.S. trade deficit is of little concern are not convincing. Regarding the first argument, it is debatable as to whether a state's competitiveness is synonymous with the competitiveness of its MNCs (see Chapter 9). In assessing U.S. trade competitiveness and employment prospects for U.S. workers, it is *not* sufficient to focus only on the sales of U.S. foreign affiliates. Regarding the second and third arguments, the United States does sometimes have higher deficits during periods of rapid economic growth, and it has been able to finance its deficits because its large economy and political stability attract foreign investors. However, a number of problems have already resulted from the long-term U.S. deficits including a protectionist backlash against U.S. liberal trade policy, a loss of U.S. manufacturing jobs and disposable income, increased leverage of foreign governments with substantial U.S. dollar holdings, and disruptive market volatility against the U.S. dollar. Indeed, the chronic U.S. current account deficits and concerns that the U.S. debt is reaching unsustainable levels are major factors explaining the depreciation of the U.S. dollar in recent years. There are also geopolitical implications, because two of the largest holders of dollar reserves—China and Russia—are U.S. rivals rather than allies. The degree to which China and Russia diversify their holdings into euros can have a major effect on the future of the U.S. dollar as the top international currency.[9] This chapter discusses the reasons for the U.S. deficits, and the rise of the euro as a rival to the U.S. dollar.

Adjustment, Financing, and the Theoretical Perspectives

In reality, states usually employ a combination of external and internal adjustment and financing measures to deal with payments deficits. Liberals, realists, and historical materialists have different preferences regarding these policies. Orthodox liberals believe that governments should adopt internal adjustment measures as a necessary form of discipline because they see payments deficits as resulting from domestic inefficiencies. They oppose external adjustment because it contributes to trade barriers and distorts economic interactions, and they oppose external financing because it permits states to delay instituting internal reforms. Realists by contrast see internal adjustment methods as posing a threat to a state's policy-making autonomy, and historical materialists believe that LDCs should not have to bear internal adjustment costs in an international system that serves DC interests. External adjustment is much more acceptable to realists and historical materialists. Realists view external measures as "fair game" in a state's efforts to improve its competitive position; for example, some analysts argue that the United States should adopt external adjustment measures because Japan and China's manipulation of "their currencies to gain an unfair competitive advantage" has "a substantial impact on exchange rates and the U.S. trade deficit."[10] Historical materialists assert that LDCs should impose import controls because of their unfavorable terms of trade with DCs and that DCs should provide LDCs with liberal financing to help alleviate their balance-of-payments problems.

THE FUNCTIONS AND VALUATION OF MONEY

Before tracing the development of monetary relations, it is important to be familiar with the concepts of *money* and *currency,* which is simply money used as a medium of exchange. Money serves three main functions:

- As *a medium of exchange,* money must be acceptable to others in payment for goods, services, or assets.
- As *a unit of account,* it places a value or price on goods, services, or assets.
- As *a store of value,* it provides a means for preserving purchasing power or wealth.

These functions depend on ideational as well as material factors, because "the key to all three of money's roles is *trust,* the reciprocal faith of a critical mass of like-minded transactors."[11] In other words, a currency can serve effectively as a medium of exchange and a store of value only if individuals are confident that it can be used in financial transactions without significantly losing its value. Currencies can be priced by setting fixed exchange rates, by free markets, or by some combination of the two. **Devaluation** occurs when a state lowers its currency's official price, and **revaluation** occurs when it raises the official price. **Depreciation** refers to a market-driven reduction in a currency's price, and **appreciation** refers to a market-driven increase in its price.

INTERNATIONAL MONETARY RELATIONS BEFORE BRETTON WOODS

There have been four monetary regimes in the modern period of international monetary relations: the classical gold standard from the 1870s to World War I; a gold exchange standard during the first part of the interwar period; the Bretton Woods system from 1944 to 1973; and a mixed system of floating and fixed exchange rates from 1973 to the present.[12] This chapter focuses mainly on the third and fourth regimes, but to understand them it is necessary to provide some background on the first two regimes.

The Classical Gold Standard (1870s to 1914)

The classical **gold standard** was a *fixed-exchange-rate* regime in which national currencies had specific exchange rates in relation to gold, and countries held their official international reserves in the form of gold. Governments were committed to converting domestic currency into gold at the fixed rate, and individuals could export and import gold obtained from official and other sources. By stabilizing national currency values, the gold standard facilitated trade and other transactions. For example, if the U.S. dollar and British pound were pegged at $35 and at £14.5 per ounce of gold, the exchange rate between the dollar and the pound would remain constant at $2.41 per £1 (35 divided by 14.5). Although some states adhered to the gold standard more closely than others, the gold standard functioned reasonably well because it was backed by British hegemony and cooperation among the major powers. Britain helped stabilize the gold standard by providing other states with public goods such as investment capital, loans, and an open market for their imports. Even more importantly, the three states at the center of the regime—Britain, France, and Germany—defended their central banks' gold reserves, maintained the convertibility of their currencies, and were willing to undergo domestic adjustments when necessary to preserve the gold standard. Thus, Western Europe and the United States generally maintained their official gold parities for about 35 years.[13] The gold standard was based on the orthodox liberal objective of promoting monetary openness and stability through the maintenance of stable exchange rates. This was a period before Keynes introduced interventionist liberal ideas to combat unemployment, and states were expected to sacrifice domestic social objectives for the sake of monetary stability. Orthodox liberals sometimes refer to the gold standard in highly idealized terms, and in 1981 President Ronald Reagan created a special commission to determine whether the United States should return to the gold standard (its recommendation was negative).[14] However, critics argue that the gold standard imposed the largest burden of adjustment in welfare and employment on the poorest people and states.

The Interwar Period (1918–1944)

World War I completely disrupted international monetary relations. After the war exchange rates floated freely, and central banks did not intervene in the foreign exchange market; but the floating rates contributed to volatile currency values, and there were efforts to restore the gold standard. By 1927 the major states established a *gold exchange standard* regime, in which central bank reserves were held in major currencies as well as gold, and each central bank fixed the exchange rate of its currency to a key currency (the British pound in the interwar period) with a fixed gold price. Although central banks had held reserve currencies in earlier years, the gold exchange standard institutionalized this practice. A gold exchange standard permits more flexibility in increasing international reserves than a gold standard because the reserves are not limited to the supply of gold. However, the gold exchange standard did not operate as planned because some states had persistent balance-of-payments deficits and others had persistent surpluses. The Great Depression of 1929 put further stress on the gold exchange standard, and in 1931 Britain suspended the convertibility of the pound sterling into gold. States gradually returned to floating their currencies, but unlike the early 1920s this was a *managed* float in which central banks intervened to deal with excessive fluctuations in exchange rates. Some theorists argue that the failure to reestablish monetary stability in the interwar period resulted from Britain's inability as a declining hegemon to stabilize policies; but others argue that the main factor was the growing reluctance of states to sacrifice *domestic* goals such as full employment for the sake of currency stability. Before World War I, voting in most states was limited, labor unions were weak, farmers were not organized, and leftist parties were restricted. Thus, governments could stabilize their currencies through policies that caused domestic hardship such as raising interest rates and taxes and decreasing government expenditures. By the end of World War I, however, the extension of suffrage, legalization of labor unions, organization of farmers, and development of mass political parties gave domestic groups more influence. It was no accident that interventionist liberalism took hold at this time, positing that some government intervention is necessary to deal with domestic economic problems. Thus, governments could no longer easily sacrifice the welfare of their citizens to maintain monetary stability.[15]

THE FORMATION OF THE BRETTON WOODS MONETARY REGIME

World War II was marked by a breakdown of monetary cooperation and a period of exchange controls, and planning for a postwar monetary regime culminated in the 1944 Bretton Woods conference. To avoid the speculative activity and volatility of currency values experienced during the free float of the 1920s, the Bretton Woods planners established a gold exchange standard in which the value of each country's currency was pegged to gold or the U.S. dollar as the key currency. A *key currency* is the currency that is most often held outside its borders by private and public actors, used globally for crossborder transactions, and purchased in the form of financial instruments such as bonds. Other states are also most likely to peg their currencies to the key currency.[16] Unlike earlier monetary regimes, the Bretton Woods system was based on the postwar interventionist liberal compromise (see Chapter 4). The postwar planners assumed that the pegged exchange rates would provide the monetary stability needed for international trade, but they also provided for some flexibility and assistance so countries could pursue domestic policies to combat inflation and unemployment. This marked a contrast with the classical gold standard, in which exchange-rate stability took precedence over domestic requirements.[17] The interventionist liberal compromise had three major elements. First, the gold exchange standard was an adjustable-peg exchange rate rather than a fixed-exchange-rate system. Although countries were to maintain the par value of their currencies in the short term, all countries other than the United States (as discussed later) could devalue their currencies under IMF guidance to correct chronic balance-of-payments problems. The IMF framework for changing currency values was designed to provide more flexibility than the classical gold standard and avoid competitive devaluations such as those of the interwar period. Second, the IMF would provide short-term loans to countries with balance-of-payments problems so they could maintain exchange-rate stability. Third, countries could impose national controls over capital flows. Speculative capital flows had led to instability during the interwar period, and the postwar negotiators feared that such speculation could undermine efforts to maintain pegged exchange rates and promote freer trade.[18]

THE INTERNATIONAL MONETARY FUND

The IMF, located in Washington, D.C., was created to stabilize exchange rates and provide member states with short-term loans for temporary balance-of-payments problems. Under the IMF Articles of Agreement, members had to peg their currencies to gold or the U.S. dollar, which was valued at $35 per ounce of gold. Members also contributed to a pool of national currencies that would be available for IMF loans to deficit countries. Each IMF member is given a *quota* based on its relative economic position, and its quota determines the size of its *subscription* or contribution to IMF resources, its voting power, and the amount it can borrow from the IMF. Under the IMF's weighted voting system, the most economically powerful states have the largest subscriptions and the most votes. At regular intervals the IMF adjusts members' quotas to accord with changes in their economic positions. IMF **conditionality** ensures that borrowers must agree to adopt specific economic policies in return for IMF funding, and the conditions become more stringent as a member borrows more from the IMF in relation to its quota. LDCs feel strong pressure to abide by IMF conditionality because they depend on IMF loans, and DCs and private banks often require the acceptance of IMF conditions before providing their own loans and development assistance. IMF officials usually require borrowers to adopt contractionary monetary and fiscal policies so they can correct their balance-of-payments problems and repay their IMF loans. However, many LDC loan recipients feel that IMF conditionality infringes on their sovereignty and does not address the basic structural problems hindering their economic development (see Chapter 11).

The highest IMF decision-making body is the *Board of Governors*. Every IMF member appoints one governor to the board, but the voting power of each governor depends on the weighted voting system. The governors are usually finance ministers or central bank heads. For example, the U.S. Governor is the Secretary of the Treasury and the alternative representative is the Federal Reserve Board Chair; the Canadian Governor is the Finance Minister and the alternate is the Governor of the Bank of Canada. The governors meet once a year at the IMF–World Bank Annual Meetings and delegate most of their powers to the *Executive Board* (or Board of Executive Directors), which also has weighted voting and is composed of 24 directors appointed or elected by the IMF members. The Executive Board is responsible for the IMF's daily business, including requests for financial assistance, economic consultations with members, and policy development. The IMF also has an *International Monetary and Financial Committee* and a *Development Committee* (jointly with the World Bank) that provide advice to the Board of Governors. The IMF *managing director,* appointed by the Executive Board for a five-year renewable term, is the top executive officer who appoints the staff and is chair of the Executive Board.[19]

The countries with the largest subscriptions and most votes in the IMF are the G5—the United States, Japan, Germany, France, and Britain. In July 2008 the G5 had 38.39 percent of the votes; the United States had 16.77 percent, followed by Japan with 6.02 percent, Germany with 5.88 percent, and France and Britain with 4.86 percent each. The G5 countries have enough votes to always appoint their own executive directors, and three other countries—China, Saudi Arabia, and Russia (with 3.66, 3.16, and 2.69 percent of the votes, respectively)—have also appointed their own executive directors. Coalitions of member states elect the other 16 executive directors every two years.[20] Although most IMF decisions are made by consensus, the weighted voting is important because members are aware "of the likely outcome [of a vote] if the negotiation breaks down."[21] Most IMF votes require a simple majority, but 70 and 85 percent majorities are required for important decisions; these special majority votes give an effective veto to the United States, the EU, and the LDCs. However, the large, amorphous group of LDCs rarely joins together to block an IMF decision. Thus, the weighted voting gives a good deal of control to the North.[22] The DCs also have the most influence in the IMF operating staff. By tacit agreement, the IMF managing director has always been European, and the World Bank president has always been American. Furthermore, in 2006, DC nationals accounted for 57.3 percent of the IMF professional staff and 70.4 percent of the managerial staff. Gender disparities are also evident. All the IMF managing directors have been men, and in 2006 men accounted for 64.3 percent of the IMF professional staff and 83.7 percent of the managerial staff.[23]

THE FUNCTIONING OF THE BRETTON WOODS MONETARY REGIME

Bretton Woods was a gold exchange regime in which the main reserves were gold and the U.S. dollar. Economists generally ask three questions about the adequacy of reserve assets in upholding a monetary regime. First, are there sufficient reserves (e.g., gold and the U.S. dollar) for **liquidity,** or financing purposes? As interdependence increases, more liquidity is needed to cover the growing number of economic transactions, but a surplus of liquidity can cause inflation and other problems. Second, is there *confidence* in the reserve assets? When countries lack confidence that an asset will retain its value, they are reluctant to hold it in their reserves. Confidence problems have led to periodic efforts to sell British pounds and U.S. dollars. And third, what *adjustment* options do countries have in dealing with balance-of-payments deficits? An effective regime should offer all deficit countries (including the top-currency country, the United States) adjustment options. The discussion that follows examines problems with liquidity, confidence, and adjustment in the Bretton Woods monetary regime.[24]

The Central Role of the U.S. Dollar

Central banks held their international reserves in gold and foreign exchange under the Bretton Woods monetary regime. However, the original attraction of gold—its scarcity—became a liability as increased trade and foreign investment led to growing demand for reserves. Most countries also preferred U.S. dollars to gold, because dollars earned interest and did not have to be shipped and stored; thus, it was vital to have sufficient U.S. dollars for global liquidity purposes. Large U.S. balance-of-trade surpluses in the late 1940s, however, contributed to a dollar shortage. To remedy this problem, the United States distributed dollars around the world from 1947 to 1958 through economic aid and military expenditures. Other countries could devalue their currencies under IMF guidance, but the dollar's value was to remain fixed at $35 per ounce of gold to ensure that the dollar would be "as good as gold." The United States agreed to exchange all dollars held by foreigners for gold at the official rate, and this seemed feasible because it had larger gold reserves than any other country. From the liberal perspective, the United States provided *public goods* by opening its market to imports, providing aid through the European Recovery Program or Marshall Plan, and supplying the U.S. dollar as the main source of international liquidity. However, the United States also benefited from having the key currency: It could avoid exchange-rate risks and transaction costs by trading and borrowing in domestic currency; it was largely exempt from the discipline the international financial system imposed on other states; and the dollar's role gave the United States more financial power, bolstering New York City as the world's financial capital. Furthermore, the United States has gained additional revenue through **seigniorage** benefits, or the difference between the cost of producing a currency and its actual face value, because such a high percentage of U.S. currency circulates outside the country.[25] Thus, U.S. policy was based on both altruism and self-interest, and others accepted U.S. leadership because of the benefits they received.

However, several changes in the late 1950s led to concerns about U.S. leadership. Although the United States had large current account surpluses because of its positive balance-of-trade, it had even larger capital account deficits because of the economic and military finance it was providing. As a result, the United States had balance-of-payments deficits beginning in 1950. U.S. payments deficits averaged $1.5 billion per year for most of the decade, but they increased rapidly in the late 1950s, and observers began to speak of a dollar glut rather than a shortage. In 1960, foreign dollar holdings exceeded U.S.

gold reserves for the first time, and European governments were reluctant to accumulate excessive dollar reserves. To some economists, the dollar's declining fortunes demonstrated basic problems with a monetary regime that relied on a single key currency. Although the need for sufficient liquidity caused the United States to supply dollars by running balance-of-payments deficits, these deficits would eventually deplete U.S. gold reserves and make it impossible for the United States to continue exchanging dollars for gold at $35 per ounce. Any U.S. actions to reduce its balance-of-payments deficit to restore confidence in the dollar would contribute to a shortage of global liquidity. The **Triffin dilemma** (named after economist Robert Triffin) refers to the problem with a monetary regime that depends on a single key currency: The *liquidity* and *confidence* functions of the currency eventually come into conflict.[26]

A second change that raised questions about U.S. leadership was the growth of the *Eurocurrency market* (or *Euromarket*). **Eurocurrencies** are national currencies traded and deposited in banks outside the home country. Although Eurocurrency activity first developed in Europe, in recent years it has expanded elsewhere. By the early 1990s banks in Europe, North America, Asia, and the Caribbean had Eurocurrency deposits totalling more than $1 trillion; over half of these were *Eurodollar* deposits held in banks outside the United States. As early as 1917 the Russian communist government deposited U.S. dollars in European banks to prevent the United States from seizing them. The Euromarket developed after World War II when the Soviet Union continued the practice of holding its U.S. dollars in Europe because of the Cold War; this also served Britain's goal of preserving London's status as a major financial center. In the 1960s the Euromarket developed further when President Lyndon B. Johnson responded to U.S. balance-of-payments deficits by limiting foreign lending by U.S. banks. U.S. companies responded by financing their foreign operations from offshore banks, which were not subject to U.S. banking legislation. The Euromarket also grew because European firms involved with international trade found it easier to use a single currency—the U.S. dollar—and because after 1973 Middle Eastern OPEC countries wanted to avoid keeping their huge dollar deposits in the United States. Eurodollars are not subject to the regulations governments impose on domestic banking activities. For example, the U.S. Federal Reserve requires banks to hold a certain percent of their deposits as reserves and impose a ceiling on interest rates they pay on deposits; but the United States does not have this control over Eurodollars. Thus, the growth of the Euromarket raised questions about U.S. control over monetary relations and created problems for monetary stability. For example, if a government tries to restrict credit to fight inflation, large firms can continue to borrow in the Eurocurrency market; and the size and speed of Eurocurrency flows can greatly destabilize foreign exchange rates and domestic interest rates. Effective regulation of the Euromarket must be multilateral, but strong competition for Eurobanking has precluded that possibility.[27]

Liberal interdependence theorists point to the role international bankers played in the expansion of the Euromarket as a result of the increase in capital mobility and global lending and borrowing. Realists note that the leading states also contributed to the growth of the Euromarket. For example, Britain allowed the Euromarket to operate without regulation to promote London as a leading financial center, and the U.S. government permitted its bankers to retain their dominance in international finance by avoiding U.S. capital controls. In view of the declining confidence in the dollar, the U.S. government also believed the Euromarket would enhance the appeal of its currency.[28] However, realists also argue that British and U.S. support for the Euromarket "may prove to have been the most important single development of the century undermining national monetary sovereignty."[29] The growth of the Euromarket combined with persistent U.S. balance-of-payments deficits posed questions about the U.S. ability to manage global monetary relations and contributed to a shift toward multilateralism.

A Shift Toward Multilateralism

A *top currency* is favored for international monetary transactions because others have confidence in the economic position of the issuing state. A *negotiated currency* does not benefit from this high degree of confidence, so the issuing state must induce others to accept its leadership. As U.S. balance-of-payments deficits increased, the dollar slipped from top-currency to negotiated-currency status, and there was a shift toward multilateral management.[30] In 1962, 10 DCs (the G10) established the *General Arrangements to Borrow (GAB)*, an agreement to lend up to $6 billion in their own currencies as supplementary resources to the IMF to cope with international monetary problems. Because the G10 had to approve each request for supplementary support, it represented a shift from unilateral U.S. toward collective management of monetary issues.[31] Another indication of the shift to multilateral management was the increased role of the Swiss-based *Bank for International Settlements (BIS)*. Although the BIS was formed to help settle German reparations after World War I, its main purpose was to promote cooperation among central banks. The BIS was controversial because of allegations that it had pro-Nazi sentiments and accepted looted gold from occupied countries; it resumed operations after returning the looted gold, but this stigma limited its role as an international financial institution. However, when there was downward pressure on the U.S. dollar in the 1960s, the BIS regained some stature by organizing mutual lines of credit among the central banks to stabilize exchange rates and the price of gold. The BIS has become the main forum for cooperation among DC central bankers, and it uses deposits it receives from the central banks to provide credit and deal with exchange-rate problems.[32]

Despite these moves toward collective management, LDCs were not represented in these groups. In 1971 the South therefore responded to the G10 by forming its own **Group of 24 (G24),** which includes finance ministers or central bank governors from the three main LDC regions—Africa, Asia, and Latin America and the Caribbean. The G24 tries to coordinate LDC monetary policies and responds to G10 reports on monetary reform, but its influence is limited because it consists of IMF borrowers.[33] Although the G10 countries have considerable economic power, there were concerns that even their resources could not defend the dollar if it came under attack as U.S. payments deficits increased. The G10 therefore took actions to bolster the dollar, and the United States tried to improve its balance of payments by reducing capital outflows. Nevertheless, U.S. gold stocks continued to fall, dollar claims against the U.S. gold supply rose, and by 1968 the dollar in effect had become inconvertible into gold.

Some observers attributed the U.S. balance-of-payments deficit to the public goods it provided such as the Marshall Plan, the U.S. dollar as the key currency, and an open market for other countries' exports; but critics argued that the United States was unwilling to balance its revenues and expenditures. For example, the U.S. Congress refused to raise taxes to pay for the Vietnam War, President Johnson refused to cut domestic social programs, and the United States had a low personal savings rate. The personal savings rate as a percentage of disposable income in 1980 was 19.2 percent for Japan, 12.3 percent for Britain, 11 percent for France, 10.9 percent for West Germany, and only 6 percent for the United States. Thus, high-saving Japan provided large-scale capital flows to the low-saving United States.[34] The U.S. payments deficit also resulted from its declining competitiveness as Western Europe and Japan recovered from the war. The Bretton Woods regime did not provide the United States with *adjustment* options, because it was the only country that could not devalue its currency.

The U.S. payments deficit was not the only problem confronting the Bretton Woods system. The national controls on capital flows were becoming less effective because investors lacked confidence in the currency exchange rates. Speculative activity in the Euromarket was especially difficult to regulate, and MNCs evaded controls through transactions among their affiliates. MNCs moved capital from one country to another to take advantage of interest rate spreads and expected exchange-rate adjustments, and this put growing pressure on states to realign their currency exchange rates. In efforts to prevent a run on their currencies, leaders often committed themselves to the established parities, severely limiting their policy options. Powerful domestic interests also prevented governments from instituting needed realignment of their currencies. Thus, modest changes in exchange rates were difficult to institute, and the monetary regime became overly rigid despite the need for flexibility.[35]

To restore financial stability, IMF members agreed in 1969 to create **special drawing rights (SDRs)** as an artificial reserve asset to provide a new source of liquidity in addition to the U.S. dollar. Created and managed by the IMF with the G10's approval, SDRs are *not* a currency. Countries use them in settling their IMF financial obligations, and the IMF creates and manages them with the G10's approval. Decisions to allocate SDRs require approval by three-fifths of the IMF members with 85 percent of the voting power, and there have been only two allocations to this point: 9.3 billion SDRs in 1970–1972 and 12.1 billion SDRs in 1979–1981. Initially, 35 SDRs were equal to $35 (U.S.) or an ounce of gold, but after the move to floating currencies (discussed later), the SDR value was determined by a basket or weighted average of currencies; since 2001 the basket has consisted of the U.S. dollar, the euro, the Japanese yen, and the British pound. Because some currencies rise while others fall in value, the SDR has served as a relatively stable unit of account for the IMF and other IOs. However, SDRs accounted for less than 1.1 percent of IMF members' nongold reserves in 2002. A major obstacle to creating more SDRs for many years was that they were allocated in proportion to a country's IMF quota, and the G5 countries received the most SDRs. The South proposed that the creation of new SDRs be linked to the transfer of resources for development, but the North argued that LDC needs for development assistance would lead to the creation of excess SDRs in liquidity terms. Furthermore, with an end to national controls on capital controls (discussed later), DCs could readily borrow on capital markets; so they do not require SDRs. However, in an April 2009 meeting the G20 (which has now become more important than the G10) responded to the global financial crisis by agreeing to a $250 billion increase in SDRs. As with the previous SDR allocations, most of the new SDRs will go to the large DC economies, but LDCs will also receive them, and richer countries can lend them to poorer countries that require assistance, such as those in Eastern and Central Europe. Although this allocation will greatly increase the number of SDRs (the details of the IMF funding have not been worked out at the time of this writing), SDRs are not likely to ever *replace* the U.S. dollar or euro as a reserve asset because "no money has ever risen to a position of international preeminence that was not initially backed by a leading economy."[36]

The Demise of the Bretton Woods Monetary Regime

By the late 1960s the Bretton Woods monetary regime had become untenable. France's President Charles de Gaulle was deliberately converting dollars into gold to bring about an end to U.S. hegemonic privilege as the key-currency state, and the United States was making it more difficult for foreign central banks to change their dollars into gold. Although U.S. foreign investment and loans had been the main source of its balance-of-payments deficits, U.S. trade competitiveness seriously declined in 1971, when it had its first balance-of-*trade* deficit since 1893. On August 15, 1971, President Richard M. Nixon therefore suspended the official convertibility of the dollar into gold and imposed a 10-percent tariff surcharge on all dutiable imports. In December 1971, the G10 countries therefore agreed to devalue the dollar by 10–20 percent vis-à-vis other major currencies through the first Smithsonian Agreement (negotiated at the Smithsonian Institution in Washington, D.C.). This did not correct the problem, however, and a second Smithsonian Agreement devalued the dollar further in February 1973.[37]

By the early 1970s the requirements for adequate reserves—liquidity, confidence, and adjustment—all presented serious problems: The U.S. balance-of-payments deficits created a crisis of confidence in the dollar; countries were therefore reluctant to hold large supplies of U.S. dollars for liquidity purposes; and the dollar could not be adequately adjusted through devaluation (the Smithsonian agreements were "too little, and too late"). With the increase of global capital flows, the Bretton Woods system of pegged exchange rates was also becoming untenable. Major IMF members tried to reform the international monetary regime, but their discussions failed because of differences among the Americans, Europeans, and LDCs; destabilizing changes such as the 1973 increase in OPEC oil prices; and Germany and France's preoccupation with establishing a *European Monetary System* (*EMS*). Thus, the Bretton Woods regime of pegged exchange rates collapsed and was replaced by a regime that permitted floating exchange rates.[38]

THE REGIME OF FLOATING (OR FLEXIBLE) EXCHANGE RATES

By 1973 the major trading nations were "living in sin," because they were ignoring the Bretton Woods ban on freely floating exchange rates.[39] The 1976 IMF meeting in Jamaica finally legalized this situation by permitting each country to either establish a par value for its currency or shift to floating rates. In a *free-floating* regime, countries do not intervene in currency markets, and the market alone determines currency values. In recent years IMF members have relied extensively on *managed floating,* in which central banks intervene to deal with disruptive conditions such as excessive fluctuations in exchange rates. Although managed floating is accepted, the IMF calls on central banks to avoid *manipulative* or *dirty floating,* which involves "manipulating exchange rates . . . in order to prevent effective balance of payments adjustment or to gain an unfair competitive advantage."[40] The current monetary regime is mixed in nature: Major DCs such as the United States, Japan, and Canada (and a number of LDCs) float their currencies; the EU members seek increased regional coordination of their policies; and many LDCs peg the value of their currencies to a key currency or basket of currencies. The choice of a pegged versus a floating currency can have distributional consequences for domestic groups in a state, and domestic as well as international factors therefore determine whether a state decides to peg or float its currency.[41] Thus, some analysts describe the current monetary system as a "nonsystem."[42]

The move to floating exchange rates had an intellectual appeal for orthodox liberals, who argued that exchange rate adjustment should occur through market pressure rather than government involvement. As early as 1953 Milton Friedman had called for "a system of exchange rates freely determined in open markets, primarily by private transactions, and the simultaneous abandonment of direct controls over exchange transactions."[43] Although some liberals feared that floating rates would lead to speculative capital flows, Friedman argued that instability during the 1930s had resulted more from fundamental economic and financial problems. Even more important, floating rates appealed to some realists as well as interventionist liberals because they permit governments to establish their own independent monetary policies in a domestic context. As capital controls were abandoned, countries were finding it increasingly difficult to set their own monetary policies under the pegged-exchange-rate regime because of the so-called *Unholy Trinity*.[44] The three elements of the Unholy Trinity are exchange-rate stability, private capital mobility, and monetary policy autonomy. Economists have found that states can attain only two of these three goals simultaneously. With pegged exchange rates and capital mobility (i.e., the integration of financial markets), a state's attempt to follow independent monetary policies can lead to capital flight and a downward pressure on the currency exchange rate until the state alters its monetary policies. For example, if domestic interest rates differ for long from global interest rates, capital flows can quickly eliminate the difference. Because most states have accepted a high degree of capital mobility (and cannot reverse this trend), the Unholy Trinity involves a trade-off between pegged exchange rates and policy autonomy. In shifting to floating exchange rates, states opted for more policy autonomy.

Although the shift to floating rates has permitted larger DCs to follow more independent monetary policies, most economists underestimated the degree to which increased capital mobility would disrupt exchange rates. As orthodox liberalism returned, the United States and Britain rejected any further attempts to control capital flows, and other DCs soon followed because countries were competing for foreign investment. The integration of financial markets, combined with technological advances, contributed to a massive growth in speculative capital flows. Thus, volatility and misalignment of currencies have been serious problems with the floating-exchange-rate regime. *Volatility* refers to the short-term instability of exchange rates. Under the floating system, unpredictable capital flows can produce highly volatile exchange rates that create uncertainty, inhibit productive investments, and interfere with international trade. *Misalignment* refers to the long-term departure of exchange rates from competitive levels. Misalignment is even more serious than volatility because it leads to prolonged changes in international competitiveness. Depending on whether a currency is under- or overvalued, misalignment gives a country substantial price advantages or disadvantages vis-à-vis its competitors.[45]

The shift to floating rates also created a crisis of purpose for the IMF because its role in stabilizing pegged exchange rates largely disappeared. The G5 and G7 discussed the floating regime outside of IMF auspices, and the G7 summits engaged in a limited degree of policy coordination to stabilize monetary relations. For example, at the 1978 Bonn Summit the United States agreed to reduce its balance-of-payments deficits, and Germany and Japan agreed to adopt expansionary economic policies to increase their demand for U.S. goods.[46] However, this limited policy coordination ended with the Reagan administration, which lowered taxes and raised spending for military-defense purposes. These policies contributed to an annual U.S. government deficit that exceeded $200 billion by the mid-1980s. To service its debt, the United States raised interest rates to attract foreign capital—but the increase in capital imports strengthened the U.S. dollar, and U.S. trade and payments deficits began to spiral out of control.

The Plaza–Louvre Accords

As its dollar appreciated and its deficits increased, the United States could no longer afford to neglect exchange rates. To lower the value of the dollar, U.S. Treasury Secretary James Baker III assembled the G5 finance ministers and central bank heads in New York City's Plaza Hotel in September 1985. The G5 agreed to raise the value of the major nondollar currencies through coordinated market intervention (i.e., by buying and selling currencies), and the United States in return promised to reduce government spending. The dollar depreciated significantly after the Plaza Agreement, and the G7 therefore met at the Louvre in Paris in February 1987 to prevent its value from slipping even further. The Plaza and Louvre accords marked a shift to managed floating, in which governments intervened to correct currency volatility and misalignment. However, the major economies have not coordinated their interventions on a consistent basis since the Louvre accord. Although policy coordination is important for maintaining currency stability, international capital flows and governments' unwillingness to accept constraints on their fiscal and monetary policies preclude such coordination. Thus, the current monetary regime is much more unstable than liberal economists had predicted.[47]

ALTERNATIVES TO THE CURRENT MONETARY REGIME

Some economists point to the problems of volatility and misalignment under the floating regime and favor a return to a pegged-exchange-rate regime.[48] However, most analysts feel that efforts "to reestablish a system of pegged but adjustable rates will . . . prove futile."[49] States would find it difficult to defend pegged exchange rates because of the rise in international financial transactions. Any effort to enforce capital controls would require policy coordination, a highly unlikely possibility; thus, the global monetary regime is likely to retain floating exchange rates. In looking to alternatives to the current regime, "the only initiative that might be held out as a serious experiment" in international monetary reform is taking place in Europe.[50] Monetary integration in Europe has global as well as regional consequences because the euro might provide an alternative to the U.S. dollar as the key international currency. It is therefore important to discuss Europe's Economic and Monetary Union (EMU), in which members substitute a common currency—the euro—for their national currencies and cede decision making to a single central agency. Chapter 8 examines the EU as a regional trade agreement, and this chapter only discusses European monetary relations. To reflect a name change in the EU, we use the term **European Community (EC)** when discussing the events from 1957 to 1992 and the term European Union (EU) when discussing events from 1993 to the present. Table 8.1 in Chapter 8 shows that the EC gradually enlarged from 6 members in 1957 to the 27-member EU in January 2007. Only 16 of the 27 EU members have to this point joined the EMU and adopted the euro as a common currency (the 16 EMU members have an asterisk in Table 8.1).

EUROPEAN MONETARY RELATIONS

The Treaty of Rome creating the EC in 1957 focused on eliminating trade barriers, but a series of events starting in the 1960s also gave concrete form to the idea of a European monetary union. In January 1999, 11 EU members formed an EMU and agreed to adopt the euro in place of their national currencies. Greece, Slovenia, Cyprus, Malta, and Slovakia later joined, and the EMU now has 16 members. (The EMU members have an asterisk in Table 8.1 in Chapter 8.) The following discussion examines the reasons the EU created an EMU, the difficulties in establishing it, and the implications of the EMU for European and global monetary relations.

From 1958 to the late 1960s, the Bretton Woods regime of pegged exchange rates provided the EC with some stability. However, two changes in the 1960s caused the EC to consider regional monetary integration: (1) Growing U.S. balance-of-payments deficits decreased confidence in the U.S. dollar and threatened exchange-rate stability. (2) Europe's rapid progress in establishing a customs union and a common agricultural policy increased the need for exchange-rate stability among EC members. At a 1969 summit meeting the six EC members asked Pierre Werner, the Luxembourg prime minister, to develop a proposal for an EMU. The 1970 Werner plan recommended that the EC countries adopt similar fiscal and monetary policies and reduce fluctuations in their currency exchange rates; one element of the plan was a "snake agreement" that limited exchange-rate fluctuations among EC currencies to a narrow band of +2.25 to −2.25 percent. However, countries with weaker currencies could not adhere to this band, and France, Ireland, Italy, and Britain soon left the snake agreement. Although global events such as the 1973–1974 oil price rise and the 1975 global recession contributed to the failure of the snake agreement, the two most important factors were the increase in capital mobility and the divergent macroeconomic policies of EC members. As discussed, it is possible for states to attain only two of the three goals of the "Unholy Trinity" (the three goals are exchange-rate stability, private capital mobility, and monetary policy autonomy). Because capital mobility was increasing, the EC members could stabilize their currency exchange rates only by sacrificing monetary policy autonomy. However, the divergent economic policies of the EC members led to differential inflation rates, and speculative capital flows against the weaker currencies split the "snake" apart.

After the failure of the "snake" agreement, the EC members launched a European Monetary System (EMS) and this time they were more successful. Kathleen McNamara argues from a constructivist perspective that a neoliberal policy consensus among EC leaders in the late 1970s induced them give up autonomous monetary policies to achieve exchange-rate stability. To become more competitive internationally, the EMS members gave priority to exchange-rate stability and inflation control over societal issues. Thus, states were "willing to rule out the use of monetary policy as a weapon against broader societal problems, such as unemployment and slow growth."[51] The EMS had two main features: an *exchange-rate mechanism (ERM)* and a *European currency unit (ECU)*. The ERM limited exchange-rate fluctuations to a +2.25 to −2.25 percent band. Central banks intervened to keep the exchange rates within these levels, and if this effort failed, a state could realign its currency after consultations with other EMS members. The ECU was a new currency based on a weighted basket of EMS currencies, which was used in cross-border banking and as a common unit of account, but not in commercial transactions. The EMS was quite success-ful in stabilizing EC exchange rates, but increased financial flows by the late 1980s put greater pressure on states, and EC members that could not keep their exchange rates within the narrow ERM band were permitted to move to a broader band of +6 to −6 percent.[52]

The EMS's drawbacks stemmed from the fact that it was only a partial monetary union, and pressures for monetary stability in Europe increased as EC integration progressed. A full monetary union would create a single European currency, and would also give Europe a greater voice in international economic negotiations. In June 1989 the Delors Committee therefore proposed a three-stage process toward EMU, involving the coordination of monetary policies, the realignment of currency exchange rates, and the creation of a single currency under a European central bank. This plan was included in the 1992 *Treaty on European Union* or *Maastricht Treaty.*[53] However, the steps toward monetary union were difficult for two major reasons. First, at Germany's insistence the Maastricht agreement had rigid requirements for developing a single currency. To join the EMU, a country's budget deficit was to be no greater than 3 percent of its GDP and its public debt no greater than 60 percent of its GDP. Only some EU countries were likely to meet these targets, and the budgetary cuts required caused considerable discontent. For example, French workers staged massive strikes in 1995 to protest planned cutbacks in social programs. Second, many Germans did not want to sacrifice the deutsche mark, which reflected the country's economic strength, for what could be a weaker euro; but Germany's Chancellor Helmut Kohl strongly supported the EMU. Other countries had dif-ferent concerns. For example, Britain wanted to preserve its sovereignty in mon-etary policy, and Britain and France were not pleased that the new European Central Bank (ECB) would be located in Frankfurt, Germany. Despite the obstacles, 11 EU members formed the EMU in 1999 and agreed to adopt the euro in place of their national currencies. (The 11 founding members were Austria, Belgium, Finland, France, Germany, Ireland, Italy, Luxembourg, the Netherlands, Portugal, and Spain.) Britain, Sweden, and Denmark chose not to join, and Greece was too weak economically. However, Greece was admitted to the EMU in 2001, Slovenia joined in 2007, Cyprus and Malta joined in 2008, and Slovakia joined in 2009.

Debate has continued over the costs and benefits of a common European currency. The benefits of a monetary union include reduced exchange-rate volatility, lower transaction costs, greater price transparency, and a better func-tioning internal market. The costs of a monetary union result mainly from the loss of the exchange rate as a policy instrument; that is, an EMU member can no longer pursue an independent monetary policy by altering its exchange rate.[54] The Nobel laureate Robert Mundell framed this debate on costs versus benefits many years earlier. Mundell argued that an **optimum currency area,** which maximizes the benefits of using a common currency, has certain characteristics: It is subject to common economic shocks, has a high degree of labor mobility, and has a tax system that transfers resources from strong to weak economic areas. Mundell's ideas have been highly influential (albeit controversial), and he has been called the "Father of the Euro." Although optimum currency area studies help frame the *economic* debate on monetary integration, *political* factors such as the existence of a regional hegemon and a sense of community also help determine whether states will join a monetary union.[55] For example, Britain has refused to join the EMU for political as well as economic reasons.

To this point, we have looked mainly at the regional implications of creation of the EMU. However, many have raised questions about the future of the U.S. dollar and whether the euro might replace it as the key international currency. The next section addresses this issue.

WHAT IS THE LIKELY FUTURE OF THE U.S. DOLLAR AS THE KEY CURRENCY?

In discussing the future of the U.S. dollar, it is important to examine its perceived benefits and drawbacks vis-à-vis other monetary reserves. When Japan was growing rapidly in the 1980s, some scholars asked whether the yen could rival the dollar as the key currency. However, rivalries and suspicions among Asian states, and Japan's economic problems since the 1990s have precluded this possibility. In accordance with its growing economic influence, China has recently moved to promote its yuan (or renminbi) globally. For example, China has signed currency swap agreements with six countries, including South Korea, Malaysia, and Argentina that would inject the yuan into foreign banking systems; and China is spreading the yuan's influence through its loans and investments in other countries. However, the yuan's influence will be limited in the short to medium term, because of the lack of development of China's financial markets, concerns about domestic political stability, and China's exchange restrictions and capital controls. Proposals to develop an Asian Currency Unit are also only in the planning stage for several reasons, including the competition and mutual suspicion between China and Japan. Thus, scholars generally agree that the euro is currently the only viable alternative to the U.S. dollar as the key international currency.[56] Others will also have a role in determining the future of the dollar, especially China, Russia, and Middle Eastern countries that have large dollar holdings in their international reserves. Thus, the dollar's future depends on a range of public and private actors with financial influence. This section begins with a discussion of the dollar versus the euro, and then examines the possible role of other actors outside the EU and the United States.

The Dollar versus the Euro

In comparing currencies, it is important to look at their three main functions, as a medium of exchange, a unit of account, and a store of value. In 2005 the dollar was used as a *medium of exchange* in 89 percent of all foreign exchange transactions, compared with 37 and 20 percent for the euro and Japanese yen. Almost two-thirds of all countries that peg their currencies today peg them to the U.S. dollar as a *unit of account* compared with one-third to the euro. The dollar is also used as a unit of account in the invoicing or pricing of almost half of all world exports. The share of dollars as a *store of value* in central bank holdings declined from 70.9 percent in 1999 to 65.7 percent in 2006, while the share of euros rose from 17.9 to 25.2 percent; but the dollar still accounts for almost two-thirds of official foreign exchange reserves. Thus, the U.S. dollar continues to be the key currency today in terms of a currency's three main functions.[57]

In assessing whether the dollar's dominance is likely to continue, economists generally look at three factors: the position of U.S. financial markets, the level of confidence in the U.S. dollar, and the importance of U.S. transactional networks.[58] First, the dollar is more likely to retain its key currency status if the United States continues to have the most developed and open financial markets. Although European financial markets could pose a challenge to U.S. dominance in this area, decentralization and fragmentation in the euro zone is a disadvantage relative to the more unified U.S. financial structure. The ECB has less supervisory capacity over EU financial markets than the U.S. Federal Reserve; and Britain, which has the most well-developed financial markets in Europe, has not adopted the euro. Confidence in U.S. financial markets was seriously tested in September 2008, when a subprime mortgage crisis expanded into a full-blown financial crisis. *Subprime lending* refers to loans to borrowers who do not qualify for market interest rates because of income level, credit history, size of the downpayment, and/or employment prospects. Subprime mortgages rose from 8 to 20 percent of U.S. mortgages from 2003 to 2006, and they became difficult to refinance when interest rates rose and housing prices dropped; thus, defaults and foreclosures sharply increased. The subprime crisis quickly became a general credit crisis, and in 10 days the United States witnessed "the nationalization, failure or rescue of what was once the world's biggest insurer . . . , two of the world's biggest investment banks . . . , and two giants of America's mortgage markets."[59] The U.S. financial crisis raises new questions about the dollar's future as the key currency, but Europe's difficulty in dealing with the financial crisis shows that the euro remains an uncertain alternative to the dollar. Although the EU has become more united in some respects, it "has a long way to go before becoming the continent-wide economic and political authority it has set out to be."[60]

Second, the U.S. dollar is more likely to remain the key currency if there is confidence that its value will remain relatively stable. The U.S. deficit and debt problems have led to a dramatic decline in the dollar's value and in the confidence level. In 2006 the U.S. trade and current account deficits exceeded $750 billion and $800 billion, respectively; this was greater than 6 percent of the U.S. GDP. Although the dollar retained its key currency status in earlier years when its value had declined, the current situation could be different because the euro is emerging as an alternative currency. The euro zone has a strong external financial position, whereas the United States now has a huge and growing foreign debt problem. Thus, the value of the euro has steadily risen vis-à-vis the dollar since 2002. When 11 EU members adopted the euro in 1999, it initially traded at a value of $1.18 (U.S.) on exchange markets. After the euro fell to 86 cents (U.S.) in January 2002, it then recovered its value and rose to $1.59 (U.S.) in July 2008. The declining value of the dollar gives governments and investors an incentive to diversify their portfolios from dollars into euros and yens. Third, in regard to U.S. transactional networks, the size of the U.S. economy and its share of global trade have ensured that the dollar is widely used in transactions across the globe. Furthermore, the widespread use of the dollar outside the United States tends to be self-perpetuating, because its use by so many others decreases transaction costs. The larger the size of a currency's transactional network, the greater are the economies of scale in using the currency. The transactional network of the euro is limited by the fact that only 16 EU members have adopted it; if the euro zone expanded to include all 27 EU members, the euro could pose more of a challenge to the dollar. In sum, in terms of economic criteria the U.S. dollar should continue to be the key currency in the short to medium term, but its dominance in the longer term is by no means certain.[61]

Political and social as well as economic factors will affect the standing of the dollar. In some respects, political factors give the dollar a definite advantage over the euro. For example, U.S. military power and political stability contribute to confidence in the dollar; confidence in the euro by contrast is decreased because of the EU's lack of political unity and the difficulty EU members have in asserting their power collectively on international political issues. In other respects, political factors give the euro an advantage. For example, the EU outperformed the United States in limiting personal and public debt and in controlling inflation. It is uncertain that U.S. government leaders will take the difficult political decisions to follow more fiscally prudent policies in the face of domestic opposition. In sum, the roles of the dollar and the euro will depend on U.S. willingness to address its current account and debt problems, and on the EU's willingness and ability to take a more assertive and unified position in the global political economy. It is also necessary to ask whether Europeans *want* to have the key currency. It is difficult to stabilize a key currency's value because other governments hold such large amounts of it in their foreign exchange reserves, and so much of the currency circulates outside the borders. Many ECB staff members feel it could be dangerous and costly if the euro became the key international currency, and they prefer to focus instead on the regional position of the euro to ensure its success as a relatively new currency. The United States of course must also be willing to take the necessary measures to remain the key currency country; for example, it must increase confidence in the dollar and resist domestic pressures to respond to its payments deficits with increased trade protectionism. China, Japan, and others would be less supportive of the dollar if the United States became a less open market for their exports.[62]

Countries with Large Foreign Reserves and the Future of the Dollar

The growing U.S. deficits have been financed by foreigners. Although much of the finance comes from private investors, an increasing amount comes from official sources, mainly central banks; from 2000 to 2006 the finance per year from official sources rose from about $35 billion to $440 billion. China and non-Chinese Asia each have about $1.2 trillion of assets; the OPEC states have $600 billion; and Russia has $400 billion due to its growing revenues from energy exports. Thus, total foreign-held U.S. dollar reserves by the end of 2006 amounted to about $5 trillion.[63] Countries with large U.S. dollar reserves will have a major effect on the future of the currency, and both economic and political factors affect their behavior. Although China, Japan, and South Korea are shifting some of their reserves from U.S. dollars to euros, it is not in their economic interests to cause a rapid decline in the U.S. dollar. They are highly dependent on the U.S. market for their exports, and U.S. consumers with a cheaper dollar would purchase less. The value of their dollar reserves would also decline along with the declining value of the dollar. Political factors also play a role in countries' support for the dollar; for example, Japan and South Korea continue to depend on U.S. military support.

However, there are also economic and political reasons why countries have begun to shift more of their dollars to other reserve currencies. Russia and the OPEC exporters are large dollar holders; they have priced their oil trade in dollars and have invested their surpluses mainly in dollar-denominated assets. However, the United States is not their main trading partner. Russia trades primarily with Europe, and the largest markets for Middle Eastern oil producers for both exports and imports are in Asia. China has also been diversifying its trade, and almost half of its exports now go to countries other than the United States, Europe, and Japan; other important export markets are mainly in Asia, but also in the Middle East and Latin America. Indeed, the United States now accounts for only about 20 percent of China's exports, and Europe recently moved above the United States as an importer of Chinese goods. As for East Asia in general, its dependence on the dollar was viewed as an important cause of the 1997 Asian financial crisis (see Chapters 10 and 11), and Japan is therefore promoting the use of the yen and considering an initiative to develop an Asian regional currency. Two of the largest holders of U.S. dollar reserves—China and Russia—are also geopolitical rivals rather than allies. U.S.–China relations today are marked by economic tensions over China's large trade surplus with the United States, China's reluctance to float its currency (the yuan or renminbi) freely against the U.S. dollar, and competition for scarce resources around the world. Political tensions relate to differences over Taiwan and over

China's support for a number of regimes that the United States opposes. China is aware that the United States prevents it from being the dominant power in the western Pacific, and it may choose to cooperate in developing an Asian currency to weaken the United States in geopolitical and economic terms. U.S.–Russian tensions have been marked by Vladimir Putin's efforts to strengthen the state and re-establish Russia's economic and political influence.

Unlike China, Russia has only a limited amount of trade with the United States. Thus, Russia was one of the first countries to begin shifting its reserves from dollars to other currencies after Putin launched an anti-dollar campaign in April 2006. For several years Russian purchases of U.S. dollar assets increased along with its growing surpluses from energy exports; but its purchases of U.S. dollar assets virtually ceased beginning in the latter part of 2006. Although Kuwait has been a close U.S. ally, in 2007 it decided to shift from pegging its currency to the U.S. dollar to pegging it to a basket of currencies; and by the end of 2006, more than 20 percent of Saudi Arabia's official assets were in nondollar currencies. OPEC members that are openly hostile to the United States such as Venezuela and Iran are taking more forthright actions to decrease their dollar reserves. China has also begun to diversify its foreign exchange holdings, and the Governor of the People's Bank of China has even proposed that the SDR should replace the dollar as the major global monetary reserve. As discussed, the top global currency must be backed by a strong economy, and this precludes the idea that a supranational currency will replace the dollar. China is likely to act cautiously on this issue, because of its large dollar holdings and its dependence on the U.S. market for its exports. [64]

In sum, the dollar continues to be the key international currency, and the only major challenger (the euro) has its own sources of weakness as well as strength. However, for economic and political reasons large holders of U.S. dollar reserves are shifting more of their reserves to other currencies. Thus, the dollar as the key currency faces an uncertain future.[65] The next section deals with the effects that large holders of reserve currencies may have on the global monetary regime through "sovereign wealth funds."

SOVEREIGN WEALTH FUNDS

Sovereign wealth funds (SWFs) are "government investment funds, funded by foreign currency reserves but managed separately from official currency reserves."[66] Whereas official reserves hold low-risk assets such as sovereign bonds, SWFs may hold equities, corporate bonds, and other assets; thus, SWFs are more important for financial markets. The rapid growth of SWFs signifies a partial return to state capitalism after decades of privatization in the West. Although SWFs have existed at least since the 1950s, their number and size have grown dramatically over the last 15 years. The main factors behind the growth of SWFs are the large asset surpluses some states have acquired due to high oil prices, financial globalization, and imbalances in the global financial system. The countries with the largest SWFs include one DC (Norway), and the emerging countries of the United Arab Emirates, Saudi Arabia, China, Kuwait, Russia, and Singapore.

The emerging countries have used their SWFs to buy stakes in Western companies and invest in areas that will reduce the effect of volatile commodity prices on their revenues and balance of payments. For example, China's SWF purchased shares in the U.S. financial firms Morgan Stanley and the Blackstone Group in 2007, and Dubai's SWF bought up shares of several Asian companies such as Sony. However, many SWFs lack transparency, and it is difficult to get reliable data 'on the size of the funds and their goals and strategies. The SWF of a democratic society such as Norway is more transparent because it has an obligation to its ultimate "shareholders," the public. However, most emerging countries are less democratic, and there is little pressure for transparency. With emerging countries growing faster than DCs and investing increasing amounts of their surpluses in the West, concerns have increased about the power and investment strategies of SWFs. For example, China's SWF has invested in major U.S. financial firms. Most countries do not have major objections to foreign *private* investment, but they are more sensitive to foreign *state* investment. The SWF issue, along with the shift of manufacturing and financial jobs away from the West, could produce rising trade tensions and protectionism. However, SWFs suffered major losses as a result of the 2008 global financial crisis, and the crisis has also caused some countries such as Russia and Qatar to use more of their SWFs for dealing with domestic economic problems. In view of their large losses, countries with SWFs are also more likely to invest more conservatively in the future.[67]

Even if SWFs prove to be less important than some analysts predicted, Asian and Middle Eastern reserve assets are likely to cause some major changes in the role of the U.S. dollar and in the IMF decision-making structure. In 2007 President Putin as leader of newly-rich Russia called for a "new architecture of international economic relations" and supported a rival candidate for IMF managing director against the EU's choice of Dominique Strauss-Kahn of France.[68] Although Strauss-Kahn was chosen for a five-year term, the IMF adopted selection procedures in 2007 which indicated that "any Executive Director may submit a nomination regardless of nationality, for the [managing director] position."[69] Under pressure from the emerging countries, the April 2009 G20 meeting to deal with the global financial crisis agreed to complete a new balance of power in the IMF by 2011, in which heads of IOs would be selected by merit and not by nationality. Thus, it is unlikely that the EU will continue to select the IMF managing director by tacit agreement.

Considering IPE Theory and Practice

In the 1940s the Bretton Woods negotiators opted for a monetary regime based on interventionist or embedded liberalism, in which states pegged their exchange rates to gold and the U.S. dollar, the IMF provided short-term loans for balance-of-payments problems, and states controlled capital flows to maintain exchange-rate stability.

However, growing U.S. balance-of-payments deficits, combined with pressures for a return to orthodox liberalism, contributed to a shift from pegged to floating exchange rates in 1973 and to a gradual freeing of capital controls. Liberal theorists point out that, with the globalization of capital flows, countries had to choose between independent monetary policies and a system of pegged exchange rates because they could not have both—the so-called "Unholy Trinity." In a bid to preserve their independence in monetary policy, the major countries shifted from pegged to floating exchange rates. In the orthodox liberal view, the shift to floating currencies and the freeing of capital flows are positive developments enabling markets to function more freely, with little interference from the state. Historical materialists by contrast see the increased capital mobility as a negative development because the fear of capital outflows can force governments to adopt policies that adversely affect the poorest and weakest in society. If governments do not adopt capital-friendly policies, MNCs and international banks can shift their funds to more welcoming locations. Thus, governments often lower their tax rates on corporate income, even if this means sacrificing social programs.[70] Increased capital mobility, according to historical materialists, also adversely affects the working class because countries with weak labor unions draw investment away from countries with stronger unions.[71] Realists often argue that the globalization of monetary and financial relations is greatly exaggerated, and they present evidence that there was more openness to capital flows before World War I than there is today.[72] To the extent that global financial flows have increased, this has occurred with the permission and sometimes encouragement of the most powerful states, and these states continue to dictate the terms for such transactions. Whereas realists are correct that powerful states supported financial globalization, liberals correctly point out that this globalization "has had unintended consequences for those who promoted it."[73] Thus, it may no longer be possible for states to regain control over the global market forces they unleashed. Attempts to restore national controls on capital flows or to restore a system of pegged exchange rates would be like putting the genie back in the bottle.

Some countries wishing to insulate themselves from global monetary instabilities are seeking regional alternatives, and the most important regional alternative is the decision of 16 EU countries to replace their currencies with the euro. Ideational as well as material factors have played a role in monetary union, because a neoliberal policy consensus among EC leaders in the late 1970s induced them

(continued)

(continued)

to give up autonomous monetary policies to achieve exchange-rate stability. As this chapter discusses, the euro has emerged as an important alternative reserve currency to the U.S. dollar. A currency's effectiveness as a medium of exchange, a unit of account, and a store of value depends on ideational as well as material factors, because individuals must be confident that the currency can be used in financial transactions without significantly losing its value. However, growing U.S. current account deficits and foreign debt have resulted in a marked depreciation of the U.S. dollar in recent years. With financial globalization, the future of the dollar depends not only on the United States and its traditional European allies, but also on the actions of a number of emerging countries with large U.S. dollar reserves such as China, Russia, and a number of OPEC countries.

This chapter has shown that the United States as the key currency country has been able to adopt policies not open to other states—such as "benign neglect" of its growing current account deficits and foreign debt. However, monetary and financial globalization is posing more limits on the policy choices of all countries today, including the United States. For example, in 2005 and 2006 the U.S. Congress sidetracked two efforts by emerging states to use their SWFs to gain control of U.S. assets: a bid by a Chinese state oil company for Unocal, the twelfth largest U.S. oil company; and a bid by Dubai to purchase a controlling stock interest in a number of U.S. ports. Congress took these actions because of concerns about the national security implications. However, the U.S. deficit and debt problems, and the credit problems posed by the 2008 financial crisis demonstrate that the United States may be less able to choose from whom, and on what terms, it receives external finance. Both the global monetary regime and the U.S. dollar as the key currency face an uncertain future.

Questions

1. What options does a country have in dealing with a balance-of-payments deficit, and what are the preferred options of the three main theoretical perspectives?
2. When did the United States first have a balance-of-payments deficit, and when did it first have a balance-of-trade deficit? Why was the Bretton Woods monetary regime unsustainable in the long term, and what role did the "Triffin Dilemma" play in the breakdown of the regime?
3. How much influence have DCs and LDCs had in the IMF decision-making structure? Do you think this is likely to change in the future?
4. What have the IMF's functions been in the global monetary regime? How did the shift from pegged to floating exchange rates affect the role of the IMF vis-à-vis the G5 and G7? Do you think that the role of the G20 is likely to increase?

5. What are the characteristics of the current global monetary regime, and in what ways has it contributed to instability? Does the "Unholy Trinity" limit the changes that IMF members could make in the current monetary regime?
6. Why was the EMU formed, and how successful has it been?
7. To what extent does the euro pose—or is likely to pose—a challenge to the U.S. dollar as the key currency? What are SDRs, are they likely to become more important, and could they pose a challenge to the U.S. dollar?
8. Do you think the U.S. deficit and debt problems pose an economic and geopolitical threat to the country? Is external financing through sovereign wealth funds and other sources a good solution for U.S. debt problems?

Further Reading

Useful historical overviews of international monetary and financial relations include Barry Eichengreen, *Globalizing Capital: A History of the International Monetary System* (Princeton, NJ: Princeton University Press, 1996); Eric Helleiner, *States and the Reemergence of Global Finance: From Bretton Woods to the 1990s* (Ithaca, NY: Cornell University Press, 1994); Harold James, *International Monetary Cooperation Since Bretton Woods* (New York: Oxford University Press, 1996); and Randall D. Germain, *The International Organization of Credit: States and Global Finance in the World-Economy* (New York: Cambridge University Press) 1997.

Two important books by Benjamin J. Cohen on monetary sovereignty and governance and the competition among currencies are *The Geography of Money* (Ithaca, NY: Cornell University Press, 1998) and *The Future of Money* (Princeton, NJ: Princeton University Press, 2004). A critique that emphasizes the disorder in global monetary and financial relations by another leading writer in the field is Susan Strange, *Mad Money: When Markets Outgrow Government* (Manchester: Manchester University Press, 1998). Studies on the governance of global finance include Tony Porter, *Globalization and Finance* (Malden, MA: Polity Press, 2005); and Michele Fratianni, Paolo Savona, and John J. Kirton, eds., *Governing Global Finance: New Challenges, G7 and IMF Contributions* (Burlington, VT: Ashgate, 2002).

Studies focusing on domestic politics and international finance include C. Randall Henning, *Currencies and Politics in the United State, Germany, and Japan* (Washington, D.C.: Institute for International Economics, 1994); and J. Lawrence Broz and Jeffry A. Frieden, "The Political Economy of International Monetary Relations," in *Annual Review of Political Science 2001* (Norwood, NJ: Ablex, 2001), pp. 317–343. On the relation between capital mobility, policy coordination, and domestic autonomy, see Michael C. Webb, *The Political Economy of Policy Coordination: International Adjustment Since 1945* (Ithaca, NY: Cornell University Press, 1995).

A book taking a constructivist approach to European monetary cooperation is Kathleen R. McNamara, *The Currency of Ideas: Monetary Politics in the European Union* (Ithaca, NY: Cornell University Press, 1998). Also recommended is Amy Verdun, ed., *The Euro: European Integration Theory and Economic and Monetary Union* (Lanham, MD: Rowman & Littlefield, 2002). On the U.S. dollar and the euro, see "At Home Abroad? The Dollar's Destiny as a World Currency," a special issue of *Review of International Political Economy* 15, no. 3 (August 2008); and C. Fred Bergsten and John Williamson, eds., *Dollar Overvaluation and the World Economy* (Washington, D.C.: Institute for International Economics, 2003).

Notes

1. Barry Eichengreen, *Globalizing Capital: A History of the International Monetary System* (Princeton, NJ: Princeton University Press, 1996), p. 3; Susan Strange, "Protectionism and World Politics," *International Organization* 39, no. 2 (Spring 1985), p. 257.
2. Benjamin J. Cohen, *The Future of Money* (Princeton, NJ: Princeton University Press, 2004), pp. 11–12.
3. Benjamin J. Cohen, *The Geography of Money* (Ithaca, NY: Cornell University Press, 1998), p. 3.
4. Susan Strange, *Casino Capitalism* (Oxford, UK: Basil Blackwell, 1986), p. 29; Benjamin J. Cohen, "Life at the Top: International Currencies in the Twenty-First Century," *Essays in International Economics,* no. 221 (Princeton, NJ: Princeton University, International Economics Section, December 2000), pp. 2–4.
5. Mordechai E. Kreinin, *International Economics: A Policy Approach,* 6th ed. (San Diego, CA: Harcourt Brace Jovanovich, 1991), pp. 123–124; Richard N. Cooper, *The Economics of Interdependence: Economic Policy in the Atlantic Community* (New York: McGraw-Hill, 1968), pp. 13–23, chs. 7–9.
6. United Nations, *World Economic Situation and Prospects 2008* (New York: United Nations, 2008), p. vii; Ernest H. Preeg, *The Trade Deficit, the Dollar, and the U.S. National Interest* (Indianapolis, IN: Hudson Institute, 2000), p. 1.
7. Joseph Quinlan and Marc Chandler, "The U.S. Trade Deficit: A Dangerous Obsession," *Foreign Affairs,* May/June 2001, p. 97.
8. William R. Cline, "The Impact of U.S. External Adjustment on Japan," and Kathryn M. Dominguez, "Foreign Exchange Intervention: Did It Work in the 1990s?" in C. Fred Bergsten and John Williamson, eds., *Dollar Overvaluation and the World Economy* (Washington, D.C.: Institute for International Economics, 2003), pp. 179, 218; Quinlan and Chandler, "The U.S. Trade Deficit," pp. 87–88; John Quiggin, "The Unsustainability of U.S. Trade Deficits," *The Economists' Voice* 1, no. 3 (2004), pp. 2–3.
9. Eric Helleiner, "Political Determinants of International Currencies: What Future for the U.S. Dollar?" *Review of International Political Economy* 15, no. 3 (August 2008), p. 370.
10. Ernest H. Preeg, "Exchange Rate Manipulation to Gain an Unfair Competitive Advantage," in C. Fred Bergsten and John Williamson, eds., *Dollar Overvaluation and the World Economy* (Washington, D.C.: Institute for International Economics, 2003), p. 270.
11. Cohen, *The Geography of Money,* p. 11; Kathleen R. McNamara, "A Rivalry in the Making? The Euro and International Monetary Power," *Review of International Political Economy* 15, no. 3 (August 2008), pp. 446–448.
12. See Kenneth W. Dam, *The Rules of the Game: Reform and Evolution in the International Monetary System* (Chicago, IL: University of Chicago Press, 1982), p. 6; Benjamin J. Cohen, *Organizing the World's Money: The Political Economy of International Monetary Relations* (New York: Basic Books, 1977), ch. 3.

13. Barry Eichengreen, *Golden Fetters: The Gold Standard and the Great Depression, 1919–1939* (New York: Oxford University Press, 1992), ch. 2, pp. 204–207.
14. Paul R. Krugman and Maurice Obstfeld, *International Economics: Theory and Policy,* 3rd ed. (New York: HarperCollins, 1994), p. 507.
15. Peter A. Gourevitch, "Squaring the Circle: The Domestic Sources of International Cooperation," *International Organization* 50, no. 2 (Spring 1996), pp. 349–373; Beth A. Simmons, *Who Adjusts? Domestic Sources of Foreign Economic Policy During the Interwar Years* (Princeton, NJ: Princeton University Press, 1994).
16. McNamara, "A Rivalry in the Making?" p. 441.
17. John G. Ruggie, "International Regimes, Transactions, and Change: Embedded Liberalism in the Postwar Economic Order," in Stephen D. Krasner, ed., *International Regimes* (Ithaca, NY: Cornell University Press, 1983), pp. 209–214; Dam, *The Rules of the Game,* p. 38.
18. Eric Helleiner, "From Bretton Woods to Global Finance: A World Turned Upside Down," in Richard Stubbs and Geoffrey R. D. Underhill, eds., *Political Economy and the Changing Global Order* (Toronto, ON: McClelland & Stewart, 1994), p. 164; J. Keith Horsefield, ed., *The International Monetary Fund 1945–1965: Twenty Years of International Monetary Cooperation, Vol. 3: Documents* (Washington, D.C.: IMF, 1969), p. 67.
19. *International Monetary Fund Annual Report—2007* (Washington, DC: IMF, 2007), pp. 60–61.
20. IMF website: http://www.imf.org/external/np/sec/memdir/eds.htm
21. John H. Jackson, *The World Trading System: Law and Policy of International Economic Relations,* 2nd ed. (Cambridge, MA: MIT Press, 1997), p. 69.
22. Marc Williams, *International Economic Organizations and the Third World* (New York: Harvester Wheatsheaf, 1994), pp. 67–68; Stephen D. Krasner, *Structural Conflict: The Third World Against Global Liberalism* (Berkeley, CA: University of California Press, 1985), pp. 138–140; Tyrone Ferguson, *The Third World and Decision Making in the International Monetary Fund: The Quest for Full and Effective Participation* (London: Pinter, 1988), pp. 90–91.
23. *International Monetary Fund Annual Report—2007* (Washington, DC: IMF, 2007), CD-ROM.
24. A group of economists identified the liquidity, confidence, and adjustment problems. See Fritz Machlup and Burton G. Malkiel, eds., *International Monetary Arrangements: The Problem of Choice: Report on the Deliberations of an International Study Group of 32 Economists* (Princeton, NJ: Princeton University International Finance Section, 1964), p. 24.
25. Charles P. Kindleberger, "Dominance and Leadership in the International Economy: Exploitation, Public Goods and Free Rides," *International Studies Quarterly* 25, no. 2 (June 1981), p. 248.
26. Robert Triffin, *Gold and the Dollar Crisis: The Future of Convertibility,* rev. ed. (New Haven, CT: Yale University Press, 1961).
27. Harold James, *International Monetary Cooperation Since Bretton Woods* (Washington, D.C. and New York: IMF and Oxford University Press, 1996), pp. 179–181.
28. Eric Helleiner, *States and the Reemergence of Global Finance: From Bretton Woods to the 1990s* (Ithaca, NY: Cornell University Press, 1994), pp. 81–100; Michael C. Webb, *The Political Economy of Policy Coordination: International Adjustment Since 1945* (Ithaca, NY: Cornell University Press, 1995), p. 16.

29. Susan Strange, *Sterling and British Policy: A Political Study of an International Currency in Decline* (London: Oxford University Press, 1971), p. 209.

30. Strange, *Sterling and British Policy,* pp. 5, 17.

31. C. Fred Bergsten and C. Randall Henning, *Global Economic Leadership and the Group of Seven* (Washington, D.C.: Institute for International Economic, 1996), pp. 22–23.

32. Hazel J. Johnson, *Global Financial Institutions and Markets* (Oxford, UK: Blackwell, 2000), p. 411; Age F. P. Bakker, *International Financial Institutions* (New York: Longman, 1996), ch. 6.

33. C. Randall Henning, "The Group of Twenty-Four: Two Decades of Monetary and Financial Cooperation Among Developing Countries," in UNCTAD, *International Monetary and Financial Issues for the 1990s—Vol. 1* (New York: United Nations, 1992), pp. 137–154.

34. Krugman and Obstfeld, *International Economics,* pp. 311–313; Marin Bronfenbrenner and Yasukichi Yasuba, "Economic Welfare," in Kozo Yamamura and Yasukichi Yasuba, eds., *The Political Economy of Japan: The Domestic Transformation,* vol. 1 (Stanford, CA: Stanford University Press, 1987), p. 100.

35. John Williamson and C. Randall Henning, "Managing the Monetary System," in Peter B. Kenen, ed., *Managing the World Economy: Fifty Years After Bretton Woods* (Washington, D.C.: Institute for International Economics, 1994), p. 89.

36. Cohen, "Life at the Top," pp. 5–6; Annys Shin and Thomas Heath, "Global Fiscal Crisis Brings Renewed Role for IMF," *Washington Post,* April 4, 2009, p. A10.

37. On President Nixon's August 1971 decision and the Smithsonian agreements, see Robert Solomon, *The International Monetary System, 1945–1981,* 2nd ed. (New York: Harper & Row, 1982), pp. 176–234.

38. On the failed negotiations, see John Williamson, *The Failure of World Monetary Reform, 1971–74* (Sunbury-on-Thames: Nelson, 1977).

39. Cohen, *Organizing the World's Money,* p. 115. The IMF permitted Canada to float its currency from 1950 to 1962 because of its "special relationship" with the United States. See Arthur F. W. Plumptre, *Three Decades of Decision: Canada and the World Monetary System, 1944–75* (Toronto, ON: McClelland and Stewart, 1977).

40. *Articles of Agreement of the International Monetary Fund,* adopted July 22, 1944 (Washington, D.C.: IMF, 1993), Article 4, section 1–iii.

41. See J. Lawrence Broz and Jeffry A. Frieden, "The Political Economy of International Monetary Relations," *Annual Review of Political Science* 4 (Norwood, NJ: Ablex, 2001), pp. 317–343.

42. Yusuke Kashiwagi, "Future of the International Monetary System and the Role of the IMF," in Bretton Woods Commission, *Bretton Woods: Looking to the Future, Background Papers* (Washington, D.C.: Bretton Woods Committee, 1994), p. C–1.

43. Milton Friedman, "The Case for Flexible Exchange Rates," *Essays in Positive Economics* (Chicago, IL: University of Chicago Press, 1953), p. 203.

44. The Unholy Trinity is derived from a model developed by Robert Mundell, and Benjamin Cohen coined the term *Unholy Trinity.* See Robert Mundell, "Capital Mobility and Stabilization Policy under Fixed and Flexible Exchange Rates," *Canadian Journal of Economics and Political Science* 29, no. 4 (November 1963), pp. 475–485; Benjamin J. Cohen, "The Triad and the Unholy Trinity: Lessons for the Pacific Region," in Richard Higgott, Richard Leaver, and John Ravenhill, eds., *Pacific Economic Relations in the 1990s: Cooperation or Conflict* (Boulder, CO: Rienner, 1993), pp. 133–158.

45. Helleiner, *States and the Reemergence of Global Finance,* pp. 115–116; John Williamson, *The Exchange Rate System,* rev. ed. (Washington, D.C.: Institute for International Economics, 1985), pp. 9–10, 39.
46. Michael Devereux and Thomas A. Wilson, "International Co-ordination of Macroeconomic Policies: A Review," *Canadian Public Policy* 15 (February 1989), pp. S23–S24.
47. Williamson and Henning, "Managing the Monetary System," p. 100. On the difficulties in bringing about policy coordination, see Webb, *The Political Economy of Policy Coordination.*
48. The Nobel laureate economist Robert Mundell has been a strong (and controversial) defender of fixed exchange rates and the gold standard as an anchor for price stability.
49. Barry Eichengreen, *International Monetary Arrangements for the 21st Century* (Washington, D.C.: Brookings Institution, 1994), p. 5.
50. Barry Eichengreen, "Prerequisites for International Monetary Stability," in Bretton Woods Commission, *Bretton Woods: Looking to the Future, Background Papers* (Washington, D.C.: Bretton Woods Committee, 1994), p. C–50.
51. Kathleen R. McNamara, *The Currency of Ideas: Monetary Politics in the European Union* (Ithaca, NY: Cornell University Press, 1998), p. 10.
52. Malcolm Levitt and Christopher Lord, *The Political Economy of Monetary Union* (London: Macmillan, 2000), pp. 29–42; Paul De Grauwe, *The Economics of Monetary Union,* 2nd rev. ed. (New York: Oxford University Press, 1994), pp. 98–102.
53. McNamara, *The Currency of Ideas,* pp. 166–170; Sylvester C. W. Eijffinger and Jakob de Haan, *European Monetary and Fiscal Policy* (Oxford, UK: Oxford University Press, 2000), pp. 4–7.
54. On the costs and benefits of a monetary union, see Eijffinger and de Haan, *European Monetary and Fiscal Policy,* pp. 16–26.
55. Robert A. Mundell, "A Theory of Optimum Currency Areas," *American Economic Review* 51, no. 4 (September 1961), pp. 657–665; C. Randall Henning and Pier C. Padoan, *Transatlantic Perspectives on the Euro* (Washington, D.C.: Brookings Institution, 2000), pp. 6–12.
56. McNamara, "A Rivalry in the Making?" p. 440; Don Lee, "China Positioning its Currency for a Run at World Supremacy," *Los Angeles Times,* April 3, 2009.
57. Helleiner, "Political Determinants of International Currencies," p. 356; McNamara, "A Rivalry in the Making?" p. 444; Cohen, *The Geography of Money,* pp. 156–161.
58. This section relies extensively on Helleiner, "Political Determinants of International Currencies," pp. 357–360.
59. "What Next?" *Economist,* September 20, 2008, p. 19.
60. Edward Cody, "No Joint European Strategy on Banks," *Washington Post,* October 5, 2008.
61. Jonathan Kirshner, "Dollar Primacy and American Power: What's at Stake?" *Review of International Political Economy* 15, no. 3 (August 2008), pp. 419–420; McNamara, "A Rivalry in the Making?" p. 439; Cohen, *The Geography of Money,* pp. 12–13.
62. Helleiner, "Political Determinants of International Currencies," pp. 360–371; McNamara, "A Rivalry in the Making?" pp. 450–451.
63. Charles R. Morris, *The Trillion Dollar Meltdown* (New York: Public Affairs, 2008), pp. 88–90.

64. Robert J. Samuelson, "China's Dollar Deception," *Washington Post,* April 6, 2009, p. A15.

65. Morris, *The Trillion Dollar Meltdown,* pp. 92–99; Paul Bowles and Baotai Wang, "The Rocky Road Ahead: China, the US and the Future of the Dollar," *Review of International Political Economy* 15, no. 3 (August 2008), pp. 335–353; Juliet Johnson, "Forbidden Fruit: Russia's Uneasy Relationship with the US Dollar," *Review of International Political Economy* 15, no. 3 (August 2008), pp. 379–398; Saori N. Katada, "From a Supporter to a Challenger? Japan's Currency Leadership in Dollar-Dominated East Asia," *Review of International Political Economy* 15, no. 3 (August 2008), pp. 399–417.

66. Lee Hudson Teslik, "Sovereign Weath Funds," Council on Foreign Relations Backgrounder, January 18, 2008, http://www.cfr.org/publication/15251

67. Stephen Jen, "Sovereign Wealth Funds: What They Are and What's Happening," *World Economics* 8, no. 4 (October–December 2007), pp. 1–7; IMF Survey online, "IMF Intensifies Work on Sovereign Wealth Funds," March 4, 2008, http://www. imf.org/external/ubs/ft/survey/so/2008/POL03408A.htm; "Sovereign Wealth Funds: From Torrent to Trickle," *The Economist,* January 24, 2009, pp. 78–79.

68. "Crisis Comes to the IMF," *Washington Post,* October 19, 2007, p. A20.

69. *International Monetary Fund Annual Report—2007* (Washington, DC: IMF, 2007), p. 61.

70. The standard rate of corporate income tax in OECD countries fell from 43 percent in 1986 to 33 percent in 1995, while the average tax rate for workers increased. See "Survey: World Economy," *The Economist,* September 20, 1997, p. 33.

71. Stephen Gill and David Law, "Global Hegemony and the Structural Power of Capital," in Stephen Gill, ed., *Gramsci, Historical Materialism and International Relations* (New York: Cambridge University Press, 1993), p. 108.

72. Paul Hirst and Grahame Thompson, *Globalization in Question: The International Economy and the Possibilities of Governance* (Cambridge, UK: Polity Press, 1996), p. 27.

73. Ethan B. Kapstein, *Governing the Global Economy: International Finance and the State* (Cambridge, MA: Harvard University Press, 1994), p. 6. See also Helleiner, *States and the Reemergence of Global Finance.*

CHAPTER 7

Global Trade Relations

Trade relations have aroused strong positive and negative emotions from the earliest times. Whereas proposals linking free trade with world peace can be traced back to the seventeenth century, trade conflicts have been common since the Middle Ages. The conflicts are often limited in scope, but sometimes they escalate and become "trade wars."[1] Societal groups today continue to express strong views about trade. For example, internationalist firms that depend on exports, imports, and multinational production pressure for global and regional trade liberalization agreements; but domestically oriented firms threatened by import competition may oppose these agreements.[2] Civil society groups also often oppose efforts to expand the authority of the WTO and regional trade agreements (RTAs) such as NAFTA. The controversy surrounding trade stems from the fact that interest groups and the broader public view their welfare as being more affected by trade policy than by monetary, investment, or financial policy. Thus, business, labor, agricultural, consumer, environmental, and cultural groups try to influence government trade policies.

The forces of globalization have had a major effect on trade relations. From 1950 to 1973, world economic output (or GDP) grew at an average annual rate of 5.1 percent while trade increased on average by 8.2 percent. From 1974 to 2007, the figures were 2.9 percent for GDP growth and 5.0 percent for trade growth.[3] Although foreign investment has increased even faster than trade, the two are closely related. MNCs have considerable influence on trade issues, and *intrafirm trade* within MNCs accounts for about one-third of total world trade. Thus, a former WTO director general has stated that "businesses now trade to invest and invest to trade—to the point where both activities are increasingly part of a single strategy to deliver products across borders."[4] This chapter discusses the postwar global trade regime and the changing role of DCs, LDCs, and transition economies in the regime. A major theme relates to the competing pressures for trade liberalization and protectionism.

TRADE THEORY

Liberal theorists view trade as a positive-sum game that provides mutual benefits to states, whereas realists see trade in more competitive terms, with each state striving to increase its exports and decrease its imports. Historical materialists view trade as a form of unequal exchange in which advanced capitalist states in the core export manufactured and high-technology goods and import raw materials and less processed goods from the periphery. Although liberal trade theory has evolved, the ideas of Adam Smith and David Ricardo are still central to the arguments for freer trade. Smith argued that the gains from free trade result from *absolute advantage,* in which all states specialize in the goods they produce best and trade with each other. For example, if France produces wine more cheaply than England and England produces cloth more cheaply than France, both states can benefit from specialization and trade. Ricardo's theory of *comparative advantage* is less intuitive and more powerful because it indicates that trade is beneficial even in the absence of absolute advantage. In his *Principles of Political Economy and Taxation,* Ricardo argued that England and Portugal could gain from trading wine for cloth even if Portugal produced *both* goods more cheaply than England.[5] Central to Ricardo's argument is the concept of **opportunity cost,** which refers to the cost of producing less of one product in order to produce more of another product. If Portugal produces wine more efficiently than cloth, it has a lower opportunity cost if it produces more wine and trades it for cloth. If England produces cloth more efficiently than wine, it has a lower opportunity cost if it produces more cloth and trades it for wine. This is the case even if Portugal produces both wine and cloth more efficiently than England.

Tables 7.1 and 7.2 use arbitrary figures to demonstrate Ricardo's theory of comparative advantage. Table 7.1 shows the bottles of wine and yards of cloth that England and Portugal produce in one day using the same number of labor hours for wine and cloth production. Ricardo assumed that labor productivity was the only factor to consider in determining comparative advantage. As Table 7.1 shows, Portugal produces 16 bottles of wine and 8 yards of cloth, while England produces 3 bottles of wine and 6 yards of cloth. Portugal

TABLE 7.1	**Production of Wine and Cloth in One Day Without Trade**	
	Bottles of Wine	**Yards of Cloth**
England	3	6
Portugal	16	8
Total	19	14

TABLE 7.2 Production of Wine and Cloth in One day With Specialization and Trade

	Bottles of Wine	Yards of Cloth
England	1 (–2)	10 (+4)
Portugal	20 (+4)	6 (–2)
Total	21	16

produces more of both products than England; but Portugal is *relatively* more efficient in wine (16) than cloth (8) production, and England is *relatively* more efficient in cloth (6) than wine (3) production. Table 7.2 shows how many bottles of wine and yards of cloth England and Portugal can produce if each specializes in producing the product with the lowest opportunity cost (wine for Portugal and cloth for England), and engages in trade. As Table 7.2 shows, if England produces two less bottles of wine, it can produce four more yards of cloth; if Portugal produces two less yards of cloth, it can produce four more bottles of wine. By specializing and engaging in trade, England and Portugal can produce two more bottles of wine (21) and two more yards of cloth (16) using the same number of labor hours. Thus, countries can benefit from specializing according to comparative advantage and engaging in trade.

Although Ricardo's theory provided a powerful liberal argument for free trade, he assumed that comparative advantage results only from differences in labor productivity. In the 1920s the Swedish liberal economists Eli Heckscher and Bertil Ohlin developed a theory to show that comparative advantage also results from other factors of production such as capital and natural resources. According to the **Heckscher–Ohlin theory,** a state has a comparative advantage in producing goods that involve intensive use of its most abundant factor of production. For example, labor is a less expensive input in a state with an abundant supply of labor and this gives labor-abundant states a cost advantage in producing labor-intensive goods; capital-rich DCs have a comparative advantage in producing capital-intensive goods, and states rich in arable land have a comparative advantage in agriculture.

Building on the Heckscher–Ohlin theory, two U.S. economists (Wolfgang Stolper and Paul Samuelson) developed a theory to explain why some domestic groups are protectionist and others are free-trade oriented. According to the **Stolper–Samuelson theory,** trade liberalization benefits abundantly endowed factors of production and hurts poorly endowed factors. For example, if state A has an abundance of labor, workers in A will favor freer trade because A will be competitive in producing labor-intensive goods for export. Although workers' wages in A will initially be low because of the abundant labor supply, as A shifts its production toward more labor-intensive goods the demand and wages for labor will increase. If state A has a shortage of arable land, farmers in A will favor agricultural protectionism vis-à-vis states where arable land is more abundant.

Thus, owners of abundant factors of production in a state support freer trade and owners of scarce factors oppose it. The Stolper–Samuelson theory helps explain why U.S. and Canadian blue-collar labor opposed NAFTA (Mexico has many more less skilled workers) and why French wheat farmers oppose agricultural trade liberalization in the WTO (the United States, Canada, Australia, and Argentina have more land for wheat production).[6]

Although the theory of comparative advantage and its offshoots provide powerful arguments for interindustry trade, they do not explain the rapid increase of *intraindustry* and *intrafirm* trade. For example, the Heckscher–Ohlin assumption that trade is most beneficial between states with different factor endowments does not explain the rapid rise of intraindustry trade among DCs with similar factor endowments. Whereas traditional trade theory assumes that goods are homogeneous, in intraindustry trade differentiated products are traded within the same industry group. For example, Germany and Japan produce auto-mobiles and trade with each other because consumers value product differentia-tion and have product preferences. Liberals theorize that intraindustry trade provides benefits such as economies of scale, the satisfaction of varied con-sumer tastes, and the production of sophisticated manufactured products.[7] The Stolper–Samuelson theory is also less applicable to intraindustry trade. It is harder to find owners of scarce factors opposing intraindustry trade because DCs with similar factor endowments often trade products that use similar factor intensities. Thus, trade negotiations have been most successful for manufactured products in which DCs engage in intraindustry trade. Trade barriers are more persistent for agricultural products traded between DCs and LDCs with different factor endowments. Much present-day trade is also *intrafirm* trade between MNC par-ent companies and their subsidiaries. Theories of the firm best explain why trade occurs between MNC affiliates (see Chapter 9).

The liberal theories to explain interindustry, intraindustry, and intrafirm trade are prescriptive as well as descriptive, because they assume that all states benefit from specialization and trade (even if they do not benefit equally). However, realists and historical materialists do not accept this assumption. Although realists generally accept trade liberalization as a part of the capitalist system, they assert that free trade is not beneficial if it jeopardizes a state's national security. Dependence on foreign states for imports of strategic goods or basic foodstuffs can become a national security threat, especially if the imports come from unfriendly or non-allied states. The national security con-cern is evident in practice as well as theory. For example, Article 21 of the GATT provides an exception to all GATT obligations for certain national secu-rity reasons such as the regulation of traffic in arms; and U.S. law permits the president to limit imports of products for national security purposes.[8] Realists (and some historical materialists) also argue that free trade may prevent LDCs from promoting industrialization. Because LDCs are late industrializers, they must limit DC industrial imports until their *infant industries* become more competitive internationally. Looking at the *relative gains* of trade based on comparative advantage, realists also believe that Ricardo's advice to Portugal did not serve its long-range interests. Portugal may have gained some short-term advantages from specializing in wine, but it became less competitive than England in the long term because cloth production was a high-growth, high-technology industry at the time. In the realist view, Portugal should have *created* a comparative advantage for itself in cloth through government assistance to the cloth industry, even if it had a "natural" comparative advantage in wine.[9] **Strategic trade theory** focuses on a state's creation of comparative advantage, referred to as *competitive advantage,* through industrial targeting. Although efforts to gain competitive advantage in trade are not new, the growing emphasis on high-technology industries provides "a fertile breeding ground for interventionist policies."[10] Strategic trade theorists argue that interventionist policies can improve a state's economic position, and they point to Japan and the East Asian NIEs as states that mobilize a limited amount of resources to create competitive advantage. However, liberals see the risks of strategic trade policy as outweighing the benefits. When a state tries to increase its competitive advantage at the expense of others according to *individual* rationality, other states retaliate and everyone is worse off as a result (see discussion of prisoners' dilemma in Chapter 4).[11] Despite the liberal warnings, the temptation to engage in strategic trade policy remains strong in an age of global competition.

Historical materialists have stronger objections to free trade than realists. As discussed in Chapter 5, Raúl Prebisch argued that LDCs in the periphery suffer from declining terms of trade with DCs in the core because of their dependence on agricultural and raw material exports. He advised LDCs to adopt import substitution policies, imposing trade barriers and producing manufactures domestically to satisfy demand previously met by imports. Dependency theorists go further, arguing that DCs in the core either underdevelop LDCs or prevent them from achieving genuine, autonomous development; thus, LDCs should decrease or sever trade ties with the core. Arghiri Emmanuel also critiques free trade in his theory of unequal exchange. He argues that wages are higher in the core than the periphery because labor is not internationally mobile and DCs specialize in higher-value-added goods. The higher wages in DCs create a larger local market for goods, encourage mechanized production, and elevate the prices of DC goods. Thus, North–South trade is an unequal exchange with LDCs paying more for their imports from high-wage DCs than they receive for their exports; that is, there is a transfer of surplus from peripheral to core countries. Although Emmanuel provides some insights on the effects of a lack of labor mobility on international prices, he fails to consider the effects of different productivity levels between core and peripheral labor or to explain why capital does not flow to low-wage areas.[12]

Despite the wide range of theoretical perspectives on trade, most DC economists and international economic organizations have adhered to liberal trade theories.

GLOBAL TRADE RELATIONS BEFORE WORLD WAR II

States have shifted between trade liberalization and protectionism throughout history. Thus, mercantilist trade restrictions gave way to freer trade when Britain lowered its import duties in 1815 and opened its borders to food imports by repealing its Corn Laws in 1846. In 1860 France and Britain signed the Cobden–Chevalier Treaty, which resulted in a network of treaties lowering tariff barriers throughout Europe. However, Britain's declining hegemony, France's defeat in the Franco-Prussian War, and the 1873–1896 depression lowered the enthusiasm for free trade; and the outbreak of World War I completely disrupted the network of European trade treaties.[13] After World War I, efforts to remove trade restrictions were unsuccessful as states reacted to harsh economic conditions by increasing their **tariffs.** Tariffs rose not only in European states recovering from the war but also in the United States, which had become a net creditor nation and the world's largest industrial power. Thus, the U.S. Congress increased import duties with the 1922 Fordney–McCumber Tariff, and after the stock market crash Congress passed the 1930 Smoot–Hawley Tariff Act, which increased average U.S. ad valorem rates on dutiable imports to 52.8 percent, the highest U.S. tariffs in the twentieth century.[14]

The question arises as to why the United States as the top economic power did not stem the rise of protectionism. Some hegemonic stability theorists believe that the United States was able but unwilling to become a hegemon until its position became more firmly established after World War II.[15] Others point to Britain's continuing influence and question whether the United States was able to establish an open economic system during the interwar period.[16] Some theorists explain U.S. protectionism in terms of domestic rather than global politics. Although the United States was the largest industrial power during the interwar period, U.S. industries feared a renewal of European competition, and U.S. agricultural groups were dismayed by a decrease in agricultural prices. The U.S. Constitution gives Congress the sole power to regulate commerce and impose tariffs, and members of Congress were highly susceptible to protectionist pressures from these groups because (unlike the president) they do not have national constituencies. Protectionist producers and workers were also politically organized and concentrated in specific industries, whereas consumer groups benefiting from freer trade were more diffuse and had little influence. Party politics also played a role in the Smoot–Hawley tariff because the Republicans who were more protectionist than the Democrats had a Senate majority at the time.[17]

The Smoot–Hawley tariff had disastrous results as other states retaliated with their own import restrictions; between 1929 and 1933, world trade declined from $35 billion to $12 billion, and U.S. exports fell from $488 million to $120 million.[18] To reverse this damage, the U.S. Congress passed the 1934 Reciprocal Trade Agreements Act (RTAA), which transferred tariff-setting authority to the president who could lower tariffs by up to 50 percent in trade negotiations with other countries. The RTAA was highly significant because for the first time it linked U.S. tariff levels to international negotiations. Instead of having Congress set tariffs on a unilateral, statutory basis, the president was given authority to establish "bargaining tariffs" through bilateral agreements.[19] From 1934 to 1945, the United States concluded bilateral trade agreements with 27 countries and lowered its tariffs by an average of 44 percent; but tariffs were so high in the early 1930s that these agreements mainly corrected earlier excesses. The Roosevelt administration's decision to lower tariffs only in exchange for similar concessions by other states (hence the name *Reciprocal Trade Agreements Act*) also limited the scope of the agreements, and many states refused to lower their tariffs. Thus, despite the RTAA agreements, protectionism continued to affect trade relations throughout the interwar period.[20]

GATT AND THE POSTWAR GLOBAL TRADE REGIME

To ensure that the effects of protectionism during the interwar period were not repeated, the United States and Britain began bilateral discussions in 1943 to lay the groundwork for postwar trade negotiations. In 1945 a U.S. State Department document formed the basis for multilateral negotiations that resulted in the Havana Charter, or charter for an international trade organization (ITO) in 1948. In addition to trade policy, the charter dealt with economic development, full employment, international investment, international commodity arrangements, restrictive business practices, and the functions of an ITO.[21] However, the Havana Charter negotiations were protracted, and 23 states began negotiations to lower tariffs before the charter was approved and ratified; in October 1947 these states signed the final act of the GATT. It was assumed that GATT would simply be folded into the ITO when it was formed, but the Havana Charter did not satisfy either U.S. protectionists or U.S. free traders. Whereas protectionists feared that ITO rules would permit low-cost imports and threaten U.S. ability to form its own trade policy, free traders believed that the charter's numerous escape clauses and exceptions would hinder trade liberalization. Thus, the U.S. Congress never ratified the Havana Charter, and GATT became an informal global trade organization by default.[22] Unlike the proposed ITO, GATT did not require ratification by the U.S. Congress because it was simply a trade agreement. Thus, countries signing GATT were *contracting parties* rather than members. (We use the term *GATT members* for the sake of brevity.) Whereas the ITO would have been a UN-specialized agency like the IMF and World Bank, GATT never gained specialized agency status; it was mainly a written code of behavior on international trade that had more limited legal obligations than the planned ITO.

Despite its informal origins, GATT gradually developed characteristics of an IO; for example, it had committees, working parties, and a small secretariat, and it made decisions that were binding on members.[23] Some analysts even argue that GATT became more effective than the IMF and World Bank because of its informality. Whereas "the strength of a formal arrangement such as the IMF is its rigidity; that of an informal, ideas-based institution such as the GATT is its adaptability."[24] GATT's strengths included its negotiations to reduce tariffs and nontariff barriers, and its steadily growing membership. However, GATT's informality was also a source of weakness in several respects. First, some trade sectors such as agriculture and textiles were largely exempt from GATT regulations. Agriculture was treated as an exception to GATT restrictions on import quotas and export subsidies, and the DCs imposed textile import quotas that contravened the spirit and rules of GATT. Second, GATT was more like a club than a formal organization, and its members could easily waive some regulations. For example, states circumvented the GATT ban on import quotas through **voluntary export restraints** (VERs), or pressure on others to "voluntarily" decrease their exports. Third, GATT's dispute settlement procedures often did not resolve trade conflicts. Fourth, growing U.S. balance-of-trade deficits caused the United States to charge that others were unfair traders. Only by enhancing GATT's authority could the United States be deterred from taking unilateral measures to ensure fair trade. Fifth, as globalization increased, many DCs wanted GATT activities to extend beyond trade in goods to trade in services, intellectual property, and investment.

By the mid-1980s, a number of trade experts therefore warned that GATT had to upgrade its regulations and dispute settlement procedures; extend its discipline to agriculture and textiles; and begin to focus on newer areas such as services and intellectual property.[25] Although the Uruguay Round negotiations began with plans to simply upgrade GATT, the decision was made during the round to replace it with the WTO. (GATT continues to exist as the largest trade agreement under the WTO.)

PRINCIPLES OF THE GLOBAL TRADE REGIME

The GATT-based trade regime marked a critical turning point because it relied on *multilateral* negotiations and the interventionist-liberal compromise. The major trading nations agreed to liberalize trade, but they also supported safeguards and exemptions to protect countries' social policies and balance of payments.[26] Despite its informal origins, GATT provided the basis for a highly developed trade regime in terms of principles, norms, rules, and decision-making procedures. The following sections discuss the trade regime principles.

Trade Liberalization

GATT promoted the *trade liberalization* principle, first by lowering *tariffs* (taxes on products passing through customs borders) and then by regulating **nontariff barriers (NTBs).** Although GATT permitted tariffs, it lowered them through rounds of multilateral trade negotiations (MTNs) As Table 7.3 shows, GATT held eight MTN rounds. Members negotiated item-by-item tariff reductions in the first five rounds, but these negotiations became too time consuming as GATT membership increased, and the sixth round (the Kennedy Round) therefore shifted to linear or across-the-board tariff reductions (there was an average 35 percent tariff reduction on all industrial goods).[27] GATT

TABLE 7.3 The Rounds of GATT and WTO Negotiations

Name	Years	Subjects Covered	Countries Participating
Geneva	1947	Tariffs	23
Annecy	1949	Tariffs	13
Torquay	1951	Tariffs	38
Geneva	1956	Tariffs	26
Dillon	1960–1961	Tariffs	26
Kennedy	1964–1967	Tariffs and antidumping measures	62
Tokyo	1973–1979	Tariffs, nontariff measures, plurilateral agreements	102
Uruguay	1986–1993	Tariffs, nontariff measures, rules, services, intellectual property, dispute settlement, trade-related investment, textiles, agriculture, creation of World Trade Organization	123
Doha (WTO)	1999–	Agriculture, services, tariffs, nontariff measures, intellectual property, dispute settlement	149

Source: WTO Focus Newsletter, no. 30, May 1998, p. 2, and other WTO information. By permission of the World Trade Organization.

prefers tariffs to import quotas because tariffs at reasonable levels permit efficient producers to increase their exports, whereas quotas set an arbitrary limit on imports. Thus, GATT Article 11 called for the "general elimination of quantitative restrictions" or import quotas. However, GATT permitted a number of exceptions to Article 11, especially for agriculture; GATT members could impose import quotas on agricultural products when they were needed to enforce domestic supply management measures. U.S. insistence on this exception stemmed from the influence of domestic agricultural groups. Viewing trade negotiations as a two-level game (see Chapter 4), DCs have often insisted that agriculture be an exception to trade liberalization agreements.[28]

As the first five GATT rounds gradually lowered tariffs, members turned to NTBs as an alternative means of protecting their producers. NTBs include a large array of measures that restrict imports, assist domestic production, and promote exports, and they are often more restrictive, ill defined, and inequitable than tariffs. NTB negotiations are also more problematic than tariff negotiations because it is difficult to measure their impact, and states tend to view NTBs as adjuncts to their domestic policies (and therefore not subject to international regulation).[29] The Kennedy Round had limited NTB negotiations, but the Tokyo Round NTB negotiations were far more extensive and resulted in NTB codes dealing with technical barriers to trade, government procurement, subsidies and countervailing duties, customs valuation, and import licensing. The NTB codes were *plurilateral* rather than multilateral agreements that bound only the signatories because most LDCs were not willing to participate. The Uruguay Round widened the agenda to include not only trade in goods but also services trade, intellectual property, and trade-related investment measures; and it began applying global trade rules to sensitive areas such as agriculture and textiles. The effects of globalization on trade were evident in the broader scope of the Uruguay Round and the increased number of participants. Table 7.3 shows that the number of participants rose from 23 in the first GATT round (Geneva) to 123 in the eighth round (Uruguay). Table 7.3 also shows that after the Dillon Round, the rounds became more lengthy and complicated. The Uruguay Round involved seven years of difficult negotiations, but it resulted in the establishment of the WTO.

IPE scholars ask *why* trade liberalization continued, despite the decline in U.S. trade hegemony. In 1953 the United States accounted for almost 30 percent of all manufactured exports, but by the late 1970s it accounted for only 13 percent. West Germany had moved into first place with 16 percent, and Japan was close behind the United States with 11 percent. Although NTBs increased during the late 1970s, trade liberalization was *not* as seriously threatened as it had been in the 1920s when Britain's trade hegemony was declining. Indeed, the Tokyo Round (1973–1979) reduced industrial tariffs to low levels and developed the NTB codes.[30] Some scholars believe that the difference between the 1920s and 1970s demonstrates the role the GATT-centered global trade regime played in upholding the trade liberalization principle even as U.S. trade hegemony declined. Others point to domestic politics to explain the differences in the 1920s and 1970s. As discussed, the U.S. Congress has the power to regulate commerce, and in the 1920s it increased tariffs in response to interest group pressures. By the 1970s, however, Congress was transferring its tariff-making authority to the president, who was more insulated from interest group pressures (this transfer began with the 1934 RTAA). Another important domestic factor stems from the forces of globalization. In the 1920s most industries had few international ties and favored protectionism to limit competition. By the 1970s, "increased economic integration of advanced industrial states into the world economy . . . altered the domestic politics of trade."[31] More firms in the 1970s depended on multinational production, exports, imports, and intrafirm trade, and they resisted protectionism despite the decline in the U.S. trade position.

Nondiscrimination

The first GATT director general referred to the *nondiscrimination* principle, as "the fundamental cornerstone" of the global trade organization.[32] The nondiscrimination principle has both external (most-favored-nation treatment) and internal (national treatment) dimensions. The unconditional

most-favored-nation (MFN) principle in Article 1 of the General Agreement stipulates that every trade advantage or privilege a GATT member gives to any state must be extended, immediately and unconditionally, to all other GATT members. The equal treatment of imports from different origins helps ensure that imports come from the lowest cost foreign suppliers. Although MFN treatment extends back to fifteenth-century Europe, the GATT-centered MFN principle is different because it is based on *multilateral* commitments and negotiations.[33] GATT permitted several exceptions to MFN treatment, the most important being the acceptance of RTAs. Members of RTAs such as the EU and NAFTA abolish tariff barriers among themselves and thus give each other more favorable treatment than they give to other GATT/WTO members. As Chapter 8 discusses, the proliferation of RTAs poses a major threat to the MFN principle.

Whereas MFN treatment prevents discrimination at a country's border, **national treatment** counters internal discrimination. The national treatment provisions in GATT Article 3 require members to treat foreign products—once they have been imported—at least as favorably as domestic products with regard to internal taxes and regulations. This provision is designed to prevent states from using domestic measures to limit foreign competition as their tariffs and other external trade barriers decline. The national treatment provision has often been tested in dispute settlement cases; for example, in 1988 a GATT panel found that the pricing and listing practices of Canadian provincial liquor boards discriminated against foreign wines and were inconsistent with Canada's national treatment obligations.[34]

Reciprocity

The **reciprocity** principle stipulates that a state benefiting from another state's trade concessions should provide roughly equal benefits in return. By ensuring that there is a balanced exchange of concessions, reciprocity limits free riding under the unconditional MFN principle. Liberal economists argue that a state gains by liberalizing its trade unilaterally as well as through negotiation. However, protectionist producers are often well organized and able to mobilize domestic opposition to unilateral trade liberalization. In *reciprocal* trade agreements, by contrast, governments can rely on support from export-oriented domestic industries that expect to gain from the agreement. The reciprocity principle also applies to new WTO members, who obtain the market access benefits resulting from earlier negotiating rounds and are expected to provide reciprocal benefits in return. In practice, the reciprocity principle ensures that tariff negotiations reflect the interests of the major trading powers. WTO members with the largest domestic markets and highest trade volumes have the most leverage because they have the greatest reciprocal concessions to offer. The United States and the EU have been the leading powers in the GATT/WTO because of the reciprocity principle, but China is rapidly gaining influence. Thus, the Kennedy Round was not completed until the United States and the

TABLE 7.4 Leading World Merchandise Traders (Excluding Intra-Eu Trade), 2007 (US$ Billions)

Rank	Exporters	Value	Rank	Importers	Value
1	EU (27)	1,695	1	United States	2,017
2	China	1,218	2	EU (27)	1,949
3	United States	1,163	3	China	956
4	Japan	713	4	Japan	621
5	Canada	418	5	Canada	390

Source: Derived from World Trade Organization Secretariat, *World Trade Report—2008* (Geneva: WTO, 2008), Appendix Table 1, p. 11.

EU reached a compromise on key issues, and in the Tokyo Round they initiated agreements before other states became involved in reaching a broader consensus. LDCs had more influence during the Uruguay Round, but even in this case U.S. agreements with the EU and Japan on agriculture were critical to ultimate success. Other than China, the most important traders in terms of reciprocal concessions to offer are DCs. Thus, Table 7.4 shows that the EU-27 was the largest merchandise exporter and the United States was the largest merchandise importer in 2007 (the figures exclude intra-EU trade). However, China ranked second as a merchandise exporter, above the United States. The large U.S. market for imports gives it considerable influence, but its lower ranking as an exporter has resulted in its balance of trade deficits. Although China ranked above the United States and Japan as a merchandise exporter in 2007, it ranked behind both countries as a commercial services exporter.[35] Even among the LDCs there is a pecking order, with more important states such as China, India, Brazil, and Mexico taking priority. Although the reciprocity principle realistically gives priority to those with the most concessions to offer, it limits the ability of smaller states to exert influence or protect their interests.[36]

Reciprocity may be either specific or diffuse. *Specific reciprocity* refers to a simultaneous exchange of strictly equivalent benefits or obligations. *Diffuse reciprocity* does not demand an immediate response to an action; it imposes a more general obligation on the recipient for repayment in the future.[37] Diffuse reciprocity can coexist with *unconditional* MFN treatment; for example, the United States and EU offered more MFN concessions than some other states to reach an agreement in the Kennedy Round, and they did not expect repayment for these concessions until the Tokyo Round. Specific (or aggressive) reciprocity is more like *conditional* MFN treatment, in which state A grants concessions to state B *only if* B promptly offers equivalent concessions to A. Realists concerned with relative gains prefer specific reciprocity, whereas liberals concerned with absolute gains accept diffuse reciprocity. Specific reciprocity is less conducive to cooperation because it is difficult to determine whether concessions are exactly equivalent; if states always demanded specific reciprocity it would be impossible to conduct multilateral negotiations. However, the United States responded to its growing balance-of-trade deficits with claims that specific reciprocity is sometimes necessary to prevent others from acting as free riders. In the 1980s, for example, the United States claimed that Japan had hidden trade barriers and demanded "results-oriented" agreements that would give it a specified share of the Japanese market in return for access to the U.S. market. However, Japan argued that its trade surpluses resulted from its competitive advantage and not from unfair trading practices.[38]

Safeguards

When GATT/WTO members negotiate reciprocal tariff reductions, the lower tariffs are "bound," meaning that they cannot unilaterally raise them at a later date (there are some exceptions for LDCs). However, the GATT/WTO includes **safeguards** that permit members to temporarily raise a duty above the maximum tariff binding to limit imports that may harm domestic producers. Safeguards were part of the interventionist liberal compromise after World War II, because they allowed states to sign international agreements without jeopardizing domestic stability. Indeed, states would not agree to trade commitments if rigid adherence was necessary in all circumstances. Safeguards also permit a state to temporarily increase protectionism without withdrawing entirely from a trade agreement.[39] We discuss here three prominent safeguard measures: the safeguards agreement, **antidumping duties (ADDs),** and **countervailing duties (CVDs).**

Article 19 of the 1947 GATT included a safeguards clause which was replaced by the WTO Agreement on Safeguards in 1995. The 1947 safeguards clause permitted a state to raise import barriers in response to "import surges" that caused, or were likely to cause, *serious* injury to a domestic industry. However, the state had to apply the safeguard action to *all* GATT members in accordance with MFN treatment, and affected states could request compensation and retaliate if compensation was not considered adequate. In view of these stringent requirements, states turned to remedies targeted at specific exporters such as VERs and antidumping actions. The WTO safeguards agreement makes it easier to take safeguard actions, but countries are still reluctant to invoke the agreement because the WTO has retained two major GATT requirements: first, the state must claim there is *serious* injury to its domestic producers, which is difficult to prove in WTO dispute settlement cases; second, the import barriers must be imposed on *all* WTO members, and this can lead to serious disputes and threats of retaliation. For example, the United States invoked the safeguards provision for certain steel products in 2001, but the EU threatened retaliation and requested that a WTO dispute settlement panel be formed. The panel ruled against the U.S. safeguards and the United States withdrew them.

Because it is so difficult to invoke the safeguards agreement, states have been more inclined to use ADDs and CVDs. Whereas safeguard provisions are designed to deal with import surges even when other states engage in fair trade,

ADDs and CVDs are imposed to counter allegedly unfair trade practices. **Dumping** occurs when a firm sells products in an export market at a lower price than it charges in the home market or below the cost of production. The WTO permits a state to impose ADDs if foreign goods are dumped and the dumping causes or threatens material injury to its domestic producers. Whereas ADDs are oriented toward private corporate practices, CVDs are a response to subsidies provided by foreign governments. The WTO permits a state to impose CVDs if another state provides trade-distorting subsidies that produce or threaten material injury to domestic producers. Unlike safeguard actions, a state imposes ADDs and CVDs in response to *material* injury (which is easier to prove than *serious* injury), and targets specific states charged with engaging in unfair trade. A state may impose ADDs and CVDs as a legitimate response to unfair foreign trade practices, but it may also use them to justify protectionist trade policies. Thus, ADD and CVD actions are highly controversial, and WTO dispute settlement panels often examine complaints about such actions. For example, the United States and Canada have been involved in many disputes over Canadian softwood lumber exports. The United States has imposed CVDs, claiming that the fees Canadian provincial governments charge private firms to harvest trees on public lands constitute a subsidy to Canadian lumber; but Canada disagrees and GATT/WTO dispute settlement panels have offered judgments on this issue on several occasions.[40] In sum, safeguards are an essential principle of the GATT/WTO, but they are controversial because a state's measures to protect its domestic producers are often viewed by others as an unjustifiable trade barrier.[41]

Development

The failed Havana Charter contained provisions on economic development that did not become part of the 1947 General Agreement, and GATT had little involvement with development issues during the 1940s and 1950s. As more LDCs joined GATT, a "development principle" began to emerge and several new GATT provisions gave LDCs special treatment that diverged from the nondiscrimination and reciprocity principles. However, development remained a subsidiary trade regime principle because the major trading nations agreed to only limited concessions to promote LDC interests.[42] LDCs were more involved in the GATT Uruguay Round than in previous rounds, and the WTO Doha Round, which began in 2001, was called the Development Round; but North–South divisions were a major factor leading to suspension of the Doha Round (see discussion later in this chapter).

FORMATION OF THE WTO

The trade regime principles were all in flux by the early 1980s, and many GATT achievements were in jeopardy. Although the GATT rounds had lowered tariffs, the liberalization principle was threatened because states were using NTBs that were not even covered by GATT rules. Furthermore, liberalization did not extend to textiles and agriculture, and GATT dispute settlement procedures were inadequate. RTAs that did not adhere to MFN treatment were also posing a threat to the nondiscrimination principle. As for the reciprocity and safeguard principles, the United States and EC were demanding specific rather than diffuse reciprocity from some trading partners, and countries were resorting to unilateral protectionist actions. LDCs had little involvement with GATT, and most of them refused to sign the Tokyo Round NTB codes. In view of GATT's shortcomings, the United States pressured for a new round of trade negotiations and GATT members agreed to launch the Uruguay Round in 1986. Although the negotiators at first focused on extending GATT's jurisdiction, in April 1990 Canada proposed that a formal WTO should replace GATT, and the EC supported this idea.[43] However, U.S. negotiators believed that plans to create a WTO would detract from the Uruguay Round's substantive negotiations and that Congress would object to a loss of U.S. sovereignty as it had with the ITO in the 1940s. In the end the United States altered its view, and the WTO replaced GATT in 1995 as the main global trade organization.[44]

In contrast to GATT, the WTO is a formal, legally constituted organization like the IMF and World Bank. GATT has reverted to its original status as an agreement for trade in goods, which the WTO oversees along with several new treaties negotiated during the Uruguay Round: the **General Agreement on Trade in Services (GATS),** the **Agreement on Trade-Related Intellectual Property Rights (TRIPs),** and the **Agreement on Trade-Related Investment Measures (TRIMs).** GATT is the most important of these agreements because trade in goods is the largest aspect of international trade. The DCs supported broadening the scope of the WTO to include the GATS, TRIPs, and TRIMs for several reasons. First, the United States wanted to redress its merchandise trade deficits by extending rules to areas such as services trade and intellectual property where it was more competitive. Second, the DCs wanted to regulate services because services trade had a 19 percent annual growth rate from 1970 to 1980 while merchandise trade grew by only 5.4 percent. Third, DCs would benefit most from the new rules because they were the major exporters of services, intellectual property and investment. Most LDCs did not want the GATS, TRIPs, and TRIMs, and the DCs agreed to tradeoffs so they could be created (see discussion later in the chapter).[45]

The *Ministerial Conference,* which is the WTO's highest authority, includes all members and can make decisions on all matters under the multilateral trade agreements (see Figure 7.1). Whereas GATT members normally met at the ministerial level only to launch or conclude new rounds of trade negotiations, the WTO Ministerial Conference meets at least every two years to increase the WTO's profile and strengthen guidance at the higher political levels. Between the Ministerial Conference meetings, the *General Council* manages WTO affairs and provides guidance to the *Councils for Trade in Goods, Trade-Related Aspects of Intellectual Property Rights,* and *Trade in Services* (see Figure 7.1). The General Council also convenes as the *Trade Policy Review Body* and the *Dispute Settlement Body* when necessary. The Trade Policy Review Body conducts regular reviews of WTO members' trade policies to increase transparency and promote trust that agreements are being enforced.

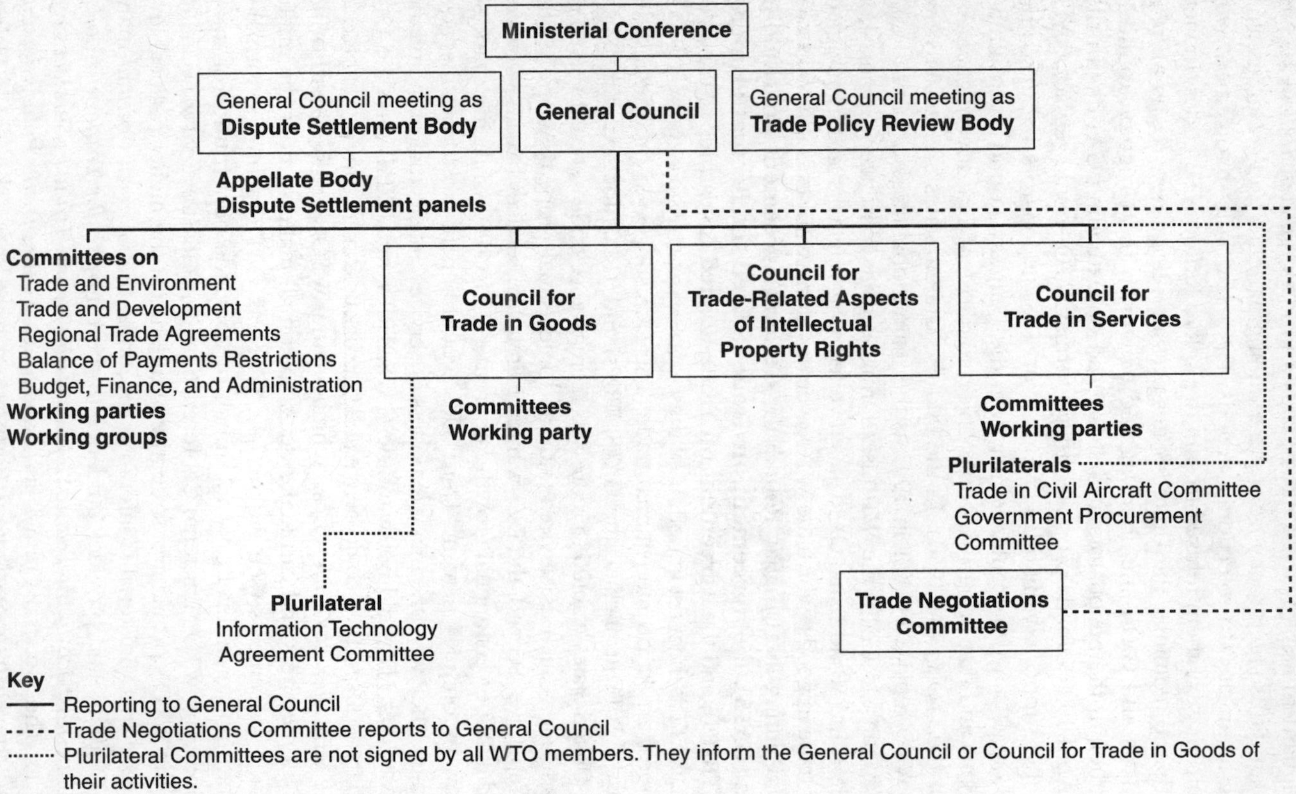

Figure 7.1 Structure of the World Trade Organization

Source: Adapted from WTO Organization Chart, Jan 15, 2007. Retrieved from WTO Web site: http://www.wto.org/english/thewto_e/whatis_e/tif_e/org2_e.htm.

Diagram content:

Ministerial Conference

General Council meeting as Dispute Settlement Body

General Council

General Council meeting as Trade Policy Review Body

Appellate Body
Dispute Settlement panels

Council for Trade in Goods

Council for Trade-Related Aspects of Intellectual Property Rights

Council for Trade in Services

Committees on
Trade and Environment
Trade and Development
Regional Trade Agreements
Balance of Payments Restrictions
Budget, Finance, and Administration
Working parties
Working groups

Committees
Working party

Committees
Working parties

Plurilaterals
Trade in Civil Aircraft Committee
Government Procurement Committee

Plurilateral
Information Technology Agreement Committee

Trade Negotiations Committee

Key
— Reporting to General Council
- - - Trade Negotiations Committee reports to General Council
······ Plurilateral Committees are not signed by all WTO members. They inform the General Council or Council for Trade in Goods of their activities.

The Dispute Settlement Body forms panels to investigate complaints and adjudicate trade disputes. A WTO member may invoke the dispute settlement procedures if another member has broken a WTO regulation or reneged on previous agreements. Dispute settlement procedures are more binding and timely under the WTO than they were under GATT. Whereas a single member (including a party to a dispute) could block the adoption of a GATT panel report, a consensus of member states is required to block a WTO panel report, a *highly* unlikely occurrence. A WTO member may appeal a dispute settlement decision to the *Appellate Body,* but if it agrees with the panel report the member must implement the recommendations or provide compensation. If a member refuses to implement a report or provide compensation, the Dispute Settlement Body can authorize the complainant to retaliate.[46]

The director-general is the GATT/WTO's chief administrative officer. Unlike the tacit agreement that the World Bank president would be American and the IMF managing director European, there was no agreement for GATT. For years the selection of GATT directors-general generated little controversy, but the issue became contentious when the WTO was formed for several reasons: the higher profile of the WTO; the tendency to appoint politicians for the WTO post unlike the officials appointed for GATT; greater U.S. assertiveness in response to its declining trade hegemony; rivalry among Europe, the United States, and Japan; and the increased assertiveness of LDCs. As Table 7.5 shows, all GATT directors-general from 1948 to 1995 were European. The United States eventually agreed to the selection of the former Italian foreign trade minister Renato Ruggiero as the first WTO director-general, but it insisted that Ruggiero serve only one four-year term and that the next WTO head be non-European. When it came time to select the next WTO director-general, most DCs other than Japan supported Mike Moore of New Zealand, and most LDCs supported Supachai Panitchpakdi of Thailand. After a protracted dispute,

TABLE 7.5 Directors-General of GATT[a] and WTO

	Years in Office	Nationality-Country
Eric Wyndham-White	1948–1968	Britain
Olivier Long	1968–1980	Switzerland
Arthur Dunkel	1980–1993	Switzerland
Peter Sutherland	1993–1995	Ireland
Renato Ruggiero	1995–1999	Italy
Mike Moore	1999–2002	New Zealand
Supachai Panitchpakdi	2002–2005	Thailand
Pascal Lamy	2005–	France

[a] The name of GATT's chief administrative officer was changed from *secretary general* to *director general* in 1965.

WTO members finally agreed that Moore and Supachai should each serve three-year terms. The current WTO director-general is Pascal Lamy from France. In contrast to the IMF and World Bank, the WTO (like GATT) is a one-nation, one-vote institution. Depending on the issue, WTO votes require a simple majority, a special majority of two-thirds or three-quarters, or unanimity. The one-nation, one-vote system gives LDCs less influence than one might expect because most decisions are made by consensus, and trade negotiations do not depend on vote-taking.[47]

THE WTO AND THE GLOBAL TRADE REGIME

The WTO was designed to be more effective and authoritative than GATT, and in some respects it has succeeded: It is a formal IO comparable in status with the IMF and World Bank; members use its binding dispute settlement system far more often than they used GATT dispute settlement; it is a more genuinely global trade organization with 153 members as of April 2009; it oversees GATS and TRIPs as well as GATT; it has made greater efforts to integrate LDCs and transition economies into the global trade regime, and it has dialogued with a number of NGOs and civil society groups. However, the WTO also has serious shortcomings, and many problems that plagued GATT continue to affect the WTO. After the Uruguay Round, liberal economists argued that a new WTO round was essential for several reasons. First, liberals believe that "*the bicycle must keep moving*. Forward momentum is essential to avoid backsliding into protectionism and mercantilism."[48] Second, GATT members agreed to conduct further negotiations on services and agriculture after the Uruguay Round was concluded, but negotiations on specific issues rarely succeed because trade-offs across issues are needed to reach agreements. Thus, a comprehensive WTO round was necessary. Third, U.S.-EU conflicts over bananas, beef hormones, and the U.S. Foreign Sales Corporation program showed the need to improve WTO dispute settlement procedures. Fourth, negotiations were needed to ensure that the growing number of RTAs were compatible with the WTO. Finally, both the South and the North had a "wish list" for changes in the global trade regime.[49]

The initial plans were to launch a new round at the Third WTO ministerial meeting in Seattle, Washington, in November 1999; but the growing scope of WTO activities elicited a strong negative reaction from civil society groups. Prenegotiations were also inadequate, and the Seattle ministerial failed mainly because the United States, EU, and LDCs had widely divergent views on critical issues. However, the September 11, 2001, terrorist attacks on the World Trade Center had a unifying effect on the United States and the EU, and under their leadership members agreed to launch the Doha Round at the fourth WTO ministerial in Doha, Qatar, in November 2001. In view of the South's disillusionment with the Uruguay Round (see the following discussion), the North agreed to the idea that the Doha Round would be "the development round." Although launching the Doha Round was a major achievement, "this first step . . . [was] in fact the smallest one."[50] WTO members papered over serious differences in launching the round, and LDCs were skeptical of assurances that this would be the "development round." The Doha Round was originally scheduled for completion in January 2005, but it was stalled by serious North–South differences, and by April 2009 there was still no Doha Round agreement. A major problem confronting the Doha Round is that the WTO membership has become so large and diverse that it is difficult to reach a consensus on contentious issues. Doha is the first WTO round of multilateral negotiations, and its failure to this point is raising serious questions about the legitimacy of the WTO. As Chapter 8 discusses, states often turn to RTAs when GATT/WTO negotiations are stalled, and the proliferation of RTAs could pose a threat to the global trade regime. Most issues at the Doha Round cannot be neatly categorized as North–South, North–North, or public–private because there are major differences *within* each of these groups. However, North–South differences pose the most serious obstacle to a Doha Round agreement. These differences can be best understood after providing some background on the South and global trade issues.

THE SOUTH AND GLOBAL TRADE ISSUES

DCs were the main participants in postwar MTNs, and LDCs were largely uninvolved. Although the Havana Charter gave some attention to LDC issues, most of these provisions were not incorporated into GATT. LDCs were also wary of participating in GATT because it did recognize their need for special and differential treatment (SDT). For many years the South therefore sought special access to DC markets and exemptions from trade regime principles and rules. In the 1980s, however, the South became more accepting of GATT's liberal economic orientation and more actively involved in the global trade regime. The following discussion identifies five stages of LDC participation in the regime:

1. *1940s to early 1960s.* LDCs had limited involvement in GATT.
2. *1960s to early 1970s.* LDCs increased their GATT membership and sought SDT.
3. *1970s to 1980.* North–South confrontation increased, and LDCs demanded a *New International Economic Order (NIEO)*.
4. *1980s to 1995.* LDCs were more willing to accept GATT's liberal economic principles.
5. *1995 to the present.* LDCs were disillusioned with the Uruguay Round and demand changes in the Doha Round.

1940s to Early 1960s: Limited LDC Involvement

LDCs were less involved in the global trade regime during the early postwar years because of their limited numbers (many were still colonies), their protectionist trade policies, and GATT's inattention to development issues. Raúl Prebisch, an Argentinian economist, argued that LDCs could not achieve high economic growth rates if they continued to depend on exports of primary products.[51] Thus, most LDCs in the 1950s adopted protectionist import substitution industrialization (ISI) policies in an effort to replace industrial imports with domestic production (see Chapter 10). With these inward-looking policies, most LDCs did not actively participate in GATT. GATT also devoted little attention to LDCs, and the only major provision dealing directly with the South was GATT Article 28, which gave LDCs some flexibility in imposing import quotas to protect their infant industries and balance of payments. Although the LDCs insisted that GATT should do more to give them SDT, they had little influence during this period.[52]

1960s to Early 1970s: Growing Pressures for Special Treatment

Two changes contributed to growing LDC pressures for special treatment: Some LDCs modified their ISI policies, and the South's bargaining power increased. By the 1960s, ISI policies resulted in serious problems, including decreased exports, dependence on intermediate imports for the production of industrial goods, and balance-of-payments deficits (see Chapter 10). Thus, LDCs became more outward-looking and demanded special treatment to promote their exports. LDCs were also better able to press their demands as their numbers increased with decolonization. In 1961 the UN General Assembly declared the 1960s to be the UN Development Decade, in 1963 the South established the G77, and in 1964 UNCTAD was formed. UNCTAD never posed a serious challenge to GATT as the main global trade organization, but it introduced a number of influential *ideas* directing attention to the role of LDCs in the global trade regime. For example, UNCTAD provided the first systematic analyses of tariff escalation, trade in services, and skilled migration flows; and an understanding reached in UNCTAD led to the introduction of a **generalized system of preferences (GSPs)** for LDCs (see discussion below). In 1965 (shortly after UNCTAD was formed) GATT members added a new Part IV to the General Agreement calling for special treatment for LDCs. Part IV was largely symbolic because it only *recommended* that DCs reduce their import barriers to LDCs, and the North actually raised its barriers to some LDC exports. For example, the North violated GATT Article 11's ban on import quotas and imposed "voluntary" restraints on the South's textile and clothing exports. A 1961 Short-Term Arrangement on Cotton Textiles was followed by several Long-Term Arrangements and Multi-Fiber Arrangements (MFAs).[53]

The South did gain a concrete concession in 1971 when DCs established GSPs for LDCs through a 10-year renewable waiver from the MFN clause.[54] The GSP lowers DC tariffs for certain LDC imports. Although some LDCs have benefited from these preferences, the North refused to accept a legal obligation to provide preferences or to bind itself to an international GSP plan. Instead, each DC established its own GSP, limited the amount of imports that could enter at lower duties, excluded sensitive products such as textiles, and reduced or eliminated its GSP for LDCs that were especially successful in increasing their exports. In view of the complexities of GSP schemes, more competitive LDCs such as the East Asian NIEs have benefited most, and the GSP has offered very few benefits to poorer LDCs. One study found that Hong Kong, South Korea, and Taiwan accounted for 44 percent of the total gains from GSP tariff reductions.[55]

1970s to 1980: Increased North–South Confrontation

OPEC's success in raising oil prices in 1973 encouraged the South to issue calls in the United Nations for an NIEO, in which LDCs would have sovereignty over their natural resources, more control over foreign investment, more development assistance, greater influence in the international economic organizations, and higher prices for their commodity exports. The North agreed to negotiate these demands because of its concerns about the price of oil, and the United Nations passed some NIEO-related resolutions.[56] However, most of these resolutions were never implemented, and the South's ability to influence the North declined sharply in the 1980s with the foreign debt crisis (see later discussion). Although the South was confronting the North in the United Nations, it participated in the 1973–1979 GATT Tokyo Round. One result of the Tokyo Round was the *enabling clause,* which "established for the first time in trade relations . . . a permanent legal basis for preferences" for LDCs.[57] The clause gave permanent legal authorization for the GSP and for preferential RTAs among LDCs. The North agreed to the enabling clause, but insisted on a "graduation" principle for states that demonstrated notable progress in development. More advanced LDCs (e.g., South Korea, Taiwan, and Brazil) whose exports threatened DC producers would have to give up special treatment and accept greater GATT discipline.[58] As discussed, most LDCs refused to participate in the Tokyo Round NTB codes for government procurement, subsidies, technical barriers to trade, import licensing, and ADDs; but the South would become far more involved in GATT in the 1980s.

1980s to 1995: More LDC Participation in GATT

LDCs initially opposed the idea of a GATT round in the 1980s because of global trade inequities and DC efforts to include services, intellectual property, and investment in the negotiations. However, their opposition softened when the North agreed to include issues of interest to them such as trade in textiles and agriculture. Unlike earlier periods, LDCs liberalized their trade policies during the 1980s and actively participated in the Uruguay Round. LDCs were also more willing to accept the reciprocity principle, and they agreed to treat the round as a **single undertaking:** Acceptance of the Uruguay Round accord meant acceptance of *all* its agreements. The single undertaking was a marked contrast to the Tokyo Round's NTB codes, in which most LDCs did not participate.[59] LDCs continued receiving SDT during the Uruguay Round, but in view of the single undertaking, they accepted "a dilution of special and differential treatment in exchange for better market access and strengthened rules."[60] LDCs also functioned less as a bloc in the Uruguay Round and joined several

North–South coalitions such as the Cairns Group of agricultural exporters that first met in Cairns, Australia, in 1986. The Cairns Group added a powerful new voice, ensuring that GATT—and the EC, United States, and Japan—would have to deal with agriculture. The founding members of the Cairns Group included eight LDCs, three DCs (Australia, Canada, and New Zealand), and one Eastern European country (Hungary). The Cairns Group continues to function and currently has 18 members.[61]

Liberals and historical materialists cite different reasons for the South's policy shift. According to liberals, LDCs began to embrace liberal economic policies for several reasons: GSP tariff preferences for the South were eroding because tariffs among DCs declined with each GATT round; the North viewed LDCs as free riders receiving special treatment and therefore marginalized them in trade negotiations; and LDCs recognized the failure of inward-looking ISI policies and began to emulate the successful East Asian export-led growth strategies (see Chapter 10).[62] Historical materialists by contrast argue that LDCs were *forced* to alter their policies. The IMF and World Bank provided structural adjustment loans to LDCs in response to the 1980s foreign debt crisis, on the condition that they decrease government spending, liberalize trade, and privatize their economies (see Chapter 11). The debtors had to liberalize their trade policies because DCs and private lenders would not extend loans to LDC debtors without the IMF's approval. Thus, one critic argues that "the current rush toward free trade follows on the heels of 10 years of structural adjustment, a logical 'next step' in the overhaul of the global economy."[63]

1995 to the Present: LDC Disillusionment with the Uruguay Round and Demands in the Doha Round

Theorists also differ regarding the Uruguay Round's effects on the South. Liberals concede that the North gained concessions from the South in intellectual property and services trade, and that DCs should do more to open their markets to LDC exports, but they argue that the Uruguay Round on balance benefited the South. LDCs gained advantages in textiles and agriculture; benefited from liberalizing their policies; and retained some SDT benefits such as flexibility in fulfilling their commitments, longer transition times to implement agreements, and technical assistance from the North.[64] Historical materialists and some interventionist liberals by contrast argue that the South gave up more than it received in the Uruguay Round. The inclusion of services trade and intellectual property was a loss for LDCs because they are less competitive in these areas; and the South's "gains" from the agreements for agriculture and textiles were limited.[65]

The outcome of the Uruguay Round in fact proved to be quite unbalanced, and the South received much less than it had expected. Although the Uruguay Round provided some "fairly significant benefits" to LDCs, they realized belatedly "that they had accepted fairly weak commitments in agriculture and textiles while making substantially stronger ones, especially in . . . intellectual property."[66] Many LDCs are highly dependent on agricultural exports and wanted significant cutbacks in the North's support for their farmers, but the Uruguay Round did little to reduce the level of agricultural subsidies and trade barriers.[67] LDC disillusionment with the Uruguay Round is evident in the Doha Round. Three areas where the South has demanded change in the Doha Round are agriculture, SDT, and technical assistance and capacity building. In agriculture, a **Group of 20** LDCs (the **G20**) led by Brazil, China, and India has called for an end to EU and U.S. agricultural export subsidies and for lower agricultural import barriers in Japan, Canada, and other DCs. (This G20 group of LDCs in trade should not be confused with the G20 group of DCs and LDCs in finance discussed in Chapters 2 and 6!) The G20 has more influence than previous LDC groupings, especially because China has now joined the WTO. The SDT issue is also contentious because LDCs found it difficult to implement their Uruguay Round obligations. The South therefore wants clarified and strengthened SDT provisions that are monitored and enforced. Regarding the third LDC demand, the North had promised technical assistance to help the South fulfill its Uruguay Round commitments, but the amount it provided was disappointing. Trade negotiations are more complicated with new issues such as services trade and intellectual property rights, and the South wants more technical and capacity building assistance from the North before it agrees to new commitments in the Doha Round. The North is also demanding changes in the Doha Round. It wants reduced LDC barriers to nonagricultural imports, and stronger agreements for services trade and intellectual property rights. Some DCs also want to extend WTO discipline to new areas such as government procurement, trade facilitation, investment, and competition policy.[68]

After seven years of sporadic negotiations, the Doha Round talks broke down in July 2008 without an agreement. Although several issues remained contentious, disagreements over agriculture were the main cause of the breakdown of the round. The Doha Round was based on the idea that DCs would give up their long-term agricultural protectionism to give more opportunities to LDC farmers, and that LDCs would reciprocate by lowering their import barriers on DC services and manufactured goods. However, the South considered the U.S. and EU offer of concessions on farm supports to be too limited. Furthermore, India and China insisted on the right to raise tariffs to protect their farmers from import surges, price declines, and other world market changes. The United States wanted the trigger for these safeguards set high because China is an important market for its agricultural exports; for example, China purchases about 40 percent of U.S. soybean exports. However, India and China insisted on lower trigger levels, and the talks broke down over this issue. Prospects for reopening the Doha Round talks in the near future are dim because of a new European Commission due in late 2009, rising opposition to farm concessions in Europe, and the rise in trade protectionism as a result of the 2008 global financial crisis.[69] At the end of this chapter, we discuss competing theoretical views of the reasons for the breakdown of the Doha Round.

THE TRANSITION ECONOMIES AND GLOBAL TRADE RELATIONS

Most centrally planned economies were not GATT members for many years. The General Agreement also devoted little attention to state trading and central planning because the Soviet Union did not even attend the Havana Charter negotiations, and it was assumed that GATT members would be free market economies. Indeed, GATT was committed to limiting government actions that interfered with market forces. As Table 7.6 shows, Czechoslovakia was a founding member and remained in GATT even after it became communist, but its membership was largely inactive. Other Eastern European states (Yugoslavia, Poland, Romania, and Hungary) joined GATT in the 1960s and 1970s. GATT admitted these CPEs under special provisions, because they excluded foreign products through administrative controls over prices and purchasing. In the late 1980s and 1990s, the requirements for membership became more rigorous, and nonmarket economies had to institute specific reforms as a condition for admission. The more stringent requirements resulted from concerns about the possible admission of China and the Soviet Union (later Russia), the revival of orthodox liberalism, and the creation of the more formal WTO. GATT's problems with its Eastern European members had only a limited

TABLE 7.6   Membership of Transition Economies in the GATT/WTO

1948	Czechoslovakia and China (founding members)
1950	Republic of China (Taiwan) withdraws from GATT
1966	Yugoslavia
1967	Poland
1971	Romania
1973	Hungary
1990	East Germany accedes to GATT due to German reunification
1993	Czech Republic, Slovak Republic
1994	Slovenia
1996	Bulgaria
1997	Mongolia
1998	Kyrgyz Republic
1999	Latvia, Estonia
2000	Albania, Croatia, Georgia
2001	Lithuania, Moldova, China
2002	Taiwan
2003	Armenia, Macedonia
2008	Ukraine

Source: http://www.org/english/thewto_e/whatis_e/tif_e/org6_e.htm

effect on the global trade regime; but Chinese and Russian membership could have significant economic and political consequences. The IMF and World Bank accepted China and Russia as members because they were loan recipients and had little influence in these weighted-voting institutions.[70] However, the major trading nations were concerned that these two states could shift the balance of power in the GATT/WTO.[71] The following sections examine GATT/WTO relations with Eastern Europe, China, and the FSU countries.

Eastern Europe and the GATT/WTO

Czechoslovakia was ousted from the IMF and the Bank shortly after it became a nonmarket economy, but it was able to remain an inactive member of GATT for many years because it was an informal IO. Table 7.6 shows that Yugoslavia, Poland, Romania, and Hungary joined GATT in the 1960s and 1970s, partly because of the GATT secretariat's goal of universal membership and the Western policy of *differentiation*. The differentiation strategy sought to contain the Soviet Union by rewarding Eastern European states that adopted more independent foreign or domestic policies. After its break with the Soviet bloc in 1948, Yugoslavia began to engage in economic decentralization and did not become a GATT member until 1966 when it had moved from protectionist policies toward the GATT model; this showed that a CPE that liberalized its policies could participate in GATT under conditions similar to those for a market economy. Unlike Yugoslavia, Poland and Romania applied to GATT when they were not yet moving toward market reform. Tariffs have little influence over the import decisions of CPEs, so they had to commit to increasing their imports in return for GATT membership. When Poland joined GATT in 1967, it agreed to increase its value of imports from GATT members by 7 percent per year, and in return it received limited MFN treatment. GATT agreed to classify Romania as an LDC, and it was therefore subject to less rigid requirements than Poland. Instead of making a specific commitment, Romania expressed a "firm intention" to increase its imports from GATT members by a prescribed amount; but this condition was virtually unenforceable. The conditions for Hungary's admission to GATT in 1973 were in between those for Yugoslavia on the one hand and Poland and Romania on the other. GATT permitted Hungary to provide tariff concessions rather than commitments to increase its imports, because it had instituted liberal economic reforms under its New Economic Mechanism. In contrast to other Eastern European states, Bulgaria's efforts to join GATT failed because it was a close Soviet ally during the Cold War, and its case became enmeshed with the issue of membership for China and Russia. It was not until 1996 that the WTO finally admitted Bulgaria.

Despite GATT's admission of Eastern European states, their acceptance was conditional. For example, the accession agreements for Poland, Romania, and Hungary permitted the EC to impose discriminatory quantitative restrictions on imports from these states; and their trade with the United States was subject to special restrictions under U.S. law. Thus, in some respects the

Eastern Europeans were second-class citizens in GATT. With the breakup of the Soviet bloc, the terms of participation for Eastern Europe were gradually normalized.[72]

China

China followed autarkic policies in 1966–1969 during the Cultural Revolution, but in the 1970s it occupied the "China seat" in the United Nations (which Taiwan had held) and expanded its commercial contacts with the West. In 1982 GATT gave China observer status, and in 1986 China indicated that it wanted to "rejoin" GATT as a full member. Compared with its rather easy takeover of the China seat in the IMF and World Bank, China's accession to the GATT/WTO was a protracted affair. The delay stemmed partly from China's ambivalence. As a member, China would have to submit to GATT rules and open its market, and it already received *de facto* MFN treatment from most states. Although the U.S. Congress held an annual vote on this issue, it had renewed China's MFN status every year. However, China decided that GATT membership would consolidate its liberalization measures and give it legal access to export markets and the GATT dispute settlement system. China had been a founding member of GATT in 1948, and it sought a resumption of membership rather than a new membership. In 1950 the Chiang Kai-shek government had sent a cable from Taiwan where it had fled withdrawing China from GATT membership, but China argued this had no legal effect because Chiang Kai-shek was no longer leading the Chinese government. However, China had not abided by GATT obligations for 35 years, and it eventually had to agree to detailed negotiations similar to those for new members.[73]

China was never admitted to GATT, and it could not join the WTO until December 2001. Several issues were central to China's accession negotiations. First was the requirement that China liberalize its economy. China had introduced a wide range of market reforms, but government intervention in the economy produced major trade distortions. The United States strongly criticized these distortions because its trade deficit with China increased from $17.8 billion in 1989 to $90.2 billion in 2001. Others also argued that China's trade policies were not based on comparative advantage, and the WTO refused to accord China the same terms as it gave to market economies. A second issue was China's status as an LDC, which would have major implications for its membership conditions. China wanted special treatment given to LDCs at similar levels of economic development, including protection for its infant industries, the GSPs, and longer transition times to implement WTO agreements. However, many WTO members argued that China should meet the same reciprocity conditions as DCs because of its size and status as a world exporter. The WTO refused to treat China as a "normal" LDC, but permitted it to phase-in reforms in some areas because it was a transition economy.[74] A third issue was China's past record in implementing agreements. In 1992, for example, the United States and China agreed to improve protection of intellectual property. Although China's policies improved to some extent, pirated intellectual property continued to be readily available in major Chinese cities.[75] Despite these contentious issues, China and Taiwan ("Chinese Taipei") became WTO members in December 2001 and January 2002, respectively.

In regard to the effects of accession on China, its automobile industry showed new signs of vitality as some of the world's top automakers moved to establish new plants there; for example, in 2002 Japan's Honda announced it would build a plant in China to produce cars specifically for export to Asian and European markets. One of the most important gains of accession is in clothing and textile exports. DC quotas on textiles and clothing were abolished in January 2005, although high tariffs remained and safeguards could be used vis-à-vis Chinese exports until 2008. In 2005 China's textiles and clothing exports to the United States and the EU increased by 43 and 44 percent, respectively. However, WTO accession also has some drawbacks for China, at least in the short term. For example, WTO membership is requiring industrial restructuring in inefficient industries with excess capacity such as aluminum, cement, light industry, petrochemicals, and steel. Although opening these sectors should generate employment in the longer term, during a transition period employment losses could be severe. In sum, accession to the WTO is having mixed effects on China, but liberals predict that the positive effects will be more important in the longer term (historical materialists disagree).[76]

The effect of China's membership on the world is important, because of the massive size and growth of the Chinese economy. As Table 7.4 shows, China became the world's second largest exporter and third largest importer in 2007. Furthermore, China's annual GDP growth has been in the 7–13 percent range for almost three decades. China's membership is also changing the balance of power in the WTO. The United States can no longer threaten China with a loss of MFN treatment, and China can use WTO dispute settlement to protect its commercial interests. China also has new respectability as a trading partner and ally on some issues in Asia, the EU, and other regions, despite ideological differences. For example, it has closer relations with the Association of Southeast Asian Nations (ASEAN), and the EU joined with China and other steel producers to challenge U.S. import levies on steel in the WTO. As discussed, China is one of the leaders in the G20, an important LDC bloc in the Doha Round.[77]

However, China's membership has also raised concerns among WTO members. Initially there was considerable enthusiasm over China's pace of liberalization, but some question how far China is willing to go in liberalizing its economy. In 2003, for example, the Deputy U.S. Trade Representative charged that some Chinese ministries "spend as much energy avoiding China's WTO obligations as living up to them . . . and intervention by Chinese government officials in the market is largely unchecked."[78] Although such criticisms may result partly from the dramatic growth of China's economy, WTO members have difficulty gaining access to the Chinese market. China applies trade barriers to many industries such as intricate registration and certification requirements for imported cosmetics, food, pharmaceuticals, and chemicals, which do not apply to local firms. Chinese exports have also been a source of concern to LDCs in some areas such as textiles and clothing. Whereas China's exports to the United States in this sector grew by 43 percent in 2005, U.S. imports from South Korea and Sub-Saharan Africa declined by 24 and 17 percent, respectively. China's exports to the EU grew by 44 percent in 2005, while EU imports from Sub-Saharan Africa, South Korea, Bangladesh, Indonesia, and Pakistan declined.[79]

Thus, there are mixed effects of China's membership for China and other economies in the WTO. Liberal economists would argue that China's membership is essential because it is a major actor in the global trade regime; without China, the WTO would not be a global trade organization. In contrast to China, Russia is still a nonmember of the WTO.

Russia

Russia is the only major economy that is not yet a WTO member. In the 1980s the Soviet Union reacted to its growing economic problems by seeking GATT observer status and quietly exploring possible membership. However, the major trading nations feared that the Soviets would politicize GATT and make it difficult to conduct trade negotiations; and U.S. officials argued that the Soviet economic system was incompatible with the trade regime principles and rules. After the breakup of the Soviet Union, Russian leaders realized that a transition to a market orientation would require more integration with the global economy. Thus, Russia lowered tariffs, quotas, and subsidies and applied for GATT membership in 1993; but negotiations have been difficult with the GATT/WTO.[80]

Russian economic conditions have been a major factor delaying membership. In the first five years after the Soviet Union's collapse, the Russian economy contracted to about half its former size. High unemployment, depreciation of the Russian rouble, and a decline in public sector spending severely affected the social safety net. The socioeconomic insecurity has taken its toll on the population, and in 2003 the male life expectancy at birth was lower in Russia than in China, Brazil, and India. Although Russia had a major setback in 1997 when a financial crisis forced it to default on its international obligations, since that time the economy has expanded, largely because of a substantial rise in global energy prices. However, the years of economic turmoil have delayed Russia's entry into the WTO.[81] A second factor delaying membership is the policies of the major trading nations. As Table 7.6 shows, the WTO admitted eight FSU states from 1998 to 2008 (the Kyrgyz Republic, Latvia, Estonia, Georgia, Lithuania, Moldova, Armenia, and Ukraine). However, as was the case for China, WTO members have imposed more stringent conditions for Russian accession because of its size and importance. A major source of friction with the West has been Russia's pricing policies for its energy exports, which can have a significant effect on competitiveness and world commodity markets. A third factor delaying membership relates to Russia's domestic policies and capacities to conclude an agreement. The number of Russians in government and business with training to deal with the trade technicalities is limited, and this has lengthened the negotiations. Russian federal and regional officials also have sharp disagreements regarding who has authority to liberalize trade, the possible results of freer trade, and the need for Russian structural reform. Furthermore, some powerful private groups in Russia fear that WTO accession would increase competition and reduce their protection and profits.[82]

The negotiation process has been intermittent. In the latter part of Yeltsin's period, Russia seemed less interested in membership; but when Vladimir Putin became president, he indicated that WTO accession was a major goal. After Russian troops entered Georgia in August 2008, the accession issue took on geostrategic as well as economic dimensions. The United States threatened to deny Russia entry into the WTO, and Putin (who had become prime minister) said Russia should abandon some of the commitments it made during the WTO accession talks. However, a month later Russia resumed accession talks and indicated that it still wanted to join the WTO. The WTO cannot claim to be a truly global trade organization without Russia, because it is a member of the G8 and is important in both security and economic terms. Russia is also more likely to liberalize its economy within the WTO, and more likely to follow disruptive economic policies if it remains an outsider.[83]

CIVIL SOCIETY AND GLOBAL TRADE RELATIONS

Civil society groups protested against the WTO even before it began operations, but the protests reached new levels at the 1999 WTO ministerial in Seattle. Whereas citizens can hold their national governments to account for their policies, to whom is the WTO accountable? Global trade governance seems far removed from accountable government, and this results in a "democratic deficit" according to civil society groups. In response to NGO pressure, the WTO has adopted some policies to increase transparency; for example, it provides more information on its website and makes derestricted documents available to the public more promptly. However, NGOs are pressuring for more significant changes, such as a role for themselves in decision making. Formally, WTO policy making operates according to a *club model,* in which only government officials and political leaders have the authority to make decisions. WTO agreements establish formal rights and obligations only for member governments, and WTO dispute settlement is formally open only to states. The club model rests on the realist perspective that the WTO functions best "when governments can speak clearly to each other without a cacophony of other voices."[84] Despite the formal limitation to governments, WTO policy making in fact often operates according to an *adaptive club model,* in which governments regularly consult with private business groups. For example, although states are the only formal participants in WTO dispute settlement, trade ministries often lack the time, expertise, and resources to gather information for WTO investigations. Thus, MNCs give governments informal advice on legal matters, assistance in preparing written submissions to panels, and advice on responses to panel questions. In a U.S.-Japanese dispute over the photographic film industry, Kodak performed these functions for the U.S. Trade Representative (USTR) office while Fuji assisted the Japanese government. Chiquita Brands International similarly helped the USTR develop its case in the U.S. dispute with the EU over its banana import regime. Instead of the adaptive club model, NGOs press for a *multistakeholder model,* in which *all* stakeholders have a role in the policy process. The involvement of a broader group of societal interests would decrease alienation from the WTO, provide alternative sources of advice to governments, and create a more democratic form of global governance. However, opponents of a multistakeholder model argue that NGOs can already participate at the domestic level, that they do not represent the national interest, and that many NGOs oppose trade liberalization. It is unlikely that the WTO will accept the multistakeholder model, because many member governments do not want their NGOs to participate independently.[85]

Some NGOs have developed innovative strategies to alter global trade relations, and a prime example is their role in the fair trade movement. *Fair trade* is a trading partnership "that seeks greater equity in international trade. It contributes to sustainable development by offering better trading conditions to, and securing the rights of, marginalized workers—especially in the South."[86] The fair trade movement emerged when church organizations began marketing handicrafts from European communities recovering from World War II. In the 1960s the movement came to focus on the unequal trade relations facing the world's poor and branched out from handicrafts to food commodities such as coffee, tea, and cocoa. Alternative trading organizations such as Oxfam and Twin Trading and cooperatives such as Equal Exchange carry out fair trade, but marketing success also depends on greater involvement of large-scale retailers and corporations bringing fair trade to the mainstream public. A major challenge facing fair trade is the inherent contradiction between its role as a social movement *against the market* challenging conventional trade practices and North–South inequalities on the one hand and its role *within the market* promoting trade between Southern producers and Northern consumers on the other. Critics warn that the expansion of fair trade as a marketing device is threatening fair trade as a social movement.[87]

TRADE AND THE ENVIRONMENT

Debates over trade and the environment are closely related to the differences in theoretical perspectives. Liberals believe that trade liberalization creates more wealth and prosperity, which gives people the incentive and ability to improve the environment. Freer trade based on comparative advantage also enables states to consume more goods with fewer resources, and contributes to the diffusion of cleaner technologies to LDCs. Orthodox liberals see efforts to inject the environment into trade discussions as interference with the market, an excuse for protectionism, and a threat to the global trade regime. Orthodox liberals also oppose the "precautionary principle," which would enable states to limit imports that pose a *possible* health risk, even in cases of scientific uncertainty. For example, the EU has relied on the precautionary principle to limit imports of beef with certain hormones and genetically modified foods from the United States and Canada. Interventionist liberals also favor market-based policies, but believe that some environmental controls are necessary when markets function imperfectly; for example, governments should address the problems of trade in hazardous wastes, dangerous chemicals, and endangered species. Institutional liberals think that the WTO should devote more attention to environmental issues, and that both global environmental regimes and the global trade regime can help address these issues. Some interventionist and institutional liberals accept the limited use of the precautionary principle, but warn that states could use it for protectionist purposes.

The greens (discussed in Chapter 5) see trade as a basic *cause* of global environmental problems. The prices of traded goods do not reflect their environmental value (e.g., in depletion of resources) and environmental pollution caused by the production process. Global trade also causes manufacturing to occur far from the point of consumption, which contributes to environmental costs of transportation. Furthermore, trade causes an unequal distribution of environmental and social problems; for example, LDCs produce the most polluting goods that depend on the unsustainable use of local natural resources, while DCs benefit from importing these products. Trade increases are also linked with the growth of consumption, which is putting pressure on the sustainability of the planet. The greens see trade as putting downward pressure on environmental standards, because states lower their environmental standards to become more cost competitive; this leads to a "race to the bottom." Thus, the greens advise states and global institutions to restrict trade when necessary to achieve environmental goals. Whereas liberals prefer voluntary environmental agreements, the greens consider trade sanctions an effective means of inducing states to adhere to environmental standards. The greens also support the use of the precautionary principle to prevent possible environmental harm.[88]

As a liberal economic trade organization, the GATT/WTO has given priority to trade over environmental goals, but there has been some change over time. Environmental protection was not a major issue when GATT was formed, and GATT did not explicitly refer to the "environment."[89] GATT Article 20 permits exceptions to GATT rules "to protect human, animal or plant life or health," and for "conservation of exhaustible natural resources." However, GATT does not consider such measures necessary if other measures are available that do not restrict trade. Many environmental problems such as global warming or dumping at sea also do not qualify for GATT exceptions because they do not fit into the terms of Article 20. The environment is a more prominent issue in the WTO. For example, the WTO Preamble's objectives include "sustainable development" and "seeking to protect and preserve the environment"; and the WTO regularly sponsors a Public Forum with civil society and private sector participants in which environmental concerns are an important focus. The WTO focuses on trade and the environment through two major routes. The first is political, with the WTO's Committee on Trade and Environment (CTE) involved in negotiation and forming a consensus among the membership. The second route is through WTO dispute settlement cases. The political route has stalled because the CTE has been unable to agree on a set of environmental recommendations, and it is virtually impossible to reach a consensus on environmental issues among the WTO members. Thus, "the relationship between trade and environment in the WTO is, in effect, being created through disputes."[90]

The GATT/WTO has had several important environmental dispute settlement cases. One of the most prominent was GATT's decisions in the tuna–dolphin case in the early 1990s. Mexico complained that the United States refused to import its tuna because of claims that Mexico's netting practices were harming dolphins, and the GATT panel decided against the United States for two major reasons. First, the national treatment obligation and GATT Article 20 indicate that states can only limit trade because of the material composition of the products (what is produced), and not because of the production and processing methods (how they are produced). The United States had not shown that the quality of Mexican tuna was inferior, and it was only objecting to the production and processing methods (which it claimed was harming dolphins). Second, the GATT/WTO does not permit a state to use extraterritorial measures to protect natural resources outside its borders, and the United States was trying to impose its domestic measures on Mexico. Prominent WTO environmental disputes have been the U.S. gasoline imports case, the shrimp–sea turtle case, the EU hormone-treated beef case, the French asbestos case, and the EU genetically modified foods case. In only one of these cases did the WTO dispute settlement panel clearly give priority to the environment over trade: The WTO panel and Appellate Body decided that France could prevent imports of Canadian asbestos on health and safety grounds.[91] (In the shrimp–sea turtle case, the decision was a partial victory for environmentalists.)

Predictably, reactions to the WTO dispute settlement cases vary in accordance with the views of the observer. Orthodox liberals believe that the market should always take priority to the environment in dispute settlement cases. Institutional liberals argue that WTO dispute settlement has ushered in "an important period of reform" in "the interplay of trade and the environment."[92] The judgments in dispute settlement cases demonstrate a gradual shift toward more recognition of environmental concerns, and the Appellate Body decisions have "inspired confidence in the adjudication process, and convinced many environmentalists that legitimate environmental measures would be permitted by the WTO."[93] Green theorists by contrast argue that when free trade and environmental regulation "come into conflict, the GATT/WTO dispute settlement system always found in favor of trade, and against national environmental regulation." The dispute settlement panelists are always trade specialists, "but never environmentalists."[94] Thus, green theorists often see the WTO as unreformable and would like replace it with a more environmentally-friendly organization.

Considering IPE Theory and Practice

This chapter shows that the forces of globalization strongly affect international trade. Internationalist firms have a major stake in an open trading system because of their reliance on multinational operations, exports, imports, and intrafirm trade. GATT was designed to deal mainly with trade in tangible goods, but this coverage proved to be too narrow. Thus, the WTO is addressing additional areas such as services, intellectual property, foreign investment, and the environment, which are closely intertwined with trade issues. Foreign direct investment and trade, for example, are highly complementary because one-third of trade is conducted among affiliates of international firms. Membership in the WTO is also becoming truly global. For years many LDCs either did not join GATT or did not fully participate in GATT negotiations. The 1980s foreign debt crisis marked a turning point, with 39 LDCs joining GATT from 1982 to 1994 (the year before the WTO was formed). The breakup of the Soviet bloc and Soviet Union were other major turning points, with many transition countries seeking membership in the GATT/WTO. As of April 2009, there were 153 members of the WTO; Russia is the only major economy that is still not a member. However, the inexorable growth of trade has also been marked by resistance and conflict,

and in July 2008 the Doha Round broke up without an agreement. This section discusses the competing theoretical views regarding the breakup of the Doha Round.

Realists attribute the Doha Round problems to the growing struggle between the North and the South, in which the South seeks both more wealth and more power in the global trade regime. The balance of power in trade is shifting from "a bipolar system driven by the United States and Europe—to a multipolar one," in which LDCs such as China, India, and Brazil have become major economies.[95] The United States, Europe, and Japan have been reluctant to accept this change in geopolitical power relationships, and until they do it will be difficult to complete a WTO round. However, China and India may also have overestimated their power when their demands resulted in the demise of the Doha Round; both North and South could benefit from a larger dose of realism. Realists also note that this is still a world of states looking after their national interest and that trade negotiations are now more complicated with 153 diverse states in the WTO. To expect such a diversity of states to achieve a consensus on all major issues is unrealistic.

Most liberals do not view the breakup of the Doha Round as a disaster, because interdependent

(continued)

(*continued*)

ties among states are not easily broken. However, the breakup of the round is a serious problem; if the bicycle does not keep moving forward, there will be a reversion to protectionism. For example, the huge subsidies in the 2008 U.S. farm bill indicates that the United States is already backsliding from its goal of freer farm trade, and resistance to decreasing farm subsidies is also increasing in Europe. Many states are shifting to more modest bilateral free trade agreements as a result of the Doha Round problems. As we discuss in Chapter 8, many liberals view RTAs as a "second-best option" after global free trade. However, some liberals warn that regional trade blocs are a divisive source in the global trade regime; for example, the noted trade specialist Jagdish Bhagwati refers to preferential trade agreements as "termites in the trading system."[96] Liberal pluralists are also attuned to the important role of domestic factors in the breakup of the Doha Round. The Doha Round negotiations were clearly a "two-level game," in which delegates had to negotiate not only with each other but with their own domestic groups. It is no accident that the talks broke down over agriculture, because this is an area where protectionist groups continue to have considerable influence. Domestic skepticism about the advantages of freer trade has grown in a number of countries, and this has been especially evident in the United States because of its traditional role as a leader in free trade. The U.S. balance-of-payments and trade deficits have resulted in a turn to protectionism among many domestic groups.

Historical materialists attribute the breakdown of the Doha Round to the realization that the WTO trade principles and rules benefit DCs and private corporations at the expense of LDCs and workers. Thus, discussion in the WTO is limited "to an approved set of topics using the language of neoliberal optimism."[97] The TRIPs agreement is a prime example of the differing views of liberals and historical materialists. The Uruguay Round agreement requires signatories to provide intellectual property rights protection; for example, WTO members must develop legislation that provides patent protection for at least 20 years. Liberals argue that most innovation occurs privately, and individuals have little incentive to engage in research and development if they do not have sufficient patent protection. Historical materialists, by contrast, argue that more than 80 percent of patents in the South are owned by foreigners, mainly by MNCs headquartered in the North. Thus, the TRIPs agreement limits and distorts trade, hinders the transfer of technology to the South, and transfers resources from the South to the North.[98] Some critical theorists argue that the WTO must become more open to a broader, more democratic organization that addresses concerns of labor, the environment, civil society groups, and LDCs. Others believe that the WTO is incapable of change, and that it should be abolished.

The breakdown of the Doha Round and the divergent views of theorists demonstrate that trade is one of the most contentious areas of IPE. Chapter 8 deals with RTAs—another aspect of trade that is of growing importance.

Questions

1. How has liberal trade theory evolved over time? (Discuss absolute and comparative advantage, and the Heckscher–Ohlin and Stolper–Samuelson theories.)
2. How do the realist concepts of competitive advantage and strategic trade theory differ from the liberal concept of comparative advantage? How do historical materialists view the liberal free trade ideas and why?
3. Is the GATT/WTO most-favored-nation principle compatible with specific reciprocity, diffuse reciprocity, and the development principle? Explain.
4. Why are safeguards an essential part of most trade agreements? What are countervailing and antidumping duties, and what must a country demonstrate to impose them?
5. How has the South's role in the GATT/WTO changed over time?
6. How has the role of transition economies in the GATT/WTO changed? What were the terms of China's admission to the WTO, and has its admission been good for China and for the WTO?
7. How much priority have GATT and the WTO given to the environment? Is free trade compatible with protection of the environment?
8. What are the similarities and differences between GATT and the WTO? What are the competing explanations for the breakdown of the Doha Round, and which explanation(s) do you think is(are) the most plausible?

Further Reading

Comprehensive studies of the GATT/WTO from a liberal economic perspective include Bernard M. Hoekman and Michel M. Kostecki, *The Political Economy of the World Trading System: From GATT to WTO*, 2nd ed. (New York: Oxford University Press, 2001); and John H. Barton, Judith L. Goldstein, Timothy E. Josling and Richard H. Steinberg, *The Evolution of the Trade Regime: Politics, Law, and Economics of the GATT and the WTO* (Princeton, NJ: Princeton University Press, 2006). Studies from a realist perspective include John A. C. Conybeare, *Trade Wars: The Theory and Practice of International Commercial Rivalry* (New York: Columbia University Press, 1987; and Laura D'Andrea Tyson, *Who's Bashing Whom? Trade Conflict in High-Technology Industries* (Washington, D.C.: Institute for International Economics, 1992). Studies from critical perspectives include Chakravarthi Raghavan, *Recolonization: GATT, the Uruguay Round and the Third World*

(New York: Zed Books, 1990); and Richard Peet, *Unholy Trinity: The IMF, World Bank and WTO* (New York: Zed Books, 2003). A study of the formal and informal institutions involved in the global trade regime is Theodore H. Cohn, *Governing Global Trade: International Institutions in Conflict and Convergence* (Burlington, VT: Ashgate, 2002).

On domestic politics and global trade, see Ronald Rogowski, *Commerce and Coalitions: How Trade Affects Domestic Political Alignments* (Princeton, NJ: Princeton University Press, 1989); Nitsan Chorev, "A Fluid Divide: Domestic and International Factors in US Trade Policy Formation," *Review of International Political Economy* 14, no. 4 (October 2007), pp. 653–689; and I.M. Destler, "U.S. Trade Politics during the Doha Round," in Isabel Studer and Carol Wise, eds., *Requiem or Revival?* (Washington, D.C.: Brookings Institution, 2007).

Studies of North–South relations and global trade include Amrita Narlikar, "Fairness in International Trade Negotiations: Developing Countries in the GATT and WTO," *World Economy* 29, no. 8 (August 2006), pp. 1005–1029; Kevin P. Gallagher, "Understanding Developing Country Resistance to the Doha Round," *Review of International Political Economy* 15, no. 1 (February 2008), pp. 62–85; Rorden Wilkinson and James Scott, "Developing Country Participation in the GATT: A Reassessment," *World Trade Review* 7, no. 3 (2008), pp. 473–510; and Ian Taylor and Karen Smith, *United Nations Conference on Trade and Development* (New York: Routledge, 2007). On "fair trade," see Laura T. Raynolds, Douglas L. Murray, and John Wilkinson, eds., *Fair Trade: The Challenges of Transforming Globalization* (New York: Routledge, 2007).

On global trade and the environment, see George Hoberg, "Trade, Harmonization, and Domestic Autonomy in Environmental Policy," *Journal of Comparative Policy Analysis: Research and Practice* 3, no. 2 (2001), pp. 191–217; and Sabrina Shaw and Risa Schwartz, "Trade and Environment in the WTO: State of Play," *Journal of World Trade* 36, no. 1 (2002), pp. 129–154.

Notes

1. A trade war is an "intense international conflict where states interact, bargain, and retaliate primarily over economic objectives directly related to the traded goods or service sectors of their economies, and where the means used are restrictions on the free flow of goods or services." See John A. C. Conybeare, *Trade Wars: The Theory and Practice of International Commercial Rivalry* (New York: Columbia University Press, 1987), p. 3.
2. Helen V. Milner, *Resisting Protectionism: Global Industries and the Politics of International Trade* (Princeton, NJ: Princeton University Press, 1988), pp. 290–291.
3. World Trade Organization, *World Trade Report—2008* (Geneva: WTO, 2008), p. 15.
4. Renato Ruggiero, "Charting the Trade Routes of the Future: Towards a Borderless Economy," address delivered to the International Industrial Conference, San Francisco, September 29, 1997, *WTO Press Release*, Geneva, Press/77, p. 4.
5. David Ricardo, *The Principles of Political Economy and Taxation* (Homewood, IL: Irwin, 1963).
6. Wolfgang F. Stolper and Paul A. Samuelson, "Protection and Real Wages," *Review of Economic Studies* 9, no. 1 (November 1941), pp. 58–73; Ronald Rogowski,

Commerce and Coalitions: How Trade Affects Domestic Political Alignments (Princeton, NJ: Princeton University Press, 1989).

7. Elhanan Helpman and Paul R. Krugman, *Market Structure and Foreign Trade: Increasing Returns, Imperfect Competition, and the International Economy* (Cambridge, MA: MIT Press, 1985), p. 3; Robert Gilpin with Jean M. Gilpin, *The Political Economy of International Relations* (Princeton, NJ: Princeton University Press, 1987), pp. 175–178.

8. John H. Jackson, *The World Trading System: Law and Policy of International Economic Relations* (Cambridge, MA: MIT Press, 2nd ed., 1997), pp. 229–232.

9. Bruce R. Scott, "National Strategies: Key to International Competition," in Bruce R. Scott and George C. Lodge, eds., *U.S. Competitiveness in the World Economy* (Boston: Harvard Business School Press, 1985), pp. 93–95.

10. Laura D'Andrea Tyson, *Who's Bashing Whom? Trade Conflict in High-Technology Industries* (Washington, D.C.: Institute for International Economics, 1992), p. 4.

11. Klaus Stegemann, "Policy Rivalry Among Industrial States: What Can We Learn from Models of Strategic Trade Policy?" *International Organization* 43, no. 1 (Winter 1989), p. 99.

12. Arghiri Emmanuel, *Unequal Exchange: A Study of the Imperialism of Trade* (New York: Monthly Review Press, 1972); Anthony Brewer, *Marxist Theories of Imperialism: A Critical Survey* (New York: Routledge, 2nd ed., 1990), pp. 200–224.

13. Edward John Ray, "Changing Patterns of Protectionism: The Fall in Tariffs and the Rise in Non-Tariff Barriers," *Northwestern Journal of International Law & Business,* 8 (1987), pp. 294–295.

14. Robert A. Pastor, *Congress and the Politics of U.S. Foreign Economic Policy, 1929–1976* (Berkeley: University of California Press, 1980), p. 78.

15. Charles P. Kindleberger, *The World in Depression 1929–1939* (Berkeley: University of California Press, 1973), pp. 291–307.

16. Stephen D. Krasner, "State Power and the Structure of International Trade," *World Politics* 28, no. 3 (April 1976), p. 338.

17. E. E. Schattschneider, *Politics, Pressures and the Tariff: A Study of Free Private Enterprise in Pressure Politics, as Shown in the 1929–1930 Revision of the Tariff* (Hamden, CT: Archon Books, 1963, same as 1935 ed.); and Pastor, *Congress and the Politics of U.S. Foreign Economic Policy,* pp. 80–84.

18. For the effects of the 1930 U.S. tariff, see Joseph M. Jones, Jr., *Tariff Retaliation: Repercussions of the Hawley-Smoot Bill* (Philadelphia: University of Pennsylvania Press, 1934).

19. I. M. Destler, *American Trade Politics,* 2nd ed. (Washington, D.C.: Institute for International Economics and Twentieth Century Fund, June 1992), pp. 14–15; Gilbert R. Winham, *The Evolution of International Trade Agreements* (Toronto: University of Toronto Press, 1992), p. 19.

20. John W. Evans, *The Kennedy Round in American Trade Policy: The Twilight of the GATT?* (Cambridge, MA: Harvard University Press, 1971), pp. 5–7.

21. Robert E. Hudec, *The GATT Legal System and World Trade Diplomacy* (New York: Praeger, 1975), pp. 7–18; and Simon Reisman, "The Birth of a World Trading System: ITO and GATT," in Orin Kirshner, ed., *The Bretton Woods–GATT System: Retrospect and Prospect After Fifty Years* (Armonk, NY: Sharpe, 1996), pp. 83–85.

22. William Diebold, Jr., "The End of the I.T.O.," *Essays in International Finance* no. 16 (Princeton, NJ: International Finance Section, Department of Economics and Social Institutions, Princeton University, October 1952), p. 2; Richard N. Gardner,

Sterling-Dollar Diplomacy in Current Perspective: The Origins and Prospects of Our International Economic Order (New York: Columbia University Press, expanded ed., 1980), pp. 348–380.

23. John H. Jackson, *World Trade and the Law of GATT* (Indianapolis, IN: Bobbs-Merrill, 1969), pp. 120–121.

24. Barry Eichengreen and Peter B. Kenen, "Managing the World Economy Under the Bretton Woods System: An Overview," in Peter B. Kenen, ed., *Managing the World Economy: Fifty Years After Bretton Woods* (Washington, D.C.: Institute for International Economics, September 1994), p. 7.

25. Bernard M. Hoekman and Michel M. Kostecki, *The Political Economy of the World Trading System: From GATT to WTO,* 2nd ed. (New York: Oxford University Press, 2001), pp. 1–3.

26. John Gerard Ruggie, "International Regimes, Transactions, and Change: Embedded Liberalism in the Postwar Economic Order," in Stephen D. Krasner, ed., *International Regimes* (Ithaca, NY: Cornell University Press, 1983), p. 212.

27. Item-by-item negotiations continued during the Kennedy Round for agricultural goods and some other sensitive products. See Hoekman and Kostecki, *The Political Economy of the World Trading System,* pp. 127–129; and Robert E. Hudec, *Enforcing International Trade Law: The Evolution of the Modern GATT Legal System* (Salem, NH: Butterworth Legal Publishers, 1993), pp. 12–13.

28. Jock A. Finlayson and Mark W. Zacher, "The GATT and the Regulation of Trade Barriers: Regime Dynamics and Functions," in Krasner, ed., *International Regimes,* pp. 282–286; William P. Avery, ed., *World Agriculture and the GATT* (Boulder, CO: Lynne Rienner, 1993).

29. Theodore H. Cohn, *The International Politics of Agricultural Trade: Canadian–American Relations in a Global Agricultural Context* (Vancouver: University of British Columbia Press, 1990), pp. 141–142.

30. Milner, *Resisting Protectionism,* p. 8.

31. Milner, *Resisting Protectionism,* p. 290.

32. Eric Wyndham-White, "Negotiations in Prospect," in C. Fred Bergsten, ed., *Toward a New World Trade Policy: The Maidenhead Papers* (Lanham, MD: Lexington Books, 1975), p. 322.

33. Charles Lipson, "The Transformation of Trade: The Sources and Effects of Regime Change," in Krasner, ed., *International Regimes,* p. 242.

34. Winham, *The Evolution of International Trade Agreements,* pp. 46–48; Hoekman and Kostecki, *The Political Economy of the World Trading System,* pp. 29–31.

35. WTO, *World Trade Report—2008* (Geneva: WTO, 2008), Appendix Table 2, p. 12.

36. Finlayson and Zacher, "The GATT and the Regulation of Trade Barriers," pp. 286–290; Gilbert Winham, *International Trade and the Tokyo Round Negotiations* (Princeton, NJ: Princeton University Press, 1986), pp. 172–175.

37. Robert O. Keohane, "Reciprocity in International Relations," *International Organization* 40, no. 1 (Winter 1986), p. 4.

38. Carolyn Rhodes, "Reciprocity in Trade: The Utility of a Bargaining Strategy," *International Organization* 43, no. 2 (Spring 1989), p. 276.

39. B. Peter Rosendorff and Helen V. Milner, "The Optimal Design of International Trade Institutions: Uncertainty and Escape," *International Organization* 55, no. 4 (Autumn 2001), pp. 829–857.

40. Gilbert Gagné and François Roch, "The US-Canada Softwood Lumber Dispute and the WTO Definition of Subsidy," *World Trade Review* 7, no. 3 (2008), pp. 547–572.

41. John H. Barton, Judith L. Goldstein, Timothy E. Josling, and Richard H. Steinberg, *The Evolution of the Trade Regime: Politics, Law, and the Economics of the GATT and the WTO* (Princeton, NJ: Princeton University Press, 2006), pp. 109–118; Bernard M. Hoekman and Petros C. Mavroidis, *The World Trade Organization: Law, Economics, and Politics* (New York: Routledge, 2007), pp. 48–51.

42. Finlayson and Zacher, "The GATT and the Regulation of Trade Barriers," pp. 293–296. On the Havana Charter's development provisions see Clair Wilcox, *A Charter for World Trade* (New York: Macmillan, 1949), pp. 140–152.

43. Minister for International Trade, "Canada Proposes Strategy for Creation of a World Trade Organization," *News Release* no. 077, External Affairs and International Trade Canada, April 11, 1990.

44. John Croome, *Reshaping the World Trading System: A History of the Uruguay Round* (Geneva: WTO, 1995), pp. 271–274, 358–361; Ernest H. Preeg, *Traders in a Brave New World: The Uruguay Round and the Future of the International Trading System* (Chicago: University of Chicago Press, 1995), pp. 113–126.

45. Theodore H. Cohn, *Governing Global Trade: International Institutions in Conflict and Convergence* (Burlington, VT: Ashgate, 2002), pp. 142–146.

46. Hoekman and Kostecki, *The Political Economy of the World Trading System,* pp. 74–98.

47. Gardner Patterson and Eliza Patterson, "The Road from GATT to MTO," *Minnesota Journal of Global Trade* 3, no. 1 (Spring 1994), p. 37.

48. C. Fred Bergsten, "Fifty Years of Trade Policy: The Policy Lessons," *World Economy* 24, no. 1 (January 2001), p. 1.

49. Jeffrey J. Schott, "The WTO after Seattle," in Jeffrey J. Schott, ed., *The WTO After Seattle* (Washington, D.C.: Institute for International Economics, 2000), pp. 8–17.

50. "Beyond Doha," *The Economist,* November 17, 2001, p. 11.

51. Raúl Prebisch, "The Economic Development of Latin America and Its Principal Problems," *Economic Bulletin for Latin America* 7, no. 1 (February 1962), pp. 1–59; Albert O. Hirschman, "The Political Economy of Import-Substituting Industrialization in Latin America," *Quarterly Journal of Economics* 82, no. 1 (February 1968), pp. 1–32; and Hollis Chenery, "The Structuralist Approach to Development Policy," *American Economic Review* 65, no. 2 (May 1975), pp. 310–316.

52. Robert E. Hudec, *Developing Countries in the GATT Legal System* (Brookfield, VT: Gower, 1987), pp. 23–24.

53. Jagdish Bhagwati, *Termites in the Trading System: How Preferential Agreements Undermine Free Trade* (New York: Oxford University Press, 2008), p. 26; Marc Williams, *Third World Cooperation: The Group of 77 in UNCTAD* (London: Pinter, 1991), pp. 89–90; Vinod K. Aggarwal, *Liberal Protectionism: The International Politics of Organized Textile Trade* (Berkeley: University of California Press, 1985), p. 8.

54. For UNCTAD's role in the GSP, see Anindya K. Bhattacharya, "The Influence of the International Secretariat: UNCTAD and Generalized Tariff Preferences," *International Organization* 30, no. 1 (Winter 1976), pp. 75–90.

55. Anne O. Krueger, *Trade Policies and Developing Nations* (Washington, D.C.: Brookings Institution, 1995), p. 41.

56. Jeffrey A. Hart, *The New International Economic Order: Conflict and Cooperation in North-South Economic Relations, 1974–77* (New York: St. Martin's Press, 1983).

57. Olivier Long, *Law and Its Limitations in the GATT Multilateral Trade System* (Dordrecht, The Netherlands: Nijhoff, 1985), p. 101.

58. Hudec, *Developing Countries in the GATT Legal System,* pp. 70–91.

59. Robert Wolfe, "Global Trade as a Single Undertaking: The Role of Ministers in the WTO," *International Journal* 51, no. 4 (Autumn 1996), pp. 690–709.

60. Quoted in Mari Pangestu, "Special and Differential Treatment in the Millennium: Special for Whom and How Different?" *World Economy* 23, no. 9 (September 2000), p. 1291.

61. Colleen Hamilton and John Whalley, "Coalitions in the Uruguay Round," *Weltwirtschaftliches Archiv* 125, no. 3 (1989), pp. 547–561; Richard A. Higgott and Andrew Fenton Cooper, "Middle Power Leadership and Coalition Building: Australia, the Cairns Group, and the Uruguay Round of Trade Negotiations," *International Organization* 44, no. 4 (Autumn 1990), pp. 589–632.

62. John Whalley, "Recent Trade Liberalisation in the Developing World: What is Behind it and Where is it Headed?" in David Greenaway, Robert C. Hine, Anthony P. O'Brien, and Robert J. Thornton, eds., *Global Protectionism* (London: Macmillan, 1991), pp. 225–253.

63. John Gershman, "The Free Trade Connection," in Kevin Danaher, ed., *Fifty Years Is Enough: The Case Against the World Bank and the International Monetary Fund* (Boston: South End Press, 1994), p. 24.

64. Bernard R. Hoekman, "Developing Countries and the Multilateral Trading System After the Uruguay Round," in Roy Culpeper, Albert Berry, and Frances Stewart, eds., *Global Development Fifty Years After Bretton Woods: Essays in Honour of Gerald K. Helleiner* (New York: St. Martin's Press, 1997), pp. 252–279.

65. Chakravarthi Raghavan, *Recolonization: GATT, the Uruguay Round and The Third World* (London: Zed Books, 1990).

66. Jayashree Watal, "Developing Countries' Interests in a 'Development Round,' " in Schott, ed., *The WTO After Seattle,* pp. 71–72.

67. Kimberley Ann Elliott, "Agricultural Reform and Trade Negotiations: Can the Doha Round Deliver?" *World Economics* 7, no. 4 (October–December 2006), p. 126.

68. Theodore H. Cohn, "The Doha Round: Problems, Challenges, and Prospects," in Isabel Studer and Carol Wise, eds., *Requiem or Revival? The Promise of North American Integration* (Washington, D.C.: Brookings Institution, 2007), pp. 147–165.

69. "Trade Talks: The Doha Round," *The Economist,* August 2, 2008, pp. 14, 71–72.

70. In 2002, China and Russia together accounted for 5.71 percent of the IMF votes and 5.58 percent of the World Bank votes. (*IMF Annual Report—2002* [Washington, D.C.: International Monetary Fund, 2002], p. 148); *World Bank Annual Report—2002* (Washington, D.C.: World Bank, 2002), p. 121.

71. John H. Jackson, *The World Trading System: Law and Policy of International Economic Relations* (Cambridge, MA: MIT Press, 1989), pp. 283–286.

72. Leah A. Haus, *Globalizing the GATT: The Soviet Union's Successor States, Eastern Europe, and the International Trading System* (Washington, D.C.: Brookings Institution, 1992); Jozef M. van Brabant, *The Planned Economies and International Economic Organizations* (New York: Cambridge University Press, 1991), pp. 199–201; Laszlo Lang, "International Regimes and the Political Economy of East–West Relations," *Occasional Paper Series 13* (New York: Institute for East-West Security Studies, 1989), pp. 35–36.

73. Chung-chou Li, "Resumption of China's GATT Membership," *Journal of World Trade Law* 21, no. 4 (1987), pp. 26–30.

74. Paul D. McKenzie, "China's Application to the GATT: State Trading and the Problem of Market Access," *Journal of World Trade* 24, no. 5 (October 1990), pp. 144–145; Harold K. Jacobson and Michel Oksenberg, *China's Participation in the IMF, the World Bank, and GATT: Toward a Global Economic Order* (Ann Arbor: University of Michigan Press, 1990), pp. 83–92.

75. Greg Mastel, "China and the World Trade Organization: Moving Forward without Sliding Back," *Law and Policy in International Business* 31, no. 3 (Spring 2000), pp. 988–991.

76. Elena Ianchovichina and Will Martin, "Trade Impacts of China's World Trade Organization Accession," *Asian Economic Review* 1, no. 1 (2006), pp. 50–51; James C. Hsiung, "The Aftermath of China's Accession to the World Trade Organization," *Independent Review* 8, no. 1 (Summer 2003), pp. 90–92.

77. Hsiung, "The Aftermath of China's Accession to the World Trade Organization," pp. 93–101; Shaun Breslin, "Power and Production: Rethinking China's Global Economic Role," *Review of International Studies* 31 (2005), pp. 737–739. On China's role in the G20 (also called the G21), see Rolf J. Langhammer, "China and the G-21: A New North-South Divide in the WTO After Cancún?" *Journal of the Asia Pacific Economy* 10, no. 3 (August 2005), pp. 339–358.

78. Breslin, "Power and Production," pp. 739–741.

79. "Inevitable Collision: Business in China," *The Economist,* February 23, 2008, pp. 82–83; WTO, *World Trade Report—2006,* pp. 14–16.

80. Brabant, *The Planned Economies and International Economic Organizations,* pp. 1–6; Harry G. Broadman, "Global Economic Integration: Prospects for WTO Accession and Continued Russian Reforms," *Washington Quarterly* 27, no. 2 (Spring 2004), pp. 79–81.

81. S. Neil MacFarlane, "The 'R' in BRICs: Is Russia an Emerging Power?" *International Affairs* 82, no. 1 (2006), pp. 43–48.

82. David A. Dyker, "Russian Accession to the WTO—Why Such a Long and Difficult Road?" *Post-Communist Economies* 16, no. 1 (March 2004), pp. 3–20.

83. Anna Smolchenko, "Put in Casts Doubt on Russia's WTO Accession," *International Herald Tribune,* August 25, 2008.

84. Daniel C. Esty, "Non-Governmental Organizations at the World Trade Organization: Cooperation, Competition, or Exclusion," *Journal of International Economic Law* 1, no. 1 (March 1998), p. 140.

85. The terminology in this section is taken from Brian Hocking, "Changing the Terms of Trade Policy Making: From the 'Club' to the 'Multistakeholder' Model," *World Trade Review* 3, no. 1 (2004), pp. 3–26. See also Jan Aart Scholte with Robert O'Brien and Marc Williams, "The WTO and Civil Society," *Journal of World Trade* 33, no. 1 (February 1999), pp. 107–123; Ngaire Woods and Amrita Narlikar, "Governance and the Limits of Accountability: The WTO, the IMF, and the World Bank," *International Social Science Journal* 170 (December 2001), pp. 572–573.

86. Laura T. Raynolds and Michael A. Long, "Fair/Alternative Trade: Historical and Empirical Dimensions," in Laura T. Raynolds, Douglas L. Murray, and John Wilkinson, eds., *Fair Trade: The Challenges of Transforming Globalization* (New York: Routledge, 2007), pp. 17–18.

87. Raynolds, Murray, and Wilkinson, eds., *Fair Trade,* chs. 1, 2, and 13; Anil Hira and Jared Ferrie, "Fair Trade: Three Key Challenges for Reaching the Mainstream," *Journal of Business Ethics* 63 (2006), pp. 107–118.

88. Clapp and Dauvergne, *Paths to a Green World,* pp. 119–134; Daniel C. Esty, *Greening The GATT: Trade, Environment, and the Future* (Washington, D.C.: 1994), pp. 35–41; Bernstein, *The Compromise of Liberal Environmentalism,* pp. 229–232.
89. Esty, *Greening the GATT,* p. 9.
90. Sabrina Shaw and Risa Schwartz, "Trade and Environment in the WTO: State of Play," *Journal of World Trade* 36, no. 1 (2002), p. 129.
91. Clapp and Dauvergne, *Paths to a Green World,* pp. 137–143.
92. Steve Charnovitz, "The WTO's Environmental Progress," *Journal of International Economic Law* 10, no. 3 (September 2007), p. 685.
93. Charnovitz, "The WTO's Environmental Progress," p. 695. On the innovative role of the WTO Appellate Body, see Noemi Gal-Or, "The Concept of Appeal in International Dispute Settlement," *European Journal of International Law* 19, no. 1 (2008), pp. 43–65.
94. Richard Peet, *Unholy Trinity: The IMF, World Bank and WTO* (New York: Zed Books, 2003), pp. 182–183.
95. Debra P. Steger, "The Culture of the WTO: Why It Needs to Change," *Journal of International Economic Law* 10, no. 3 (September 2007), p. 487.
96. Bhagwati, *Termites in the Trading System.*
97. Peet, *Unholy Trinity,* p. 199.
98. For contending views on this issue, see Krueger, *Trade Policies and Developing Countries,* pp. 52–54; Raghavan, *Recolonization: GATT, the Uruguay Round and the Third World,* pp. 114–141; and Croome, *Reshaping the World Trading System,* pp. 130–138.

CHAPTER 8

Regionalism and the Global Trade Regime

The formation of GATT after World War II demonstrated strong support for multilateral trade liberalization, but regionalism also emerged as a significant force with the creation of a number of regional trade agreements (RTAs). Some scholars see RTAs as "stepping stones" while others see them as "obstacles" to global free trade. This chapter examines why RTAs are formed and how they are affecting the global trade regime. Economists describe RTAs as existing at five levels of integration (see Figure 8.1):

1. *Free trade area.* Member states eliminate tariffs and other restrictions on substantially all trade with each other, but each member can have its own trade policies toward nonmember states. Thus, a free trade area poses less of a threat to national sovereignty and is more acceptable to states with politically sensitive relationships. More than 90 percent of RTAs today are free trade agreements (FTAs). The *North American Free Trade Agreement* (*NAFTA*) is an important example of an FTA.

2. *Customs union (CU).* A CU has the same characteristics as an FTA *plus* a common external tariff (CET) toward outside states. The CU normally creates institutions to administer the common tariff, and the CU members have less ability to make independent decisions. When six states (France, West Germany, Italy, Belgium, the Netherlands, and Luxembourg) formed the European Economic Community (EC) as a CU in 1957, Britain was unwilling to join because it wanted to retain its Commonwealth preference system. To join the EC, Britain would have to raise its tariffs with Commonwealth countries to the same levels as the CET. Instead of joining the EC, Britain formed the European Free Trade Association (EFTA) with six other states in 1960 (Austria, Denmark, Norway, Portugal, Sweden, and Switzerland). Britain retained its Commonwealth preferences because the

	Free trade area (FTA)	Customs union (CU)	Common market	Economic union	Political union
Removal of all tariffs among members	X	X	X	X	X
Common external tariff		X	X	X	X
Free movement of factors (labor and capital)			X	X	X
Harmonization of economic policies				X	X
Political unification					X

FIGURE 8.1   Stages of Regional Economic Integration

EFTA was only an FTA. However, Britain's trade gradually became more oriented toward EC members, and in 1973 it joined the EC and agreed to phase out its Commonwealth preferences. Compared with FTAs, the number of CUs is relatively small; the most important CU is the European Union (EU). (We use the term EC from 1957 to 1992, and EU after 1992 to reflect the name change in 1993.)

3. *Common market.*   A common market has the same characteristics as a CU *plus* the free mobility of factors of production (labor and capital) among members. The increased labor mobility induces common market members to establish similar health, safety, educational, and social security standards so that no country's workers have a competitive advantage. Successful common markets are rare because they require high levels of integration; the EU is a common market.

4. *Economic union.*   An economic union has the characteristics of a common market, *and* it harmonizes members' industrial, regional, transport, fiscal, and monetary policies. A full economic union also includes a monetary union with a common currency. As discussed, 16 EU members have formed the Economic and Monetary Union (EMU) and adopted the euro as their common currency.

5. *Political union.*   A political union has the characteristics of an economic union and also harmonizes members' foreign and defense policies. A fully developed political union is more like a federal political system than an agreement among sovereign states.

It is important to note that these levels of integration are *models* that do not fully describe reality. NAFTA, for example, is at level 1 as an FTA; but its provisions also require more openness toward foreign investment identified with level 3 (a common market). Furthermore, some RTAs in the South that describe themselves as CUs and common markets have not actually reached those levels. FTAs are much more common than CUs, because they do not require difficult negotiations over a CET. Today there are only two major CUs, the EU and Mercosur, and Mercosur in fact has not yet become an effective CU (see discussion in this chapter). Despite the shortcomings of these levels of integration, they provide general guidance to the stages states go through as they become more integrated. This is especially true for the EU, the most advanced of the RTAs.

REGIONALISM AND THE IPE THEORETICAL PERSPECTIVES

In some cases multilateralism and regionalism are competing approaches to trade. Whereas multilateralism contributes to global trade liberalization, regionalism may divide the world into competing trade blocs. However, "open regionalism" can break down national trade barriers and serve as a stepping stone rather than an obstacle to global free trade. RTAs following open regionalism abolish barriers on substantially all trade within the RTA and lower trade barriers to outsiders. MNCs often use open regionalism and multilateralism as complementary strategies to promote market forces and increase their competitiveness in the global economy.

Liberal economists see multilateralism as the best possible route to trade liberalization because it breaks down regional as well as national barriers. Liberals often support open RTAs as a "second-best" route to trade liberalization when global trade negotiations fail, but they consider closed RTAs as a threat to global free trade. Liberals are also concerned that the recent trend toward forming numerous bilateral FTAs is producing overlapping FTAs that undermine "transparency and predictability in international trade relations."[1] Although liberals acknowledge that RTAs may harm some groups such as displaced workers, they believe that the efficiency gains from open regionalism outweigh the costs incurred. Liberals do not view power disparities as a problem for smaller states in RTAs because they assume that all states benefit from open RTAs. Indeed, liberals argue that small states benefit more than large states because of economies of scale and increased demand for their exports. In contrast to liberals, realists and historical materialists believe that RTAs have important distributional effects, with some states and groups benefiting *at the expense of* others. Realists argue that the larger partner in an RTA either does not permit the smaller partner to receive greater benefits or expects "side payments" in return. These side payments exceed any economic benefits the smaller partner receives from gains in market access and economies of scale. For example, Canada and Mexico sought free trade with the United States partly to gain more assured access to the large U.S. market. The United States, however, expected side payments in such areas as foreign investment, services trade, and access to natural resources—especially energy.[2] Thus, realists expect the distribution of benefits in RTAs to reflect the asymmetries of power, wealth, and technology among member states. Historical materialists see MNCs and transnational capital as the main beneficiaries of RTAs, and the working class and poorest groups in the North and the South as the main losers. MNCs can locate their production in states with the lowest wages, environmental standards, and taxes and export freely to other states in the RTA. Historical materialists also believe that some RTAs permit states in the core (in association with transnational capital) to exploit states in the periphery.

This chapter begins with a discussion of regionalism and its relationship to globalization. It then examines the historical development of RTAs; the reasons states form RTAs; the institutional relationship between the WTO and RTAs; and trade regionalism in Europe, the Western Hemisphere, and East Asia.

REGIONALISM AND GLOBALIZATION

Regionalism is a difficult term to define because it often connotes both geographic proximity and a sense of cultural, economic, political, and organizational cohesiveness.[3] To compound the confusion, about one-third of the FTAs currently being negotiated are cross-regional, and the WTO includes these in its list of RTAs. For example, the EU has bilateral FTAs with Mexico, Chile, South Africa, and some Middle Eastern states; the United States has bilateral FTAs with Singapore, Chile, Israel, and Jordan; and Singapore has bilateral FTAs with New Zealand, Japan, EFTA, Australia, and the United States. Some scholars argue that the term *preferential trade agreements* better captures this wide range of agreements among states in different geographic regions.[4] However, we use "RTAs" because it is the preferred term of IOs such as the WTO. Some countries in Asia have strong regional economic ties that are not associated with RTAs. This chapter therefore includes discussion of cross-regional as well as regional RTAs and of trade regionalism not limited to RTAs.

In some respects, globalization limits the growth of regionalism. As interdependence increases, financial crises, trade wars, and environmental degradation require management at the global level. Multilateral institutions such as the WTO, IMF, and World Bank are better equipped than regional organizations to deal with these problems. Globalization also promotes linkages among regions as well as states, and in this sense it can undermine both national and regional cohesiveness. However, globalization may also stimulate the growth of regionalism. States must often rely on institutions above the national level to deal with global interdependence issues, but IOs with large, diverse memberships may be unable to identify common interests and sanction defectors.[5] Thus, regional institutions composed of like-minded states may be more effective than larger multilateral institutions in dealing with cross-national problems. Globalization also contributes to increased competition, and states and MNCs can often improve their global competitiveness by organizing regionally. For example, European MNCs have improved their global competitiveness by using the EU as a regional platform, and U.S. MNCs have benefited from the existence of NAFTA. Finally, globalization is closely associated with neoliberalism, which favors a shift in authority from the state to the market. The market pressures weaken state barriers and contribute to the growth of private and public linkages at both the regional and global levels. Thus, regionalism and globalization can be both conflictual and complementary.[6]

A HISTORICAL OVERVIEW OF RTAs

From the seventeenth century to World War II, there were many RTA proposals involving colonies, provinces, and states, and some of the agreements resulted in political as well as commercial unions. Examples of early integration efforts were an 1826 CU between England and Ireland; an 1833 customs treaty establishing a German *Zollverein* among splinter states; and an 1854 Canada–U.S. Reciprocity Treaty removing all tariffs on natural products. Early agreements in the South included a 1910 South African Customs Union among the Union of South Africa, Bechuanaland, Basutoland, and Swaziland, and a 1917 CU between the British colonies of Kenya, Uganda and Tanganyika.[7] However, regional integration in its modern form did not develop until after World War II with the creation of the EC. This chapter deals with the two major waves of regionalism during the postwar period.

The First Wave of Regionalism

In 1949 the Soviet Union signed a treaty with Bulgaria, Czechoslovakia, Hungary, Poland, and Romania establishing the *Council for Mutual Economic Assistance (CMEA)*. Although CMEA members engaged in technical cooperation and joint planning, state-centered central planning precluded any moves toward regional economic integration.[8] Thus, most writers view the first wave of regionalism as beginning with the formation of the EC in 1957 and EFTA in 1960.[9] Regionalism then spread to Latin America and Africa during the 1960s. However, RTAs in the South were designed mainly to provide larger markets and economies of scale for LDC production of industrial goods through import substitution policies. By the early 1970s, the first wave of regionalism proved to be largely unsuccessful outside Europe, because the South's attempts to promote import substitution at the regional level led to numerous problems. Only a limited number of industries were willing to locate in Southern RTAs, and they were concentrated in the larger, more advanced LDCs. This unequal distribution of benefits led to disputes among member states; in the East African Common Services Union, for example, Tanzania and Uganda were resentful that the major industries were concentrated in Kenya. Some Southern RTAs tried to allocate industries among members by bureaucratic means rather than the market, but this led to economic inefficiencies and further conflict.

RTAs in the first wave (the 1950s to 1960s) also had some other characteristics. First, they were plurilateral rather than bilateral; that is, they were formed among at least three states. Second, all members of an RTA were from the same geographic region. Third, the RTAs were either among DCs (North–North) or among LDCs (South–South). For example, six European states formed the EC, and four Central American states formed the Central American Common Market. Fourth, the United States as global hegemon firmly supported multilateral trade, would not join RTAs, and generally opposed them. The United States made an exception in supporting the EC because it saw an economically strong Western Europe as essential to the Cold War struggle with the Soviet Union.[10]

The Second Wave of Regionalism

The second wave of regionalism, which began in the 1980s, is proving to be much more widespread and durable than the first wave. The most notable part of the second wave has been the rapid creation of RTAs since the creation of the WTO. GATT/WTO members are to notify the organization of all RTAs in which they participate. Notifications refer to both the creation of new RTAs and the accession of new states to an RTA (e.g., the 2007 accession of Romania and Bulgaria to the EU). From 1948 to 1994 GATT received 124 notifications of RTAs (relating to trade in goods), and from 1995 to July 2007 the WTO received notifications of 256 additional RTAs covering trade in goods or services.[11] Many states are making RTAs the centerpiece of their commercial policy, and for some WTO members preferential trade now accounts for more than 90 percent of their total trade.[12]

What accounts for the greater significance of the second wave? First, the EU has broadened and deepened the integration process. Table 8.1 shows that the number of EU members increased to 27 in 2007. The EU also created a monetary union and 16 EU members have adopted the euro as a common currency. Second, the United States reversed its policy of refusing to join FTAs, and has formed them with a growing number of countries. Third, NAFTA was the first reciprocal RTA between DCs (the United States and Canada) and an LDC (Mexico). This marked a change from the RTAs in the first wave which were all either North–North or South–South. Fourth, the second wave is marked by a proliferation of bilateral RTAs, unlike the plurilateral RTAs of the first wave. Fifth, many of the bilateral RTAs are between states that are not in the same geographic region. Finally, there has been a revival of South–South RTAs, and about 35 percent of RTAs currently in force are among LDCs. These RTAs are no longer based on import substitution policies and more open to global market forces. However, the integration process in South–South RTAs is usually slower than it is in North–North RTAs.[13]

EXPLANATIONS FOR THE RISE OF REGIONAL INTEGRATION

Realists, liberals, and historical materialists emphasize different factors in explaining the rise of regional integration. Whereas realists look to security and power relationships, liberals focus on the growth of interdependence, and historical materialists emphasize the role of transnational capital.

Realist Explanations

Some realists see regional integration as a response to changing security and power relationships. For example, the U.S.–Soviet bipolar system after World War II was more conducive to European regional integration than a multipolar

TABLE 8.1   Expanding Membership of the European Union

Year of Membership	Members	GDP^a (PPP^b) Percentage Addition	GDP per Capita as Percentage of Existing Average
1957	France*, West Germany, Italy*, Belgium*, the Netherlands*, Luxembourg*		
1973	Britain, Denmark, Ireland*	31.9	95.5
1979	Greece*	1.8	48.4
1986	Spain*, Portugal*	11.0	62.2
1990	Germany unified*		
1995	Austria*, Finland*, Sweden	6.5	103.6
2004	Cyprus*, Czech Republic, Estonia, Hungary, Latvia, Lithuania, Malta*, Poland, Slovakia*, Slovenia*	9.1	46.5
2007	Bulgaria, Romania		33.3

^{a}Gross domestic product

^{b}Purchasing power parity

*Members of the EMU

Sources: Table in "A Club in Need of a New Vision," *The Economist,* May 1, 2004, p. 26; David M. Wood and Birol A. Yeşilada, *The Emerging European Union,* 3rd ed. (New York: Pearson Longman, 2004), pp. 1–8.

system for several reasons. First, European integration progressed because most EC members were also members of the NATO alliance, and "tariff cuts are more likely between allies than between states belonging to different military coalitions."[14] Second, under the bipolar system the U.S. and Soviet superpowers assumed the main responsibilities in the security sphere, and this enabled Western Europe to focus on regional economic integration.[15] Third, the emergence of the United States and Soviet Union as the only superpowers also gave Europeans an *incentive* to form the EC. With European states facing the loss of their colonies, integration was necessary if they were to retain some influence in the bipolar world. Fourth, although the United States generally opposed RTAs during the 1950s and 1960s, it supported the EC because it viewed economic recovery in Western Europe as essential to meeting the Soviet security threat. Indeed, U.S. insistence that Europeans *jointly* administer U.S. Marshall Plan aid resulted in the formation of the **Organization for European Economic Cooperation (OEEC)** in 1948. The OEEC also oversaw moves toward the convertibility of European currencies and the integration of West Germany in Western Europe; this laid the foundations for the eventual formation of the EC.[16]

When the Soviet Union collapsed and the Cold War ended in the early 1990s, realists such as John Mearsheimer argued that cooperation among EU members would no longer be necessary to counter the Soviet threat. Thus, EU integration would falter as each EU member would begin to focus on its relative gains vis-à-vis the other members.[17] However, realists looking at other states and regions in the 1980s and 1990s predicted that regional integration would increase. After World War II, the United States as global hegemon used its power and resources to support an open multilateral trade regime centered in GATT. As U.S. economic hegemony declined, it was less willing to continue providing this support, and it sought to regain its economic leverage by joining RTAs such as NAFTA. U.S. participation in RTAs was a major factor contributing to the rise of regional integration in the second wave.[18] Some realists also pointed out that security considerations explain the formation of some North–South bilateral FTAs in recent years. For example, Singapore and South Korea sought bilateral FTAs with the United States partly to maintain a continued U.S. presence in East Asia as a counterbalance to China, Japan, and North Korea.[19] In the European case, the formation of the EMU and the expansion of the EU to 27 members raise serious doubts about Mearsheimer's prediction that European integration would falter with the end of the Cold War, but there are also signs of disarray in the EU today (see discussion in this chapter).[20]

Liberal Explanations

Liberals have been the main contributors to regional integration theory. We discuss liberal theory on the *deepening* of integration from a free trade area to a CU, common market, and economic union in the section of this chapter on Europe. The following discussion summarizes liberal views concerning the reasons why states form RTAs. Liberal assertions include the following:

- International institutions at the regional as well as global levels are created to support a liberal economic order. Thus, there were close linkages between the liberalism of the postwar era and the creation of the IMF, World Bank, GATT, and new RTAs.
- RTAs are created to promote peace among countries within a region. For example, France, West Germany, Italian, the Netherlands, Belgium, and Luxembourg formed the European Coal and Steel Community (ECSC) in 1951 to integrate their coal and steel resources. The main purpose was to integrate France and West Germany's coal and steel resources and prevent them from renewing their age-old conflicts. The six ECSC members expanded their agreement in 1957 to form the EC. (This liberal assertion draws partly on David Mitrany's *theory of functionalism,* which states that "international economic and social cooperation is a major prerequisite for the ultimate solution of political conflicts and the elimination of war.")[21]
- RTAs are formed to provide a larger market for member countries' products. The agreement to form the EC was based partly on an understanding among the two largest members that the EC would provide a market for

France's agricultural goods and West Germany's industrial products. A major attraction of NAFTA for the two smaller partners (Canada and Mexico) was the free trade access they would have to the large U.S. market for their exports.

- RTAs are formed to promote freer foreign investment flows. For example, a major reason Mexico joined in forming NAFTA was its need for more foreign investment from the United States; and the United States supported NAFTA partly to liberalize foreign investment flows in the region.
- RTAs are formed to compensate for the inadequacies of the multilateral trade regime. GATT/WTO negotiations have encountered numerous problems, and RTAs are often a more feasible route to freer trade because they involve smaller groups of like-minded states. Thus, the number of RTAs has increased most rapidly when there are problems with global trade negotiations (such as the Uruguay and Doha Rounds). States also sometimes seek RTAs because they can provide a positive demonstration effect for the GATT/WTO; for example, the 1988 Canada–U.S. Free Trade Agreement (CUSFTA) included provisions on trade in services and agriculture before GATT addressed these issues.[22]
- RTAs are formed because of pressures from domestic groups. Interdependence and globalization have caused many private firms to become more dependent on trade and shift their operations from the national to multinational level. These internationalist firms pressure for freer regional as well as global trade. Regionalism often improves the competitiveness of international firms, because they can develop economies of scale and benefit from "the larger regional markets as their base rather than just the home market."[23]
- RTAs are formed as part of a "two-level game," in which political leaders can use the requirements of the RTA to bring about domestic changes. For example, one reason Canada sought the CUSFTA was "to constrain the more subtle new instruments of protectionism. More open borders would expose Canadian firms to greater international competition and encourage them to restructure and modernize."[24]

Historical Materialist Explanations

Historical materialists, like liberals, see MNCs and other sources of transnational capital as having a central role in the creation of RTAs. Unlike liberals, however, historical materialists believe that RTAs permit MNCs to locate their production facilities in states with the lowest taxes, wages, and environmental standards and then export freely within the RTA. Whereas the capitalist class benefits from the growth of regionalism, domestic labor suffers because capital can move more easily to low-wage regions and states. Historical materialists also attribute the development of RTAs to the desire of powerful states to seek regional hegemony. As its global economic hegemony declined, the United States sought to recoup its losses by establishing its hegemony more firmly on a regional basis.

Thus, some critics charge that NAFTA was "designed to fit Canada and Mexico into the American model of development, on terms amenable to American corporations."[25]

THE GATT/WTO AND RTAs

The United States as the postwar global hegemon strongly opposed preferential agreements that would interfere with an open multilateral trade regime. However, Britain wanted to preserve its discriminatory imperial preferences, and a number of states wanted to establish RTAs. The U.S. views largely prevailed, and GATT Article 1 calls for unconditional MFN treatment. However, GATT Article 24 permits countries to form FTAs and CUs that do not adhere to MFN treatment, as long as these agreements meet specific conditions.[26] In line with the liberal view that open RTAs offer a second-best route to trade liberalization, Article 24 sanctions the formation of CUs and FTAs but seeks to ensure that they are more trade creating than diverting.[27] An examination of the rationale for Article 24 is crucial to understanding the WTO's relationship with RTAs. Before discussing Article 24, it is necessary to describe the ways in which RTAs are trade creating and trade diverting.

Trade Diversion

RTAs produce some trade diversion because the elimination of intraregional trade barriers shifts some imports from more efficient outside suppliers to less efficient regional suppliers. Furthermore, the freeing of trade within an RTA increases competition in member countries' markets. Inefficient industries may lobby for increased external trade barriers to shift the adjustment burden onto countries outside the RTA. Thus, trade diversion can result when RTAs raise protectionist barriers against outsiders. Investment diversion may also occur when MNCs put branch plants inside an RTA to take advantage of the tariff-free zone instead of producing in the least-cost location and shipping goods to the region.

A CU may be more trade diverting in some respects than an FTA. Even if external tariffs do not increase on the average when a CU is formed, protectionism may increase if the CU imposes antidumping and countervailing duties in response to pressure from import-competing industries. In view of the CET, such duties can limit imports to the entire CU area. Antidumping and countervailing duties pose less of a problem for outsiders in an FTA because each FTA member levies its own tariffs, and industries cannot pressure for areawide protection. Whereas antidumping and countervailing duties are a special problem in CUs, **rules of origin** may have serious trade-diverting effects in FTAs. Because each FTA member has its own external tariffs, FTAs require rules of origin to prevent importers from bringing goods in through the lowest duty member and then shipping them duty-free to other FTA members. The rules of origin determine whether products have undergone enough processing within the FTA to qualify for the trade preferences. It is difficult to formulate these rules because many goods are manufactured with components from a number of countries. Domestic firms often pressure FTAs for stiffer rules of origin, which can become a form of trade protectionism against outsiders. Rules of origin are a less significant issue for CUs because of the CET.[28] Trade diversion depends on external as well as internal political dynamics. When an RTA is formed, nonmember states have the incentive to establish their own RTAs to "better defend themselves against the discriminatory effects of *other* regional groups."[29] Furthermore, regional trade blocs such as the EU can become larger as pressure from disadvantaged nonmember firms triggers "membership requests from countries that were previously happy to be nonmembers."[30] This proliferation of regionalism increases fragmentation of the global trade regime.

Trade Creation

The main source of trade creation in RTAs is the increased trade among members, which shifts demand from less efficient domestic suppliers to more efficient regional suppliers. When firms within the region become more competitive as a result of the RTA, they are also more likely to support freer trade at the global as well as regional levels. Furthermore, RTAs often achieve a deeper level of integration than multilateral agreements because negotiations occur among a smaller number of like-minded partners. RTAs may therefore have a positive demonstration effect on multilateral trade negotiations. For example, the inclusion of agriculture, services, and intellectual property in the NAFTA provided a stimulus for negotiating these issues in the GATT Uruguay Round.

GATT Article 24 and RTAs

GATT Article 24 seeks to ensure that RTAs result in more trade creation and less trade diversion. *To increase trade creation,* Article 24 stipulates that FTAs and CUs are to eliminate tariffs on "substantially all" trade among the members within a "reasonable" time period. (GATT granted waivers from the substantially all trade requirement for the ECSC in 1952 and the Canada–U.S. Auto Pact in 1965.) The GATT founders believed that a requirement to remove all tariffs in RTAs would limit preferential agreements with only partial trade liberalization such as those that contributed to protectionism during the 1930s. RTAs that remove all internal trade barriers are also more likely to serve as stepping stones to multilateral free trade. *To decrease trade diversion,* Article 24 stipulates that an RTA should not raise tariffs on the average to countries outside the agreement. Whereas individual members of an FTA are not to raise their average level of duties, the CET of a CU may not "on the whole" be higher than the duties of the member states' before the CU was established. These provisions are designed to limit reductions in imports from nonmembers as a result of the RTA.[31] Although GATT Article 24 *seems* to regulate RTAs, it is necessary to ask how effective it has been in practice.

The Effectiveness of GATT Article 24

When countries formed an RTA, GATT established a working party to determine whether it met the Article 24 conditions. However, these working parties had only limited influence over RTAs. GATT's regulations for RTAs were drafted with smaller agreements in mind, such as the Benelux CU negotiated by Belgium, the Netherlands, and Luxembourg in 1944. In 1957, however, the EC members were unwilling to wait for GATT approval before proceeding with economic integration because of the size and importance of the EC. Negotiating the Treaty of Rome had been a difficult process, and EC members would not readjust the treaty to satisfy GATT.[32] In the end, GATT acceded to EC demands and never finished examining the Treaty of Rome, even though it had reached no consensus on the treaty's consistency with Article 24. GATT's acquiescence in this case limited its authority over subsequent RTAs. Thus, GATT working parties had little success in changing RTAs after member states negotiated them. Whereas GATT was notified about early agreements such as the EC before they entered into force, some later agreements such as NAFTA entered into force before a working party was even formed to examine them.[33]

It is not surprising that GATT had little influence over RTAs after they were negotiated. Governments had already engaged in extensive bargaining and were reluctant to reopen negotiations in response to outside criticism. GATT working parties could only try to embarrass RTA members with allegations of noncompliance and encourage them to comply with the guidelines in the future. However, GATT did influence decision making *at earlier stages* by setting broad parameters for conducting the regional negotiations. For example, the diplomats negotiating the EC and some FTAs

> were operating under instructions to make maximum efforts to comply with GATT rules, and the actual results of these negotiations testify that a quite important degree of GATT compliance was achieved. Except for agriculture . . . and except for the EC's relationship with former colonies, the . . . developed-country agreements . . . were essentially GATT-conforming. To be sure, GATT was unable to do anything further once the agreements were signed and deposited in Geneva.[34]

Some analysts note that GATT was less effective because Article 24 requirements that RTAs cover "substantially all" trade, do not become more restrictive "on average" to outsiders, and be fully implemented in a "reasonable length of time" are subject to multiple interpretations. In view of the imprecise wording, working parties were reluctant to give RTAs unqualified approval. By 1994, only 6 of 69 working parties had reached a consensus that particular RTAs conformed to Article 24, and only 2 of these 6 RTAs are still operative.[35] In most cases, working parties simply noted that members had divergent views regarding the RTA's conformity with GATT. However, GATT never explicitly concluded that an RTA did *not* meet the legal requirements! Article 24 also does not adequately address such issues as rules of origin and antidumping and countervailing duties, which may increase regional protectionism toward outsiders.[36] To improve the regulation of RTAs, an Understanding on the Interpretation of Article 24 (UR Understanding) and a GATS article on regional trade in services (Article 5) were concluded in the GATT Uruguay Round.[37] The WTO also established a *Committee on Regional Trade Agreements* (*CRTA*) in 1996. Although the Uruguay Round agreements and CRTA have dealt with some GATT Article 24 shortcomings, many problems remain. For example, divisions persist on the interpretation of concepts such as the "substantially all trade" requirement (many RTAs exclude agriculture), and the Uruguay Round negotiators did not decide how to deal with restrictive rules of origin in FTAs. In 2006 a negotiating group agreed on a new mechanism to ensure that the WTO receives early notification of new RTAs; but this mechanism may not become permanent because of the breakdown of the Doha Round.[38]

Special Treatment for LDCs

Although GATT Article 24 was to apply to all RTAs, LDCs receive special treatment in this area.

RTAs AMONG LDCs The GATT/WTO is more lenient in its approach to RTAs among LDCs. For example, GATT did not object to the formation of the LAFTA in 1960, even though it "did not even approach the requirements of total integration."[39] After Part IV on trade and development was added to GATT in 1965, LDCs sometimes invoked it when forming RTAs that did not meet Article 24's substantially all trade requirement. When the 1979 enabling clause established a permanent legal basis for LDC preferences, it became the main legal basis for LDCs forming questionable RTAs. The enabling clause permits LDCs to form RTAs that cover a limited range of products and lower rather than eliminate tariffs. Any RTA is eligible for special treatment under the enabling clause, as long as the RTA does not include any DC members. For example, Mercosur was notified to GATT under the enabling clause, not Article 24 (see discussion below).[40] Despite the GATT/WTO's permissiveness, recent LDC moves toward trade liberalization have inevitably affected their RTAs. The negative experience of LDCs with import substitution policies, combined with IMF and World Bank pressure on LDC debtors to liberalize, have caused RTAs among LDCs to become more outward looking.

THE EU ASSOCIATION AGREEMENTS WITH LDCs As discussed in Chapter 7, DCs unilaterally established a generalized system of preferences (GSPs) for LDCs. The EU association agreements with LDCs by contrast are *jointly* negotiated preferential agreements. When the EC was formed in 1957, the Treaty of Rome provided associate status to France's African Overseas Territories.[41] The EC's enlargement when Britain, Denmark, and Ireland joined in 1973 (see Table 8.1) necessitated a change because of Britain's relationship with

Commonwealth LDCs. In 1975, the nine EC members concluded the first **Lomé Convention** (Lomé I) with 46 *African, Caribbean, and Pacific* countries (the *ACP* countries); three more Lomé Conventions followed in 1979, 1984, and 1989 (eventually with 71 ACP states). In the Lomé Conventions the EC offered preferential access for ACP products to its market *without requiring reciprocity* for EC goods. A number of GATT members argued that the Lomé system was not a genuine FTA because it was nonreciprocal. GATT Article 24 provides an exception to MFN treatment *only* for RTAs that follow the reciprocity principle. Furthermore, the 1979 enabling clause permits DCs to provide trade preferences only if *all* LDCs have access to these preferences. The enabling clause does *not* sanction EU discrimination in favor of its ex-colonies at the expense of other LDCs. Although the EU insisted that the association agreements contributed to LDC economic development, external events increased the pressures for change. For example, in 1994 Mexico accepted reciprocal free trade with the DCs (the United States and Canada) in NAFTA.[42] The value of the Lomé Conventions to ACP countries was also questioned because ACP benefits from the EC trade preferences declined as MFN tariffs were reduced in the GATT negotiations, the EC limited imports of some ACP products, and the nonreciprocal preferences enabled ACP states to maintain inefficient production structures. Thus, the ACP states' share of the EU market fell from 6.7 percent in 1976 to 3 percent in 1998, with more than 60 percent of ACP exports concentrated in only 10 primary products. Historical materialists also described EU nonreciprocal preferences "as a form of neocolonialism that perpetuates the production of . . . products not compatible" with the long-term interests of the ACP states.[43] Even in the EU there were pressures for change because the nonreciprocable tariff preferences with ACP states complicated the EU's relations with other LDCs.

In view of the pressures for change, the EU and ACP states negotiated the more WTO-compatible *Cotonou Agreement* (or *New Partnership Agreement*) in 2000. The Cotonou Agreement stipulates that the ACP nonreciprocal tariff preferences will continue until 2008, when ACP–EU *reciprocal* "economic partnership" agreements will gradually replace them over a 10- to 12-year period. Although supporters of this change argue that the ACP states will benefit by liberalizing their trade policies, critics argue that EU–ACP nonreciprocal relations must continue because of the lower level of development of the ACPs.[44]

The following sections focus on the EU and NAFTA, the two most important RTAs today; Mercosur, the largest RTA among LDCs; and East Asian regionalism because of the growing importance of Asia in the global political economy.

THE EUROPEAN UNION

Postwar regional integration has been mainly in Europe, with European states as parties to 76 of the 109 RTAs formed from 1948 to 1994.[45] In 1951, six states (Belgium, France, West Germany, Italy, Luxembourg, and the Netherlands) formed the ECSC and then established the EC and the European Atomic Energy

Community (Euratom) in 1957 (see Table 8.1). In 1959, seven states (Austria, Britain, Denmark, Norway, Portugal, Sweden, and Switzerland) formed the EFTA. These states would not join the EC because it required a degree of policy coordination that threatened Britain's Commonwealth preference system and the nonaligned policies of states such as Sweden and Switzerland. As Table 8.1 shows, the EC gradually added some former members of EFTA. In 1993 the EC's name was changed to the EU to symbolize the extension of the community from trade and economic matters to a much broader range of activities under the Maastricht Treaty. Thus, the term "EC" is used when discussing events from 1957 to 1992, and "EU" is used for events from 1993 to the present.

As discussed, the EU is an economic union, and 16 of the 27 EU members have disgarded their national currencies and adopted the euro (see Table 8.1). The EU's institutional structure differentiates it from other RTAs at a lower level of integration. The *European Commission* represents general EU interests rather than those of any particular member state, and the powers of the *European Court of Justice (ECJ)* are greater than those of other international courts. The EU is therefore a "supranational" organization that operates above the level of the nation-state in some areas. However, the *Council of Ministers* (or *Council of the European Union*) is the EU's primary decision-making body and the most powerful EU institution in day-to-day politics. The fact that the Council of Ministers are foreign ministers representing their governments is a reminder that the EU (despite its supranationality) is still beholden to its member states. Other important institutions of the EU are the *European Parliament* and *European Council* (of Heads of State and Government). In sum, the EU's unique institutional structure gives it more authority than other IOs, but ensures that it remains subject to considerable control by its member states.[46]

The Deepening of European Integration

The EC began with considerable enthusiasm in 1957, but the integration process slowed in the 1960s and 1970s due to actions of France's President Charles de Gaulle and international events such as the collapse of the Bretton Woods monetary regime, the OPEC oil crisis, and the onset of recession. Although Britain joined the EC in 1973, it opposed the development of strong EC supranational institutions, and the 1970s were marked by "Eurosclerosis" (i.e., stagnation) and a loss of faith in the EC's vitality.[47] In the early 1980s, EC members became acutely aware of their lack of competitiveness vis-à-vis the United States and Japan. Divisions within the EC due to differential taxation, border inspections, domestic subsidies, and limits to market access were a major source of the problem. Thus, the EC sought to create a unified European market with more competitive firms based on specialization and economies of scale. The EC Commission President Jacques Delors was a significant force behind the negotiation of the 1986 *Single European Act (SEA)*, which was designed to abolish nontariff barriers, liberalize trade in services, and facilitate the free movement of capital and labor by 1992 (see Table 8.2).

TABLE 8.2   The Deepening of European Integration

Year	Event	Description
1951	European Coal and Steel Community (ECSC)	• Six states integrate their coal and steel resources
1957	Treaty of Rome	• Establishes the European Economic Community (EC)
1986	Single European Act (SEA)	• To free the movement of goods, services, and labor
		• Commitment to form a monetary union (EMU)
1992	Treaty on European Union (or Maastricht Treaty)	• Commitment to form an EMU, common foreign and security policy, common social policy
		• Renames the EC the European Union (EU)
1999	Creation of the Euro	• 11 EU states adopt the euro as a common currency. The number increases to 16 states by early 2009

The SEA also included a commitment to monetary union, and the European Council established the Delors Committee to propose a plan for this purpose. The committee proposed a three-stage process toward a monetary union, and negotiations subsequently resulted in the *Treaty on European Union* (or *Maastricht Treaty*) in December 1991 (see Table 8.2). Although the proposed EMU was the centerpiece of the Maastricht Treaty, the treaty also sought to establish a European federal political system with common social, foreign, and security policies. A large segment of public opinion was initially hostile to the Maastricht Treaty, and this forced European governments to confront the problem of legitimizing an integration process in which EU bureaucrats were largely removed from the populace.[48] Because the EMU is discussed in Chapter 6, this section focuses on the Maastricht Treaty's commitment to cooperation on foreign and security policy and social policy.

The Maastricht Treaty describes the EC as the first pillar, and a common foreign and security policy as the second pillar of the EU. On security, the Treaty reflected "a delicate balance between a French view that sought to develop security policy in the Union through the European Commission and a British view that sought to enhance the Western European Union in order to strengthen NATO."[49] Although the long-term cooperation between the EU and NATO (the North Atlantic Treaty Organization) on security and defense policy will depend on future negotiations, the EU will depend on NATO in the near to medium term. Divisions on security issues ranging from the former Yugoslavia to the Middle East and the response to terrorism raise questions as to whether the EU can in fact develop a common security policy. The other Maastricht Treaty area involves social policy toward organized labor, a welfare state, and migration into the EU. For example, the EU Council of Ministers was given authority to make decisions by qualified majority vote on working conditions and worker health and safety. Social issues are highly sensitive because of political divisions in Europe between conservatives and social democrats, and management has occurred more through informal agreements. Of the Maastricht Treaty's broad goals for deepening integration, the objective of forming an EMU has been the most successful, and 16 EU members have adopted the euro as a common currency.[50] Although Table 8.2 shows that European integration has deepened over the years, we have discussed some of the obstacles to the integration process. As the next section discusses, the widening of European integration is also putting strains on the deepening process.

The Widening of European Integration

As Table 8.1 shows, the EU expanded from 6 to 27 members in several enlargements. While increasing its membership, the EU also extended associate linkages with the ACP states and other LDCs. Whereas the deepening of integration has often been a response to economic conditions, the recent widening was "thrust on the EU by the failure of communism in Europe."[51] This section focuses on the accession of 12 Central and Eastern European countries (CEECs) to the EU in 2004 and 2007.

The Soviet Union was hostile to the EC when it was formed in 1957, and insisted that the Council for Mutual Economic Assistance (CMEA) be the vehicle for EC economic contacts with Eastern Europe. However, the EC preferred to negotiate bilateral agreements with Eastern European states and some of them broke ranks with the Soviet position. For example, the EC granted the GSP to Romania in 1972, and Romania and the EC signed a trade and cooperation agreement in 1980. As economic conditions in the East worsened, the Soviets became more dependent on economic linkages with the West and softened their position; thus, a 1988 EC–CMEA agreement sanctioned EC negotiations with individual Eastern European states. After the breakup of the Soviet bloc, the EU negotiated a number of "Europe agreements" with Eastern Europeans. However, the EU offered the Eastern Europeans only limited trade concessions, and they began to apply for full membership in the EU.[52]

An obstacle to admitting the Eastern Europeans was the disparity in economic development between the CEECs and most EU members. Ten CEECs that signed Europe agreements with the EU had only one-fourth of the purchasing power of the EU average, and about 20 percent of their workers had agricultural jobs compared with only 6 percent of EU workers.[53] Thus, an EU Commission report warned that admission of the CEECs would cause firms to move eastward because of lower labor costs in Eastern Europe, migration from the CEECs due to higher wages in Western Europe, and a sharp increase in the population eligible for EU social and economic development funds. However, official EU statements described enlargement as "a political necessity and a historic opportunity."[54] Both the CEECs and the EU saw some advantages from enlargement. The CEECs felt that EU and NATO membership would give them security vis-à-vis Russia and that access to EU capital, technology, and markets would help close the economic gap with the West. EU members believed that stable CEECs would provide a buffer against political instability, the CEECs would provide the EU with cheaper workers and investment opportunities, and enlargement would enhance the EU's influence. From a realist perspective, the EU would "not be able to withstand competition from . . . America and Asia unless it expands its economic area and market."[55]

Ten CEECs were admitted to the EU in May 2004. Although this was the largest expansion in the number of states, Table 8.1 shows that it was not the most important in GDP terms. Whereas the 1973 accession of Britain, Denmark, and Ireland added 31.9 percent to the EC's GDP, the 2004 accession of the 10 CEECs added only 9.1 percent to the EU's GDP. A major factor accounting for this difference is the lower incomes of the 10 CEECs. Thus, the last column of Table 8.1 shows that the per capita GDP of Britain, Denmark, and Ireland was 95.5 percent of the EC average when they joined in 1973. The per capita GDP of the 10 CEECs was by contrast only 46.5 percent of the EU average when they joined in 2004. When Bulgaria and Romania joined the EU in 2007, their incomes were only a third of the EU average. Romania and Bulgaria together increased the EU's population by 6.5 percent, but added only 1 percent to the EU's economic output. The CEECs have also had much greater difficulties than the Western European EU countries in responding to the 2008 global financial crisis.[56]

Widening need not hinder the deepening of integration, and sometimes they occur together. However, the large number of states involved in the 2004 and 2007 enlargements and their lower level of economic development contributed to a diversity of interests that was "harder to contain within a single framework."[57] The failure to ratify a new EU constitutional treaty in 2005 and a revised version (the Treaty of Lisbon) in 2008 exemplifies the problem. In 2005 French voters rejected the constitution for several reasons, including economic insecurity and unemployment, hostility to political leaders, and concerns that the constitution would move the EU further toward liberal orthodoxy. However, French voters were also reacting to the growing size and diversity of the EU. They were concerned that the large EU bureaucracy was removed from the populace, that they would lose jobs to lower cost labor in the CEECs, and that France's influence in the EU was declining. Several other states, including Turkey and Croatia, are candidates for possible admission, and a major task for the EU is to strike the proper balance between the widening and deepening of integration.[58]

Theoretical Perspectives and the EU

Theory on the deepening of integration is most relevant to the EU, because of its advanced level of integration. We discuss here three theoretical approaches: neofunctionalism, liberal intergovernmentalism, and constructivism.

NEOFUNCTIONALISM Theorists generally ask why European states have chosen to pool substantial elements of their sovereignty in the EU. *Neofunctionalists* see integration in one economic sector as creating pressures for further integration. For example, the six ECSC members found that the integration of their coal and steel resources would have only limited benefits without also coordinating their transportation systems for moving the coal and steel. Thus, neofunctionalists believe that regional integration has an expansive logic, in which integration of one economic sector creates pressures for *spillover* into related sectors. Spillover can also contribute to the deepening of integration from an FTA to a CU, common market, and economic union. Whereas functionalists see spillover as an automatic process, neofunctionalists see political activism by interest-driven actors as also necessary. First, integration in an area (in this case coal and steel) results in increased transactions and in new interest organizations (representing business, labor, and consumer groups) at the regional level. These interests exert political pressure for deeper integration. Second, the supranational bureaucracy (the High Authority in the ECSC or the European Commission in the EU) has a vested interest in expanding its authority through the deepening of integration over a wider range of sectors. Thus, Ernst Haas describes integration as "the process whereby political actors in several distinct national settings are persuaded to shift their loyalties, expectations and political activities toward a new center, whose institutions possess or demand jurisdiction over the pre-existing national states."[59]

Neofunctionalism had considerable influence on the study of regional integration, but its influence varied over the years. The expansion of integration from the ECSC to the EC seemed to support neofunctionalism, but numerous problems during the 1960s and 1970s (De Gaulle's actions and Euroschlerosis) raised questions about the expansive logic of the theory. Neofunctionalist ideas such as "spillover" had somewhat of a revival with the SEA, the Treaty of Maastricht, and the creation of the EMU, and neofunctionalist theory continues to influence the study of integration. However, few scholars call themselves neofunctionalists today because the theory has been subject to numerous criticisms. First, the tortuous path of European integration demonstrates conflicting pressures for integration and diversity, and there is no certainty that "spillover" will occur. Second, neofunctionalists tended to ignore the growing gap between elites on the one hand and voters and consumers on the other. The average citizen has been more skeptical of European integration than the elites, and this is evident from the failed referendums on a new EU constitution. Contrary to what Haas predicted, citizens have *not* shifted their "loyalties, expectations and political activities toward a new center." Third, critics argue that the member states, rather than interest groups and the EU institutions, have the main power in the EU. States resist further integration when it does not fit with their national objectives.[60]

LIBERAL INTERGOVERNMENTALISM Whereas neofunctionalists emphasize societal interests and supranational institutions, liberal intergovernmentalists consider states (central governments) to be the most important actors. For liberal intergovernmentalists, member states remain free to choose how the EU functions. Andrew Moravcsik is the founder of liberal intergovernmentalism, which is "liberal" in its view of governments as bringing together domestic interest groups within a state, and "intergovernmentalist" in its emphasis on the central role of states (which also shows the influence of realism). According to this theory, the EU rests on a series of bargains between member states, which are self-interested and rational in pursuing outcomes that serve their economic interests. Major policy decisions reflect the preferences of national governments rather than supranational institutions, and each state's preferences reflect the balance of its domestic economic interests. Conflict may arise between states with different preferences, and the status quo changes only when states (especially the largest ones) agree to acceptable compromises. Intergovernmentalists seek to explain how national interests are reconciled in intergovernmental bargains, and they see the EU as occupying "a permanent position at the heart of the European landscape" only because of decisions by member states.[61] The members support the EU supranational institutions as a means of enforcing intergovernmental bargains. Thus, European integration is reversible in many respects, and always will be. While neofunctionalists are criticized for underemphasizing the role of national governments, liberal intergovernmentalists are criticized for overemphasizing their role. Moravcsik focuses on a series of "grand bargains" between governments, but devotes less attention to the EU's day-to-day politics. Governments cannot monitor daily activities, and this gives institutions such as the EU commission considerable discretion to make decisions that may differ from government preferences. Neofunctional theory also emphasizes the fact that state bargains may have "unintended consequences" in giving more discretion than expected to the supranational institutions. Liberal intergovernmentalism devotes too little attention to these unintended consequences.

CONSTRUCTIVISM Neofunctionalists and liberal intergovernmentalists emphasize the role of material factors such as interests in the integration process. Constructivists by contrast focus on the role of ideas, norms, and identity. In studying European integration, we need to understand not only the interactions of the EU with member states and domestic and transnational interest groups, but also the effects of national self-image, identity, and views of the integration process. For example, compliance with EU principles and rules often depends less on EU sanctions and rewards than on whether a country sees itself as law abiding. Some EU states are noted for implementing EU laws even when there is strong domestic opposition to them. Compliance with EU rules also depends on the development of a European identity within societies of the member states, and this can only occur if there is some EU compatibility with the core elements of national identity. Furthermore, assessments of the integration process require some understanding of the developing European identity. If various European groups do not view some states such as Turkey as being "European," they might oppose their joining the EU even if they meet the objective criteria for membership. Although constructivists correctly alert us to the importance of of ideas, norms, and identities, critics argue that they have not yet developed shared theoretical principles and research strategies for studying the integration process.[62]

THE NORTH AMERICAN FREE TRADE AGREEMENT

Regionalism in the Western Hemisphere is more heterogeneous than it is in Europe. Efforts to form a *Free Trade Area of the Americas* for the entire hemisphere were a failure, and the most important FTA in the Western Hemisphere continues to be the NAFTA. As discussed, the United States would not participate in comprehensive RTAs from the 1940s to the early 1970s and instead focused on developing a strong GATT-based multilateral trade regime. However, a reversal of U.S. policies combined with greater openness to free trade in Canada and Mexico resulted in the creation of the CUSFTA in the 1980s and NAFTA in the 1990s.

The Formation of NAFTA

Moves toward Canada–U.S. free trade have a long history, and a noted historian observed that one economic issue in Canada "comes close to rivalling the linguistic and race question for both longevity and vehemence, and this is, of course, the question of free trade with the United States."[63] In 1854, the two countries concluded a Reciprocity Treaty providing for free trade in natural products such as grains, meat, dairy products, and fish. However, the United States abrogated the treaty in 1866 because of its negative trade balance with Canada, increased Canadian duties on U.S. manufactures, and the British role in the U.S. Civil War. Efforts to revive free trade in 1911 and 1948 were unsuccessful, but the 1965 Canada–U.S. Auto Agreement provided for free trade in automobiles and parts (the two states received a GATT waiver from the Article 24 requirement that FTAs should cover substantially all trade). In 1988 the two states established their first comprehensive FTA, the CUSFTA; when Mexico, the United States, and Canada signed NAFTA in 1992, it superseded CUSFTA.

The question arises as to why these FTAs were formed after so many years. The United States reversed its policy on RTAs with the 1974 U.S. Trade Act, which permitted the president to "initiate negotiations for a trade agreement with Canada to establish a free trade area."[64] However, Canada and Mexico requested the negotiations that resulted in CUSFTA and NAFTA. Canada and Mexico had become increasingly dependent on trade with the United States and cross-border production with U.S. companies, and both countries were seeking to increase their competitiveness by becoming less protectionist. When the United States responded to its balance of payments deficits in the mid-1980s with increased protectionism, both countries viewed an FTA as necessary to gain more assured access to the U.S. market and to solidify their domestic reforms. Mexico was also concerned about Canada's more favored position as a U.S. trader due to the Canada–U.S. FTA, and as an LDC Mexico viewed an FTA as essential for attracting more U.S. foreign investment. The United States as a major economic power was more concerned about global trade linkages, and it decided to conclude CUSFTA and NAFTA largely because of frustration with the slow pace of the GATT Uruguay Round. Negotiating RTAs, in the U.S. view, would induce the EU and Japan to offer concessions in the GATT negotiations. Regionalism also has a tendency to breed more regionalism, and the EU's enlargement and consolidation in the SEA gave the United States another reason to join RTAs. Furthermore, the United States became less committed to multilateralism as the sole option and more open to participating in RTAs as its trade hegemony declined. The United States also wanted Canada and Mexico to ease their regulations on foreign investment and natural resources, and it was willing to open its market to Canadian and Mexican goods in return. The private sector in all three countries also provided a major impetus for the formation of NAFTA. High levels of cross-border intraindustry trade in intermediate goods and possible gains from economies of scale induced producers in key sectors such computers, autos, electronics, and machinery to pressure for an RTA.[65]

NAFTA as a Free Trade Agreement

Unlike the EU, NAFTA has remained a free trade agreement. All three countries have been skeptical of EU-type supranational institutions that would impinge on national sovereignty, and the U.S. Congress has long resisted agreements that interfere with U.S. trade policy (see Chapter 7 on the United States and the planned ITO). However, Mexico and Canada as the two smaller NAFTA members realized that further integration in some areas was necessary to protect their interests, even if it infringed on their sovereignty. For example, Canada considers U.S. antidumping and countervailing duty laws to be highly protectionist, and favors either the elimination of ADDs and CVDs among the NAFTA members or a common code to define which subsidies are permissible. However, the United States sees the use of ADDs and CVDs as its sovereign prerogative, and NAFTA dispute settlement panels can only decide whether a country's decision to levy a CVD is made in accordance with its own law; the panels *cannot* assess the fairness of each country's laws. As the less-developed NAFTA member, Mexico views some aspects of EU integration as useful for decreasing asymmetries in wealth and power. When Vicente Fox became Mexico's president in 2000, he proposed that North American integration extend to the free movement of labor as well as goods and services; and he also proposed that a development fund be established to upgrade infrastructure throughout North America. The United States and Canada, however, did not support these proposals, and NAFTA continues to have a minimal institutional framework. Thus, the NAFTA approach depends on the market to facilitate integration and decrease inequalities of wealth over the long term.[66] As an FTA, NAFTA has detailed rules of origin in key sectors such as automobiles to prevent imports from entering the free trade area via the member with the lowest tariffs.

The private sector has been an important force behind NAFTA, which has moved further than the WTO in services trade, intellectual property rights, and dispute settlement procedures. In dispute settlement, NAFTA's highly contentious Chapter 11 gives private investors access to binding international arbitration if they believe that a host government's investment measures do not adhere to national treatment. This contrasts with WTO dispute settlement cases where only states can be directly involved in dispute settlement. Business firms are not the only private actors that have helped shape NAFTA. The controversy surrounding NAFTA before U.S. ratification provided an opportunity for civil society groups to ensure that two side agreements would be included: the *North American Agreement on Labor Cooperation* and the *North American Agreement on Environmental Cooperation*. The environmental side agreement seeks to ensure that the NAFTA members cooperate on environmental issues, that each member enforces its domestic environmental laws, and that a mechanism exists for settling environmental disputes. The side agreement also established a *Commission on Environmental Cooperation (CEC)* to conduct studies on environmental behavior of NAFTA members, hear complaints, and settle disputes. However, the institutions formed to implement the two side agreements have only limited authority and funding to perform their activities; this reflects the fact that NAFTA is mainly a trade and investment agreement that has not developed EU-type supranational institutions. Whereas the EU is committed to upward harmonization of regulations regarding air and water pollution, waste management, and climate change, the NAFTA members retain their rights to establish their own levels of environmental protection.[67]

In sum, the NAFTA negotiators included some innovative features in such areas as services and agricultural trade, investment, and dispute settlement. However, NAFTA has remained an FTA with a minimal degree of institutionalization.

The IPE Theoretical Perspectives and NAFTA

NAFTA is controversial in all three countries, and the controversy is reflected in the divisions among and within the IPE theoretical perspectives.

LIBERALISM Liberal economists often praise NAFTA for being an open RTA that serves as a stepping stone to multilateral free trade. The NAFTA negotiations demonstrated that the United States might opt for regionalism as an alternative to multilateralism, and the EU and Japan were therefore more willing to compromise during the GATT Uruguay Round. NAFTA also had a positive demonstration effect on the WTO in services trade, investment, and intellectual property rights, and it goes beyond the WTO in these areas. For example, NAFTA follows a "negative list" approach to national treatment for trade in services, which puts the onus on each NAFTA member to identify services it wants to exclude from national treatment; all services a country does not list are automatically included. The General Agreement on Trade in Services (GATS), by contrast, takes a "positive list" approach; that is, national treatment applies only to sectors specifically included in a member's list of commitments. Liberals acknowledge that NAFTA has produced both winners and losers, and that some workers and businesses will not benefit. However, they assert that the rewards from NAFTA greatly exceed the costs, and that trade among the NAFTA countries has increased more than threefold since the agreement entered into force. Liberals also often praise NAFTA for its market orientation, and note that it is the first North–South FTA that does not give special treatment to LDC members (Mexico).[68]

Despite this generally positive assessment, liberals also point to NAFTA problems. For example, liberals sometimes criticize restrictions that continue to limit trade and investment, and increased security measures since September 11, 2001 that make it more difficult to move goods and people across borders. The border restrictions pose problems for businesses operating on a regional basis that require timely delivery of materials for the production process. Liberals also consider rules of origin to be a common protectionist device in FTAs, and they argue that NAFTA has highly restrictive rules of origin for such products as automobiles, textiles and apparel, and color televisions. Recognizing that the growth of interdependence requires more policy coordination, many liberals favor a deepening of the integration process; for example, some liberals propose the development of a CET among NAFTA members.[69] Differences, of course, exist between liberals. For example, orthodox liberals view NAFTA's environmental and labor side agreements as nontrade issues that can be used to impose protectionist trade barriers, whereas interventionist liberals believe that these side agreements may help correct market imperfections; and some liberals such as Jagdish Bhagwati are more critical of the proliferation of RTAs than others. Differences also exist between liberals in different countries. For example, some U.S. liberals call on the NAFTA countries to develop a North American energy security policy that promotes regional production and trade, and the buildup of a strategic reserve. However, Canadian and Mexican liberals tend to treat such proposals with more skepticism. Despite these differences, *most* liberals generally favor NAFTA, arguing that it is more trade creating than trade diverting. For example, one study finds that NAFTA has "contributed to an explosion of exports and imports between the U.S. and Mexico, producing gains from trade as specified by the theory of comparative advantage"; and another study concludes that "NAFTA remains vital to maintaining trade and investment in the three countries and helps anchor the economic health of the North American marketplace."[70]

REALISM AND HISTORICAL MATERIALISM   Realists and historical materialists emphasize NAFTA's asymmetries in power and levels of economic development.

Thus, realists reject the liberal view that smaller states often benefit from FTAs more than larger states because of economies of scale and increased exports. From the realist perspective, the United States as the larger partner expects its benefits from free trade to outweigh those of the smaller partners. For example, Canada sought free trade with the United States to gain more assured access to the U.S. market. In return for granting free trade, the United States expected various side payments, including less Canadian regulation of U.S. foreign investment, greater U.S. access to Canadian energy, and a services trade agreement. The United States also expected Mexico to grant access to its market for U.S. agricultural goods and to give up claims as an LDC to special treatment.[71] Realists also argue that NAFTA has a detrimental effect on national sovereignty. For example, NAFTA's Chapter 11 gives investors access to binding international arbitration if they believe that a host government is violating NAFTA's investment provisions on national treatment. Whereas liberals view Chapter 11 as an innovative mechanism that permits foreign enterprises to prevent states from discriminating against them, realists see it as "a vehicle for investors to harass governments whose policies they dislike."[72]

Historical materialists argue that NAFTA is shifting power to the capitalist class and against labor groups. For example, NAFTA enables MNCs to avoid labor and environmental standards in Canada and the United States by relocating production in Mexico. As capital leaves the United States and Canada, wages and employment in these countries decline. Some historical materialists use the terms *core* and *periphery* to designate social position and class rather than geographic location, arguing that NAFTA has relegated many U.S. and Canadian workers to peripheral status. For example, one study concludes that "the emergence of Mexico as the first-ranked exporter of clothing to the United States as a result of NAFTA has been accompanied by dramatic growth of garment maquiladora employment south of the border and a dramatic decline in the garment industry north of the border, especially among manual, direct production workers."[73] The losses for U.S. and Canadian workers, according to historical materialists, do not result in comparable gains for Mexican workers. For example, NAFTA is destroying the livelihoods of Mexican peasants because U.S. corn, which benefits from government subsidies, is being freely exported to Mexico. Historical materialists thus argue that NAFTA is increasing poverty and inequality between the rich and poor in all three states. Some Gramscian theorists assert that a coalition of labor, environmental, consumer, and women's groups could form a counterhegemonic bloc based on opposition to the domination of corporate capital in NAFTA. A counterhegemonic bloc would replace the current corporate view of liberalization in North America with a more democratic, participatory model.[74]

ENVIRONMENTALISM NAFTA deals more explicitly with the environment than the GATT/WTO; it mentions the environment in the preamble and main text of the agreement, and it has an environmental side agreement. During the negotiation of NAFTA, there were serious disagreements over the environmental provisions. The critical environmental greens such as Greenpeace, Public

Citizen, and the Sierra Club argued that the negotiation process favored corporate interests and that the provisions gave priority to trade liberalization over environmental concerns. For example, the greens charged that NAFTA's investor–state dispute resolution provisions (Chapter 11) opened a new legal channel for private investors to contest a state's environmental policies. At the other end of the spectrum, some business groups expressed concerns that the environmental side agreement would interfere with free trade and result in costly new regulations. Liberal environmental groups such as the World Wildlife Fund, Environmental Defense, and National Resources Defense Council took a position between these two extremes. Some of these groups were disappointed that the environmental side agreement did not establish procedures to encourage the upward harmonization of environmental standards. However, they viewed trade liberalization as a positive objective, and were generally supportive of the efforts to include environmental provisions in NAFTA. To this point, the results of the NAFTA provisions have in fact been mixed. For example, U.S. environmental standards have not declined and Mexican environmental rules have improved under NAFTA. However, Canadian and Mexican imports of toxic waste from the United States have increased since NAFTA, and critics argue that NAFTA has contributed to the devastation of Mexican agriculture and the introduction of toxic chemicals in the countryside. In view of these mixed results, it is not surprising that the controversy continues. Whereas more critical greens see NAFTA as beyond repair, interventionist liberals believe that the NAFTA environmental provisions can be upgraded by adopting stronger provisions,. Thus, two prominent liberals argue that "it makes more sense to tackle the shortcomings than to lament the existence of an FTA, as many environmentalists do, or to overlook the problems, as a very few diehard free trade advocates might. With the necessary tuning, NAFTA can become a trade agreement that both environmentalists and free traders appreciate."[75]

In sum, NAFTA remains highly contentious in all three member states. However, NAFTA is likely to remain a central agreement in view of the high degree of interdependence in the region, the growing importance of the EU, and the failure to conclude the WTO Doha Round.

MERCOSUR

RTAs in Latin America during the 1960s and 1970s were generally inward looking, but there was a revival of Latin American regionalism in the mid-1980s on a more open basis. The largest and most successful of these newer RTAs is *Mercosur,* or the "Common Market of the Southern Cone." As of November 2008, Mercosur had four members (Argentina, Brazil, Paraguay, and Uruguay), five associate members (Chile, Bolivia, Peru, Colombia, and Ecuador), and one country with its membership pending (Venezuela). Although Venezuela signed a membership agreement in 2006, Brazil and Paraguay had not yet ratified the agreement.[76]

In 1988 Argentina and Brazil signed an agreement that led to the 1991 Treaty of Asunción (TOA) to establish Mercosur. The TOA timetable for the members (Argentina, Brazil, Paraguay, and Uruguay) included the formation of an FTA from 1991 to 1994, a CU in 1995, and eventually a common market; this schedule was unusual for Latin America, where most integration plans included only vague promises. Mercosur's significance also stemmed from the importance of its two largest members, Brazil and Argentina. In 2008 Mercosur encompassed a population of about 250 million, a GDP of $1.1 trillion, and an area larger than the continental United States. Many observers were skeptical about Mercosur because of Latin America's history of inward-looking development policies and the long-term enmity between Brazil and Argentina. However, most Latin American LDCs were active participants in the GATT Uruguay Round, and the Argentine and Brazilian presidents supported integration because of their neoliberal economic strategies and their belief that integration would strengthen their position vis-à-vis the United States and the EU.[77]

The integration process was quite dynamic from 1991 to 1995 as tariffs were gradually eliminated and a number of business firms began to organize their production and sales on a regional basis. However, Brazil and Argentina introduced new tariffs and NTBs after 1995, and intra-Mercosur exports as a share of total exports declined. Although most merchandise trade within Mercosur is now duty-free, rules do not extend to services trade, government purchases, and many NTBs and administrative barriers. The automotive sector, which accounts for about 25 percent of intra-Mercosur trade, is subject to managed trade in which a Mercosur state can export only as much as it imports from a partner state. Mercosur has also not achieved its goal of establishing a CU with a CET. To maintain a CET, no member state can negotiate bilaterally with outside states. However, Argentina, Uruguay, and Paraguay have been tempted to engage in bilateral negotiations, and in 2007 Uruguay signed a trade and investment agreement with the United States that could lead to a bilateral FTA.[78]

International, regional, and national factors account for the problems. First, Mercosur members as LDCs are highly vulnerable to international developments. Latin American LDCs had the highest debts during the 1980s foreign debt crisis, and in 1997 the combined debt of the four Mercosur states amounted to 29 percent of their GNPs. The Mexican and East Asian financial crises in the 1990s also contributed to the loss of markets for Latin American exports and a marked decrease in the prices of primary commodities (see Chapter 11). Second, in 2005 intra-Mercosur trade accounted for only 13 percent of the members' total trade. The dependence on trade with external actors such as the United States and the EU limits the actions members can take to consolidate Mercosur. Third, there is a high level of asymmetry, with Brazil accounting for about 70 percent of Mercosur's GDP. Although Brazil has been a strong force behind Mercosur, it is less dependent than other Mercosur members on the regional market. To ensure that Mercosur does not infringe on its sovereignty, Brazil has opposed a strong dispute-settlement body.[79] Fourth, Mercosur has devoted little attention to the harmonization of macroeconomic policies. In 1991 Argentina pegged its peso to the U.S. dollar, whereas Brazil adjusted its exchange rate to account for inflation. After Brazil devalued its currency in 1999,

Argentina's trade balance with Brazil sharply deteriorated and many companies moved operations from Argentina to Brazil. By 2001, Argentina had a massive foreign debt and defaulted on its loans partly because its peso was pegged to the U.S. dollar. When Argentina devalued its currency in 2002, this eliminated a major source of trade conflict with Brazil. Fifth, Venezuela signed an agreement to join Mercosur in 2006, but Brazil and Paraguay have not yet ratified the agreement. Venezuela's role as a major oil exporter and its Caribbean ports could provide some important benefits to Mercosur. However, some members fear that Hugo Chavez's anti-Americanism would upset Mercosur's internal balance and regional trade relations.[80]

Realists see Mercosur as contributing to security as well as economic ties; Argentina and Brazil have upgraded their military cooperation, with joint military exercises and annual meetings between their joint chiefs of staff. Realists also argue that Mercosur strengthens its members' bargaining power vis-à-vis the United States and the EU.[81] Liberals favor widening the scope of Mercosur's trade liberalization and predict that domestic business groups will continue to see Mercosur as a means of attracting global investment. Historical materialists argue that Mercosur resulted from IMF pressure on Latin Americans to liberalize their policies and that Mercosur incorporates its members "within the world capitalist system while preserving their subordinate status in the system."[82]

EAST ASIAN REGIONALISM

East Asia was late in forming RTAs, and in 2000 preferential trade arrangements accounted for only 5.6 percent of merchandise imports in Asia, compared with 64.7 percent for Western Europe, 41.4 percent for North America, 37.2 percent for Africa, and 18.3 percent for Latin America (excluding Mexico).[83] RTAs were less important in East Asia for several reasons, including the protectionist and interventionist industrial policies of many Asian states, East Asian memories of Japanese militarism in the 1930s, concerns about dominance by China, and U.S. military and economic influence in the region. However, East Asians have developed strong regional linkages without formal institutions. Intraregional trade has increased because many East Asian states have dynamic, rapidly growing economies, and because their diversity in size, per capita income, and natural resources provides opportunities for specialization. Informal East Asian linkages also increase the competitiveness of the region's firms in global markets. Thus, the internationalization of the East Asian production process contributed to the region's ability to market high-quality goods at competitive prices. Whereas Japan provided capital and high-technology goods, East Asian NIEs provided some highly sophisticated goods and services, and lower-wage countries such as China, Indonesia, and Vietnam provided labor-intensive assembly operations. Despite their preference for informal regionalism, East Asians became more interested in forming RTAs because of the exclusionary aspects of the EU and NAFTA, the 1997 East Asian financial crisis, and the problems in the WTO Doha Round.[84]

The *ASEAN Free Trade Area* (*AFTA*) was the first political attempt to form a plurilateral FTA (more than two countries) in Asia. Indonesia, Malaysia, the Philippines, Singapore, and Thailand established ASEAN in 1967 as a political organization to promote peace, stability, and economic growth. In 1992 these five states and Brunei (the ASEAN-6) formed the AFTA, and four more states joined later: Vietnam in 1995, Laos and Myanmar in 1997, and Cambodia in 1999. The goal was to achieve a free trade area by 2002 among the ASEAN-6 and to include the four newer members later. The ASEAN countries formed AFTA to increase their intraregional trade; to bargain as a bloc with the United States, China, Japan, and the EU; and to attract more foreign investment as a larger unified market.[85] AFTA has lowered tariffs and has accelerated some of its trade liberalization objectives; for example, the ASEAN-6 moved their goal of achieving an FTA forward from 2008 to 2002. However, the AFTA provisions have loopholes and it is uncertain that all intra-AFTA tariff barriers will be eliminated. AFTA has four lists of products under its tariff reduction scheme: an *inclusion list,* a *temporary exclusion list,* a *sensitive list,* and a *general exceptions list* consisting of products that are permanently excluded. AFTA has delayed trade liberalization for some products because they are politically sensitive. For example, AFTA has accepted Malaysia's delay in reducing tariffs on automobiles, the Philippines' delay for petrochemical products, and Indonesia's delay for some agricultural products. Furthermore, the four newest AFTA members are at a lower level of development and have left many products off the inclusion list.

Several factors explain AFTA's delays in trade liberalization. First, like Mercosur, the AFTA members as LDCs are highly vulnerable to global changes, and the 1997 Asian financial crisis contributed to economic and political instability. Second, intra-AFTA exports accounted for 23.5 percent of total AFTA exports (for the ASEAN-6) in 2005, and AFTA members' largest markets are outside the RTA. Third, AFTA members range from high-income Singapore to upper-middle-income Malaysia, lower-middle-income Thailand, Philippines, and Indonesia, and low-income Laos, Cambodia, Myanmar, and Vietnam. As Table 8.3 shows, there is a stark income divide between the original AFTA-6 members, and the four countries that joined later. Whereas Singapore and Brunei had PPP-adjusted per capita GDPs of $37,360 and $25,191, respectively in 2007, the figures for Myanmar and Laos were $2,193 and $2,840, respectively. The low-income countries need more time to adjust to trade liberalization and assistance to move toward market reform. Third, although the emphasis of many Asian states on informal procedures may contribute to solidarity, there is less political commitment to formal trade liberalization.[86]

Liberal economists disagree among themselves regarding AFTA's progress toward free trade. Some liberals focus on what AFTA has accomplished to date, arguing that "most of Southeast Asia is now close to full realization of free trade."[87] Others focus more on the development divide among AFTA members and on the products excluded from tariff reductions, and conclude that AFTA's progress toward free trade is limited. Whereas some analysts attribute the free trade obstacles to the four less-developed members (Laos, Cambodia,

TABLE 8.3 Per Capita GDP of AFTA[a] Members, 2007 (US$, PPP[b])

Countries	Per Capita GDP
ASEAN-6	
Brunei	$25,191
Indonesia	4,931
Malaysia	14,256
The Philippines	5,918
Singapore	37,360
Thailand	10,678
ASEAN-4	
Cambodia	$3,778
Laos	2,840
Myanmar	2,193
Vietnam	3,836

[a] ASEAN Free Trade Area

[b] PPP Purchasing Power Parity *Source:* ASEAN, "Basic ASEAN Indicators," http://www.aseansec.org/19226.htm

Myanmar, and Vietnam), others argue that "what has slowed down ASEAN economic integration has been the foot-dragging by some of the ASEAN-6."[88] These assessments show that analysts within the same perspective can have major disagreements. Realists focus on ASEAN's history before AFTA and point out that the ASEAN countries emphasize security as much as trade and finance. This explains the ASEAN-6's willingness to accept Vietnam, Cambodia, Laos, and Myanmar, which have a minor economic role but can pose a serious risk to regional security. Realists also emphasize non-institutional aspects of Asian regionalism, and note that Japan was less interested in establishing an RTA than in "using its Asian production alliance in part as a platform from which to continue supplying high-technology products to Western markets."[89] More recently, China "has become the center for assembling parts mainly manufactured in other Asian countries and transferred primarily through intra-industry trade, for export to extra-regional markets, especially the United States."[90]

Realists are correct to point out that East Asia lacks a broadly encompassing RTA comparable with the EU and NAFTA. Although AFTA has made some progress in liberalizing trade, it is too small by itself to be of major importance. ASEAN's embryonic arrangement with Japan, China, and South Korea (referred to as ASEAN+3) seems to be "the most credible and realistic vehicle to advance the form and substance of regional cooperation in East Asia."[91] However, a region-wide FTA in Asia comparable with the EU and NAFTA is a possibility only in the distant future.

Considering IPE Theory and Practice

During the postwar period, there were two major waves of regionalism, the first in the 1950s and 1960s and the second since the mid-1980s. Globalization has acted as a stimulus to the second wave, and it has been more enduring than the first wave. The most contentious issue in the current wave of regionalism is whether RTAs serve as stepping stones or obstacles to global free trade. This is a debate mainly within liberalism and shows that some of the major debates in IPE are among theorists within the same perspective. Liberals generally agree that multilateralism is the best route to trade liberalization and that *open* RTAs are a second-best option because they divert some imports from more efficient outside suppliers to less efficient regional suppliers. However, some liberals believe that RTAs today pose a serious threat to an open multilateral trade regime while others believe that RTAs can coexist beneficially with multilateralism.

The most notable theorist taking the first position is Jagdish Bhagwati, who describes RTAs as "termites" that are "eating away at the multilateral trading system."[92] Bhagwati prefers the term *preferential trade agreements* (PTAs) to *free trade agreements* (FTAs), because it highlights the fact that the trade arrangements are discriminatory rather than a form of free trade. (He also notes that PTAs is a more accurate term than RTAs, which are often between states in different geographic regions.)[93] Bhagwati and others in the first group present a number of arguments to show that RTAs pose a threat to the global trade regime, including the following:

- The discriminatory nature of RTAs is incompatible with MFN treatment, a basic principle of the global trade regime.
- The special exemption for RTAs among LDCs under the enabling clause allows LDCs to engage in discrimination without any discipline.
- The recent proliferation of bilateral FTAs is bringing chaos to the global trade regime, with different rules and tariff rates for each FTA; Bhagwati likens this to a "spaghetti bowl."
- FTA rules of origin are very complex, because states are members of overlapping FTAs, and MNCs source components from many different countries; the rules of origin are also a disguised form of protectionism.
- Many bilateral FTAs are between poor and rich countries, and their "most troubling aspect . . . is the exercise of virtually unconstrained political and economic power by the United States and EU to secure concessions from developing (and developed) countries."[94]

(continued)

(*continued*)

• RTAs divert valuable resources away from multilateral negotitions such as the Doha Round.

The second group of liberals agree that RTAs can sometimes create problems such as trade diversion. However, they describe some plurilateral FTAs such as NAFTA as more trade creating than many bilateral FTAs, and they believe that trade regionalism can coexist beneficially with global trade liberalization. In a study of NAFTA at the time of its creation, Gary Clyde Hufbauer and Jeffrey J. Schott concluded (in 1993) that "on balance . . . the trade created by growth in the NAFTA region should more than offset the trade diverted in particular sectors."[95] More than 10 years later, Hufbauer and Schott came to similar conclusions, pointing to a number of empirical studies that "on balance . . . find that NAFTA tends to promote trade creation more than trade diversion." Although the authors criticize NAFTA for its restrictive rules of origin, they nevertheless conclude that the agreement has been a "success."[96] Theorists have also described some other FTAs in positive terms. For example, some observers found a "general increase in ASEAN exports to both ASEAN partners and the rest of the world after the AFTA implementation," and concluded that "AFTA had been trade creating rather than trade diverting."[97] Arguments of theorists in the second group include the following:

• FTAs contribute to economies of scale and a division of labor based on comparative advantage.
• Trade creation is likely to be greater than trade diversion if the FTA members are already major trading partners.
• RTAs allow members to overcome disagreements at the regional level, which helps reduce the complexity of the WTO negotiations.
• By promoting deeper integration at the regional level, RTAs lead the way for multilateral trade negotiations. For example, NAFTA liberalized trade in services and agriculture before the GATT/WTO.[98]

How can these two groups of liberal theorists have such divergent views regarding the effects of RTAs on the global trade regime? Although they often base their findings on empirical studies,

the recent literature on examining RTA trade impact shows that different studies come out with different trade effects for the same RTAs. This is due to the use of different estimation methods, different databases and time periods to measure these trade effects.[99]

The theorists in the two groups also often use different

methodologies. In the first group, Bhagwati uses historical analysis to show that political factors resulted in the exceptions the GATT/WTO provides to RTAs. In the second group, many analysts focus on specific RTAs for which they have a strong affinity. For example, Hufbauer and Schott believe that NAFTA should go beyond free trade to establish a CET, strengthen its institutions, and promote closer cooperation on monetary policy. In sum, empirical studies have contributed greatly to our understanding of the effect of RTAs on multilateral trade. However, the diversity of findings cannot be explained only by differences in methodologies; they also depend on nonmaterial factors such as the assumptions and values of the theorists.

Chapters 7 and 8 have focused on trade, but the relationship between trade and investment are closely related; for example, RTAs affect regional production, intraindustry specialization, and the location of firms.[100] Thus, a former WTO director general notes that "businesses now trade to invest and invest to trade—to the point where both activities are increasingly part of a single strategy to deliver products across borders."[101] The next chapter deals with the issue of MNCs and foreign investment.

Questions

1. What are the differences between an FTA, CU, common market, and economic union? Do any RTAs fit completely within one of these models of integration?
2. How do realists, liberals, and historical materialists explain the rise of regional integration?
3. In what ways can RTAs be trade diverting and trade creating? Do you think that RTAs are stepping stones or obstacles to global trade liberalization, and why do you think liberal theorists cannot agree on this issue?
4. What conditions does GATT Article 24 impose on RTAs? How successful has the GATT/WTO been in regulating RTAs?
5. In what ways do LDCs receive special treatment as members and associate members of RTAs? Does Mexico receive special treatment in NAFTA?
6. In what ways is the EU a unique RTA? What are the neofunctionalist, liberal intergovernmentalist, and constructivist theoretical approaches to economic integration, and why are they applied mainly to Europe?
7. Why has NAFTA not resulted in integration above the level of an FTA? What are the liberal, realist, historical materialist, and environmentalist views of NAFTA?
8. What special problems do FTAs among LDCs such as Mercosur and AFTA have in achieving regional integration? Why is East Asian regionalism less institutionalized than regionalism in Europe and North America, and do you think that this will change over time?

Further Reading

A useful examination of changes in regionalism and the relation between RTAs and the WTO is Jo-Ann Crawford and Roberto V. Fiorentino, "The Changing Landscape of Regional Trade Agreements," Discussion Paper 8 (Geneva: WTO, 2005), http://www.wto.org/english/res_e/booksp_e/discussion_papers8_e.pdf. A clearly written assessment of the economic benefits and costs of regionalism is a World Bank Policy Research Report entitled *Trade Blocs* (Washington, D.C.: World Bank, 2000). A book that strongly posits the case against RTAs from a liberal perspective is Jagdish Bhagwati, *Termites in the Trading System: How Preferential Agreements Undermine Free Trade* (New York: Oxford University Press, 2008). A general examination of the ways governments deal with environmental issues in RTAs is Organization for Economic Cooperation and Development, *Environment and Regional Trade Agreements* (Paris: OECD, 2007).

On the EU and integration theory, see Ben Rosamond, *Theories of European Integration* (New York: St. Martin's Press, 2000); and Andrew Moravcsik, *The Choice for Europe: Social Purpose and State Power from Messina to Maastricht* (Ithaca, NY: Cornell University Press, 1998). Good introductions to the EU include Steve Wood and Wolfgang Quaisser, *The New European Union: Confronting the Challenges of Integration* (Boulder, CO: Lynne Rienner, 2008); and Elizabeth Bomberg, John Peterson, and Alexander Stubb, *The European Union: How Does it Work?*, 2nd ed. (New York: Oxford University Press, 2008). On the EU and LDCs, see Martin Holland, *The European Union and the Third World* (New York: Palgrave, 2002).

Two useful collections of readings on integration in the Western Hemisphere are Joseph A. McKinney and H. Stephen Gardner, eds., *Economic Integration in the Americas* (New York: Routledge, 2008); and Isabel Studer and Carol Wise, eds., *Requiem or Revival?: The Promise of North American Integration* (Washington, D.C.: Brookings Institution, 2007). A detailed examination of the negotiation of NAFTA is Maxwell A. Cameron and Brian W. Tomlin, *The Making of NAFTA: How the Deal Was Done* (Ithaca, NY: Cornell University Press, 2000). An assessment of NAFTA from a liberal perspective is Gary C. Hufbauer and Jeffrey J. Schott, *NAFTA Revisited: Achievements and Challenges* (Washington, D.C.: Institute for International Economics, 2005). An assessment from a critical perspective is Isidro Morales, *Post-NAFTA North America: Reshaping the Economic and Political Governance of a Changing Region* (New York: Palgrave Macmillan, 2008). On Mercosur, see Riordan Roett, ed., *Mercosur: Regional Integration, World Markets* (Boulder, CO: Lynne Rienner, 1999).

On Asian economic integration, see Edward J. Lincoln, *East Asian Economic Regionalism* (Washington, D.C.: Brookings Institution, 2004). On the recent proliferation of bilateral trade agreements in the Asia-Pacific, see Vinod K. Aggarwal and Shujiro Urata, eds., *Bilateral Trade Agreements in the Asia-Pacific: Origins, Evolution, and Implications* (New York: Routledge, 2006).

Notes

1. Jo-Ann Crawford and Robert V. Fiorentino, "The Changing Landscape of Regional Trade Agreements," Discussion Paper 8 (Geneva: WTO Secretariat Staff, 2005), p. 1. For competing views on the current trend toward regionalism, see Yoram Z. Haftel,

"From the Outside Looking In: The Effect of Trading Blocs on Trade Disputes in the GATT/WTO," *International Studies Quarterly* 48, no. 1 (March 2004), pp. 121–142; Valentin Zahrnt, "How Regionalization Can Be a Pillar of a More Effective World Trade Organization," *Journal of World Trade* 39, no. 4 (2005), pp. 671–699.

2. Gerald K. Helleiner, "Considering U.S.–Mexico Free Trade," in Ricardo Grinspun and Maxwell A. Cameron, eds., *The Political Economy of North American Free Trade* (Montreal: McGill-Queen's University Press, 1993), pp. 50–51.

3. Andrew Hurrell, "Explaining the Resurgence of Regionalism in World Politics," *Review of International Studies* 21 (1995), p. 333. For the difficulty in defining a region, see Bruce M. Russett, *International Regions and the International System: A Study in Political Ecology* (Chicago, IL: Rand McNally, 1967).

4. For example, see Jagdish Bhagwati, *Termites in the Trading System: How Preferential Agreements Undermine Free Trade* (New York: Oxford University Press, 2008).

5. Mancur Olson, *The Logic of Collective Action: Public Goods and the Theory of Groups* (Cambridge, MA: Harvard University Press, 1965).

6. Hurrell, "Explaining the Resurgence of Regionalism in World Politics," pp. 345–347.

7. Fritz Machlup, *A History of Thought on Economic Integration* (New York: Columbia University Press, 1977).

8. Michael Kaser, *Comecon: Integration Problems of the Planned Economies* (London: Oxford University Press, 1965).

9. The European Economic Community's name was changed, first to the European Community, and then to the European Union.

10. Jagdish Bhagwati, "Regionalism and Multilateralism: An Overview," in Jaime de Melo and Arvind Panagariya, eds., *New Dimensions in Regional Integration* (New York: Cambridge University Press, 1993), pp. 28–29.

11. WTO, "Regional Trade Agreements: Facts and Figures," http://www.wto.org/english/tratop_e/region_e/regfac_e.htm.

12. World Trade Organization, *Understanding the WTO,* 3rd ed. rev. (Geneva: WTO, October 2005), pp. 67–68; Crawford and Fiorentino, "The Changing Landscape of Regional Trade Agreements."

13. Bhagwati, "Regionalism and Multilateralism," pp. 29–31.

14. Joanne Gowa, "Bipolarity, Multipolarity, and Free Trade," *American Political Science Review* 83, no. 4 (December 1989), p. 1248.

15. Kenneth N. Waltz, *Theory of International Politics* (Reading, MA: Addison-Wesley, 1979), p. 70.

16. In 1960 the OEEC became the OECD, which also includes non-Europeans. See Theodore H. Cohn, *Governing Global Trade: International Institutions in Conflict and Convergence* (Burlington, VT: Ashgate, 2002), pp. 37–41.

17. John J. Mearsheimer, "Back to the Future: Instability in Europe After the Cold War," *International Security* 15, no. 1 (Summer 1990), pp. 5–56.

18. Hurrell, "Explaining the Resurgence of Regionalism in World Politics," pp. 341–342; Joanne Gowa, "Bipolarity, Multipolarity, and Free Trade," *American Political Science Review* 83, no. 4 (December 1989), pp. 1245–1256.

19. Bhagwati, *Termites in the Trading System,* p. 44.

20. Mark A. Pollack, "International Relations Theory and European Integration," *Journal of Common Market Studies* 39, no. 2 (June 2001), pp. 222–223; and John J. Mearsheimer, "Back to the Future: Instability in Europe After the Cold War," *International Security* 15, no. 1 (1990), pp. 47–48.

21. Inis L. Claude, Jr., *Swords into Plowshares: The Problems and Progress of International Organization,* 4th ed. (New York: Random House, 1971),

p. 379; David Mitrany, *A Working Peace System* (Chicago, IL: Quadrangle Books, 1966).

22. Bernard M. Hoekman and Michel M. Kostecki, *The Political Economy of the World Trading System: The WTO and Beyond,* 2nd ed. (New York: Oxford University Press, 2001), pp. 347–352. On GATT's problems, see Clyde V. Prestowitz, Jr., Alan Tonelson, and Robert W. Jerome, "The Last Gasp of GATTism," *Harvard Business Review* 69, no. 2 (March–April 1991), pp. 130–138.

23. Marc L. Busch and Helen V. Milner, "The Future of the International Trading System: International Firms, Regionalism, and Domestic Politics," in Richard Stubbs and Geoffrey R. D. Underhill, eds., *Political Economy and the Changing Global Order* (Toronto: McClelland & Stewart, 1994), p. 270.

24. Michael Hart, *A North American Free Trade Agreement: The Strategic Implications for Canada* (Halifax, NS: Institute for Research on Public Policy, 1990), pp. 45–46.

25. Duncan Cameron, "Introduction," in Duncan Cameron and Mel Watkins, eds., *Canada Under Free Trade* (Toronto: Lorimer, 1993), p. xxi.

26. General Agreement on Tariffs and Trade, *Text of the General Agreement* (Geneva: GATT, July 1986), Article 24.

27. Although Jacob Viner coined the terms *trade creation* and *trade diversion* after GATT Article 24 was written, these terms summarize the article's intent. See Jacob Viner, *The Customs Union Issue* (New York: Carnegie Endowment, 1950), pp. 41–55.

28. Hoekman and Kostecki, *The Political Economy of the World Trading System,* pp. 350–363; Robert Z. Lawrence, *Regionalism, Multilateralism, and Deeper Integration* (Washington, D.C.: Brookings Institution, 1996), pp. 41–42.

29. Gardner Patterson, *Discrimination in International Trade, The Policy Issues: 1945–1965* (Princeton, NJ: Princeton University Press, 1966), pp. 146–147.

30. Richard E. Baldwin, "A Domino Theory of Regionalism," in Richard Baldwin, Pertti Haaparanta, and Jaakko Kiander, eds., *Expanding Membership of the European Union* (New York: Cambridge University Press, 1995), p. 45.

31. Bhagwati, "Regionalism and Multilateralism," pp. 25–26; World Trade Organization Secretariat, *Regionalism and the World Trading System* (Geneva: WTO, April 1995), p. 7.

32. Robert E. Hudec, *The GATT Legal System and World Trade Diplomacy* (New York: Praeger, 1975), pp. 195–196; J. Michael Finger, "GATT's Influence on Regional Arrangements," in Jaime de Melo and Arvind Panagariya, eds., *New Dimensions in Regional Integration* (New York: Cambridge University Press, 1993), pp. 136–137.

33. WTO Secretariat, *Regionalism and the World Trading System,* pp. 12–13.

34. Robert E. Hudec, "Discussion," in Jaime de Melo and Arvind Panagariya, eds., *New Dimensions in Regional Integration* (New York: Cambridge University Press, 1993), p. 152.

35. The only two active agreements are the Caribbean Community and Common Market (CARICOM) and the Czech and Slovak Republics Customs Union.

36. WTO Secretariat, *Regionalism and the World Trading System,* pp. 16–17; Gary C. Hufbauer and Jeffrey J. Schott, *NAFTA: An Assessment,* rev. ed. (Washington, D.C.: Institute for International Economics, 1993), p. 112.

37. WTO, *The Results of the Uruguay Round of Multilateral Trade Negotiations—The Legal Texts* (Geneva: World Trade Organization, 1994), pp. 31–34, 331–332.

38. Robert E. Hudec and James D. Southwick, "Regionalism and WTO Rules: Problems in the Fine Art of Discriminating Fairly," in Miguel R. Mendoza, Patrick Low, and Barbara Kotschwar, eds., *Trade Rules in the Making: Challenges in Regional and Multilateral Negotiations* (Washington, D.C.: Brookings Institution, 1999), pp. 49–74; "Lamy Welcomes WTO Agreement on Regional Trade Agreements," *WTO News Items,* July 10, 2006.
39. Hudec, *The GATT Legal System and World Trade Diplomacy,* pp. 205–206.
40. Olivier Long, *Law and Its Limitations in the GATT Multilateral Trade System* (Dordrecht, The Netherlands: Nijhoff, 1985), p. 101; Sam Laird, "Regional Trade Agreements: Dangerous Liaisons?" *World Economy* 22, no. 9 (1999), p. 1196.
41. Martin Holland, *The European Union and the Third World* (London: Palgrave, 2002), pp. 25–32.
42. Matthew McQueen, "ACP-EU Trade Cooperation after 2000: An Assessment of Reciprocal Trade Preferences," *Journal of Modern African Studies* 36, no. 4 (1998), p. 669; Richard Gibb, "Post-Lomé: The European Union and the South," *Third World Quarterly* 21, no. 3 (2000), pp. 457–467.
43. Bonapas F. Onguglo, "Developing Countries and Trade Preferences," in Rodriguez Mendoza, Patrick Low, and Barbara Kotschwar, eds., *Trade Rules in the Making: Challenges in Regional and Multilateral Negotiations* (Washington, D.C.: Brookings Institution, 1999), p. 119.
44. Francis A. S. T. Matambalya and Susanna Wolf, "The Cotonou Agreement and the Challenges of Making the New EU-ACP Trade Regime WTO Compatible," *Journal of World Trade* 35, no. 1 (2001), pp. 123–144.
45. WTO Secretariat, *Regionalism and the World Trading System,* pp. 27–29; André Sapir, "EC Regionalism at the Turn of the Millennium: Toward a New Paradigm?" *World Economy* 23, no. 9 (September 2000), p. 1135; and Thomas C. Fischer, *The United States, the European Union, and the "Globalization" of World Trade* (Westport, CT: Quorum Books, 2000), p. 75.
46. On the EU institutions, see Elizabeth Bomberg, John Peterson, and Alexander Stubb, *The European Union: How Does it Work?* 2nd ed. (New York: Oxford University Press, 2008), pp. 45–70.
47. Stephen George and Ian Bache, *Politics in the European Union* (New York: Oxford University Press, 2001), pp. 87–104; Andrew Moravcsik, "Negotiating the Single European Act," in Robert O. Keohane and Stanley Hoffmann, eds., *The New European Community: Decisionmaking and Institutional Change* (Boulder, CO: Westview Press, 1991), p. 41.
48. Stephen George, "The European Union, 1992 and the Fear of 'Fortress Europe,'" in Andrew Gamble and Anthony Payne, eds., *Regionalism and World Order* (New York: St. Martin's Press, 1996), pp. 21–54.
49. Stuart Croft, "Guaranteeing Europe's Security? Enlarging NATO Again," *International Affairs* 78, no. 1 (January 2002), p. 101. On the EU and security policy, see Robert E. Hunter, *The European Security and Defense Policy: NATO's Companion or Competitor?* (Santa Monica, CA: RAND, 2002).
50. Michael H. Abbey and Nicholas Bromfield, "A Practitioner's Guide to the Maastricht Treaty," *Michigan Journal of International Law* 15, no. 4 (Summer 1994), pp. 1329–1357.
51. Fischer, *The United States, the European Union, and the "Globalization" of World Trade,* p. 136.

52. Enzo R. Grilli, *The European Community and the Developing Countries* (New York: Cambridge University Press, 1993), pp. 7–8, 296–316.

53. Erik Faucompret and Jozef Konings, "The Integration of Central and Eastern Europe in the European Union," *Journal of World Trade* 33, no. 6 (December 1999), pp. 121–127; Pier C. Padoan, "The Changing European Political Economy," in Richard Stubbs and Geoffrey R. D. Underhill, eds., *Political Economy and the Changing Global Order* (Toronto: McClelland & Stewart, 1994), pp. 340–342.

54. Quoted in "Arguments for Enlargement," *The Economist,* August 3, 1996, p. 41.

55. EC Economic and Social Council document, quoted in David M. Wood and Birol A. Yeşilada, *The Emerging European Union,* 3rd ed. (New York: Longman, 2004), p. 118.

56. See Amy Verdun and Osvaldo Croci, eds., *Institutional and Policy-Making Challenges to the European Union in the Wake of Eastern Enlargement* (Manchester, UK: Manchester University Press, 2004).

57. "A Divided Union," in "A Survey of the European Union," *Economist,* September 25, 2004, p. 4.

58. "A Severe Crise d'Identité," *The Economist,* May 28, 2005, pp. 27–29; Alex Warleigh-Lack, *European Union: The Basics,* 2nd ed. (New York: Routledge, 2009), pp. 101–112.

59. Ernst Haas, *The Uniting of Europe: Political, Social and Economical Forces 1950–1957* (London: Stevens & Sons, 1958), p. 16.

60. Ben Rosamond, *Theories of European Integration* (New York: St. Martin's Press, 2000), pp. 50–73.

61. Andrew Moravcsik, *The Choice for Europe: Social Purpose and State Power from Messina to Maastricht* (Ithaca, NY: Cornell University Press, 1998), p. 501.

62. Clive Archer, *The European Union* (New York: Routledge, 2008), pp. 8–17; Young J. Choi and James A. Caporaso, "Comparative Regional Integration," in Walter Carlsnaes, Thomas Risse, and Beth A. Simmons, eds., *Handbook of International Relations* (Thousand Oaks, CA: SAGE, 2002), pp. 485–491.

63. Jack L. Granatstein, "Free Trade Between Canada and the United States," in Dennis Stairs and Gilbert R. Winham, eds., *The Politics of Canada's Economic Relationship with the United States,* vol. 29, Royal Commission on the Economic Union and Development Prospect for Canada (Toronto: University of Toronto Press, 1985), p. 11.

64. "U.S. Trade Act of 1974, as amended (Public Law 93-618)," Title VI, section 612, in *Legislation on Foreign Relations Through 1989* (Washington, D.C.: U.S. Government Printing Office, 1990), p. 456.

65. John Whalley, "Regional Trade Arrangements in North America: CUSTA and NAFTA," in Jaime de Melo and Arvind Panagariya, eds., *New Dimensions in Regional Integration* (New York: Cambridge University Press, 1993), pp. 352–353; Carol Wise, "Unfulfilled Promise: Economic Convergence under NAFTA," in Isabel Studer and Carol Wise, eds., *Requiem or Revival? The Promise of North American Integration* (Washington, D.C.: Brookings Institution, 2007), p. 28.

66. Isabel Studer, "Obstacles to Integration: NAFTA's Institutional Weaknesses," in Isabel Studer and Carol Wise, eds., *Requiem or Revival? The Promise of North American Integration* (Washington, D.C.: Brookings Institution, 2007), pp. 53–58.

67. Wise, "Unfulfilled Promise," pp. 29–32; Jennifer Clapp and Peter Dauvergne, *Paths to a Green World: The Political Economy of the Global Environment* (Cambridge, MA: MIT Press, 2005), pp. 150–153.

68. Bernard Hoekman and Pierre Sauvé, "Liberalizing Trade in Services," *World Bank Discussion Papers,* no. 243 (Washington, D.C.: World Bank, 1994).

69. Jeffrey J. Schott, "Trade Negotiations among NAFTA Partners: The Future of North American Economic Integration," in Studer and Wise, eds., *Requiem or Revival?* p. 86.

70. Willem Thorbecke and Christian Eigen-Zucchi, "Did NAFTA Cause a 'Giant Sucking Sound'?" *Journal of Labor Research* 23, no. 4 (Fall 2002), p. 647; Alan S. Alexandroff, Gary C. Hufbauer, and Krista Lucenti, "Still Amigos: A Fresh Canada-US Approach to Reviving NAFTA," C.D. Howe Institute, The Border Papers, no. 274, September 2008, p. 1.

71. Helleiner, "Considering U.S.-Mexico Free Trade," pp. 50–51.

72. Jon R. Johnson, *The North American Free Trade Agreement—A Comprehensive Guide* (Aurora, ONT: Canada Law Book, 1994), p. 512; Mark MacKinnon, "NAFTA Members to Talk Reform," *Toronto Globe and Mail,* April 10, 2001, p. B1.

73. David Spener and Randy Capps, "North American Free Trade and Changes in the Nativity of the Garment Industry Workforce in the United States," *International Journal of Urban and Regional Research* 25, no. 2 (June 2001), p. 320.

74. Mark E. Rupert, "(Re) Politicizing the Global Economy: Liberal Common Sense and Ideological Struggle in the US NAFTA Debate," *Review of International Political Economy* 2, no. 4 (Autumn 1995), pp. 679–681.

75. Gary C. Hufbauer and Jeffrey J. Schott, *NAFTA Revisited: Achievements and Challenges* (Washington, D.C.: Institute for International Economics, 2005), p. 183; Gary C. Hufbauer and Jeffrey J. Schott, *NAFTA: An Assessment,* rev. ed. (Washington, D.C.: Institute for International Economics, 1993), pp. 157–163; Clapp and Dauvergne, *Paths to a Green World,* pp. 151–152; Alexandroff, Hufbauer, and Lucenti, "Still Amigos," pp. 17–19.

76. Mario E. Carranza, "Mercosur and the End Game of the FTAA Negotiations: Challenges and Prospects after the Argentine Crisis," *Third World Quarterly* 25, no. 2 (March 2004), p. 325; Clay Risen, "Latin America's Free Trade Market Struggles," *World Trade,* June 2008, pp. 52–54.

77. Jeffrey Cason, "On the Road to Southern Cone Economic Integration," *Journal of Interamerican Studies and World Affairs* 42, no. 1 (2000), pp. 23–28; Heinz G. Preusse, "Mercosur—Another Failed Move Towards Regional Integration?" *World Economy* 24, no. 7 (July 2001), pp. 911–914; Riordan Roett, "Introduction," in Riordan Roett, ed., *Mercosur: Regional Integration, World Markets* (Boulder CO: Lynne Rienner, 1999), pp. 1–5.

78. Mario E. Carranza, "Can Mercosur Survive? Domestic and International Constraints on Mercosur," *Latin American Politics and Society* 45, no. 2 (Summer 2003), p. 94; Francesco Duina and Jason Busbaum, "Regional Trade Agreements and the Pursuit of State Interests: Institutional Perspectives from NAFTA and Mercosur," *Economy and Society* 37, no. 2 (2008), pp. 201–202.

79. Rafael A. Porrata-Doria, Jr., *MERCOSUR—The Common Market of the Southern Cone* (Durham, NC: Carolina Academic Press, 2005), p. 41.

80. Rafael A. Lecuona, "Economic Integration: NAFTA and Mercosur, a Comparative Analysis," *International Journal of World Peace* 16, no. 4 (December 1999), pp. 41–42; Lia V. Pereira, "Toward the Common Market of the South: Mercosur's

Origins, Evolution, and Challenges," in Riordan Roett, ed., *Mercosur: Regional Integration, World Markets* (Boulder, CO: Lynne Rienner, 1999), pp. 7–13; Michael Mecham, "Mercosur: A Failing Development Project?" *International Affairs* 79, no. 2 (March 2003), pp. 377–379; Risen, "Latin America's Free Trade Market Struggles," pp. 53–54.

81. Carranza, "Can Mercosur Survive? Domestic and International Constraints on Mercosur," p. 74.

82. Donald G. Richards, "Dependent Development and Regional Integration: A Critical Examination of the Southern Cone Common Market," *Latin American Perspectives* 24, no. 6 (November 1997), p. 133.

83. World Trade Organization, *World Trade Report—2003* (Geneva: WTO, 2003), p. 48.

84. Miles Kahler, *International Institutions and the Political Economy of Integration* (Washington, D.C.: Brookings Institution, 1995), pp. 107–108; Lawrence, *Regionalism, Multilateralism, and Deeper Integration,* pp. 80–86; Edward J. Lincoln, *East Asian Economic Regionalism* (Washington, D.C.: Brookings Institution, 2004), pp. 159–193.

85. Helen Cabalu and Cristina Alfonso, "Does AFTA Create or Divert Trade?" *Global Economy Journal* 7, no. 4 (2007), pp. 1–3; Lincoln, *East Asian Economic Regionalism,* pp. 168–169.

86. Linda Low, "Multilateralism, Regionalism, Bilateral and Crossregional Free Trade Arrangements: All Paved with Good Intentions for ASEAN?" *Asian Economic Journal* 17, no. 1 (2003), pp. 67–84; Emiko Fukase and Will Martin, "Free Trade Area Membership as a Stepping Stone to Development: The Case of ASEAN," *World Bank Discussion Paper,* no. 421 (Washington, D.C.: World Bank, 2001), pp. 10–11.

87. Cabalu and Alfonso, "Does AFTA Create or Divert Trade?" p. 5.

88. Rofolfo C. Severino, "The ASEAN Developmental Divide and the Initiative for ASEAN Integration," *ASEAN Economic Bulletin* 24, no. 1 (2007), p. 38.

89. Walter Hatch and Kozo Yamamura, *Asia in Japan's Embrace: Building a Regional Production Alliance* (New York: Cambridge University Press, 1996), p. 36; Eul-Soo Pang, "AFTA and MERCOSUR at the Crossroads: Security, Managed Trade, and Globalization," *Contemporary Southeast Asia* 25, no. 1 (April 2003), p. 129.

90. Donald C. Hellman, "A Decade after the Asian Financial Crisis," *Asian Survey* 47, no. 6 (November/December 2007), pp. 843–844.

91. Quoted in Hellman, "A Decade after the Asian Financial Crisis," p. 843.

92. Bhagwati, *Termites in the Trading System,* p. xii.

93. Bhagwati, *Termites in the Trading System,* p. 18.

94. Frederick M. Abbott, "A New Dominant Trade Species Emerges: Is Bilateralism a Threat?" *Journal of International Economic Law* 10, no. 3 (September 2007), p. 583.

95. Hufbauer and Schott, *NAFTA,* p. 113.

96. Hufbauer and Schott, *NAFTA Revisited,* p. 24.

97. Cabalu and Alfonso, "Does AFTA Create or Divert Trade?" p. 12.

98. Paul Wonnacott and Mark Lutz, "Is There a Case for Free Trade Areas?" in Jeffrey J. Schott, ed., *Free Trade Areas and U.S. Trade Policy* (Washington, D.C.: Institute for International Economics, 1989), pp. 69–72; Valentin Zahrnt, "How Regionalization can be a Pillar of a More Effective World Trade Organization," *Journal of World Trade* 39, no. 4 (August, 2005), pp. 671–699; Matthew Schaefer, "Ensuring that Regional Trade Agreements Complement the WTO System: US

Unilateralism a Supplement to WTO Initiatives?" *Journal of Internatinal Economic Law* 10, no. 3 (September 2007), pp. 585–603.

99. Cabalu and Alfonso, "Does AFTA Create or Divert Trade?" p. 3.
100. See for example Walid Hejazi and Peter H. Pauly, "How Do Regional Trade Agreements Affect Intra-Regional and Inter-Regional FDI?" in Lorraine Eden and Wendy Dobson, eds., *Governance, Multinationals and Growth* (Northhampton, MA: Edward Elgar, 2005), pp. 176–208; and Ho Y. Kim, "Impact of Trade Liberalization on the Location of Firms: NAFTA and the Automobile Industry," *Annals of Regional Science* 37 (2003), pp. 149–173.
101. Renato Ruggiero, Director General of the World Trade Organization, "Charting the Trade Routes of the Future: Towards a Borderless Economy," address delivered to the International Industrial Conference, San Francisco, September 29, 1997, *World Trade Organization Press Release* (Geneva: Press/77), p. 4.

CHAPTER 9

Multinational Corporations and Global Production

The largest MNCs are in many respects the main agents of globalization. They produce and distribute goods and services across national borders; plan their operations on a global scale; and spread ideas, tastes, and technology throughout the world. MNCs are normally considered to be firms that control productive assets in more than one country. MNC parent firms in *home* countries acquire foreign assets by investing in affiliate or subsidiary firms in *host* countries. This is **foreign direct investment (FDI),** which involves management rights and control. **Portfolio investment,** by contrast, is investment without control; it involves the purchase of bonds, money market instruments, or stocks simply to realize a financial return. The growing presence of MNCs testifies to their role as agents of globalization. In 2007, 79,000 MNCs and their 790,000 foreign affiliates provided over $15 trillion in FDI stock. International production is also fairly concentrated. The world's 100 largest MNCs, based mainly in the North, represent 0.13 percent of the total number of MNCs. However, they account for about 10 percent of the foreign assets, 16 percent of the sales, and 12 percent of the employment of all MNCs. A new aspect of global FDI is the emergence of sovereign wealth funds as direct investors. As discussed in Chapter 6, SWFs are government investment vehicles that are managed separately from a country's official reserves. They amount to about $5 trillion today and can play a complementary role to MNCs as sources of foreign investment. However, most SWFs have been invested in U.S. and European government bonds with ownership shares of less than 10 percent (only investment above the 10-percent level is classified as FDI). Because SWFs account for only 0.6 percent of total FDI flows, this chapter focuses on the role of MNCs in providing FDI.[1]

Although FDI has declined in some years (e.g., in 1982–1983 and 2000–2003), FDI inflows have generally grown much faster than trade or income.

From 1985 to 1999, the growth rates of global GDP, exports, and FDI inflows were 2.5, 5.6, and 17.7 percent, respectively.[2] The growing importance of MNCs has caused some analysts to argue that the critical problem in IPE "is the tension between states and multinationals, not states and markets."[3] However, MNCs receive less attention because many scholars place primary emphasis on relations among governments. Limited amounts of reliable data also pose an obstacle to the study of MNCs. As private enterprises, MNCs are reluctant to provide information about themselves and adept at obscuring their activities. This problem is compounded by the fact that IOs regulate monetary, trade, and development activities but not foreign investment. Furthermore, MNCs evoke strong positive and negative reactions; in debates about MNCs it is common for "anecdote to replace data" and "the witty phrase to replace analysis."[4]

Liberals believe that the mobility of MNCs gives them a major advantage over national governments, which are bound to specific territories. In this age of globalization, MNCs and private banks are therefore "the major weavers of the world economy."[5] Historical materialists also refer to the growing power of MNCs, but they see corporate managers as a transnational class that maintains and defends the capitalist system. Liberals and historical materialists also differ over the effects of MNCs. Liberals believe that FDI contributes to increased efficiency by stimulating innovation, competition, economic growth, and employment. MNCs also provide countries with numerous benefits, such as capital, technology, managerial skills, and marketing networks. Historical materialists, by contrast, view MNCs as predatory monopolists that overcharge for their goods and services, limit the flow of technology, and create dependency relationships with LDC host countries. MNCs also have a negative impact on home countries by imposing downward pressures on labor and environmental standards. Realists are more inclined than other theorists to downgrade the political importance of MNCs. They argue that the most powerful states have considerable control over their MNCs and that MNCs retain close ties with their home governments.[6]

DEFINITIONS AND TERMINOLOGY

Controversy exists not only over the effects of MNCs but even over definitions and terminology. MNCs are usually defined as firms that control assets in at least two countries, but the Harvard Multinationals Project developed in the 1960s limited the MNC label to firms with subsidiaries in at least six countries.[7] Those who favor such restrictive definitions see the important investment issues as relating to the largest firms that establish a number of foreign affiliates as part of a global strategy; but restrictive definitions are problematic because they exclude enterprises on a rather arbitrary basis. This chapter adopts the more expansive definition of MNCs as firms that operate in two or more countries. An enterprise that does business in more than one country is not necessarily an MNC. To qualify, a firm must possess at least one FDI project in which it has a degree of management rights or control. A firm can undertake FDI in a host country in two forms: *greenfield investment,* or the creation of new facilities and productive assets by foreigners; and *mergers and acquisitions* (*M&As*), or the purchase of stocks in an existing firm with the purpose of participating in its management. In a cross-border merger, the assets and operations of two firms belonging to different countries are combined to establish a new legal entity. In an acquisition, a local firm becomes an affiliate or subsidiary of a foreign firm. During the past decade, most growth in international production has occurred through M&As rather than greenfield investment, and acquisitions are much more common than mergers.[8]

Although the definition of FDI may seem straightforward, there are disagreements over what constitutes "control." Until the 1960s, the U.S. Department of Commerce defined FDI as involving an equity capital stake of at least 25 percent. However, the department subsequently lowered this to 10 percent, and IOs such as the IMF and OECD use the 10-percent figure for statistical purposes. In reality, the share of equity required for control varies in different circumstances. If ownership of a company is widespread among many shareholders, a small amount of equity may be sufficient to exercise control, but if ownership is more concentrated among a few shareholders, a larger amount of equity may be needed to exercise control. The important point is that a shareholder can exercise control without holding a majority of shares. Foreign affiliates may be minority-owned (10–50 percent of equity), majority-owned (more than 50 but less than 100 percent), or wholly owned (100 percent) subsidiaries.[9]

Differences exist not only over definitions but also over the use of the term MNC. The United Nations and a number of scholars prefer the term *transnational* to multinational because the ownership and control of most firms is not really multinational. Instead, a firm normally extends its operations from a single home country across national frontiers. Most MNCs are in fact *ethnocentric* or home country oriented, with directives flowing from the headquarters to the affiliates and much of the MNCs' R&D located in the home country. However, a small but growing number of MNCs are *geocentric* or *stateless;* they adopt a worldwide approach and are not closely tied to any single state. Strategic alliances among MNCs from different states further complicate the task of associating an MNC with a home government; they may take the form of production-sharing agreements, or collaborative research and networking arrangements. Finally, MNCs can sometimes gain entry into a foreign country only by agreeing to form *joint ventures* with local firms; joint ventures are increasingly common in LDCs and transition states. This text uses the term MNC simply to signify that a firm has ongoing managerial and productive activities in more than one country.[10]

WHY DO FIRMS BECOME MNCs?

John Dunning developed a seminal theory explaining that firms decide to engage in FDI for reasons of ownership, location, and internalization, and the following discussion draws partly on his ideas.[11] To understand why firms become MNCs, it is important to distinguish between horizontal and vertical integration. A *horizontally integrated MNC* extends its operations abroad by producing the same product or product line in its foreign affiliates. Firms engage in **horizontal integration** to defend or increase their market share. Although a firm's exports from the home country may initially meet the foreign demand for products and services, the firm may have to set up a subsidiary to compete with new local suppliers. The MNC can compete more effectively with local firms through its affiliates because they have lower transportation costs and become more aware of the market's special characteristics; and labor costs are lower if a DC firm produces directly in LDC markets. Firms also engage in horizontal integration because of foreign government policies. When a government's tariffs and NTBs limit exports from a firm's home country, it may establish foreign operations to get behind the trade barriers. For example, when the United States imposed voluntary export restraints on Japanese automobile imports in the 1980s, Honda became the first Japanese firm to produce them in the United States. National and subnational governments also provide investment incentives to encourage firms to locate production facilities in their territories. Furthermore, FDI sometimes complements exports by stimulating the export of intermediate goods for use by foreign affiliates.[12]

A *vertically integrated MNC* geographically separates the different stages of production, with the outputs of some affiliates serving as inputs to other affiliates. Firms engage in **vertical integration** to gain the benefits of comparative advantage in the production process. For example, an electronics firm can lower production costs by locating assembly operations in low-wage LDCs, chip production in an NIE such as Singapore, and high-end R&D operations in California. Vertically integrated MNCs can also gain control of uncertain transactions with different owners at various stages of the production process by *internalizing* them within the firm. Firms opt for *backward integration* when raw materials and other production inputs they require are not readily available or have high transaction costs. Examples of backward integration include steel firm investments in iron ore operations, oil company investments in the extraction of crude oil, and rubber manufacturer investments in natural rubber plantations. Backward integration also enables MNCs to gain control over the quality of inputs. For example, three vertically integrated MNCs accounted for 60 percent of the banana export trade during the 1980s, because bananas are highly perishable and require specific handling and ripening conditions. The motivations for *forward vertical integration* are similar: to reduce uncertainty and transaction costs and to ensure the quality of goods and services that reach the consumer.[13] Another reason firms engage in vertical integration is to limit competition. When a small number of MNCs control the raw materials for an industry, they can impose substantial barriers to the entry of new rival firms. MNCs also engage in vertical integration to limit government scrutiny of their activities. For example, MNCs sometimes manipulate their **transfer prices** (the prices an MNC's affiliates charge each other for internal sales of goods and services) without detection by governments. Transfer prices help an MNC efficiently manage its internal operations and monitor the performance of its affiliates; but they can also enable an MNC to shift its reported profits from high-tax to low-tax countries (and thus avoid paying some taxes) by raising or lowering the prices charged by each affiliate. In 1993 the U.S. Internal Revenue Service ruled that Nissan Motor Company used transfer prices to underreport its U.S. income, and Nissan had to pay the United States about $150 million.[14]

Firms that become MNCs must have the ability as well as incentive to make the transition. Innovations in communications, transportation, and technology have enabled firms to internationalize, and they are more successful if they can "think globally" and "act locally." On the one hand, large MNCs have major advantages such as economies of scale, brand-name reputation, and access to global financing and inputs such as raw materials. On the other hand, MNCs operate in a world of states in which they must adhere to national laws and cater to the demands of local consumers.[15]

THE HISTORICAL DEVELOPMENT OF FDI

Although the rapid expansion of MNCs is a post–World War II phenomenon, some scholars trace MNC origins to the transborder business operations of medieval banks in fifteenth-century Florence. During the sixteenth to eighteenth centuries, international trading companies such as the English, Dutch, and French East India Companies and the Hudson's Bay Company also coordinated cross-border business activities. In the nineteenth century, firms that are commonly considered to be MNCs were involved in investments in a number of countries; thousands of these MNCs existed by the time of World War II.[16] A number of factors have affected the growth—and sometimes the contraction—of MNC activity during different periods:

- MNC activity increases when advances in communications, transportation, and technology facilitate MNC control over foreign operations.
- Rapid economic growth often stimulates MNC expansion, while depressed economic conditions have the opposite effect.
- MNC expansion depends on national and international rules and events. For example, the rules protecting private property encouraged FDI, whereas major wars had a depressing effect.
- Capital liberalization leads to increased FDI; capital and exchange controls discourage such activity.
- FDI often expands during periods of trade protectionism because MNCs shift production abroad to circumvent the trade barriers.[17]

The following discussion focuses on three periods: pre–World War II, the mid-1940s to mid-1980s, and the mid-1980s to the present.

The Pre–World War II Period

Earlier studies found that portfolio investment accounted for most of the long-term capital flows during the nineteenth and early twentieth centuries. However, as economists refined their definitions, they upgraded their estimate of foreign *direct* investment flows. Indeed, some studies indicate that FDI accounted for up to 45 percent of British foreign investment in 1913 and 1914.[18] As the first country to industrialize, Britain was the main force behind the dramatic growth of FDI during the nineteenth century. Although there were no government guarantees or international institutions to provide safeguards, investments were fairly secure for several reasons: Economic risk was lower under the pre–World War I gold standard because currencies were convertible and exchange rates were fairly stable; political risk was lower because a large share of European investment was in colonial territories operating under home country rules; there were no major restrictions on capital flows; and wars during this period were limited in scope. The nineteenth century was also a period of rapid advances in rail and sea transport and communications, which facilitated the management of FDI over long distances. Although FDI continued to increase in the twentieth century, there was an investment downturn after World War I because of global economic and political instability. For example, a number of countries began to impose restrictions on inward FDI, the Soviet Union nationalized foreign property, and the gold exchange standard was suspended. FDI contracted further during the Great Depression and World War II, and MNCs accounted for a smaller share of world economic activity in 1949 than in 1929. It was not until after World War II that the vigorous growth of MNCs and FDI would resume.[19]

The Mid-1940s to Mid-1980s

The United States overtook Britain as the leading source of FDI after World War II. As Table 9.1 shows, U.S. firms accounted for 47.1 percent of FDI outward stock in 1960, compared with Britain's 18.3 percent. FDI rapidly expanded under U.S. leadership because the North experienced a sustained period of economic growth from 1950 to 1973; there were major improvements in international transportation and communications; and most DCs relaxed their controls over FDI after their currencies became convertible. (A notable exception was Japan, which continued to restrict foreign investment flows.) Since the late 1960s, the U.S. share of outward FDI has declined steadily, partly because of Japan and Germany's rapid economic growth as they recovered from the war. Thus, Table 9.1 shows that the U.S. share of total outward FDI stock fell from 47.1 percent in 1960 to 32.3 percent in 1985, whereas Japan's share rose from 0.7 to 6.0 percent, and West Germany's share rose from 1.2 to 8.1 percent. Table 9.1 also shows that DCs were the source of most FDI flows: 99 percent in 1960 and 90 percent in 1985. However, MNCs based in the South increased their share of outward FDI stock from only 1 percent in 1960 to 10 percent in 1985. Most of this FDI came from more

TABLE 9.1 Outward FDI Stock (U.S.$ Billions)

	1960 Value	1960 %	1975 Value	1975 %	1985 Value	1985 %	1990 Value	1990 %	2000 Value	2000 %	2007 Value	2007 %
United States	31.9	47.1	124.2	44.0	238.4	32.3	430.5	24.1	1,316.2	21.4	2,791.3	17.9
Japan	0.5	0.7	15.9	5.7	44.0	6.0	201.4	11.3	278.4	4.5	542.6	3.5
Germany[a]	0.8	1.2	18.4	6.5	59.9	8.1	151.6	8.5	541.9	8.8	1,236.0	7.9
Britain	12.4	18.3	37.0	13.1	100.3	13.6	229.3	12.8	897.8	14.6	1,705.1	10.9
France	4.1	6.1	10.6	3.8	37.8	5.1	112.4	6.3	445.1	7.2	1,399.0	9.0
Italy	1.1	1.6	2.0	3.3	16.6	2.2	60.2	3.4	180.3	2.9	520.1	3.3
Canada	2.5	3.7	3.5	10.4	43.1	5.8	84.8	4.7	237.6	4.5	520.7	3.3
Total G7[b]	53.3	78.7	219.8	77.9	540.1	73.1	1,267.9	71.0	3,897.3	63.4	8,714.8	55.9
Total DCs[c]	67.0	99.0	275.4	97.7	664.9	90.0	1,640.4	91.9	5,265.1	85.6	13,042.2	83.6
Total	67.7		282.0		738.8		1,785.3		6,148.2		15,602.3	

[a]The 1960–1985 data are for West Germany.

[b]G7 = Group of Seven

[c]DCs = developed countries

Source: Centre on Transnational Corporations, *Transnational Corporations in World Development: Trends and Prospects* (New York: UN, 1988), Table 1.2, p. 24 (1960 and 1975 data); UNCTAD, *World Investment Report 2004* (New York: UN, 2004), Annex Table B.4, p. 382 (1985 data); UNCTAD, *World Investment Report 2008* (New York: UN, 2008), Annex Table B.2, p. 257 (1990, 2000, and 2007 data).

prosperous LDCs in Asia and Latin America and from OPEC states. The five largest LDC sources of outward FDI stock in 1985 were Brazil, South Africa, Argentina, Singapore, and Hong Kong.[20]

Whereas the U.S. outward FDI stock was declining, Table 9.2 shows that the U.S. share of inward FDI stock increased from 12 percent in 1980 to 19 percent in 1985. Japan was the only DC that maintained an extremely low share of inward FDI stock, at 0.5 percent in 1985, because governmental, societal, and cultural factors limited its investment flows. Thus, the DCs were the largest recipients as well as providers of FDI, accounting for 58.6 percent of inward FDI stock in 1985. Although the South had received over 60 percent of total FDI before World War II, this figure fell during the postwar period because of LDC demands for more control over their natural resources in the 1970s, the LDC foreign debt crisis in the 1980s, a gradual shift in FDI from primary products to manufacturing, and an increase in technology-related investment in the North. Among the LDCs, the most prosperous and resource-rich states received the most FDI. Thus, Table 9.2 shows that the share of FDI stock directed to Africa, which has many of the LLDCs, declined from 4.6 percent in 1980 to only 3.5 percent in 1985. Asian and Latin American LDCs, by contrast, received 30 and 8.2 percent of total inward FDI stock in 1985. The five largest LDC recipients of inward FDI stock in 1985 were Hong Kong, Brazil, Indonesia, Saudi Arabia, and Mexico. The Central and Eastern European socialist states (including the Soviet Union) received almost no FDI from 1975 to 1985.[21] Thus, DCs were directing most FDI in the mid-1980s to each other, and many LDCs were marginalized.

The 1980s to the Present

As discussed, FDI flows have declined in some years such as 1982–1983, and 2001–2003. However, FDI flows since the 1980s have *on average* increased faster than at any time since the nineteenth century. Table 9.3 shows that inward and outward FDI stock as a share of the GDPs of developed economies increased from 4.9 and 6.2 percent in 1980 to 27.2 and 33.9 percent in 2007. A number of factors account for the rapid growth of FDI. Most important, the reemergence of orthodox liberalism gave MNCs more freedom to expand their activities because of deregulation, privatization, and an end to restrictions on capital flows. Furthermore, the breakup of the Soviet bloc opened up large new areas for FDI as the transition economies instituted market reforms, and China also became a major FDI recipient. Another factor in the FDI expansion was the problems with international trade. The protracted Uruguay and Doha Round negotiations, combined with the use of NTBs, caused many MNCs to extend their activities abroad to circumvent trade barriers. Finally, significant advances in information and transportation technologies enabled MNCs to extend their global network.[22]

An important feature of FDI is the degree to which it has been concentrated in the "Triad"—the United States, the EU, and Japan. From 1985 to 2002, the triad accounted for about 80 percent of the world's outward FDI stock and

TABLE 9.2 Inward FDI Stock (U.S.$ Billions)

	1980		1985		1990		2000		2007	
	Value	%	Value	%	Value	%	Value	%	Value	%
DCs[a]	390.7	56.4	569.7	58.6	1,412.6	72.8	3,987.6	68.9	10,458.6	68.9
United States	83.0	12.0	184.6	19.0	394.9	20.3	1,256.9	21.7	2,093.0	13.8
Japan	3.3	0.4	4.7	0.5	9.9	0.5	50.3	0.9	132.9	0.9
Germany[b]	36.6	5.2	36.9	3.8	111.2	5.7	271.6	4.7	629.7	4.1
Britain	63.0	9.1	64.0	6.6	203.9	10.5	438.6	7.6	1,347.7	8.9
France	25.9	3.7	36.7	3.8	97.8	5.0	259.8	4.5	1,026.1	6.7
Italy	8.9	1.3	19.0	2.9	60.0	3.1	121.2	2.1	364.8	2.4
Canada	54.2	7.8	64.7	6.7	112.8	5.8	212.7	3.7	520.7	3.4
LDCs[c]	302.0	43.6	402.5	41.4	528.6	27.2	1,738.3	30.0	4,246.7	27.9
Africa	32.0	4.6	33.8	3.5	59.0	3.0	152.6	2.6	393.4	2.6
Asia and Oceania	218.3	31.5	287.3	30.0	359.1	18.5	1,082.7	18.7	2,713.3	17.8
Latin America and Caribbean	50.4	7.3	80.1	8.2	110.5	5.7	502.9	8.7	1,140.0	7.5
Total	692.7		972.2		1,941.3		5,786.7		15,210.6	

[a]DCs = developed countries

[b]1980 and 1985 data are for West Germany

[c]LDCs = less developed countries.

Source: UNCTAD, *World Investment Report 2004* (New York: UN, 2004), Annex Table B.3, pp. 376–380 (1980 and 1985 data); UNCTAD, *World Investment Report 2008* (New York: UN, 2008), Annex Table B.2, pp. 257–260 (1990, 2000, and 2007 data).

TABLE 9.3 Share of Inward and Outward FDI Stock as a Percent of GDP[a]

	1980	1985	1990	1995	2000	2007
DCs[b]						
Inward	4.9	6.2	8.2	8.9	16.2	27.2
Outward	6.2	7.3	9.6	11.3	21.3	33.9
United States						
Inward	3.0	4.4	6.9	7.3	12.8	15.1
Outward	7.8	5.7	7.5	9.5	13.4	20.2
Japan						
Inward	0.3	0.3	0.3	0.6	1.1	3.0
Outward	1.8	3.2	6.6	4.5	6.0	12.4
Germany						
Inward	3.9	5.1	7.1	7.8	14.3	19.0
Outward	4.6	8.4	8.8	10.5	28.5	37.3
Britain						
Inward	11.8	14.1	20.6	17.6	30.4	48.6
Outward	15.0	22.0	23.2	26.9	62.3	61.5
France						
Inward	3.8	6.9	7.1	12.3	19.6	40.1
Outward	3.6	7.1	9.1	13.2	33.5	54.7
Italy						
Inward	2.0	4.5	5.3	5.8	11.0	17.3
Outward	1.6	3.9	5.2	8.8	16.4	24.7
Canada						
Inward	20.4	18.4	19.6	21.1	29.3	36.5
Outward	8.9	12.3	14.7	20.3	32.8	36.5

[a]GDP = gross domestic product

[b]DCs = developed countries

Source: UNCTAD, *World Investment Report 2003* (New York: UN, 2003), Annex Table B.6, pp. 278–279 (1980–1995 data); UNCTAD, *World Investment Report 2008* (New York: UN, 2008), Annex Table B.3, pp. 261–271 (2000 and 2007 data).

for 50–60 percent of the inward FDI stock. U.S. firms have shown a strong preference for investing in Europe, intra-European investment has accelerated, and Japan and Western European countries have invested heavily in the United States. Clusters of non-Triad states also have strong FDI links with each Triad member. Table 9.4 shows that the nine largest host countries for FDI from 1985 to 1995 were also included among the largest home countries for FDI (i.e., countries in bold type) and that all but one of these nine (China) is an advanced industrial state. The only important home country for FDI that is not also an important host country is Japan. Although Japan has eased some

TABLE 9.4 Leading Host Economies for FDI (Cumulative Inflows, 1985–1995)[a]

Rank	Country	FDI (U.S.$ Billions)
1	United States	477.5
2	United Kingdom	199.6
3	France	138.0
4	China	130.2
5	Spain	90.9
6	Belgium–Luxembourg	72.4
7	Netherlands	68.1
8	Australia	62.6
9	Canada	60.9
10	Mexico	44.1
11	Singapore	40.8
12	Sweden	37.7
13	Italy	36.3
14	Malaysia	30.7
15	Germany	25.9
16	Switzerland	25.2
17	Argentina	23.5
18	Brazil	20.3
19	Hong Kong	17.9
20	Denmark	15.7

[a]Economies in bold are also among the 20 leading home economies for FDI.

Source: World Trade Organization Annual Report 1996, vol. 1, Trade and Foreign Direct Investment, p. 47, Table 4.1. Copyright © World Trade Organization 1996. By permission of the World Trade Organization.

of its formal impediments to inward FDI, a number of informal barriers remain. As Table 9.2 shows, Japan accounted for only 0.9 percent of inward FDI stock in 2007—well below the shares for other G7 countries.[23]

Despite the continued predominance of the DCs, there have been some notable changes in outward FDI since the 1980s. First, the United States lost its dominant position as a source of FDI. As Table 9.1 shows, the U.S. share of outward FDI stock fell from 44 percent in 1975 to 17.9 percent in 2007. Second, there were erratic changes in Japan's share of FDI outflows. As Table 9.1 also shows, Japan's share of outward FDI rose dramatically from 6 percent in 1985 to 11.3 percent in 1990. A strong Japanese yen as a result of the 1985 Plaza accord, combined with trade barriers on Japanese goods such as voluntary export restraints, forced Japanese firms to invest and produce more abroad.[24] However, Table 9.1 also shows that Japan's share of outward FDI fell back to 3.5 percent in 2007. Persistent economic recession and the financial problems of major Japanese banks (see Chapter 11) led to changes in the corporate strategies of many Japanese MNCs, which found it difficult to expand abroad.[25] Table 9.3 shows that Japan's outward FDI stock accounted for only 12.4 percent of its GDP in 2007, the lowest share of any G7 country. Third, as Table 9.1 shows, the DC share of outward FDI stock fell from 91.9 percent in 1990 to 83.6 percent in 2007. Thus, LDCs increased their share of outward FDI stock, and Asian economies have been the most active investors. South Korea, Singapore, Taiwan, and China (including Hong Kong) accounted for more than two-thirds of FDI outflows from the LDCs in 2004.[26]

There have also been some notable changes in inward FDI since 1980. First, Table 9.2 shows that the U.S. share of inward FDI stock steadily increased from 12 percent in 1980 to 21.7 percent in 2000. However, the U.S. share declined to 13.8 percent in 2007; this is concerning because inward FDI has become important for the future of U.S. prosperity. Although the U.S. share of inward FDI has fluctuated since 2000, economists attribute the general downward trend to several factors: The U.S. dollar was overvalued, and this elevated the cost of producing in the United States; some other countries gave more incentives to MNCs to engage in offshore production; U.S. corporate taxes were higher than taxes in some other locations; and MNCs had growing concerns about U.S. economic prospects. Second, Canada was the only G7 country whose share of inward FDI stock fell in all of the years listed in Table 9.2; overall, the Canadian share fell from 7.8 percent in 1980 to 3.4 percent in 2007. The U.S. share of Canada's inward FDI has declined from about 80 percent in 1980 to 60 percent today, and this decrease is linked to the creation of CUSFTA and NAFTA. Before free trade, U.S. MNCs often located inside Canada to avoid paying tariffs; but under NAFTA, a U.S. firm can produce in the United States (or Mexico) and freely export to Canada. Canada has not attracted more FDI from sources other than the United States for a variety of reasons related to productivity, labor costs, taxes, and the increase in value of the Canadian dollar in recent years. Third, the DC share of inward FDI stock has declined, and the LDC share has increased (to a limited extent) in recent years. Table 9.2 shows that the DC share of inward FDI fell from 72.8 percent in 1990 to 68.9 percent in 2007, whereas the LDC share rose from 27.2 percent to 27.9 percent during the same period. As Table 9.4 shows, a small group of rapidly growing LDCs, including China, Mexico, Singapore, Malaysia, Argentina, Brazil, and Hong Kong, were among the 20 leading host economies for FDI between 1985 and 1995. China and India stand out as major candidates for inward FDI because they offer MNCs a huge supply of cheap labor, and, in terms of numbers, they are the two largest consumer markets in the world. However, from 1998 through 2003, China had aggregate FDI inflows of $280 billion while India's inflows were only $18 billion. Although China's figure is inflated because it includes FDI inflows from Hong Kong and Taiwan, and from some mainland Chinese firms, China nevertheless attracts much more FDI than India. As some analysts discuss, China has moved quickly to adopt economic initiatives and reforms, while India has delayed in removing regulatory practices that MNCs consider burdensome. However, India is attracting more FDI in some areas such as outsourcing contracts that provide business services for foreign companies.[27] In contrast to the more prosperous LDCs, most Sub-Saharan African LDCs have been marginalized. Table 9.2 shows that Africa accounted for only 2.6 percent of inward FDI stock in 2007, compared with 17.8 percent for Asia and 7.5 percent for Latin America. Fourth, FDI has become a significant part of the privatization process in transition economies in Eastern Europe and the FSU.[28]

Although MNC influence has generally increased, the following sections examine their effects on home and host states. Most of the discussion of host state–MNC relations is devoted to the LDCs, and much of the discussion of home state–MNC relations focuses on the advanced industrial states.

MNC–HOST COUNTRY RELATIONS: DETERMINANTS AND EFFECTS OF FDI

We earlier discussed the reasons firms decide to become MNCs, but it is also important to examine why firms direct FDI to one host state rather than another. For example, analysts disagree as to whether MNCs are more likely to invest in LDCs with democratic or authoritarian governments. Some authors assume that democratic LDCs attract more FDI, because democratic institutions impose constraints on governments that decrease political risks and preserve MNCs' private property rights. Other authors assume that authoritarian LDCs attract more FDI, because autocratic leaders can repress labor unions, drive down wages, and shield MNCs from popular pressures for environmental controls. Scholars have conducted empirical studies to determine which of these views is correct, but the results have been inconclusive. For example, one study found that "regime type . . . seems to have little impact on foreign investors"; a second study found that "empirically the results prove rather conclusive—democracies attract more FDI"; and a third study found that "in fifteen Latin American countries for the period of 1981 to 1996 . . . abuse of civil liberties and political rights . . . had a positive and statistically significant effect on inflows of U.S. FDI."[29] A major problem is that authors use different measures of regime type; is democracy based on elections, the rights of workers and peasants, freedom of the press, or economic rights and privileges? Thus, more research is needed to determine which types of countries attract more FDI. There are also debates in the literature on the *effects* of FDI on host states. Orthodox liberals see MNCs as contributing to LDC development by providing external capital, new technologies, and modern ideas that replace traditional social values. They assume that states have different factor endowments and that foreign investment goes to areas where it is most needed or in shortest supply. Thus, inward FDI compensates for inadequate local savings, export earnings, or foreign aid; tax revenues from MNC profits supplement local taxes; and MNCs fill LDC needs for imported technology. Although liberals acknowledge that a strong MNC presence may initially result in more income inequality, they attribute this to the positive effect of MNCs on income growth in general. This inequality is a temporary price to be paid for economic success, and the market will help bring about economic convergence in the longer term.[30]

The first major challenge to orthodox liberal views came from two economists, Stephen Hymer (a Marxist) and Charles Kindleberger (a liberal). They argued that FDI cannot simply be equated with the movement of capital from home to host countries, because MNCs often get financing for FDI by borrowing funds in host countries. Although FDI supporters see free markets as promoting open competition, Hymer and Kindleberger noted that MNCs are oligopolistic; they lack certain advantages that local firms possess, but gain competitiveness by creating an oligopolistic environment. For example, an MNC can raise barriers to the entry of firms through its use of new technologies, economies of scale, and privileged access to global finance. Thus, Hymer wrote that "the industries in which there is much foreign investment tend to be concentrated industries, while the industries in which there is little or no foreign investment tend to be unconcentrated."[31] Drawing on some of Hymer's ideas, dependency theorists argued that MNCs appropriate local capital rather than bringing in new capital, prevent local firms from participating in the most dynamic sectors of the economy, increase income inequalities in the host country, and use capital-intensive technologies that contribute to unemployment. MNCs also undermine the host government and society by co-opting local elites, imposing political and economic pressure (often with the help of the MNC's home country), and altering consumer tastes and habits. Although Latin American and East Asian NIEs are industrializing, MNCs prevent these states from achieving autonomous development; thus, one study claims that MNCs in Brazil keep "the innovative side of their businesses as close to home as possible" and ensure that "the industrialization of the periphery will remain partial."[32]

Many studies indicate that MNC effects on host states are neither as positive nor as negative as neoliberal and dependency theorists maintain and that a host state's options vary under different circumstances. For example, one factor affecting a host state's options is the amount of competition among investors; a host state has greater leverage if it has more investors to choose from. Although states have become more dependent on investment, the diversity of investment sources has also increased because U.S. MNCs have become less dominant and there are more European, Japanese, and Southern MNCs. The *obsolescing bargain* is another factor that causes a host state's relations with MNCs to change over time. A host state has a weak bargaining position before an MNC enters it because the MNC can pursue other options and the host state must provide incentives to attract the initial investment. The MNC's bargaining power stems from its sophisticated technology, brand-name identification, access to capital, product diversity, and ability to promote exports. Thus, the initial investment agreement favors the MNC. After the investment is made, however, the host state has more bargaining leverage because the MNC commits itself to immobile resources. The host state can treat these resources as a "hostage," and it gains bargaining, technological, and managerial skills through spinoffs from the foreign investment. Thus, the host state may try to renegotiate the original bargain and gain more favorable terms with the MNC.[33]

The obsolescing bargain is more applicable in some cases than in others; for example, it is more likely to apply to projects that require large fixed investments. Such projects initially give foreign investors considerable leverage, but later the fixed investments can become hostage to the host state. MNCs with smaller fixed investments can more easily withdraw from the host state. Another factor is the type of technology used; MNCs using new sophisticated technologies that are unavailable to the host state may be less vulnerable to aggressive host state policies at a later date. A third factor is the importance of marketing or product differentiation through advertising. When a firm's sales depend on brand identification and consumer loyalty, it is in a stronger position vis-à-vis the host state. These three factors—fixed investments, new technologies, and brand identification—help predict whether an industry will be subject to the obsolescing bargain. For example, the obsolescing bargain is less applicable to manufacturing industries that are less dependent on host state resources, rely on advanced technologies, and manufacture brand-name products familiar to consumers. The obsolescing bargain is more applicable to natural resource industries that involve large fixed investments and familiar technologies. In these industries, nationalizations have been more common, and host states have been more successful in demanding higher taxes, more processing of goods, joint marketing, and the employment of local people in management.[34]

Although investments are subject to uncertainties such as the obsolescing bargain and political unrest in host states, MNCs employ various strategies to offset these risks. For example, an MNC can decrease its vulnerability to host states by vertical integration, that is, by placing the various stages of production in different states. MNCs can also avoid strong pressures from a host state by establishing alliances with the local private sector in joint ventures or other arrangements. When an MNC becomes more firmly established in a host state, it can gain political and economic support by creating linkages with local suppliers, distributors, and consumers. One indication of MNC success in countering risks is the fact that host states tend to be more restrained than they were in the past; for example, nationalizations of MNC affiliates have generally not occurred since the mid-1980s. State-to-state interactions can also affect MNC–host state relations, and one analyst argues that "the traditional bargaining model of MNC–host developing country relations" should be replaced with "a two-tier, multi-party bargaining process."[35] As a result of first-tier bargaining between the host and home states, MNCs have had more influence in second-tier bargaining with host states. For example, DC home states have induced LDC host states to liberalize their policies toward FDI through bilateral investment agreements (discussed later in this chapter) and conditions attached to IMF and World Bank structural adjustment loans. In assessing MNC–host state bargaining relationships, we must therefore also consider the role of other actors such as home states, IOs, and NGOs.

HOST COUNTRY POLICIES TOWARD MNCs

Host state policies toward MNCs vary widely, ranging from nationalizations to efforts to attract MNCs with concessions and incentives; and many states have an "attraction-aversion dilemma" in their approach to FDI. For example, governments may welcome FDI in some sectors while limiting or blocking it in others (e.g., in defense industries). States also may try to impose obligations such as performance requirements on MNCs to maximize the benefits of FDI. Some federal governments follow restrictive policies toward foreign investment, while their subnational governments (e.g., states or provinces) compete with one another to attract FDI. Although states seek the capital, technology, and organizational skills of MNCs, they may try to preserve large segments of the domestic market for local firms. The issue becomes even more complicated when a country's verbal statements courting FDI differ from the experiences of foreign investors.[36] The following sections discuss Southern and Northern host state policies.

The South

The South imposed very few restrictions on MNCs before World War I. Colonial territories were open to investment from the imperial powers, and independent Latin American LDCs generally accepted the liberal view that foreign investment would further their economic development. Russia's nationalization of its oil industry after the 1917 revolution had an impact on LDC attitudes, with some shifting to more nationalist policies during the interwar period. However, the South's adoption of restrictive policies was more notable after World War II. In extreme cases, communist regimes in China, North Korea, North Vietnam, and Cuba nationalized Western assets. In other cases, many newly independent states sought limits on FDI to preserve their national sovereignty. FDI often bred hostility because it involved foreign control over LDCs' natural resources and public utilities and was associated with the former colonial powers. However, LDCs had limited ability to pressure for a greater share of FDI benefits because they lacked experience in dealing with MNCs and had few sources of external finance. From 1946 to 1959, U.S. MNCs accounted for more than two-thirds of all new foreign-owned subsidiaries in the South.[37]

In the 1960s and 1970s, LDCs had more leverage and were more activist for several reasons. The growing number of non-U.S. MNCs gave the LDCs alternative sources of finance; FDI was often in natural resources, which were subject to the obsolescing bargain; dependency theorists encouraged the South to exert more pressure on MNCs; and LDCs increased their managerial, administrative, and technical abilities to regulate MNC behavior. Thus, nationalization of foreign firms became widespread in the petroleum and mining industries. LDCs also posed a major challenge to liberal economic views of FDI in the United Nations. In the 1950s and 1960s, the liberal approach to FDI emphasized national treatment, compensation to MNCs for infringement of their privileges, and the right of MNCs to seek support from their home countries. By the late 1960s, LDCs were pressuring instead for agreements to restrict the rights of MNCs, permit discrimination in favor of national firms, and give host state institutions the authority to resolve investment disputes. OPEC's success in raising oil prices in 1973 gave the LDCs more influence, and the UN General Assembly passed resolutions on FDI despite objections of the North such as the 1974 NIEO Declaration calling on host states to unilaterally apply rules to resident MNCs. However, these resolutions were largely symbolic, and the United Nations failed to reach an agreement on a comprehensive code of conduct for MNCs (discussed later in this chapter).[38]

By the late 1970s, the South shifted to a more conciliatory position for several reasons:

- The nationalization of large-scale petroleum and mining industries was largely completed.
- LDC experience with nationalizing natural resource industries was disappointing because of declining productivity, failure to introduce new technologies, and continued dependence on MNCs for marketing products.
- LDC militancy caused MNCs to shift some of their investments from the South to DCs with natural resources such as Australia, Canada, and the United States.
- The 1980s foreign debt crisis and world recession led to cutbacks in bank loans to LDCs, and the South's fear of exploitation by MNCs was replaced by concern that its inward FDI was declining.

Many LDCs therefore adopted more open policies toward MNCs during the 1980s. Mexico, for example, liberalized its policies and participated in drafting the NAFTA provisions for freer foreign investment. The most significant change was in the policies of transition economies, especially China. Although China was largely closed to FDI from the 1950s to 1970s, it became more welcoming to FDI in the late 1970s and even granted foreign investors special treatment not available to domestic firms. Thus, China soon became the largest LDC host country for FDI.[39] Although LDCs adopted more welcoming policies, some governments imposed local content and export requirements on MNCs and pressured them to enter into joint ventures with local firms. The East Asian NIEs, for example, welcomed investment but attached a number of conditions to inward FDI. However, most LDCs and transition economies as well as DCs are currently seeking to attract FDI. Of the 1,035 changes in FDI laws of countries from 1991 to 1999, 974 were more favorable and only 61 were less favorable to FDI. Most new measures by LDCs and transition economies reduce restrictions on foreign entry and offer incentives such as lower taxes to promote investment in priority industries. FDI is the largest source of external finance for LDCs, and during financial crises LDCs have found FDI to be more stable than other capital flows. Whereas investment ratings and short-term financial considerations influence access to bank lending and portfolio investment, FDI responds more to underlying economic fundamentals.[40]

It is important to note that the poorest LDCs find it difficult to attract FDI even when they liberalize their investment policies. For example, most Sub-Saharan African LDCs adopted policies to encourage FDI, partly under pressure from IMF and World Bank structural adjustment loans (see Chapter 11). However, low economic growth rates, civil conflicts, political crises, and high indebtedness levels have adversely affected their FDI inflows. As Table 9.2 shows, Africa's share of inward FDI stock was only 2.6 percent in 2007, compared with 17.8 and 7.5 percent for Asia and Latin America, respectively.

The North

MNC investments have on average focused more on natural resources and lower technology manufacturing in the South, and on higher technology production in the North. MNCs also loom larger in LDC than DC economies, and DCs are often major home as well as host countries for FDI; thus they are reluctant to restrict incoming FDI. Despite these differences, DC policies have also shifted over time.

The United States, Western Europe, and Canada imposed very few controls on foreign firms during the nineteenth century, largely because of liberal attitudes fostered by British hegemony. Western Europe followed more open policies than the United States toward FDI after World War I, but their positions reversed after World War II when the United States emerged as the global hegemon. Indeed, the Europeans adopted more restrictive policies in the 1960s largely because of concerns about the dominance of American MNCs. In his book *The American Challenge,* the French writer Jean-Jacques Servan-Schreiber attributed the success of U.S. MNCs to the dynamism of American society, and he called on Europe to reform its educational, industrial, and social policies, and focus on establishing its own MNCs.[41] In response, European governments promoted national champions in key industries by subsidizing research, encouraging mergers, and increasing procurement from national firms; and they demanded that foreign MNCs contribute to job creation and export promotion. France in particular screened inward FDI and rejected more FDI proposals than other European states. Canada also began a screening process in the 1970s because 50 percent of its manufacturing output and 70 percent of its oil production were foreign controlled. As Table 9.3 shows, inward FDI accounted for 20.4 percent of Canada's GDP in 1980, compared with only 11.8 percent for Britain, 3.8 percent for France, 3 percent for the United States, and 0.3 percent for Japan. In 1974 Canada created a Foreign Investment Review Agency (FIRA) to determine whether foreign takeovers were of "significant benefit" to the country, and in 1980 it developed a National Energy Program (NEP) to increase Canadian ownership in the oil and gas industry. These policies produced major tensions with the United States.[42] However, Japan had the most interventionist DC policy. Table 9.2 shows that Japan's inward FDI accounted for only 0.4 percent of total inward FDI stocks in 1980, compared with 12 percent for the United States and 9.1 percent for Britain. Japan's low level of inward FDI resulted partly from the difficulty Western MNCs had in adapting to its cultural and linguistic differences, but Japan's investment restrictions also played a critical role. Dating back to the sixteenth century, Japan's international economic controls resulted from fear of foreign intervention and pride in its distinct economy and society. During the 1930s, Japan developed policies to extract benefits from foreign investment, such as access to capital and technology, while avoiding the drawbacks of foreign control; and after World War II Japan continued to restrict FDI inflows.[43]

In contrast to the restrictions of the 1970s, most DCs began to seek FDI in the mid-1980s for several reasons. First, states viewed FDI restrictions as less legitimate because of the phasing out of global capital controls and the reemergence of orthodox liberalism. Second, states viewed FDI as a remedy for increased global competitiveness and unemployment. The average unemployment rate in OECD countries rose from 3.3 percent in 1973 to 8.6 percent in 1983, and governments placed considerable value on the jobs FDI could provide. DCs also began to view inward FDI as a means of enhancing their competitiveness, and they offered financial incentives and tax concessions to attract MNCs. A third factor in the policy shift was the change in the country composition of FDI. As other DCs joined the United States as important home countries for FDI, they favored fewer restrictions on MNCs. For example, the EC was ambivalent about a 1981 U.S. proposal that GATT should compile an inventory of host countries' trade-related investment measures; but when European MNCs increased their outward FDI, they began to favor greater discipline over host countries and supported the U.S. position in the GATT Uruguay Round.[44] Japan also felt pressure to ease its inward FDI restrictions as its outward investment increased. Although Japan had removed most legal obstacles to inward FDI by the 1980s, intangible barriers continue to limit the role of foreign firms. Foreign M&As are less common in Japan because shareholders with ties to the firms' management and members of *keiretsus* (groups with extensive cross-shareholdings) hold most of the stock of Japanese firms. For example, of the 584 M&As involving Japan in 1992, 165 were Japanese firms acquiring other Japanese firms, 165 were Japanese firms acquiring foreign firms, and only 32 were foreign firms acquiring Japanese firms. It is also difficult to develop new FDI projects because of the costs and complexities of doing business in Japan, exclusionary business practices of the *keiretsus,* and bureaucratic practices that discriminate against foreign firms. Japan is adopting policies to encourage more openness, and foreign takeovers of Japanese firms are gradually increasing. However, Table 9.3 shows that inward FDI accounted for only 3.0 percent of Japan's GDP in 2007.[45]

A fourth reason for more open investment policies was the pressure imposed by the United States. Canada and Mexico as U.S. neighbors felt this pressure most strongly. For example, the Canadian Liberal government loosened the controls on inward FDI it had instituted through FIRA and the NEP because of U.S. protests and a U.S. challenge in GATT. The Progressive Conservative government elected in 1984 then rescinded the NEP and replaced FIRA with Investment Canada, which did more to encourage than review inward FDI. Subsequently, the CUSFTA and NAFTA led to further liberalization of Canadian (and Mexican) foreign invest-ment regulations. It is important to note that Canada's position on inward FDI was also changing because Canada was becoming a more important *source* of FDI. As Table 9.3 shows, in 2007 Canada's outward FDI stock accounted for the same percentage of its GDP (36.5 percent) as its inward FDI stock.[46]

As the main advocate of open investment policies, it is ironic that the United States adopted somewhat more restrictive policies in the 1980s and 1990s. This policy shift resulted from the relative decline of its economic hege-mony and its increased role as a host country for FDI. Table 9.3 shows that inward FDI accounted for only 3 percent of U.S. GDP in 1980 and 4.4 percent in 1985. However, U.S. inward FDI rose to 6.9 percent of GDP in 1990 and to 15.1 percent by 2007. Some congressional leaders warned that foreign investors were acquiring U.S. high-technology firms and that the U.S. military was depending more on foreign-controlled suppliers. Thus, U.S. policies became more interventionist with a number of proposed and actual legislative changes. Most important was the Exon-Florio amendment to the 1988 Omnibus Trade and Competitiveness Act, which enables the president to block foreign mergers or acquisitions of U.S. firms that pose a possible danger to national security. The authority to implement Exon-Florio rests with an interagency Committee on Foreign Investment in the United States (CFIUS). The U.S. Congress did not pass some more extreme proposals, and the CFIUS and U.S. presidents have implemented the Exon-Florio amendment with con-siderable moderation. However, an administration could limit inward FDI if it chose to liberally interpret the national security clause in Exon-Florio. Despite the Exon-Florio amendment, the United States continues to support liberal foreign investment policies in international forums. For example, the United States was the main force behind the TRIMs negotiations in the GATT Uruguay Round and negotiations for a Multilateral Agreement on Investment in the OECD. The North in general supports liberalization, and most DC regulatory changes in recent years have been investment friendly.[47]

MNC–HOME COUNTRY RELATIONS

The number of major home countries for MNCs has always been small. Western Europe was the source of about 80 percent of FDI before World War I, and Britain accounted for the largest share. The United States, Britain, and the Netherlands accounted for 65–75 percent of outward FDI stock between World War I and 1980. Although the sources of FDI became more diverse after 1980, six DCs accounted for about 75 percent of the total in the early 1990s—the United States, Britain, Germany, France, Japan, and the Netherlands. Some LDCs and transition economies have become more important as sources of FDI, and the value of outward FDI stock from these countries reached $1.4 trillion in 2005.[48] Despite the increase in FDI from LDCs and transition economies, Table 9.1 shows that DCs still accounted for 83.6 percent of outward FDI stock in 2007. This discussion of FDI–home country relations therefore focuses mainly on the North.

The effects of FDI on a home country depend on the characteristics of both the home country and its MNCs. Realists often focus on the home country's characteristics, differentiating between rising and declining hegemons. Outward FDI seemed to have numerous benefits and few costs for Britain and the United States as rising hegemons in the nineteenth and twentieth centuries, because it did not hurt the interests of powerful domestic groups. As a hegemonic state declines, however, some important domestic groups begin to perceive outward FDI as having negative effects. For example, during the 1970s U.S. labor groups began to argue that U.S. FDI was exporting jobs and contributing to unemployment.[49] Whereas some theorists focus on the home country's characteristics, others examine the MNC. Some analysts, for example, argue that more MNCs are becoming "stateless" and developing interests that diverge from those of their home countries. Thus, American oil companies became less closely identified with the U.S. national interest after the 1973 energy crisis, and European oil companies refused to give their home markets preferential deliveries during the Arab oil embargo. Whether policy makers focus on the characteristics of the state or the MNC, questions about the costs as well as benefits of FDI to home countries have increased in recent years. This section begins with a discussion of home country policies toward MNCs. It then examines two contentious questions in regard to home country–MNC relations: (1) What are the costs and benefits of FDI for labor groups in the home country? and (2) What is the relationship between the competitiveness of a home country and the competitiveness of its MNCs?

Home Country Policies Toward MNCs

Home countries normally view outward FDI as an indication of economic and political strength and as beneficial to their competitiveness. Thus, they usually give their MNCs favored treatment and try to protect them from hostile actions by foreigners, especially when the MNCs operate in strategic industries. However, governments sometimes associate outward FDI with a decrease in home country exports, a decline in the country's industrial base, and losses in domestic employment. In such circumstances, home countries may try to stem the flow of outward FDI. Some governments also view their MNCs as tools of foreign policy and may attempt to monitor, control, or restrain their outward FDI in the interests of the home economy.

THE PRE–WORLD WAR II PERIOD   During the nineteenth and early twentieth centuries, home countries supported their corporations and protected them vis-à-vis foreigners. For example, in the colonial period European states sometimes intervened militarily to ensure that their companies developed and prospered. During the interwar years, European home countries provided subsidies and other assistance to support airlines, shipping firms, and oil companies that were closely tied to their strategic interests. In the 1930s, the Japanese army occupied Chinese plants and gave Japanese companies control over their management. The United States also was sometimes willing to support its companies' interests in Latin America with military force. However, governments at times took actions to limit outward FDI; for example, the Nazi government in Germany had to approve all new FDI, and it only rarely gave its approval. Although the U.S. government was concerned that outward FDI could transfer technology and employment to foreign countries, it adopted no policies to restrict FDI outflows before World War II.[50]

EARLY POSTWAR PERIOD   In the 1950s to 1970s, the United States as the hegemonic power both protected its MNCs and pressured them for political and economic reasons. For example, in 1962 the U.S. Congress passed the Hickenlooper Amendment, which threatened to withhold development assistance from LDCs that nationalized American MNC affiliates without providing adequate compensation. The United States also viewed its MNCs as tools of foreign policy. For example, the U.S. government used its Trading with the Enemy Act and Foreign Assets Control Legislation in the 1960s and 1970s to limit the trade of U.S. subsidiaries with China, Cuba, North Vietnam, and North Korea. Host governments for U.S. subsidiaries in Canada, Europe, and Latin America considered these policies an infringement of their sovereignty, and they often adopted laws to counter the U.S. legislation. The United States also tried to control corporate behavior in response to its growing balance-of-payments deficits. In the 1960s, the government called on U.S. MNCs to limit capital outflows to their foreign affiliates; in the 1970s, the government created the Domestic International Sales Corporation (DISC) program, which provided tax incentives to encourage MNCs to export from the United States instead of from abroad.[51]

Although European governments recovering from World War II were concerned that outward FDI would adversely affect their balance of payments, they did little to either encourage or restrict outward FDI in the 1950s and 1960s. Japan was the only major economy that systematically restricted outward FDI for about two decades after World War II. In its efforts to keep scarce capital at home for postwar reconstruction, Japan scrutinized FDI projects and approved only those that would increase exports, provide access to raw materials, and pose no threat to Japanese producers. Thus, Table 9.1 shows that Japan accounted for only 0.7 percent of outward FDI stock in 1960. Japan did not begin to liberalize its controls on outward FDI until the late 1960s, when its balance-of-trade surpluses were rapidly increasing.[52]

1980s TO THE PRESENT   The United States did less to limit dealings with communist countries as the Cold War declined, but it sometimes acted in response to international events. In the early 1980s, for example, Western Europe and the Soviet Union agreed to construct a natural gas pipeline; Western European firms were to provide equipment for the pipeline's construction in return for future deliveries of Soviet natural gas. After Poland declared martial law in December 1981, the United States retaliated against the Soviet Union by imposing an embargo on materials produced by U.S. companies that were to be used in constructing the pipeline. The United States not only prohibited subsidiaries of U.S. MNCs from exporting equipment and technology to the Soviet Union, but also ordered foreign companies not to export goods produced with technology acquired under licensing agreements with U.S. companies. The Reagan administration's opposition to the pipeline stemmed from concerns that Western Europe would become dependent on Soviet gas exports, and that these exports would provide the Soviet Union with hard currency to strengthen its economy. However, planning for the pipeline was already at an advanced stage, and Britain, France, West Germany, and Italy ordered their resident firms to ignore the U.S. restrictions and provide the goods and technology to the Soviet Union. A number of firms, such as Dresser-France (a U.S. subsidiary) and licensees of General Electric in Britain, Italy, and West Germany, complied with the European orders. The United States initially imposed penalties on these firms, but the Europeans did not back down; eventually the U.S. sanctions were removed and the European sales proceeded.[53] Since the breakup of the Soviet Union, U.S. extraterritorial actions have been aimed mainly at Cuba. For example, the 1996 Helms–Burton Act penalizes *foreign* companies for doing business in Cuba if they use assets or property of U.S. MNCs (or individuals) that were nationalized after the 1959 Cuban Revolution; but foreign governments indicated that their companies would not abide by this legislation.[54]

Other home countries have been less inclined than the United States to take such blatant political actions to control MNC behavior. However, Japan and Western Europe have established close linkages with their MNCs to achieve common *economic* objectives; the United States by contrast has maintained more of an arm's length relationship between business and government (the U.S. defense and oil industries are notable exceptions). Realists argue that the United States should counter the actions of Japan and Europe by developing an industrial policy to support its MNCs, especially in high-technology areas; this would involve assessing competitive trends in high-technology industries and shifting federal R&D funds from military uses to dual-use and economic areas. The United States has pursued some limited industrial policy initiatives but not to the same extent as Japan and some European countries. In contrast to industrial policy measures, liberals support dependence on the market and on firms that are the lowest cost suppliers, regardless of their nationality.[55]

The Effects of MNCs on Labor Groups in Home Countries

A major controversy regarding the impact of MNCs on *home* countries relates to whether or not foreign production causes a loss of exports and jobs at home. The debate began in the 1970s when the American Federation of Labor–Congress of Industrial Organizations (AFL-CIO) reversed its liberal trade policy position and called for limits on imports and on FDI by American firms. In the early 1990s, U.S. labor groups opposed NAFTA because of concerns that MNCs would shift their operations to Mexico. The assumption of the AFL-CIO and other U.S. labor groups is that workers in the home country are likely to lose their jobs when a U.S. firm switches from exporting to serving foreign markets through subsidiaries. Other DCs have also been concerned about FDI and the loss of jobs. For example, a 1993 report to the French Senate argued that outward FDI was a major cause of unemployment among factory workers, Japanese policy makers warned that unemployment resulted from the relocation of plants to other Asian countries, and Germany was concerned about the employment effects of industries relocating in Eastern Europe.[56]

Liberals generally dismiss these concerns, arguing that U.S. FDI "tends in the aggregate to create rather than destroy U.S. job opportunities in high-wage, export-oriented industries."[57] Although outward FDI destroys some jobs in the home country, "it creates others, and the jobs thus gained tend to pay higher wages than the jobs lost."[58] Thus, liberals often present evidence that MNCs have a better record than domestic firms in job creation, worker salaries, export performance, and technological innovations in the home country. Liberals also reject the idea that home country workers suffer as a result of the transfer of MNC activities to LDC subsidiaries with lower wages and standards. For example, one liberal study argues that investment by U.S. firms in Mexico as a result of NAFTA "creates U.S. jobs, both in the short run, by boosting U.S. exports of capital goods, and in the long run, by establishing channels for the export of U.S. intermediate components, replacement parts, and associated goods and services."[59] Realists and historical materialists by contrast emphasize the negative effects of outward FDI on employment stemming from export substitution and intrafirm imports. *Export substitution* results when production of a subsidiary in country B substitutes for exports from the parent firm in country A, or when exports from the subsidiary in B to a third country (C) substitute for goods and services that A formerly supplied to C. *Intrafirm imports* are goods and services that the home country imports from foreign affiliates of a parent firm. Realists argue that export substitution and intrafirm imports reduce production and employment in the home country, and historical materialists add that the mobility of capital and MNCs puts immobile workers at a disadvantage. The constant threat that MNCs will "outsource" jobs to subsidiaries in low-wage countries forces workers in the home country to accept lower salaries, health benefits, pensions, and job security. MNCs from this perspective benefit both by exploiting low-cost labor in LDC host countries and by reducing labor costs in DC home countries. Critical theorists reject the liberal view that workers in the home country will be compensated for the loss of manufacturing jobs with the growth of skilled service positions by arguing that MNCs are now even exporting more skilled positions to lower salary locations.[60]

Despite numerous studies on MNCs, it is difficult to find unequivocal evidence supporting one side or the other on this issue. A major problem confronting empirical researchers is that we cannot know whether a specific firm's exports would have been maintained if it had *not* established foreign subsidiaries. Firms that establish foreign affiliates are often more competitive, and workers in a less competitive firm may lose jobs whether at home or abroad. Creation of foreign production facilities can also be both job displacing and job creating for workers in the home country, depending on whether an MNC is able to expand and diversify its production facilities. With all the variables involved, it may be easier to determine the impact of FDI on specific jobs in specific firms than to provide a broader view of the impact on aggregate employment and exports. Finally, most analysts would agree that FDI in LDCs is more likely to adversely affect less skilled than more skilled workers in DC home countries. The "fairness" of this situation depends not only on our economic views, but also on our political and social views. Thus, the controversy over the effects of FDI on workers in home countries shows no signs of abating.[61]

Competitiveness and Home Country–MNC Relations

Another contentious issue is whether a state's competitiveness is closely linked with the competitiveness of its MNCs, or whether MNCs have worldwide interests that differ from the interests of their home countries. Realists argue that a state's MNCs have a major impact on its competitiveness because its "standard of living in the long term depends on its ability to attain a high and rising level of productivity in the industries in which its firms compete."[62] For example, Canada has a good standard of living despite the high degree of foreign ownership in its manufacturing industry; but it can never have the highest standard because the best jobs and R&D are located in the home country.[63] Liberals by contrast often argue that MNCs seek profitable opportunities around the world and "are becoming disconnected from their home nations."[64] They see U.S. competitiveness as depending more on U.S. workers' education and skills than on U.S. corporate ownership; if Americans have the requisite training, foreign MNCs will employ U.S. workers. Thus, U.S. Senator Lamar Alexander asserted that the American auto industry was earlier defined as "the Big Three companies in Detroit. Now the definition is any company that makes a substantial number of cars and trucks in the U.S. and has a big payroll here, pays big taxes here and buys supplies here."[65] Some liberals go even further and assert that we are entering a "borderless world" in which a corporation's nationality no longer makes a difference.[66] An analyst's position on competitiveness affects their policy prescriptions. Whereas realists argue that governments should pursue industrial policies to promote their own

MNCs in high-technology areas, interventionist liberals believe that govern-ments should focus more on upgrading their workers' skills so that MNCs of any nationality will want to do business, invest, and pay taxes there.[67]

Some evidence indicates that large MNCs are becoming more global in their operations and outlook and less closely tied to their home countries. For example, the sales of foreign affiliates of U.S. firms were four times greater than U.S. merchandise exports between 1988 and 1990; U.S. foreign affiliates accounted for 43 percent of their parent companies' total profits in 1990; and U.S. firms increased their foreign R&D spending by 33 percent, compared with an increase of only 6 percent in the United States from 1986 to 1988. National boundaries are also becoming blurred as some MNCs spread their head office functions and list their shares in stock exchanges in several countries. For example, Shell and Unilever have headquarters in Britain and the Netherlands, and Astra-Zeneca has its headquarters in one state and conducts most of its R&D in another state. Asea Brown Boveri was formed from a merger of Sweden's ASEA and Switzerland's Brown Boveri, moved its headquarters from Stockholm to Zurich, has Swiss, German, and Swedish managers, and does its business in English. The increase of cross-border M&As and cross-holding of shares are additional complications in defining an MNC's nationality, and inte-grated production systems make it difficult to determine a product's origins. MNCs can insulate themselves from national policies and conditions by sourc-ing inputs, information, and personnel from around the world. For example, an automobile manufactured by Ford may be assembled in Britain with inputs from all over Europe, from designs produced in the United States, and from stages of processing in various locations. In this age of globalization, liberals argue that the highest priority should be "to provide competitive conditions for businesses in general in the country rather than only for the country's firms in particular."[68]

Despite the blurring of nationalities, realists note that *most* MNCs are home country based and that a state's competitiveness is linked with the com-petitiveness of its MNCs. R&D is a major factor promoting competitiveness, and MNCs tend to keep much of their R&D activity at home. In 1984, for example, the ratio of R&D to sales for industrial machinery and equipment firms in Canada was only 40 percent of the U.S. ratio, and much of this difference resulted from the high degree of foreign ownership in Canadian industry. Although U.S. MNCs are more willing than Japanese MNCs to invest in R&D abroad, even U.S. companies spent only 8.6 percent of their R&D funding in foreign countries in 1988.[69] One factor in a country's competitiveness is its abil-ity to maintain a positive trade balance, and U.S. affiliates of Japanese firms are more likely than U.S. firms to import goods and services into the United States. R&D funding is also essential for developing new technologies, and the control of high-technology industries can affect a country's national security. Although a state's competitiveness is tied to the competitiveness of its firms, there are important national differences. For example, U.S. MNCs tend to favor their home country less than Japanese and German MNCs. Studies show that U.S.

MNCs are more interested in the financial returns on investments, whereas Japanese MNCs emphasize market share; U.S. MNCs are more willing to invest in overseas R&D than Japanese MNCs; and German and Japanese MNCs put more emphasis than U.S. MNCs on exporting from the home country. Thus, Robert Reich's question as to whether "our MNCs" look after "our national interests" may be more relevant for U.S. MNCs than for Japanese and German MNCs.[70]

A REGIME FOR FDI: WHAT IS TO BE REGULATED?

Despite the global influence of MNCs, the principles, norms, and rules for foreign investment are more rudimentary than those for trade and monetary relations; and no IO has a role in a "foreign investment regime" comparable to the WTO's role in the global trade regime. Most government policies on MNCs are formulated at the national level, but the transnational nature of MNCs makes these policies inadequate. The main obstacle to forming a foreign investment regime is the lack of consensus on what should be regulated—the MNC, the host state, or the home state. The prominent role of private actors (MNCs and multinational banks) as sources of investment capital also makes international regulation a difficult and contentious issue. According to orthodox liberals, investment agreements should regulate host state behavior and provide maximum protection against nationalization, performance requirements, and other impediments to MNC operations in the global marketplace. Home countries should also be able to intervene on behalf of their MNCs to counter host country actions that inhibit investment flows. Realists and historical materialists, by contrast, see host country restrictions on foreign investment as perfectly legitimate. Realists argue that state intervention is necessary to ensure that FDI does not conflict with the national interest and national security, and historical materialists believe that investment agreements should regulate MNCs rather than host states.

The United States as the global hegemon provided much of the regulatory activity for foreign investment in the 1950s and 1960s. U.S. policy sought to protect FDI flows against host country actions such as nationalization and to ensure that MNC behavior did not conflict with the West's Cold War objectives. European states concluded **bilateral investment treaties (BITs)** in the 1960s, that helped protect their investments in LDCs (BITs are discussed later in this chapter). In the 1970s, attention shifted to developing international regulations for FDI, and some economists called for the creation of "a General Agreement for the International Corporation."[71] Several events in the 1970s contributed to the view that this agreement should regulate the behavior of MNCs; for example, currency speculation by MNCs posed a threat to the Bretton Woods pegged exchange rates, and some DCs such as France and Canada began to screen foreign investment because of concerns about the influence of U.S. MNCs.[72] Thus, one U.S. author argued that "global corporations must be regulated to restore sovereignty to government" because the MNC is "not accountable to any public authority that matches it in geographical reach."[73] The South took the main initiative in the 1970s, pressuring for UN regulation of MNCs rather than host states. As a result, the United Nations set up a Commission on Transnational Corporations in 1974 with a mandate to develop a binding Code of Conduct for MNCs. LDCs also engaged in nationalizations in the 1960s and 1970s, and OPEC actions to gain more control over oil pricing and production posed a threat to the international oil companies. To counter these developments, the OECD ministers sought more balance than the United Nations in recognizing the responsibilities of host states as well as MNCs. Thus, the OECD's 1976 Declaration and Decisions on International Investment and Multinational Enterprises included guidelines for the behavior of both MNCs and host states.[74]

By the late 1970s, it was evident that the North would not agree to the South's demands for a UN Code of Conduct for MNCs, and several factors contributed to a shift back to emphasis on controlling the behavior of host states. For example, the South's share of inward FDI was declining because of the foreign debt crisis, concerns about LDC political and economic stability, and the emphasis on high-technology investment in the North. Thus, LDCs followed less interventionist policies toward MNCs as their needs for capital inflows increased. As the North's bargaining power increased, it began forging a consensus during the 1980s that a regime should facilitate increased FDI flows and that host state (not MNC) behavior should be regulated. Before examining the multilateral efforts to regulate investment, the next section provides some background on BITs.

BILATERAL INVESTMENT TREATIES

Bilateral treaties to protect and promote foreign investment have a long history. In the eighteenth century, the United States, Japan, and some Western European states concluded bilateral treaties that dealt with investment as well as trade, maritime, and consular relations. When the GATT-based multilateral trade regime was formed after World War II, countries began to conclude separate BITs. The first BIT was ratified in 1959, and most of the earlier treaties were between DCs and LDCs. With the breakup of the Soviet bloc, many Eastern European countries signed BITs with DCs and LDCs, and the number of BITs between LDCs increased as some LDCs became more important home countries for FDI. BITs are the most widely used international agreement for protecting FDI; they are designed mainly to protect the legal rights of foreign owned or controlled subsidiaries, and they do not impose obligations on MNCs. Most BITs call on host states to provide national treatment to MNC subsidiaries, which ensures that they are treated at least as favorably as domestic firms. Other provisions include the right of MNCs to repatriate profits, and the right to "fair" compensation in cases of expropriation. The treaties also prohibit host country performance requirements committing MNCs to export goods produced in the host country or to purchase goods and services locally, and they have dispute resolution procedures that can provide MNCs with compensation in cases of hostile host country actions. Some of the more recent BITs refer to social and environmental concerns and the host country's right to regulate FDI. On balance, however, BITs continue to give priority to the rights of MNCs.[75]

From the South's perspective, BITs with the North are one-sided because they impose obligations on the host state to protect foreign investment without any corresponding obligations on the home country or the MNC. However, many LDCs have agreed to sign BITs because they assume this is necessary to attract needed foreign investment. Even in the 1970s, when LDCs called for a New International Economic Order, they participated in BITs for pragmatic reasons to attract FDI. The 1980s foreign debt crisis resulted in a sharp reduction in commercial bank loans, and LDC debtors therefore became more dependent on foreign investment for development finance (see Chapter 11). Thus, many more LDCs and transition economies concluded BITs in the 1980s. The total number of BITs increased from 167 in the late 1970s to 385 in 1989, and BITs increased even more rapidly during the 1990s as DC foreign aid declined. By 2007, 179 countries had concluded 2,608 BITs.[76] Despite the willingness of LDCs to sign BITs, several studies find "little evidence that BITs have stimulated additional investment."[77] LDCs with weak domestic institutions are not likely to gain from signing BITs, because BITs act as a complement rather than as a substitute for domestic governance. Thus, many countries in Sub-Saharan Africa have difficulties in attracting FDI even when they sign BITs.

From the North's perspective, BITs provide a "second best solution in the absence of a universal investment agreement."[78] Other than some regional agreements such as NAFTA, BITs continue to be the best means to regulate the treatment of foreign investors by LDC host countries. However, the rapid increase in the number of BITs is resulting in "a wide range of non-uniform and inconsistent arrangements that could become increasingly inefficient, complex, and non-transparent."[79] International and regional organizations also have foreign investment provisions, and the following sections focus on efforts to establish regulations in the United Nations, the EU and NAFTA, the GATT/WTO, and the OECD.

UNITED NATIONS

As discussed, concerns were raised about MNC effects on the national sovereignty of host states in the 1960s and 1970s. A high-profile case involving the International Telephone and Telegraph Corporation (ITT) and Chile brought the issue of regulating MNCs to UN attention. ITT was concerned that Salvador Allende, the Marxist candidate in Chile's 1970 presidential election, would nationalize its Chilean affiliate without compensation. As a result, ITT tried to prevent Allende's election and have him removed from power after he was elected, and also tried to involve the U.S. Central Intelligence Agency and U.S. Information Agency in its activities. When ITT's actions became public in 1972 through published documents of a syndicated columnist, a U.S. Senate subcommittee investigated the case and released a report on *The International Telephone and*

Telegraph Company and Chile, and the UN secretary general appointed a Group of Eminent Persons to examine the impact of MNCs.[80] In 1974 the UN group's report condemned "subversive political intervention" by MNCs such as ITT in Chile, and called for the development of a code of conduct for governments and MNCs.[81] The United Nations then established a *Commission on Transnational Corporations* to develop a comprehensive information system on MNC activities and a code of conduct, and a *UN Center on Transnational Corporations (UNCTC)* to serve as its secretariat. An intergovernmental working group began preparing a draft code of conduct and submitted its report to the commission in 1982, but a long period of negotiations followed because of fundamental disagreements among UN members. For example, there was no consensus on whether the code should be a set of voluntary guidelines or have the force of law. Most LDCs and socialist states supported the draft code because it sought to prevent MNC tax evasion, restrictive business practices, and transfer pricing. The DCs as leading home states for MNCs, by contrast, argued that the draft code did not deal with host state treatment of MNCs. After years of sporadic negotiations, the United Nations abandoned its efforts to form a consensus on a code of conduct for MNCs in 1992; the UNCTC was dissolved in 1993 and replaced by a less proactive Division on Transnational Corporations and Investment within UNCTAD.[82]

UNCTAD has developed expertise on foreign investment issues, and its annual *World Investment Reports* and *Trade and Development Reports* are highly regarded. However, UN efforts since 1993 have been limited to promoting *voluntary* standards of behavior for MNCs. At the 1999 World Economic Forum in Davos, UN Secretary General Kofi Annan proposed that a Global Compact be established. The compact comprises principles on human rights, labor standards, and the environment, and participating MNCs are to work with the United Nations in partnership projects and report on steps they take to further the compact's principles. Although the International Chamber of Commerce has pledged to work with UN agencies to implement the Global Compact and some MNCs have lent their support, the response of MNCs has been highly uneven. Unlike a regulatory code of conduct, the compact is purely voluntary, and there are serious questions as to whether it can alter MNC behavior.[83]

REGIONAL APPROACHES: THE EU AND NAFTA

Regional agreements often include investment as well as trade provisions, partly because of the failure of multilateral institutions to develop a strong foreign investment regime; this section focuses on two important examples: the EU and NAFTA. As a common market, the EU provides for the free movement of capital and protection of FDI among the member states. Thus, the European Commission has legal authority to monitor and regulate MNC activities to ensure that there is a "level playing field." The EU has also been concerned that European MNCs are not large enough to compete with American and Japanese MNCs, and its policy toward MNCs is therefore "two-edged, encouraging multinational activity in a transnational European market, while seeking to remedy the concerns caused by this activity by specific binding measures of containment."[84] In view of the high level of EU integration, its method of dealing with FDI is less likely to serve as a model for future efforts to develop a multilateral foreign investment regime.

The investment provisions in NAFTA Chapter 11 "carry forward on a trilateral basis all of the key provisions of U.S. bilateral investment treaties."[85] For example, NAFTA commits its three members to provide MFN and national treatment to foreign investors; to ban all new export performance, local content, and technology transfer requirements; and to phase out most existing performance requirements within 10 years. NAFTA also commits governments to compensate investors in cases of expropriation, which it defines in very broad terms. Most liberal economists believe that "open investment policies should be the norm," with limited exceptions for issues such as national security.[86] Liberals applaud NAFTA for its significant advances in freeing investment flows, but criticize the sectoral exceptions that prevent NAFTA from completely liberalizing North American investment.[87] For example, the United States excludes its maritime industry, Canada exempts its cultural industries, and Mexico excludes its energy and rail sectors. Liberals also point out that the NAFTA rules of origin include complex procedures that may disadvantage outside firms wishing to enter North America. However, NAFTA Chapter 11 goes much further than multilateral agreements in liberalizing investment flows. Realists and critical theorists, by contrast, view the NAFTA investment provisions as threatening national sovereignty and the ability of environmental and labor groups to protect their interests. In the view of critical theorists, the NAFTA rules increase capital mobility and give the capitalist class greater leverage vis-à-vis labor. For example, MNCs can transfer their operations from the United States and Canada to Mexico to benefit from lower labor costs and environmental standards, contributing to a competitive "race to the bottom."[88] Realists argue that NAFTA's limits on the use of performance requirements prevent host countries from gaining positive spinoffs from foreign investment. Canada and Mexico have imposed performance requirements to ensure that foreign investment contributes to local employment and the growth of exports. By preventing these measures, NAFTA makes it difficult for host countries to channel foreign investment to further their national objectives.[89]

Liberals and realists also have different views of NAFTA Chapter 11 investment dispute resolution provisions, which permit private investors to obtain relief directly from governments for alleged NAFTA violations. NAFTA Chapter 11 stipulates that disputes between an investor from a NAFTA state and a NAFTA member may be settled, if the investor chooses, by binding international arbitration. In the WTO, by contrast, only governments have "standing" in dispute settlement cases, and investors must be represented by governments in settling their claims. In the liberal view, "these procedures have the merit of distancing investment disputes from the political arena. An investor who feels that it has suffered damage . . . by a NAFTA country can pursue its claim without having to involve its government." Realists by contrast believe that the procedures "provide a vehicle for investors to harass governments whose policies they dislike."[90] By giving MNCs legal standing in investment disputes with governments, realists see the NAFTA provisions as posing a direct threat to national sovereignty. It is important to add that the Canadian and U.S. governments have also expressed reservations about the outcome of some NAFTA dispute settlement cases that favored investors. Both countries want to ensure that the protection of investors' rights "does not threaten the ability of governments to regulate in the public interest."[91]

THE GATT/WTO TO THE OECD AND BACK TO THE WTO

The WTO is a natural institution to deal with FDI because of the close relationship between foreign investment and trade. However, FDI is the "neglected twin" of trade because it has been much less subject to multilateral negotiations and institution building.[92] The proposed ITO of the 1940s contained some controversial FDI-related topics, and this was a major factor in the U.S. rejection of the Havana Charter. As a result, GATT did not deal with investment issues for many years until they emerged on the Uruguay Round agenda. The Uruguay Round resulted in the TRIMs, which was incorporated into the WTO. Although the TRIMs is an important beginning in recognizing the relationship between trade and investment, it is largely symbolic because many LDCs are reluctant to accept limits on their policies in this area. Thus, TRIMs does not impose major new restraints on government actions vis-à-vis FDI; it only bans certain investment-related measures that are inconsistent with GATT/WTO provisions. The GATS and the TRIPs also contain some investment provisions, but the WTO investment provisions do not provide a comprehensive body of rules for FDI; they are not designed specifically with investment in mind and are scattered throughout the agreement.[93]

Instead of conducting investment negotiations in the WTO, the DCs began negotiations in the OECD in 1995. The OECD seemed to be a natural venue for developing a *Multilateral Agreement on Investment* (*MAI*) because OECD countries account for such a large share of FDI inflows and outflows. The OECD also had long-term experience with investment issues: In 1961 it adopted two codes to liberalize capital flows, and in 1976 it issued a Declaration on International Investment and Multinational Enterprises.[94] The United States wanted a comprehensive and binding MAI, and it was frustrated that LDCs had opposed even the limited TRIMs agreement. Most OECD members are capital exporters, and the United States assumed that they would agree to an MAI. However, there was no consensus that the OECD was the best venue for the negotiations. The EU Commission preferred the WTO as a venue because it wanted the agreement to bind non-OECD countries, which were a growing destination for FDI. Canada also favored the WTO as a venue because NAFTA already dealt with its most important investment relationship (the United States), and it wanted an MAI to benefit Canadian MNCs in the South. Despite these differences, the MAI negotiations began in the OECD for several reasons: Many LDCs in the WTO opposed negotiations on investment issues; and some EU members preferred to negotiate for themselves in the OECD rather than expanding the EU Commission's mandate by going to the WTO. (The EU Commission represents EU members in the WTO, but not the OECD.) To allay concerns about the exclusivity of the MAI negotiations, the OECD indicated that non-OECD countries would be consulted.[95]

The OECD negotiations addressed three major issues: protection for foreign investors, liberalization of investment, and dispute settlement procedures. The investment protection talks focused on compensation for expropriation of property, freedom of investors to transfer profits and dividends out of host countries, and fair and equitable treatment for foreign investors. The investment liberalization talks focused on host country obligations to limit performance requirements and provide MFN and national treatment to foreign investors. The dispute settlement talks focused on procedures investors as well as states could take to submit complaints for binding international arbitration. Although BITs and NAFTA already dealt with many of these issues, the MAI would be multilateral and more comprehensive than previous agreements. Despite early progress in the talks, the negotiating group requested a one-year extension of its mandate in May 1997 because of significant national differences. For example, France and Canada wanted to exempt culture from the agreement to protect their arts and media sectors; the EU and Canada resented the U.S. Helms–Burton law that could be used to sanction foreign companies for investing in Cuba, Iran, and Libya; and OECD members disagreed as to whether environmental and labor measures should be included. These differences gave outside critics such as civil society groups and LDCs the opportunity to organize opposition to an agreement. Although LDCs had become more open to foreign investment after the 1982 foreign debt crisis, they resented their exclusion from the OECD negotiations, and they feared that an MAI would limit host government rather than MNC practices. Indeed, most OECD members seemed "to agree that an MAI should not impose any obligations on firms but that it should be binding on governments."[96] This position resulted from the North's opposition to the South's efforts to develop a UN code of conduct for MNCs and from the growing neoliberal support for free foreign investment and capital flows. In the South's view by contrast, the 1990s Asian financial crisis demonstrated the need for regulation of capital and foreign investment (see Chapter 11). LDCs feared that an MAI would threaten their autonomous development.[97]

A coalition of NGOs launched the most effective opposition to the MAI, arguing that it would threaten human rights, labor and environmental standards, and LDC development. They believed that the MAI would result in a race to the bottom among countries willing to lower their labor and environmental standards to attract foreign investment. A crucial turning point occurred when Ralph Nader and his consumer advocacy group acquired a draft copy of the MAI and put it on the Internet. Using a variety of websites, NGOs mobilized a strong opposition composed of human rights, consumer advocacy, and labor and environmental groups. Gramscian theorists would argue that the NGOs organized a counterhegemony, which used the Internet "with incredible effectiveness to derail a planned . . . pact designed to increase globalization."[98] Problems also mounted within the OECD when France withdrew from the negotiations in October 1998 because of concerns about culture and the threat to national sovereignty; this forced a suspension of the OECD negotiations. The failure of the MAI negotiations shows that the OECD is not well-suited to negotiating binding agreements on sensitive issues. Instead it should focus on providing advice and analysis and concluding nonbinding accords.

Even before the MAI talks collapsed, the EU and Japan tried to revive the investment issue at the WTO's first Ministerial meeting in 1996 when they pressured for negotiation of the so-called Singapore issues: trade facilitation, trade and competition, government procurement, and investment. However, the South was adamantly opposed to negotiating these issues, and the impasse was eventually resolved by the decision that only one of the Singapore issues (trade facilitation) would be negotiated in the Doha Round. Any current work the WTO does on investment will therefore be separate from the multilateral trade negotiations.[99] A major obstacle to negotiation of an MAI under the WTO is the wide divergence of views on the issue. Liberal economists want an MAI to regulate host state behavior and establish a level playing field for foreign investors with uniform rules for market access. Realists and critical theorists, by contrast, strongly oppose regulations on host states. They fear that a strong WTO agreement would enable MNCs to move operations to states with low environmental, labor, and consumer safety standards; ban performance requirements that states use to promote development; prevent restrictions on the repatriation of profits and removal of capital from the host country; and restrict a host country's ability to sanction irresponsible MNC behavior. In view of these differences, governments have not established an effective foreign investment regime, and private actors are having a greater role in regard to FDI issues.

PRIVATE ACTORS

In view of the lack of multilateral mechanisms to regulate MNCs, private actors have become involved with promoting *corporate social responsibility* (CSR). NGOs representing consumer, environmental, religious, and other groups have pressured MNCs to engage in socially responsible behavior, and MNCs have engaged in a degree of voluntary self-regulation of their behavior. This section discusses the role of NGOs and civil society groups, and the "considering IPE theory and practice" section that follows examines the CSR concept from different theoretical perspectives.

As discussed in Chapter 2, NGOs and civil society groups may be conformist, reformist, or rejectionist.[100] Conformists largely endorse MNC behavior and do not favor restrictions on their activities, reformists believe that MNCs can and should be reformed with some regulation, and rejectionists believe that MNCs are not reformable. NGO reformists prefer to promote responsible MNC behavior without engaging in ideological confrontation. For example, reformist environmental strategies include ecoconsumerism or NGO campaigns to purchase products from ecologically minded firms, partnerships between NGOs and business firms to make production methods more environmentally responsible, and codes of conduct that call on business firms to voluntarily engage in socially conscious behavior.[101] Rejectionist NGOs seek to expose and punish irresponsible corporate behavior and are less willing to engage in compromise and dialogue. Rejectionist NGO strategies include consumer boycotts to publicly expose and punish environmental abuses, monitors to track and disseminate information about MNCs' destructive activities, and counterinformation to refute MNC claims. Some rejectionists aim to develop a counterhegemony to "confront the hegemonic formation of globalization," which includes MNCs.[102] Some NGOs employ reformist and rejectionist strategies simultaneously. For example, Greenpeace worked with companies to develop ozone-friendly refrigerators at the same time as it was encouraging consumers to boycott Shell Oil Company over its alleged involvement with state suppression in Nigeria. In efforts to avoid negative NGO campaigns and government regulations, many MNCs have become proactive in developing their own regulatory frameworks and collaborating with reformist NGOs. For example, MNCs that collaborate with environmental groups may gain a reputation for being environmentally responsible and draw on the expertise of environmental NGOs in reforming their practices. Instead of binding commitments at the international level, business firms and associations have supported voluntary agreements as an alternative. Thus, the International Chamber of Commerce endorsed 16 principles on the environment known as the *Business Charter on Sustainable Development* before the 1992 UN Conference on Environment and Development in Rio de Janeiro, Brazil.

The question arises as to how effective NGOs have been in altering MNC behavior. MNCs have different levels of vulnerability to NGO strategies. Oil companies, for example, are less vulnerable to NGO pressure because governments depend on MNCs' access to oil technology, expertise, and distribution networks. NGOs also have limited monitoring capabilities; although they direct their campaigns and protests at certain high-profile companies, they permit other companies to be free riders. Overall, it is likely that MNCs have not changed significantly as a result of NGO activities and that NGOs do not substitute for adequate multilateral regulation.

Considering IPE Theory and Practice

As discussed, liberals, realists, and historical materialists have widely divergent views regarding MNCs. Liberals view MNCs as positive agents of change that contribute to efficiency and stimulate innovation, economic growth, and employment. Realists believe that host states should be able to impose performance requirements and other regulations on MNCs to promote industrial development and protect the national interest. Historical materialists argue that MNCs overcharge for their goods and services, create dependency relationships with LDC host states, and pose a threat to labor groups and the environment in home as well as host states. In this section, we discuss competing theoretical views of CSR, a concept to which most leading MNCs are now directing some attention.

CSR evokes a wide divergence of views, both within and between the IPE theoretical perspectives, and there is no consensus on a definition of the concept. Three common definitions of CSR are

- the responsibility of a corporation to "operate ethically and in accordance with its legal obligations and to strive to minimize any adverse effects of its operations and activities on the environment, society and human health"
- "actions that appear to further some social good, beyond the interests of the firm and that which is required by law"
- "the contribution that a company makes in society through its core business activities, its social investment and philanthropy programs, and its engagement in public policy."[103]

The first definition describes CSR as operating ethically but also in accordance with the law, the second emphasizes the fact that CSR goes *beyond* obeying the law, and the third does not even mention the law. CSR can mean different things to researchers and practitioners, and to companies, NGOs, consumers, and governments; and it may include such activities as corporate governance, philanthropy, environmental management, labor rights, community development, and animal rights. Some orthodox liberals have rejected the CSR concept as irrelevant to MNCs and their basic objectives. For example, Milton Friedman asserts that "there is one and only one social responsibility of business—to use its resources and engage in activities designed to increase its profits so long as it . . . engages in open and free competition, without deception or fraud."[104] However, orthodox liberals today (i.e., neoliberals) would find it more difficult to dismiss CSR than Friedman did in 1962 when he wrote this passage, because so many private and public groups now support the CSR concept. Thus, many neoliberals (including MNC and industry representatives) give credence to the CSR principle, but say that it should be voluntary rather than regulated; regulation would stifle innovation and hurt national competitiveness. MNCs should be able to develop their own policies on CSR problems and through peer pressure collectively increase standards. Regulation is also unnecessary because MNCs are aware that there are financial benefits in being socially responsible.[105]

At the other extreme from neoliberals are critical theorists who

(*continued*)

(*continued*)

view the CSR concept as a contradiction in terms, because the MNC "remains . . . a legally designated 'person' designed to valorize self-interest and invalidate moral concern." The ideal model of the corporation from this perspective "compels executives to prioritize the interests of their companies and shareholders above all others and forbids them from being socially responsible—at least genuinely so."[106] These critical theorists basically agree with orthodox liberals such as Friedman that the CSR concept has little or no relevance for MNCs, but unlike the orthodox liberals they view this in highly negative terms. Whereas some critical theorists reject the possibility that MNCs can be socially responsible, others argue that the CSR concept can only have meaning if it is subject to mandatory regulation; a voluntary approach would not lead to responsible corporate behavior. For example, one NGO has argued that "the image of multinational companies working hard to make the world a better place is often just that—an image. . . . What's needed are new laws to make businesses responsible for protecting human rights and the environment wherever they work."[107]

In between the more extreme orthodox liberal and critical views are a wide range of interventionist liberals who see CSR as a viable concept that can depend on a combination of government regulation and voluntary involvement. For example, Jagdish Bhagwati argues that "in the main, voluntary codes must characterize what corporations should do . . . and mandatory codes must address what they should not do."[108] MNC self-regulation can supplement but not substitute for government responsibility to set and maintain standards of behavior. However, government regulation cannot resolve all CSR issues, because the law has many gray areas, and MNCs should be expected to follow the spirit as well as the letter of the law. When legal standards are unclear or difficult to enforce, other factors such as corporate culture or pressure from consumer groups and NGOs may also be important. According to interventionist liberals, MNCs will have the motivation to engage in CSR for a number of reasons. For example, companies often view CSR as part of good financial management, because unethical firms tend to be unsustainable in the long term. As part of good financial management, CSR can both contribute to society and increase the profitability of participating firms. Some interventionist liberals also refer to "strategic CSR" as "good works that are also good for business."[109]

In sum, there is a wide divergence of theoretical views on CSR as there are on other aspects of MNCs. As discussed, it is difficult to build a good body of empirical research in this area because of the private nature of MNCs, and because so many researchers have strongly-held views. As one researcher in this area states, "one of the very few generalizations that accurately characterize FDI and MNCs is that their benefits have been exagger- ated by advocates and their harm has been exaggerated by crit- ics."[110] The next chapter addresses another subject on which there is a diversity of strongly held views: international development.

Questions

1. How do liberals, realists, and historical materialists differ in their views of what should be regulated in a foreign investment regime?
2. Do liberals, realists, and historical materialists believe that the nationality of an MNC makes a difference? Do you think that the competitiveness of a country is closely tied with the competitiveness of its MNCs?
3. Why does a business firm choose to become horizontally integrated? Why does a firm choose to become vertically integrated?
4. In what ways have the major host and home countries for FDI changed over time? What are SWFs and do they represent a significant change in the sources of foreign investment?
5. What are some of the major effects of MNCs on home and host states? Do you think that the effects have on the average been more positive or negative?
6. What is the role of BITs, NAFTA, the United Nations, the WTO, and the OECD in regulating FDI?
7. Why was the decision made to negotiate an MAI in the OECD, and was this a wise decision? Do you think that more regulation of FDI is possible?
8. Have NGOs had an impact on the behavior of MNCs? What is CSR, and what are the competing theoretical views regarding the value of the concept?

Further Reading

Important general studies of MNCs and FDI include Geoffrey Jones, *Multinationals and Global Capitalism: From the Nineteenth to the Twenty-first Century* (New York: Oxford University Press, 2005); Stephen D. Cohen, *Multinational Corporations and Foreign Direct Investment: Avoiding Simplicity, Embracing Complexity* (New York: Oxford University Press, 2007); Nathan M. Jensen, *Nation-States and the Multinational Corporation: A Political Economy of Foreign Direct Investment* (Princeton, NJ: Princeton University Press, 2006); and Grazia Ietto-Gillies, *Transnational Corporations and International Production: Concepts, Theories and Effects* (Northampton, MA: Edward Elgar, 2005).

A useful book on theories of the MNC is Mats Forsgren, *Theories of the Multinational Firm: A Multidimensional Creature in the Global Economy* (Northampton, MA: Edward Elgar, 2008). Two studies that discuss MNCs in positive terms are Edward M. Graham, *Fighting the Wrong Enemy—Antiglobal Activists and Multinational*

Enterprises (Washington, D.C.: Institute for International Economics, 2000); and Jagdish Bhagwati, *In Defense of Globalization* (New York: Oxford University Press, 2004), Chapter 12. Two useful studies of corporate social responsibility are Jennifer A. Zerk, *Multinationals and Corporate Social Responsibility: Limitations and Opportunities in International Law* (New York: Cambridge University Press, 2006); and Josep M. Lozano, Laura Albareda, and Tamyko Ysa, *Government and Corporate Social Responsibility: Public Policies beyond Regulation and Voluntary Compliance* (New York: Palgrave Macmillan, 2008). Strong critiques of MNCs include Joel Bakan, *The Corporation: The Pathological Pursuit of Profit and Power* (New York: Penguin, 2004); and James Petras and Henry Veltmeyer, *Multinationals on Trial: Foreign Investment Matters* (Burlington, VT: Ashgate, 2007). A realist study arguing that an MNC's nationality makes a difference is Paul N. Doremus, William W. Keller, Louis W. Pauly, and Simon Reich, *The Myth of the Global Corporation* (Princeton, NJ: Princeton University Press, 1998).

On emerging LDCs and transition economies as both host and home countries for FDI, see H. S. Kehal, *Foreign Investment in Rapidly Growing Countries: The Chinese and Indian Experiences* (New York: Palgrave Macmillan, 2005); Karl P. Sauvant, ed., *The Rise of Transnational Corporations from Emerging Markets: Threat or Opportunity?* (Northampton, MA: Edward Elgar, 2008); and Andrea Goldstein, *Multinational Companies from Emerging Economies* (New York: Palgrave Macmillan, 2007).

Notes

1. United Nations Conference on Trade and Development (UNCTAD), *World Investment Report 2008* (New York: United Nations, 2008), overview and ch. 1.
2. Giorgio B. Navaretti and Anthony J. Venables, *Multinational Firms in the World Economy* (Princeton, NJ: Princeton University Press, 2004), p. 3.
3. Lorraine Eden, "Bringing the Firm Back In: Multinationals in International Political Economy," in Lorraine Eden and Evan H. Potter, eds., *Multinationals in the Global Political Economy* (New York: St. Martin's Press, 1993), p. 26.
4. Ethan B. Kapstein, "We Are US: The Myth of the Multinational," *The National Interest* (Winter 1991–1992), p. 55.
5. DeAnne Julius, "International Direct Investment: Strengthening the Policy Regime," in Peter B. Kenen, ed., *Managing the World Economy: Fifty Years After Bretton Woods* (Washington, D.C.: Institute of International Economics, 1994), p. 269.
6. Robert W. Cox, *Production, Power, and World Order: Social Forces in the Making of History* (New York: Columbia University Press, 1987), pp. 358–359; Nathan M. Jensen, *Nation-States and the Multinational Corporation: A Political Economy of Foreign Direct Investment* (Princeton, NJ: Princeton University Press, 2006), pp. 28–34; Stephen D. Krasner, "Power Politics, Institutions, and Transnational Relations," in Thomas Risse-Kappen, ed., *Bringing Transnational Relations Back In: Non-State Actors, Domestic Structures and International Institutions* (New York: Cambridge University Press, 1995), p. 279.
7. Raymond Vernon, *Sovereignty at Bay: The Multinational Spread of U.S. Enterprises* (New York: Basic Books, 1971), p. 11.
8. UNCTAD, *World Investment Report 2000* (New York: United Nations, 2000), pp. 99–136; Grazia Ietto-Gillies, *Transnational Corporations and International Production: Concepts, Theories and Effects* (Northampton, MA: Edward Elgar,

2005), pp. 11–31; Geoffrey Jones, *Multinationals and Global Capitalism: From the Nineteenth to the Twenty-First Century* (New York: Oxford University Press, 2005), pp. 4–14.

9. Edward M. Graham and Paul R. Krugman, *Foreign Direct Investment in the United States,* 3rd ed. (Washington, D.C.: Institute for International Economics, 1995), pp. 9–11; Geoffrey Jones, *The Evolution of International Business: An Introduction* (London: Routledge, 1996), pp. 4–6.

10. Howard V. Perlmutter, "The Tortuous Evolution of the Multinational Corporation," *Columbia Journal of World Business* 4, no. 1 (January–February 1969), p. 11. Although most political scientists and U.S. scholars prefer the term *MNC,* economists, business professors, and British scholars often use the term *multinational enterprise* (*MNE*). An "enterprise" includes "a network of corporate and non-corporate entities in different countries joined together by ties of ownership." See UN Department of Economic and Social Affairs, *Multinational Corporations in World Development* (New York: United Nations, 1973), p. 4; Eden, "Bringing the Firm Back In," p. 55.

11. Relevant studies by John H. Dunning include *International Production and the Multinational Enterprise* (Boston, MA: Allen & Unwin, 1981); *Explaining International Production* (Boston, MA: Unwin Hyman, 1988); *Multinational Enterprises and the Global Economy* (Reading, MA: Addison-Wesley, 1993).

12. Laura D'Andrea Tyson, "They Are Not Us: Why American Ownership Still Matters," *The American Prospect* 4 (Winter 1991), p. 42; Keith Head and John Ries, "Exporting and FDI as Alternative Strategies," *Oxford Review of Economic Policy* 20, no. 2 (2004), pp. 409–423.

13. Jean-François Hennart, "The Transaction Cost Theory of the Multinational Enterprise," in Christos N. Pitelis and Roger Sugden, eds., *The Nature of the Transnational Firm* (London: Routledge, 1991), pp. 143–151.

14. Graham and Krugman, *Foreign Direct Investment in the United States,* p. 83. On transfer pricing, see Alan M. Rugman and Lorraine Eden, eds., *Multinationals and Transfer Pricing* (London: Croom Helm, 1985).

15. Lorraine Eden, "Thinking Globally—Acting Locally: Multinationals in the Global Political Economy," in Lorraine Eden and Evan H. Potter, eds., *Multinationals in the Global Political Economy* (New York: St. Martin's Press, 1993), pp. 1–2.

16. Alfred D. Chandler, Jr., and Bruce Mazlish, eds., *Leviathans: Multinational Corporations and the New Global History* (New York: Cambridge University Press, 2005).

17. Jones, *The Evolution of International Business,* pp. 23–25.

18. Peter Svedberg, "The Portfolio-Direct Composition of Private Foreign Investment in 1914 Revisited," *The Economic Journal* 88 (December 1978), pp. 763–777; Thomas A. B. Corley, "Britain's Overseas Investments in 1914 Revisited," *Business History* 36, no. 1 (January 1994), pp. 71–88.

19. Julius, "International Direct Investment," pp. 272–273; Edward M. Graham, *Global Corporations and National Governments* (Washington, D.C.: Institute for International Economics, 1996), pp. 25–26, 136–140.

20. UNCTAD, *World Investment Report 2004* (New York: UN, 2004), pp. 382–385.

21. UNCTAD, *World Investment Report 2004,* pp. 376–380.

22. Jones, *The Evolution of International Business,* pp. 52–59.

23. Peter J. Buckley and Mark Casson, *The Future of the Multinational Enterprise,* 2nd ed. (London: Macmillan, 1991), p. 11; UNCTAD, *World Investment Report 2003* (New York: UN, 2003), p. 23.

24. Dennis J. Encarnation, *Rivals Beyond Trade: America versus Japan in Global Competition* (Ithaca, NY: Cornell University Press, 1992), p. 5; and Kiyoshi Kojima, *Direct Foreign Investment: A Japanese Model of Multinational Business Operations* (New York: Praeger, 1978), pp. 1–18.

25. UNCTAD, *World Investment Report 1999* (New York: United Nations, 1999), p. 42.

26. Andrea Goldstein, *Multinational Companies from Emerging Economies: Composition, Conceptualization and Direction in the Global Economy* (New York: Palgrave Macmillan, 2007), pp. 11–12.

27. Stephen D. Cohen, *Multinational Corporations and Foreign Direct Investment: Avoiding Simplicity, Embracing Complexity* (New York: Oxford University Press, 2007), pp. 161–164; Harbhajan S. Kehal, ed., *Foreign Investment in Rapidly Growing Countries: The Chinese and Indian Experiences* (New York: Palgrave Macmillan, 2005).

28. Charles P. Lewis, *How the East Was Won: The Impact of Multinational Companies on Eastern Europe and the Former Soviet Union* (New York: Palgrave Macmillan, 2005); *Transnational Corporations* issue 20, no. 3 (December 2001) on "Privatization and Greenfield FDI in Central and Eastern Europe: Does the Mode of Entry Matter?"

29. Glen Biglaiser and Karl DeRouen, Jr., "Economic Reforms and Inflows of Foreign Direct Investment in Latin America," *Latin American Research Review* 41, no. 1 (February 2006), p. 69; Jensen, *Nation-States and the Multinational Corporation*, p. 22; John P. Tuman, "Regime Type, Rights, and Foreign Direct Investment in Latin America: A Brief Comment," *Latin American Research Review* 41, no. 2 (June 2006), p. 184.

30. Grazia Ietto-Gillies, *International Production: Trends, Theories, Effects* (Cambridge, MA: Blackwell, 1992), pp. 78–84.

31. Stephen H. Hymer, *The International Operations of National Firms: A Study of Direct Foreign Investment* (Cambridge, MA: MIT Press, 1976), p. 100.

32. Peter Evans, *Dependent Development: The Alliance of Multinational, State, and Local Capital in Brazil* (Princeton, NJ: Princeton University Press, 1979), p. 37; Mark Herkenrath and Volker Bornschier, "Transnational Corporations in World Development—Still the Same Harmful Effects in an Increasingly Globalized World Economy?" *Journal of World-Systems Research* 9, no. 1 (Winter 2003), pp. 105–139.

33. Vernon, *Sovereignty at Bay*, pp. 46–59; Ravi Ramamurti, "The Obsolescing 'Bargaining Model'? MNC-Host Developing Country Relations Revisited," *Journal of International Business Studies* 32, no. 1 (2001), p. 25.

34. Stephen J. Kobrin, "Testing the Bargaining Hypothesis in the Manufacturing Sector in Developing Countries," *International Organization* 41, no. 4 (Autumn 1987), pp. 609–638; Theodore H. Moran, "Multinational Corporations and the Developing Countries: An Overview," in Theodore H. Moran, ed., *Multinational Corporations: The Political Economy of Foreign Direct Investment* (Lexington, MA: Heath, 1985), pp. 3–24.

35. Ramamurti, "The Obsolescing 'Bargaining Model'? MNC-Host Developing Country Relations Revisited," p. 23.

36. William A. Stoever, "Attempting to Resolve the Attraction–Aversion Dilemma: A Study of FDI Policy in the Republic of Korea," *Transnational Corporations* 11, no. 1 (April 2002), pp. 49–76.

37. Jones, *The Evolution of International Business*, pp. 288–291.

38. Stephen J. Kobrin, "Expropriation as an Attempt to Control Foreign Firms in LDCs: Trends from 1960 to 1979," *International Studies Quarterly* 28, no. 3

(September 1984), pp. 337–342; Stephen D. Krasner, *Structural Conflict: The Third World Against Global Liberalism* (Berkeley, CA: University of California Press, 1985), pp. 176–195.

39. Kobrin, "Expropriation as an Attempt to Control Foreign Firms in LDCs," p. 338; Graham, *Global Corporations and National Governments*, pp. 17–20.

40. UNCTAD, *World Investment Report 2000*, pp. 6, 7, 17–18.

41. Jean-Jacques Servan-Schreiber, *The American Challenge*, transl. Ronald Steel (New York: Atheneum, 1979). The book was first published in 1967.

42. Stephen Clarkson, *Canada and the Reagan Challenge: Crisis and Adjustment, 1981–85*, updated ed. (Toronto: James Lorimer & Company, 1985), pp. 3–113; Barbara Jenkins, *The Paradox of Continental Production: National Investment Policies in North America* (Ithaca, NY: Cornell University Press, 1992), pp. 113–117.

43. Mark Mason, *American Multinationals and Japan: The Political Economy of Japanese Capital Controls, 1899–1980* (Cambridge, MA: Council on East Asian Studies, Harvard University, 1992), pp. 243–247.

44. Jones, *The Evolution of International Business*, pp. 280–281; A. E. Safarian, "Host Country Policies Towards Foreign Direct Investment in the 1950s and 1990s," *Transnational Corporations* 8, no. 2 (August 1999), p. 105.

45. Paul N. Doremus, William W. Keller, Louis W. Pauly, and Simon Reich, *The Myth of the Global Corporation* (Princeton, NJ: Princeton University Press, 1998), pp. 77–78; Robert Z. Lawrence, "Japan's Low Levels of Inward Investment: The Role of Inhibitions on Acquisitions," in Kenneth Froot, ed., *Foreign Direct Investment* (Chicago, IL: University of Chicago Press, 1993), pp. 85–107; C. Fred Bergsten and Marcus Noland, *Reconcilable Differences? United States–Japan Economic Conflict* (Washington, D.C.: Institute for International Economics, 1993), pp. 79–82.

46. Jenkins, *The Paradox of Continental Production*, pp. 117–121; Clarkson, *Canada and the Reagan Challenge*, pp. 83–113; and Tom Keating, *Canada and World Order: The Multilateralist Tradition in Canadian Foreign Policy* (Don Mills: Oxford University Press, 2002), pp. 195–196.

47. Edward M. Graham and Michael E. Ebert, "Foreign Direct Investment and US National Security: Fixing Exon-Florio," *The World Economy* 14, no. 3 (September 1991), pp. 245–268; Edward M. Graham and Paul R. Krugman, *Foreign Direct Investment in the United States* (Washington, D.C.: Institute for International Economics, 1995), pp. 126–132.

48. UNCTAD, *World Investment Report 2006* (New York: UNCTAD, 2006), p. 105.

49. Robert Gilpin, *U.S. Power and the Multinational Corporation: The Political Economy of Foreign Direct Investment* (New York: Basic Books, 1975), p. 62.

50. UNCTC, *Transnational Corporations in World Development—Trends and Prospects* (New York: United Nations, 1988), p. 240; Jones, *The Evolution of International Business*, pp. 219–220.

51. Robert T. Kudrle, "The Several Faces of the Multinational Corporation: Political Reaction and Policy Response," in W. Ladd Hollist and F. LaMond Tullis, eds., *An International Political Economy* (Boulder, CO: Westview Press, 1985), pp. 176–177; Jack N. Behrman and Robert E. Grosse, *International Business and Governments: Issues and Institutions* (Columbia, SC: University of South Carolina Press, 1990), pp. 82–85.

52. Jones, *The Evolution of International Business*, pp. 221–222.

53. Gary C. Hufbauer and Jeffrey J. Schott, "The Soviet-European Gas Pipeline: A Case of Failed Sanctions," in Theodore H. Moran, ed., *Multinational Corporations: The Political Economy of Foreign Direct Investment* (Lexington, MA: Heath, 1985), pp. 219–245.

54. Paul Lewis, "Cuba Trade Law: Export of U.S. Ire and Politics," *New York Times,* March 15, 1996, pp. C1, C3; "Biter Bitten: The Helms-Burton Law," *The Economist,* June 8, 1996, p. 45.

55. Robert B. Reich, "Who Is Us?" *Harvard Business Review* 90, no. 1 (January–February 1990), pp. 59–60; Vernon, *Sovereignty at Bay,* pp. 214–215; Laura D'Andrea Tyson, *Who's Bashing Whom? Trade Conflict in High-Technology Industries* (Washington, D.C.: Institute for International Economics, 1992), pp. 289–295.

56. Cohen, *Multinational Corporations and Foreign Direct Investment,* pp. 217–218; Jamuna P. Agarwal, "Effect of Foreign Direct Investment on Employment in Home Countries," *Transnational Corporations* 6, no. 2 (August 1997), pp. 1–2.

57. Edward M. Graham, *Fighting the Wrong Enemy—Antiglobal Activists and Multinational Enterprises* (Washington, D.C.: Institute for International Economics, 2000), p. 83.

58. Graham, *Fighting the Wrong Enemy,* p. 83.

59. Gary C. Hufbauer and Jeffrey J. Schott, *NAFTA: An Assessment,* rev. ed. (Washington, D.C.: Institute for International Economics, 1993), p. 19; Peter Enderwick, *Multinational Business and Labour* (London: Croom Helm, 1985).

60. Agarwal, "Effect of Foreign Direct Investment on Employment in Home Countries," pp. 3–4; James Petras and Henry Veltmeyer, *Multinationals on Trial: Foreign Investment Matters* (Burlington, VT: Ashgate, 2007), pp. 116–118.

61. Cohen, *Multinational Corporations and Foreign Direct Investment,* pp. 217–222.

62. Michael E. Porter, *The Competitive Advantage of Nations* (New York: Free Press, 1990), p. 2; Tyson, "They Are Not Us," pp. 37–49.

63. Lester Thurow, *Head to Head: The Coming Economic Battle Among Japan, Europe, and America* (New York: Morrow, 1992), p. 201.

64. Robert B. Reich, *The Work of Nations: Preparing Ourselves for 21st-Century Capitalism* (New York: Vintage Books, 1991), p. 8.

65. Sholnn Freeman, "Detroit Waves Flag That No Longer Flies: Congress Embraces Jobs, Growth Created by Foreign Carmakers," *Washington Post,* August 19, 2006, p. A01.

66. Kenichi Ohmae, *The Borderless World: Power and Strategy in the Interlinked Economy* (New York: HarperPerennial, 1991), p. 10.

67. Reich, *The Work of Nations,* p. 163; Ohmae, *The Borderless World,* p. 194.

68. UNCTAD, *World Investment Report 2000,* pp. 20–21; Robert B. Reich, "Who Do We Think They Are?" *The American Prospect* 4 (Winter 1991), p. 51.

69. Fred Lazar, "Corporate Strategies: The Costs and Benefits of Going Global," in Robert Boyer and Daniel Drache, eds., *States Against Markets: The Limits of Globalization* (London: Routledge, 1996), p. 285; Louis W. Pauly and Simon Reich, "National Structures and Multinational Corporate Behavior: Enduring Differences in the Age of Globalization," *International Organization* 51, no. 1 (Winter 1997), p. 13.

70. Robert B. Reich, "Who Is Us?" *Harvard Business Review* 90, no. 1 (January–February 1990), pp. 59–60; Pauly and Reich, "National Structures and Multinational Corporate Behavior," pp. 1–30.

71. Paul M. Goldberg and Charles P. Kindleberger, "Toward a GATT for Investment: A Proposal for Supervision of the International Corporation," *Law and Policy in International Business* 2 (Summer 1970), pp. 295–325.
72. Christopher J. Maule and Andrew Vanderwal, "International Regulation of Foreign Investment," *International Perspectives,* November/December 1985, p. 22.
73. Vernon, *Sovereignty at Bay,* p. 249.
74. OECD, *International Investment and Multinational Enterprises: Review of the 1976 Declaration and Decisions* (Paris: Organization for Economic Cooperation and Development, 1979).
75. On BITs, see UNCTAD, *Bilateral Investment Treaties in the Mid-1990s* (New York and Geneva: United Nations, 1998); Mary Hallward-Driemeier, "Do Bilateral Investment Treaties Attract Foreign Direct Investment? Only a Bit . . . and They Could Bite," Policy Research Working Paper 3121, The World Bank, August 2003; Paul B. Christy III, "Negotiating Investment in the GATT: A Call for Functionalism," *Michigan Journal of International Law* 12, no. 4 (Summer 1991), pp. 754–763; and UNCTAD, *World Investment Report 2003,* pp. 89–91.
76. UNCTAD, *World Investment Report 2003,* p. 89; UNCTAD, *World Investment Report 2008,* pp. 14–15.
77. Hallward-Driemeier, "Do Bilateral Investment Treaties Attract Foreign Direct Invesment? Only a Bit . . . and They Could Bite," p. 22.
78. UNCTAD, *Bilateral Investment Treaties in the Mid-1990s,* p. 4.
79. Sherif H. Seid, *Global Regulation of Foreign Direct Investment* (Burlington, VT: Ashgate, 2002), p. 55.
80. U.S. Senate, "The International Telephone and Telegraph Company and Chile, 1970–1971," in George Modelski, ed., *Transnational Corporations and World Order* (San Francisco, CA: W.H. Freeman, 1979), pp. 226–244.
81. United Nations, "Report of the Group of Eminent Persons to Study the Impact of Multinational Corporations on Development and on International Relations," in George Modelski, ed., *Transnational Corporations and World Order* (San Francisco, CA: W.H. Freeman, 1979), pp. 323, 330.
82. UNCTC, *The United Nations Code of Conduct on Transnational Corporations* (New York: United Nations, September 1986), pp. 1–6; R. Alan Hedley, "Transnational Corporations and Their Regulation: Issues and Strategies," *International Journal of Comparative Sociology* 40, no. 2 (May 1999), pp. 218–221.
83. Georg Kell and John G. Ruggie, "Global Markets and Social Legitimacy: The Case for the 'Global Compact,'" *Transnational Corporations* 8, no. 3 (December 1999), pp. 101–120.
84. John Robinson, *Multinationals and Political Control* (New York: St. Martin's Press, 1983), p. 44.
85. Jon R. Johnson, *The North American Free Trade Agreement—A Comprehensive Guide* (Aurora: Canada Law Book, 1994), p. 275.
86. Graham, *Global Corporations and National Governments,* p. 47.
87. Alan M. Rugman and Michael Gestrin, "A Conceptual Framework for a Multilateral Agreement on Investment: Learning from the NAFTA," in Pierre Sauvé and Daniel Schwanen, eds., *Investment Rules for the Global Economy* (Toronto: C.D. Howe Institute, 1996), p. 170.
88. Fred Lazar, "Investment in the NAFTA: Just Cause for Walking Away," *Journal of World Trade* 27, no. 5 (October 1993), pp. 28–29.

89. Gilbert Gagné and Jean-Frédéric Morin, "The Evolving American Policy on Investment Protection: Evidence from Recent FTAs and the 2004 Model BIT," *Journal of International Economic Law* 9, no. 2 (May 2006), p. 357; Gilbert Gagné, "The Investor-State Provisions in the Aborted MAI and in NAFTA," *Journal of World Investment* 2, no. 3 (September 2001), pp. 489–501.

90. Johnson, *The North American Free Trade Agreement—A Comprehensive Guide,* p. 512.

91. Gagné and Morin, "The Evolving American Policy on Investment Protection," p. 358.

92. De A. Julius, *Foreign Investment: The Neglected Twin of Trade,* Occasional Papers no. 33 (Washington, D.C.: Group of Thirty, 1991).

93. Stephen Young and Ana T. Tavares, "Multilateral Rules on FDI: Do We Need Them? Will We Get Them? A Developing Country Perspective," *Transnational Corporations* 13, no. 1 (April 2004), pp. 2–3; Cohen, *Multinational Corporations and Foreign Direct Investment,* pp. 260–261.

94. On the OECD's long-term experience with international investment, see OECD, *International Investment Perspectives* (Paris: Organization for Economic Cooperation and Development, 2002), pp. 197–205.

95. Elizabeth Smythe, "Your Place or Mine? States, International Organizations and the Negotiation of Investment Rules," *Transnational Corporations* 7, no. 3 (December 1998), pp. 85–120.

96. Edward M. Graham and Pierre Sauvé, "Toward a Rules-Based Regime for Investment: Issues and Challenges," in Pierre Sauvé and Daniel Schwanen, eds., *Investment Rules for the Global Economy* (Toronto: C.D. Howe Institute, 1996), p. 135.

97. Elizabeth Smythe, "The Multilateral Agreement on Investment: A Charter of Rights for Global Investors or Just Another Agreement?" in Fen O. Hampson and Maureen A. Molot, eds., *Canada Among Nations 1998: Leadership and Dialogue* (Toronto: Oxford University Press, 1998), pp. 239–277.

98. Peter Morton, "MAI Gets Tangled in Web," *The Financial Post,* October 22, 1998, p. 3.

99. Pierre Sauvé, "Multilateral Rules on Investment: Is Forward Movement Possible?" *Journal of International Economic Law* 9, no. 2 (2006), pp. 326–327.

100. Jan A. Scholte with Robert O'Brien and Marc Williams, "The WTO and Civil Society," *Journal of World Trade* 33, no. 1 (1999), pp. 112–116.

101. Peter Newell, "Environmental NGOs, TNCs, and the Question of Governance," in Dimitris Stevis and Valerie J. Assetto, eds., *The International Political Economy of the Environment: Critical Perspectives* (Boulder, CO: Lynne Rienner, 2001), pp. 85–107.

102. Robert W. Cox, "Civil Society at the Turn of the Millennium: Prospects for an Alternative World Order," *Review of International Studies* 25 (1999), p. 26.

103. Jennifer A. Zerk, *Multinationals and Corporate Social Responsibility: Limitations and Opportunities in International Law* (New York: Cambridge University Press, 2006), pp. 31–32; Abagail McWilliams and Donald Siegel, "Corporate Social Responsibility: A Theory of the Firm Perspective," *Academy of Management Review* 26, no. 1 (January 2001), p. 117; World Economic Forum (WEF), "Follow-up Questionnaire on the World Economic Forum CEO States," http://www.weforum.org/pdf/GCCI/GCCI_CEO_Questionnaire.pdf. (The WEF defines "global corporate citizenship," which is often used interchangeably with CSR.)

104. Milton Friedman with Rose D. Friedman, *Capitalism and Freedom* (Chicago, IL: University of Chicago Press, 1962), p. 133.
105. Michael Blowfield and Jedrzej G. Frynas, "Setting New Agends: Critical Perspectives on Corporate Social Responsibility in the Developing World," *International Affairs* 81, no. 3 (2005), p. 499; Zerk, *Multinationals and Corporate Social Responsibility,* pp. 32–34.
106. Joel Bakan, *The Corporation: The Pathological Pursuit of Profit and Power* (New York: Penguin, 2004), pp. 28, 35.
107. Quoted in Kenneth M. Amaeshi and Bongo Adi, "Reconstructing the Corporate Social Responsibility Construct in *Utlish,*" *Business Ethics* 16, no. 1 (January 2007), p. 13.
108. Jagdish Bhagwati, *In Defense of Globalization* (New York: Oxford University Press, 2004), p. 191.
109. Geoffrey P. Lantos, "The Boundaries of Strategic Corporate Social Responsibility," *Journal of Consumer Marketing* 18, no. 7 (2001), p. 595.
110. Cohen, *Multinational Corporations and Foreign Direct Investment,* p. 16.

CHAPTER 10

International Development

The Bretton Woods system and its institutions have been credited with contributing "to almost unprecedented global economic growth."[1] However, a large percentage of people living in the South have received little benefit from this growth. Poverty, hunger, and disease are prevalent in much of the world, and the gap between the richest and poorest states is growing; per capita income in all regions of the South (except South Asia and East Asia) declined relative to per capita income in the North between 1980 and 2001. In 2001 more than 1.1 billion people in the world were living on less than $1 a day. LDC economic development problems are also often accompanied by social problems such as inadequate health and educational facilities, low literacy rates, and high infant mortality rates. For example, 24 percent of children in Mali will not reach age 5 compared with less than 1 percent of American children; and the average American born between 1975 and 1979 has completed more than 14 years of school compared with less than 2 years of school for the same cohort in Mali.[2]

Despite the South's socioeconomic problems, there are major differences in economic development among LDCs. As Table 10.1 shows, East Asian and Latin American NIEs are middle- to high-income economies. For example, in 2006 Singapore and Hong Kong, China, had per capita GNIs (at purchasing power parity rates) of $43,300 and $39,200, respectively; OPEC members Kuwait and Saudi Arabia had per capita GNIs of $48,310 and $22,300, respectively; and the per capita GNIs for Mexico and Argentina were $11,990 and $11,670, respectively. In stark contrast, Table 10.1 shows that the poorest African and Asian states such as Liberia, Congo D.R., Nepal, and Bangladesh had GNIs per capita of $260, $270, $1,010, and $1,230, respectively. In addition to their higher incomes, Table 2.2 in Chapter 2 shows that East Asia and Latin America rank higher than other LDC regions on human development

TABLE 10.1   GNI^a Per Capita (PPP^b U.S. $)—Southern Economies—2006

Higher and Middle-Income

East Asian NIEs		OPEC Members		Latin American NIEs	
Singapore	$43,300	Kuwait	$48,310	Mexico	$11,990
Hong Kong, China	39,200	Saudi Arabia	22,300	Argentina	11,670
South Korea	22,990	Iran	9,800	Brazil	8,700

Low-Income

Africa		Asia	
Ethiopia	$630	Tajikistan	$1,560
Burundi	320	Cambodia	1,550
Congo D. R.	270	Bangladesh	1,230
Liberia	260	Nepal	1,010

^{a}GNI = gross national income

^{b}PPP = purchasing power parity

Source: World Bank, *World Development Indicators 2008* (Washington, D.C.: World Bank, 2008), pp. 14–16.

indicators. For example, life expectancy in 2005 was 72.8 and 71.7 years for Latin America and the Caribbean and East Asia and the Pacific, respectively; life expectancy in South Asia and Sub-Saharan Africa, by contrast, was 63.8 and 49.6 years, respectively.

The development rate also differs in the LDC regions. As we discuss in Chapter 11, an international debt crisis erupted in the 1980s which had a serious effect on development in many LDCs. From 1980 to 1989, East Asia's average annual economic growth rate was 6.2 percent, whereas Sub-Saharan Africa and Latin America and the Caribbean had *negative* economic growth rates (of −1.2 and −0.4 percent). More recently, rapid economic growth in China and, to a lesser extent, India is evident from overall poverty figures. For example, from 1981 to 2001 the number of people living in extreme poverty (i.e., on less than $1 U.S. per day) fell from 634 million to 212 million in China and from 382 million to 359 million in India. In marked contrast, the numbers living in extreme poverty increased by almost 90 million in Sub-Saharan Africa between 1990 and 2001 and by more than 14 million in Europe and Central Asia between 1981 and 2001; in Sub-Saharan Africa a major factor was the high incidence of HIV/AIDS, and in Europe and Central Asia there was economic disruption resulting from the breakup of the Soviet bloc and Soviet Union.[3]

Despite these regional differences, the South in general lacks wealth and power vis-à-vis the North. In view of its vulnerabilities, the South is ambivalent about its relations with the North. Although LDCs look to the North for trade, foreign investment, development assistance, and technology transfers, they fear that these linkages increase their dependence and threaten their autonomy. The KIEOs (the IMF, World Bank, and WTO) have helped the South gain access to external finance and export markets, but LDCs believe that some KIEO policies inhibit their development efforts, and they resent the North's dominance in these organizations.[4] This chapter assesses the strategies LDCs have pursued to promote their economic development, such as import substitution, socialism, and export-led growth. In accordance with the revival of orthodox liberalism, LDCs in recent years have shifted to more open economic policies. However, current development policies fall short in meeting the needs of the poorest and most disadvantaged (e.g., LDC women and children) and in looking after the needs of the future as well as the present (e.g., in preserving the environment). As background for examining the LDC economic development strategies, this chapter first discusses the IPE theoretical perspectives; the role of official development assistance (ODA); and the functions of the World Bank, which "enjoys a unique position as a generator of ideas about economic development."[5]

IPE PERSPECTIVES AND NORTH–SOUTH RELATIONS

This section briefly summarizes the main tenets of the IPE perspectives as they relate to North–South relations. (For a more detailed discussion, see Chapters 3–5.) Realists in the North, preoccupied with the issues of power and influence, tend to ignore the economic interests of poorer countries in the South. In the realist view, "Third World states want power and control as much as wealth," and it is only when LDCs pose a challenge to the North's predominance that most realists take notice.[6] In the 1970s realist scholars looked at OPEC's increased leverage in raising oil prices and at LDC efforts to gain more power and wealth through an NIEO; in the 1980s and 1990s, realists focused on the challenge the East Asian developmental state model posed to the North; and in more recent years realists have been interested in emerging powers such China, India, and Brazil. Despite the lack of realist attention to poverty in the South, realist ideas have had considerable influence on LDC policies. For example, Alexander Hamilton and Friedrich List argued that late industrializers (the United States and Germany at the time) required more government involvement if they were to "catch up" with Britain—the leading state. LDC development strategies such as import substitution and export-led growth draw on Hamilton and List's ideas calling for a larger role for the state in promoting economic development.

Liberals believe that interdependence has widespread benefits, and they often see North–South linkages as providing even more benefits to the South than to the North. LDC economic problems in the liberal view stem more from inefficient domestic policies than from their dependent position in the global economy. Thus, LDCs that follow open economic policies and increase linkages with the North are more likely to achieve successful development.

Although all liberals encourage LDCs to follow open, market-oriented policies, interventionist liberals (also called reformist liberals) recognize that North–South inequalities can put LDCs at a disadvantage. Whereas orthodox liberals emphasize equal treatment and reciprocity, interventionist liberals call on the North to consider the special needs of the South. However, interventionist liberals believe that the necessary changes can occur within the existing capitalist order, and they share the faith of other liberals in private enterprise and the market.

As historical materialists, dependency theorists reject the liberal view that LDC economic problems result mainly from inefficient domestic policies. In the dependency view, capitalist states in the core of the global economy either "underdevelop" LDCs in the periphery or prevent them from attaining genuine, autonomous development. Class linkages also play a role, with elites in the South (the "comprador" class) collaborating with foreign capitalists in the North to reinforce the pattern of LDC dependency. Because some LDCs such as East Asian and Latin American NIEs were successfully industrializing, world-system theorists modified the dependency argument by introducing a third category of countries, the semiperiphery. Countries may move upward (or downward) from the periphery to the semiperiphery or even the core, but this only rarely occurs. Whereas some historical materialists call for a redistribution of resources from the core to the periphery, others believe that the core will never willingly transfer resources; thus, they call for a social revolution in the South and/or a severing of contacts with the North. The solution for disadvantaged groups, according to Gramscian theorists, is the development of a counterhegemony.

OFFICIAL DEVELOPMENT ASSISTANCE

Development assistance or **foreign aid** refers to grants, loans, or technical assistance that donors provide to recipients on concessional rather than commercial terms. **Concessional loans** (or *soft loans*) have lower interest rates, longer grace periods, and longer repayment periods than *commercial loans* (or *hard loans*). Private actors such as NGOs and foundations (such as the Bill and Melinda Gates Foundation) provide some valuable foreign aid, but by far the largest share of aid is **official development assistance (ODA)** provided by governments. To qualify as ODA, a loan must have a *grant element* of at least 25 percent. The grant element refers to the loan's financial terms, or the interest rate, maturity period, and grace period (the interval before the first repayment of a loan); and it ranges from 0 for a loan at 10 percent interest to 100 percent for a grant that requires no repayment.[7] Scholars have widely divergent views regarding the motivations for aid-giving. Most liberals acknowledge that donors provide ODA partly to gain commercial benefits, but they argue that this aid can be a positive-sum game that also helps promote socioeconomic and political development of recipients. Realists often see aid as a policy tool that donors developed to influence recipients in the bipolar Cold War, and that they now use to support the war on terrorism. Critical

theorists view aid in highly negative terms as perpetuating dependency relations, promoting the integration of the South in the unequal global market,
and failing to deal with serious problems such as environmental degradation.[8]
In reality, all of these theoretical views have some merit. Donors sometimes
provide aid for humanitarian and development reasons, but they also seek to
promote their own political and economic interests.

Regardless of the motivation for foreign aid-giving, it is important to ask
whether it is *necessary* and whether it is *effective* in decreasing poverty and
promoting economic development. Critics often point out that LDCs acquire
much more revenue from private capital flows and merchandise exports than
from aid. In 1977, private capital flows to LDCs exceeded ODA by a 2-to-1
ratio, and from 1990 to 1996 private international finance to LDCs increased to
more than six times ODA flows. In 2002 two Oxfam staff members wrote that
compared with aid, trade "has far more potential to benefit the poor. If developing countries increased their share of world exports by just five percent, this
would generate $350 billion—seven times as much as they receive in aid."[9]
However, private capital and trade are adequate substitutes for aid for only
some LDCs. Most private capital to LDCs goes to China and about 10 other East
Asian and Latin American countries, and very little goes to the least developed
countries (LLDCs) or for areas such as health and education. Private capital
can also be withdrawn rapidly from LDCs, as demonstrated in the 1990s East
Asian financial crisis (see Chapter 11). The poorest LDCs are least likely to
benefit from international trade, and the WTO Doha Round was suspended
partly because the North was unwilling to end its trade restrictions in areas
such as agriculture that are important to the South. Thus, aid continues to be
important for poorer LDCs and for sectors such as health and education.[10]
Jeffrey Sachs, one of the strongest advocates of the necessity of foreign aid for
the poorest LDCs, argues that "when poverty is very extreme, the poor do not
have the ability—by themselves—to get out of the mess." They become trapped
with low or negative economic growth rates because "they are too poor to
save for the future and thereby accumulate the capital...that could pull them
out of their current misery."[11] Sachs sees foreign aid as providing the answer,
and in his 2005 book *The End of Poverty,* he recommended a doubling of aid in
2006 and almost another doubling by 2015. However, many critics such as
William Easterly question the effectiveness of aid-giving. Easterly points out
that many LDCs have developed economically without large amounts of
foreign aid, and that aid does not necessarily promote development. Indeed,
"the typical African country received more than 15 percent of its income from
foreign donors in the 1990s," but this "surge of aid was not successful in
reversing or halting the slide in growth of income per capita."[12] Easterly
believes that aid can sometimes be useful when it is accompanied with a
piecemeal, bottom-up approach to development. However, he strongly criticizes the top-down planning approach of most large development agencies,
and he attributes LDC problems more to corruption and bad government than
to a lack of foreign aid. The Sachs–Easterly debate shows that (as with other

IPE issues) some of the major debates are often within the same theoretical perspective—in this case both Sachs and Easterly are liberal economists. As with many of these debates, the reality is somewhere in between. Both Sachs's external constraints (lack of capital) and Easterly's internal constraints (bad government) can interfere with development. Regardless of the overall merits of foreign aid, ultimately the amount provided depends on the aid donors, not on the LDC recipients. After briefly discussing the trends, determinants, and effects of aid-giving, this chapter focuses mainly on the development strategies of the LDCs.

In the 1950s and 1960s, the North provided ODA to promote economic growth in the South, and in 1970 the United Nations resolved that the DCs should provide net ODA amounting to 0.7 percent of their GNP (most countries did not meet this objective).[13] However, this aid was often provided for security and commercial reasons, and the main security issue after World War II was the Cold War. Although the Soviet Union and its Warsaw Pact allies provided about 10 percent of aid during much of the Cold War period, the members of the OECD's Development Assistance Committee (DAC) provided almost 90 percent. The DAC continues to provide most of the aid today, but China has also become an important aid provider, especially in Sub-Saharan Africa. Table 10.2 shows the net ODA of DAC members as a percent of their GNI. As the bottom line in Table 10.2 shows, after an initial decline from 1960 to 1970, ODA stayed in the 30 percent range from 1970 to 1990, but by 2000 the ODA level had fallen to 0.22 percent of GNI. Most notable was the decline of U.S. aid from 0.21 percent of its GNI in 1990 to 0.10 percent of its GNI in 2000. The United States had been the largest aid donor (despite the low percent of its aid relative to its GNI), but Japan took over first place for much of the 1990s. Cold War security concerns were a major motivation for U.S. aid in the 1945–1990 period, and the collapse of the Soviet Union was the most important factor accounting for its decline. Geostrategic security issues are also a major factor accounting for a degree of revival of foreign aid since 2001. As Table 10.2 shows, total ODA as a percent of GNI increased from 0.22 to 0.46, and U.S. aid increased from 0.10 to 0.18 percent of its GNI. The most important security factor was the terrorist attack on New York's World Trade Center on September 11, 2001. Increased ODA has been part of an effort to combat terrorism, on the theory that poverty can contribute to extremism and violence.[14]

Commercial factors have also played a role in the level and destination of aid-giving, and commercial factors became more important with the return of orthodox liberalism. As ODA declined in the 1980s and 1990s, the substantial increase of foreign investment fueled "the belief that the financing needs of developing countries could be met by a reliance on the markets."[15] As discussed, however, private investment cannot substitute for ODA to the least developed countries because it is speculative and volatile, rarely deals with the environment and other social concerns, and is concentrated in LDCs with higher incomes or with mineral and oil resources. A major indication of commercial factors is the widespread use of *tied aid*, in which a donor country ties a percentage of its bilateral aid to purchases

TABLE 10.2   Net Official Development Assistance of DAC[a] Members as a Percent of GNI[b]

	1960	1970	1980	1990	2000	2006
Australia	0.38	0.59	0.48	0.34	0.27	0.30
Austria	—	0.13	0.23	0.25	0.23	0.47
Belgium	0.88	0.48	0.50	0.46	0.36	0.50
Canada	0.19	0.43	0.43	0.44	0.25	0.29
Denmark	0.09	0.38	0.74	0.94	1.06	0.80
Finland	0	0	0.22	0.63	0.31	0.40
France	1.38	0.65	0.63	0.60	0.30	0.47
Germany	0.31	0.32	0.44	0.42	0.27	0.36
Greece	—	—	—	—	0.20	0.17
Ireland	0	0	0.16	0.16	0.29	0.54
Italy	0.22	0.16	0.17	0.31	0.13	0.20
Japan	0.24	0.23	0.32	0.31	0.28	0.25
Luxembourg	0	0	0	0.21	0.71	0.89
The Netherlands	0.31	0.63	0.97	0.92	0.84	0.81
New Zealand	0	0	0.33	0.23	0.25	0.27
Norway	0.11	0.33	0.87	1.17	0.76	0.89
Portugal	1.45	0.45	0	0.25	0.26	0.21
Spain	0	0	0	0.20	0.22	0.32
Sweden	0.05	0.37	0.78	0.91	0.80	1.02
Switzerland	0.04	0.14	0.24	0.32	0.34	0.39
United Kingdom	0.56	0.37	0.35	0.27	0.32	0.51
United States	0.53	0.31	0.27	0.21	0.10	0.18
Total	**0.52**	**0.34**	**0.37**	**0.33**	**0.22**	**0.46**

[a]DAC = Development Assistance Committee of the OECD

[b]GNI = gross national income

Source: OECD, *Development Co-operation* (Paris: OECD, various years).

from its own producers and the employment of its technical experts. In 2005, about 49 percent of total aid was tied to procurement in the donor country. Commercial motives have similarly been important to most donors such as France, which "has given overwhelmingly to its former colonies," and to Japan, which directed almost three-quarters of its ODA during 1998–2002 to Asian recipients.[16]

Despite the strategic and commercial motives for aid, ODA also serves an important function in addressing the needs of poorer LDCs for development finance. As discussed, the United Nations set a goal in 1970 that DC donors should increase net ODA to at least 0.7 percent of their GNPs. In 2000 the United Nations established eight *Millennium Development Goals* (*MDGs*) to be achieved by 2015, which include DC commitments in aid, trade, and debt relief.[17] The increase in ODA from 0.22 percent of GNI in 2000 to 0.46 percent in 2006 (Table 10.2) is partly a result of the MDGs. However, the emphasis donors place on commercial and political-security objectives tends to make ODA a volatile and unpredictable source of funding for long-term development needs. Although aid has revived somewhat, it is not meeting the UN development goals. As Table 10.2 shows, in 2006 only five donors had met the 0.7 percent of GNI goal set in 1970: Denmark, Luxembourg, the Netherlands, Norway, and Sweden. Japan's aid ranking declined because of its economic problems since the late 1990s, and it is now the third largest aid donor after the United States and Britain; both the United States and Japan ranked very low in 2006 in terms of aid as a percent of GNI (0.18 percent for the United States and 0.25 percent for Japan). Some even argue that aid has in fact not revived since 2000, because 28 percent of ODA went for debt relief in 2005. It is questionable whether much of this debt would have been repaid, and thus whether it represents a real addition to ODA (see Chapter 11). In addition to being an unreliable source of funding, the effects of ODA are in dispute. Whereas donors often provide aid for commercial and security purposes, recipients are often accused of corruption and of redirecting aid for other purposes; and there is considerable debate over the ability of LLDCs to absorb large amounts of aid effectively. Most LDCs would therefore be well advised to devote considerable attention to alternative strategies to promote development. Thus, most of this chapter focuses on the development strategies of LDCs. The next section focuses on the World Bank, which is not only a major source of multilateral development finance but also has considerable influence over LDC development strategies.[18]

THE WORLD BANK GROUP

The World Bank ("the Bank") has a major effect on LDC development strategies because of its dominant role "as a non-private lender, as a research and idea-generating unit, and as a provider of advice to the Third World."[19] DAC members prefer to give most of their ODA bilaterally, or directly to recipient countries; in 2006, they gave 74 percent of their ODA bilaterally and 26 percent through multilateral channels. (**Multilateral aid** is foreign assistance in which donor governments provide funding through IOs whose policies are collectively determined.) The World Bank Group is the largest lender of multilateral funds for international development, but its influence also stems from "its role as a rating agency for others"; its lending decisions, data collection, and analyses have a strong influence on bilateral donors, regional development banks, and private investors.[20] The Bank also contributes to the evolution of ideas, and debates on development are often "framed in terms of 'pro or anti' World Bank positions."[21] Thus, the Bank forms the core of an **epistemic community** or "a network of professionals with recognized expertise and competence in a particular domain and an authoritative claim to policy-relevant knowledge within that domain or issue-area."[22] Recognized expertise is a source of power in today's knowledge-based world-economy, and several factors account for the Bank's influence in generating ideas on development: The Bank affects the terms on which LDCs gain access to development finance and international capital markets, it has the largest group of development economists and research budget of any development organization, and the global media direct attention to Bank reports. The following discussion examines the Bank as an IO and the views of its proponents and critics.

Located in Washington, D.C., the Bank is actually a bank group composed of five institutions (see Figure 2.1 in Chapter 2). The first institution, the *International Bank for Reconstruction and Development (IBRD)*, was planned at the 1944 Bretton Woods conference. The DCs at Bretton Woods established the IMF to deal with monetary and balance of payments issues, and the decision to also form the IBRD was "something of an afterthought."[23] The DCs expected the IBRD to give priority to European reconstruction over Southern development, and Harry Dexter White of the U.S. Treasury Department even suggested that the new institution be called the Bank for Reconstruction. Although the negotiators responded to LDC protests by pledging that the IBRD would give "equitable" consideration to reconstruction and development, the first IBRD loans in 1947 went to France, the Netherlands, and Denmark for European reconstruction. It was not until the United States established the European Recovery Program or Marshall Plan for Western Europe in 1948 that the IBRD shifted its focus to development.[24]

The Bank, like the IMF, is a weighted voting institution. Each member has a capital subscription (or quota) based on its economic strength, which determines its financial contribution to the Bank and its number of votes. The G5 countries have the largest subscriptions and number of votes; in June 2008 the G5 had 37.4 percent of the votes in the IBRD policy-making bodies; the United States led with 16.4 percent, followed by Japan, Germany, Britain, and France, with 7.9, 4.5, 4.3, and 4.3 percent, respectively.[25] Members pay only 10 percent of their subscriptions to the IBRD and hold the remaining 90 percent as callable capital if needed to meet the IBRD's financial obligations. The IBRD receives most of its funds for development loans from borrowing on world capital markets. The principal U.S. bond-rating services give IBRD bonds a triple-A credit rating, because LDCs have a good record in repaying its loans and its members provide financial backing if necessary with their callable capital. To make its bonds attractive to purchasers, the IBRD must pay market interest rates on the funds it borrows, and it therefore charges near-conventional interest rates on loans to LDCs. Since IBRD loans are not concessional enough to qualify as ODA, the OECD introduced the concept of **official development finance (ODF)** to recognize their developmental value. The IBRD's quasi-commercial loans are considered to be ODF because it extends them for development purposes, it accompanies the loans with economic and technical advice, and LDCs receive the loans on better terms than they could obtain from borrowing directly on capital markets (LDCs deemed uncreditworthy cannot even borrow on capital markets).

To be a Bank member, a state must also join the IMF and provide it with detailed information about its economy. This requirement deterred most Communist states from joining the Bank for many years, even though they would have liked to receive Bank loans (see Table 11.3 in Chapter 11). The *board of governors* is theoretically the main policy-making body in the Bank (and the IMF). Every Bank member has one governor, but the governors have different numbers of votes based on the weighted voting system. The governors meet only once a year to review the Bank's operations and policies, admit new members, and amend the Articles of Agreement, and they delegate most of their functions to a 24-member *board of executive directors* (or *executive board*). The executive board, which also has weighted voting, is responsible for approving all Bank loan proposals and developing the Bank's general policies. Whereas the G5 countries have enough votes to appoint their own executive directors, coalitions of members elect the other executive directors every two years. (China, Saudi Arabia, and Russia also have appointed their own executive directors, but they have fewer votes than the G5 countries.) Elected executive directors must cast the votes of their entire coalition group as a unit.

Early in the Bank's history, the United States and other DCs gave the president and staff considerable discretion in daily operations because of the lack of Communist members, the Bank's weighted voting system, and the dominant position of DCs on the professional staff. The staff also has a degree of autonomy from governments because the IBRD receives most of its funds from financial markets (dependence on financial markets has other costs). Several factors also give the Bank staff more autonomy vis-à-vis the executive board: The executive directors lack analytical support to monitor the staff's management of a broad range of complex issues; the frequent rotation of executive directors puts them at a disadvantage in relation to staff members who are career civil servants; and although the executive board can reject a staff loan proposal, only the Bank president can decide whether to propose a loan. Despite the staff's prerogatives, its autonomy has limits, and the United States and some other DCs have scrutinized Bank actions more closely in recent years (see discussion later in this chapter).[26]

The IBRD was the only Bank group institution until the *International Finance Corporation (IFC)* was created in 1956 (see Figure 2.1 in Chapter 2). Reflecting the Bank group's liberal economic orientation, the IFC encourages private business and investment in LDCs, and it is the largest multilateral source of loans and equity financing for private-sector projects in the South. Whereas the IBRD provides loans only to governments or with a government guarantee, the IFC directs loans to private ventures in LDCs, and it may not even accept a government guarantee. The IFC also invests in equity shares of corporations, brings foreign and domestic partners together in joint ventures, and persuades commercial banks to lend to LDCs partly through joint financing deals with banks as co-lenders. Like the IBRD, the IFC charges near-commercial rates on its loans. During the 1980s, the U.S. Reagan administration's emphasis on the private sector elevated the IFC's importance, and it reported net profits of $142 million in fiscal 1992–1993. In view of these profits and the high interest rate on IFC loans, critics question whether the IFC is a money-making or philanthropic institution. However, the IFC argues that it provides technical, financial, and environmental advice for private-oriented development projects.[27]

The *International Development Association (IDA)*, which became the third Bank group institution in 1960, was formed in response to the South's complaints that poorer LDCs could not pay the high interest rates on IBRD loans. The South also opposed the Bank's weighted voting system, and throughout the 1950s it demanded a soft-loan agency in which it would have greater control. The North finally agreed to create the IDA in 1960, but it insisted that IDA be under World Bank auspices with its weighted voting system. Although the IDA and IBRD are legally and financially distinct, they share the same staff and their projects must meet the same criteria. The IDA provides soft loans or "credits" to LDC governments with no interest, 10-year grace periods, and 35- to 40-year maturities. (The IDA also provides a small share of its funds as grants to some low-income countries in "debt distress."[28]) Unlike IBRD and IFC loans, IDA credits meet the criteria for Official Development Assistance (ODA). LDCs and transition economies are categorized in three groups in terms of eligibility for loans: States with stronger economies such as Argentina, Brazil, Mexico, Malaysia, Thailand, Iran, Egypt, Poland, Russia, and China are only eligible for IBRD loans; states with somewhat weaker economies such as India, Pakistan, Bolivia, and Azerbaijan are eligible for a blend of IBRD and IDA funds; and states with the weakest economies such as Bangladesh, Vietnam, Honduras, Tanzania, Kenya, Ethiopia, and Nigeria are only eligible for IDA credits.[29] The interest-free terms of IDA credits give it no basis for borrowing on capital markets, and it therefore depends on replenishments by DC governments every three years. Other donors often wait for the United States to pledge funds before making their own pledges, and the U.S. Congress sometimes delays approval of IDA contributions. Orthodox liberal views that LDCs should rely on private capital rather than IDA "handouts" pose a constant threat to its finances. Despite the importance of IDA credits to poorer LDCs, nonconcessional lending accounts for almost three-fourths of the Bank group's loan agreements.

The other two Bank group institutions—the *International Center for Settlement of Investment Disputes (ICSID)* and the *Multilateral Investment Guarantee Agency (MIGA)*—encourage the flow of private foreign investment to LDCs and transition economies. The ICSID was formed in 1966 to provide facilities for conciliation and arbitration of disputes over FDI. The need for a neutral international forum arose because foreign investors fear that host country courts will not be impartial, and host countries fear that foreign courts will threaten their sovereignty. The MIGA was created in 1988 to provide guarantees to foreign investors for noncommercial risks, such as currency inconvertibility, expropriation, war, and civil disturbances, and to help LDCs and transition economies disseminate information on investment opportunities.[30]

It is important to note that the Bank has considerable influence over bilateral as well as multilateral aid. Donor governments consider Bank reports a key source of data and analysis on development issues, and the Bank also chairs a number of aid consortia and **consultative groups** which enable DC donors to avoid duplication and coordinate their bilateral aid-giving. However, LDCs believe that consultative groups permit donors to exert collective pressures on a recipient government because only one recipient and its major donors attend each meeting.[31] As the most important multilateral development institution, the Bank also provides a model for regional banks such as the Inter-American, African, and Asian Development Banks and the European Bank for Reconstruction and Development (EBRD). Like the World Bank, these regional banks usually raise funds on international capital markets and lend at near-commercial interest rates; they also have IDA-type soft-loan affiliates that raise funds from government subscriptions. Whereas the World Bank focuses on larger projects and programs, the regional banks support smaller development projects at the regional level.[32]

The United States is the most important Bank member, and there are several indications of its influence. First, the United States has more votes than any other member. Second, English is the Bank's only working language, reflecting its location in Washington, D.C. The U.S. view that a single working language contributes to efficiency contrasts with the view of many other states that cultural and ethnic diversity dictates the need for more than one working language in IOs.[33] Third, the Bank president has always been American, and the executive directors accept the U.S. government's nominee for the position. Whereas the U.S. Treasury Department handles most matters related to U.S. involvement in the Bank, the White House nominates Bank presidents and "invariably chooses candidates with connections to the U.S. political establishment."[34] However, U.S. influence has declined in some respects. For example, the share of the Bank's outstanding securities held in the United States has steadily decreased and U.S. voting power in the Bank has fallen from about 40 percent of the total to less than 17 percent.

Despite the decline in U.S. influence, it continues to be the most important Bank member for several reasons:

- The United States continues to be the only country with sufficient voting power (over 15 percent) to veto amendments to the Bank Articles of Agreement and decisions to increase the Bank's capital.
- Other DCs have been willing to let the United States take "the lead—and the heat—for doing what they wanted anyway," and they are unwilling to jeopardize their relations with the United States on this issue.[35] Japan and Europe have been more interested in controlling regional institutions such as the EBRD in Europe.
- The United States has considerable structural or soft power in the Bank, enabling it to induce "other countries to *want* what it wants."[36] This soft power depends on U.S.-based civil society actors such as academics, think tanks, and NGOs with ready access to the Bank in Washington, D.C.
- The creation of IDA in 1960 gave the United States a source of influence it did not have over the IBRD. The U.S. threat to withhold IDA replenishments may be its most important source of pressure, and in some cases this threat is explicitly linked with U.S. objections to specific Bank policies.[37]

Despite the influence of the United States and other DCs, the Bank sometimes asserts its autonomy on issues and uses its expertise to influence foreign aid officials in the DCs. Thus, the United States and the Bank have "a complex, evolving relationship that is part symbiosis, part two-way influence, and part struggle over the Bank's autonomy of action."[38]

Instead of detailing the arguments for and against Bank policies, this chapter briefly outlines some salient issues raised by critics and supporters. The strongest critics are historical materialists on the left and orthodox liberals on the right. Historical materialists accuse the Bank of enriching DC exporters and MNCs at the expense of LDCs, and of "prying state control" from LDC "nationalists and socialists who would regulate international capital's inroads."[39] Some orthodox liberals, by contrast, see the Bank as having "an evident interest in ever-increasing multinational aid" and advise it to "impose a greater check on the staff's tendency to be 'state enthusiasts.'"[40] Those who defend the Bank consider it inevitable "that the Bank should be subjected to severe criticism from the ideologues of both left and right."[41] As this chapter discusses, the Bank has in fact often disregarded challenges to its liberal free market approach to development, and it has been more willing to criticize government failure than market failure. During the 1980s and 1990s, the Bank used its **structural adjustment loans** (**SALs**) to pressure LDCs to adopt orthodox liberal policies.[42] Only recently has the Bank become more aware of the need to cushion vulnerable groups and states from unrestrained market pressures. Other criticisms of the Bank range from its patronizing attitude toward the United Nations Development Program (UNDP) and the regional development banks; its highly centralized structure in Washington, D.C., with too little staff time spent in the field; and the priority it gives to large project commitments with fast-disbursing loans over project supervision, implementation, and evaluation. In fairness to the Bank, as the largest multilateral development institution it is sometimes a target of criticism regardless of its policies. For example, some critics charge that the Bank is too slow to change its policies in response to civil society pressures and changing LDC requirements. However, when the Bank alters its policies, others charge that it is embracing "the latest fads in development thinking regardless of their substantive merits."[43] The Bank, like other IOs, is also largely a creature of its member states; for example, the Bank's ability to increase loans to the poorest LDCs depends on the North's willingness to provide IDA replenishments. We now turn to a discussion of LDC development strategies.

LDC DEVELOPMENT STRATEGIES

Most development economists in the early postwar period were "surprisingly sceptical about the benefits of free trade and capital movements."[44] The decline in the North's demand for imports during the 1930s Depression had caused world prices for Latin American commodity exports to collapse, and John Maynard Keynes' interventionist liberalism had more appeal to development economists than orthodox liberalism. Interventionist liberals accepted the idea that LDCs required more government intervention in their economies than DCs. The apparent success of Soviet central planning in the 1930s also contributed to support for "statism," or a greater role for the state in the economy. This skepticism of free trade and emphasis on statism provided the setting for the ISI strategy after World War II. As we will discuss, ISI was ultimately unsuccessful and has been replaced by other development strategies in subsequent years. The remainder of this chapter focuses on the succession of LDC development strategies since World War II.

IMPORT SUBSTITUTION INDUSTRIALIZATION

The ideas of several major economists influenced Southern development strategies during the early postwar period. As discussed, development strategies drew on Keynesian interventionist liberalism. Although Keynes focused mainly on government involvement in the North, his ideas contributed to the view that LDC governments should also do more to promote economic development. Second, development strategies drew on the ideas of Raúl Prebisch and Hans Singer. In 1950, Prebisch and Singer separately published studies arguing that the North–South income gap was growing because of a long-term decline in the prices of primary products (raw materials and agricultural goods). To close the gap, LDCs should decrease their emphasis on producing primary products and focus on industrialization.[45] According to the Prebisch-Singer thesis, demand for industrial goods such as automobiles and televisions rises as income increases, but the same does not apply to primary products. Indeed, the North's demand for raw materials may even decline as technological advances lead to the discovery of substitutes (such as synthetic rubber for natural rubber). Thus, LDCs that depend on primary product exports suffer from declining terms of trade. When LDCs increase the production of primary products to gain more revenue, the surplus stocks in fact result in lower prices and more poverty. Prebisch argued that *import substitution industrialization (ISI)* would permit LDCs to produce manufactured goods they had previously imported. In the 1950s Prebisch began to use the terms *center* and *periphery,* and his writings formed the core of Latin American structuralism. Although Prebisch's structuralism was a *precursor* to dependency theory, it was reformist and more optimistic than dependency theory that the South could catch up with the North through protectionism and state-promoted industrialization.[46]

Realists such as Hamilton and List had supported policies similar to ISI for late industrializers, and some LDCs had developed ISI policies as a short-term response to the Great Depression. However, the South did not adopt ISI as a long-term development strategy until after World War II. Central to ISI was the argument that LDCs should promote industrial growth through protectionist barriers and subsidies for their infant industries. LDCs could compete with the DCs only by emphasizing industrial development (and deemphasizing agriculture). In the 1950s and 1960s LDCs in Latin America, Asia, and Africa followed ISI policies, and import substitution "emerged as the new gospel for Third World industrialization."[47] The World Bank generally supported ISI during the 1950s even though it was a realist development strategy with strong nationalist overtones, because the Bank was also affected by postwar interventionist liberal views that the state should have an important role in development. The Bank's approach to development placed considerable emphasis on industrialization, which meant ISI in the 1950s, and it provided funding for major infrastructure projects such as transportation and communications facilities and power projects that LDCs needed to industrialize.[48]

Initially, ISI seemed to provide major gains for the South. For example, Latin America had healthy industrial growth rates in the 1940s and 1950s, India's steel production increased by six times from 1951 to 1966, and some African states such as Ghana also registered industrial gains. International conditions were favorable to ISI, because LDCs benefited from prosperity and growth in North America and Western Europe. Furthermore, the "green revolution" led to the development of high-yielding grains in the 1950s that increased agricultural output in Asian LDCs and masked the fact that ISI was promoting industrialization at the expense of agriculture. Despite the initial success of ISI, problems developed in LDCs during the 1960s and 1970s. The global food crisis of the 1970s exposed ISI weaknesses, as inclement weather and Soviet crop shortfalls led to greatly increased demand for food imports, and global food stocks fell to their lowest levels in 20 years. The food crisis had its severest effects on the South because many LDCs had limited ability to purchase foodstuffs on global markets at inflated prices.[49] When OPEC drastically raised oil prices in 1973, a number of LDC oil importers such as India were doubly hit by the food and energy crises. These external stresses exposed a number of weaknesses in ISI as a development strategy. First, the global food crisis pointed to the pitfalls in emphasizing industrialization at the expense of agriculture. The neglect of agriculture contributed to poverty in the countryside, the need for food grain imports, and the stagnation of agricultural exports. The LDC share of world agricultural exports fell from 44 percent in 1955 to 32 percent in 1970, and the decline in revenue exacerbated LDC balance-of-payments deficits. Second, despite its emphasis on promoting self-sufficiency, ISI *increased* the South's dependence on the North. In view of their shortages of capital and foreign exchange, LDCs encouraged inward FDI as part of their ISI policies to promote industrialization. Thus, MNCs established subsidiaries behind the LDC trade barriers; this helps explain why the U.S. government supported ISI as part of "its vigorous efforts to secure favorable conditions for U.S. foreign direct investment."[50]

The most serious weakness of ISI was its inability to promote industrial competitiveness. Industrialization proceeded well under an "easy" first stage, but the second stage of ISI was more difficult. In the first stage, LDCs replaced nondurable consumer imports such as shoes, household products, and clothing with domestic production. LDCs have a sizable domestic market for these labor-intensive goods, and they do not require large amounts of capital investment, advanced technology, or a network of component suppliers. However, LDCs had to move to a second stage to maintain high industrial growth rates, replacing imports of intermediate goods (e.g., petrochemicals and steel) and producer and consumer durables (e.g., refrigerators and automobiles) with domestic production. These second-stage products were more difficult to produce because they are capital intensive and depend on economies of scale and higher levels of technology. LDCs had to import technology and inputs to produce these goods, and the cost of the imports outweighed any savings from locally producing the final goods. Finally, the emphasis on capital-intensive production concentrated development gains in a small segment of the population in industrial enclaves, and unemployment became a major problem; thus, ISI exacerbated the income inequalities within LDCs.[51] LDCs pursuing second-stage ISI experienced a slower growth of primary product exports, greater dependence on imports, and a failure to increase manufactured exports. In response to their balance-of-payments problems, LDCs sought external loans, aid, and investment and turned increasingly to trade protectionism. Liberal economists therefore began to argue that "an import substitution policy tends to be less and less successful the longer it continues,"[52] and the World Bank also changed its views. By the late 1960s, "the financing of profitable import-substituting industry by IFC and Bank-financed development finance companies" was giving way "to a more discriminating policy of industrial financing."[53] Even Prebisch expressed concerns that "the proliferation of industries of every kind in a closed market has deprived the Latin American countries of the advantages of specialization and economies of scale."[54] Prebisch hoped that regional trade agreements would provide economies of scale so that Latin American LDCs could continue to industrialize under ISI. However, Latin American regionalism during the 1970s was unsuccessful (see Chapter 8).

Many Latin American and South Asian states nevertheless continued with second-stage ISI because protectionist domestic groups limited their ability to institute policy change.[55] It was not until the 1980s foreign debt crisis that most LDCs finally shifted from ISI to a more outward-oriented development strategy (see the following discussion). Although many LDCs persisted with ISI during the 1960s and 1970s, some sought alternatives. A second group of LDCs turned to socialist central planning based on the Soviet Union model, but they encountered many problems. A third group, the East Asian NIEs, changed from ISI to export-led growth strategies at a fairly early stage, and experienced far more impressive economic growth rates than other LDCs. Thus, the development community began to look positively at export-led growth as an alternative strategy to promote economic development.

SOCIALIST DEVELOPMENT STRATEGIES

During the 1960s, scholars challenged ISI from both the right and the left, and many left-leaning scholars turned to dependency theory (see Chapter 5). Dependency theorists argued that ISI did not do enough to restructure peripheral-core relations and that the South could promote autonomous development only by turning to socialism and severing linkages with the North. A small number of LDCs including China, North Korea, Cuba, Ethiopia, Mozambique, Vietnam, Laos, Cambodia, and Burma opted for socialist central planning.[56] The socialist development strategies were patterned after the Soviet model, with state central planning largely replacing market signals in allocating resources and setting production targets, wages, and prices. LDCs taking the socialist route often reduced socioeconomic inequities more than nonsocialist LDCs by providing better access to health care and education, improving the status of women, and opening parks and other facilities to the public. However, the socialist LDCs encountered serious economic problems, because China was the only one of them with sufficient size and resources to engage in central planning on the Soviet/Eastern European model. LDCs lacked the communications and transportation infrastructure for central planning and a well-trained bureaucracy to design and monitor the plans. LDCs also encountered many of the same problems that plagued the Soviet Union and Eastern Europe. Thus, central planners were more successful in setting production targets and increasing output than in ensuring the quality of output and the efficient use of resources. Western aid and investment policies also did not make the task of these LDCs easier. World Bank and U.S. Agency for International Development (AID) officials believed that foreign aid should at least partly promote private enterprise, and most LDCs following a socialist development model therefore were not major beneficiaries of Western development assistance.

Mozambique was a prime example of an LDC facing problems because of its socialist policies. Shortly after gaining independence in 1975, Mozambique tried to loosen its linkages with South Africa's apartheid government and follow a socialist development path. However, the state lacked the capacity to intervene massively in the economy to achieve its egalitarian and socialist objectives. In agriculture, for example, Mozambique established communal villages and about 2,000 state farms to supply most of the country's food, but agricultural production fell drastically because farmers preferred family plots over communal farming, and the government could devote only limited resources to the state farms and communal villages. Although Mozambique tried to promote cooperation with the West as well as socialist states, the U.S. Congress refused to offer it foreign aid from 1975 to 1984. The South African government also launched a destabilization campaign against Mozambique because of its support for refugees and liberation movements in southern Africa. By late 1983, Mozambique had shortfalls in local production, food for the population, and foreign exchange. Thus, the government defaulted on its debts and became a major recipient of international aid. In response to debt-rescheduling negotiations with the IMF and World Bank,

Mozambique agreed to introduce orthodox liberal reforms. Several other LDCs following socialist policies had similar experiences, and when the Soviet bloc collapsed in the 1980s and 1990s, the socialist LDCs could no longer look to it for economic and military support. Thus, very few LDCs currently follow socialist strategies, and even the holdouts such as Cuba are seeking closer ties with the capitalist world.[57]

EXPORT-LED GROWTH

The East Asian NIEs—South Korea, Taiwan, Singapore, and Hong Kong—adopted **export-led growth** strategies that were far more successful than the socialist and ISI strategies in the 1970s and 1980s. In examining export-led growth, it is best to discuss South Korea and Taiwan, because Singapore and Hong Kong are so small geographically, and Hong Kong was a British crown colony before it was incorporated into mainland China. In the 1950s Taiwan and South Korea adopted ISI policies, which resulted in large balance-of-payments deficits and did not succeed in decreasing their dependence on primary commodity exports. Thus, Taiwan and South Korea followed Japan's example in the 1960s and shifted from ISI to a policy of encouraging the growth of manufactured exports. While maintaining moderate protection of domestic producers, they promoted exports with tax incentives, export credits, export targets, and duty-free imports of inputs required by exporters. Taiwan and South Korea also adopted other measures such as abandoning minimum wage legislation to encourage increased employment in export-oriented industries. During the early 1980s, Southeast Asian economies such as Malaysia, Indonesia, and Thailand followed a similar path and switched to export-led growth strategies. Thus, Hong Kong, Singapore, South Korea, and Taiwan were "first-tier" Asian NIEs, and Malaysia, Indonesia, and Thailand were "second-tier" Asian NIEs. The change to export-led growth had a dramatic effect on economic performance. For example, South Korea's GDP grew at an average annual rate of more than 8 percent during the 1960s, and its exports rose from about $31 million in 1960 to $882 million in 1970. In the 1960s most South Korean and Taiwanese industrial exports required relatively little capital and large amounts of unskilled labor, but industrial wages gradually increased and there was a structural transformation as the two economies began producing sophisticated industrial goods with highly skilled labor. By the late 1980s, Taiwan and South Korea were the tenth and thirteenth largest world exporters of manufactures, respectively.[58]

The East Asian successes of the 1960s to 1980s were often compared with the experiences of the Latin American NIEs—Argentina, Brazil, Chile, and Mexico.[59] Although the Latin Americans began to provide some incentives for exports in the 1960s, their policies continued to be based mainly on ISI. Thus, the first two columns of Table 10.3 show that per capita GDP growth rates were much higher for East Asian than Latin American NIEs. Whereas South Korea's GDP per capita of $747 was well *below* the per capita GDPs of all four Latin American NIEs in 1963, by 1988 South Korea's per capita GDP of $4,094

TABLE 10.3 GDP[a] Per Capita and Export/GDP Ratios

	GDP Per Capita		Export/GDP Ratios	
	1963	1988	1963	1988
East Asian NIEs[b]				
Hong Kong	$2,247	$11,952	39.0	51.1
South Korea	747	4,094	2.3	35.4
Singapore	1,777	11,693	124.5	164.2
Taiwan	980	4,607	15.3	51.8
Latin American NIEs				
Argentina	$2,949	$3,474	10.0	10.2
Brazil	1,400	3,424	6.0	9.5
Chile	3,231	3,933	11.6	31.9
Mexico	2,312	3,649	5.1	11.9

[a]GDP = gross domestic product

[b]NIES = newly industrializing economies

Source: Bela Balassa, Policy Choices for the 1990s (London: Macmillan, 1993), pp. 57, 59.

was *above* the figures for the Latin Americans. The change was even more dramatic for Hong Kong and Singapore, with their per capita GDPs soaring above $11,000 by 1988. The last two columns of Table 11.3 show that export-led growth policies led to much higher export-to-GDP ratios. Whereas South Korea's export-to-GDP ratio of 2.3 was well below the Latin American figures in 1963, its export-led growth policies resulted in a ratio of 35.4 in 1988, exceeding the ratios of the Latin American NIEs. The 1988 export-to-GDP ratios for Singapore (164.2), Taiwan (51.8), and Hong Kong (51.1) were much higher than the Latin American ratios. There were also striking differences in the composition of exports, with Taiwan, South Korea, and Hong Kong *each* producing more manufactured exports than all of Latin America by the late 1980s.[60]

The East Asian NIEs had a few years of reduced growth during the 1980s foreign debt crisis (see Chapter 11), but they did not have to seek debt rescheduling and soon adjusted their economies and resumed rapid growth rates. Although the East Asians had about the same debt-to-GDP ratios as other oil importers, their debt-to-export ratios were much lower. Their healthy export positions, combined with large infusions of foreign investment (especially from Japan), provided sufficient revenue so they could continue their debt payments without depending on IMF and World Bank loans. The Latin Americans following ISI, by contrast, were more severely affected by the debt crisis and had to seek substantial IMF and World Bank funding.[61] As discussed later, the East and Southeast Asian economies encountered economic problems which became starkly evident in the late 1990s. However, just as ISI had been the "gospel" for LDC industrialization in the 1950s, export-led growth emerged as the new gospel for many development specialists from the 1970s to the early 1990s. Although there was a general consensus that export-led growth was more successful than ISI, scholars disagreed on the reasons for the East Asians' success.

IPE Perspectives and the East Asian Experience

Liberals, realists, and historical materialists had different explanations for the success of East Asian export-led growth in the 1960s to 1980s. Liberal economists argued that East Asia's economic performance was strong because export-led growth was "outward-oriented" as opposed to Latin America's "inward-oriented" ISI strategy. The East Asians were open to freer trade and competition because they did not have "the mistrust of markets and private entrepreneurship that motivates large-scale doctoring in other Asian countries and in African and South American countries."[62] Thus, liberals attributed the East Asians' success to their adoption of the open market policies of Western DCs. Realists by contrast saw the key to the East Asian performance as the existence of a strong **developmental state** that had "a fundamental role in engineering economic growth, development and success in these countries."[63] Although Hamilton and List had argued that late industrializers required state intervention to catch up with more advanced states (see Chapter 3), it was not until the early 1980s that Chalmers Johnson coined the phrase "developmental state" in regard to Japan and the East Asian NIEs.[64] Realists attributed several characteristics to the East Asian developmental state:

- It provided extensive guidance to the market, controlling investment flows, promoting the development of technology, and protecting selected infant industries.
- It identified development as its main objective, encouraging citizens to increase investment rather than consumption and using repression if necessary to enforce its priorities.
- It invested heavily in education to give people the skills to be globally competitive.
- It depended on a highly skilled, technocratic bureaucracy that was committed to instituting economic reforms.

ISI and export-led growth both depended on government intervention, but realists argued that these policies differed in two respects: (1) The East Asian developmental state focused mainly on export industries, whereas ISI focused on industrialization mainly to meet domestic demand. (2) ISI protected all local industries, whereas the developmental state supported a small number of key industries most likely to succeed.

Unlike liberals and realists, world-system theorists believed that the NIEs were not in fact achieving genuine economic development. Although the NIEs were in the semiperiphery, they were simply "more advanced exemplars of dependent development," still dependent on states in the core.[65] Thus, André Gunder Frank argued that NIEs producing end products such as shirts, radios, or automobiles were "simply increasing their dependent integration into a worldwide division of labor...in which they are allocated the least remunerative and technologically obsolete contribution."[66] A fourth group of theorists explained the East Asian success in terms of *political culture,* or widely shared social values that affect a state's political economy. They argued that the realist focus on the state was insufficient because "the nature of...society is important in determining whether or not state policies are effective."[67] The political cultures of Japan, China, and the East Asian NIEs are influenced by Confucian philosophy, which is highly supportive of an economic development model based on collective values, respect for authority, hard work and enterprise, strong kinship ties in entrepreneurship, and a benevolent state staffed by highly educated individuals. Thus, Confucianism was a key factor explaining the success of Japan and the East Asian NIEs in promoting economic development.[68]

Most analysts opted for the realist model of the strong developmental state as the best explanation for East Asia's rapid economic growth. However, the Asian financial crisis of the late 1990s raised serious questions about all of these models and demonstrated "how rapidly an informed consensus can change."[69]

The Asian Financial Crisis

In 1993 the World Bank issued a report on *The East Asian Miracle* which examined the region's "remarkable record of high and sustained economic growth" from 1965 to 1990, and a number of analysts began to refer to the East Asian "miracle economies."[70] As our earlier discussion indicated, economists could not agree on a satisfactory explanation for the East Asian success, and the term *miracle* implied that "the phenomenon was beyond purely scientific explanation."[71] Although East Asia's rapid growth continued into the 1990s, by 1996 there were signs of slower export growth, lower earnings, and surplus industrial capacity. For example, problems emerged in Thailand's real estate and financial sector, several large South Korean enterprises or *chaebol* failed, and the Japanese economy continued to stagnate. In 1997 a financial crisis developed when Thailand allowed its baht currency to float, some other Asian economies followed the Thai example, and their currencies depreciated sharply. Thailand, Indonesia, Malaysia, and South Korea were the economies affected most by the crisis. Foreign investors lost confidence in their currencies, and the most severely affected economies had to seek IMF and World Bank loans. By 1999 the worst part of the financial crisis was over, and the region began to recover as U.S. and European demand for East Asian exports increased. Although there was growing confidence in the future of East Asian economic growth, the economies have been slow to institute some needed economic reforms, and they continue to be vulnerable to changing economic conditions.[72] The following discussion examines the reasons for the East Asian shift from "miracle" to "meltdown" status and the effects of the financial crisis on international development strategies. (Chapter 11 discusses the effects of the financial crisis on the IMF's role and the need for a new international financial architecture.)

The East Asian economic problems in 1997 caused some analysts to question whether the "miracle" was over or whether it had even occurred, and economists that had tried "to find a fully convincing explanation" for the rapid East Asian growth "now struggled to explain the 'meltdown.'"[73] Historical materialists had questioned whether the East Asian economies were achieving genuine, autonomous development, and they believed that the financial crisis added weight to their arguments. The East Asian NIEs grew more rapidly than other LDCs for most of the 1970s and 1980s, but this was fragile and dependent development. Although the strong developmental state contributed to East Asian economic growth, this growth was highly dependent on U.S. and Japanese policies. Taiwan and South Korea had special linkages with the United States because of their strategic location vis-à-vis the Soviet Union and China; thus, the United States provided them with military and economic aid and opened its market to their exports while permitting them to follow protectionist policies. East Asian economic growth also stemmed from special linkages with Japan. Japanese colonialism had created the social foundations for industrialization in East Asia, but also the basis for dependency relations. When the Japanese yen increased in value as a result of the 1985 Plaza Agreement (see Chapter 6), Japanese companies invested in East Asian subsidiaries to take advantage of cheaper costs of production. These Japanese investments helped East Asia avoid the worst effects of the debt crisis that ravaged Latin America and Africa during the 1980s (see Chapter 11). Beginning in the late 1980s, however, East Asia's dependence on the United States and Japan began to have some major drawbacks. For example, the United States responded to its growing balance-of-payments deficits by becoming more protectionist, and South Korea and Taiwan offered concessions because of fears that the United States would retaliate against what they considered to be "unfair" trade practices. With the breakup of the Soviet bloc and the decline of the Cold War, the United States was also less willing to supply large amounts of aid to South Korea and Taiwan. In sum, changes in the United States' economic and strategic position made it less willing to provide the East Asian NIEs with support. East Asian development was also fragile because of the region's dependence on Japan. Although East Asian industrial exports to the West were increasing, the goods were often produced by Japanese subsidiaries, designed in Japan, composed of imported Japanese components, and dependent on Japanese technology. For example, South Korea's automobile industry depends on Japanese auto parts and advanced technology. When

Samsung, a large Korean industrial conglomerate, received government approval to enter the auto industry in 1994, it planned to "import all of the advanced technology it needs from Nissan" in Japan.[74] Whereas the East Asians had large trade surpluses with the West, they had growing trade deficits with Japan. The depreciation of the Japanese yen relative to the U.S. dollar in the 1990s put downward pressure on East Asian currencies, many of which were pegged (at least partly) to the U.S. dollar. As Japanese exports became more competitive and Japanese markets absorbed a declining share of East Asian exports, problems of indebtedness and lack of competitiveness in the region increased. The financial crisis began when Thailand had to float its baht currency in 1997 (the baht had previously been pegged to a basket of currencies, with the U.S. dollar the most important).[75]

Although historical materialists were correct in pointing to East Asian dependence on the United States and Japan as one source of the financial crisis, realists and liberals consider them to be unduly negative. As discussed, East Asia had largely recovered from the financial crisis by 2000, and there was renewed confidence in economic growth in the region. Even if the East Asian NIEs had not been miracle economies, they *had* developed rapidly for several decades, and their economic development has resumed. It is therefore important to discuss the liberal and realist perspectives. In 1968, Samuel Huntington argued that authoritarian governments provided stability and order in developing societies and that democracy was a luxury to be introduced at a later time.[76] For a number of years, authoritarian East Asian developmental states limited individual freedom, but realists point out that these governments oversaw some marked improvements in economic growth and prosperity. Liberals by contrast attributed the East Asian financial crisis to the pervasive role of governments and government–business linkages in the region. In their view, the 1990s financial crisis revealed that authoritarian developmental states were not as efficient and immune to political pressure as realist writers maintained. For example, the one-party authoritarian states and close government–business linkages contributed to widespread nepotism, and the operation of banks and access to credit depended more on political connections than on market forces. Thus, lenders and foreign investors expanded credit without sufficient safeguards to risky borrowers, and huge sums were spent for questionable building and real estate projects without clear sources of financing. These inefficiencies challenged the realist contention that East Asian authoritarian states facilitated the development process.

Whereas liberals questioned the benefits of developmental states, realists questioned liberal claims that the East Asians benefited from economic interdependence. Indeed, realists (and also historical materialists) argued that "the process of deeper financial integration constituted a necessary condition" for the East Asian financial crisis.[77] Most East Asian economies had opened their capital accounts, and the region received a dramatic increase of international capital inflows during the early 1990s. The financial crisis resulted from the vulnerability of these economies to the massive reversal of these capital flows. Deeper financial integration also contributed to a contagion effect in which creditors engaged in speculative attacks on currencies, not because of economic fundamentals but because of the actions of other creditors.[78] Realists, historical materialists, and some liberals also charged that the liberal economic emphasis on composite statistics such as the growth in GDP and per capita GDP led to an overestimation of East Asian development. Some economists warned that increased labor and capital inputs rather than increased efficiency explained much of the rapid East Asian economic growth in the 1980s and early 1990s. Thus, Paul Krugman has argued in reference to the East Asian economies that

> sustained growth in a nation's per capita income can only occur if there is a rise in output *per unit of input*. Mere increases in inputs, without an increase in the efficiency with which those inputs are used—investing in more machinery and infrastructure—must run into diminishing returns; input-driven growth is inevitably limited.[79]

Environmentalists have also argued that rapid East and Southeast Asian economic growth is not sustainable in the long term. In Indonesia, logging practices are contributing to a deforestation rate of 2.4 million hectares per year; in the Malaysian state of Sarawak, loggers have removed 30 percent of the forest area in 23 years; and in Vietnam, resources are being exported with little concern for social and environmental consequences.[80] As discussed in Chapter 5, *sustainable development* is a policy that "meets the needs of the present without compromising the ability of future generations to meet their own needs."[81] LDCs often argue they cannot afford to divert resources from their immediate development to pay the costs for environmentally friendly policies, and they point out that DCs did not adopt sustainable policies when they were developing and that the North produces more pollution than the South. However, East Asians will not be able to sustain their economic growth rates in the long term if they disregard the effects of environmental degradation.

The export-led growth model has a number of strengths, and the East Asian developmental state outperformed other LDCs according to most economic indicators in the 1970s and 1980s. However, the financial crisis demonstrated that the export-led growth strategy also has weaknesses. The IMF, World Bank, and most industrial states strongly supported another development strategy in response to the 1980s foreign debt crisis and the 1990s Asian financial crisis: the orthodox liberal model.

THE REVIVAL OF ORTHODOX LIBERALISM

Two characteristics are critical for the effective functioning of the developmental state: a highly skilled technocratic bureaucracy and close cooperation among major economic groups such as agriculture, business, and labor. However, most LDCs "lack the highly professional merit-based bureaucracies and the tradition of cooperation between key economic actors that would permit them to replicate the East Asian model."[82] Developmental states also have been rather authoritarian in guiding the economy and controlling labor, business, and other private groups; but today globalization pressures are causing democracy (in a political sense) to spread throughout the world. The most important constraint on replicating the developmental state model was the revival of orthodox liberalism. In line with the new orthodoxy, critics charge that the IMF and World Bank viewed "the market rational/market ideological approach" as "the only correct course for development."[83] The shift to the right by British Prime Minister Margaret Thatcher and U.S. President Ronald Reagan in the late 1970s and 1980s resulted in a strong attack on realist or statist development strategies in the South. Thus, the Reagan administration, the U.S. Treasury, the Federal Reserve, and the international financial institutions responded to the 1980s foreign debt crisis by becoming powerful advocates of what later became known as the **Washington consensus.** The Washington consensus refers to the belief that "the combination of democratic government, free markets, a dominant private sector and openness to trade is the recipe for prosperity and growth."[84] (This is not what John Williamson meant by the term when he coined it in 1989.[85]) In applying the Washington consensus to the 1980s debt crisis, the IMF and the Bank imposed several conditions on their SALs, including requirements that recipients control inflation, decrease government spending, balance their budgets, privatize state-owned enterprises, deregulate financial and labor markets, and liberalize their trade and investment policies.

Structural Adjustment and the Theoretical Perspectives

A number of LDC debtors implemented World Bank and IMF–financed *structural adjustment programs* (*SAPs*) during the 1980s, and the South became "a laboratory for a huge experiment" in promoting economic development through orthodox liberalism.[86] Studies of the effects of SAPs in Sub-Saharan Africa demonstrate the wide range of views regarding the effects of structural adjustment. For example, one study concluded that "the performance of poor compliers deteriorates over time and is significantly worse than the performance of countries that comply" with the SAP conditions; a second study found that LDCs that followed World Bank structural adjustment policy conditions most closely "failed to grow as quickly as several less compliant African economies during the same period"; and a third study argued that SAPs "over the past decade are leading to the destruction of the [African] continent...with the failure of the state being an immediate outcome and environmental deterioration being devastating in the long run."[87] In view of these conflicting perceptions, this section briefly discusses SAPs and the theoretical perspectives.

Historical materialists believe that SAPs are not "simply an innocuous remedial package for sustained growth and development," but "an almost deliberate scheme for the perpetuation of export dependency...and reproduction of existing conditions of global inequality."[88] It is unrealistic to expect the World Bank and IMF to design SAPs to alleviate the South's problems because they caused the LDC debt problems in the first place. Whereas historical materialists are the harshest critics of structural adjustment, orthodox liberals are the strongest supporters. They believe that SAPs provide the necessary prescriptions and discipline based on the Washington consensus to deal with LDC debt problems. Interventionist liberals agree with orthodox liberals that SAPs are often necessary to combat domestic inefficiencies and corruption in LDCs; but they are more receptive to state interventionism and believe that the World Bank and IMF should be more sensitive to the effect of SAPs on the poorest groups and states.[89] Realists view the World Bank and IMF's emphasis on downsizing government through privatization, deregulation, and trade liberalization as misguided because late industrializers *require* government intervention to catch up with the leading powers. Despite these differing perceptions, many analysts would agree that SAPs had some serious problems in the 1980s and 1990s. After referring to some strengths of the SAPs, a discussion of their problems follows.

Structural Adjustment and Questions About Orthodox Liberalism

The World Bank's SAPs were most effective in middle-income LDCs that export manufactures, such as Brazil, Morocco, the Philippines, South Korea, Thailand, and Uruguay. These states had more developed institutions for implementing policy reforms and better resilience in dealing with the disruptions resulting from structural adjustment policies. Thus, liberal studies indicate that SAPs in middle-income LDCs contributed to lower government budget deficits, increased export earnings, more financing for private investment, and greater economic growth and efficiency. However, the effects of SAPs on the poorest LDCs and the poorest groups within LDCs were a more contentious issue. The Bank endorsed liberal economic views that benefits from the efficient allocation of resources under free markets would "trickle down" to the poor. However, critics rejected this trickle-down theory and argued that the poorest groups had to bear the largest share of the adjustment burden. The persistence or exacerbation of poverty in low-income LDCs and the poorest within LDCs gave credence to these criticisms and eventually forced the Bank to alter its approach.[90] Critics also charged that the emphasis of SAPs on privatization and deregulation did not address the need for effective LDC governments and that the Bank's "top-down" approach to structural adjustment did not address the need for local participation in "owning" policies and implementing reforms. The following sections examine these criticisms by focusing on an LDC region and a group within LDCs in which the effects of SAPs have been controversial: the Sub-Saharan African states and LDC women. We then discuss the World Bank's attempts to address the problems by altering its policies.

Structural Adjustment and Sub-Saharan Africa

Some of the strongest criticisms of structural adjustment relate to its effects on Sub-Saharan Africa ("Africa" in this section). More than two-thirds of African states received SALs in the 1980s, which has been described as a lost decade for Africa because economic growth and industrial and agricultural production stagnated, unemployment increased, and per capita incomes and investment declined. As Chapter 2 discusses, the UNDP ranks states according to a human development index based on per capita income, adult literacy rate, education, and life expectancy. In 2001, 19 of the 31 states with the lowest per capita GNPs were African; this adds weight to the findings of a study by the UN Program of Action for African Recovery and Development that although SAPs registered a few gains, "for the majority of African states, there has not been even a hint of recovery."[91]

Liberal economic analysts argue that SAPs are often blamed for problems caused by general economic deterioration. Thus, the World Bank and IMF were simply reacting to the foreign debt crisis, which resulted from inefficient LDC economic policies and global economic changes such as the 1970s oil crisis. Furthermore, many African problems such as political instability, civil wars, and famine are difficult to resolve, and African economic conditions would be even worse without IMF and World Bank SAPs. The Bank and IMF market-led prescriptions are the best strategies for bringing about adjustment and growth, because state-led strategies such as ISI were unsuccessful.[92] However, critics argue that SAPs in Africa put too much emphasis on market-oriented policies and impose the largest costs on the poorest groups and states. IMF and World Bank demands that LDC debtors privatize, deregulate, and downgrade the role of the government ignore the fact that the public sector provides a critical source of employment for African LDCs. As government capacity declines, infrastructure such as transportation and communications and services such as health care and education also suffer. Furthermore, the emphasis on privatization does not address the fact that private firms are unwilling or unable to supply public goods required for development. LDCs rely on government to provide resources for education and other aspects of human capital necessary for industrialization and competitiveness. Critics also oppose the emphasis SAPs put on trade liberalization. Although Latin American and East Asian LDCs reap some benefits from freer trade, there are few benefits for lower income African and Asian LDCs. Domestic industries in Latin America and East Asia can often compete with growing imports because these states have sheltered their industrial producers for lengthy periods. African LDCs, by contrast, are only beginning to industrialize and require protection for their infant industries. World Bank and IMF market-based prescriptions harm Africa because most African LDCs are at an early stage of development and require a substantial role for the government.[93]

Structural Adjustment and LDC Women

Another criticism of IMF and World Bank SAPs is that they have disregarded gender issues. Gender inequality and the exploitation of women are evident in almost all societies, and it is therefore not possible for SAPs to be gender neutral. By disregarding the subsidiary role of women, these programs reinforce male bias and exacerbate the problems confronting LDC women. The positions of LDC women vary widely as a result of diverse cultural values, historical factors, levels of economic development, and types of government. Women in the same society may also occupy vastly different positions depending on their social class and ethnicity. Nevertheless, it is possible to generalize about the challenges facing most LDC women:

- In the household, women spend more time than men on unpaid subsistence work such as child care, food production and preparation, health care, and education.
- Outside the home, more women than men work in the informal sector of the economy, which has little government regulation. Most informal-sector workers are service providers such as food stall operators, market traders, messengers, and shoe shiners, whose earnings are well below those in the formal sector.
- In the formal sector, women are more concentrated in lower skilled, lower wage occupations, and they often receive lower salaries than men for doing the same work.
- Women are more important in agricultural labor and less important in industry than men. In Africa, women produce about 90 percent of the food but are less important in the production of export crops.
- In view of women's lower wages in the formal sector and their overrepresentation in agriculture, the informal sector, and household work, women tend to have lower incomes than men. Households where women are the sole breadwinners are among the poorest groups in LDCs.[94]

World Bank policy prescriptions are based on macroeconomic concepts relevant for the economy as a whole rather than individual firms or households. The Bank gives little attention to the effect of its structural adjustment policies on women's work because much of women's time is spent doing unpaid subsistence work in the household, which does not appear in production statistics. For example, SAPs usually call for cutbacks in government spending, leading to decreased public funding for health, education, and water and sanitation facilities. Thus, much of the burden of health care and education shifts to the community and household, where women have most of the responsibilities. The World Bank and IMF also often pressure LDCs to lower government deficits by phasing out food subsidies. The higher food costs force women to use cheaper foods that take longer to prepare, such as coarse grain and root crops, and to bake at home rather than purchasing bread. Furthermore, hospitals may cut their costs by shifting care to the unpaid economy of the household. Whereas the Bank views cutbacks in government spending as an indication of increased efficiency, the costs are simply shifted to the unpaid economy, where women do most of the work.[95]

Even if women worked only in the household, the off-loading of government services and subsidies would place unreasonable burdens on them. The need for income, however, "has forced women into the labour force to protect their families' survival."[96] Thus, the share of women in the total labor force rose in Asia from 29 percent in 1950 to 33.8 percent in 1985, and in Latin America from 18 to 24.2 percent. Women have often fared poorly in the labor force under SAPs. In Africa, for example, farmers are paid higher prices to encourage them to produce more crops for the export market. However, men tend to produce the cash crops, and women produce the subsistence food crops. Men also market most of the crops produced, and women do not benefit from the increased prices because men often keep most of the revenue for themselves.[97] In sum, critics argue that SAPs affect women adversely in their multiple roles as mothers, household managers, community leaders, and wage earners. To confront the problems that SAPs pose for LDC women, it is necessary to dispel the myth that such programs are gender neutral.

ANOTHER SHIFT IN DEVELOPMENT STRATEGY?

In the late 1980s and 1990s, the World Bank became more responsive to criticisms of its structural adjustment policies and reassessed its orthodox liberal approach to development. To determine whether there has been another shift in the Bank's development strategy, it is necessary to discuss the Bank's reassessment of its approach to the role of the state in development, the poorest LDCs and groups within LDCs, and the "top-down" imposition of conditionality based on the Washington consensus. The Bank's reassessment can be divided into two periods: from the late 1980s to 1994 and from 1995 to the present.

The Late 1980s to 1994

In the late 1980s to 1994, the Bank began to reassess its approach to the role of the state in development and to the poorest LDCs and most vulnerable groups. The Bank did not want to veer too far from its market oriented views, but it began to recognize that the state would have to play a significant role in dealing with protracted problems in the least developed countries. The evolution in Bank thinking was evident in its 1991 *World Development Report,* which acknowledged that "governments need to do more in those areas where markets cannot be relied upon" such as health, education, family planning, and poverty alleviation. However, the 1991 report adhered to the position that state intervention had to be market conforming to have a positive developmental impact, and that "governments need to do less in those areas where markets work, or can be made to work."[98] Japan, as an important aid donor and foreign investor, reacted negatively to the 1991 report and the liberal orthodoxy that had come to dominate Bank thinking. The Japanese government insisted that the Bank give more recognition to the East Asian developmental state model, because it could not "be expected to fund a set of policies, and an underlying ideology" that denied "its own experience of having been heavily interventionist."[99] As a result, the Bank published a 1993 policy research report on *The East Asian Miracle: Economic Growth and Public Policy* (henceforth, "the report") examining the reasons East Asia had such "a remarkable record of high and sustained economic growth."[100] The report recognized the value of government intervention in some circumstances, noting that Japanese, Korean, and Taiwanese government policies of allocating credit to high-priority activities "may have been beneficial."[101] (Some observers saw this as a necessary concession to Japan's Ministry of Finance, which financed the report.[102]) Most of the report, however, questioned the value of government-directed industrial policy, indicated that the East Asian model might not be successful elsewhere, and cautioned that the East Asian successes should not "be taken as an excuse to postpone needed market-oriented reform."[103] The report also claimed that Malaysia, Thailand, and Indonesia (unlike the Northeast Asian economies) achieved rapid economic growth without an industrial policy and that other LDCs should emulate Southeast Asia. In sum, the Bank's approach to the state's role in development did not change significantly during the early 1990s. Although the report gave more recognition than previous Bank studies to government involvement in East Asian development, it attributed the East Asian success mainly to a liberal market-friendly approach.

The Bank also began to focus more on the poorest LDCs and most vulnerable groups. It is possible to identify four phases of thought in the Bank (and the foreign aid community) on poverty reduction.[104] In the first phase from 1945 to the late 1960s, the Bank financed large infrastructure projects to provide LDCs with transportation and communication facilities, port development, and power projects. Bank officials believed that large transfers of capital and technology would contribute to industrial development, employment, and a reduction of poverty. This is the trickle-down approach to development aid, which assumes that prosperity will "eventually trickle down from the top, alleviating the problem of poverty at the bottom."[105] Although LDCs achieved rapid economic growth in the 1960s, the large capital-intensive projects bypassed the neediest and increased income disparities within LDCs. Thus, Bank President Robert McNamara ushered in the second phase in the 1970s, with a commitment to reducing poverty. Although the focus on **basic needs** was only partly fulfilled in practice, the Bank developed projects that provided health, educational, and family-planning services to the poor; gave special attention to women and the poorest LDCs; and increased lending for agricultural and rural development, low-cost urban housing and slum rehabilitation, and primary and nonformal education.[106] However, alleviating poverty by targeting the poor was more difficult than anticipated, and orthodox liberals argued that the basic needs approach distracted attention from the need to promote economic growth. Thus, disillusionment with the basic needs approach along with significant global changes in the 1980s—the foreign debt crisis and the return of orthodox liberalism—ushered in the third phase of the Bank's approach to poverty. The third phase in the 1980s was similar to the first phase in the 1950s and 1960s when the Bank relied on trickle-down theories of poverty reduction, but the third phase put much more emphasis on orthodox liberal reforms. SAPs during the 1980s were conditioned on the implementation of orthodox liberal policies such as privatization, deregulation, and trade liberalization, and the basic needs of vulnerable groups were largely forgotten. Throughout the 1980s, there was growing pressure on the Bank to consider the distributional effects of structural adjustment. For example, a 1987–1988 United Nations Children's Fund (UNICEF) study entitled *Adjustment with a Human Face* argued that it was necessary to include a "poverty alleviation dimension" in adjustment programs.[107] This pressure eventually resulted in a fourth phase of Bank thinking on poverty, which began in the late 1980s.

The fourth phase is similar to the second phase in which the Bank devoted more attention to basic human needs and poverty reduction. For example, in 1989 the Bank acknowledged that "Sub-Saharan Africa has now witnessed almost a decade of falling per capita incomes and accelerating ecological degradation" and that there was a need for "special measures…to alleviate poverty and protect the vulnerable."[108] The Bank also devoted its 1990 *World Development Report* to poverty and began to redesign its SAPs to decrease adverse effects on the poor.[109] One indication of the Bank's renewed interest in poverty reduction was its increased attention to **microfinance.** Microfinance refers to the provision of low-cost, short-term financial services, mainly savings and credit, to poor households that do not have access to traditional financial institutions. In the late 1970s, there was growing recognition that the lack of access to financial services prevented the working poor from improving their lives. A number of microfinance institutions (MFIs) were established at this time to lend money to the poor; the most well-known of these was the *Grameen Bank,* which Professor Muhammad Yunus established in Bangladesh in 1976. In the 1990s, the donor agencies began to view microfinance as a key strategy in poverty reduction, and in 1993, the World Bank provided an initial grant of $2 million to support international replication of the Grameen Bank model.[110] Microfinance had appeal to many critical as well as liberal theorists. Whereas leftists liked "the 'bottom-up' aspects, attention to community, focus on women, and…the aim to help the underserved," rightists liked "the prospect of alleviating poverty while providing incentives to work, the nongovernmental leadership, the use of mechanisms disciplined by market forces, and the general suspicion of ongoing subsidization."[111]

However, tension continued to exist in the Bank between pressures for orthodox liberal reforms on one hand and concerns with the state and poverty on the other. In December 1994, the Bank had to directly confront the shortcomings of its development approach when Mexico—a model of economic management according to the Western policy establishment—encountered a serious financial crisis and appealed for emergency loans. Mexico had implemented an economic strategy based largely on the Bank model and had signed the NAFTA with the United States and Canada. The Bank was also subject to criticisms that it was more interested in loan approval than development effectiveness and accountability, that it was lending to corrupt governments such as the Suharto regime in Indonesia, and that it was devoting too little attention to social and environmental effects of its projects.[112] On the fiftieth anniversary of the Bretton Woods agreements in 1994, NGOs launched a "Fifty Years Is Enough" campaign, which strongly criticized the Bank for failing to alleviate poverty and promote environmentally sustainable development. At the same time, the Bank faced new challenges to its financial influence. Whereas private capital flows to LDCs increased from $40.9 billion in 1990 to $256 billion in 1997, multilateral and bilateral development assistance declined from 57 to only 15 percent of all net financial flows to LDCs. Thus, the Bank had to alter its approach to development if it was to continue to be an effective development institution.[113]

1995 to the Present

James Wolfensohn was appointed the new Bank President in June 1995, and he "promised to revolutionize the Bank and finish the...business of internal reform long overdue."[114] In some respects Wolfensohn acted to update the Bank and prepare it for a role in the twenty-first century. For example, Wolfensohn devoted attention to the issues of corruption, HIV/AIDS, the role of women, and the role of the Bank in the information revolution. Corruption had been a taboo subject in the Bank because it could be interpreted as interference in politics, but Wolfensohn argued that corruption interfered with development and therefore had to be a Bank concern. Despite resistance from many Bank member states as well as Bank staff, Wolfensohn also increased the Bank's involvement in HIV/AIDs programs. Furthermore, Wolfensohn focused considerable attention on upgrading the role of women in the Bank's professional staff and in LDCs, and he pressed the Bank staff to take more leadership as a source of information on development ideas. In addition to updating the Bank, Wolfensohn's appointment of Joseph Stiglitz as senior vice-president and senior economist of the Bank signaled a change in the Bank's approach to poverty reduction, the state's role in development, and the top-down imposition of conditionality. Stiglitz, who was formerly chair of the U.S. Council of Economic Advisors, had called for limits to privatization and a stronger state role in development. Although some critics argued that Stiglitz was merely repackaging orthodox liberal ideas, most believed that he sought genuine changes in Bank policy.[115]

In regard to the state, the Bank's 1997 *World Development Report* argued that state minimalism "is at odds with the evidence of the world's development success stories," and described development as requiring "an effective state, one that plays a catalytic, facilitating role, encouraging and complementing the activities of private businesses and individuals."[116] The report also indicated that Africa had to "rebuild state effectiveness...through an overhaul of public institutions, reassertion of the rule of law, and credible checks on abuse of state power."[117] However, the report warned against state-dominated development and called for "a contraction of the role of the state" in South Asia, because overregulation was "both a cause and effect of bloated public employment and the surest route to corruption."[118] Regarding poverty, in 1995 the Bank initiated the creation of a *Consultative Group to Assist the Poorest (CGAP)*, a multi-donor effort to increase the resources for microfinance. The Bank also consulted about 60,000 poor people in more than 50 states for a *Voices of the Poor* study, and the theme of the Bank's 2000–2001 *World Development Report* was "Attacking Poverty."[119] A third change was Wolfensohn's introduction of a *Comprehensive Development Framework (CDF)* in 1999. The CDF took a more holistic approach than structural adjustment, emphasizing the linkages among the economic, social, and institutional aspects of development. Unlike the coercive conditionality of structural adjustment, the CDF was a consultative framework for development finance that emphasized partnership among the Bank, recipient governments, and civil society.[120]

Despite the Bank's expressed intentions to move away from the Washington consensus, there are reasons to question the degree to which it is actually shifting policy. First, it is easier for the Bank to verbally support new objectives than to implement them in practice. To satisfy critics, the Bank has broadened its objectives to include poverty reduction, governance, democratic development and human rights, women in development, the environment, corruption, and microfinance; these are all positive objectives, but they have overloaded the Bank's agenda.[121] Second, global events have constrained the Bank's ability to alter its strategies. For example, the 1997 *World Development Report* on the need for an effective state was released shortly before the East Asian financial crisis. Orthodox liberals argued that the crisis demonstrated the weakness of East Asia's developmental state model, and Japan's economic problems added weight to their arguments. A third reason for constraints on the Bank was the reaction of its members, especially the United States. Stiglitz asked a development economics professor—Ravi Kanbur—to oversee the writing of the 2000–2001 *World Development Report* on attacking poverty, but the United States, the Bank, and the IMF charged that the draft report gave too little emphasis to economic growth. Some Bank members also had other criticisms, such as viewing the Bank's CDF as "a capitulation to NGOs."[122] Stiglitz and Kanbur eventually left the Bank in response to the criticisms, and at the end of Wolfensohn's term, Paul Wolfowitz replaced him as the next Bank president.

Wolfowitz was Bank president for only two years (June 2005 to June 2007) in a period marked by controversy. He came to the Bank amid strong protests over his role as a key architect of U.S. military operations in Iraq and Afghanistan. During his tenure, Wolfowitz alienated many Bank staff members by attempting to run the Bank through personal aides and by remaining too closely tied to U.S. policies. He tried to continue Wolfensohn's campaign against corruption in LDCs, but his actions were taken "without sufficient consultation and engagement of the World Bank staff or...its Board and shareholders."[123] Thus, there was little sympathy for him when he was accused of offering special favors to a Bank employee with whom he had a special relationship, and he was forced to resign. Despite wide calls for an open selection process, the United States wanted to continue appointing the Bank president, and Europeans supported this because of their wish to continue appointing the IMF Managing Director. In July 2007, Robert Zoellick, former U.S. Trade Representative and Deputy Secretary of State, became the next Bank president.

Although Zoellick has done much to smooth tensions in the Bank related to his predecessor, he will have to continue redefining the Bank's role if it is to continue to influence development policy. A number of LDCs—especially in Latin America—are dissatisfied with the Washington consensus and are reassessing their own development strategies. In the 1980s, there was great hope that Latin America's acceptance of market economics and democracy, combined with the United States' decreasing emphasis on security matters, would result in closer and more cooperative linkages. For example, there were predictions that a Free Trade Area of the Americas (FTAA) would bring about unprecedented convergence in the Western Hemisphere. However, the FTAA talks collapsed and there has been a backlash in some Latin American countries "against the predominant trends of the last 15 years: free-market reforms, agreement with the United States on a number of issues, and the consolidation of representative democracy."[124] A major reason for this change was that political and economic reform in Latin America did not achieve the desired results. China, India, and Malaysia had economic growth rates well above those of Latin America, which continued to be the world's most unequal region in the distribution of wealth. Defenders of the Washington consensus attribute Latin America's economic problems to poor policy decisions and the inadequate implementation of liberal reforms.[125] However, critics of the Washington consensus point to the pitfalls of an unrestrained free market, the dislocations associated with privatization and trade liberalization, and the environmental costs of orthodox liberal reform. Whereas historical materialists want to expand the domain of the state in development, interventionist liberals argue that the state and the market complement each other. Thus, they call for a post-Washington consensus, in which the state would help overcome market failure, and open markets and democratic governance would help prevent state failure.[126] Two left-wing currents have emerged in Latin America. The more extreme current in Venezuela and Bolivia is populist, nationalist, and stridently anti-American. The more moderate current in Chile, Uruguay, and Brazil emphasizes social policy within a market framework, welcomes economic linkages with the United States, and rarely takes disagreements with the United States "to the brink."[127] Interventionist liberals argue that willingness to accept a post-Washington consensus based on state-market complementarity may encourage the moderate current in Latin America and in other parts of the South.

Considering IPE Theory and Practice

The postwar period has generally been marked by prosperity and economic growth for DCs of the North, but this has not been the case for the poorer LDCs and peoples in the South. This chapter examines the strategies LDCs have used in attempts to promote their economic development and discusses the important role the World Bank has played as the largest multilateral development organization in framing debates on these strategies. The discussion of ISI, socialist, export-led growth, and orthodox liberal models provides some basis for drawing conclusions about the most appropriate development strategies.

First, all the development strategies have shortcomings, and one is unlikely to find the "perfect" strategy. Development is a more difficult and complex process than Walt Rostow had indicated in *The Stages of Economic Growth*.[128] Rostow's claim that an LDC's growth would become self-sustaining when it reached the "takeoff stage" raised false hopes that economic development was a readily achievable and irreversible process. As new development strategies emerge, there is always the danger of raising unrealistic expectations. For example, some analysts argue that "too much is claimed for microfinance, and that expectations are grossly exaggerated."[129] Despite the advantages of microfinance in reaching the poor, it is criticized for encouraging poor households to accept loans they may not be able to service, and for focusing on credit and loans when people have more need for savings and insurance. Microfinance also has limitations in reaching the poor. Although the 1997 Microcredit Summit in Washington, D.C. launched a nine-year goal of reaching 100 million of the world's poorest families, microfinance levels have fallen far short of this goal. Thus, no development strategy may be adequate by itself, and LDCs may need to employ a combination of strategies.

Second, whereas liberal prescriptions for economic growth emphasize the need for domestic changes, historical materialists focus on the need to alter international relations (e.g., relations of dependency). In reality, economic development is a complex process that requires *both* domestic and international changes. Only a small number of LDCs such as the East Asian NIEs and more recently China and India have been able to meet both the domestic and international requirements for rapid economic development; the 1990s East Asian financial crisis shows that such rapid growth may be subject to setbacks (see Chapter 11). A third related point is that the same development strategy is neither feasible nor desirable for all LDCs. Although East and Southeast Asian LDCs achieved impressive economic growth rates through export-led growth, it is unlikely that many other LDCs could emulate their experience. The East Asian NIEs' success resulted from a confluence of favorable external and domestic circumstances, such as U.S. and Japanese support and the presence of highly skilled, technocratic government bureaucracies. These characteristics are often lacking in poorer African and Asian LDCs. The return to liberal orthodoxy in the 1980s has also prevented many LDCs from following state-led growth policies. Instead, IMF and World Bank SAPs have pressured LDC debtors to engage in deregulation, privatization, and other measures to downsize the role of the state.[130]

Fourth, negative experiences with IMF and World Bank SAPs have pointed to the pitfalls of focusing on the economic aspects of development without looking sufficiently at the social and human aspects. Thus, the UNDP began publishing a *Human Development Report* in 1990 to emphasize that there is "no automatic link between growth and human development."[131] The human development approach assesses development not only in terms of a country's per capita GDP growth but also in terms of life expectancy; health and sanitation; education; employment; and the income, gender, and rural–urban gaps. The IMF and World Bank also at first overlooked the environmental implications of SAPs. They simply assumed that by stimulating market-oriented reforms SAPs would lead to improved environmental management. However, critics argued that IMF and World Bank prescriptions such as currency devaluation and the removal of trade and investment restrictions would increase unsustainable exports of natural resources and pollution-intensive foreign investment in LDCs.[132] In response to these criticisms, the Bank has increased its efforts to understand the linkages between economic development on the one hand and human development and the environment on the other.

Fifth, an economic development strategy should strike a realistic balance between the state and the market. Whereas ISI policies emphasize state intervention and give too little consideration to market signals, orthodox liberalism disregards the fact that late industrializers require an active role for the state. East Asian governments were adept at using state–market interactions to their advantage, and this enabled them to register some striking economic gains. However, the East Asians also sometimes substituted "political whim…for proper risk assessment for commercial activities," and their failure to provide adequate banking regulations helped precipitate the 1990s financial crisis.[133] The East Asian experience shows the importance of finding the amount and type of government regulation that will ensure economic stability and the proper functioning of market signals. Sixth, an economic development strategy should take account of North–South differences in wealth and power. Between 1980

(*continued*)

(*continued*)

and 2001, per capita income in all regions of the South except South Asia and East Asia and the Pacific declined relative to per capita income in the North, and the debt and financial crises were a reminder of the degree to which the South is still dependent on the North. Although Northern linkages in trade, foreign investment, and other economic areas are critical to the South, development strategies should provide the South with some special and differential treatment and give it some room for independent action (within the limits of global interdependence). One possible route to greater self-sufficiency is through establishing more South–South economic linkages.[134]

Finally, the Washington consensus has *not* become the only broadly-accepted approach to economic development today. As discussed, negative experiences with IMF and World Bank SAPs raised awareness that the unrestrained market is not the answer to LDC problems. The East Asians also did not totally abandon their developmental state export-led growth model after the 1990s financial crisis. It is important to note that "contrary to expectations all these countries rapidly returned to levels of growth comparable to those prior to the crisis," and that they have "become more involved in the global financial and trading systems without fully converging to the Washington consensus norms."[135] Thus, we are in a post-Washington consensus period in which most scholars believe that market discipline must be mediated by some state involvement. In sum, the realist, liberal, and critical perspectives all have something important to say regarding development strategies. Furthermore, there is no single best development strategy for all LDCs because of major differences among these states and their positions in the world. A variety of development strategies will be pursued in the future, as they have been in the past.

Questions

1. Why do the DCs give official development assistance (ODA), and why have the ODA levels fluctuated over the years? What are some of the debates regarding the effectiveness of aid-giving?
2. Why has the World Bank group been so important in a development context, and how influential has the United States been in the Bank group?
3. What are the five main institutions of the World Bank group, and what functions do they perform?
4. How would you compare the effectiveness of import substitution and export-led growth strategies? Do you think that other LDCs could pursue export-led growth strategies as effectively as the East Asian NIEs?

5. What are structural adjustment loans, and how have they affected LDCs, women, and the poorest groups in LDCs?
6. What is the Washington consensus, and what form do you think a post-Washington consensus should take?
7. How has the World Bank attempted to change its approach to development, and how successful has it been?
8. What do you think is the best approach to development, and why?

Further Reading

Three prominent books that take diverse approaches to development and aid-giving are Jeffrey D. Sachs, *The End of Poverty: Economic Possibilities of Our Time* (New York: Penguin, 2005); William Easterly, *The White Man's Burden* (New York: Penguin, 2006); and Paul Collier, *The Bottom Billion* (New York: Oxford University Press, 2007). A study with good articles on development assistance is Tony Addison and George Mavrotas, *Development Finance in the Global Economy: The Road Ahead* (New York: Palgrave Macmillan, 2008). On the millennium development goals, see Fantu Cheru and Colin Bradford, Jr., eds., *The Millennium Development Goals: Raising the Resources to Tackle World Poverty* (New York: Zed Books, 2005).

Important general studies of the World Bank that take a generally positive approach include Devesh Kapur, John P. Lewis, and Richard Webb, *The World Bank: Its First Half Century, Vol. I: History* (Washington, D.C.: Brookings Institution Press, 1997); and Katherine Marshall, *The World Bank: From Reconstruction to Development to Equity* (New York: Routledge, 2008). More critical studies of the Bank include Jonathan R. Pincus and Jeffrey A. Winters, eds., *Reinventing the World Bank* (Ithaca, NY: Cornell University Press, 2002); and Eric Toussaint, *The World Bank: A Critical Primer* (Ann Arbor, MI: Pluto Press, 2008). On the regional development banks, see Volume 5 in a series on multilateral development banks: Roy Culpeper, *Titans or Behemoths?* (Boulder, CO: Lynne Rienner, 1997). Other books in the series are on the African, Asian, Caribbean, and Inter-American Development Banks.

Useful general studies of major development issues and strategies are John Rapley, *Understanding Development: Theory and Practice in the Third World* (Boulder, CO: 1996); and Damien Kingsbury, et al., *International Development: Issues and Challenges* (New York: Palgrave Macmillan, 2008). On the realist approach to North–South relations and development strategies, see Stephen D. Krasner, *Structural Conflict: The Third World Against Global Liberalism* (Berkeley, CA: University of California Press, 1985); and Robert Wade, *Governing the Market: Economic Theory and the Role of Government in East Asian Industrialization* (Princeton, NJ: Princeton University Press, 1990). On the Washington Consensus and its aftermath, see Ben Fine, Costas Lapavitsas, and Jonathan Pincus, eds., *Development Policy in the Twenty-First Century: Beyond the Post-Washington Consensus* (London: Routledge, 2001); and Pedro-Pablo Kuczynski and John Williamson, eds., *After the Washington Consensus: Restarting Growth and Reform in Latin America* (Washington, D.C.: Institute for International Economics, 2003). For competing studies on microfinance, see Bernd Balkenhol, ed., *Microfinance and Public Policy* (New York: Palgrave Macmillan, 2007); and Thomas Dichter and Malcolm Harper, eds., *What's Wrong with Microfinance?* (Bourton, UK: Practical Action Publishing, 2007).

Notes

1. Bretton Woods Commission, *Bretton Woods: Looking to the Future* (Washington, D.C.: Bretton Woods Committee, 1994), p. B3.
2. UN Department of Economic and Social Affairs, *The Inequality Predicament: Report on the World Social Situation 2005* (New York: United Nations, 2005), pp. 47–51; World Bank, *World Development Report 2006* (Washington, D.C.: Oxford University Press, 2006), p. 56; Howard Handelman, *The Challenge of Third World Development* (Upper Saddle River, NJ: Prentice Hall, 1996), pp. 3–10.
3. World Bank, *World Development Report 1991* (New York: Oxford University Press, 1991), pp. 2–3; UN, *The Inequality Predicament,* pp. 50–55, 68–71.
4. Stephan Haggard, *Developing Nations and the Politics of Global Integration* (Washington, D.C.: Brookings Institution, 1995), p. 1.
5. Robert Wade, "Japan, the World Bank, and the Art of Paradigm Maintenance: The East Asian Miracle in Political Perspective," *New Left Review* 217 (May/June 1996), p. 5.
6. Stephen D. Krasner, *Structural Conflict: The Third World Against Global Liberalism* (Berkeley, CA: University of California Press, 1985), p. 3.
7. OECD, *Development Co-operation Report 2007* (Paris: Organization for Economic Cooperation and Development, 2008), p. 231.
8. Alberto Alesina and David Dollar, "Who Gives Foreign Aid to Whom and Why?" *Journal of Economic Growth* 5, no. 1 (March 2000), pp. 33–63; Ngaire Woods, "The Shifting Politics of Foreign Aid," *International Affairs* 81, no. 2 (2005), p. 394; Tomohisa Hattori, "Reconceptualizing Foreign Aid," *Review of International Political Economy* 8, no. 4 (Winter 2001), p. 634.
9. Kevin Watkins and Penny Fowler, *Rigged Rules and Double Standards: Trade, Globalization and the Fight Against Poverty* (Boston: Oxfam International, 2002), p. 8.
10. Janet Hunt, "Aid and Development," in Damien Kinsbury, et al., *International Development: Issues and Challenges* (New York: Palgrave Macmillan, 2008), pp. 92–95.
11. Jeffrey D. Sachs, *The End of Poverty: Economic Possibilities for Our Time* (New York: Penguin, 2005), pp. 56–57.
12. William Easterly, *The White Man's Burden* (New York: Penguin, 2006), p. 45.
13. This recommendation is contained in *Partners in Development—Report of the Commission on International Development* (New York: Praeger, 1969), p. 152.
14. Peter Burnell, "Foreign Aid Resurgent: New Spirit or Old Hangover?" in Tony Addison and George Mavrotas, eds., *Development Finance in the Global Economy: The Road Ahead* (New York: Palgrave Macmillan, 2008), pp. 24–33; Woods, "The Shifting Politics of Foreign Aid," p. 397.
15. Sylvanus I. Ikhide, "Reforming the International Financial System for Effective Aid Delivery," *World Economy* 27, no. 2 (February 2004), p. 149.
16. Alesina and Dollar, "Who Gives Foreign Aid to Whom and Why?" p. 55; Woods, "The Shifting Politics of Foreign Aid," p. 401; Hunt, "Aid and Development," p. 81.
17. "UN Millennium Development Goals," http://www.un.org/millenniumgoals.
18. Hunt, "Aid and Development," pp. 78–80.
19. Gustav Ranis, "The World Bank Near the Turn of the Century," in Roy Culpeper, Albert Berry, and Frances Stewart, eds., *Global Development Fifty Years After Bretton Woods* (New York: St. Martin's Press, 1997), p. 73.

20. Ranis, "The World Bank Near the Turn of the Century," p. 73.
21. Wade, "Japan, the World Bank, and the Art of Paradigm Maintenance," p. 5.
22. Peter M. Haas, "Introduction: Epistemic Communitites and International Policy Coordination," *International Organization* 46, no. 1 (Winter 1992), p. 3.
23. Barry Eichengreen and Peter B. Kenen, "Managing the World Economy under the Bretton Woods System: An Overview," in Peter B. Kenen, ed., *Managing the World Economy: Fifty Years After Bretton Woods* (Washington, D.C.: Institute for International Economics, 1994), p. 6.
24. Edward S. Mason and Robert E. Asher, *The World Bank Since Bretton Woods* (Washington, D.C.: Brookings Institution, 1973), pp. 52–53; Robert E. Wood, *From Marshall Plan to Debt Crisis: Foreign Aid and Development Choices in the World Economy* (Berkeley, CA: University of California Press, 1986), p. 29.
25. World Bank, *World Bank Annual Report 2008* (Washington, D.C.: World Bank, 2008), CD-ROM.
26. Devesh Kapur, "The Changing Anatomy of Governance of the World Bank," in Jonathan R. Pincus and Jeffrey A. Winters, *Reinventing the World Bank* (Ithaca, NY: Cornell University Press, 2002), pp. 54–59.
27. International Finance Corporation, *IFC Annual Report 1995* (Washington, D.C.: International Finance Corporation, 1995), pp. 5–6; "Hey, Big Lender," *The Economist,* April 23, 1994, pp. 81–82.
28. A. Geske Dijkstra, *The Impact of International Debt Relief* (New York: Routledge, 2008), pp. 118–119.
29. *World Bank Annual Report 2008,* CD-ROM.
30. Ibrahim F. I. Shihata, *MIGA and Foreign Investment: Origins, Operations, Policies and Basic Documents of the Multilateral Investment Guarantee Agency* (Boston, MA: Nijhoff, 1988).
31. Anne O. Krueger, Constantine Michalopoulos, and Vernon W. Ruttan, with Keith Jay, *Aid and Development* (Baltimore, MD: Johns Hopkins University Press, 1989), pp. 106–108.
32. Roy Culpeper, *Titans or Behemoths? The Multilateral Development Banks* (Boulder, CO: Lynne Rienner, 1997).
33. Theodore Cohn, "Developing Countries in the International Civil Service: The Case of the World Bank Group," *International Review of Administrative Sciences* 41, no. 1 (1975), pp. 47–56.
34. Stephen Fidler, "Who's Minding the Bank?" *Foreign Policy* 126 (September/October 2001), p. 41; Miles Kahler, *Leadership Selection in the Major Multilaterals* (Washington, D.C.: Institute for International Economics, 2001), pp. 42–49.
35. Kapur, "The Changing Anatomy of Governance of the World Bank," pp. 58–64.
36. Joseph S. Nye, Jr., "Soft Power," *Foreign Policy* 80 (Fall 1990), p. 166.
37. Thomas B. Andersen, Henrik Hansen, and Thomas Markussen, "US Politics and World Bank IDA-Lending," *Journal of Development Studies* 42, no. 5 (July 2006), pp. 772–794.
38. William Ascher, "The World Bank and U.S. Control," in Margaret P. Karns and Karen A. Mingst, eds., *The United States and Multilateral Institutions* (Boston, MA: Unwin Hyman, 1990), p. 115.
39. Cheryl Payer, *The World Bank: A Critical Analysis* (New York: Monthly Review Press, 1982), p. 20.
40. Peter T. Bauer, *Reality and Rhetoric: Studies in the Economics of Development* (London: Weidenfeld and Nicolson, 1984), p. 70; Kalman Mizsei, "The Role of the Bretton Woods Institutions in the Transforming Economies," in Bretton Woods

Commission, *Bretton Woods: Looking to the Future* (Washington, D.C.: Bretton Woods Committee, 1994), p. C–103.

41. Robin Broad, "Research, Knowledge, and the Art of 'Paradigm Maintenance': The World Bank's Development Economics Vice-Presidency (DEC)," *Review of International Political Economy* 13, no. 3 (August 2006), pp. 390–393; Robert L. Ayres, *Banking on the Poor: The World Bank and World Poverty* (Cambridge, MA: MIT Press, 1983), p. 15.

42. Ranis, "The World Bank Near the Turn of the Century," p. 76.

43. Fidler, "Who's Minding the Bank?" p. 45.

44. Stephan Haggard, ed., *The International Political Economy and the Developing Countries,* vol. I (Brookfield, VT: Edward Elgar, 1995), p. xv.

45. Raúl Prebisch, *The Economic Development of Latin America and Its Principal Problems* (New York: UN Economic Commission for Latin America, 1950), pp. 1–59; Hans W. Singer, "The Distribution of Gains Between Investing and Borrowing Countries," *American Economic Review* 40, no. 2 (May 1950), pp. 473–485.

46. Anil Hira, *Ideas and Economic Policy in Latin America: Regional, National, and Organizational Case Studies* (Westport, CT: Praeger, 1998), ch. 3.

47. Ozay Mehmet, *Westernizing the Third World: The Eurocentricity of Economic Development Theories* (London: Routledge, 1995), p. 78; John Rapley, *Understanding Development: Theory and Practice* (Boulder, CO: Lynne Rienner, 1996), pp. 27–34.

48. Luiz C. B. Pereira, "Development Economics and the World Bank's Identity Crisis," *Review of International Political Economy* 2, no. 2 (Spring 1995), pp. 215–217; Devesh Kapur, John P. Lewis, and Richard Webb, *The World Bank: Its First Half Century,* vol. 1 (Washington, D.C.: Brookings Institution, 1997), p. 451.

49. Rapley, *Understanding Development,* pp. 27–36; Theodore Cohn, *Canadian Food Aid: Domestic and Foreign Policy Implications* (Denver, CO: University of Denver Graduate School in International Studies, 1979), pp. 25–27.

50. Sylvia Maxfield and James N. Nolt, "Protectionism and the Internationalization of Capital: U.S. Sponsorship of Import Substitution Industrialization in the Philippines, Turkey and Argentina," *International Studies Quarterly* 34, no. 1 (March 1990), p. 50.

51. Anne O. Krueger, *Trade Policies and Developing Nations* (Washington, D.C.: Brookings Institution, 1995), pp. 3–10, 33–44; Stephan Haggard, *Pathways from the Periphery: The Politics of Growth in the Newly Industrializing Countries* (Ithaca, NY: Cornell University Press, 1990), pp. 9–14.

52. Anne O. Krueger, "The Effects of Trade Strategies on Growth," *Finance and Development* 20, no. 2 (June 1983), p. 8.

53. Mason and Asher, *The World Bank Since Bretton Woods,* pp. 378–379.

54. Raúl Prebisch, *Towards a Dynamic Development Policy for Latin America* (New York: United Nations, 1963), p. 71.

55. Bela Balassa, "The Process of Industrial Development and Alternative Development Strategies," in Bela Balassa, ed., *The Newly Industrializing Countries in the World Economy* (New York: Pergamon Press, 1981), pp. 5–16.

56. Joseph L. Love, "The Origins of Dependency Analysis," *Journal of Latin American Studies* 22 (February 1990), pp. 143–160. This section draws partly on Rapley, *Understanding Development,* pp. 44–47.

57. James H. Mittelman and Mustapha K. Pasha, *Out from Underdevelopment Revisited: Changing Global Structures and the Remaking of the Third World,* 2nd ed. (London: Macmillan, 1997), pp. 181–214.

58. John M. Page, "The East Asian Miracle: An Introduction," *World Development* 22, no. 4 (1994), p. 619; Robert Wade, *Governing the Market: Economic Theory and the Role of Government in East Asian Industrialization* (Princeton, NJ: Princeton University Press, 1990), p. 34.
59. Arnold C. Harberger, "Growth, Industrialization and Economic Structure: Latin America and East Asia Compared," in Helen Hughes, ed., *Achieving Industrialization in East Asia* (New York: Cambridge University Press, 1988), pp. 164–194; Haggard, *Pathways from the Periphery,* chs. 3–7; Bela Balassa, *Policy Choices for the 1990s* (London: Macmillan, 1993), pp. 56–67.
60. Wade, *Governing the Market,* p. 34.
61. Krueger, *Trade Policies and Developing Nations,* pp. 20–23.
62. Staffan B. Linder, *The Pacific Century: Economic and Political Consequences of Asian-Pacific Dynamism* (Stanford, CA: Stanford University Press, 1986), p. 31; Bela Balassa, *The Newly Industrializing Countries in the World Economy* (New York: Pergamon Press, 1981), pp. 6–24.
63. Ronen Palan and Jason Abbott, with Phil Deans, *State Strategies in the Global Political Economy* (London: Pinter, 1996), p. 78.
64. Chalmers Johnson, "Introduction—The Taiwan Model," in James C. Hsiung et al., eds., *Contemporary Republic of China: The Taiwan Experience 1950–1980* (New York: Praeger, 1981), pp. 9–18; Chalmers Johnson, *MITI and the Japanese Miracle: The Growth of Industrial Policy, 1925–1975* (Stanford, CA: Stanford University Press, 1982).
65. Peter Evans, *Dependent Development: The Alliance of Multinational, State, and Local Capital in Brazil* (Princeton, NJ: Princeton University Press, 1979), p. 33.
66. Quoted in William Nester, "The Development of Japan, Taiwan and South Korea: Ends and Means, Free Trade, Dependency, or Neomercantilism?" *Journal of Developing Societies* 6 (1990), p. 206.
67. Cal Clark and Steve Chan, "MNCs and Developmentalism: Domestic Structure as an Explanation for East Asian Dynamism," in Thomas Risse-Kappen, ed., *Bringing Transnational Relations Back In: Non-State Actors, Domestic Structures and International Institutions* (New York: Cambridge University Press, 1995), p. 125.
68. Lucian W. Pye with Mary W. Pye, *Asian Power and Politics: The Cultural Dimensions of Authority* (Cambridge, MA: Belknap Press, 1985), ch. 3.
69. Christopher Lingle, "What Ever Happened to the 'Asian Century'?" *World Economic Affairs* 2, no. 2 (Spring 1998), p. 32.
70. World Bank, *The East Asian Miracle: Economic Growth and Public Policy* (New York: Oxford University Press, 1993), p. 1.
71. Graham Bird and Alistair Milne, "Miracle to Meltdown: A Pathology of the East Asian Financial Crisis," *Third World Quarterly* 20, no. 2 (1999), p. 421.
72. Stephan Haggard, *The Political Economy of the Asian Financial Crisis* (Washington, D.C.: Institute for International Economics, 2000), p. 3; Shahid Yusuf, "The East Asian Miracle at the Millennium," in Joseph E. Stiglitz and Shahid Yusuf, eds., *Rethinking the East Asian Miracle* (New York: Oxford University Press, 2001), pp. 1–4.
73. Bird and Milne, "Miracle to Meltdown," p. 422.
74. Walter Hatch and Kozo Yamamura, *Asia in Japan's Embrace: Building a Regional Production Alliance* (New York: Cambridge University Press, 1996), p. 37.
75. Walden Bello and Stephanie Rosenfeld, *Dragons in Distress: Asia's Miracle Economies in Crisis* (San Francisco, CA: Institute for Food and Development Policy, 1990), pp. 3–10; Jim Glassman and Pádraig Carmody, "Structural

Adjustment in East and Southeast Asia: Lessons from Latin America," *Geoforum* 32, no. 1 (February 2001), pp. 79–80.

76. Samuel P. Huntington, *Political Order in Changing Societies* (New Haven, CT: Yale University Press, 1968).

77. Haggard, *The Political Economy of the Asian Financial Crisis,* p. 4.

78. Stephan Haggard and Andrew MacIntyre, "The Political Economy of the Asian Economic Crisis," *Review of International Political Economy* 5, no. 3 (Autumn 1998), p. 405.

79. Paul Krugman, "The Myth of Asia's Miracle," *Foreign Affairs* 73, no. 6 (November/December 1994), p. 67.

80. Walden Bello, "Overview of Current Economic, Strategic and Political Developments in Southeast and South Asia," *Focus Files* (Bangkok, Thailand, October 1997), p. 3.

81. World Commission on Environment and Development, *Our Common Future* (New York: Oxford University Press, 1987), p. 8.

82. Handelman, *The Challenge of Third World Development,* p. 228.

83. Palan and Abbott, *State Strategies in the Global Political Economy,* p. 99.

84. Christopher L. Gilbert and David Vines, "The World Bank: An Overview of Some Major Issues," in Christopher L. Gilbert and David Vines, eds., *The World Bank: Structure and Policies* (New York: Cambridge University Press, 2000), p. 16.

85. John Williamson, "Democracy and the 'Washington Consensus,'" *World Development* 21, no. 8 (August 1993), pp. 1329–1336.

86. Rapley, *Understanding Development,* p. 76.

87. Farhad Noorbakhsh and Alberto Paloni, "Structural Adjustment and Growth in Sub-Saharan Africa: The Importance of Complying with Conditionality," *Economic Development and Cultural Change* 49, no. 3 (April 2000), pp. 479–509; cited in Bob Milward, "The Heavily Indebted Poor Countries and the Role of Structural Adjustment Policies," in *Developments in Economics: An Annual Review* (Lancashire, UK: Causeway Books, 2001), p. 38; J. Barry Riddell, "Things Fall Apart Again: Structural Adjustment Programmes in Sub-Saharan Africa," *Journal of Modern African Studies* 30, no. 1 (1992), p. 67.

88. Gloria Thomas-Emeagwali, "Introductory Perspectives: Monetarists, Liberals and Radicals: Contrasting Perspectives on Gender and Structural Adjustment," in Gloria Thomas-Emeagwali, ed., *Women Pay the Price: Structural Adjustment in Africa and the Caribbean* (Trenton, NJ: Africa World Press, 1995), p. 5.

89. Thomas-Emeagwali, "Introductory Perspectives," pp. 3–4.

90. James H. Weaver, "What Is Structural Adjustment?" in Daniel M. Schydlowsky, ed., *Structural Adjustment: Retrospect and Prospect* (Westport, CT: Praeger, 1995), pp. 12–13; Barend A. de Vries, "The World Bank's Focus on Poverty," in Jo M. Griesgraber and Berhard G. Gunter, eds., *The World Bank: Lending on a Global Scale* (London: Pluto Press, 1996), pp. 68–69.

91. Quoted in Julius O. Ihonvbere, "Economic Crisis, Structural Adjustment and Africa's Future," in Gloria Thomas-Emeagwali, ed., *Women Pay the Price: Structural Adjustment in Africa and the Caribbean* (Trenton, NJ: Africa World Press, 1995), p. 137; World Bank, *World Development Report 2003* (New York: Oxford University Press, 2003), pp. 234–235.

92. For a defense of World Bank SAPs in Africa, see Elliot Berg, "African Adjustment Programs: False Attacks and True Dilemmas," in Daniel M. Schydlowsky, ed., *Structural Adjustment: Retrospect and Prospect* (Westport, CT: Praeger, 1995), 89–107.

93. Rapley, *Understanding Development,* pp. 83–92; Riddell, "Things Fall Apart Again: Structural Adjustment Programmes in Sub-Saharan Africa," pp. 53–68.
94. Frances Stewart, "Can Adjustment Programmes Incorporate the Interests of Women?" in Haleh Afshar and Carolyne Dennis, eds., *Women and Adjustment Policies in the Third World* (New York: St. Martin's Press, 1992), pp. 22–24.
95. Diane Elson, "Male Bias in Macro-Economics: The Case of Structural Adjustment," in Diane Elson, ed., *Male Bias in the Development Process* (Manchester, UK: Manchester University Press, 1991), pp. 175–178.
96. Stewart, "Can Adjustment Programmes Incorporate the Interests of Women?" p. 27.
97. Elson, "Male Bias in Macro-Economics," p. 173; Stewart, "Can Adjustment Programmes Incorporate the Interests of Women?" p. 22.
98. World Bank, *World Development Report 1991,* p. 9.
99. Ben Fine, "Neither the Washington nor the Post-Washington Consensus: An Introduction," in Ben Fine, Costas Lapavitsas, and Jonathan Pincus, eds., *Development Policy in the Twenty-First Century: Beyond the Post-Washington Consensus* (London: Routledge, 2001), p. 12.
100. World Bank, *The East Asian Miracle: Economic Growth and Public Policy* (New York: Oxford University Press, 1993), p. 1.
101. World Bank, *The East Asian Miracle,* p. 274.
102. K. S. Jomo, "Rethinking the Role of Government Policy in Southeast Asia," in Joseph E. Stiglitz and Shahid Yusuf, eds., *Rethinking the East Asian Miracle* (New York: Oxford University Press, 2001), p. 462.
103. World Bank, *The East Asian Miracle,* p. 26.
104. Ravi Kanbur and David Vines, "The World Bank and Poverty Reduction: Past, Present and Future," in Christopher L. Gilbert and David Vines, eds., *The World Bank: Structure and Policies* (New York: Cambridge University Press, 2000), pp. 87–107.
105. Mohammed H. Malek, "Towards an Integrated Aid and Development Programme for Europe," in Mohammed H. Malek, ed., *Contemporary Issues in European Development Aid* (Brookfield, VT: Avebury, 1991), p. 142.
106. OECD, *Twenty-five Years of Development Co-operation: A Review—1985 Report* (Paris: Organization for Economic Cooperation and Development, November 1985), p. 49; Ayres, *Banking on the Poor,* pp. 4–6; Anthony Bottrall, "The McNamara Strategy: Putting Precept into Practice," *ODI Review* 1 (1974), pp. 70–80.
107. Giovannia A. Cornia, Richard Jolly, and Frances Stewart, eds., *Adjustment with a Human Face, Vol. 1: Protecting the Vulnerable and Promoting Growth* (Oxford, UK: Clarendon Press, 1987), p. 7.
108. World Bank, *Sub-Saharan Africa: From Crisis to Sustainable Growth, a Long-Term Perspective Study* (Washington D.C.: World Bank, 1989), pp. 17, xi. See also Ihonvbere, "Economic Crisis, Structural Adjustment and Africa's Future," pp. 138–147.
109. See World Bank, *World Development Report 1990, "Poverty"* (New York: Oxford University Press, 1990).
110. Paul B. McGuire and John D. Conroy, "The Microfinance Phenomenon," *Asia-Pacific Review* 7, no. 1 (2000), pp. 90–93; Alex Counts, *Small Loans, Big Dreams* (Hoboken, NJ: John Wiley, 2008), pp. 201–206.
111. Jonathan Morduch, "The Microfinance Promise," *Journal of Economic Literature* 37, no. 4 (December 1999), p. 1570.
112. Bruce Rich, "The World Bank under James Wolfensohn," in Jonathan R. Pincus and Jeffrey A. Winters, *Reinventing the World Bank* (Ithaca, NY: Cornell University Press, 2002), pp. 27–29.

113. John Pender, "From 'Structural Adjustment' to Comprehensive Development Framework: Conditionality Transformed?" *Third World Quarterly* 22, no. 3 (2001), p. 402; Rich, "The World Bank under James Wolfensohn," p. 28.

114. Rich, "The World Bank under James Wolfensohn," p. 26.

115. Pender, "From 'Structural Adjustment' to Comprehensive Development Framework," pp. 402–403; Guy Standing, "Brave New Words? A Critique of Stiglitz's World Bank Rethink," *Development and Change* 31, no. 4 (2000), pp. 737–763.

116. World Bank, *World Development Report 1997* (New York: Oxford University Press, 1997) foreword, p. iii.

117. World Bank, *World Development Report 1997,* p. 14.

118. World Bank, *World Development Report 1997,* p. 14.

119. Kanbur and Vines, "The World Bank and Poverty Reduction," p. 88; McGuire and Conroy, "The Microfinance Phenomenon," p. 93.

120. Katherine Marshall, *The World Bank: From Reconstruction to Development to Equity* (New York: Routledge, 2008), pp. 49–52; World Bank, *World Development Report 1999/2000* (New York: Oxford University Press, 2000), pp. 21–23.

121. Kapur, "The Changing Anatomy of Governance of the World Bank," p. 69.

122. Fidler, "Who's Minding the Bank?" p. 46; Robert Wade, "Showdown at the World Bank," *New Left Review* 7 (January/February 2001), p. 132; Robert H. Wade, "US Hegemony and the World Bank: The Fight over People and Ideas," *Review of International Political Economy* 9, no. 2 (May 2002), p. 212.

123. Marshall, *The World Bank,* p. 57.

124. Jorge G. Castañeda, "Latin America's Left Turn," *Foreign Affairs* 85, no. 3 (May/June 2006), pp. 28–29.

125. Peter Kingstone, "After the Washington Consensus: The Limits to Democratization and Development in Latin America," *Latin American Research Review* 41, no. 1 (February 2006), p. 155; and Pedro-Pablo Kuczynski and John Wlliamson, eds., *After the Washington Consensus: Restarting Growth and Reform in Latin America* (Washington, D.C.: Institute for International Economics, 2003).

126. Duncan Green, *Silent Revolution: The Rise and Crisis of Market Economics in Latin America* (New York: Monthly Review Press, 2003); Javier Santiso, *The Political Economy of Emerging Markets: Actors, Institutions and Financial Crises in Latin America* (New York: Palgrave Macmillan, 2003).

127. Castañeda, "Latin America's Left Turn," p. 35.

128. Walt W. Rostow, *The Stages of Economic Growth: A Non-Communist Manifesto* (Cambridge, UK: Cambridge University Press, 1960).

129. Malcolm Harper, "Some Final Thoughts," in Thomas Dichter and Malcolm Harper, eds., *What's Wrong with Microfinance?* (Bourton, UK: Practical Action Publishing, 2007), p. 257.

130. Rapley, *Understanding Development,* pp. 135–154.

131. United Nations Development Program, *Human Development Report 1996* (New York: UNDP, 1996), p. 1.

132. Jennifer Clapp and Peter Dauvergne, *Paths to a Green World: The Political Economy of the Environment* (Cambridge, MA: MIT Press, 2005), pp. 196–210.

133. Lingle, "What Ever Happened to the 'Asian Century'?" p. 33.

134. Rapley, *Understanding Development,* pp. 155–157. See also Elizabeth Parsan, *South-South Trade in Global Development* (Brookfield, VT: Avebury, 1993).

135. Donald C. Hellmann, "A Decade After the Asian Financial Crisis," *Asian Survey* 47, no. 6 (November/December 2007), p. 836.

CHAPTER 11

Foreign Debt and Financial Crises

An international debt crisis erupted in the early 1980s that was "one of the most traumatic international financial disturbances" of the twentieth century.[1] Debt crises had occurred in the nineteenth century, and widespread defaults on loans in the 1930s had severely disrupted capital flows to Latin America and Southern and Eastern Europe. However, the world was unprepared for the 1980s debt crisis, which threatened the international banking system and many LDCs. This chapter focuses mainly on the origins and effects of the 1980s debt crisis and the strategies adopted to deal with it. The latter part of the chapter discusses the East and Southeast Asian (henceforth "Asian") financial crisis of the late 1990s, which resulted in the collapse of some currencies and a sharp decrease in capital formation and economic output; and the subprime mortgage financial crisis of 2007–2008, which resulted from a speculative bubble in the U.S. housing market that eventually resulted in a global credit crunch and financial failures in many countries. Whereas the economic development aspects of the Asian financial crisis are discussed in Chapter 10, this chapter compares the debt and financial crises and discusses the international management of debt and financial problems.

WHAT IS A DEBT CRISIS?

As discussed in Chapter 6, a country has a current account deficit when its payments abroad are greater than those it receives. A government that finances rather than adjusts to its deficits must borrow from external credit sources and/or decrease its foreign exchange reserves. If the government continues to borrow, it may be burdened with growing foreign debts. The severity of a country's debt problem depends not only the size of the debt but also on whether the country has the ability and commitment to service its debt repayments. A "debt crisis" occurs when a state lacks sufficient foreign exchange to make the interest and/or principal payments on its debt obligations. Debt crises vary in severity and in the measures required to resolve them. If the debt problem is temporary, the state has a *liquidity* problem: It may defer some payments or obtain a new loan to meet its repayment commitments and then repay later on terms acceptable to the creditors. If the debt problem is unsustainable, the state has a *solvency* problem. In this case, the debtor can regain its creditworthiness only if its creditors reduce the interest or principal payments on its debt. Debt crises may begin as liquidity problems and become solvency problems.[2] In addition to these objective measures of a debt crisis, there are also more subjective definitions. For example, the North defined the 1980s debt crisis as a threat to "the stability of the international financial system" resulting from "widespread difficulties in servicing the mountain of developing country debt." The South, by contrast, defined the debt crisis as "a crisis of development" which began "for some developing countries after the first oil shock."[3]

A number of scholars have compared the debt crises of the 1930s and 1980s.[4] One difference relates to the lending mechanisms. Most lending to Latin America in the 1920s occurred through the bond markets, and when LDCs defaulted on their debts in the 1930s, the losses were fragmented among many individual bondholders. By contrast, most lending to middle-income LDCs in the 1970s was private bank lending, and when the debtor countries threatened to default on their loans in the 1980s, the losses were more concentrated in the largest commercial banks. In 1982 the nine largest U.S. banks had loans outstanding to 17 highly indebted states amounting to 194 percent of the banks' capital and reserves, and a major debt default would have affected the core of the banking system. Northern states and international institutions also had a greater role in the 1980s debt crisis for several reasons. First, creditor governments felt more pressure to intervene in the 1980s crisis because of the threat posed to the international banking system. Second, international institutions that deal with debt problems were almost nonexistent during earlier periods. During the 1980s, by contrast, the IMF pressured private banks to continue lending to LDC debtors, and debtor countries to alter their economic policies. Third, there was no hegemon to deal with the 1930s debt crisis, but the United States filled this position in the 1980s. The United States and IMF orchestrated the response in the 1980s, and the World Bank, the Paris and London Clubs, and the Bank for International Settlements (BIS) had supporting roles.[5]

It is important to be familiar with the terminology used in regard to foreign debt. *Debt restructuring* agreements alter the terms between the creditor and debtor for servicing a debt, and can take two different forms. First, *debt rescheduling* agreements defer debt service payments and apply longer maturities to the deferred amount. Debt rescheduling is more likely to be effective if a debtor has a liquidity problem. Second, *debt relief, debt forgiveness,* or *debt reduction* agreements decrease the overall debt burden; that is, they include an element of debt reduction or forgiveness. They are more likely to be concluded when a debtor state has a solvency problem.[6] As the following discussion shows, debt rescheduling was the main form of debt restructuring in the earlier years of the debt crisis, but there was a shift to debt relief for highly indebted low-income LDCs in later years.

THE ORIGINS OF THE 1980s DEBT CRISIS

The debt crisis began in August 1982, when Mexico announced that it could no longer service its public sector debt obligations. This produced shock waves because Mexico had an external debt of about $78 billion, $32 billion of which was owed to commercial banks. However, earlier warning signs of a possible debt crisis had been largely ignored. A number of LDCs, including Zaïre, Argentina, Peru, Sierra Leone, Sudan, and Togo, were involved in debt rescheduling negotiations from 1976 to 1980, and the South's external debt had increased sixfold to $500 billion between 1972 and 1981. Foreign debt was also a growing problem in Eastern Europe, and Poland's debt had reached serious proportions by 1981. After Mexico's 1982 announcement, the debt crisis spread rapidly as private creditor banks moved to decrease their loan exposure to other LDC borrowers. Thus, 25 LDCs requested a restructuring of their commercial bank debt by late 1982, and in 1983 the World Bank reported that "almost as many developing countries have had to reschedule loans in the last two years as in the previous twenty-five years."[7] Partly because of their divergent perspectives, analysts attribute the 1980s debt crisis to a variety of factors, including unexpected changes in the global economy, irresponsible behavior of lenders, irresponsible behavior of debtors, and the South's dependence on the North.

Unexpected Changes in the Global Economy

Some observers attribute the debt crisis to unexpected changes in the global economy. The first external shocks occurred in the early 1970s, when grain and oil prices sharply increased. Major surpluses of wheat and grain had accumulated during the 1960s, leading to a decline in international food prices and production cutback programs in grain-exporting countries such as the United States and Canada. As a result of the cutbacks, the world's grain supply was highly vulnerable to inclement weather and unexpected crop shortfalls in the Soviet Union. In 1972 and 1973 global food stocks fell to their lowest level in 20 years, food grain prices sharply increased, and the volume of food aid was drastically reduced.[8] Oil prices also increased sharply when the Arab OPEC countries limited supplies after the October 1973 Middle East war. Whereas LDC oil and food importers were doubly hit by the food and oil crises, the OPEC states accumulated huge "petrodollar" reserves, which they deposited in the largest commercial banks; and the banks recycled the petrodollars through loans to middle-income LDCs. Thus, from 1974 to 1979 non-OPEC LDCs received about 60 percent of their external finance from commercial bank credits.[9]

Another doubling of OPEC oil prices in 1979 (the "second oil shock") led to additional private bank loans to oil-importing LDCs, and the banks also offered loans to some oil-exporting LDCs to help develop their industries and diversify their economies. The second oil shock contributed to a severe economic contraction in the North and a sharp decline in the North's demand for the South's commodity exports, which made it difficult for LDCs to earn foreign exchange to service their debts. The South's problems were compounded when the U.S. Reagan administration raised interest rates to limit inflation resulting from the 1979 oil price increases and to facilitate U.S. borrowing abroad to cover its huge federal budget deficits. The creditor banks were providing short-term loans to LDCs at variable interest rates, and the impact of the higher interest rates on LDC debt levels was rapid and severe.[10] It may seem odd that the debt crisis began with Mexico—an oil exporter. However, oil-exporting LDCs had also borrowed private funds to launch ambitious development projects without anticipating that oil prices would fall sharply after 1979. Thus, unexpected global economic changes in the 1970s and 1980s contributed to external debt problems for LDC oil exporters as well as importers.

Both commercial banks and debtor states often favor this external shocks explanation for the debt crisis because it awards "primary responsibility to economic policy shifts beyond their control."[11] However, external shocks do not explain why East and Southeast Asian debtors fared so much better than Latin American debtors (see the following discussion). Thus, the policies of lenders and borrowers must also be considered as explanations for the crisis.

Irresponsible Behavior of Lenders

Historical materialists and some interventionist liberals consider irresponsible behavior of creditor banks to be a major cause of the debt crisis. Because banks in New York, London, and elsewhere had a surfeit of OPEC petrodollars, they aggressively increased their loans to the South without giving due attention to the creditworthiness of borrowers or the activities they were financing. The large commercial banks charged extremely low interest rates because of inflationary conditions and the competition among lenders, and they did not give LDCs adequate signals as to when to stop borrowing. After LDC debtors had become overly dependent on commercial bank loans, interest rates rose sharply in the early 1980s, and this heightened the severity of the debt crisis. Thus, the "loan pushing" by commercial banks encouraged "debtor countries to increase their liabilities."[12] Critics also argue that Northern governments and the IMF shared responsibility for the bank overlending. After the first oil shock in 1973, the DCs adopted policies that encouraged the flow of private bank funds to the South; for example, central banks in the G10 states provided assurances that they would assist banks recycling petrodollars if they encountered financial difficulties. The IMF also introduced new lending programs for LDC oil importers such as the 1974 oil facility, which encouraged private banks to upgrade their lending activities. Furthermore, the gradual lifting of capital controls (discussed in Chapter 6) eased the process by which U.S. and Western European banks could recycle petrodollars to the South. From this perspective, creditor banks, DCs, and the IMF shared responsibility for overlending, which was a major cause of the debt crisis.[13]

Irresponsible Behavior of Borrowers

Many liberal theorists, especially orthodox liberals, attribute primary responsibility for the debt crisis to the behavior of borrowing states. They argue that LDCs chose to borrow from private banks in the 1970s to avoid the conditionality requirements of IMF loans. Unlike the IMF, private banks were not inclined (and did not have legal authority) to impose policy conditions on their loans to sovereign governments. Basic IMF principles—that indebted governments should not have unlimited access to balance-of-payments financing and should undergo adjustment measures—were jeopardized because private funds were so accessible. Thus, the IMF warned that

> Access to private sources of balance of payments finance may . . . in some cases permit countries to postpone the adoption of adequate domestic stabilization measures. This can exacerbate the problem of correcting payments imbalances, and can lead to adjustments that are politically and socially disruptive when the introduction of stabilization measures becomes unavoidable.[14]

Liberals point out that LDC governments sometimes secretly seek IMF conditionality to help them push through unpopular economic reforms. As Robert Putnam notes, international negotiations are a two-level game that may enable "government leaders to do what they privately wish to do, but are powerless to do domestically"; for example, in Italy's negotiations with the IMF, "domestic conservative forces exploited IMF pressure to facilitate policy moves that were otherwise infeasible internally."[15] Uruguay also found an IMF agreement useful in its efforts to impose painful, unpopular economic austerity measures. IMF conditionality raised the cost to domestic interests of opposing economic reform "because a rejection was no longer a mere rejection of . . . [Uruguay's] president, but also of the IMF."[16] In most cases, however, LDC governments were inclined to follow the path of least resistance and seek private bank loans without instituting necessary reforms.

In addition to imprudent borrowing, liberals also attribute the debt crisis to the domestic policies of borrowing states. Although some LDCs used commercial bank loans to finance productive investments and economic growth, a number used the funds to make poor investments, increase public expenditures, import luxury consumer goods, and pay off corrupt officials. Some LDCs reacted to the debt crisis in a timely manner with readjustment policies, but many others demonstrated unwillingness or inability to change. Liberal economists often contrast the strong economic performance of Asian debtors such as

South Korea and Indonesia during the 1980s with the weak performance of Latin American debtors. (A notable exception was the weak performance of the Philippines.) Whereas Latin Americans employed protectionist import substitution policies, East Asians adopted outward-oriented export-led growth policies that put them in a stronger position because exports provided foreign exchange for servicing their debts.[17] Thus, Table 11.1 shows that the three largest debtors were Latin American when the debt crisis erupted in 1982; the debts of Brazil, Mexico, and Argentina exceeded $92, $86, and $43 billion, respectively. Table 11.1 shows that South Korea, Indonesia, and the Philippines also had substantial debts in 1982, exceeding $37, $24, and $24 billion, respectively; but the stronger export position of the Asians (except the Philippines) enabled them to service their debts better than the Latin Americans. To assess a country's ability to service its debt, economists use the **debt service ratio,** which measures the ratio of a country's interest and principal payments on its debt to its export income. The lower the debt service ratio (and debt-to-export ratio), the more favorable are the prospects that a country will meet its debt obligations. Table 11.1 shows that the debt service ratios of Malaysia and Indonesia were as low as 10.7 and 18.1 percent in 1982, while the debt service ratios of Brazil and Chile were as high as 81.3 and 71.3 percent.

Those who question the orthodox liberal view that LDC behavior was the main factor explaining the debt crisis point out that LDC governments with good

TABLE 11.1 Total Debt, and Debt Indicators, 1982 (U.S.$ in Millions)

	Total Debt	Debt/Exports (%)	Debt Service Ratio[a] (%)
Latin America			
Argentina	43,634	447.3	50.0
Brazil	92,990	396.1	81.3
Chile	17,315	335.9	71.3
Colombia	10,306	204.3	29.5
Mexico	86,019	311.5	56.8
Peru	10,712	255.9	48.7
Venezuela	32,153	159.8	29.5
East and Southeast Asia			
Indonesia	24,734	116.3	18.1
Republic of Korea	37,330	131.6	22.4
Malaysia	13,354	93.4	10.7
Philippines	24,551	297.8	42.6
Thailand	12,238	130.0	20.6

[a]Debt service ratio: the ratio of a country's interest and principal payments to its export income
Source: World Bank, *World Debt Tables 1992–93, Vol. 2: Country Tables* (Washington, D.C.: IBRD, 1992).

intentions often lacked the political capacity and support to institute necessary economic reforms. They also charge that orthodox liberals ignore the fact that the debt crisis was *systemic* in nature; "the simultaneous onset of the crisis in more than forty developing countries" indicates that some contributing factors were external and largely beyond LDCs' control.[18] Furthermore, Asian LDCs such as Thailand, Malaysia, Indonesia, and South Korea, which liberals identified as following responsible policies during the 1980s debt crisis, experienced a severe financial crisis in the late 1990s (see later discussion).

The South's Dependence on the North

Historical materialists argue that the 1980s debt crisis stemmed not only from proximate factors, but also from the long-term structural nature of capitalism. Thus, dependency and world-system theorists view debt crises as extreme instances of a "debt trap" that exploits LDCs in the periphery and binds them to DCs in the core. Some writers draw linkages between debt crises and the legacy of colonialism. The colonial powers established a division of labor in which the colonies provided agricultural products and raw materials to the metropole and served as markets for the metropole's manufactures. This pattern still characterizes the export and import structures of many LDCs, preventing them from earning the foreign exchange necessary for development. Although some LDCs are industrializing, they cannot escape from their indebtedness because they remain dependent on the core for technology and finance.[19] Historical materialists also point to foreign aid as a cause of debt crises because more than half of all official development assistance (ODA) is disbursed as loans. A substantial share of World Bank financing is disbursed as *hard loans* with high interest rates and shorter repayment periods (see Chapter 10). Development assistance is another mechanism for transferring surpluses from the periphery to the core, because a large share of foreign aid is required simply to cover LDC repayments of past aid disbursements. Historical materialists conclude that public as well as private external finance perpetuates LDC dependency:

> If they seek official help on softer than commercial terms, they have to accept outside scrutiny . . . and accept conditions which doom their efforts at industrial, diversified development. If they accept suppliers' credits on commercial terms in order to go through with their cherished projects, they are caught anyway when the payments come due before they are able to meet them.[20]

Like other interpretations of the debt crisis, critics question the views of historical materialists. Liberals argue that dependency theorists attribute LDC debt problems solely to external causes beyond their control and avoid looking at the *domestic* sources of LDC problems—traditional attitudes, domestic inefficiencies, corrupt political leaders, and a reluctance to follow liberal economic policies. It is safe to conclude that *all* the preceding views on the origins of the debt crisis have some validity. Unexpected food and oil price increases during the 1970s encouraged LDCs to increase their borrowing, and the world recession after the 1979 oil price increases added to the debt load of many LDCs. Although these unexpected global changes made the debt crisis more likely, irresponsible behavior of commercial banks, DCs, and LDCs exacerbated the crisis. Furthermore, the South's long-term structural dependence on the North increased the vulnerability of LDCs to protracted debt problems. A Mexican finance minister identified the multiple causes of the debt crisis and the widespread failure to foresee it, when he stated,

> The origin of the debt itself is clearly traceable to a decision by both developing and developed countries that . . . resulted in the channeling of tens of billions of dollars to the debtor community of today. . . . The whole world congratulated itself on the success, smoothness, and efficiency with which the recycling process was achieved. *We all were responsible.*[21]

THE FOREIGN DEBT REGIME

Before discussing the world reaction to the 1980s debt crisis, we describe the foreign debt regime that monitored and managed the crisis. A debt regime was more evident in the 1980s than in the 1930s because a global hegemon (the United States) and an institutional framework (the IMF and World Bank) existed to deal with the 1980s crisis. The mechanisms for coping with a debt crisis before World War II included unilateral actions by the creditors or debtors and two-party solutions in which debtors and creditors negotiated agreements. Postwar debt settlements, by contrast, have been three-party affairs involving IOs such as the IMF and World Bank and informal groups such as the Paris and London Clubs. The United States has acted as a third-party hegemon in the postwar period, pressuring for debt settlements and coordinating settlement efforts. In recent years the members of the G7/G8 summits have acted to supplement U.S. hegemony by taking collective responsibility for dealing with foreign debt issues.[22]

Some regimes encompass only one sector or issue while others are broader in scope, and specific regimes are nested within more diffuse regimes; for example, the textile and agricultural trade regimes are nested within the global trade regime.[23] Although the global trade regime principles, norms, and rules provide a general framework, textile and agricultural trade have their own unique characteristics and have been treated as exceptions by the GATT/WTO. This chapter views the 1980s foreign debt regime as a specific regime nested within a more diffuse balance-of-payments financing regime because foreign debt crises are a specific, more extreme type of balance-of-payments problem.[24] Although creditors and debtors have negotiated agreements throughout the postwar period, pressures resulting from the 1980s debt crisis produced more coordinated, longer-term efforts to establish rules and decision-making procedures that we normally associate with an international regime. A basic principle of the balance-of-payments financing regime is that an adequate but not unlimited amount of financing should be available to states to deal with their balance-of-payments deficits. A second principle is that those providing the financing may attach conditions to it to ensure that recipient states correct their balance-of-payments problems.[25] The balance-of-payments regime principle of conditional lending was threatened in the 1970s because private banks recycled petrodollars as loans to debtor countries with minimal conditions and very low interest rates. Although these bank loans were readily available to middle-income countries (MICs) and NIEs during the 1970s, low-income countries (LICs) lacked creditworthiness and remained dependent on loans from the IMF and donor governments. Thus, Table 11.2 shows that private bank loans in 1980 accounted for only 6 percent of LIC debt but for 38 percent of MIC debt and 65 percent of NIE debt. ODA, by contrast, accounted for 67 percent of LIC debt in 1980 but for only 25 percent of MIC debt and 4 percent of NIE debt. The willingness of private banks to provide finance to the more creditworthy LDCs limited the IMF's ability to set conditions for these borrowers.

However, private banks responded to the 1980s debt crisis by quickly limiting their loan exposure, and the MICs and NIEs therefore had to look to the IMF, World Bank, and government aid agencies for assistance with their growing debt problems. This dependence on official financing provided the IOs and the U.S. government with considerable leverage in establishing the foreign debt regime. As with the pre-1970s balance-of-payments regime, the basic principle of the debt regime revolved around conditionality—the provision of new loans and debt rescheduling were contingent on the debtor countries' commitment to market-oriented reforms. However, the 1980s debt regime differed from the pre-1970s regime in some important respects. First, the IMF (with U.S. backing) adopted a new role when it pressured private commercial banks in the 1980s to continue providing loans to debtor LDCs. Second, creditor groups such as the Paris and London Clubs met much more frequently in the 1980s and 1990s than in earlier periods. Third, both the IMF and World Bank provided structural adjustment loans to indebted LDCs and transition economies. These SALs were conditioned on more demanding requirements—that loan recipients adopt orthodox liberal reforms such as deregulation, privatization, and greater openness to trade and foreign investment. The following sections discuss two other groups of actors in the global debt regime—the transition economies of Eastern Europe and the FSU that became debtors along with the LDCs, and the Paris and London Clubs that coordinated the actions of creditors. The changing roles of the IMF and World Bank in the foreign debt regime are examined later in the chapter.

The IMF, World Bank, and Transition Economies

Chapter 2 noted that the Soviet bloc countries were not IMF and World Bank members for most of the early postwar period. Before examining the role of

TABLE 11.2 Total Debt, and Share of Debt Based on ODA and Private Bank Loans for Nonoil LDCS

Income Group	1971			1975			1980			1982		
	Total Debt[a]	ODA (%)	Private Banks (%)	Total Debt	ODA (%)	Private Banks (%)	Total Debt	ODA (%)	Private Banks (%)	Total Debt	ODA (%)	Private Banks (%)
LICs	$18	74	2	$40	73	7	$ 86	67	6	$110	69	6
MICs	$25	45	14	$40	33	29	$107	25	38	$144	24	39
NIEs	$32	16	38	$72	9	60	$192	4	65	$266	3	67

ODA = official development assistance

LICs = low-income countries

MICs = middle-income countries

NIEs = newly industrializing economies

[a]Total debt figures in billions.

Source: External Debt of Developing Countries—1982 Survey, p. 34. Copyright © OECD, 1982. By permission of the Organization for Economic Cooperation and Development.

these countries in the foreign debt regime, this chapter discusses how they joined these institutions; a country cannot join the World Bank ("the Bank") without first becoming a member of the IMF. As Table 11.3 shows, Yugoslavia was a member of the IMF and the Bank from the time they were established. This is not surprising in view of Yugoslavia's defection from the Soviet Bloc in 1948 and its moves to develop a nonaligned foreign policy. Yugoslavia was also adopting worker self-management and market socialist policies that were more compatible with the liberal economic orientation of the Bretton Woods institutions. In contrast to Yugoslavia, Poland and Czechoslovakia left the IMF and the Bank in 1950 and 1954 (Czechoslovakia was expelled for not paying its dues), because membership in these institutions conflicted with their status as satellite countries in the Soviet bloc. Table 11.3 shows that Romania joined these institutions in 1972. Although Romania was still a Soviet bloc member, it

TABLE 11.3 Membership of Transition Economies in the IMF and World Bank

	IMF	World Bank
1946	Poland, Czechoslovakia, Yugoslavia, and China (founding members of IMF and World Bank)	
1950	Poland withdraws from IMF and World Bank	
1954	Czechoslovakia ousted from IMF and World Bank	
1972	Romania	Romania
1980	People's Republic of China (PRC) replaces Taiwan in IMF and World Bank	
1982	Hungary	Hungary
1986	Poland	Poland
1990	Czech and Slovak Federal Republic, Bulgaria	Bulgaria
1991	Albania, Lithuania	Albania, Czech and Slovak Federal Republic
1992–1997	Russian Federation, other FSU[a] Republics, Croatia, Slovenia, Macedonia, Czech Republic, Slovak Republic, Bosnia and Herzegovina (IMF and World Bank)	
2000	Serbia/Montenegro (IMF and World Bank)	
2007	Montenegro (IMF and World Bank) (Serbia continues membership of former Serbia/Montenegro)	

[a]FSU = former Soviet Union

Sources: International Monetary Fund, *Annual Report of the Executive Board* (Washington, D.C.: IMF, various years); World Bank, *Annual Report* (Washington, D.C.: World Bank, various years).

had distanced itself politically from the Soviet Union and viewed the Soviet-led Council for Mutual Economic Assistance (CMEA) as hindering its development. As an IMF and Bank member, Romania could receive their loans, upgrade its economic relations with the West, and further its political objectives. Despite Romania's slow moves toward economic reform and its sizable foreign debt, it became a member of these IOs without going through a transition phase. Western states disregarded these economic issues because Romania's membership produced new divisions within the Soviet bloc. Although Romania provided sensitive economic information to the IMF and the Bank, they agreed not to disclose this information in their statistical reports.[26]

The case of the People's Republic of China (PRC) was also atypical. The IMF and the Bank treated the China case as a representation rather than a new membership issue, and in 1980 they permitted the PRC to take the China seat from Taiwan. The PRC's decision to "return" to the Bretton Woods institutions in 1980 followed a radical change in its policies. Mao Zedong had adopted an inward self-reliance policy in the 1950s to early 1960s, and China's policies became even more autarkic from 1966 to 1969 during the Cultural Revolution. However, the Cultural Revolution created so many political and economic problems that China began to adopt more open policies. China's commercial contacts with the North increased, and the UN General Assembly voted to seat the PRC delegation in 1971. After Mao's death in 1976 and the arrest of cultural revolutionaries, the PRC launched the Four Modernizations program to increase economic productivity and develop a more active role in the global economy. Thus, China viewed membership in the IMF and the Bank as a means of gaining access to capital for its development. Several factors facilitated China's reentry application in the negotiations, including active U.S. support and a compromise agreement on the Taiwan issue.[27] After the PRC's takeover of the China seat in 1980, Hungary and Poland requested accession in 1981. Unlike Romania, Hungary was much closer to meeting the IMF's normal economic requirements. Hungary's New Economic Mechanism (NEM) had increased its economic decentralization, outward economic orientation, and international competitiveness in the late 1960s; and in the 1970s and 1980s it introduced other economic reforms. Hungary sought IMF membership to safeguard these reforms and get assistance with its foreign debt, which resulted partly from its development plans. Poland's debt problems were much more serious, because it had borrowed in international financial markets during the 1970s instead of introducing meaningful economic reform. Poland needed to reassure the financial community that it was committed to servicing its debt in the early 1980s, and IMF membership would be helpful in this regard. Although Hungary was admitted to the IMF and the Bank in 1982, Poland's application was stalled by its imposition of martial law in 1981; it was not until 1986 that Poland was admitted to the Bretton Woods institutions (see Table 11.3).[28]

Poland was the last Eastern European country to become an IMF and Bank member before upheaval in the Soviet bloc transformed East–West relations.

Mikhail Gorbachev's attempts to revive the Soviet economy through economic restructuring (*perestroika*) and political openness (*glasnost*) failed, but his policies contributed to a series of revolutionary changes. These included the disintegration of Communist regimes in Eastern Europe in 1989, the unification of Germany in 1990, and the independence of the Baltic states and formal dissolution of the Soviet Union in 1991. Czechoslovakia and Bulgaria joined the IMF and the Bank in 1990 and 1991, but the most significant change was the accession of Russia and other FSU republics in 1992 and 1993. Russia was facing an economic crisis, and the IMF and Western donors offered it a $24 billion assistance package in return for its commitment to decrease its budget deficit and inflation rate.[29]

The Bretton Woods institutions have worked together to help the transition economies move toward market reform. The IMF has taken the lead in this process, estimating financing needs, providing policy advice, and setting conditions for reform. The Bank has offered technical assistance and funding for infrastructure, the development of market incentives, the privatization of state monopolies, and the creation of a legal framework for the emerging private sector. However, tensions have existed between the transition economies and the Bretton Woods institutions because of their different economic outlooks. The addition of so many new members has also put pressure on IMF and Bank resources, and LDCs sometimes charge that the transition economies receive better treatment. These charges seem to have some validity. For example, one study revealed that Romania, Poland, and Hungary received more IMF loans than expected on the basis of economic criteria; and Russia was able to borrow more funds in relation to its IMF quota than other countries when it joined the IMF in 1992.[30] This favored treatment demonstrates that security as well as economic factors affect IMF lending decisions. However, the charges of favored treatment do not seem to apply to all transition economies; for example, a 1990 study concluded that the IMF and the Bank did not give special treatment to China.[31] Despite the charges of special treatment, the membership of transition economies has enhanced the universality of the Bretton Woods institutions.

The Paris and London Clubs

Three types of negotiations occurred between creditors and debtors to deal with the 1980s debt crisis. First, the IMF and World Bank agreed to provide SALs to debtor governments in exchange for the debtors' commitment to follow prescribed policies to deal with their balance-of-payments problems. The other two types of negotiations involved meetings between the debtors and less formal creditor groups: the Paris and London Clubs. The **Paris Club** is an informal group of creditor governments, which in most cases are OECD members. The **London Clubs** (also called *private creditor committees* and *bank advisory committees*) are composed of the largest commercial banks. The Paris and London Clubs have no charters or formal institutional structures, and their memberships vary with each rescheduling negotiation. The ad hoc nature of these clubs stems from the creditors' view that negotiations should be low profile and that debt reschedulings should be unusual occurrences. Thus, the Paris Club has no legal status or written rules, no voting procedure (decision making occurs by consensus), and no regular office (meetings are usually held in the French Ministry of Finance). The Paris Club's origins stem from a 1956 meeting of 12 European creditor states to negotiate a rescheduling of Argentina's foreign debt. Argentina was in arrears to the governments, and the meeting provided a multilateral rescheduling forum instead of uncoordinated bilateral reschedulings. Paris Club meetings were originally limited in number, but they became much more frequent as debt problems increased. Thus, the Paris Club concluded more than twice as many agreements in the 7 years from 1978 to 1984 as it did in the previous 22 years, and the 1978 to 1984 agreements deferred $27 billion of debt service obligations. Participants in Paris Club meetings include the debtor government; the main creditor governments; and representatives of the IMF, the Bank, UNCTAD, and regional development banks. The Paris Club emphasizes three basic principles in its deliberations— imminent default, conditionality, and burden sharing:

- The *imminent default principle* is designed to limit debt rescheduling to states with a serious, justifiable need. To avoid unnecessary negotiations, the Paris Club will not even consider a request unless the debtor has substantial external payments arrears and is likely to default on its payments.
- The *conditionality principle* stems from the creditor governments' concerns that the debtor services its debts on schedule. Thus, the debtor must conclude an IMF arrangement with conditionality requirements before the Paris Club will agree to negotiate. In the rare cases where the debtor was not an IMF member at the time of rescheduling (e.g., Poland, Cuba, and Mozambique), the Paris Club established its own conditionality.
- The *burden sharing principle* requires all creditor states to provide relief in proportion to their loan exposure to the debtor state. This principle helps avoid the problem of free riding, and it applies to creditor banks as well as states. Thus, the Paris and London Clubs cooperate with each other.[32]

The London Clubs received their name because many of their meetings were held there in the 1980s. Like the Paris Club agreements, a single debtor and its creditors negotiate London Club agreements, and the debtor must normally commit to IMF adjustment policies. However, whereas a relatively small number of states can agree to reschedule loans at Paris Club meetings, the coordination problems for the far more numerous private creditors are more complicated. Private creditors coordinate their activities by establishing bank advisory committees for the various debtor countries which the largest international banks (those holding the most loans outstanding) attend. The international banks on each committee bargain with each other and with the debtor country to establish the debt rescheduling terms and then present the agreement to smaller creditor banks for ratification. Although the largest creditors would like to limit their loan exposure to a troubled debtor, they realize that the debtor state could default if all creditors withheld loans. The major international banks have a common interest in successful debt restructuring because of their high loan exposure and their long-term interest in the stability of international capital markets. Smaller creditor banks, by contrast, have fewer loans at risk and less interest in maintaining the international credit system; thus, they are reluctant to ratify restructuring agreements that require them to provide additional loans. Because smaller creditor banks often think on the basis of individual rationality (see prisoners' dilemma in Chapter 4), there is a danger that all banks could defect and that massive debtor default could disrupt the international banking system. To prevent a Pareto-deficient outcome, the large international banks pressure the smaller banks to avoid free riding and participate in the debt restructuring agreements.[33] As discussed in the next section, this system of private creditor committees worked effectively in earlier years but was insufficient to deal with the 1980s debt crisis.

Historical materialists and LDC debtors are often critical of the Paris and London Clubs. When a single debtor meets with all its major creditors at the bargaining table, the creditors can exert stronger pressures on the debtor state. The case-by-case approach of the Paris and London Clubs also prevents debtors from developing a united front, and it ignores the systemic nature of the 1980s debt crisis by operating on the assumption that each debtor's situation can be treated individually. Furthermore, historical materialists criticize the two clubs for their emphasis on IMF conditionality as a prerequisite for negotiations.[34] Thus, at the UNCTAD V conference in 1979 the G77 sought to replace the Paris and London Clubs with an international debt commission more attuned to LDC interests. Although the creditor governments agreed to invite an observer from UNCTAD to future Paris Club negotiations, it did not agree to create an international debt commission. Thus, the creditors continue to set the rules and procedures for Paris and London Club negotiations.

STRATEGIES TO DEAL WITH THE 1980s DEBT CRISIS

The debt crisis was more prolonged than expected, and the creditor states and international institutions gradually adopted more activist policies as milder measures proved to be insufficient. The United States and the IMF were two of the main actors involved in devising and implementing strategies. Although the IMF had lost some importance with the collapse of the pegged exchange rate system and the increase in private bank lending in the 1970s, the 1980s debt crisis placed it "back at the center of the international financial system, first as a coordinator in a crisis, and then . . . as a source of information, advice, and warning on the mutual consistency of national policies."[35] The IMF's central role stemmed largely from the U.S. administration's view that multilateral institutions could best implement DC policies on debt issues. Unlike the United States, the IMF could exert pressure on LDC debtors and private banks without causing major protests over U.S. government interference. When G7 summit meetings began to address international debt issues in the late 1980s, the major economic powers to a degree replaced U.S. hegemony with collective responsibility for LDC debt problems.[36]

The international debt strategies had three major objectives: to prevent the collapse of the international banking and financial systems; to restore capital market access for debtor countries; and to minimize economic dislocation and restore economic growth in debtor states. The strategies to achieve these objectives can be divided into four phases:

1. Emergency loans and private "involuntary" loans to debtor states (1982–1985).
2. The Baker Plan, which continued the private involuntary lending and put new emphasis on official lending (1986–1988).
3. The Brady Plan, which emphasized debt reduction agreements (1989–1994).
4. Initiatives for the poorer LDCs (1996 to the present).

Emergency Measures and Involuntary Lending: 1982–1985

The United States, the IMF, and other creditors first reacted to the debt crisis with a "firefighting" strategy, providing short-term emergency loans to Mexico, Brazil, and other LDCs to avert a 1930s-style financial collapse. The BIS provided some bridging finance to LDC debtor states until IMF loans were approved.[37] This emergency lending was followed by a medium-term strategy, in which the IMF induced private banks to engage in *involuntary lending* (politely termed *concerted lending* in official circles). Involuntary lending refers to "the increase in a bank's exposure to a borrowing nation that is in debt-servicing difficulty and that, because of a loss of creditworthiness, would be unable to attract new lending from banks not already exposed in the country."[38] Before the debt crisis, the London Clubs were quite successful because the largest international banks induced smaller banks to engage in involuntary lending when necessary in debt restructuring agreements. Only nine states had to restructure their commercial debts from the mid-1970s to 1982, so interbank coordination was sufficient to manage the debt situation. Although the IMF helped supervise debtor economic policies, its involvement was quite limited during this period. However, the 1982 Mexican debt crisis drastically altered the debt management system. The large international banks were unable to cope with the massive scope of the debt crisis, and many small banks in the U.S. Southwest with loans outstanding to Mexico were unwilling to increase their loan exposure. Thus, the IMF had to intervene:

> In November 1982, the Fund's Managing Director . . . took the unprecedented step of establishing mandatory levels of forced private lending before the IMF would sign a stabilization agreement with Mexico. This bold action, repeated in the Brazilian case, was a turning point in the treatment of sovereign debt. It staked out a new leadership role for the Fund, and a new relationship between the Fund and private banks.[39]

The IMF also insisted that debtor states develop adjustment programs as the price for debt rescheduling and new lending. Thus, realists argue that creditor *states* operating through the IMF managed the debt crisis; the crisis posed such a major threat to the international financial system that only states could mobilize sufficient resources to deal with it. Furthermore, only official pressures could induce banks to continue lending to debtors and force debtors to meet conditionality requirements. Liberals, by contrast, emphasize the IMF's role as an international institution in managing the debt crisis, and they reject the realist view that the IMF was simply following creditor state instructions. The IMF and creditor states in these early years assumed that the debt crisis was a short-term problem stemming from the temporary inability of LDCs to service their debts. However, many LDCs could not resolve their debt problems even after adjusting their policies. Although the early firefighting tactics dealt with the immediate crisis, economic activity and investment in most debtor states declined, and adjustment programs in LDCs hindered their economic growth. Private commercial banks were also reducing their loan exposure despite IMF pressures, and this forced the IMF to assume an increasing share of the lending risk. When James A. Baker III became U.S. Secretary of the Treasury in 1985, he therefore adopted a more structured approach to the debt crisis.

The Baker Plan: 1986–1988

In 1985 Secretary Baker provided a formula for dealing with the debt crisis and extended debt repayments over a longer period; but he did not change basic assumptions about the best strategy to follow. As was the case in the 1982–1985 period, the **Baker Plan** underestimated the insolvency problem confronting many LDCs and did not offer any debt forgiveness. Instead, the Baker Plan emphasized the postponement of debt payments, the provision of new loans, and changes in debtor country policies. This strategy rested on the assumption that "debtor countries could grow their way out of debt and could expand their exports enough to reduce their relative debt burdens to levels compatible with a return to normal credit market access."[40] The Baker Plan focused mainly on 17 middle-income heavily indebted LDCs as the target group for international debt measures. As Table 11.4 shows, 12 of the "Baker-17" states were Latin American and Caribbean, and the list did not include low-income LDCs that were heavily indebted to official (rather than private) creditors.[41] Table 7.4 lists these 17 countries in order of their gross external debt in 1985, shortly before the Baker Plan was instituted. As the table shows, the four countries with the highest debts in 1985 (Brazil, Mexico, Argentina, and Venezuela) were all Latin American. However, a country's debt servicing abilities also depend on its debt service ratio (see Table 11.1) and its debt as a share of GNI. Table 11.4 shows that the LDCs with the highest gross external debts ranked well below some poorer and smaller LDCs in terms of debt as a percent of GNI. Thus, external debt as a percent of GNI for the three largest debtors in 1985, Brazil, Mexico, and Argentina, was 50.3, 55.2, and 84.2 percent, respectively. The debtors on the list

TABLE 11.4 Gross External Debt and External Debt as a Percent of GNI for the Baker-17 Countries, 1985 and 1997 (U.S.$ in Millions)

	1985		1997	
	Debt	**EDT/GNI (%)**[a]	**Debt**	**EDT/GNI (%)**[a]
Brazil[b]	106,148	50.3	198,023	23.8
Mexico[b]	96,867	55.2	148,702	38.3
Argentina[b]	50,946	84.2	128,411	44.8
Venezuela[b]	35,334	—	35,797	41.5
Philippines	26,622	89.1	45,683	53.4
Former Yugoslavia	22,251	48.2	10,968	—
Chile[b]	20,384	143.3	22,809	31.4
Nigeria	19,550	25.1	28,455	83.7
Morocco	16,529	136.6	20,195	62.6
Peru[b]	12,884	85.3	29,265	50.6
Colombia[b]	14,245	42.6	31,800	30.5
Cote d'Ivoire	9,745	154.2	15,609	158.1
Ecuador[b]	8,703	77.4	15,419	81.8
Bolivia[b]	4,805	176.6	5,237	68.0
Costa Rica[b]	4,401	120.8	3,476	27.6
Jamaica[b]	4,068	234.9	3,920	56.9
Uruguay[b]	3,919	89.7	6,710	31.8

[a]EDT/GNI (%): Total external debt as a percentage of gross national income
[b]Latin American and Caribbean countries

Source: World Bank, *World Debt Tables, 1992–93, Vol. 2: Country Tables* (Washington, D.C.: IBRD, 1992); World Bank, *Global Development Finance 2002, Vol. 2: Country Tables* (Washington, D.C.: IBRD, 2002).

with the highest debt-to-GNI ratios were Jamaica (234.9 percent), Bolivia (176.6 percent), and Cote d'Ivoire (154.2 percent).

Although the Baker Plan focused mainly on middle-income LDCs and underestimated the severity of the debt problem, it recognized that the debt crisis was becoming a longer-term issue. Thus, the Baker Plan shifted emphasis from short-term balance-of-payments adjustment to long-term structural change and the resumption of economic growth in LDC debtor states. Thus, the World Bank and Inter-American Development Bank (IDB)—with their longer-term loans—assumed a more central role. The Baker Plan proposed that the multilateral development banks double their lending to $20 billion over three years and that the private banks also lend $20 billion. In return, the debtors were to liberalize their trade and investment policies and privatize state firms. These reforms marked a major change from Latin America's protectionist import substitution policies.

Despite its positive features, the Baker Plan encountered major obstacles because of unexpected changes in the global economy. For example, international oil prices collapsed shortly after the Baker Plan was announced; this upset the recovery plans of oil-exporting debtor states such as Mexico and gave oil-importing LDCs less incentive to adopt economic reforms necessary for their recovery. The Baker Plan also did not achieve adequate results in terms of LDC economic growth, and many LDC debtors refused to comply with IMF conditionality requirements (e.g., Brazil declared a moratorium on paying its debts in 1987). Furthermore, commercial banks sought to reduce their loan exposure, and the lending risks continued to shift from private banks to governments and multilateral agencies. The multilateral development banks also disbursed less funding than the Baker Plan had anticipated, and debt repayments began to exceed the funding LDCs received in new loans. The net transfer of financial resources to LDCs fell from +\$29 billion in 1982 to −\$34 billion by 1987, and the net resource transfer to the Baker-17 countries fell from +\$11 billion to −\$17 billion during the same period.[42] In sum, debtors experienced serious economic problems during the Baker Plan period because their debt repayments greatly exceeded their access to new financing. From 1981 to 1988, real per capita income in most South American LDCs declined in absolute terms, and living standards in many LDCs fell to levels of the 1950s and 1960s. Thus, some analysts refer to the 1980s as a "lost development decade." Although the Baker Plan's failure resulted partly from unforeseen events such as the collapse of international oil prices, critical theorists view the plan as an "attempt to maintain the fiction that the debt crisis was only temporary and could be surmounted if all parties cooperated."[43] Many debtors were caught in a vicious circle in which their debt burdens hindered their economic growth, and their slow growth prevented them from overcoming their debt problems.[44]

The Brady Plan: 1989–1997

The Baker Plan's failure to promote economic recovery raised concerns about U.S. exports to Latin America and about the effects of continued debt problems on the revival of democratic governments in the region. Riots in Caracas, Venezuela, in February 1989 in reaction to government austerity measures provided further evidence that the Baker Plan was insufficient. In March 1989, U.S. Treasury secretary Nicholas Brady sanctioned the idea of *debt reduction,* or forgiving some LDC debts to commercial banks, referred to as the **Brady Plan.** After the major economic powers resolved their differences on this issue at the July 1989 G7 summit, the IMF adopted the Brady Plan; from that time on, the G7 finance ministers became much more involved in foreign debt issues. Mexico was the first LDC to conclude a Brady Plan debt reduction agreement because it had the largest debts, was liberalizing its economy, had a good track record of adjustment, and was strategically important to the United States.[45]

Like the Baker Plan, the Brady Plan handled debt on a case-by-case basis, with each debtor negotiating separately with its creditors, and it linked the easing of credit terms with the debtor's acceptance of IMF and Bank conditions for liberal economic reform. However, the Baker Plan had rejected debt reduction on the grounds that banks would not lend to countries if they failed to pay their debts, and that LDCs would be able to repay loans if the debt repayment period was extended. The Brady Plan, by contrast, recognized that some highly-indebted LDCs could not regain creditworthiness and that extending the debt repayment period without debt reduction had not returned the debtors to economic growth. The Brady Plan stipulated that U.S. private banks that reduced the principal or interest on LDC debt would receive guarantees of repayment on the remaining portion of debt. The IMF and the Bank would help finance these guarantees, and Japan also committed funds for this purpose. Brady Plan agreements were concluded for 12 LDCs from 1990 to 1994, and for 5 more LDCs from 1995 to 1997.[46] Although the Brady Plan was an improvement over the Baker Plan, it did not resolve all the debt problems of the Baker-17 countries. Table 11.4 compares the external debt for the Baker-17 in 1985 (the year before the Baker Plan was instituted) and in 1997 (the last year that a Brady Plan agreement was concluded). As Table 11.4 shows, the external debt for all but three of the Baker-17 (Yugoslavia, Costa Rica, and Jamaica) increased from 1985 to 1997. Most of these countries were Latin American, and the total foreign debt of Latin America's states increased from $425 billion in 1987 to more than $600 billion in 1997. In 1997, Latin America was paying about 30 percent of its export earnings to service its debts, and it owed about 45 percent of its combined GNI to foreign creditors. However, a country's creditworthiness depends more on its debt-to-GNI ratio than on its foreign debt, and the Brady Plan helped restore the creditworthiness of most of the Baker-17 countries. As Table 11.4 shows, the external-debt-to-GNI ratio was lower in 1997 than in 1985 for most countries other than Nigeria, Cote d'Ivoire, and Ecuador. (IMF data were not available for Venezuela and the former Yugoslavia.)

The Brady Plan's greatest shortcoming was that it dealt only with commercial bank debt. It offered little to low-income LDCs because most of their debt was to governments and international financial institutions. Thus, 11 of the 17 Brady Plan agreements were concluded with the Baker-17 group (mainly middle-income LDCs), and 2 of the agreements were with Eastern European countries (Poland and Bulgaria). In the 1990s the debt situation was far worse for the low-income LDCs, and after the Brady Plan helped restore the creditworthiness of the Baker-17, "the G7 finally mustered enough political will in the mid-1990s to tackle the debt problems of the poorest countries."[47]

Initiatives for the Poorest LDCs

The total external debt of Sub-Saharan African countries increased from $56.2 billion (U.S.) in 1980 to $147 billion in 1990, and their external debt service payments (interest and principal) on long-term loans rose from $4.5 billion to $11.1 billion. Thus, by the early 1990s it was evident that the poorest, heavily indebted LDCs needed more debt relief. The 1996 G7 summit in Lyon, France, addressed this problem by establishing the **Heavily Indebted Poor Countries (HIPC) Initiative,** a plan to alleviate the debts of the poorest LDCs to multilateral institutions. The IMF and the Bank had previously refused to permit debt rescheduling of their loans because this could damage their high credit ratings, and the presence of the IMF director general and World Bank president at the Lyon G7 summit facilitated agreement on the HIPC initiative.[48] The HIPC initiative was designed to reduce the debts of eligible countries to a sustainable level so they could service them without incurring loan arrears or hindering their economic development. The HIPC countries have high debt-to-export ratios, high debt-to-GNI ratios, and low enough incomes to be eligible for soft loans from the Bank group's International Development Association (IDA) (see Chapter 10). Forty-one countries initially met these criteria: 33 in Sub-Saharan Africa and the other 8 in the Americas and Asia. The HIPC program involved a demanding two-stage process, with each stage lasting up to three years. During the first stage, the HIPC country had to implement an IMF and Bank-supported economic reform program. If the IMF and the Bank determined that debt relief was insufficient, the country entered the second stage, where it received some debt relief and financial support from bilateral and commercial creditors and the multilateral institutions. The HIPC initiative was therefore a slow process, and the debt situation of many of the poorest LDCs was not improving. The costs of the debt crisis were also not spread evenly *within* debtor states, and the poorest and most vulnerable people were the most adversely affected.[49]

A London-based civil society organization with worldwide connections called *Jubilee 2000* responded to the debt problems of low-income LDCs with a debt forgiveness campaign. Jubilee 2000 is composed of mainly religious but also some secular NGOs from around the world. Beginning in 1998, Jubilee 2000 called for full debt relief for low-income LDCs by the year 2000 and outlined proposals to accelerate the HIPC process, increase assistance levels, and broaden the eligibility criteria. The rapid economic relief offered to more prosperous LDCs affected by the 1997 Asian financial crisis showed that DCs could move swiftly when foreign investment and the stock market were affected, and Jubilee 2000 demanded similar treatment for low-income LDCs. Jubilee 2000 also engaged in mass demonstrations; for example, it formed a human chain of 50,000 people around the convention center at the 1998 G7 summit. In response, the 1999 G7 summit agreed to establish an *enhanced HIPC initiative,* and the IMF and the Bank adopted the major elements of the G7 proposal. The enhanced initiative more than doubled the amount of debt relief and made the HIPC initiative faster (LDCs received debt relief more quickly), broader (it applied to more countries), and deeper (it permitted more debt relief). However, the poorest LDCs continued to have serious indebtedness problems. For example, the countries with the highest external debt as a percent of GNI in the 2001–2003 period were low-income LDCs such as Sao Tome and Principe (723 percent), Liberia (603 percent), Guinea-Bissau (369 percent), the Republic of the Congo (242 percent), the Democratic Republic of the Congo (222 percent), Mauritania (218 percent), and Sierra Leone (216 percent). In 2005, the World Bank listed 27 of the low-income LDCs as "severely indebted," 17 as "moderately indebted," and only 14 as "less indebted."[50] Although the Bank also listed a number of middle-income LDCs as severely and moderately indebted, most of them had reestablished their creditworthiness as a result of the Baker and Brady plans.

In view of the continuing problems of the poorest LDCs, the 2005 G8 Summit proposed that they be eligible for 100 percent cancellation of their debt owed to the major multilateral lenders. The IMF and World Bank refined this proposal and established the **Multilateral Debt Relief Initiative (MDRI)** in 2006. IMF members with low per capita incomes that have their debts reduced under the Enhanced HIPC Initiative are eligible to have the rest of their debt to the IMF, World Bank, and African Development Bank cancelled under the MDRI.[51] Despite the gradual expansion of debt relief programs for the low-income LDCs, it remains to be seen whether they can overcome the internal and external structural problems underlying their debt problems. It is therefore necessary to look at the overall effectiveness of the debt reduction strategies.

Assessing the Effectiveness of the Debt Strategies

The international debt strategies had three main objectives: to prevent the collapse of the international banking system, to restore capital market access for the debtors, and to restore economic growth in the debtor countries. The Baker and Brady plans were most successful in achieving the first two objectives. In regard to the first objective, by the late 1980s "the banks were no longer in the serious jeopardy that they faced at the outset of the debt crisis."[52] From 1982 to 1992, the loan exposure of U.S. banks to the Baker-17 highly indebted countries fell from 130 percent of the banks' capital and reserves to only 27 percent; the loan exposure of French banks fell from 135 to 23 percent. In regard to the second objective, Latin American debtors were able to return to the international financial markets far more rapidly after the 1980s debt crisis than after the 1930s crisis. Liberal economic theorists view these two criteria as the most important for assessing the effectiveness of the debt strategies, and they therefore believe that the Baker and Brady plans were fairly successful.[53] Some liberals question whether debt reduction for the poorest LDCs in the HIPC and MDRI initiatives is necessary, because the two main liberal objectives of the debt strategies have been achieved,. They argue that debt reduction is "too easy to get" and simply relieves "countries' immediate budget constraint, allowing them to persist with bad economic policies."[54] Historical materialists and some interventionist liberals by contrast see the third objective—restoring economic growth in LDC debtor countries—as the most important, and they considered the Baker and Brady plans to be largely ineffective. For example, one critic argued that the IMF and major creditor states were concerned with increasing "the immediate payment capacity of the debtor nations and not their development."[55] Historical materialists also believe that the debt strategies required more sacrifice from LDCs than from DCs and international bankers, and they therefore argue that "the debt crisis is by no means over yet; a banking crisis may have been tidied up, but a development crisis is in full swing."[56]

The Baker and Brady plans did in fact have serious shortcomings in regard to the third objective of restoring LDC economic growth. This was especially true for the low-income LDC debtors that were not on the Baker-17 list. As discussed, the Baker and Brady plans focused on debt to commercial banks, and they did not provide relief for debt to the IMF and World Bank. Because the poorest LDCs were highly dependent on IMF and Bank loans, the Baker and Brady plans were of little use to them. The North should be credited for gradually developing more assertive debt strategies, shifting from debt rescheduling under the Baker Plan to debt reduction under the Brady Plan to debt relief for the poorest LDCs under the HIPC and MDRI initiatives. However, it always took a new crisis before the IMF, the Bank, and DCs upgraded their debt relief efforts, and it remains to be seen whether the new initiatives will deal with the debt problems of the poorest LDCs. The HIPC and MDRI initiatives recognize that debt relief is sometimes necessary, but successful debt management requires more than debt reduction. It "depends on a country's ability to achieve high growth and foreign-exchange generation—thereby containing debt-to-GDP, debt-to-exports and debt-to-revenues at reasonable ('sustainable') levels."[57]

TRANSITION ECONOMIES AND FOREIGN DEBT

To this point, we have discussed the effects of the debt crisis on LDCs. However, the transition economies in Eastern Europe and the FSU were also foreign debtors in the 1980s and 1990s. The Soviet bloc countries contended with many of the same economic problems as the South, including balance-of-payments deficits, declining terms of trade, and stagnating economic growth. The need for financing also caused Soviet bloc countries to look to the IMF and World Bank for support. Thus, Hungary and Poland joined these institutions in the 1980s, partly to deal with their growing debt problems. Eastern Europeans borrowed heavily on international financial markets in the 1970s to finance industrial investment. However, the oil price shocks, poor investment decisions, economic inefficiency, lack of export competitiveness, and high interest rates on their foreign debt created severe economic problems. Thus, Eastern Europe experienced a debt crisis as early as 1981 when an acute foreign exchange shortage forced Poland to negotiate a rescheduling of its debt with official and private creditors. Poland had financed an ambitious industrial investment program with external funding, but its exports were insufficient to service its debt.[58]

Like the South, Eastern European countries followed different strategies to deal with their foreign debt; the two basic strategies were referred to as the Polish and Czech-Hungarian models. The Polish model involved large debt buildup followed by repeated debt reschedulings and eventually official debt reduction, partly based on political considerations. Poland's debt to the Western DCs increased from $7.6 billion in 1975 to $22.1 billion in 1980, and in 1981 it had the highest debt and debt service ratio in the Soviet bloc. Poland's growing economic problems resulted in severe economic austerity measures and the formation of the anti-Communist Solidarity Movement, and when the Polish government responded to the Solidarity Movement by imposing martial law in December 1981, the West imposed trade sanctions and suspended debt repayment talks. Although private banks agreed to refinance some Polish debt, Western governments did not resume rescheduling negotiations on official debt until Poland ended martial law in 1983.

From 1981 to 1990, Poland had seven reschedulings of its commercial bank debt and five reschedulings of its official debt. When a democratically elected government replaced the communists and began to promote structural change in early 1990, the West gave Poland assistance under the Brady Plan. Western governments, which held two-thirds of Poland's debt, offered a 50-percent forgiveness of its official bilateral debt at Paris Club negotiations in 1991; the Paris Club had previously offered a maximum forgiveness of only 33 percent to LDCs. Under pressure from the G7, commercial banks also agreed to reduce Poland's private debt by 45 percent. Bulgaria followed the Polish model, and the private banks agreed in principle to a substantial reduction of Bulgaria's debt in late 1993 (most of Bulgaria's debt was private). Czechoslovakia and Hungary were also affected by the debt crisis, but unlike the Polish–Bulgarian model they tried to maintain their creditworthiness with more prudent economic policies. For example, in 1981 Hungary had the highest per capita debt in the Soviet bloc and the second highest debt service ratio after Poland. However, Hungary joined the IMF and the Bank in 1982 and instituted ambitious economic reforms. As a result of their more prudent policies, Hungary and Czechoslovakia did not require the debt relief measures that were offered to Poland and Bulgaria.[59]

As with the LDCs, the differing debt strategies of transition economies stemmed partly from domestic economic and political factors. For example, Poland's large debt buildup followed political events that prevented the government from taking decisive action to deal with its debt problems. Wladyslaw Gomulka's removal as first secretary of the Polish Communist party in 1970 resulted in decentralization of the party and divisions within the top political leadership. When serious economic problems resulted from high oil prices and declining exports in the late 1970s, workers were able to resist austerity moves because Poland's political leadership was so fractured. The leaders attempted to raise prices and hold down wages, but massive strikes by workers forced them to reverse these moves. An austerity program was introduced in 1981 when the military took control in Poland and dominated the Solidarity Movement; but that resulted in hardship and further protests.[60] In contrast to

Poland, domestic politics contributed to more prudent economic policies in Hungary. Although Hungary instituted some austerity measures, it also adopted reforms to increase economic efficiency and give profits and prices a larger role in resource allocation. The suppression of the 1956 Hungarian revolt had led to several developments that contributed to these economic reforms. For example, Hungary turned from one-person leadership to collective leadership, which introduced a limited market mechanism and a more balanced development strategy. Hungarian supporters of economic reform also "sought not to weaken the [Communist] party but to use it to pursue their particular economic goals."[61] When Hungary confronted debt problems, its earlier reforms enabled it to meet its debt service obligations much more effectively than Poland.

Despite the different development strategies of Eastern Europeans, their debt problems also resulted from external events largely beyond their control. For example, they suffered economically from increased dependence on imports from nonsocialist states, the collapse of the Soviet bloc's CMEA in 1991, and deteriorating terms of trade as the Soviet Union ended subsidized oil exports. Bulgaria is a prime example of a state affected by external events: The breakup of CMEA had major consequences for Bulgaria because of its export dependence on the Soviet Union, the Gulf War adversely affected Bulgaria's exports to Iraq, and the war in Yugoslavia disrupted Bulgarian export routes to Western Europe. The structural transition to market-oriented economies produced further instability in Eastern Europe, and domestic output fell by almost 25 percent in 1990 and 1991. Thus, a combination of internal and external factors contributed to Eastern Europe's foreign debt problems.

THE IMF, THE WORLD BANK, AND THE DEBT CRISIS

The IMF and World Bank had a central role in the 1980s debt crisis, and the crisis altered the relationship between these two institutions as they adopted new overlapping functions. This was not the original intention of the Bretton Woods negotiators, who wanted the IMF and the Bank to have separate functions; thus, they excluded specific references to the South in the IMF Articles of Agreement and assigned the development function to the Bank. Whereas the IMF was to provide short-term loans to *any* country with balance-of-payments problems, the Bank was to provide long-term loans for reconstruction and development. (The South was later mentioned in the second amendment to the IMF Articles of Agreement.) The only direct linkage between the two organizations was that membership in the IMF was a prerequisite for Bank membership. However, the Bank began to infringe on IMF territory in the 1960s. Diverging from its practice of providing loans for specific development projects, the Bank provided *program lending* to India for balance-of-payments support; and it linked its loans with conditions that India should reform its policies. The Bank justified its actions by asserting that India's balance-of-payments deficit resulted from long-term development problems. However, the IMF argued that the Bank's balance-of-payments funding with conditionality infringed on its functions. In 1966 the two organizations signed an agreement to avoid further overlap, but it did not fully differentiate their responsibilities.[62]

Several changes in the 1970s increased the overlap between the IMF and Bank functions. First, the IMF lost its role of stabilizing exchange rates when the Bretton Woods system of pegged exchange rates collapsed. The IMF's other function of providing loans, in which there is potential overlap with the Bank, therefore became more prominent. Second, the IMF initially provided loans to all countries, but by the late 1970s it was lending almost exclusively to LDCs—the same countries receiving Bank loans. Third, although the Bank's Articles of Agreement (Article 3, Section 4) state that it should provide loans for specific projects "except in special circumstances," some LDCs needed development funding for purposes other than specific projects. In 1971, the Bank therefore decided that program loans of the type they had provided to India in the 1960s were appropriate under some circumstances. The Bank's program loans to finance commodity imports have distinct similarities with IMF loans for balance-of-payments purposes.[63] However, the main reason for increased overlap was the 1980s foreign debt crisis. The IMF's short-term loans for balance-of-payments problems with 3- to 5-year repayment periods were inadequate for LDCs with longer-term debt problems, and it therefore began to provide *medium-term* SALs with repayment periods of 5–10 years. The Bank's long-term loans for development projects with repayment periods of 15–20 years were also not what LDC debtors required to deal with more immediate balance-of-payments problems, and like the IMF, the Bank provided medium-term SALs to debtor countries. Although the IMF still provided short-term balance-of-payments loans and the Bank provided long-term development loans, they *both* were now providing medium-term SALs to indebted countries.[64]

The greater overlap of IMF and Bank functions has increased both conflict and the need for collaboration. The overlap also raises questions as to whether two institutions are necessary, and the *Economist* predicted in 1991 that a merger between the two "makes sense, and in time it will happen."[65] Despite this prediction, the IMF and the Bank both perform important functions. First, the Bank group is composed of five institutions, and it is already too large for efficient management (see Chapter 10); joining the Bank and the IMF would compound the problems related to size. Second, development issues are highly complex, and a range of institutions are needed to provide advice and loans. Although historical materialists argue that IMF and Bank policies are virtually identical, liberal economists point to IMF–Bank disputes as an indication of competing perspectives. Third, IMF and Bank responsibilities extend well beyond providing loans to LDCs. Although the IMF's monetary role declined when the pegged exchange rate regime collapsed, the IMF continues to advise states on monetary issues, and it could play a more important role in future monetary and financial issues. As discussed in Chapter 10, the Bank is a source of economic expertise on development issues. Finally, the breakup of the Soviet bloc, the financial crises, and the economic problems in Sub-Saharan Africa provide sufficient economic challenges for both institutions. Whereas the IMF has coordinated actions to deal with Eastern European and FSU debt and the Asian financial crisis, the Bank has coordinated aid efforts in Sub-Saharan Africa.[66]

Although IMF–Bank collaboration is partly designed to avert institutional conflict, the South is highly suspicious of these moves. Historical materialists and the debtors often criticize IMF conditionality as an unwarranted infringement on LDC sovereignty, and they argue that the liberal economic conditions on IMF and World Bank loans hinder LDC development. Moves toward IMF–Bank collaboration concern the South because of possible *cross-conditionality,* in which an IMF decision that a loan applicant is uncreditworthy also prevents the applicant from receiving Bank funding. Although the IMF and the Bank rule out cross-conditionality in a formal, legal sense, they sometimes practice it informally.[67] Critics also charge that IMF and Bank SALs put the onus of adjustment on LDC debtors and vulnerable groups within LDCs, even though the North shared responsibility for the debt crisis. The SAL prescription for improving LDC balance of payments is to reduce spending for social services, lower wages, produce more for export than for local consumption, and end subsidies for local industries. However, poorer LDC women who manage the household are the most severely affected by IMF and Bank pressures for a reduction in funding for public services. Thus, poorer women pay the price for structural adjustment programs through increased unpaid work and a deterioration of health and nutrition.[68] IMF and Bank officials argue that structural adjustment aimed at market efficiency and decreased public sector involvement can be compatible with social welfare goals, but they have not convinced their critics.

THE 1990s ASIAN FINANCIAL CRISIS

This section discusses the 1990s East and Southeast Asian financial crisis (or the Asian financial crisis). Of particular interest are the challenges the crisis posed to the IMF and international financial stability and the proposals that emerged to improve the "international financial architecture." Chapter 10 discusses the crisis in the context of international development. As discussed, international bank lending to LDCs sharply declined during the 1980s as a result of the foreign debt crisis. In the 1990s, private capital flows to middle-income LDCs increased again, but there was a change in the source of this capital. Whereas commercial bank lending was of primary importance in the 1970s and 1980s, *portfolio investment,* or the purchase of stocks, bonds, and money market instruments by foreigners, was much more important in the 1990s. *Foreign direct investment,* or the foreign ownership or control of assets, also increased during the 1990s (see Chapter 9). Indeed, the net private capital flows to 29 "emerging market economies" increased from $35 billion in 1990 to $334 billion in 1996. (Emerging market economies are LDCs able to attract private capital flows.[69]) This revival of capital flows resulted from LDC economic reforms in response to the debt crisis, the success of the Brady Plan debt reductions, higher interest rates in the South, and a freeing of capital controls on investment in LDCs. However, some economists expressed concerns that these capital flows were volatile and "could be reversed easily."[70] Their concerns were soon realized when capital inflows to Mexico halted rather suddenly in 1994. This section devotes primary attention to the 1997–1999 Asian financial crisis because "it was the sharpest financial crisis to hit the developing world since the 1982 debt crisis."[71]

The Asian financial crisis began in Thailand in July 1997, when there was a massive run on its currency, the *baht*. The roots of this crisis can be traced to the early 1990s, when capital inflows to Thailand rose dramatically even though the country's economic and financial conditions were deteriorating; Thailand's current account deficit was increasing, its property prices were declining, and Thai banks were incurring a sizable foreign currency debt. Like other East Asian currencies, the baht was pegged to the U.S. dollar, and Thai exports became less competitive when the dollar's exchange rate rose against the Japanese yen. Thus, Thailand had to allow its baht to float because of downward pressure on the currency. Despite government efforts to bolster the baht, capital outflows caused the currency to lose 48.7 percent of its value over the next six months, and this resulted in a sharp decrease in the country's assets and growth. After the baht began to depreciate, the currencies of other Asian countries such as Indonesia, South Korea, Malaysia, the Philippines, and Singapore also came under severe downward pressure. All of these countries experienced rapid outflows of capital, depreciation of their currencies, and dramatic declines in their stock markets. Most of these countries also had recessions, banking crises, and lower economic growth rates. Thus, Thailand, Indonesia, and South Korea had to seek IMF and World Bank loans to bolster their currencies and economies. The economic problems also led to political problems, with major demonstrations resulting in the resignation of Indonesia's President Suharto, and transfers of power in Thailand, South Korea, and the Philippines.[72]

The main concerns of the 1980s debt crisis had related to the overall indebtedness and high debt-service ratios of many LDC governments. However, in the Asian financial crisis the debts of governments such as Thailand, Indonesia, and South Korea to private and official creditors were relatively small. Domestic banks and private companies in Asia, by contrast, had borrowed heavily from foreign creditors, and they owed large amounts when capital flows were reversed. The Asian governments had the difficult and expensive tasks of overhauling insolvent banking systems and restructuring corporate debt. In sum, while the 1980s debt crisis resulted from "unsustainable current account deficits and poor macroeconomic fundamentals," the "Asian crisis was essentially a 'capital account crisis.' "[73] As Chapter 10 discusses, the financial crisis proved to be only a temporary setback, and the Asian economies have generally resumed their rapid rate of growth. However, there were concerns that financial crises could recur because of the increased capital flows. Thus, the major DC governments proposed a number of reforms to strengthen global governance in finance, or the *international financial architecture*.[74]

The annual G7 summits played an important role in the architecture exercise, which began in 1995 in response to the Mexican financial crisis and evolved in response to the Asian crisis and a financial crisis in Russia. The architecture exercise led to the creation of new IMF lending facilities, efforts to strengthen the financial infrastructure in LDCs and transition economies, and a debate regarding the role of the IMF and its conditionality requirements. Major objectives were to develop better strategies to prevent and resolve financial crises. *Crisis prevention* involved identifying vulnerable countries before they experienced crises and fostering compliance with international standards to produce financial stability. *Crisis resolution* involved reforming IMF policies and involving private creditors in efforts to resolve financial problems of LDCs and transition economies.[75] Prescriptions for the best measures to reform the international financial architecture depend on one's theoretical perspective, and the following discussion compares the views of four groups:

1. Orthodox liberals.
2. Those combining orthodox and institutional liberalism.
3. Those combining interventionist and institutional liberalism.
4. Historical materialists.[76]

As discussed in Chapter 4, orthodox liberals promote freedom of the market to function with minimal interference from the state. Thus, liberals such as Milton Friedman see the problems with international finance as stemming from inadequate domestic institutions and policies, not from the freeing of capital flows. From this perspective, the 1994 Mexican peso crisis resulted from an overvalued exchange rate and inadequate attention to the country's trade and budget deficits and foreign debt; the 1997 Asian financial crisis stemmed from inaccurate financial reporting, pegged exchange rates, and banks offering questionable loans to businesses with political connections. Freer global capital flows were not responsible for the Asian financial problems. On the contrary, capital flows maximize efficiency because they are directed to countries with balanced budgets, stable markets, and low inflation rates. International regulation to limit risky behavior in capital markets would be harmful, and all capital controls should be abolished. Some economists believe that *a lender of last resort* is necessary for states with financial problems and that the IMF could perform this function if it had more financial resources. A lender of last resort "is an institution that is willing and able to supply unlimited amounts of short-term credit to financial institutions when they are threatened by a creditor panic."[77] However, orthodox liberals argue that the best way to prevent capital flight and speculative attacks on a state's currency is to eliminate the problem of **moral hazard.** Moral hazard refers to the idea that protection against risk encourages a person or state to engage in riskier behavior. If a lender of last resort exists, states facing financial crises are more likely to engage in risky and irresponsible behavior because they can always count on the lender to rescue them. Some orthodox liberals criticize the IMF and the Bank for contributing to moral hazard by providing development assistance, debt bailouts, and balance-of-payments support.

The second group of scholars combines orthodox and institutional liberalism. Like the first group, they believe that inadequate domestic policies are the main factors increasing a country's vulnerability to financial crises, and that the Asian financial crisis stemmed more from "crony capitalism" or overly close connections between business groups and governments than from financial contagion. Unlike the first group, however, they see an important role for international financial institutions such as the IMF and World Bank in ensuring that LDCs and transition economies follow transparent, liberal economic policies. Thus, they favor strong IMF conditionality requirements to ensure that states are subject to the discipline of the marketplace and IMF policies that "legitimize financial liberalization" and block "tendencies to move toward increased state regulation of international financial flows."[78]

The third group of scholars combines interventionist and institutional liberalism. As liberals, they assume that the failure of countries to follow liberal economic policies interferes with efficiently functioning markets. As *interventionist* liberals, however, they feel that *unrestrained* markets are not beneficial and that measures must be taken to protect society (see Chapter 4). In finance, currency traders often buy and sell for profit without taking account of fundamental economic conditions, and this produces unnecessary volatility in capital flows and foreign exchange markets. Thus, financial markets are likely to perform better when regulated. The third group also emphasizes the need for a well-funded international lender of last resort. Without such a lender, financial crises may increase and detract from global economic efficiency and development in LDCs and transition economies.[79] Many theorists in this group have been actively involved in the debate regarding the international financial architecture. For example, some members of this group responded to the Asian financial crisis by supporting the *Tobin tax,* which Nobel Laureate James Tobin first proposed in 1972. Tobin's proposal called for "an internationally uniform tax on all spot conversions of one currency into another, proportional to the size of the transaction."[80] Although Tobin recommended a tax of only 1 percent, he believed that it would discourage short-term speculative capital flows and generate revenue that could be used for purposes such as combating international poverty. Many supporters of the Tobin tax argue that it would help reduce the risk of global financial crises and provide the international community with some of the profits flowing from international capital mobility. However, critics of the Tobin tax range from orthodox liberals who insist there is nothing wrong with the financial markets, to others who argue that such a tax would not be effective. Whereas currency traders in times of crisis would disregard a small tax, a larger tax would seriously interfere with financial markets.[81] As institutional as well as interventionist liberals, the third group proposes numerous reforms in IMF and World Bank transparency, accountability, and conditionality requirements. They also support the idea that the IMF should become a lender of last resort.[82]

The fourth group of scholars are historical materialists who view the Asian financial crisis as another example of the corrupting power of international capital. Unlike interventionist liberals, they think that the IMF and the Bank are unreformable, and (like some orthodox liberals) they therefore favor the abolition of these institutions. For example, one study concludes that "the international financial institutions require Third World countries to adopt policies that harm the interests of working people."[83] Until recently, the second group (orthodox and institutional liberals) had the most influence in discussions of the international financial architecture.[84] However, the third group (interventionist and institutional liberals) has been gaining more influence as a result of the global financial crisis which began in the first decade of the twenty-first century.

THE GLOBAL FINANCIAL CRISIS—2008 TO ?

The global financial crisis is different from the 1980s debt crisis and the 1990s Asian financial crisis because it began in the North rather than the South, specifically in the United States. However, there are similarities between these crises, regardless of their origins. As discussed, the global financial crisis began with a subprime crisis in the U.S. housing market that resulted in a global credit crunch and financial failures in many countries. U.S. housing prices and home ownership increased dramatically in the late 1990s, and investing in a house seemed to be a means of gaining financial security. Relatively low interest rates contributed to increases in house prices and in mortgage financing. A substantial share of this mortgage financing was through subprime mortgages, which are mortgages for borrowers who do not qualify for market interest rates because of income level, credit history, size of the downpayment, and/or employment prospects. The high prices made it profitable to build houses, but this resulted in an oversupply and U.S. house prices began to fall in mid-2006 at an accelerating rate. Lower "teaser" mortgage rates that mortgage lenders had initially provided to entice possible homeowners were also coming up for renewal at higher rates. Many subprime borrowers who could not pay the higher rates had to default on their loans, and they ended up owing more than the value of their houses because of the declining prices. The U.S. subprime crisis has had serious repercussions around the globe, because the subprime mortgages were packaged and sold to investors in many countries. The credit crisis has also led to defaults in other areas besides housing such as automobile loans and credit card payments.[85]

What are some of the similarities between the subprime crisis and the previous two crises? Although the subprime crisis began in the United States, one can draw some parallels between U.S. subprime borrowers and LDCs in the previous two crises, because subprime borrowers (like LDCs) are poorer and more vulnerable to financial distress. Critical theorists pointed to "loan pushing" by international banks recycling OPEC petrodollars as a cause of the 1980s debt crisis, and mortgage pushing by highly assertive mortgage lenders was a cause of the current crisis. As with the international banks in the 1970s, the mortgage lenders did little to assess borrowers' ability to repay their loans, and they encouraged people who were credit risks to borrow in the subprime mortgage market. Subprime lenders also sought to persuade legislators to forgo regulations restricting lending to borrowers with poor credit ratings. For example, one of the largest U.S. subprime lenders (Ameriquest Mortgage Company) reportedly spent more than $20 million on political donations. Rating agencies such as Moody's, Standard and Poor's (S&P), and Fitch issued some warnings about emerging problems in the subprime market, but critics argue that their warnings were too little and too late. U.S. House Committee hearings on the subprime crisis have pointed to possible conflicts of interest because of services that the rating agencies provide to mortgage lenders.[86] Mortgage buyers also bear some responsibility for the subprime crisis just as LDC borrowers bore some responsibility for the 1980s debt crisis. Many mortgage buyers were overly complacent about their personal debts, accustomed to living beyond their means, and inclined towards having unrealistic expectations. As Robert Shiller points out, mortgage buyers as well as sellers were susceptible to an irrational "contagion of ideas" that the housing boom would continue indefinitely. As was the case with the 1980s debt crisis and the 1990s financial crisis, this contagion of ideas seemed to blind both the credit agencies and those in responsible positions such as Alan Greenspan of the Federal Reserve, Ben Bernanke of the Council of Economic Advisers, and President George W. Bush to the severity of the emerging problems.[87] Although the 2008 global financial crisis began in the North, the resulting credit crunch has been felt strongly in the South. Thus, many LDCs have turned to the IMF for assistance, as they did in the 1980s debt crisis and the 1990s Asian financial crisis.

We can also find similarities between the possible solutions to the three crises. As with the 1980s debt crisis and the 1990s financial crisis, it is first necessary to have a "firefighting strategy" to deal with the immediate problems created by the bursting of the housing bubble and its aftermath. An immediate problem in all three of the crises was the inability or reluctance of banks and other lending agencies to provide credit and finance. In the 2008 global crisis, DCs and some LDCs and transition economies have instituted huge bailout programs for their banks and other institutions. As with the Asian financial crisis, there is a debate between those calling for even more assistance and those warning that too much assistance could encourage risk taking because of "moral hazard." After the immediate problems are dealt with, there is the more difficult problem of restructuring the financial system to prevent a recurrence of the problems. In the 1990s financial crisis, many referred to this as reforming the "international financial architecture." In the current crisis, there is a need for greater transparency and tighter regulation of the banking and financial industry.

Despite the similarities, there are also some major differences between the previous crises and the 2008 global financial crisis. First, whereas the G7/G8 provided the political support for dealing with the earlier debt and Asian financial crises, the G20 is having a more important role in dealing with the 2008 crisis. This is an indication of the growing power of some emerging countries such as the BRIC economies, and of some shift in economic power from the West to Asia. Second, a major cause of the 2008 crisis is the imbalance of foreign exchange reserves, with the United States having a massive foreign debt, and emerging countries such as China, South Korea, and some OPEC members having growing reserves. Thus, IMF lending resources will now depend more on some emerging countries, and they are demanding a greater role in IMF and World Bank decision making. In an April 2009 meeting, the G20 agreed to complete a new balance of power in the IMF by 2011, with some changes in the weighted voting, and in the selection of the IMF and World Bank heads on the basis of merit and not by nationality. Third, the 1990s Asian financial crisis resulted in strong criticisms of the IMF to the point where some observers were questioning the future of the organization. The 2008 crisis has given the IMF a new sense of purpose, because the G20 has decided to give it a substantial increase in resources to deal with the financial problems of poorer countries. Finally, the 2008 crisis more than the previous crises has raised questions about the adequacy of the unrestrained market, and there has been a noted shift back toward interventionist liberalism with similarities to the post–World War II period.

Considering IPE Theory and Practice

What is the relevance of the IPE theoretical perspectives for the 1980s foreign debt crisis? Most observers agree that unexpected changes such as the food and oil crises of the 1970s were a major cause of the debt crisis. However, orthodox liberals also see imprudent borrowing and inefficient domestic policies of LDCs as major causes. Historical materialists focus instead on the irresponsible behavior of commercial banks and creditor governments and the long-term dependency of LDCs. In response to the debt crisis, DCs, the IMF and the World Bank induced, the debtors to adopt liberal economic policies, and views sharply differ regarding the effects of these debt strategies. Liberal economists argue that the strategies were quite successful, because they prevented the collapse of the international banking system and restored capital market access for many indebted states. Although the debtors' policy changes caused hardship for some groups and individuals, the long-term effects of the shift to economic openness benefited LDCs and transition economies. Realists and historical materialists, by contrast, argue that liberals ignore the effect of inequality among states on the debt issue. Although globalization facilitated the *transmission* of liberal values to the DCs, these values were *imposed on* LDC debtor states.[88] Furthermore, historical materialists argue that the debt strategies required far more sacrifice from LDC debtors than from international banks and that IMF and World Bank conditionality requirements served the needs of international capital. IMF requirements that debtors reduce social expenditures, increase exports, remove restrictions on capital flows, and devalue their currencies had a negative impact on the poorest and weakest societal groups.

Assessments of the 1990s Asian financial crisis, like the 1980s debt crisis, depend on one's theoretical perspective. Orthodox liberals attributed the Asian financial crisis mainly to inefficient domestic policies, and they opposed international controls on capital flows. Whereas some extreme orthodox liberals argue that the IMF and the Bank should be abolished because they contribute to moral hazard, others encourage these institutions to strengthen their conditionality requirements to ensure that LDCs and transition economies are subject to market discipline. Interventionist liberals by contrast see some degree of control over capital flows as necessary and argue for institutional reforms making the IMF and the Bank more transparent and accountable. In contrast to orthodox liberals, interventionist liberals also call for a lender of last resort. The harshest critics of international capital flows are historical materialists, who argue that the IMF and the Bank are agents of international capital and are unreformable. Interventionist liberals were the most supportive of developing a new international financial architecture that would ensure adequate transparency and regulation of domestic and international financial systems, provide sufficient international official liquidity in crisis conditions, and create mechanisms for orderly debt management and development finance. However, progress in developing a new financial architecture has been limited, largely because of differences between DCs on the one hand and LDCs and transition economies on the other.[89]

The lack of financial reforms was a major factor contributing to the 2008 global financial crisis, which differed from the previous two crises because it originated in the North, in particular in the United States. As with the previous two crises, there are competing views of the causes of the U.S. subprime mortgage crisis, with some casting blame on the subprime lenders and the rating agencies, others blaming the subprime borrowers, and still others referring to the lack of regulation in global financial relations. There is also a lack of agreement on the best means of dealing with the crisis, with some warning that bailing large banks and corporations out will lead to "moral hazard" and others warning that the banks and corporations are "too big to fail." As with the 1990s, the subprime mortgage crisis has led to calls for major financial reforms. The main global actors failed to establish a new international financial architecture after the 1990s financial crisis, and it remains to be seen whether they will be more successful in reforming the domestic and international financial systems after the 2008 global financial crisis.

Questions

1. What are the liberal and historical materialist views regarding the causes of the 1980s foreign debt crisis?
2. Do liberals and historical materialists believe that the debt strategies have successfully dealt with the worst aspects of the debt crisis? Do you feel that debt reduction is necessary or that it contributes to moral hazard?
3. How did the 1980s debt crisis differ from the 1990s Asian financial crisis? What are the similarities and differences between the 2008 global financial crisis and the two earlier crises discussed in this chapter?
4. What are the views of orthodox, institutional, and interventionist liberals and historical materialists regarding the best means for reforming the international financial architecture? Was a new financial architecture developed as a result of the 1990s Asian financial crisis?
5. What is the relationship among the London Clubs, the IMF, and the Paris Club in dealing with foreign debt? Why do you think some of the most important institutional groupings such as the Paris Club, the London Clubs, the G7/G8, and the G20 are so informal?
6. What were the strengths and weaknesses of the Baker Plan, Brady Plan, and HIPC and MDRI Initiatives? How do you explain the fact that the Baker and Brady plans did not address the problems of the poorest LDC debtors?
7. What are the competing theoretical views of the causes, and remedies for, the 2008 global financial crisis? Which of these views do you find most convincing? Do you think that the 2008 global financial crisis is likely to have an effect on U.S. economic hegemony?
8. How have the roles of the IMF and World Bank, and the relationship between these two institutions, changed as a result of the foreign debt and financial crises?

Further Reading

Good recent books on the foreign debt crisis include Lex Rieffel, *Restructuring Sovereign Debt: The Case for Ad Hoc Machinery* (Washington, D.C.: Brookings Institution Press, 2003); Chris Jochnick and Fraser A. Preston, eds., *Sovereign Debt at the Crossroads: Challenges and Proposals for Resolving the Third World Debt Crisis* (New York: Oxford University Press, 2006); Christian Barry, Barry Herman, and Lydia Tomitova, eds., *Dealing Fairly with Developing Country Debt* (Malden, MA: Blackwell, 2007); and A. Geske Dijkstra, *The Impact of International Debt Relief* (New York: Routledge, 2008).

Books on global and development finance that deal with both debt and financial crises include Tony Addison and George Mavrotas, eds., *Development Finance in the Global Economy: The Road Ahead* (New York: Palgrave Macmillan, 2008); Stephen Spratt, *Development Finance: Debates, Dogmas and New Directions* (New York: Routledge, 2009); Martin Wolf, *Fixing Global Finance* (Baltimore, MD: Johns Hopkins University Press, 2008); and Tony Porter, *Globalization and Finance* (Malden, MA: Polity Press, 2005).

On national responses to the 1990s Asian financial crisis, see T. J. Pempel, ed. *The Politics of the Asian Economic Crisis* (Ithaca, NY: Cornell University Press, 1999). On the financial crisis and the need to develop new international financial arrangements, see Leslie E. Armijo, ed., *Debating the Global Financial Architecture* (Albany, NY: State University of New York Press, 2002); Peter B. Kenen, *The International Financial Architecture: What's New? What's Missing?* (Washington, D.C.: Institute of International Economics, 2001); Ben Thirkell-White, *The IMF and the Politics of Financial Globalization: From the Asian Crisis to a New International Financial Architecture?* (New York: Palgrave, 2005); Karl Kaiser, John J. Kirton, and Joseph P. Daniels, eds., *Shaping a New International Financial System: Challenges of Governance in a Globalizing World* (Burlington, VT: Ashgate, 2000); and Dilip K. Das, *Asian Economy and Finance: A Post-Crisis Perspective* (New York: Springer, 2005). On the need to reform the IMF, see Edwin M. Truman, ed., *Reforming the IMF for the 21st Century* (Washington, D.C.: Institute for International Economics, 2006).

On the subprime mortgage crisis, see Robert Shiller, *The Subprime Solution: How Today's Global Financial Crisis Happened, and What to Do about It* (Princeton, NJ: Princeton University Press, 2008); and Charles R. Morris, *The Trillion Dollar Meltdown* (New York: Public Affairs, 2008).

Notes

1. William R. Cline, *International Debt Reexamined* (Washington, D.C.: Institute for International Economics, 1995), p. 1.
2. Lex Rieffel, *Restructuring Sovereign Debt: The Case for Ad Hoc Machinery* (Washington, D.C.: Brookings Institution, 2003), pp. 9–16.
3. Miles Kahler, "Politics and International Debt: Explaining the Crisis," *International Organization* 39, no. 3 (Summer 1985), p. 357.
4. Barry Eichengreen and Richard Portes, "Dealing with Debt: The 1930s and the 1980s," in Ishrat Husain and Ishac Diwan, eds., *Dealing with the Debt Crisis: A World Bank Symposium* (Washington, D.C.: World Bank, 1989), pp. 69–86; and Barry Eichengreen and Peter H. Lindert, eds., *The International Debt Crisis in Historical Perspective* (Cambridge, MA: MIT Press, 1989).
5. Stuart Corbridge, *Debt and Development* (Oxford, UK: Blackwell, 1993), p. 25; Barbara Stallings, *Banker to the Third World: U.S. Portfolio Investment in Latin America, 1900–1986* (Berkeley, CA: University of California Press, 1987), pp. 313–314.
6. Rieffel, *Restructuring Sovereign Debt,* pp. 22–23.
7. *World Bank Annual Report—1983* (Washington, D.C.: World Bank, 1983), p. 34; John T. Cuddington, "The Extent and Causes of the Debt Crisis of the 1980s," in Ishrat Husain and Ishac Diwan, eds., *Dealing with the Debt Crisis: A World Bank Symposium* (Washington, D.C.: World Bank, 1989), p. 15; World Bank, *World Debt Tables 1992–1993,* vol. 1 (Washington, D.C.: World Bank, 1992), pp. 41–45.
8. Theodore H. Cohn, *Canadian Food Aid: Domestic and Foreign Policy Implications* (Denver, CO: University of Denver, Graduate School of International Studies, 1979), pp. 25–26.
9. Charles Lipson, "The International Organization of Third World Debt," *International Organization* 35, no. 4 (Autumn 1981), p. 611; Benjamin J. Cohen, "Balance-of-Payments Financing: Evolution of a Regime," in Stephen D. Krasner, ed., *International Regimes* (Ithaca, NY: Cornell University Press, 1983), p. 329.

10. Albert Fishlow, "Lessons from the Past: Capital Markets During the 19th Century and the Interwar Period," *International Organization* 39, no. 3 (Summer 1985), p. 433.
11. Kahler, "Politics and International Debt," pp. 358–359.
12. Stallings, *Banker to the Third World,* pp. 184–186.
13. Ethan B. Kapstein, *Governing the Global Economy: International Finance and the State* (Cambridge, MA: Harvard University Press, 1994), pp. 60–69.
14. *IMF Annual Report—1977* (Washington, D.C.: International Monetary Fund, 1977), pp. 40–41.
15. Robert D. Putnam, "Diplomacy and Domestic Politics: The Logic of Two-level Games," *International Organization* 42, no. 3 (Summer 1988), p. 457.
16. James R. Vreeland, "Why Do Governments and the IMF Enter into Agreements? Statistically Selected Cases," *International Political Science Review* 24, no. 3 (2003), pp. 338–339.
17. Jeffrey Sachs, "External Debt and Macroeconomic Performance in Latin America and East Asia," in William C. Brainard and George L. Perry, eds., *Brookings Papers on Economic Activity,* vol. 2 (Washington, D.C.: Brookings Institution, 1985), pp. 523–535.
18. Sachs, "External Debt and Macroeconomic Performance in Latin America and East Asia," p. 526; Lewis W. Snider, "The Political Performance of Third World Governments and the Debt Crisis," *American Political Science Review* 84, no. 1 (December 1990), pp. 1263–1280.
19. Cheryl Payer, *The Debt Trap: The IMF and the Third World* (Middlesex, UK: Penguin, 1974), pp. 45–49; Peter Körner, Gero Maass, Thomas Siebold, and Ranier Tetzlaff, *The IMF and the Debt Crisis: A Guide to the Third World's Dilemma* (London: Zed Books, 1986), pp. 30–31; Peter Evans, *Dependent Development: The Alliance of Multinational, State, and Local Capital in Brazil* (Princeton, NJ: Princeton University Press, 1979).
20. Payer, *The Debt Trap,* p. 48.
21. Jesús Silva-Herzog, "The Costs for Latin America's Development," in Robert A. Pastor, ed., *Latin America's Debt Crisis: Adjusting to the Past or Planning for the Future?* (Boulder, CO: Lynne Rienner, 1987), p. 33.
22. Peter H. Lindert and Peter J. Morton, "How Sovereign Debt Has Worked," in Jeffrey D. Sachs, ed., *Developing Country Debt and Economic Performance, Vol. 1: The International Financial System* (Chicago, IL: University of Chicago Press, 1989), pp. 66–77; Nicholas Bayne, *Hanging in There: The G7 and G8 Summit in Maturity and Renewal* (Burlington, VT: Ashgate, 2000), p. 38.
23. Vinod K. Aggarwal, *Liberal Protectionism: The International Politics of Organized Textile Trade* (Berkeley, CA: University of California Press, 1985); Theodore H. Cohn, "The Changing Role of the United States in the Global Agricultural Trade Regime," in William P. Avery, ed., *World Agriculture and the GATT, International Political Economy Yearbook,* vol. 7 (Boulder, CO: Lynne Rienner, 1993), pp. 17–38.
24. On the balance-of-payments financing regime, see Cohen, "Balance-of-Payments Financing," pp. 315–336.
25. Cohen, "Balance-of-Payments Financing," pp. 319–323.
26. Valerie J. Assetto, *The Soviet Bloc in the IMF and the IBRD* (Boulder, CO: Westview Press, 1988), pp. 186–187; Jozef M. van Brabant, *The Planned Economies and International Economic Organizations* (New York: Cambridge University Press, 1991), p. 126.

27. Harold K. Jacobson and Michel Oksenberg, *China's Participation in the IMF, the World Bank, and GATT: Toward a Global Economic Order* (Ann Arbor, MI: University of Michigan Press, 1990), pp. 46–52.

28. Klaus Schröder, "The IMF and the Countries of the Council for Mutual Economic Assistance," *Intereconomics* 2 (March/April 1982), pp. 88–90; Marie Lavigne, "Eastern European Countries and the IMF," in Béla Csikós-Nagy and David G. Young, eds., *East–West Economic Relations in the Changing Global Environment* (London: Macmillan, 1986), pp. 300–304.

29. Leah A. Haus, *Globalizing the GATT: The Soviet Union's Successor States, Eastern Europe, and the International Trading System* (Washington, D.C.: Brookings Institution, 1992), p. 104.

30. Assetto, *The Soviet Bloc in the IMF and the IBRD,* p. 50.

31. Jacobson and Oksenberg, *China's Participation in the IMF, the World Bank, and GATT,* p. 128; William Feeney, "Chinese Policy in Multilateral Financial Institutions," in Samuel S. Kim, ed., *China and the World: Chinese Foreign Policy in the Post-Mao Era* (Boulder, CO: Westview Press, 1984), p. 274; Richard W. Stevenson, "In Borrowing from the I.M.F., Did Yeltsin Get a Sweetheart Deal?" *New York Times,* March 3, 1996, p. A5.

32. Alexis Rieffel, *The Role of the Paris Club in Managing Debt Problems* (Princeton, NJ: Princeton University, Essays in International Finance, no. 161, December 1985), pp. 4–14; Barry Herman, "The Players and the Game of Sovereign Debt," in Christian Barry, Barry Herman, and Lydia Tomitova, eds., *Dealing Fairly with Developing Country Debt* (Malden, MA: Blackwell, 2007), pp. 25–28.

33. Charles Lipson, "International Debt and International Institutions," in Miles Kahler, ed., *The Politics of International Debt* (Ithaca, NY: Cornell University Press, 1986), pp. 222–226; Charles Lipson, "Bankers' Dilemmas: Private Cooperation in Rescheduling Sovereign Debts," in Kenneth A. Oye, ed., *Cooperation Under Anarchy* (Princeton, NJ: Princeton University Press, 1986), pp. 200–225.

34. See Cheryl Payer, *Lent and Lost: Foreign Credit and Third World Development* (London: Zed Books, 1991), pp. 52–56.

35. Harold James, *International Monetary Cooperation Since Bretton Woods* (New York: Oxford University Press, 1996), p. 347.

36. Benjamin J. Cohen, "International Debt and Linkage Strategies: Some Foreign-policy Implications for the United States," *International Organization* 39, no. 4 (Autumn 1985), p. 722.

37. Paul Krugman, "LDC Debt Policy," in Martin Feldstein, ed., *American Economic Policy in the 1980s* (Chicago, IL: University of Chicago Press, 1994), pp. 692–694; Age F. P. Bakker, *International Financial Institutions* (New York: Longman, 1996), pp. 95–96.

38. William R. Cline, *International Debt and the Stability of the World Economy* (Washington, D.C.: Institute for International Economics, 1983), p. 74.

39. Lipson, "Bankers' Dilemmas," p. 223; Lipson, "International Debt and International Institutions," pp. 220–227.

40. William R. Cline, "The Baker Plan and Brady Reformulation: An Evaluation," in Ishrat Husain and Ishac Diwan, eds., *Dealing with the Debt Crisis: A World Bank Symposium* (Washington, D.C.: World Bank, 1989), p. 177.

41. Corbridge, *Debt and Development,* p. 65.

42. Edwin M. Truman, "U.S. Policy on the Problems of International Debt," *Federal Reserve Bulletin* 75, no. 11 (November 1989), p. 730; Richard E. Feinberg and

Delia M. Boylan, "Modular Multilateralism: North–South Economic Relations in the 1990s," in Brad Roberts, ed., *New Forces in the World Economy* (Cambridge, MA: MIT Press, 1996), p. 45.

43. Payer, *Lent and Lost,* p. 97.

44. Paul R. Krugman, "Debt Relief Is Cheap," *Foreign Policy* 80 (Fall 1990), pp. 141–152.

45. Ross P. Buckley, "The Facilitation of the Brady Plan: Emerging Markets Debt Trading from 1989 to 1993," *Fordham International Law Journal* 21, no. 5 (1998), p. 1805; Bayne, *Hanging in There,* pp. 64–65; Rieffel, *Restructuring Sovereign Debt,* pp. 164–177.

46. Jeffrey Sachs, "Making the Brady Plan Work," *Foreign Affairs* 68, no. 3 (Summer 1989), pp. 87–92; Rieffel, *Restructuring Sovereign Debt,* pp. 170–171.

47. Rieffel, *Restructuring Sovereign Debt,* p. 178; David Roodman, "Creditor Initiatives in the 1980s and 1990s," in Chris Jochnick and Fraser A. Preston, eds., *Sovereign Debt at the Crossroads: Challenges and Proposals for Resolving the Third World Debt Crisis* (New York: Oxford University Press, 2006), pp. 23–26.

48. Bichaka Fayissa, "Foreign Debt, Capital Inflows, and Growth: The Case of the Sub-Sahara African Countries (SSACs)," *Scandinavian Journal of Development Alternatives and Area Studies* 16, nos. 3 & 4 (September and December 1997), p. 253; Bayne, *Hanging in There,* p. 123.

49. U.S. General Accounting Office, "Status of the Heavily Indebted Poor Countries Debt Relief Initiative," GAO/NSIAD-98-229, September 1998, pp. 5–8, 27; Gerardo Esquivel, Felipe Larraín, and Jeffrey D. Sachs, "Central America's Foreign Debt Burden and the HIPC Initiative," *Bulletin of Latin American Research* 20, no. 1 (January 2001), p. 2.

50. World Bank, *Global Development Finance, vol. I—2005* (Washington, D.C.: World Bank, 2005), pp. 166–169.

51. Tony Addison, "Debt Relief: The Development and Poverty Impact," in Tony Addison and George Mavrotas, eds., *Development Finance in the Global Economy: The Road Ahead* (New York: Palgrave Macmillan, 2008), p. 220.

52. Cline, *International Debt Reexamined,* p. 70.

53. Cline, *International Debt Reexamined,* pp. 70–76; "Summary of Discussion on LDC Debt Policy," in Martin Feldstein, ed., *American Economic Policy in the 1980s* (Chicago, IL: University of Chicago Press, 1994), p. 737.

54. Nancy Birdsall and Brian Deese, "Beyond HIPC: Secure, Sustainable Debt Relief for Poor Countries," in Fantu Cheru and Colin Bradford, Jr., eds., *The Millennium Development Goals: Raising the Resources to Tackle World Poverty* (New York: Zed Books, 2005), p. 139.

55. Ricardo Ffrench-Davis, "External Debt, Adjustment, and Development in Latin America," in Richard E. Feinberg and Ricardo Ffrench-Davis, eds., *Development and External Debt in Latin America: Bases for a New Consensus* (South Bend, IN: University of Notre Dame Press, 1988), p. 31.

56. Richard E. Feinberg, "Latin American Debt: Renegotiating the Adjustment Burden," in Feinberg and Ffrench-Davis, eds., *Development and External Debt in Latin America,* pp. 57–58; and Corbridge, *Debt and Development,* p. 85. William Cline argues from a liberal economic perspective that the debt strategies did not favor the banks over the debtor countries. See Cline, *International Debt Reexamined,* pp. 255–262.

57. Addison, "Debt Relief," p. 217.

58. Valerie J. Assetto, *The Soviet Bloc in the IMF and the IBRD* (Boulder, CO: Westview Press, 1988), pp. 189–190; Cline, *International Debt Reexamined,* p. 360.

59. Cline, *International Debt Reexamined,* pp. 360–367; Assetto, *The Soviet Bloc in the IMF and the IBRD,* pp. 163–179.

60. Matthew Evangelista, "Domestic Structure and International Change," in Michael W. Doyle and G. John Ikenberry, eds., *New Thinking in International Relations Theory* (Boulder, CO: Westview Press, 1997), pp. 212–214; Kazimierz Poznanski, "Economic Adjustment and Political Forces: Poland Since 1970," *International Organization* 40, no. 2 (Spring 1986), pp. 455–488.

61. Ellen Comisso and Paul Marer, "The Economics and Politics of Reform in Hungary," *International Organization* 40, no. 2 (Spring 1986), p. 422.

62. Joseph Gold, "The Relationship Between the International Monetary Fund and the World Bank," *Creighton Law Review* 15 (1982), pp. 509–510; Richard E. Feinberg, "The Changing Relationship Between the World Bank and the International Monetary Fund," *International Organization* 42, no. 3 (Summer 1988), p. 547; Jacques Polak, "The World Bank and the IMF: The Future of Their Coexistence," in Bretton Woods Commission, ed., *Bretton Woods: Looking to the Future* (Washington, D.C.: Bretton Woods Committee, 1994), p. C–149.

63. Hiroyuki Hino, "IMF-World Bank Collaboration," *Finance & Development* 23, no. 3 (September 1986), p. 11.

64. Jacques J. Polak, *The World Bank and the International Monetary Fund: A Changing Relationship,* Brookings Occasional Papers (Washington, D.C.: Brookings Institution, 1994).

65. "Survey: The IMF and the World Bank," *The Economist,* October 12, 1991, p. 48.

66. James, *International Monetary Cooperation,* p. 326; Polak, *The World Bank and the International Monetary Fund,* pp. 44–45.

67. Feinberg, "The Changing Relationship Between the World Bank and the International Monetary Fund," pp. 552–556; Polak, *The World Bank and the International Monetary Fund,* pp. 16–17.

68. Diane Elson, "From Survival Strategies to Transformation Strategies: Women's Needs and Structural Adjustment," in Lourdes Benería and Shelley Feldman, eds., *Unequal Burden: Economic Crises, Persistent Poverty, and Women's Work* (Boulder, CO: Westview Press, 1992), pp. 26–48; Gita Sen and Caren Grown, *Development, Crises, and Alternative Visions: Third World Women's Perspectives* (New York: Monthly Review, 1987), pp. 62–63.

69. Rieffel, *Restructuring Sovereign Debt,* pp. 190–192.

70. Stijn Claessens and Sudarshan Gooptu, "Can Developing Countries Keep Foreign Capital Flowing In?" *Finance and Development* 31, no. 3 (September 1994), p. 64; Susan Schadler, "Surges in Capital Inflows: Boon or Curse?" *Finance and Development* 31, no. 1 (March 1994), pp. 20–23.

71. Steven Radelet and Jeffrey Sachs, "The Onset of the East Asian Financial Crisis," in Paul Krugman, ed., *Currency Crises* (Chicago, IL: University of Chicago Press, 2000), p. 105.

72. T. J. Pempel, ed., *The Politics of the Asian Economic Crisis* (Ithaca, NY: Cornell University Press, 1999), pp. 1–2; Stephan Haggard, *The Political Economy of the Asian Financial Crisis* (Washington, D.C.: Institute for International Economics, 2000), pp. 3–7.

73. Dilip K. Das, *Asian Economy and Finance: A Post-Crisis Perspective:* (New York: Springer, 2005), p. 243.

74. U.S. Treasury Secretary Robert Rubin coined the *architecture* term in 1998. See Peter B. Kenen, *The International Financial Architecture: What's New? What's Missing?* (Washington, D.C.: Institute for International Economics, 2001), p. 1.
75. Kenen, *The International Financial Architecture,* pp. 87–123.
76. This section uses different categories but draws extensively from Leslie E. Armijo, "The Political Geography of World Financial Reform: Who Wants What and Why?" *Global Governance* 7, no. 4 (October–December 2001), pp. 379–396; and Leslie E. Armijo, ed., *Debating the Global Financial Architecture* (Albany, NY: State University of New York Press, 2002). See also Ben Thirkell-White, *The IMF and the Politics of Financial Globalization: From the Asian Crisis to a New International Financial Architecture?* (New York: Palgrave, 2005).
77. Kenen, *The International Financial Architecture,* p. 57.
78. Susanne Soederberg, "The Emperor's New Suit: The New International Financial Architecture as a Reinvention of the Washington Consensus," *Global Governance* 7, no. 4 (October–December 2001), p. 460.
79. Armijo, "The Political Geography of World Financial Reform," pp. 385–390.
80. James Tobin, "A Proposal for Monetary Reform," *Eastern Economic Journal* 4 (1978), p. 155.
81. For arguments for and against the Tobin tax, see Barry Eichengreen, *Toward a New International Financial Architecture* (Washington, D.C.: Institute for International Economics, 1999), pp. 88–90; and Alex C. Michalos, *Good Taxes* (Toronto: Dundurn Press, 1997).
82. Examples of the voluminous literature on this subject include Shelendra D. Sharma, "Constructing the New International Financial Architecture: What Role for the IMF?" *Journal of World Trade* 34, no. 3 (2000), pp. 47–70; Ngaire Woods, "Making the IMF and the World Bank More Accountable," *International Affairs* 77 (2001), pp. 83–100; Tony Porter, "The Democratic Deficit in the Institutional Arrangements for Regulating Global Finance," *Global Governance* 7, no. 4 (October–December 2001), pp. 427–439; and Graham Bird and Joseph P. Joyce, Remodeling the Multilateral Financial Institutions," *Global Governance* 7, no. 1 (January–March 2001), pp. 75–93.
83. Vincent Lloyd and Robert Weissman, "How International Monetary Fund and World Bank Policies Undermine Labor Power and Rights," *International Journal of Health Services* 32, no. 3 (2002), pp. 433–442.
84. Armijo, "The Political Geography of World Financial Reform," pp. 389–393.
85. Robert Shiller, *The Subprime Solution: How Today's Global Financial Crisis Happened, and What to Do about It* (Princeton, NJ: Princeton University Press, 2008), pp. 1–9; Michel G. Crouhy, Robert A. Jarrow, and Stuart M. Turnbull, "The Subprime Credit Crisis of 2007," *Journal of Derivatives* 16, no. 1 (Fall 2008), pp. 81–84; Charles R. Morris, *The Trillion Dollar Meltdown* (New York: Public Affairs, 2008).
86. Crouhy, Jarrow, and Turnbull, "The Subprime Credit Crisis of 2007," pp. 84–87.
87. Shiller, *The Subprime Solution,* pp. 39–47.
88. See Anthony Hurrell and Ngaire Woods, "Globalisation and Inequality," *Millennium* 24, no. 3 (1995), pp. 447–470.
89. Spratt, *Development Finance,* pp. 291–295.

PART FOUR

Concluding Comments

The last three decades of the twentieth century and the beginning of the twenty-first century have been marked by a series of unexpected and disruptive developments in global politics and economics. Some of the most notable developments have been the food and oil crises in the 1970s; the foreign debt crisis in the 1980s; the breakup of the Soviet bloc and Soviet Union during the 1980s and 1990s; the Asian financial crisis of the late 1990s; the terrorist attacks on New York and Washington, D.C., in September 2001; and the global financial crisis of 2008. As globalization has increased, economic and security events in one part of the world are having a greater impact on distant areas, and predictions about the future of the global economy have become more hazardous. However, the historical and theoretical focus of this book enables us to speculate about current and possible future changes in the twenty-first century. Relying on the major themes of this book, Chapter 12 examines contemporary trends in the global political economy.

Current Trends in the Global Political Economy

This book provides a comprehensive approach to the study of IPE, introducing students to the main theoretical perspectives and substantive issue areas. The realist, liberal, and critical perspectives have evolved and influenced each other over time, and some theoretical approaches such as hegemonic stability theory and regime theory draw upon more than one of these perspectives. Constructivist theory, feminist theory, environmental theory, and approaches that focus on domestic–international linkages are contributing to further changes in the study of IPE. To help link theory and practice, this book focuses on three themes central to the study of IPE: globalization, North–North relations, and North–South relations. Issues related to Eastern Europe and the FSU are subsumed under these three themes because the Cold War has ended and the transition economies are becoming increasingly integrated in the capitalist global economy. Whereas the more developed transition states such as the Czech Republic and Hungary have levels of development comparable with some DCs, poorer transition states such as Moldova and Tajikistan face economic problems comparable with those of LDCs. This concluding chapter examines where we are with these themes of globalization, North–North relations, and North–South relations and speculates about the future.

GLOBALIZATION

Globalization is a process that involves the broadening and deepening of interdependence among societies and states throughout the world. *Broadening* refers to the geographic extension of linkages to encompass virtually all major societies and states, and *deepening* refers to an increase in the frequency and intensity of interactions. This book does *not* adopt an extreme view of globalization that we are entering a "borderless world" where MNCs are losing their national identities and states are losing their distinctiveness.[1] Thus, globalization affects some states and regions more than others, threatens the state's autonomy in some respects but gives the state some new roles and does not prevent it from making policy choices, and contributes to fragmentation and conflict as well as unity and cooperation. Although states and societies were highly interdependent during the nineteenth and early twentieth centuries, globalization is more encompassing today than it was at any time in the past. Advances in technology, communications, and transportation are facilitating the globalization process as never before; the role of MNCs in generating FDI, trade, and technology is unprecedented; the capitalist economic system is spreading throughout the globe; and international economic organizations are becoming truly universal in membership.

Realists, liberals, and critical theorists have widely divergent views of globalization. Realists emphasize the importance of the state and often question whether globalization has significantly increased. Although realists acknowledge that interdependence is increasing in some areas, they see this as occurring only with the permission or encouragement of the most powerful states. Liberals, by contrast, view globalization as a significant force that is eroding state control, and they see the growth of interdependence as a positive development. Whereas realists believe that globalization occurs at the whim of the state, liberals see such factors as technological change and advances in communications and transportation as being beyond state control. Liberals also argue that domestic and transnational societal actors such as internationalist firms are a major force behind the increase of globalization.[2] Many critical theorists, like liberals, see globalization as having a significant impact, but they often view this in negative terms. For example, historical materialists argue that globalization has negative consequences for lower classes and poorer states in the periphery. Some Gramscian theorists assert that globalization is leading to the development of a "transnational historic bloc" composed of the largest MNCs, international banks, international economic organizations, and international business groups in the most powerful capitalist states. A crucial element of this historic bloc is the power and mobility of transnational capital, which is putting national groups such as labor unions on the defensive. The only way to counter this historic bloc is to develop a counterhegemony composed of disadvantaged labor, human rights, women's, environmental, consumer, and development groups. This counterhegemonic bloc would seek to replace the current corporate view of liberalization with a more democratic, participatory model based on socialism.[3]

Globalization and Triadization

Globalization is in many respects more akin to "triadization." The integrative processes are most intense among three major regions that contain most of the world's DCs: Europe, North America, and East Asia.[4] Countries in these three regions are the main sources of foreign investment, and they direct most of their FDI to each other. In 2007, the DCs accounted for 83.6 percent of total outward FDI stock and for 68.9 percent of inward FDI stock (see Tables 9.1 and 9.2 in Chapter 9). China is the only LDC that now vies with the largest DCs as a leading home as well as host country for FDI, and China is of course in East Asia (see Table 9.4). Europe, North America, and East Asia also dominate global trade flows. In 2007 the leading merchandise exporters were the EU(27), China, the United States, Japan, and Canada, and the leading merchandise importers were the United States, the EU(27), China, Japan, and Canada (see Table 7.4).[5] Despite the continuing importance of triadization, there are important power shifts occurring within the triad with the relative decline of U.S. economic hegemony. Conflict within the triad on a wide range of security and economic issues has also increased in recent years. These changes within the triad and the implications for the global political economy are discussed later in this chapter (under North–North relations).

Problems have also arisen with areas outside the triad, where states and other actors have sometimes reacted negatively to feelings of subordination and marginalization. As discussed in Chapter 10, Latin America is one of those areas. In the 1980s there was hope that the United States' decreasing emphasis on security issues, combined with Latin America's turn toward market liberalism and democracy, would lead to more cooperative linkages. However, the United States devoted much less attention to Latin America after the September 11, 2001, terrorist attacks. Subsequently, efforts to establish a Free Trade Area of the Americas (FTAA) collapsed, some Latin American states have turned against democratic practices and market liberalism, and the question has arisen as to whether the United States is "losing Latin America."[6] Like Latin America, Russia has also felt marginalized, particularly by the United States and the European Union. As Russia's economy has revived with revenues from energy and other commodity exports, Russia has adopted more hostile policies to the West on a range of issues, and has demanded a greater role in international political and economic institutions. The other BRIC economies (Brazil, India, and China), like Russia, are demanding that the North share decision making with them on major global economic issues. Another problem area outside the triad is the Middle East and North Africa; there has been continued strife among states in the region, and growing tensions between Islamic and Western practices.[7] Of all the regions, Sub-Saharan Africa (henceforth, Africa) has been the most marginalized. Most of the LLDCs are African, and Africa's trade and investment flows have been very limited. For example, Africa accounted for only 2.6 percent of inward FDI stock in 2007, compared with 17.8 percent for Asia and Oceania and 7.5 percent for Latin America and the Caribbean (see Table 9.2). The HIV/AIDS virus has also had a devastating effect on Africa. Most the 3 million people who died from HIV/AIDS in 2004 were from LDCs, and 70 percent of them were in Africa.[8] Thus, triadization has had a negative effect on a number of marginalized areas.

Globalization and the State

Liberals see globalization as causing state authority to leak "away upwards, sideways, and downwards."[9] Internationally, states must share authority with MNCs and international institutions; domestically, central governments must share authority with NGOs and regional and local authorities. For example, globalization has constrained the ability of DCs to continue providing the social welfare benefits that citizens came to expect during the 1950s to 1970s, and neoliberalism has made such social expenditures seem less legitimate. Globalization also limits the ability of states to regulate the national economy. For example, the massive growth of international capital flows has contributed to volatility and misalignment in currency exchange rates. These exchange rate fluctuations interfere with the state's ability to promote economic regulation and stability. Orthodox liberals view the increased capital flows as a favorable development because financial markets impose necessary discipline on states, and global capital moves to the most productive locations. Interventionist liberals agree that increased capital flows are beneficial, but caution that states and IOs must adopt some regulatory policies to limit the volatility of capital flows. Historical materialists see increased capital mobility as a negative development because the fear of capital outflows can induce governments to adopt policies that adversely affect the poorest and weakest in society. If states do not adopt capital-friendly policies, MNCs and international banks can shift their funds to more welcoming locations. Thus, MNCs locate their production facilities in states with the lowest wages, taxes, and environmental standards.

Realists are more inclined than other theorists to argue that reports of the state's decline have "been greatly exaggerated."[10] They argue that the increase in global financial flows has occurred with the permission or encouragement of the most powerful states and that these states continue to dictate the terms for such transactions. Some realists also argue that globalization has "enabling" as well as "constraining" effects on the state. Thus, many states have "increased direct tax yields, maintained or expanded social spending, and devised more complex systems of trade and industrial governance in order to cope with deepening integration."[11] The impressive economic growth rates of some states are closely related to their success in fostering a symbiotic relationship with the competitive marketplace. Although the state must vie with a range of nonstate actors, it continues to be the most important actor in the global political economy.

The validity of the positions of different theorists depends partly on the states they are examining. Thus, the largest DCs on average have more policy-making autonomy than many LDCs vis-à-vis major private actors and international institutions. For example, the 1990s Asian financial crisis demonstrated that LDCs are especially vulnerable to the freeing of capital flows. East and Southeast Asian states had opened their economies to capital flows in the years leading up to the crisis, and a surge of bank lending and portfolio investment contributed to risky and ill-advised investments in the region. When these states encountered economic problems, there was a "rush of international capital out of the region in 1997—a movement that was more frenzied than its mad rush to get into the area in earlier years."[12] Although domestic political and economic factors in the Asian economies contributed to the financial crisis, a major external factor was *contagion,* or "the spread of currency and asset market problems from one market to another."[13] As investor concerns spread, even sound financial institutions were adversely affected. Thus, one Asian currency after another was depreciated, states experienced liquidity crises, and the IMF became deeply involved in providing finance. Even an IMF deputy managing director acknowledged that the "factors contributing to contagion suggest it has been excessive—and that a way should be found to moderate it."[14] Thus, a consensus developed that LDCs and transition economies should not open their capital markets too rapidly because it may be difficult for them to make adequate adjustments. Although major DCs are less vulnerable than most LDCs to financial globalization, the contagion effects of the 2008 global financial crisis show that capital volatility can also have a strong effect on DCs. It is difficult for states to coordinate their policies on regulating capital mobility for several reasons:

- States often give priority to their own national concerns over the need for policy coordination.
- It is questionable whether governments have the will to regain control over capital and foreign investment movements in the present climate of neoliberalism.
- Although there is general agreement that LDCs must be more careful in liberalizing capital flows, there is a lack of consensus on proposals for reform (see Chapter 11).

Thus, some aspects of globalization such as the freeing of capital flows pose a major challenge to the ability of states to regulate global market forces.

Globalization, Inequality, and Poverty

The World Bank has compiled a large body of statistics on global equality and poverty, but critics from both the Right and Left often take issue with the Bank's methodology and findings. These criticisms show that it is difficult to interpret the statistics on inequality and poverty, and that a researcher's theoretical perspective often affects their methodology and findings. For example, one researcher argues that poverty is not the same as inequality and that inequality matters when people compare their income or wealth with others in their society. He strongly criticizes the Bank's methodology of putting "all the households in the world onto one chart to measure worldwide inequality of incomes":

What sense does it make to put a household in Mongolia alongside a household in Chile, one in Bangladesh, another in the United States, and still another in the Congo? These households do not belong to a 'society' in which they compare themselves with the others, and so a measure that includes all of them is practically a meaningless construct.[15]

Another researcher argues that "deep methodological flaws in the Bank's poverty measurement methodology suggest that its figures may be quite inaccurate and that both the incidence and the trend may be worse than reported." This researcher believes that the UNDP, which found greater increases in poverty than the Bank, has "a more plausible poverty measurement methodology."[16]

Although the statistics are sometimes conflicting, it seems that globalization and liberalization in combination have contributed to greater inequalities among and within many states. Thus, the World Bank reports that the average income in the richest 20 states is 37 times higher than the average income in the poorest 20 states—a gap that has doubled in the past 40 years. The growing inequalities are most evident between the North and South. Thus, the OECD states' share of the global GDP rose from 66 percent in 1970 to 78 percent in 1995. Whereas the real per capita GDP of the LDCs rose from $936 in 1980 to $1,417 in 2000, the increase for the DCs was from $20,397 to $30,557. Inequality has also increased within many DCs and LDCs. From 1979 to 1997, unemployment in the EU more than doubled to 11 percent. Although the employment picture was healthier in the United States, the income gap between the rich and poor was widening. In 1995 the real family income of the top 5 percent of the U.S. population was 130 percent higher than the 1973 level, while the real family income of the bottom 20 percent in 1995 stayed at the 1973 level. Income inequality has also increased in many LDCs and transition economies. For example, in 1997 the UNDP reported that a falling share of national income was going to the poorest 20 percent of people in several Latin American states (Argentina, Chile, the Dominican Republic, Ecuador, Mexico, and Uruguay) and that income distribution had worsened in 16 of 18 states in Eastern Europe and the FSU (excluding Estonia, Latvia, and Lithuania). The World Bank reported that inequality in China was much greater at the end of the 1990s than it had been in the early 1980s.[17]

How do IPE theorists interpret the statistics on inequality? Liberals recognize that globalization may contribute to inequality in the short term, but they believe that efficiency gains can reduce poverty even when inequality increases. Thus, one liberal asserts that "globalization does not appear to exacerbate poverty and may indeed contribute toward its reduction," and another argues that "globalization . . . has improved the lot of hundreds of millions of poor people around the world."[18] The data on poverty give some support to the liberal view, but the findings are somewhat ambiguous. For example, the number of people living in extreme poverty (less than $1 a day) declined between 1987 and 1998, but resulted mainly from growth in China and India. In most other areas such as Africa, Eastern Europe, and Central Asia, extreme poverty was increasing. Furthermore, the UNDP reports that the number of chronically malnourished people increased from 800 million in 1990 to 850 million in 1995.[19] Liberals also differentiate the short from the long term, arguing that globalization will reduce inequality over time. For example, one liberal asserts that "the late-comers to modern economic growth tend to catch up with the early-comers"; and another argues that "the economic gap between South Korea and industrialized countries . . . has diminished in part because of global markets."[20] Liberals believe that the poorest LDCs such as North Korea and Myanmar will never become rich by isolating themselves from global markets.

Realists and historical materialists, by contrast, believe there are long-term losers as well as winners from globalization. Historical materialists see globalization as benefiting the most powerful capitalist states and MNCs in the core at the expense of peripheral states and vulnerable societal groups. Realists argue that the most powerful states have control over the pace and direction of globalization and that they use the globalization process "to reinforce their position and their relative power." Globalization for less powerful states, by contrast, "is a process which is happening to them and to which they must respond."[21] Realists also assert that the policies of states, and their positions in the global economy, can make a difference. For example, some Asian LDCs such as China, India, Bangladesh, and Vietnam have reduced poverty to some extent while liberalizing their trade and investment policies. Variations among LDCs in the concentration of land ownership, the degree to which production is labor intensive, and other factors can influence the way in which globalization affects the distribution of wealth. In sum, theorists have a wide range of views on the relationship between globalization, inequality and poverty.

Globalization and Democracy

Many liberals believe that globalization is promoting democracy throughout the world. Indeed, they can point to the spread of liberal democratic practices such as constitutional guarantees, freedom of speech, open elections, and multiparty systems in southern Europe during the 1970s, Africa and Latin America during the 1980s, and the transition economies of Eastern Europe and the FSU during the late 1980s and 1990s. However, historical materialists and some interventionist liberals note that the poorest individuals in the South lack employment, education, and health facilities. The economic right to an adequate standard of living is more important to these people than Northern-oriented political rights such as free speech and democratic elections. Furthermore, income inequalities resulting from globalization contribute to disparities in political influence that limit opportunities for democratic policy making. These economic inequalities help explain the recent backlash against previous gains in representative democracy in some Latin American and African LDCs. Latin America and Africa have had the highest levels of income inequality, and "the situation deteriorated even further" in the 1980s and 1990s.[22] Even in the North, globalization critics argue, political rights mean little to the poorest individuals who lack housing, employment, and other basic amenities.[23]

Critics also argue that globalization is transferring control from democratically accountable governments to MNCs, international banks, and IOs. IMF, World Bank, and WTO decisions and policies are having a growing effect on individuals and groups within states. However, whereas national governments are accountable to domestic groups and individuals through periodic elections, international institutions lack such accountability. Thus, some scholars ask whether IOs such as the IMF, World Bank, and WTO are "accountable to those whom they directly affect."[24] Liberal supporters of globalization argue that democratization has occurred in the KIEOs in some important respects. For example, KIEO transparency has increased through the publication of minutes, decisions, and documents, and the KIEOs have upgraded their relations with NGOs. Critics by contrast argue that KIEO accountability has not increased in significant areas, and they refer to the gap between national and international governance as a "democratic deficit."[25]

Globalization and Civil Society

As discussed, globalization has contributed to the growth of civil society groups committed to social change. As discussed, there are three types of civil society groups: *Conformists* largely endorse the behavior of the KIEOs and private actors such as MNCs; *reformists* accept the existence of the KIEOs and MNCs but believe that they should and can be reformed; and *transformists* or *rejectionists* see the KIEOs and MNCs as unreformable, and want to downsize or abolish them. Reformists rely mainly on cooperative strategies to alter the behavior of the KIEOs and MNCs, whereas rejectionists engage in ideological—and sometimes physical—confrontation. Conformists and reformists are liberals, with reformists favoring embedded liberalism that takes account of the social effects of the market. Rejectionists, like historical materialists, are committed to transforming the capitalist system. Some NGOs employ reformist and rejectionist strategies simultaneously; for example, Greenpeace worked with companies to develop ozone-friendly refrigerators at the same time as it encouraged consumers to boycott Shell Oil because of its alleged involvement with state suppression in Nigeria.[26]

In recent years, reformists and rejectionists have organized protests against the WTO, World Bank, IMF, G8, MNCs, and other entities that they view as purveyors of globalization. In opposing globalization, civil society groups have taken advantage of some of globalization's trappings such as the World Wide Web to convey their ideas. As discussed in Chapter 9, the web was especially useful to protestors against the proposed MAI because it "facilitates networked sociopolitical relationships in important new ways, it (potentially) increases NGOs' organizational effectiveness and political significance, and it helps to foster more broadly participatory (transnational) political processes."[27] The question arises as to whether a "global civil society" is likely to develop a counterhegemony in opposition to globalization in Gramscian terms.[28] Civil society groups have had influence in certain cases such as their opposition to the proposed MAI, and a number of IOs and MNCs have responded to civil society pressures by opening communication with NGOs. However, it is highly unlikely that a global civil society will establish a counterhegemony for several reasons. First, most civil society groups are conformists (a "silent majority") that may be dissatisfied with some aspects of the global economic order, but are not sufficiently dissatisfied to attempt to institute major changes. Many conformists are also beneficiaries of the current global order. Second, civil society groups have a diverse range of objectives, and they often find it easier to agree on what they are against than on what type of world order they favor. A third obstacle to the development of a counterhegemony relates to differences in strategies and tactics; that is, reformists and rejectionists have divergent views regarding the legitimacy of violent protests. Finally, the terrorist attacks of September 11, 2001, have had a chilling effect on the activities of some civil society groups. In sum, civil society groups have had some influence in inducing international institutions and MNCs to alter top-down modes of decision making, but one should not overestimate the effect they are likely to have on the global political economy.

Globalization and "Newer Issues": The Environment, Migration, and Illegal Activity

Most IPE theorists associate globalization with the liberalization of trade, foreign investment, and capital flows. However, it is difficult to separate these explicitly economic processes from the effects of globalization on a variety of "newer" socioeconomic processes and issues. This section examines the effects of globalization on three of these issues: the environment, migration, and illegal activity.

THE ENVIRONMENT   Liberals see globalization as a positive force for the environment because it creates the wealth needed to pay for environmental improvements. Globalization contributes to economic growth that enables countries to afford environmental protection programs. Many liberals acknowledge that economic growth may contribute to environmental problems such as pollution from industries and the cutting of forests in the short term. In the longer term, however, growth is necessary to pay for environmental protection. Thus, one theorist asserts that "the overall historical pattern in industrial countries in the last century has been one of increasing and then decreasing emissions over time."[29] Orthodox liberals believe that such improvements will occur naturally with the functioning of free and open markets. For example, if there are fewer market distortions, we will be less likely to undervalue a natural resource. Interventionist and institutional liberals see a greater role for the state and IOs in ensuring that development does not pose major damage to the environment. Liberals also are optimistic about solving global environmental problems through cooperation and technological advances. For example, they have lauded the success in reducing the amount of chlorofluorocarbons (CFCs) released into the atmosphere. CFCs were used in refrigerators, aerosols, insulation, and solvents, but scientists discovered that they were depleting the ozone layer which protects us from harmful ultraviolet sun rays. As a result of the 1987 Montreal Protocol on Substances that Deplete the Ozone Layer and subsequent amendments, the global community has significantly lowered CFC production.[30]

In contrast to liberals, critical environmental theorists—the greens— attribute many environmental problems to globalization. They argue that globilization is contributing to a type of economic growth that results in environmental pollution and overconsumption of natural resources. For example, they cite figures to show that global water consumption, deforestation, and pollutants such as carbon dioxide emissions from automobiles are increasing exponentially. Some greens see the world's growing population as the main factor behind the environmental problems. Others see the main factor as global inequality, which results in overconsumption by the wealthy and the relegation of the more polluting forms of production to poorer areas and LDCs. Many greens focus specifically on capitalist globalization, which "undermines the quest for an ecologically and socially sustainable future. The constant threat of international capital flight strips individual governments of important domestic regulatory powers."[31] Unlike liberals, the greens view the success in reducing production of CFCs as an exception, and they argue that global progress on most environmental issues under the capitalist form of globalization has been extremely limited.[32]

Realists are less involved in debates over globalization and the environment because of their preoccupation with security issues. However, it is useful to discuss what the realist position would be on this issue. Realists assume that the largest states can use globalization to improve their power positions vis-à-vis weaker states, and unlike the liberals and greens they argue that globalization has not systematically undermined state control. Indeed, globalization increases only when states permit it to increase. Realists would argue that the environmental effects of globalization depend more on the actions of states than on the market and international institutions. The main issue to realists would be whether states establish mechanisms to protect the environment, and whether they are willing to transfer some authority to international environmental institutions.

Theorists from each of these perspectives have a point. As the greens point out, globalization-generated economic growth can result in environmental pollution and the overconsumption of resources. However, economic stagnation and poverty also pose environmental risks. Thus, liberals are correct in noting that economic growth can create the wealth necessary for dealing with environmental problems. Realists are also correct that environmental protection will ultimately depend more on the actions of states than on the market or international institutions. Whether states have the motivation and ability to cooperate to protect the environment is another matter.

MIGRATION   It is quite common for individuals, societal groups, and states to support some aspects of globalization they view as beneficial and to oppose other aspects of globalization that pose a real or presumed threat to them. Whereas many states and societal groups support freer trade and capital flows, they are much more resistant to the cross-border movement of people. Indeed, there are growing signs of anti-immigrant sentiment in a number of DCs. An EU public opinion survey in 1993 found that 52 percent of respondents thought there were too many immigrants, and a 1993 *New York Times*/CBS national telephone survey reported that 61 percent of Americans favored a decrease in the number of immigrants, compared with 42 percent in a 1977 Gallup poll.[33] The September 11, 2001, terrorist attacks on the World Trade Center and the Pentagon added greatly to U.S. concerns about migration.

Although states and societal groups regulate cross-border migration because of valid concerns about illegal immigration and terrorism, they may also impose limits for more questionable reasons. For example, less skilled DC workers sometimes oppose immigration because of concerns that immigrants are taking away their jobs. There is no conclusive empirical evidence of a linkage between immigration from LDCs on the one hand and increased unemployment among semiskilled and unskilled workers in DCs on the other. Indeed, some analysts argue that migrants often enter low-wage occupations that do not attract the local population, that many migrants are self-employed and create their own jobs, and that migration can stimulate growth and thus reduce unemployment.[34] Nevertheless, DC labor groups often express concerns about the effects of migration on employment. Hostility to immigrants is heightened by groups with less legitimate objectives linked with extreme nationalism, racism, and suspicion of those who are different.

Despite these negative societal attitudes, the politics of immigration is complex, and there are also countervailing tendencies. For example, the market demand for certain types of foreign workers sometimes makes it difficult for political leaders to limit immigration. Newly naturalized immigrants also can form a large voting constituency, and the Clinton administration adopted a plan in 1996 that gave citizenship to more than 1 million people. These new citizens provided Clinton with an important source of votes for his reelection.[35] Most IPE scholars who write about globalization do not even discuss migration because "no other issue remains so much under the thrall of states and so resistant to globalizing effects."[36] Nevertheless, as globalization increases, migration pressures will grow along with the pressures for other types of international interactions.

ILLEGAL ACTIVITY   In addition to migration and the environment for IPE specialists should address the effects of globalization on illegal activity. Indeed, one analyst refers to "the five wars of globalization" as "the fights against the illegal trade in drugs, arms, intellectual property, people, and money."[37] For example, the annual trade in illicit drugs is estimated at $400 billion, or about 8 percent of world trade; illicit trade accounts for about 20 percent of the total small arms trade; the piracy rate of business software is as high as 60 percent in Greece and South Korea; and estimates of the volume of global money laundering (hiding, moving, and investing assets obtained by criminal activity) range from 2 to 5 percent of the world's GNP. Although states often benefit from more rapid communication and transportation, so do criminal networks. Furthermore, privatization, deregulation, and the growth of international trade and investment have made it more difficult for states to control global criminal activity. Governments and international institutions must develop the skills, laws, and mechanisms to address these issues.

NORTH–NORTH RELATIONS

The second theme of this book relates to the interactions among DCs of the North. The issue of international economic management has been mainly a North–North issue because only the Northern states have had the wealth and power to look after the management of the global economy. However, some emerging states such as the BRIC economies (Brazil, Russia, India, and China) are posing a challenge to the North's supremacy. This book discusses two factors contributing to international economic management: hegemony and international institutions.

The Current State of U.S. Hegemony

This book provides a mixed picture of the current state of U.S. hegemony. On the one hand, the United States continues to demonstrate a number of strengths as a global hegemon. With the breakup of the Soviet bloc, the United States has emerged as the unchallenged military power in the world. As long as the threat of violent conflict persists, a state with hegemony in security matters will also have a degree of power over economic and other nonsecurity areas. The U.S. dollar continues to serve as the main international currency, and the United States has the most votes in the IMF and World Bank. The United States has also had a considerable amount of co-optive power (i.e., structural or soft power): It is often successful in getting "other countries to *want* what it wants."[38] For example, Part III shows that the United States had a central role in setting the agenda for the GATT Uruguay Round negotiations and in guiding DC policies on a range of issues extending from liberalizing capital flows to the foreign debt crisis and international development. On the other hand, Part III provides a number of indications of U.S. hegemonic decline. The U.S. dollar shifted from top-currency to negotiated-currency status in the 1960s, and the United States has had chronic balance-of-trade deficits, serious foreign debt problems, and greater dependence on external capital. Furthermore, U.S. soft power has declined in recent years. Although U.S. military predominance increased with the breakup of the Soviet bloc, even traditional U.S. allies have resented its unilateral actions on security issues. This resentment has increased in response to the Bush administration's dismissive approach to states and IOs that disagree with its policies. These unilateral tendencies increased after the understandable outrage against the September 11, 2001, terrorist attacks on U.S. soil. The United States has also diverged from its customary role as a prime supporter of liberalization in some key economic areas such as trade. As a result of this shift in the U.S. international posture, its soft power has declined.[39]

Despite the conflicting assessments of U.S. hegemony, there is no doubt that the United States continues to be a major global economic power. Thus, the World Economic Forum's 2008–2009 *Global Competitiveness Report* concludes that "notwithstanding the present financial crisis, the United States continues to be the most competitive economy in the world."[40] Although the report expresses concerns about the U.S. banking sector and macroeconomic weaknesses, it asserts that the United States has highly innovative companies, an excellent university system that collaborates with business in R&D, and the largest domestic economy in the world. The report refers to U.S. economic weaknesses, such as its banking sector; its costs to combat terrorism, crime, and violence; and most importantly its fiscal deficits and growing public indebtedness. However, the report concludes that the United States continues to be the most competitive country overall. Some may question the accuracy of these competitive ratings in view of the failure of rating agencies such as Moody's and Standard and Poor's (S&P) to foresee the U.S. subprime credit crisis. However, one should not underestimate U.S. economic power. The next section discusses whether there are possible competitors as hegemons.

Is There a Candidate to Replace the United States as Global Hegemon?

In the late 1980s, many analysts took a positive view of Japan's hegemonic prospects. For example, one scholar wrote that "if any country surpasses the United States as the world's leading economic power, it will be Japan."[41] By the mid-1990s, however, most analysts saw Japan as lacking the military power and ideological appeal of a hegemon and as unwilling to assume the responsibility of global leadership. During the late 1990s, the Asian financial crisis raised further questions about Japan's hegemonic potential. Many hoped that Japan would set an example of reform because it shared some economic problems with other Asian states such as failing banks, questionable bookkeeping methods, and corrupt interlocking corporate relationships.[42] However, political indecisiveness and inflexible economic and social practices prevented Japan from adopting bold policies to reform the economy. Japan continues to have a major competitive edge in business innovation and sophistication, and its economy has shown definite signs of recovery until recently. However, Japan has been one of the DCs most severely affected by the 2008 global financial crisis, and it is highly unlikely that it will replace the United States as a global hegemon.

Some writers see the EU as a possible hegemon, and one economist predicts that "future historians will record that the twenty-first century belonged to the House of Europe."[43] The EU's global reach has expanded with the admission of 12 Central and Eastern European states, and the associate membership of the ACP (Africa, Caribbean, and Pacific) states gives the EU considerable influence among LDCs. The euro is becoming more important and it could eventually replace the U.S. dollar as the key international currency. The EU was also the largest global merchandise exporter in 2007, and second after the United States as a global importer (see Table 7.4). However, the EU is an unlikely hegemon unless it becomes a more cohesive unit. Only 16 of the 27 EU members have replaced their national currencies with the euro, and Britain continues to refuse to join the monetary union. In trade, divisions on issues such as agriculture have prevented the EU from adopting a more important leadership role, and EU members have many disagreements on global security issues. The 2008 global financial crisis has created additional divisions within the EU. Whereas wealthy EU members such as France, Germany, and Britain have moved to protect their economies, some of the Central and Eastern European members have had to seek loans from the IMF. These divisions pose a major obstacle to the EU becoming a global hegemon.

A third possibility is that China could become the global hegemon. China's average annual growth rates of 9.7 percent since the late 1970s have enabled it to develop and diversify its economy, reduce poverty, and raise the standard of living. China has one of the largest economies in the world, and it is second to the United States in the size of the domestic and export market available to companies located in its territory; this has given it great opportunities to upgrade its efficiency and economies of scale.[44] In 2007 China was the second largest merchandise exporter after the EU, and the third largest importer after the United States and the EU (see Table 7.4); and China's current account balance of *plus* $238.5 billion in 2006 was a stark contrast with the U.S. current account balance of *minus* $856.7 billion. China has had persistent trade surpluses with the United States, and this has been a source of growing friction between the two countries. Japan is also concerned about China's growing economic influence in Asia at the same time as it depends on China as a growing market for its exports. China's expanding power reaches beyond economic areas, and its official statistics report a double-digit annual increase in the defense budget since 1989. The U.S. Pentagon has asserted that these "officially published figures substantially underreport actual expenditures for national defense."[45] Despite the impressive changes in China, as an LDC it is more vulnerable than the major DCs to economic and political instabilities. Whereas some parts of China are experiencing rapid growth, the western and northeastern regions of the country have widespread poverty, with about 128 million people living on less than $1 per day and many lacking adequate clean water and health and education facilities. Such inequalities are a source of political instability, and demonstrations and protests have increased as a result of the 2008 global financial crisis. The 2008–2009 *Global Competitiveness Report* indicates that "China is reaching a critical point in its development, when it can no longer rely solely on the abundance of low-cost inputs to sustain growth," and that one should not underestimate "the enormous challenges that face China in maintaining its competitiveness, in view of sustaining its rapid growth and moving up the value chain."[46] Despite China's enormous potential, in the short to medium term it is unlikely that it will assume hegemonic status.

Although China alone is unlikely to challenge U.S. hegemony in the short to medium term, some analysts see a definite shift in power in recent years from North America and Europe to Asia. One indication of this shift is the massive buildup of foreign exchange reserves in Asia, especially in China, Japan, and South Korea. These three economies wanted to accumulate reserves as an insurance policy against another Asian financial crisis, and they were able to amass reserves because of their large current account surpluses. Thus, the reserves of China, Japan, and South Korea now exceed $2 trillion, and together they now own about 50 percent of the U.S. national debt.[47] Thus, the major East Asian economies are posing a significant challenge to U.S. economic hegemony. Another overlapping challenge comes from the emerging BRIC economies, which "have all historically espoused conceptions of international order that challenged those of the liberal developed West."[48] A final possibility is the Gramscian idea that MNCs and internationally mobile capital may be vying with the state today for global hegemony.[49]

The Role of International Institutions

Institutional liberals believe that interdependence and globalization create a need for international institutions "to deal with the ever more complex dilemmas of collective action."[50] Thus, international regimes and organizations have been an important part of IPE since the end of World War II. Although the North has the largest role in maintaining these regimes and IOs, emerging states are demanding a greater role. The IMF, World Bank, and GATT/WTO are the most important international economic institutions (the KIEOs). Whereas liberals see them as beneficial organizations that promote economic efficiency and openness, realists view them as creatures of the most powerful member states, and historical materialists see them as instruments the capitalist core states use to exploit weaker states in the periphery. This section assesses the current and possible future influence of the KIEOs.

The KIEOs have adapted to changing economic circumstances by altering their functions, and they are likely to continue having important roles in global economic management. As discussed in Chapter 6, the IMF lost one of its two main functions—looking after the pegged exchange rate system—when the major economic powers shifted to floating exchange rates in 1973. The IMF also became a less essential source of loans for middle-income LDCs in the 1970s when private banks recycled large sums of petrodollars to the South. During the 1980s, however, the IMF regained its stature when it took the lead role (along with the United States) in managing the LDC foreign debt crisis. The IMF also provided funding for transition economies after the breakup of the Soviet bloc, and it took the lead responsibility for dealing with the 1990s Asian financial crisis. Although the South resented the intrusive conditions the IMF attached to its structural adjustment loans, the IMF was secure as long as it retained the confidence of the North. However, the 1990s financial crisis marked a turning point because DC economists and policy makers began to attack IMF stabilization programs in South Korea, Indonesia, Russia, and elsewhere. For example, critics charged that the IMF imposed the same conditions on loans to South Korea as it had imposed on foreign debtors in the 1980s, despite major differences in the two cases. South Korea's foreign debt was low and its problems stemmed mainly from a temporary lack of liquidity.

In the early twenty-first century, LDCs such as Brazil, Argentina, and Indonesia that benefited from surging commodity prices were able to forgo IMF loans and the strict demands that accompany them. Thus, IMF lending fell to $16 billion in 2007, and some analysts asserted that the IMF was declining.[51] However, the 2008 global financial crisis contributed to an acute shortage of capital flows, and the G20 decided in April 2009 to give the IMF a central role in dealing with the crisis (see Chapter 11). Despite the criticisms of the IMF, most analysts believe that abolishing the organization is not the answer and that emphasis should be placed on refocusing it.[52] The IMF provides official financing, and if it were dismantled another similar organization would probably be invented. A restructured IMF that gives more influence to the emerging economies, tempers its conditionality requirements for loans, and recognizes the important role of governments as well as the market is likely to continue to have an important role in the future. The IMF will focus some of its efforts on monitoring global currency imbalances and the rise of SWFs, and serving as a consultant on fiscal decisions and financial crises. Although the IMF is uncertain about the proper macroeconomic solutions, it is not alone in lacking definitive answers; many economists failed to foresee the 1980s debt crisis, the 1990s financial crisis, and the 2008 global financial crisis. It is therefore likely that the IMF will continue to adapt its functions to meet changing circumstances.

The World Bank initially provided long-term loans for European reconstruction and LDC development; when the Bank lost its reconstruction function, it shifted entirely to development. The Bank's importance stems partly from the fact that it is the largest source of multilateral finance for LDC development. The Bank also chairs a number of aid consortia and consultative groups where DC donors can coordinate their bilateral aid-giving. However, ODA as a percent of donor countries' GNIs steadily declined from 1960 to 2000 (see Table 10.2) for several reasons: Aid agencies encountered obstacles in promoting economic development; the end of the Cold War removed the security rationale for providing aid; and states cut spending in an increasingly competitive global environment. The United States and other donors were also more reluctant to replenish funding for the Bank group's soft-loan affiliate, the IDA. As Table 10.2 shows, ODA as a percent of GNI increased again after 2000, but this increase was mainly due to the fact that donor states are counting the funds they provide for debt forgiveness as aid. Thus, the Bank's importance depends on much more than its roles as an aid coordinator and as a source of development finance.

The 1980s foreign debt crisis gave the Bank as well as the IMF new functions to perform. However, both the IMF and Bank began to provide SALs to debtor states, and the IMF rather than the Bank was given responsibility for coordinating the response to the foreign debt crisis. As the IMF and Bank functions increasingly overlapped, questions were raised about whether the Bank was redundant. Still another problem confronting Bank officials has been the high degree of controversy surrounding their efforts to alter the institution's policy outlook and mode of operation (see Chapter 10). However, the Bank group has been highly adaptable. As discussed in Chapter 10, Sub-Saharan Africa is currently facing a development crisis, and the Bank group is the IO with the most economic resources and technical expertise to deal with the crisis. Thus, the Bank group's soft loan arm, the *International Development Association,* has been closely involved in providing assistance for the debt forgiveness programs. Another arm of the Bank group, the *International Finance Corporation,* has an important role in promoting private enterprise in LDCs. The Bank group also includes two institutions (the *International Center for Settlement of Investment Disputes* and the *Multilateral Investment Guarantee Agency*) that deal with investment issues. Most important, the Bank has carved out for itself "a unique position as a generator of ideas about economic development."[53]

The WTO is in some respects the most important KIEO, but it too is in an uncertain position because of the suspension of the Doha Round. Unlike the IMF and World Bank, which impose conditions on LDC and transition economy borrowers, the WTO establishes rules for almost all the world's major trading nations. The WTO moved closer to becoming a universal membership organization when China joined, and Russia should become a member in the future. The WTO's predecessor, the GATT, became a permanent organization only by default when the proposed ITO was not approved, but the GATT's informal nature permitted it to be highly adaptable. Although GATT negotiations were initially designed to lower tariffs, the trade organization also began to negotiate NTB reductions in the 1960s, and it expanded these negotiations at the Tokyo Round. The Uruguay Round was the most complex and ambitious GATT negotiation, resulting in agreements not only for trade in goods, but also for trade in services, intellectual property, and trade-related investment measures. Most important, the Uruguay Round created the WTO, a formal organization with a much wider range of regulatory functions than GATT.

Despite the WTO's importance, there are some major threats to its legitimacy. Whereas the GATT oversaw eight rounds of multilateral trade negotiations, major differences led to the breakdown of the first round of WTO negotiations, the Doha Round, in July 2008. The Doha Round was to be "the development round," but North–South divisions were the main obstacle to completion of the round. In addition to North–South divisions over substantive issues, tensions also exist over the South's effort to upgrade its influence in the WTO. There were also major differences within the North and within the South, and a major question is whether the WTO with its 153 members has become so large and diverse that it is difficult to reach a consensus on contentious issues. Another challenge to the WTO relates to dispute settlement. The WTO has a much stronger dispute settlement system than the GATT, but it is uncertain whether major trading powers such as the United States, the EU, Japan, and China would accept a series of major dispute settlement decisions against them. One of the most important challenges relates to the increase of regional trade agreements, which occurs whenever there is stalemate in the global trade organization (as is the case currently). Although some RTAs such as the EU and NAFTA may serve as stepping stones to global free trade, the recent proliferation of bilateral FTAs threatens to fragment the global trade regime. Most recently, the 2008 global financial crisis has contributed to a rise in trade protectionism that poses an additional obstacle to the revival of the Doha Round. In sum, the WTO, like the IMF and the Bank, faces serious governance challenges.

NORTH–SOUTH RELATIONS

The South accounted for almost 65 percent of the total world population in 1950, and by 1996 the South's population had climbed to almost 80 percent of the world total. Furthermore, a number of transition economies are now receiving foreign debt and development financing and thus have characteristics in common with the South. Despite the growing population of the South, it has relatively little influence in setting the agenda and making decisions regarding the global political economy. Some LDCs and transition economies are experiencing some economic success and pressuring for more influence in the world's economic forums. For example, emerging countries such as the China, Russia, Kuwait, United Arab Emirates, and Saudi Arabia have accumulated large foreign reserves and SWFs, often from sales of oil and commodities, which enhance their influence under current conditions of capital shortages. Groups of LDCs such as the East Asian NIEs, BRIC economies, and OPEC countries all have members that are being viewed as economic "success stories." However, these success stories tend to mask the degree of poverty affecting many LDCs today. For example, the *overall* figures indicate that the number of people living in extreme poverty (on less than $1 per day) declined from 1981 to 2001. However, the numbers in extreme poverty in China and India fell dramatically, while the numbers increased in Sub-Saharan Africa, Europe, and Central Asia.[54] The United Nations has identified 50 LDCs as "least developed" because they have extremely low per capita incomes, literacy rates, and shares of manufacturing; almost all these countries are in Sub-Saharan Africa and South Asia. Poverty also has a differential impact on societal groups in the South, with women and children most severely affected. Furthermore, globalization tends to marginalize the weakest states and societal groups, even as it is contributes to growth in many stronger states. For example, the poorest LDCs, which have 20 percent of the world's population, saw their share of world trade fall from about 4 percent in 1960 to less than 1 percent in 1990. Private investment flows to the South increased from $5 billion in 1970 to $173 billion in 1994, but about 75 percent of this investment went to only 10 LDCs, mainly in East and Southeast Asia and Latin America.[55] The data on the poorest LDCs and societal groups indicate that development strategies have had only limited success. The following discussion examines how the concept of development is changing and considers whether there is a "best" path to development.

Changing Concepts of Development

During the 1950s and 1960s, economic development was usually equated with the growth of a country's GDP and per capita income. Orthodox liberals argued that Western industrial states with high per capita incomes had achieved successful development, and that LDCs could acquire similar wealth if they followed the path set by the North. Orthodox liberals were not concerned about redistributing wealth to the poorest LDCs and groups because the benefits from the efficient allocation of resources under free markets would "eventually trickle down from the top, alleviating the problem of poverty at the bottom."[56] Although the South experienced unprecedented economic growth during the 1960s, unemployment, poverty, and the gap between rich and poor were increasing. Thus, a number of development specialists rejected the orthodox liberal view that growth would trickle down to the poor and called for conscious efforts to redistribute income and meet basic human needs for health, education, food, and clean water. From this perspective, GDP and per capita income are not the only important development indicators, and human development indicators such as health and sanitation, literacy rates, education, employment, the position of women and children, and rural–urban disparities must also be considered. The human development approach demonstrates that development must be measured "through investment in people and not just in machinery, buildings, and other physical assets."[57] Another change in the development concept came from those concerned about environmental degradation. Of particular importance is the *sustainable development* concept, which was popularized by some NGOs in the early 1980s and received multilateral approval in the 1987 report of the World Commission on Environment and Development (the Brundtland Report). The Brundtland Report describes sustainable development as a policy that "meets the needs of the present without compromising the ability of future generations to meet their own needs."[58] Sustainable development is a controversial concept because of South's views that LDCs cannot afford to divert resources from their immediate development needs to the environment, the North did not adopt sustainable policies when it was developing, and the North produces more pollutants than the South. If the North expects the South to follow environmentally friendly policies, it must be willing to compensate the South with financial resources.[59]

The prevailing concepts of development have a major effect on policy making, so it is essential that we opt for a broad rather than narrow concept of development for two reasons:

- Experience shows that rapid economic growth does not necessarily enrich people's lives and may increase income gaps and poverty under some circumstances. A broader concept of development includes not only economic growth but also human development, poverty reduction, and environmental protection.
- As interdependence increases, the form of development can have major implications for the entire globe. For example, the World Bank estimates that more than 2 million people in China die each year from the effects of air and water pollution and that this pollution extends far beyond China's boundaries. Aside from the United States, China is the largest source of greenhouse gases linked to global warming, and China and India are the two fastest growing sources of these gases.[60]

In an age of globalization, we can no longer afford to adopt a development concept that is limited to economic growth. Thus, the North must assist LDCs that lack the capacity to transfer scarce resources from economic growth to other crucial objectives such as sustainability and the reduction of poverty.

Is There a "Best" Development Strategy?

Chapter 10 discussed several major development strategies, including ISI, socialist development, export-led growth, orthodox liberalism, and "bottom-up" strategies such as microfinance. Liberals, realists, and historical materialists disagree as to which strategy is best, and sometimes they even disagree as to the strategy a state is following. For example, when East Asian economies were growing rapidly under the export-led growth model in the 1970s and 1980s, liberals attributed their success to their outward market orientation; realists attributed their success to the existence of a strong developmental state that promoted an effective industrial policy; and historical materialists argued that the East Asians were still dependent and not as successful as the realists and liberals assumed. Experience indicates that *none* of the development strategies is always the best and that every strategy has strengths and weaknesses. Furthermore, in view of the diverse nature of the South, the best strategy for one LDC may not be feasible for another. A brief recounting of the strengths and weaknesses of various development strategies will help reinforce these points.

As discussed in Chapter 10, many LDCs adopted ISI as a development strategy during the 1950s and 1960s. The easier first stage of ISI resulted in economic growth and industrialization in a number of LDCs. However, LDCs in Latin America and elsewhere that continued on to a second stage of ISI encountered growing problems with balance-of-payments deficits, uncompetitive industries, and increased dependence on external finance. In response to the problems with ISI, some LDCs adopted more extreme inward-looking policies and followed the socialist planning model of the Soviet Union. Central planning contributed to increased industrial production in some LDCs, but even larger states such as

China were plagued by inefficiencies, low-quality production, and lack of competitiveness. Smaller LDCs lacking in resources such as North Korea, Cuba, Ethiopia, Mozambique, Vietnam, and Burma were even less effective in instituting central planning. Although these states registered some gains in health care and education and reduced socioeconomic inequalities, socialist central planning in LDCs was largely unsuccessful.[61]

The East Asian NIEs, which followed the Japanese model and turned from import substitution to export-led growth policies in the 1960s, were the most successful group of LDCs in increasing their economic growth during the 1960s to 1980s. Although liberals and realists often agreed that other LDCs should learn from the East Asian example, they had different interpretations of the reasons for these countries' successes. The realists were probably more accurate in their interpretations: the East Asian NIEs (other than Hong Kong) had strong developmental states that provided extensive guidance to the market, controlled investment flows, promoted the development of technology, and protected selected infant industries. A financial crisis during the 1990s, however, demonstrated that the developmental state was not as efficient and immune to political pressures as was earlier assumed. Thus, the crisis stemmed partly from the failure of governments to develop adequate regulations for banking and other financial institutions. It also became evident that the East Asians had benefited from a unique set of circumstances in which the United States and Japan gave them favored treatment in aid, trade, and foreign investment. Thus, the East Asians had dependent linkages with the United States and Japan, and when these two countries' policies changed in the 1990s, the East Asian states were highly vulnerable. Environmentalists also raised questions about the sustainability of rapid economic growth in East Asia, because little action was taken to prevent environmental degradation. In the late 1990s the East Asian financial crisis resulted in rapid outflows of capital, recessions, banking crises, and lower economic growth rates. Thus, many analysts who had viewed the East Asians as "miracle economies" were now questioning the export-led growth model. As discussed, the East Asians recovered quite rapidly from the 1990s financial crisis, and resumed their growth rates. However, the decreased demand for imports in the United States and elsewhere as a result of the 2008 global financial crisis has raised new questions about the wisdom of relying too heavily on an export-led growth model.

During the 1980s, the debt crisis and IMF and World Bank SALs ushered in yet another Southern development strategy based on neoliberalism (a return to orthodox liberalism). In marked contrast to import substitution and export-led growth, neoliberalism emphasized decreased government spending, privatization, deregulation, and open trade and foreign investment policies. The SALs to middle-income LDCs had some positive effects in reducing government budget deficits, increasing export earnings, and enhancing economic efficiency and growth. However, IMF and World Bank SALs had negative effects on the poorest LDCs in Sub-Saharan Africa and Asia and on vulnerable groups in LDCs such as women and children. Critics argued that structural adjustment programs underestimated the need to involve the state in development and to maintain social, health, and educational programs for vulnerable groups. However, supporters of neoliberalism asserted that LDCs would benefit from liberalizing their economies and following the path of Western Europe and North America.[62]

In view of the global spread of orthodox liberalism, the question arises as to whether we have reached the "end of history" for Southern development strategies and whether liberalism has become the only acceptable path to follow.[63] This is clearly not the case. As discussed in Chapter 10, several Latin American states have reacted against orthodox liberalism, partly because of the stark inequalities between rich and poor, and this reaction could spread to other LDC regions. Even the World Bank has acknowledged that SALs will succeed only if they take account of the need for strong, stable LDC governments and include some distributional goals to assist the poorest and most vulnerable groups. As realists since Friedrich List have noted, strategies that provide an active role for the government may be necessary for states at earlier stages of development if they are to catch up with the leading states. Two events in the twenty-first century have caused a revival of interest in the value of development strategies that have an important role for the government as well as the market. First was the rapid revival of the East Asian NIEs after the 1990s financial crisis. Despite the problems with depending too heavily on export-led growth, the East Asian developmental state model addresses the need to involve the state as well as the market in the development process. Second, the United States and other countries have reacted to the global financial crisis by depending on governments to stimulate economies with massive increases in public expenditures and tax cuts; some refer to this as an "undeniable shift to Keynes."[64]

In sum, we have *not* reached the end of history in terms of development strategies. The best strategy is likely to include realist and historical materialist as well as liberal characteristics, and the best strategy for some LDCs may not necessarily be the best strategy for others.

A FINAL WORD ON IPE THEORY AND PRACTICE

This book combines theory and practice in the study of IPE, and devotes considerable attention to the three traditional IPE perspectives of realism, liberalism, and historical materialism. As Chapters 3–5 show, these perspectives remain relevant because they have not been static; they have interacted with each other and evolved over time. However, the dramatic global changes outlined in this book have revealed a need to supplement the traditional perspectives with "new theoretical categorizations."[65] Thus, we also focus on some theoretical perspectives that are newer to IPE such as constructivism, feminism, and environmentalism. Each perspective has its own strengths and weaknesses, and a familiarity with a range of perspectives is necessary to gain a better understanding of the relation between IPE theory and practice. IPE theory will of course continue to evolve as it has in the past.

IPE as a university discipline only began to develop in the 1970s, and IPE theorists have made great strides since that time. In focusing on IPE issues, however, these theorists have often ignored security issues just as security theorists have ignored IPE. It is time that theorists devote more attention to the important linkages between IPE and security issues. The globalization phenomenon points to yet another direction theorists should follow: the development of theories that explore domestic–international interactions. With globalization, the sensitivity and vulnerability of national economies to changes in capital, foreign investment, and trade flows have dramatically increased, and policies that were traditionally considered to be domestic can have a major impact on outsiders. The major IPE perspectives have devoted too little attention to domestic–international interactions.[66] This book introduces students to a range of theoretical approaches and applies these theories to substantive IPE issue areas. As an international relations theorist has stated, "to think theoretically one must be constantly ready to be proven wrong,"[67] and this book shows that all theoretical perspectives are partly correct and partly incorrect in their assessments of a wide range of IPE issues. It is only through formulating and reformulating our theories that we can address anomalies and increase our understanding of the global political economy.

Notes

1. The term *borderless world* derives from Kenichi Ohmae, *The Borderless World: Power and Strategy in the Interlinked Economy* (New York: HarperPerennial, 1990).
2. Helen V. Milner, *Resisting Protectionism: Global Industries and the Politics of International Trade* (Princeton, NJ: Princeton University Press, 1988).
3. Stephen Gill and David Law, "Global Hegemony and the Structural Power of Capital," in Stephen Gill, ed., *Gramsci, Historical Materialism and International Relations* (New York: Cambridge University Press, 1993), pp. 93–124; Mark E. Rupert, "(Re) Politicizing the Global Economy: Liberal Common Sense and Ideological Struggle in the US NAFTA Debate," *Review of International Political Economy* 2, no. 4 (Autumn 1995), pp. 679–681.
4. Riccardo Petrella, "Globalization and Internationalization: The Dynamics of the Emerging World Order," in Richard Boyer and Daniel Drache, eds., *States Against Markets: The Limits of Globalization* (London: Routledge, 1996), pp. 77–78.
5. UNCTAD, *World Investment Report 2003* (New York: United Nations, 2003), pp. 257–262; and Bernard M. Hoekman and Michel M. Kostecki, *The Political Economy of the World Trading System: The WTO and Beyond,* 2nd ed. (New York: Oxford University Press, 2001), pp. 9–10.
6. Peter Hakim, "Is Washington Losing Latin America?" *Foreign Affairs* 85, no. 1 (January/February 2006), pp. 39–53.
7. See Mary A. Tétreault and Robert A. Denemark, eds., *Gods, Guns & Globalization: Religious Radicalism & International Political Economy* (Boulder, CO: Lynne Rienner, 2004).
8. United Nations Development Program, *Human Development Report 2005* (New York: Published for UNDP, 2005), p. 26.
9. Susan Strange, "The Defective State," *Daedalus* 124 (Spring 1995), p. 56.
10. Shalendra D. Sharma, "The Many Faces of Today's Globalization: A Survey of Recent Literature," *New Global Studies* 2, no. 2 (2008), p. 3.
11. Linda Weiss, "The State-augmenting Effects of Globalisation," *New Political Economy* 10, no. 3 (September 2005), p. 352; "Realism vs Cosmopolitanism:

A Debate between Barry Buzan and David Held, Conducted by Anthony McGrew," *Review of International Studies* 24, no. 3 (July 1998), p. 394.

12. Walden Bello, "East Asia: On the Eve of the Great Transformation?" *Review of International Political Economy* 5, no. 3 (Autumn 1998), p. 426.

13. Stephan Haggard and Andrew MacIntyre, "The Political Economy of the Asian Economic Crisis," *Review of International Political Economy* 5, no. 3 (Autumn 1998), p. 383.

14. Stanley Fischer, "Lessons from a Crisis," *The Economist,* October 3, 1998, p. 27.

15. Jagdish Bhagwati, *In Defense of Globalization* (New York: Oxford University Press, 2004), p. 67.

16. Thomas Pogge, "Reframing Economic Security and Justice," in David Held and Anthony McGrew, eds., *Globalization Theory: Approaches and Controversies* (Malden, MA: Polity Press, 2007), pp. 212–213.

17. World Bank, *World Development Report 2000/2001* (New York: Oxford University Press, 2001), p. 3; Michael W. Doyle, "The Liberal Peace, Democratic Accountability, and the Challenge of Globalization," in David Held and Anthony McGrew, eds., *Globalization Theory: Approaches and Controversies* (Malden, MA: Polity Press, 2007), pp. 197–198; United Nations Development Programme, *Human Development Report—1997,* pp. 88–89; World Bank, *World Development Report 2006* (New York: Oxford University Press, 2005), p. 45.

18. Doyle, "The Liberal Peace, Democratic Accountability, and the Challenge of Globalization," p. 197; Joseph S. Nye, Jr., "Globalization's Democratic Deficit: How to Make International Institutions More Accountable," *Foreign Affairs* 80, no. 4 (July/August 2001), p. 3.

19. Doyle, "The Liberal Peace, Democratic Accountability, and the Challenge of Globalization," p. 197; Pogge, "Reframing Global Economic Security and Justice," p. 213.

20. Walt W. Rostow, *Why the Poor Get Richer and the Rich Slow Down* (Austin, TX: University of Texas Press, 1980), p. 259; Nye, "Globalization's Democratic Deficit," p. 3.

21. Andrew Hurrell and Ngaire Woods, "Globalisation and Inequality," *Millennium* 24, no. 3 (1995), p. 458.

22. United Nations Department of Economic and Social Affairs, *The Inequality Predicament: Report on the World Social Situation* 2005 (New York: United Nations, 2005), p. 49.

23. Ian Robinson, "Globalization and Democracy," *Dissent* (Summer 1995), pp. 374–377. On globalization and democracy, see David Held, *Democracy and the Global Order: From the Modern State to Cosmopolitan Governance* (Cambridge, UK: Polity Press, 1995).

24. Ngaire Woods and Amritar Narlikar, "Governance and the Limits of Accountability: The WTO, the IMF, and the World Bank," *International Social Science Journal* 170 (December 2001), p. 569.

25. For differing views on this issue, see Tony Porter, "The Democratic Deficit in the Institutional Arrangements for Regulating Global Finance," *Global Governance* 7 (2001), pp. 427–439; Woods and Narlikar, "Governance and the Limits of Accountability"; and Nye, "Globalization's Democratic Deficit."

26. Jan A. Scholte, "Civil Society and Democracy in Global Governance," *Global Governance* 8 (2002), pp. 281–304.

27. Craig Warkentin and Karen Mingst, "International Institutions, the State, and Global Civil Society in the Age of the World Wide Web," *Global Governance* 6, no. 2 (April–June 2000), p. 240.

28. Robert W. Cox, "Civil Society at the Turn of the Millennium: Prospects for an Alternative World Order," *Review of International Studies* 25 (1999), pp. 3–28.
29. Robert Mendelsohn, "Globalization and the Environment," in Ernesto Zedillo, ed., *The Future of Globalization: Explorations in the light of Recent Turbulence* (New York: Routledge, 2008), p. 391.
30. Jennifer Clapp and Peter Dauvergne, *Paths to a Green World: The Political Economy of the Global Environment* (Cambridge, MA: MIT Press, 2005), pp. 26–31; Mendelsohn, "Globalization and the Environment," pp. 384–385.
31. Ken Conca, "Beyond the Statist Frame: Environmental Politics in a Global Economy," in Fred P. Gale and R. Michael M'Gonigle, eds., *Nature, Production, Power: Towards an Ecological Political Economy* (Northampton, MA: Edward Elgar, 2000), p. 141.
32. Clapp and Dauvergne, *Paths to a Green World,* pp. 32–40.
33. Myron Weiner, *The Global Migration Crisis: Challenge to States and to Human Rights* (New York: HarperCollins, 1996), p. 3.
34. Keith Griffin, "Nine Good Reasons to Love Labor Migration," *UC Mexus News,* California Institute for Mexico and the United States, p. 2.
35. "Immigration: Suspicious Minds," *The Economist,* July 4, 1998, p. 25.
36. Malcolm Waters, *Globalization* (London: Routledge, 1995), p. 89.
37. Moisés Naím, "The Five Wars of Globalization," *Foreign Policy* no. 122 (January/February 2003), p. 29. See also Nigel Morris-Cotterill, "Money Laundering," *Foreign Policy* no. 124 (May/June 2001), pp. 16–22; and Michel Schiray, "Introduction: Drug Trafficking, Organized Crime, and Public Policy for Drug Control," *International Social Science Journal* 53, no. 169 (2001), pp. 351–358.
38. Joseph S. Nye, Jr., "Soft Power," *Foreign Policy* 80 (Fall 1990), p. 166; Susan Strange, *States and Markets,* 2nd ed. (London: Pinter, 1994), p. 29.
39. On the changing U.S. position on international trade see Theodore H. Cohn, *Governing Global Trade: International Institutions in Conflict and Convergence* (Burlington, VT: Ashgate, 2002).
40. Xavier Sala-I-Martin, et al., "The Global Competitiveness Index: Prioritizing the Economic Policy Agenda," in Klaus Schwab and Michael E. Porter, *The Global Competitiveness Report 2008–2009* (Geneva: World Economic Forum, 2008), p. 8, http://www.weforum.org/pdf/GCRO8/GCRO8.pdf.
41. Ronald A. Morse, "Japan's Drive to Pre-Eminence," *Foreign Policy* 69 (Winter 1987–1988), pp. 3–21.
42. "Japan on the Brink," *The Economist,* April 11, 1998, pp. 15–17; Ron Bevacqua, "Whither the Japanese Model? The Asian Economic Crisis and the Continuation of Cold War Politics in the Pacific Rim," *Review of International Political Economy* 5, no. 3 (Autumn 1998), pp. 410–423.
43. Lester Thurow, *Head to Head: The Coming Economic Battle Among Japan, Europe, and America* (New York: Morrow, 1992), p. 258.
44. On China's growing economic strength see, for example, Daniel W. Bromley and Yang Yao, "Understanding China's Economic Transformation," *World Economics* 7, no. 2 (April-June 2006), pp. 73-95; and Barry Eichengreen and Hui Tong, "How China is Reorganizing the World Economy," *Asian Economic Policy Review* 1, no. 1 (June 2006), pp. 73-97.
45. Quoted in Akiho Tanaka, "Global and Regional Geo-strategic Implications of China's Emergence," *Asian Economic Policy Review* 1, no. 1 (June 2006), pp. 182–183.
46. Sala-I-Martin, et al., "The Global Competitiveness Index," pp. 27–28.
47. Donald C. Hellmann, "A Decade after the Asian Financial Crisis," *Asian Survey* 47, no. 6 (November/December 2007), p. 844.

48. Andrew Hurrell, "Hegemony, Liberalism and Global Order: What Space for Would-be Great Powers?" *International Affairs* 82, no. 1 (2006), p. 3.

49. Stephen Gill, "Global Finance, Monetary Policy and Cooperation among the Group of Seven, 1944–1992," in Philip G. Cerny, ed., *Finance and World Politics: Markets, Regimes and States in the Post-hegemonic Era* (London: Elgar, 1993), p. 105.

50. Hurrell, "Hegemony, Liberalism and Global Order," p. 6.

51. Anthony Faiola, "As Global Wealth Spreads, the IMF Recedes," *Washington Post,* May 24, 2008.

52. Martin Feldstein, "Refocusing the IMF," *Foreign Affairs* 77, no. 2 (March/April 1998), pp. 20–33.

53. Robert Wade, "Japan, the World Bank and the Art of Paradigm Maintenance: The East Asian Miracle in Political Perspective," *New Left Review* 217 (May/June 1996), p. 5.

54. World Bank, *World Development Report 1991* (New York: Oxford University Press, 1991), pp. 2–3; UN, *The Inequality Predicament,* pp. 50–55, 68–71.

55. World Bank, *World Development Report 1990* (New York: Oxford University Press, 1990), pp. 1–2; United Nations Development Programme, *Human Development Report 1996* (New York: Oxford University Press, 1996), pp. 8–9.

56. Mohammed H. Malek, "Towards an Integrated Aid and Development Programme for Europe," in Mohammed H. Malek, ed., *Contemporary Issues in European Development Aid* (Brookfield, VT: Avebury, 1991), p. 142.

57. Wilfred L. David, *The Conversation of Economic Development: Historical Voices, Interpretations, and Reality* (Armonk, NY: Sharpe, 1997), p. 177.

58. World Commission on Environment and Development, *Our Common Future* (New York: Oxford University Press, 1987), p. 8.

59. See Maurice F. Strong, "Achieving Sustainable Global Development," in the South Centre, *Facing the Challenge: Responses to the Report of the South Commission* (London: Zed Books, 1993), pp. 305–313.

60. Nicholas D. Kristof, "Across Asia, a Pollution Disaster Hovers," *New York Times,* November 28, 1997, pp. A1, A10.

61. John Rapley, *Understanding Development: Theory and Practice in the Third World* (Boulder, CO: Lynne Rienner, 1996), pp. 44–47.

62. See Walter R. Mead, "Asia Devalued," *New York Times Magazine,* May 31, 1998, pp. 38–39.

63. See Francis Fukuyama, "The End of History?" *The National Interest* 16 (Summer 1989), pp. 3–18.

64. Chris Giles and Ralph Atkins, "The Undeniable Shift to Keynes," *Financial Times,* December 29, 2008.

65. Thomas J. Biersteker, "Evolving Perspectives on International Political Economy: Twentieth-Century Contexts and Discontinuities," *International Political Science Review* 14, no. 1 (January 1993), p. 27.

66. Robert O. Keohane and Helen V. Milner, eds., *Internationalization and Domestic Politics* (New York: Cambridge University Press, 1996); and Helen V. Milner, *Interests, Institutions, and Information: Domestic Politics and International Relations* (Princeton, NJ: Princeton University Press, 1997).

67. James N. Rosenau, "Thinking Theory Thoroughly," in James N. Rosenau, *The Scientific Study of Foreign Policy,* rev. ed. (London: Pinter, 1980), p. 30.

GLOSSARY

absolute advantage   A country has an absolute advantage in a particular good if it can produce that good at a lower cost than another country. See *comparative advantage*.

antidumping duties (ADDs)   Duties a country imposes on imported goods if it determines that the goods are being dumped and that this is causing or threatening material injury to its domestic producers. See *dumping*.

appreciation   A market-driven increase in the value or price of a currency. See *depreciation*.

Association of Southeast Asian Nations (ASEAN)   Established in 1967 with the objectives of promoting peace, stability, and economic growth in the region, ASEAN currently has 10 Southeast Asian countries as members. ASEAN was mainly a political organization for many years, but in 1992 the ASEAN Free Trade Area (AFTA) was formed. AFTA has made only limited progress toward total free trade.

Baker Plan   A plan proposed by U.S. Secretary of the Treasury James A. Baker III in 1985 to deal with the LDC foreign debt crisis. The plan emphasized the postponement of some debt payments, the provision of new IMF and World Bank loans as an incentive for continued lending by private banks, and structural changes in debtor country policies.

balance of payments   A summary record of all international economic transactions that a country has, normally over a one-year period. The most important components of the balance of payments are the *current account* and the *capital account*.

Bank for International Settlements (BIS)   The oldest international financial institution, formed in 1930 to oversee German war reparations. Located in Basel, Switzerland, the BIS is the main forum for cooperation and consultation among central bankers in the OECD countries. It helps deal with exchange-rate problems and provides credit to central banks that lack liquidity. The BIS responded to the 1980s debt crisis by providing "bridging" finance until IMF and World Bank loans were available and by adopting measures to increase confidence in the international banking system.

basic needs   A foreign aid approach that focuses on the poorest people among and within LDCs. The basic needs (or basic human needs) approach became prominent in the 1970s and marked a shift from the emphasis on GNP growth in the 1960s. It focused on aid for basic health, education, family planning, rural development, and services to the poor; the increased involvement of women in development programs; and special attention to the problems of the least developed countries.

bilateral aid   Foreign assistance that flows directly from a donor to a recipient government. The largest percentage of official development assistance is given bilaterally. See *foreign aid, multilateral aid,* and *official development assistance*.

bilateral investment treaties (BITs)   Bilateral treaties normally negotiated between DCs and LDCs to promote and protect foreign investment. BITs generally uphold the MFN and national treatment principles, often prohibit host country performance requirements, and require prompt and adequate compensation in the event of nationalization.

Brady Plan   A plan that U.S. Secretary of the Treasury Nicholas Brady proposed in 1988 after the Baker Plan proved to be insufficient to deal with the foreign debt crisis. The Brady Plan introduced the idea that debt relief or reduction was necessary for some LDCs with severe and protracted debt problems.

Bretton Woods system   Bretton Woods, New Hampshire, was the location of the July 1944 meetings to establish the postwar economic order. The IMF and International Bank for Reconstruction and Development (or World Bank) were established at Bretton Woods, as was the monetary regime of pegged exchange rates. This regime ended in 1973, when major countries shifted to flexible exchange rates.

Canada–U.S. Free Trade Agreement (CUSFTA)   Concluded in 1988, the CUSFTA resulted from a U.S. decision that it would participate in RTAs, and from Canada's desire to gain more assured access to the U.S. market. The NAFTA replaced the CUSFTA in 1994. See *North American Free Trade Agreement*.

capital account An item in the balance of payments that records the amount a country lends to and borrows from nonresidents. Countries often finance their current account deficits with a net inflow of capital or a surplus in their capital accounts. Transactions in the capital account include *foreign direct investment* and *portfolio investment*.

capital market A capital market consists of institutions in a country (e.g., the stock exchange, banks, and insurance companies) that match supply with demand for long-term capital. Unlike a capital market, a money market deals with shorter term loanable funding. The World Bank floats bonds on the capital markets of developed states to acquire funds for lending purposes.

capital A factor of production, along with land and labor. Capital consists of physical assets such as equipment, tools, buildings, and other manufactured goods that can generate income and financial assets such as stocks. Marxists view capital in social and political as well as economic terms and emphasize capital's exploitation of labor in the capitalist system.

central bank A public authority responsible for managing a country's money supply and for regulating and controlling its monetary and financial institutions and markets. Most countries rely on a central bank for such regulatory activities.

civil society A wide range of nongovernmental, noncommercial groups that seek to either reinforce or alter existing norms, rules, and social structures.

common market The third stage of regional integration, which has the characteristics of a customs union *plus* the free mobility of factors of production (capital and labor). See *customs union, economic union,* and *free trade area*.

comparative advantage A country has a comparative advantage in producing good A if it can produce A at a *relatively* lower cost than other goods, even if it does not have an absolute advantage in producing any good. Comparative advantage is a powerful liberal economic theory justifying specialization and free trade.

competitiveness The U.S. President's Commission on Industrial Competitiveness defines competitiveness as "the degree to which . . . [a state] can, under free and fair market conditions, produce goods and services that meet the tests of international markets while simultaneously expanding the real income of its citizens."

concessional loans (or *soft loans*) Loans that have lower interest rates, longer grace periods, and longer repayment periods than commercial or hard loans.

conditionality A concept closely associated with the IMF and also with World Bank SALs. To receive IMF loans above a certain level, borrowers must explicitly agree to follow a prescribed set of policies. These policies typically include decreased government spending, increased government revenues, devaluation, deregulation, and privatization.

constructivism A social theory that examines the role of collectively held ideas in IR. Constructivists believe that reality is socially constructed and that our interests and identities become established as *social facts*. In IR and IPE, constructivism is concerned with conceptualizing the relationship between *agents* (states) and *structures* (the international system).

consultative group A group of donor states that provide bilateral development assistance to a particular recipient. Donors use consultative groups to coordinate their bilateral aid-giving and to exert collective pressure on recipient states.

countervailing duties (CVDs) Duties a country imposes on imported goods if it determines that the goods benefit from trade-distorting subsidies that cause or threaten material injury to its domestic producers.

current account An item in the balance of payments; records a country's trade in goods and services with foreigners, investment income and payments, and gifts and other transfers paid to and received from foreigners.

customs union (CU) The second stage of regional integration in which the member countries eliminate tariffs on all (or substantially all) trade with each other and develop a common external tariff toward outsiders.

debt service ratio (or debt-to-export ratio) The ratio of a country's interest and principal payments on its debt to its export income; often used to assess a country's ability to repay its foreign debt. During the 1980s, East Asian NIEs had stronger export positions than Latin American NIEs and were better able to service their foreign debts.

dependency theory A historical materialist development theory that sees the world as hierarchically organized, with the leading capitalist states in the core of the global economy exploiting the poorer states in the periphery.

depreciation A market-driven reduction in the value or price of a currency. See *appreciation*.

devaluation A reduction in the official rate at which one currency is exchanged for another. When a country devalues its currency, the prices of its imported goods and services rise while its exports become less expensive to foreigners. A country can therefore gain some trade advantages through devaluation of its currency. See *revaluation*.

developmental state A term Chalmers Johnson used in the early 1980s to describe Japan and the East Asian NIEs. Realists believe that the East Asian developmental state provided extensive guidance to the market, identified development as its primary objective, invested heavily in education, and depended on a highly skilled technocratic bureaucracy. The 1990s East Asian financial crisis raised questions about the efficacy of the developmental state.

dumping Selling a product in an export market at a price lower than is charged in the home market or below the cost of production.

economic union The fourth stage of regional integration, which has the characteristics of a common market and harmonizes the industrial, regional, fiscal, monetary, and other economic policies of member countries. A full economic union also involves the adoption of a common currency.

economism An overemphasis on the importance of the economic sphere along with an underemphasis on the autonomy of the political sphere.

endogenous growth theory Posits that technological change is not simply the result of fortunate breakthroughs in the quest for new knowledge that are exogenous to the factors of production determining economic growth. Instead, technological knowledge is an endogenous factor of production along with labor and capital that gives DCs and their firms major advantages over LDCs.

epistemic community A group of professionals with acknowledged expertise and a recognized claim to policy-relevant knowledge in a particular issue area.

Eurocurrencies National currencies traded and deposited in banks outside the home country, usually (but not only) in Europe. Eurocurrencies are most often U.S. dollars, or eurodollars. International firms and national governments often use the Eurocurrency market for deposits and loans because the transactions are free of most government regulations.

European Coal and Steel Community (ECSC) Six Western European states (Belgium, France, West Germany, Italy, Luxembourg, and the Netherlands) formed the ECSC in 1951. Although the ECSC integrated the members' coal and steel resources, it was formed mainly to prevent France and Germany from renewing their age-old rivalries. In 1957 the ECSC members expanded the integration process by forming the *European Community*.

European Community (EC) A regional integration agreement formed in 1957 by six Western European states. The EC's economic goals were to establish a customs union and a common market. The EC also established a complex institutional structure, including a Commission, Council of Ministers, European Court of Justice, and European Parliament. Membership in the EC increased to 12 states by 1986, and in 1993 the EC was superseded by the *European Union*.

European Union (EU) The EU became the successor to the EC in 1993, largely as a result of the "Europe 92" program. Europe 92 was designed to complete the creation of a single market by removing the remaining fiscal, nontariff, technical, and other barriers to trade. The EU has widened and deepened the integration process in Europe. As for widening, EU membership increased to 27 members in 2007. As for deepening, 16 EU members have joined in an economic and monetary union (EMU) with a common currency (the euro).

exchange rates The number of units of one currency that can be exchanged for a unit of another currency. See *fixed exchange rates* and *floating exchange rates*.

export-led growth An economic development strategy that emphasizes the production of industrial goods for export. Export-led growth is commonly associated with the economic success of the East Asian NIEs. See *import substitution industrialization*.

fiscal policy   Fiscal policy affects the economy through changes in taxes and government spending. A government that uses fiscal policy to deal with a balance-of-payments deficit lowers government expenditures and raises taxes to withdraw purchasing power from the public. See *monetary policy*.

fixed exchange rates   In a fixed-exchange-rate system, currencies are given official exchange rates, and governments regularly take actions to keep the market rates of their currencies close to the official rates.

floating exchange rates (or flexible exchange rates)   In a floating-exchange-rate system, the supply and demand for each currency in the foreign exchange market determine its exchange rate. With *free-floating exchange rates,* governments do not intervene and the market alone determines currency valuations. With *managed floating,* central banks intervene to deal with disruptive conditions such as excessive fluctuations in exchange rates. Although managed floating is considered legitimate, the IMF calls on central banks to avoid *dirty floating;* that is, a government's manipulation of exchange rates to prevent balance-of-payments adjustment or to give it an unfair competitive advantage.

foreign aid   The transfer of resources to recipient countries for the stated purpose of promoting their welfare and economic development. The greatest share of foreign aid is official development assistance, but nongovernmental organizations also provide aid. According to the Development Assistance Committee of the OECD, only grants that do not require repayment and concessional loans with a grant element of at least 25 percent qualify as foreign aid. See *concessional loans, bilateral aid, multilateral aid,* and *official development assistance*.

foreign direct investment (FDI)   Foreign investment that involves the ownership and control of assets. The foreign residents are usually MNCs that have management rights or control in a branch plant or subsidiary. FDI may occur through the creation of new productive assets by foreigners (greenfield investment) or through the purchase of stock in an existing firm. See *portfolio investment*.

free trade area   The first stage of regional integration, in which the member states are to eliminate tariffs on all (or substantially all) trade with one another. However, each member state can levy its own tariffs and follow its own trade policies toward nonmembers.

General Agreement on Tariffs and Trade (GATT)   A provisional treaty that became the main global trade organization in 1948 by default when a planned International Trade Organization was not formed. GATT served as a written code of behavior and as a venue for multilateral trade negotiations and trade dispute settlement cases. When the WTO was formed in 1995, GATT reverted to its original status as a treaty to regulate trade in goods.

General Agreement on Trade in Services (GATS)   The GATS was established during the GATT Uruguay Round and is a treaty under the WTO. It begins the process of creating principles and rules for policies affecting access to service markets.

generalized system of preferences (GSP)   During the 1970s, the DCs agreed to establish a GSP in response to LDC demands. Under the GSP, individual DCs can waive MFN treatment and give preferential treatment to specific imports from LDCs. Thus, the import duties for some LDC products are lower than those levied on DC products.

global governance   Formal and informal arrangements that provide a degree of order and collective action above the state in the absence of a global government. See *governance*.

gold standard   A monetary system in which central banks fix the value of their currencies in terms of gold and hold international reserves in gold. A gold standard regime existed from the 1870s to 1914, and there were attempts to restore it after World War I. In a *gold exchange standard* (e.g., the Bretton Woods regime), central banks hold their international reserves in two forms—gold and foreign exchange—in any proportion they choose.

governance   Formal and informal processes and institutions that organize collective action.

gross domestic product (GDP)   The total value of goods and services produced within a country's borders during a given year. GDP counts income in terms of where it is earned rather than who owns the factors of production.

gross national income (GNI)   Virtually identical with the GNP. The GNI measures the income produced by the GNP rather than the value of the product itself.

gross national product (GNP) The total value of goods and services produced by domestically owned factors of production during a given year. GNP counts income according to who owns the factors of production rather than where the income is earned.

Group of 20 (G20) There are two G20s: (1) The G20 finance ministers and central bank governors hold an annual summit to discuss key issues in the global economy, and also meet on extraordinary occasions such as the November 2008 meeting to address the global financial crisis. This G20 consists of the G8, Australia, Turkey, the EU, and nine LDCs. (2) A G20 in trade consists of 20 LDCs led by Brazil, China, and India that has called for an end to EU and U.S. agricultural export subsidies and for lower agricultural import barriers in Japan, Canada, and other DCs.

Group of 24 (G24) The G77 formed the G24 in 1972 to represent LDC interests on international monetary issues. The G24 consists of eight finance ministers or central bank governors from each of the main LDC regions—Africa, Asia, and Latin America.

Group of 77 (G77) The principal group representing the South's economic interests in negotiations with the North. The G77 derives its name from the 77 LDCs that formed the group in 1964, but it now has 130 members.

Group of Eight (G8) The G8 includes the G7 members plus Russia. Although Russia is a full member of the G8, it does not participate fully in the G7's trade and financial deliberations.

Group of Five (G5) The G5 includes the finance ministers and central bank governors of the largest developed economies: the United States, Japan, Germany, France, and Britain. It has played a major role at times in coordinating monetary and other economic policies.

Group of Seven (G7) The G5 plus Italy and Canada. The G7 includes the seven largest industrial democracies, which account for about two-thirds of global output.

Group of 10 (G10) The G10 includes the DCs that established the General Arrangements to Borrow with the IMF in 1962. Eleven countries are now G10 members—the G7 plus the Netherlands, Belgium, Sweden, and Switzerland. In addition to providing supplementary finance, the G10 discusses important matters related to the international monetary regime.

Heckscher–Ohlin theory Postulates that comparative advantage is determined by the relative abundance and scarcity of factors of production (land, labor, and capital). Thus, capital-rich states (usually DCs) should specialize in capital-intensive production, and states with an abundance of cheap labor (many LDCs) should specialize in labor-intensive production.

hegemonic stability theory Asserts that a relatively open and stable international economic system is more likely to exist when a hegemonic state is willing and able to lead. The hegemonic state may manage the global economic system through coercion, persuasion, and the provision of public goods. See *hegemony* and *public goods*.

hegemony Leadership, preponderant influence, or dominance in the international system, usually (but not always) associated with a particular state. Gramscian theorists use the term in a cultural sense to connote not only dominance but also the complex of "ideas" social groups use to legitimize their authority.

Heavily Indebted Poor Countries (HIPC) Initiative An initiative proposed in 1996 to provide debt relief for HIPCs. Unlike the Baker and Brady plans, the HIPC Initiative provided relief for the debt of low-income LDCs to the IMF and World Bank. An enhanced HIPC Initiative established in 1999 increased the amount of debt relief and provided it more rapidly. See *Baker Plan, Brady Plan,* and *multilateral debt relief initiative*.

horizontal integration A horizontally integrated MNC extends its operations abroad by producing the same product or product line in affiliates in different countries. Firms often engage in horizontal integration to defend or increase their market share. See *multinational corporation* and *vertical integration*.

human development index (HDI) The UNDP's measure of human development based on life expectancy at birth; the adult literacy rate; primary, secondary, and tertiary school enrollments; and the PPP-adjusted per capita GDP.

import substitution industrialization (ISI) A strategy to promote economic development by replacing industrial imports with domestic production through trade protectionism and government assistance to domestic firms. Many LDCs followed ISI policies in the 1950s and 1960s.

infrastructure   The underlying framework of facilities, equipment, institutions, and installations crucial for the growth and functioning of an economy. Examples of infrastructure include transportation systems, public utilities, finance systems, laws and law enforcement, education, and research.

instrumental Marxism   A form of Marxism that sees formal government institutions as responding in a passive manner to the interests and pressures of the capitalist class. See *structural Marxism.*

International Monetary Fund (IMF)   An international financial organization formed in 1944 to uphold the Bretton Woods system of pegged exchange rates (until the move to floating rates in 1973) and to provide countries with short-term loans for balance-of-payments problems. The IMF has had a leading role in dealing with the 1980s foreign debt crisis and the 1990s financial crisis.

liquidity   The ease with which an asset can be used at a known price in making payments. Cash is the most liquid form of an asset.

Lomé Convention   Trade and aid agreements between the EU and 71 African, Caribbean, and Pacific (ACP) countries that have associate status in the EU. In 2000, the Lomé Convention was replaced by the more WTO-compatible Cotonou Agreement.

London Clubs   Informal groups in which the largest private creditor banks engage in debt rescheduling negotiations with individual LDC debtor countries. The London Clubs have no formal structure or specific location for their meetings; they are also called "bank advisory committees" or "creditor committees." See *Paris Club.*

macroeconomics   A branch of economics that deals with the behavior of the economy as a whole. For example, macroeconomics is concerned with overall levels of employment, growth, production, and consumption. It examines such issues as monetary and fiscal policy, the banking system, trade, and the balance of payments.

market economy   An economy in which the market coordinates individual choices to determine the types of goods and services produced and sold as well as the methods of production.

market   A coordinating mechanism where sellers and buyers exchange goods, services, and factors of production at prices and output levels determined by supply and demand.

mercantilism   A policy of states from the sixteenth to eighteenth centuries to increase their relative power and wealth largely by maintaining a balance-of-trade surplus.

Mercosur   Mercosur, or the Southern Common Market Treaty, was formed in March 1991 when Argentina, Brazil, Paraguay, and Uruguay agreed to eventually establish a common market. Venezuela signed a membership agreement in 2006, but its membership has still not been finalized.

microfinance   The provision of low-cost, short-term financial services, mainly savings and credit, to poor households that do not have access to traditional financial institutions.

monetary policy   Monetary policy influences the economy through changes in the money supply. A government uses monetary policy to deal with a balance-of-payments deficit when its central bank limits public access to funds for spending purposes and makes such funds more expensive.

moral hazard   The idea that protection against risk encourages a person or state to engage in riskier behavior. For example, if a lender of last resort exists, states facing financial crises are more likely to engage in risky behavior because they can count on the lender to rescue them.

most-favored-nation (MFN) treatment   A principle stipulating that every trade advantage, favor, privilege, or immunity a WTO member gives to any state must be extended to all other WTO members. A major exception to MFN treatment is provided for regional integration agreements.

multilateral aid   A type of foreign assistance in which donor governments provide funding through international organizations (such as the World Bank) whose policies are collectively determined. See *bilateral aid, foreign aid,* and *official development assistance.*

multilateral debt relief initiative (MDRI)   The IMF and World Bank established the MDRI in 2006. Low-income LDCs that have their debts reduced under the Enhanced HIPC Initiative are eligible to have the rest of their debt to the IMF, World Bank, and African Development Bank cancelled under the MDRI. See *heavily indebted poor countries initiative.*

multinational corporation (MNC) An enterprise that owns and controls facilities for production, distribution, and marketing in at least two countries. Also referred to as a transnational corporation or multinational enterprise.

national treatment A principle stating that all WTO members should treat foreign products—after they have been imported—as favorably as domestic products with regard to internal taxes and other internal charges and regulations.

New International Economic Order (NIEO) LDC proposals for extensive international economic reform and DC concessions presented to the United Nations in the 1970s. These included LDC demands for control over their economies and natural resources, control over foreign investment, more development assistance, greater access to DC markets, and higher prices for LDC commodity exports. The North ultimately rejected most of these demands.

nontariff barriers (NTBs) A large array of measures other than tariffs that limit imports, assist domestic production, and promote exports. As tariffs declined in each round of GATT negotiations, NTBs became relatively more important. NTBs are often more restrictive, ill-defined, and inequitable than tariffs.

North American Free Trade Agreement (NAFTA) An FTA formed in 1994 by the United States, Canada, and Mexico. NAFTA's importance stems from the inclusion of the United States, the comprehensive nature of the agreement, and the fact that it was the first reciprocal FTA among DCs and an LDC. Unlike the WTO, NAFTA does not give special and differential treatment to the LDC member (Mexico).

official development assistance (ODA) Flows of foreign aid to LDCs and multilateral institutions from official government agencies. See *bilateral aid, foreign aid,* and *multilateral aid.*

official development finance (ODF) Nonconcessional or "hard" loans the IBRD provides to LDCs and transition economies. Although the IBRD's quasi-commercial loans are not concessional enough to be ODA, they are classified as ODF because the IBRD extends them for development purposes, it accompanies the loans with economic and technical advice, and LDCs receive the loans on better terms than they could obtain from borrowing directly on capital markets.

opportunity cost The cost of producing less of one product in order to produce more of another product.

optimum currency area A concept developed by Robert Mundell, an optimum currency area is a region that maximizes the benefits of using a common currency. Regions that are optimum currency areas are subject to common economic shocks, have a high degree of labor mobility, and have a tax-transfer system that relocates resources from economically strong to weak areas.

Organization for Economic Cooperation and Development (OECD) An organization of 30 mainly DCs located in Paris, France. The OECD conducts policy studies on economic and social issues, serves as a forum for DCs to discuss members' economic policies and promote cooperation, and sometimes is a forum for negotiation or prenegotiation.

Organization for European Economic Cooperation (OEEC) An organization of Western European states formed in 1948, that developed a program to distribute Marshall Plan funds and facilitated moves toward currency convertibility and trade liberalization. In 1960 the OEEC was replaced by the OECD, which also has non-European DCs as full members.

Pareto-optimal outcome A condition in which no actor can be made better off without making someone else worse off. A Pareto-deficient outcome is one in which all actors prefer another outcome to the equilibrium outcome. See *prisoners' dilemma.*

Paris Club An informal grouping of DC creditor governments that meets with individual LDC debtor governments to negotiate debt-rescheduling agreements. The Paris Club normally meets in the French Ministry of Finance, but it has no legal status or written rules, no voting procedure, and no formal organizational structure.

political union Has the characteristics of an economic union and also harmonizes members' foreign and defense policies. A fully developed political union is more like a federal political system than an agreement among sovereign states.

politicism An overemphasis on politics and power and an underemphasis on economic structures and processes.

portfolio investment The purchase of stocks, bonds, and money market instruments by foreigners for the purpose of realizing a financial return; it does not result in foreign management, ownership, or legal control.

prisoners' dilemma A game often used in international relations to examine situations in which individual rationality induces a state to "cheat" regardless of the actions taken by others. Such individually rational actions can produce a Pareto-deficient outcome, hence the "dilemma" in prisoners' dilemma. See *Pareto-optimal outcome.*

public goods Also called *collective goods,* these are *nonexcludable* (all states have access to them) and *nonrival* (any state's use of the good will not decrease the amount available for others). Liberals believe that hegemons often provide public goods. A major problem is the existence of *free riders* because noncontributing states (or individuals) can benefit from the provision of public goods.

purchasing power parity (PPP) The number of units of a country's currency needed to buy the same amount of goods and services in the domestic market as a U.S. dollar can buy in the United States.

rational choice Rational choice analysis assumes that individuals have goals and some freedom of choice and that they take actions they believe will achieve their goals. Individuals are "utility maximizers" who seek to optimize their self-interest by weighing the expected costs versus benefits of their actions. Rational choice analysis favors propositions presenting simplified versions of the real world that can be tested through quantitative methods.

reciprocity The principle that a country benefiting from another country's trade concessions should provide roughly equal benefits in return. *Specific reciprocity* requires concessions of equivalent value between two actors within a strict time period. *Diffuse reciprocity* is less demanding, with more flexibility in terms of equivalence of value and the time period for granting reciprocal concessions. The WTO upholds the diffuse reciprocity principle.

regime A form of institution dealing with a specific area of international relations, in which actors' expectations converge around a set of principles, norms, rules, and decision-making procedures. *International organizations* are more concrete and formal institutions than regimes and are often embedded within regimes. For example, the WTO is embedded within the global trade regime.

revaluation An increase in the official rate or value at which one currency is exchanged for another. See *devaluation.*

rules of origin Regulations to prevent importers from bringing goods into a free trade area through member states with lower duties and then shipping them to partner states with higher duties. Rules of origin sometimes provide an excuse for protectionism.

safeguards Term usually applied to actions states can take to counter unexpected import surges that cause, or are likely to cause, serious injury to domestic industry. The Uruguay Round Agreement on Safeguards provides rules for taking such actions.

seigniorage The profit and advantages a "seigneur" or sovereign power gains from issuing money. The term usually refers to the influence and power a hegemon acquires as a result of its position as the top-currency state.

single undertaking Indicates that acceptance of an agreement requires acceptance of all its parts. The GATT Uruguay Round agreement was a single undertaking because it required LDCs to accept all parts of the agreement; this differed from the NTB Tokyo Round codes, in which most LDCs did not participate.

sovereign wealth funds (SWFs) Government investment funds that are funded by foreign currency reserves but managed separately from official currency reserves. Whereas official reserves hold low-risk assets such as sovereign bonds, SWFs may hold equities, corporate bonds, and other assets; thus, SWFs are more important for financial markets. There are concerns about the geopolitical implications of SWFs.

special drawing rights (SDRs) Artificial international reserves created and managed by the G10 and used among central banks. SDRs have been issued in only limited amounts, and efforts to have them supplement (or replace) the U.S. dollar as the main international reserve have been unsuccessful.

state   A sovereign, territorial political unit.

Stolper–Samuelson theory   Posits that trade liberalization benefits abundantly endowed factors of production and hurts poorly endowed factors of production in a state. Building on the Heckscher–Ohlin theory, Stolper–Samuelson helps explain why some domestic groups are free-trade oriented and others are protectionist.

strategic trade theory   A realist theory that a state can successfully engage in industrial targeting to alter its comparative or "competitive" advantage vis-à-vis other states. In deciding on intervention strategies, a state tends to favor industries with advantages in research and development, technology, economies of scale, and market power.

structural adjustment loans (SALs)   Medium-term balance-of-payments financing the World Bank and IMF provide to LDCs. To receive such loans, LDCs must agree to institute structural reforms.

structural Marxism   Structural Marxists view the state as relatively autonomous vis-à-vis direct political pressure from capitalists, but they believe that the state acts in the long-term interests of the capitalist class.

sustainable development   A policy that recognizes the complementarity between economic development and environmental conservation. NGOs endorsed sustainable development in the early 1980s, and the Brundtland Commission gave it multilateral approval in 1987. According to the Brundtland Commission, sustainable development "meets the needs of the present without compromising the ability of future generations to meet their own needs."

tariffs   Taxes levied on products that pass through a customs border. Although tariffs are usually imposed on imports, they may also apply to exports. Import tariffs are most often used as a means of protectionism, but they may also be levied for revenue purposes.

terms of trade   The relative prices of a country's exports and imports. During the 1940s and 1950s, structuralists such as Raúl Prebisch argued that there was unequal exchange between the core and periphery, marked by deteriorating terms of trade for LDCs in the periphery. LDCs were therefore advised to follow ISI policies.

Trade-Related Intellectual Property Rights (TRIPs)   An agreement that establishes minimum standards of protection for copyrights, patents, and other types of intellectual property; provides for remedies available to members to protect these rights; and extends some basic GATT principles to intellectual property. The TRIPs agreement was concluded during the GATT Uruguay Round and is part of the WTO.

Trade-Related Investment Measures (TRIMs)   The TRIMs is a rather weak and narrowly defined agreement to impose some discipline over trade-related investment issues. The TRIMs agreement prohibits host countries from imposing local content requirements on FDI, but it does not address many other issues such as a host country's export performance requirements.

transfer prices   Prices that a business firm uses for the internal sale of goods and services among its divisions (i.e., for intrafirm trade). Transfer prices help an MNC efficiently manage its internal operations, but an MNC may artificially raise or lower these prices to shift its reported profits from high-tax to low-tax countries.

transnational advocacy networks (TANs)   TANs include actors working internationally on an issue, who are bound together by shared values and frequent exchanges of information and services. TANs advocate for value-laden causes, and they are important in some economic areas such as trade, development, and foreign debt issues. NGOs have a central role in most TANs, but they may also include social movements, the media, labor unions, consumer groups, religious institutions, intellectuals, and various branches of government.

Triffin dilemma   The Triffin dilemma referred to the conflict between the "liquidity" and "confidence" functions of the U.S. dollar as the top currency under the Bretton Woods regime. Continued balance-of-payments deficits created a confidence problem in the U.S. dollar, but if the United States reduced its payments deficits, there would be a shortage of U.S. dollars for liquidity purposes.

United Nations Conference on Trade and Development (UNCTAD) A permanent organ of the UN General Assembly, created in 1964 as a result of the South's dissatisfaction with international economic organizations such as GATT. UNCTAD is mainly concerned with promoting the South's trade and development interests.

vertical integration A vertically integrated MNC controls production of goods and services at different stages of the production process, with some of its affiliates' output serving as inputs to other affiliates. Firms become vertically integrated to avoid uncertainty, reduce transaction costs, and limit competition. See *horizontal integration*.

voluntary export restraints A practice states used to circumvent the GATT Article 11 ban on import quotas by pressuring other states to "voluntarily" decrease their exports of specific products.

Washington consensus Refers to the neoliberal belief that countries can best achieve economic growth through free markets, a dominant private sector, democratic government, and trade liberalization.

World Bank group Consists of five multilateral institutions that provide development finance to LDCs and transition economies. These include the International Bank for Reconstruction and Development (formed at Bretton Woods in the 1940s), International Finance Corporation (formed in 1956), International Development Association (created in 1960), International Centre for the Settlement of Investment Disputes (formed in 1966), and Multilateral Investment Guarantee Agency (formed in 1988).

World Economic Forum (WEF) The WEF is a private institution that has become a venue in which business executives, political leaders, and multilateral institutions discuss global socioeconomic and political problems. The WEF's core members are the top 1,200 global firms and banks in terms of global sales or capital. In addition to its annual meeting in Davos, Switzerland, the WEF holds regional summits and issues influential publications.

World Trade Organization (WTO) The main global trade organization, formed as the successor to GATT in 1995. Agreements under the WTO include the General Agreement on Tariffs and Trade (GATT), General Agreement on Trade in Services (GATS), Agreement on Trade-Related Intellectual Property Rights (TRIPs), and Agreement on Trade-Related Investment Measures (TRIMs).

world-system theory World-system theorists reject the view of modernization theorists that states in the periphery have problems because they follow traditional practices. They argue that problems in the periphery stem from capitalism, a global system for organizing economic activities. To explain the fact that some states in the periphery have been developing, world-system theorists introduced the concept of the "semiperiphery."

INDEX

Note: Page reference with *f* And *t* notation refer to a figure and table on that page respectively

419